JANE'S
FIGHTING SHIPS
1906/7

JANE'S FIGHTING SHIPS 1906/7

A Reprint of the 1906/7 Edition of Fighting Ships

Edited by

FRED T. JANE

ARCO PUBLISHING COMPANY, INC.
New York

First published by Sampson Low Marston in 1906

This edition published 1970 by ARCO PUBLISHING COMPANY, INC.
219 Park Avenue South, New York, N.Y. 10003

Library of Congress Number 69-14519
ARCO Book Number 668-02019-9

Printed in Great Britain

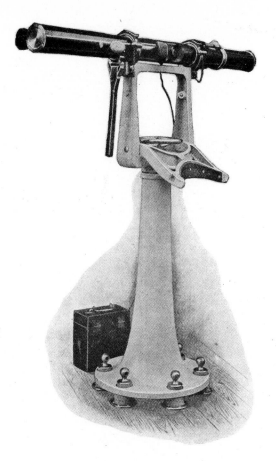

Rangefinders
For Naval, Fortress,
and Field use.

BARR & STROUD'S PATENTS

Electric

Transmitters

and Receivers.

ANNIESLAND, GLASGOW, SCOTLAND.

Walker's Patent Ship-Logs.

THE TAFFRAIL REGISTER AND CONNECTION BOX.

THE CHART-ROOM REGISTER.

Walker's Patent "NEPTUNE" Electric Ship-Log.

By the use of this instrument, the distance run, as indicated by the Log Register on the Taffrail, is also recorded on a dial in the Chart Room or in any other part of the vessel as desired, thus enabling the Officer of the Watch to take the Log reading himself, instead of having to rely upon the care and accuracy of a seaman sent aft for the purpose.

ALSO MAKERS OF THE

" Cherub," " Cherubal," " Tom Bowling," " Rocket," and " Harpoon " Logs.

Thomas Walker & Son, 58, Oxford Street, Birmingham.

FIGHTING SHIPS.

A CHANNEL FLEET SPEED RACE.   DUNCANS BEATING SWIFTSURES.

ELECTRIC LIGHTING AND POWER PLANTS

FOR

SHIPS, HARBOURS, GOVERNMENT DOCKYARDS, FORTS, LIGHTHOUSES, & ORDNANCE WORKS.

As supplied to the British and Indian Governments, the Admiralty, and the War Office; the Belgium and Egyptian Governments, and Steamship Companies.

ARC LAMPS.   PROJECTORS.   STEAM DYNAMOS.
ELECTRIC CAPSTANS.
AMMUNITION HOISTS AND ASH HOISTS.

INDIA. BURMAH.
NEW ZEALAND.
JAPAN.
NORWAY.
WESTERN AUSTRALIA.

CROMPTON & COMPANY, LTD.,
Head Office: SALISBURY HOUSE, LONDON WALL LONDON, ENGLAND.

EGYPT.
SOUTH AFRICA.
NEW SOUTH WALES.
CHILI.
ARGENTINA.

FIGHTING SHIPS.

PART I.—THE NAVIES OF THE WORLD: the Great Powers in Order of Strength; the Coast Defence Navies in Geographical Order.

PART II.—Special contributions by Admiral Sir John O. Hopkins, G.C.B., Rear-Admiral Nebogatoff, I.R.N., Rear-Admiral Wiren, I.R.N., Colonel Cuniberti, R.I.N., C. de Grave Sells, M.Inst.C.E., Commander Hovgaard, R.D.N., H. Reuterdahl, U.S.N.I., and others.

FOUNDED AND EDITED BY

FRED T. JANE.

PUBLISHED FOR THE NAVAL SYNDICATE

BY

SAMPSON LOW, MARSTON & CO., Ltd.,

LONDON, E.C.

1906.

(NINTH YEAR OF ISSUE.)

PRINTED BY NETHERWOOD, DALTON & CO., PHŒNIX WORKS, FOLLY HALL, HUDDERSFIELD.

PREFACE.

REVOLUTION is thick upon the naval world, and there has never been an edition of this book in which so many alterations have had to be made. In the British Navy the advent of fire-control stations, in the Japanese the removal of fighting tops, in the French, German, Dutch, Norwegian and other fleets the addition of top-gallant masts almost *en bloc* means changes in appearance of the most marked description. This of course has necessitated innumerable fresh photographs and silhouettes, and also the changing of any number of plans—the principle of this book being to show in the elevation the ship rigged as she actually is, and not as she was originally contemplated to be.

Very careful attention has been devoted to the silhouette-identification pages, and well nigh half the silhouettes of last year have been replaced by new ones. The making of a satisfactory silhouette of a warship is a work of extreme difficulty, and one for which photography is often of very little assistance and sometimes almost the reverse. All are familiar with those instantaneous photographs of horse racing once so popular; undeniably correct but also undeniably unlike galloping horses as seen by the human eye. Something of the same sort obtains with ship silhouettes : to be of any real service they have to express the ship not only as she actually is, but also the ship as she strikes the ordinary observer who always is mentally comparing her with other vessels. This necessitates some slight accentuation of peculiarities. Salient points have to be seized upon and emphasised. For instance, the two ships of the *Powerful* class are most easily to be differentiated from other four funnelled cruisers by the fact that the two amidship funnels are rather close together instead of equally spaced. This fact is obvious in any photograph that is carefully inspected, but not at all obvious unless looked for. Some slight accentuation of the peculiarity is necessary in a silhouette if obviousness is to be secured. A suitable silhouette has therefore to be a very slight caricature, and it is not always possible to hit off the likeness the first time. Silhouettes which seemed lacking in the necessary qualities have been replaced in this issue. In addition, the continual changes in rig now going on have demanded much attention.

It is with some regret that changes have been made in the arrangement of the identification silhouettes. Experiments have, however, indicated weak points in the arrangement by which battleships and cruisers were differentiated. There are now so many cruisers which seen alone from a distance could be mistaken for possible battleships that the old arrangement often necessitated the consultation of two pages. This was unsatisfactory. Now, therefore, all navies have the silhouettes grouped by funnels alone.

Although on board a warship a vessel like the *Prinz Adalbert* is not very likely to be confounded with the *Deutschland*, such an error is quite easy on board a merchant ship, unless the two silhouettes are in direct comparison. One of the prime objects in designing this identification system was to enable it to be used by any merchant vessel in wartime. Hence the need of simplicity. I have to thank several officers interested in signalling for much kind assistance and advice in this matter.

In pursuit of the same ideal the silhouette index at the end of the book has been entirely re-done and re-arranged. This index is now designed to be used wherever the nationality of a ship sighted is unknown. She will be found grouped with all other vessels at all like her and so can very quickly be picked out. When nationality is known then the larger identification silhouette can be at once employed.

The re-arrangement of the silhouettes has necessitated a change in the identification letters. After much thought it has been decided to use one unchanging first hoist for each nation to indicate each important ship or class of ships by a single letter, and unimportant ships by double letters which " read in." The double letters for individual ships have been done away with as an unnecessary complication never likely to be really necessary.

A re-arrangement of pages has been necessitated by the fact that the United States Navy is now very superior to the French. The salving of the Port Arthur fleet has added many extra pages to Japan, and the annihilation of the Baltic Fleet has considerably attenuated the space given to Russia. The Japanese Navy has also made an advance in the position accorded to it. Though Germany disposes of 15 modern battleships some of these are of such small account (the *Kaisers* for instance) that there is little question that the ten best Japanese battleships are very nearly equal to them, while there is no question of the superiority either in number or in individual units of the Japanese armoured cruisers. The Japanese Navy is indeed very little behind the French in *material*.

In previous years ships have been grouped at the end of the ship pages, classed in parallel lines of equal value with point values assigned. The arrival on the scene of the *Dreadnought* entirely upsets the old arrangement. Many correspondents have interested themselves in an attempt to give her a unit of value in comparison with other vessels, but it has generally been considered impossible to carry this assigning of points beyond a certain stage except as regards the stage or two immediately below. It is easy to assign something like the relative ratios to the *King Edward* and *Dreadnought*. It can also be done between the *King Edward* and *Majestic*, *Majestic* and *Cressy*, *Cressy* and *Devonshire*, etc., but when applied between the *Dreadnought* and *Devonshire*, the ratios logical over two or three groups appear farcical. What could the *Devonshire* do, or a number of *Devonshires* in point value equal to the *Dreadnought*? There is about one chance in a hundred of a torpedo hit, which would in all probability do no harm.

PREFACE.

Similarly it may be asked what the *Majestics* could do. It is difficult to see how half a dozen of them could prevent the *Dreadnought* from steaming out of effective range of their guns and sinking them one by one.

In view of the secrecy with which it has been considered desirable to surround the *Dreadnought*, no detailed plan of this ship is given, but merely an outline of her probable appearance and such details concerning her as are common property.

In the Comparative Tables, as re-arranged this year, special attention has been devoted to the long-range accuracy that is POSSIBLE with the guns, which really means chance of hitting at all, and to speed as the all-important factor that admits of choosing the range. Displacement and armour have then come in for consideration, but modernity of design in the guns has counted higher than anything else.

It has been deemed advisable to omit Stations of Ships this year. So many changes are in progress or contemplated that no list would be even moderately accurate a couple of months hence.

A table of building programmes for 1906-07 and for the three preceding years has been introduced in a form convenient for instant reference and this will be a new permanent feature.

The majority of the contributors to Part II are so well-known and their articles of such special interest that no introduction of them is required here.

In conclusion I have to thank an unprecedented number of correspondents who have been kind enough to send me photographs from all quarters of the world, and to point out the unfortunately large number of misprints in the 1905 Edition. I have specially to thank Messrs. F. McMurtrie and J. Richmond for their carefully scheduled lists which have materially lightened my labours in this direction. Free from misprints, I fear the present edition is not—in a work of this nature it is practically impossible to avoid a few—but I hope a material improvement will be found.

FRED T. JANE.

Tressillian House,
Southsea, Portsmouth.

A few REPRINTS of certain of the articles in Part II can be obtained from the publishers:—

SAMPSON LOW, MARSTON & Co.,

Paternoster Row, London, E.C.

(Tastefully bound in Paper Covers.)

THE WAR ARTICLES - - -	5/-
PROGRESS OF WARSHIP ENGINEERING -	3/6
COLONEL CUNIBERTI'S ARTICLE - -	2/6
GENERAL SILHOUETTE INDEX - -	2/6

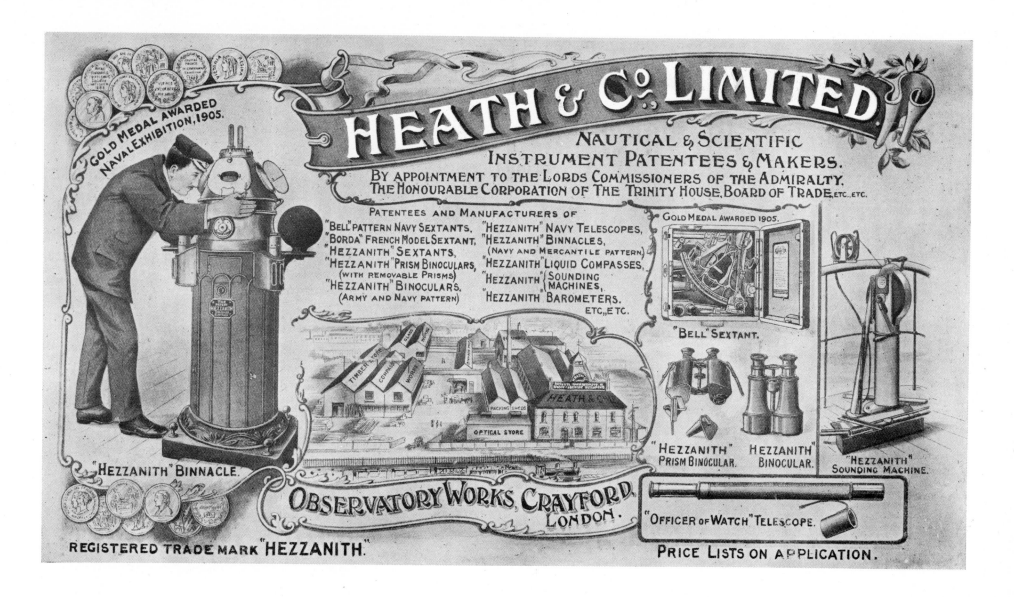

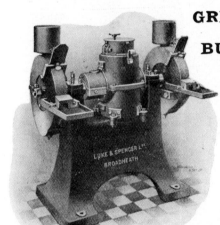

CONTENTS.

CONTENTS.

J. SAMUEL WHITE & COMPANY LTD.,
SHIPBUILDERS & ENGINEERS, EAST COWES, I. o. W.

SPECIALTIES:
TORPEDO VESSELS UP TO 36 KNOTS. | WATER TUBE BOILERS AND FEED REGULATORS (WHITE-FORSTER TYPE).
TURBINES (PARSONS' PATENT). | STEAM, PETROL, AND OIL DRIVEN LAUNCHES AND LIFEBOATS.

COMPLETION BERTHS SHEWING TORPEDO VESSELS UNDER CONSTRUCTION AND REPAIRS AT J. SAMUEL WHITE & CoS WORKS

All guns that can be regarded as "armour piercers" are notated with some variation of the letter A.

Note.—It must be understood that all these comparisons are *approximate* and solely designed for *war* work. The fractional proving ground penetrations will be found on the Gun Tables at the beginning of each navy.

Powder. M.D. Cordite or Cordite.	Same as M.D. Cordite.	Nitro-cellulose.	Nitro-cellulose.	Nitro-cellulose.	Nitro-cellulose.	Cordite.	"Ammonal."	Powder	Armour Penetrations with *capped* A.P. (shading as uniform in all plans).	
Gun Nota-tions. BRITISH.	FRENCH.	U.S.A.	GERMAN.	JAPANESE.	RUSSIAN.	ITALIAN.	AUSTRIAN.	Gun Nota-tions.	Direct impact at 5000. Average battle penetration at 3000 yards.	Direct impact at 7000. Average battle penetration at 5000 yards.
AAAAA 12 in. XI. (m. '04).	12 in. (m. '02).	12 in., IV. (m. '04).	*New* 12 in.	12 in., 45 cal. (m. '04).	......	......	......	**AAAAA**	*aaaaa*	*aaaa*
AAAA 12 in. IX. (M.D. cordite)	12 in. (m. '96). 13·4 in. (m. '87). 12 in. (m. '93-96).	12 in., III. (m. '99). •• ••	11 in., 50 cal. (*new*).	12 in., 40 cal.	12 in., 40 cal. (m. '00).	12 in. (m. '00).	......	**AAAA**	*aaaa* =superior to 12″ K.C.	*aaa*
AAA 12 in. IX. (*with cordite*) 12 in. VIII. 10 in., 45 cal. 9·2 X., 50 cal.	13·4 in. (m. '93 & m. '97). 12 in. (m. '93 & m. '87). 10·8 in. (m. '93-'96). 9·4 in. (m. '02). 9·4 in. (m. '93-'96).	10 in., III. (m. '99). 13 in., I. & II.	11 in. (m. '01).	12 in. (Fuji). 12·6 in. Canet. 10 in., 45 cal.	10 in., 45 cal.	17 in., 29 cal. 10 in., 45 cal.	......	**AAA**	*aaa* =·10-12″ K.C.	*aa*
AA 13·5 in. 9·2 in., IX., 45 cal.	13·4 in. (m. '84). 10·8 in. (m. '93). 9·4 in. (m. '96). 7·6 in. (m. '02).	......	9·4 in. (m. '99).	......	12 in., 35 cal. 9 in., 45 cal.	13·5 in. 17 in., 27 cal. 17 in., 26 cal. 10 in., 40 cal.	9·4 in. (m. '01).	**AA**	*aa* =9-8″ K.C.	*a*
A 9·2 in., VIII., 40 cal. 7·5 in., II., 50 cal. 7·5 in., I., 45 cal.	14·5 in. 10·8 in. (m. '87). 9·4 in. (m. '93). 7.6 in. (m. '93-'96).	12 in., I. 8 in., V. (m. '99).	9·4 in. (m. '95). 8·2 in. (m. '03).	8 in., 45 cal.	6 in., 45 cal.	8 in., 45 cal.	9 4 in. (m. '94). 12 in. (m. '80), 35 cal. 7·6 in , 42 cal., Skoda.	**A**	*a* =7-6″ K.C., or 7-8½″ K.N.C.	*b*
B 10 in., 29 tons.	13·4 in. (m. '84 & m. '81). 7·6 in. (m. '93 & m. '87). 6·4 in. (m. '02).	7 in., I. (m. '99). 10 in., 35 cal.	11 in., 40 cal. (*old*). 8·2 in. 40 cal. 6·7 in.	8 in., 40 cal.	9 in., 35 cal.	......	9·4 in., 35 cal. (m. '86).	**B**	*b* =5″ K.C. or about 6″ K.N.C.	*c*
C 9·2 in. (*old*). 6 in., IX. & X., 50 cal.	10·8 in. (m. '84). 6·4 in. (m. '96).	6 in., VI. (m. '99), 50 cal. 10 in., 30 cal.	11 in., 35 cal. 9·4 in., 35 cal.	6 in. (m. '04). 6 in., 50 cal.	12 in., 30 cal. 6 in., 45 cal. (m. '00).	100 tons, M.I.	......	**C**	*c* =4½° K.C. or 5″ K.N.C	*d*
D 6 in. VII. & VIII., 45 cal.	6·4 in., *light* (m. '91). 9·4 in. (m. '84).	8 in., III., 40 cal.	......	12 in. Krupp (*old*).	......	......	......	**D**	*d* =4″ K.C. or K.N.C. or about 9″ iron.	*e*
E 6 in., Q.F., 40 cal.	6·4 in. (m. '87). 5·5 in. 3·9 in. (m. '92). 3·9 in. (m. '91).	8 in., 35 cal. 5 in., V. (m. '99). 4 in., VII. (m. '99).	6 in., 40 cal. 10·2 in., 26 cal. (*old*). 9·4 in., 30 cal. (*old*).	6 in. 40 cal. 10·2 in. *old* Krupp.	6 in., 45 cal. (*older*). 4·7 in., 45 cal. (m. '00). 9 in. (*old*).	6 in., 40 cal.	6 in., 40 cal. (m. '01).	**E**	*e* =about 6″ iron.	*f*
F 4·7 in. 4 in. 12 pdr., 18 cwt. 12 pdr., 12 cwt. 14 pdr.	3·9 in. (m. '81). 9 pdr. (65 m/m.)	8 in., 30 cal. 6 in., 40 cal. 5 in., R.F., 40 cal. 5 in., I. 4 in., I.-VI. 3 in., 14 pdr.	4·1 in., 40 cal. 6 in., 35 cal. 3·4 in., 24 pdr. 4·1 in., 35 cal. 3·4 in., 15½ pdr.	4·7 in., 40 cal. 6 in. (*old*). 4·7 in. (*old*). 3 in. 14 pdr. 3 in. 12 pdr.	4·7 in. (*older*). 6 in., 35 cal. 3 in. 12 pdr.	*Old* 6 in., 40 cal. 4 in., 45 cal. 4·7 in.	6 in., 40 cal. (m. '94). 4·7 in., 40 cal. 6 in., 35 cal. (m. '80 & '86). 4·7 in. (m. '87). 3 in. 12 pdr.	**F**	*f* =about 4″ iron.	

1. Add or subtract a grade of armour for each 2000 yards difference in range.
2. For penetration *uncapped* add 2000 yards to the actual range (*i.e.*, deduct a grade).
3. For penetrations at angles *well over* 30° *normal* add 2000 yards to the "average battle penetrations" (*i.e.*, deduct a grade).

GLOSSARY OF TECHNICAL TERMS.

	ENGLISH.		FRENCH.		GERMAN.		ITALIAN.		RUSSIAN.		RUSSIAN.		SPANISH.		SWEDISH.
31	Funnels	31	Cheminées	31	Schornsteine	31	Fumaioli	31	Трубы	31	Trubi	31	Chimeneas	31	Skorstenar
32	Guns	32	Artillerie	32	Geschütze	32	Cannoni	32	Орудія	32	Orudiia	32	Cañones	32	Kanoner
33	Hoods	33	Carapaces	33	Cupoles	33	Scudi	33	Покрышки	33	Pokrishki	33	Carapachos	33	Kapor
34	Kts. (Knots)	34	Noeuds	34	See-milen	34	Nodi	34	Узелъ	34	Uzell	34		34	Knop
35	Length	35	Longeur	35	Länge	35	Lunghezza	35	Длина	35	Dlina	35	Eslora	35	Längd
36	Liquid Fuel	36	Combustile liquide	36	Petroleum	36	Combustibile liquido	36	Жидкое топлнво	36	Jhidkoe toplivo	36	Combustibile liqu:do	36	Flytande bränsle
37	Lower deck	37	Faux pont	37	Zwischen-deck	37	Ponte inferiore	37	Нижняя палуба	37	Nijhniaia paluba	37	Cubierta baja	37	Trossdäck
38	Machinery	38	Machines	38	Maschinen	38	Machinaria	38	Механизмъ	38	Mekhanizm	38		38	Maskineri
39	Main-deck	39	Pont de batterie	39	Batterie deck	39	Ponte principale	39	Главная палуба	39	Glavnaia paluba	39	Cubierta principal	39	Batteridäck
40	Masts	40	Mâts	40	Masten	40	Alberi	40	Мачты	40	Machti	40	Palos	40	Master
44	Port (side)	44	Babord	44	Backbord [Maschinen	44	Sinistra	44	Лѣвый	44	Lievii	44	Babor	44	Babord
45	Protection to vitals	45	Protection des	45	Protektion an Schutz der	45	Protezione delle parti	45	Защнта	45	Zastchita	45	Protection de las partes	45	Skydd för vitala delar
46	Ram	46	Eperon [machines	46	Ramsporn	46	Sperone [vitali	46	Таранъ	46	Tarann	46	Espolon [vitales	46	
47	Screens	47	Ecrans	47	Splitter-traversen	47	Schermi	47	Шнрмы	47	Shirmi	47	Mante!ete	47	Splinterskärmar
48	Shields	48	Boucliers.	48	Schützschildern	48	Scudi	48	Щнтъ	48	Stchit	48	Mantelete	48	Kanonskärmar
49	Speed	49	Vitesse	49	Geschwindigkeit	49	Velocita	49	Скорость хода	49	Skorost khoda	49	Velocidad	49	Fart
50	Starboard	50	Tribord	50	Steuerbord	50	Dritta	50	Правая сторона	50	Pravaia storona	50	Estribor	50	Styrbord
51	Stern	51	Arrière	51	Heck	51	Poppa	51	Корма	51	Korma	51	Popa	51	Akter
52	Submarine	52	Sousmarin	52	Untersee-Boote	52	Sottomarino	52	Подводная-лодка	52	Podvodnaia lodka	52	Submarino	52	Undervattens
53	Submerged	53	Submergé	53	Unterwasser	53	Subacqueo	53	Подводный	53	Podvodnii	53	Sumerfido	53	Undervattens
54	Torpedo	54	Torpille	54	Torpedo	54	Siluro	54	Мина	54	Mina	54	Torpedero	54	Torpedo
55	Torpedo boat	55	Torpilleur	55	Torpedo boot	55	Torpediniera	55	Миноносецъ	55	Minonosets	55	Torpedero	55	Torpedbat
56	Torpedo tubes	56	Tubes lance torpille	56	Torpedo lancier-röhre	56	Tubi lancia siluri	56	Минные апараты	56	Minnie aparati	56	Tubos lanza torpedos	56	Torpedtuber
57	Tons	57	Tons	57	Tonnen	57	Tonnelate	57	Тонны	57	Tonni	57	Toneladas	57	Ton
58	Trials	58	Essais	58	Probefahrten	58	Prove	58	Испытанія	58	Ispitaniia	58	Pruebas	58	Proftur
59	Turrets	59	Tourelles	59	Thürme	59	Torri	59	Башня	59	Bashnia	59	Torres	59	Rörliga torn
60	Upper deck	60	Pont de gaillards	60	Oberdeck	60	Ponte superiore	60	Верхняя палуба	60	Verkhniaia paluba	60	Cubierta alta	60	Öfre däck
61	Water line	61	Flotation	61	Wasserlinie	91	Linea d'acqua	61	Ватеплиннія	61	Vaterliniia	61	La linea de flotacion	61	Vattenlinie

JAPANESE.
(pronounce as French.)

61	Water line (Suishen)	水線
60	Upper deck (Johanpan)	上甲板
59	Turrets (Yihoto)	圍砲塔
58	Trials (Shi Unten (Kokoromi Unten))	試運轉
57	Tons	噸
56	Torpedo tubes (Suirai Hatsushakuan)	水雷發射管
55	Torpedo boat (Suirai-Tei)	水雷艇
54	Torpedo (Suirai)	水雷
53	Submerged (Suichu)	水中
52	Submarine (Shen-sui)	潜水
51	Stern (Kambi)	艦尾
50	Starboard (side) (Ugen)	右舷
49	Speed (Sokurioku)	速力
48	Shields (Tate)	楯
47	Screens (Kukusho)	スクルー
46	Ram (Shoto)	撞頭
45	Protection to vitals (Yobu-Bogio)	要部防禦
44	Port (side) (Sagen)	左舷
43	Normal (Kitei)	規定
42	m/m (Millimetre)	ミリメーター
41	M. (Metre)	メーター
40	Masts (Hobashira)	檣
39	Main (-deck) (Chukan-pan)	中甲板
38	Machinery	機械
37	Lower (-deck) (Gekan-pan)	下甲板
36	Liquid fuel (Yokitai-Nemrio)	液体燃料
35	L. (Length) (Nagasa)	長
34	Kts. (Knots)	節
33	Hoods (Hogai)	砲蓋
32	Guns (How)	砲
31	Funnels (Yentotsu or Entotsu)	烟突

18

GLOSSARY OF TECHNICAL TERMS.

	ENGLISH.	FRENCH.	GERMAN.	ITALIAN.	RUSSIAN.	RUSSIAN.	SPANISH.	SWEDISH.
1	Above water	Au dessus de l'eau	Ober wasser	Sopracqua	Надводные	Nadvodnie		Öfvervattens
2	Armour	Cuirasse	Panzer	Corazzato	Броня	Bronia	Coraza Blindage	Pansar
3	Armoured cruiser	Croiseur cuirassé	Gepanzerter Kreuzer	Incrociatore corazzati	Броненосный-крейсеръ	Bronenosnii-kreiser	Crucero acorazado	Pansarkryssare
4	Ahead	Avant	Vorwärts	A prora (davanti)	Впередъ	Vpered	A proa	Framat
5	Astern	Arrière	Rückwärts	A.poppa	Назадъ	Nazad	A popa	Back
6	Amidships	Au milieu	Mittschiffs	Al centro	Въсерединну	Vseredinu	Crujia	Midskepps
7	Barbettes	Barbettes	Brustwerk	Barbette	Барбеты	Barbeti	Torres-barbetas	Barbettorn
8	Bases (of barbettes)	Au dessous la tourelle	Trunk (Schacht)	Piattoforme	Внизу	Vnizu	Platformas	Fasta torn
9	Battery	Batterie	Batterie	Batteria	Баттарея	Battereya	Bateria	Batteri
10	Battleship	Cuirassé d'escadre	Schlachtschiff	Nave da battaglia	Броненосецъ	Bronenosets	Acorazado	Slagskepp
11	Beam	Largeur	Breite	Larghezza	Ширина	Shirina	Manga	Bredd
12	Belt	Ceinture	Gürtel	Cintura	Поясъ	Poyass	Faja	Gördelpansar (citadel
13	Bow	Avant	Bug	Prora	Носъ	Noss	Proa	Bog [eller gördel)
14	Boilers	Generateurs	Kessel	Caldaie	Котлы	Kotli	Calderas	Ångpannor
15	Bulkheads	Traverses	Querwände	Paratie	Переборки	Pereborki	Mamparos	Tvärpansar
16	Bridge	Pont	Brücke	Ponte di comando	Мостъ	Most	Puente	Brygga
17	Bunkers	Soutes	Bunker	Carbonili	Угольные ящики	Ugolnie yastchiki	Carboneras	Kolboxar
18	Capacity	Approvisement	Capacität	Capacita	Поннѣчение	Poinyestchenie	Capacidad	Kapacitet
19	Casemates	Casemates	Casematten	Casamette	Казематъ	Kazemat	Casamatas	Kasematter
21	Coal	Charbon	Kohlenvorrat	Carbone	Уголь	Ugol	Carbon	Kol
22	Complement	Équipage	Besatzung	Equipaggio	Комплектъ	Kompleki	Dotacion	Besättningsstyrka
23	C.T. (conning tower)	Block-haus (C.T.)	Commando Turm	Torre di comando	Рулевая башня	Roolevaia bashnia	Torse o' redueto de	Styrtorn
24	Cruiser	Croiseur	Kreuzer	Incrociatore	Крейсеръ	Kreiser	Crucero [mando	Kryssare
25	Deck	Pont	Deck	Ponte	Палуба	Palooba	Cubierta	Däck
26	Destroyer	Contre-torpilleur	Zerstörer	Caccia-torpediniere	Контръ-миноносецъ	Kontr-minonosets	Caratorpedenos	Jagare
27	Displacement	Déplacement	Deplacement	Dislocamento	Водоизмѣщеніе	Vodoizmiestchenie	Desplazamient	Deplacement
28	Draught	Tirage	Tiefgang	Immersione	Углубленіе	Ooglooblenie	Puntal	Djupgaende
29	Ends	Extrémités	Ends	Estremita	Край	Krai		Stäfvar
30	Fighting tops	Hunes	Marsen	Coffe militari	Пушечный марсъ	Poostchechnii mars	Cofas militares	Militärmaster

30	29	28	27	26	25	24	23	22	21	20	19	18	17	16	15	14	13	12	11	10	9	8	7	6	5	4	3	2	1
{Fighting tops Sheito-Shorou	{Ends Hashi	{Draught Kissui	{Displacement Hai-sui-Tonsu	{Destroyer Kuchiku-tei	{Deck Kanpan	{Cruiser Junyo-Kan	C. T. (Conning tower) Shireito	{Complement Teiin	{Coal Shekitan	{c/m (Centi-metre)	{Casemates Kuku-Hodai	{Capacity Yorio	{Bunkers Shekitanko	{Bridge Kankio	{Bulkheads Kakuheki	{Boilers Kikan	{Bow Kanshu	{Belt Kotai	{Beam Haba	{Battleship Shemo-Kan	{Battery Hodai	{Bases (of Barbettes, etc.) Hoto-no-Kibu	{Barbettes Roloto	{Amidships Chuō	{Astern Tomo / Ahead Omote	{Armoured Cruiser Kotetsu-Junyo-Kan	{Armour Kotetsu	{Above water
戰鬪檣樓	両端	吃水	排水噸數	驅逐艦	甲板	巡洋艦	司令塔	定員	石炭	センチメーター	穹窖砲臺	容量	石炭庫	艦橋	隔壁	汽罐	艦首	甲帶	巾	戰鬪艦	砲臺	砲塔の基部	露砲塔	中央	艦後 艦前	甲鐵巡洋艦	甲鐵	水上

FIGHTING SHIPS IDENTIFICATION OF WARSHIPS SIGNAL SYSTEM.

THIS system is put forward to allow of any merchantman being used as a war-scout without being supplied with naval signalmen—a copy of FIGHTING SHIPS being the sole requisite. However unfamiliar the merchantman may be with warships, the arrangement of the identification silhouettes is such that should any error be made, the receiver by a glance at the identification silhouettes can at once estimate it. Special notes of the chances of error are also made.

INSTRUCTIONS.

In the identification silhouettes on the index page of each navy, letters are assigned to each navy, and to each *class* of ships or series of ships practically identical in appearance.

PREPARATIVE.

The ship wishing to communicate by this code hoists a CONE under her ensign. The significance of this signal is—*following signals are by F.S. Code and refer to warships that I have sighted.* This should be kept up all the time that signalling by this system is going on.

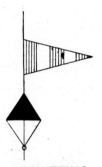

ANSWERING.

Hoist the INTERNATIONAL CODE FLAG with a CONE below it. This signifies *I am able to understand the F.S. Code, and am ready to take in your message in International Code.*

This is to be kept up the whole of the time the signalling is being received. In case there is any difficulty in reading the signals, then this answering signal is to be lowered to the dip. This signifies "*Repeat Message.*"

PROCEDURE.

The ships communicating then proceeds as follows:

First hoist.—The identification signal for the nationality of ship or ships sighted.

Second hoist.—Identification letters of ships that it is desired to indicate.

Signals to be hoisted where they can be best seen.

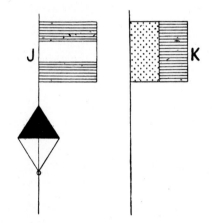

First hoist.   *Second hoist.*

The significance of this signal is:—"*I have sighted the Japanese warship (J cone) Fuji (K).*"

NOTES.

If several ships of one class are to be indicated, a numeral should be hoisted *under* the cone of the first hoist. *Any flag under a cone has numerical significance and no numeral flag is required.* (*See Examples*).

If several ships of two or more classes are to be indicated, the necessary signals for two or three classes can be made as per example with a long tack between each combination.

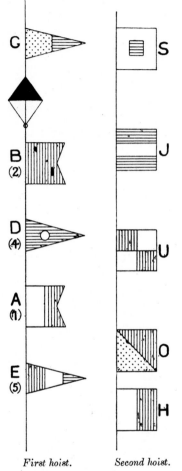

First hoist.   *Second hoist.*

The significance of this signal is:—"*I have sighted a fleet of German warships, consisting of the following vessels:*—

    2 Braunschweig class,
    4 Wittelsbach class,
    1 Prinz Adalbert class,
    5 Siegfried class."

The special nationality signals are:

A cone,	Austro-Hungarian.
B „	British.
C „	Chilian.
D „	Danish.
E „	Argentine.
F „	French.
G „	German.
H „	Dutch.
I „	Italian.
J „	Japanese.
K „	Chinese.
M „	Swedish.
N „	Norwegian.
P „	Portuguese.
R „	Russian.
S „	Spanish.
T „	Turkish.
U „	United States.
Z „	Brazilian.
X „	*Unknown Nationality.*

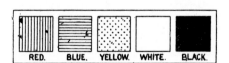

(Key to colour symbols used in these illustrations).

SUBSTITUTES.

Substitutes for use with this code are:

1st substitute.—INTERNATIONAL CODE FLAG.

2nd substitute.—OWN ENSIGN.

3rd substitute.—PILOT-BOAT FLAG or PILOT JACK.

4th substitute.—A ball.

(*See examples on next page*).

SIGNAL SYSTEM.

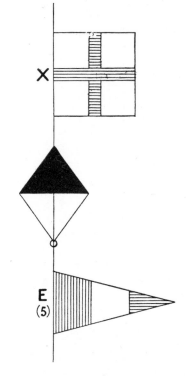

The significance of this signal is "*I have sighted a German squadron, consisting of 7 Siegfried class, 2 Roon class, 2 Bremen class.*"

TO CEASE COMMUNICATION.

The hauling down of the CONES indicate that F. S. code signalling is completed, and any further signals will be in International Code in the usual manner.

This applies to communications as to latitude and longitude of ships sighted, course, etc., etc., etc.

SIGNALS OF SPECIAL SIGNIFICANCE.

Doubt.—(1) Any hoist *at the dip* signifies that the sender is uncertain as to the accuracy of the information that he is imparting.

(2.) If unable to recognise the nationality of the fleet sighted, the sender hoists the special signal provided (**X** cone) with, below it the numeral for ships sighted. (*Single hoist*).

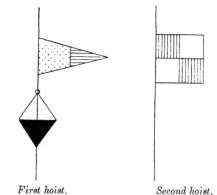

(3.) If able to recognise nationality, but unable to identify any ship or ships, the cone in the first hoist is hoisted *upside down*, and in the second hoist the identification letter or letters of the ship silhouette *most like the unknown vessel.*

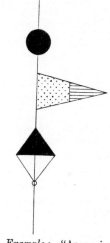

First hoist.　　　Second hoist.

The significance of this signal is "*I have sighted an unknown German vessel more like the P. Adalbert class than any other.*"

(4). The special signal for a flotilla of torpedo craft is a **T** immediately following the nationality letter and superior to the cone. For submarines an **S**.

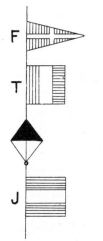

Example: *Single hoist only.*

The significance of this signal is "*I have sighted a flotilla of 10 French Torpedo boats.*"

SPECIAL SIGNALLING BETWEEN WARSHIPS.

When for any reason warships wish to use this Code between themselves, the JACK is to be hoisted instead of the ENSIGN in conjunction with the CONE for the Preparative.

The significance of this signal is that the Service Flags will be used instead of International Code Flags.

The usual service alphabetical flags and numeral pennants will then be used, together with the proper service substitutes when required.

Otherwise the general directions given above to be adhered to.

GENERAL NOTE.

In order to prevent confusion between this and the 1905 system, till 31st December, 1906, every first hoist should begin with a ball, to indicate that the 1906 system is in use. On and after 1st January, 1907, this ball will not be required.

Example : "Answering."

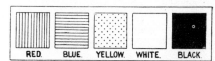

(Key to colour symbols used in these illustrations.)

LONG DISTANCE SIGNAL SYSTEM.

LONG DISTANCE SYSTEM.

Cones, balls or square flags may be used *indifferently* : significance is entirely a matter of *position.**

There are six positions.   These are :

(1.) *In a ship end on* :
1 and 2 ends of topsail yard.
3 and 4 ends of lower yard.
5 and 6 at the dip from lower yard.
(well clear of the bridge).

(2.) *In a ship broadside on.* The triatic stay takes the place of the topsail yard. Positions 3 and 4 about the level of the tops. Positions 5 and 6 just clear of the upper works. (Keep well clear of the masts and rigging).

* This system is based upon the fact that at great distances it is impossible to distinguish with certainty a ball from a cone—hence the absence of significance in objects.

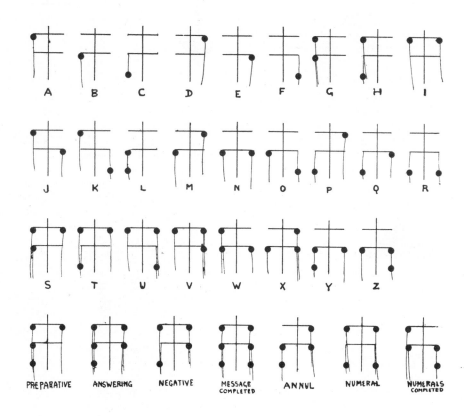

PROCEDURE.

Hoist preparative.—On the answering being made haul down preparative and proceed with the signal, not more than one letter being made at a time.

The alphabet is as per accompanying illustration.

Signals are of course always to be made so that they *are read* as they appear here.

The combination need not be made up of the same object : thus the preparative may be made up of two cones, a square flag and a ball instead of four balls, cones or square flags.

A cone at the *masthead* always has the significance of the cone in the flag signal identification system and denotes nationality signals about to be made. Hauling down this cone indicates that remaining signals do not denote nationality.

For the cone in the nationality signals, hoist the NUMERAL combination, and NUMERALS COMPLETED when the equivalent of the first hoist is completed.

Pennants are not to be used as objects, but, when the distance is very great or the light poor a long pennant may be flown from the lower yard (or at level with the fore-top) so as more clearly to indicate the positions.

NIGHT SIGNALLING.

Use *red* or *white* lamps with a *green* lamp for the long pennant.

DIXON BROS. & HUTCHINSON, L^{TD.}

SOUTHAMPTON, ENGLAND . .

'TELEPHONE No. 389.

TELEGRAMS:
   "CYLINDER, SOUTHAMPTON."

CODE: A.B.C.

Designers and Builders of all classes of

MOTOR LAUNCHES, with Motors complete.

NAVAL LAUNCHES, SHIPS' BOATS, .

YACHTS' BOATS, PLEASURE CRAFT, .

BOTH FOR RACING AND CRUISING.

ONLY HIGH-CLASS WORK UNDERTAKEN . . . .

MODERN BOAT SLIP FOR HAULING-UP AND REPAIRS.

THE PARSONS MARINE STEAM TURBINE

Suitable for Vessels of the Mercantile Marine, Yachts and War Vessels of about 15 knots speed and upwards.

H. M. S. "AMETHYST"—SPEED ATTAINED 23·63 KNOTS.

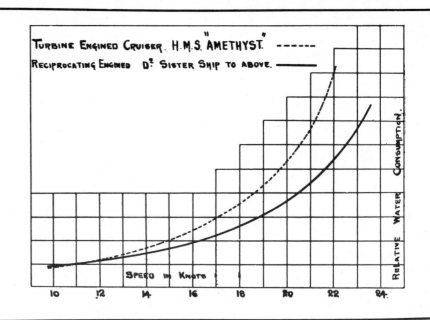

ADVANTAGES OF TURBINE SYSTEM:

Absence of Vibration.

Increased Economy of Coal Consumption.

Reduced Cost of Attendance on Machinery.

Reduced Consumption of Oil and Stores.

Reduced Diameter of Propellers, gives increased facilities for Navigating in Shallow Water and reduces Racing of Propellers.

THE PARSONS PATENT VACUUM AUGMENTOR.

The higher the condenser vacuum the greater the efficiency of the turbine. The Parsons Vacuum Augmentor will maintain a very high vacuum, practically equal to the limit imposed by the temperature of the cooling water, without any increase in the size of the air pump.

The Augmentor consists of a small steam jet placed in the contracted portion of a pipe led from the bottom of the condenser. The jet draws air from the condenser and delivers it to the air pump through a small auxiliary cooler. By this means the air in the condenser is reduced to a negligible quantity, and the vacuum in the condensers can be higher than in the air pump, thus increasing the efficiency of the machinery by from 5 to 8%.

For further particulars apply to

The Parsons Marine Steam Turbine Co. Ltd.,

TELEGRAPHIC ADDRESS:
" TURBINIA," WALLSEND.

Turbinia Works, WALLSEND-ON-TYNE.

ALPHABETICAL INDEX.

D

ALPHABETICAL INDEX.

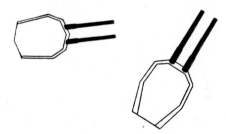

BRITISH FLEET.

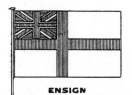

ENSIGN   JACK   ADMIRAL   VICE ADMIRAL   REAR ADMIRAL

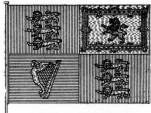 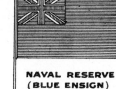 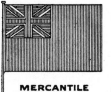 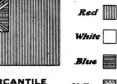

ROYAL STANDARD   NAVAL RESERVE (BLUE ENSIGN)   MERCANTILE ENSIGN (RED ENSIGN)

Red ▦
White ☐
Blue ▦
Yellow ▦

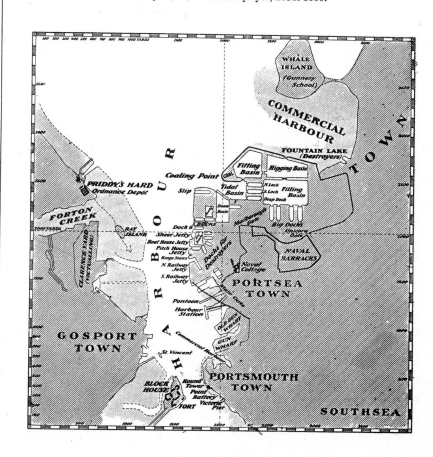

ROSYTH		
	to	knots.
Aberdeen	...	95
Dover	...	473
Helder	...	360
Hull	...	260
Kronstadt	...	1345
Newcastle	...	130
Portsmouth	...	570
Sheerness	...	458
Wilhelmshaven		445

SHEERNESS		
	to	knots.
Dover	...	45
Dunkirk	...	70
Helder	...	190
Hull	...	200
Kronstadt	...	1200
Newcastle	...	328
Portsmouth	...	150
Wilhelmshaven		270

PORTSMOUTH		
	to	knots.
Barbadoes	...	3600
Berehaven	...	375
Brest	...	226
Cherbourg	...	72
Devonport	...	155
Gibraltar	...	1200
Lorient	...	331
New York	...	3080
Pernambuco	...	3900

Portland	...	55
Wilhelmshaven		620

DEVONPORT		
	to	knots.
Berehaven	...	375
Brest	...	140
Cape of Good Hope	...	5890
Cherbourg	...	110
Gibraltar	...	1050
Lorient	...	233
New York	...	2905
Portland	...	100
Queenstown	...	292
Rochefort	...	370
Toulon	...	1764

GIBRALTAR		
	to	knots.
Ajaccio	...	1000
Algiers	...	420
Berehaven	...	1170
Biserta	...	875
Brest	...	953
Devonport	...	1050
Malta	...	980
Oran	...	225
Toulon	...	713

MALTA		
	to	knots.
Aden	...	2320
Ajaccio	...	450
Biserta	...	430

Constantinople	...	702
Port Said	...	920
Sevastopol	...	1000
Spezia	...	580
Suda Bay	...	575
Suez	...	1010
Toulon	...	612

ADEN		
	to	knots.
Batavia	...	3950
Beira	...	2824
Bombay	...	1652
Cape Town	...	4450
Colombo	...	2100
Delagoa Bay	...	3340
Devonport	...	4350
Durban	...	3650
Karachi	...	1470
Mauritius	...	2600
Suez	...	1310
Tamatave	...	2290
Zanzibar	...	1770

COLOMBO		
	to	knots.
Bombay	...	900
Calcutta	...	1240
Devonport	...	6450
Fremantle (W.A.)	...	3105
Karachi	...	1400
Penang	...	1280
Rangoon	...	1207

Singapore	...	1600
Sydney(N.S.W.)		5450

SINGAPORE		
	to	knots.
Bangkok	...	820
Batavia	...	500
Devonport	...	8020
Hong Kong	...	1430
Manila	...	1320
Saigon	...	648

HONG-KONG		
	to	knots.
Devonport	...	9450
Kiao-chau	...	1270
Manila	...	650
Nagasaki	...	1067
Port Arthur	...	1415
Saigon	...	930
Shanghai	...	870
Ta-kau (Formosa)		340
Vladivostock	...	1927
Wei-hai-wei	...	1470
Yokosuka	...	1620

CAPE OF GOOD HOPE		
	to	knots.
Ascension	...	2395
Durban	...	812
Falkland Isles		4800
Fremantle (W.A.)	...	4850
Hobart	...	5527

Madagascar	...	1800
Port Elizabeth		428
Portsmouth	...	5960
St. Helena	...	1710
Teneriffe	...	4470

ESQUIMAULT		
	to	knots.
Honolulu	...	2410
San Francisco	...	750
Seattle	...	76
Yokosuka	...	4300

SYDNEY (N.S.W.)		
	to	knots.
Adelaide	...	1076
Auckland	...	1280
Batavia	...	4476
Brisbane	...	510
Cape of Good Hope	...	6157
Colombo	...	5450
Devonport (via Cape)		12,047
Hobart	...	630
Melbourne	...	570
Singapore	...	4980
Wellington, (N.Z.)	...	1234

29

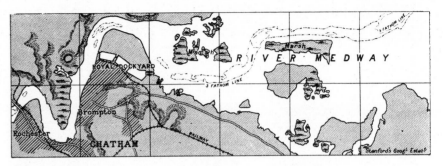

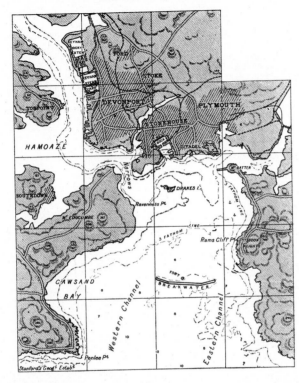

Divided into 2000 yard squares.

Soundings in fathoms.

Heights in feet.

2. DEVONPORT and KEYHAM. At *Devonport*—two big slips, three small. Dry docks:— No. 3, able to take any 15,000 ton battleship, 430 × 93 × 34¾ feet, and three others, of which one (Long Dock) can take a second class cruiser; other two suitable for small craft only. At *Keyham*—No slips. New basin, 35½ acres, depth, 32½ft. Tidal basin, 10 acres, depth, 32ft. Docks in New Extension :—

Entrance lock, able to take any ship, size 730 × 95 × 44 feet.
No. 5 (double)   ,,   ,,   ,,   745 × 95 × 32 ,,
,, 6 (double)   ,,   ,,   ,,   741 × 95 × 44 ,,
,, 4   ,,   any battleship ,, 460 × 95 × 32 ,,

In the old part of the yard there are three docks, of which one (Queen's) can take a second class cruiser; the others small craft only. Total employees for the two yards, about 6000.

3. CHATHAM. Three building slips. Three large closed basins. Dry docks :—
New dock, able to take any ship,   size, 800 × 100 × 33 feet.
No. 8   ,,   ,, battleship, ,, 456 × 82 × 33   ,,
,, 7   ,,   ,,   ,,   ,, 456 × 82 × 32½ ,,
,, 6   ,,   ,,   ,,   ,, 456 × 80 × 32½ ,,
,, 5   ,,   ,,   ,,   ,, 456 × 80 × 32½ ,,
North Lock ,,   ,,   ,,   ,, 477 × 94½ × 34½ ,,
South Lock ,,   ,,   ,,   ,, 479 × 84½ × 33 ,,
There are four other docks suitable only for small craft (Nos. 1, 2, 3, 4). Total employees about 6000.

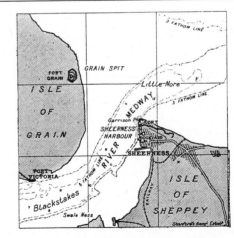

4. SHEERNESS. No slips. One small basin. Dry docks :—Five, all small, and able to take small craft only. Destroyer base.

BRITISH HOME DOCKYARDS AND NAVAL HARBOURS.

(All maps divided into 2000 yard squares. Soundings in fathoms. Heights in feet).

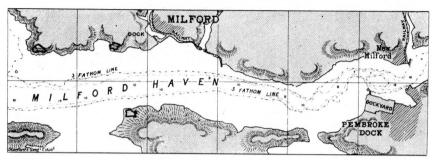

5. PEMBROKE.   Building yard.   Two large slips.   Dry docks:—One, able to take a second class cruiser, 404 × 75 × 25¼ feet.

6. HAULBOWLINE.   No slips.   Dry docks:—
    Entrance, able to take any warship,   size 720 × 94 × 32½ feet.
    No 1.   „   „   battleship, „   425 × 94 × 32½ „

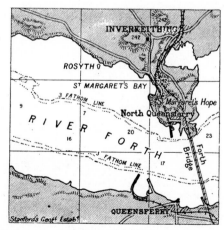

7. ROSYTH (constructing).   One dock to take any warship, *pro.*   Large basin (365 × 460) *constructing.*

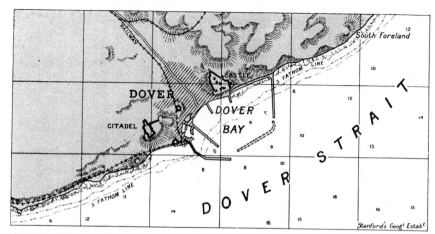

DOVER (*building*).   New harbour, 610 acres; depth of 30 feet at low water over half the area. E. entrance, 1 cable; W. entrance, 800 feet.   Coaling station.   Well fortified.

    Moorings for 16 battleships, 5 large cruisers, 7 *Counties*, 4 small cruisers, and for destroyers.

Other Naval Harbours in Home Waters.

BEREHAVEN.   Good anchorage.

PORTLAND.   Base for Channel Fleet.   1500 acres of enclosed harbour; minimum depth, 30 feet.   Coaling station.   N. and E. entrances 700 feet wide.   Impregnable fortifications.

SCILLY (*projected* harbour of refuge).   The anchorage is moderately good.   The entrance is very narrow, difficult and dangerous.   Fortifications are being erected.

LOUGH SWILLY (harbour of refuge).   Very moderately fortified.   Good anchorage.

KINGSTOWN (DUBLIN), TORBAY, FALMOUTH, are other commodious anchorages used by fleets.   Only the first has any forts.

BRITISH COMMERCIAL HARBOURS AND BIG PRIVATE SHIPBUILDING FIRMS.

British Private Docks, at Home and Abroad, able to take Large British Warships.

HEBBURN (Floating),	able to take	*Drake* or *Duncan*,	size, 700 × 90 × $28\frac{1}{2}$ feet.
SUNDERLAND (No. 3) (bldg.)	able to take	any warship,	,, *700 × 80 × 35* ,,
TILBURY (No. 1)	,,	*County* class	,, 868 × 70 × 35 ,,
SOUTHAMPTON (No. 5)	,,	any warship	,, 745 × 91 × 35 ,,
,, (No. 6)	,,	,,	,, 800 × 90 × 33 ,,
,, (No. 3)	,,	*Duncan* or *Cressy*	,, 516 × 80 × $27\frac{1}{4}$,,
MILFORD (Dry dock)	,,	*County* class	,, 600 × 70 × 34 ,,
LIVERPOOL (Canada Graving)	,,	any warship	,, 925 × 94 × 32 ,,
BIRKENHEAD (S. dock)	,,	*Drake* or *Duncan*	,, 720 × 100 × $28\frac{1}{2}$,,
GLASGOW (Clyde Trust, No. 3)	,,	*County* class	,, 865 × 83 × $26\frac{1}{2}$,,
BELFAST (No. 1) (bldg.)	,,	any warship	,, *750 × 95 × 32* ,,
(No. 2) ,,	,,	,,	,, *750 × 96 × $32\frac{1}{2}$* ,,
COLOMBO (Dry dock)	,,	,,	,, 600 × 85 × 32 ,,
HALIFAX (N.S.) Graving	,,	,,	,, 600 × 89 × 30 ,,
AUCKLAND (N.Z.) Calliope dock	,,	*Cressy* class	,, 500 × 80 × 33 ,,

---

Principal Commercial Harbours.

(In order of importance, with tons of shipping clearing).

London (8 million); Cardiff ($6\frac{3}{4}$ million); Liverpool ($6\frac{1}{2}$ million); Newcastle and district ($4\frac{1}{2}$ million); Hull ($2\frac{1}{4}$ million); Glasgow (2 million); Southampton ($1\frac{1}{2}$ million); and Newport, Blyth, Swansea, Sunderland, Leith, Dover, Kirkcaldy, Grimsby, Middlesbrough, Grangemouth (all doing about 1 million); Harwich, Manchester, Bristol, Goole, Hartlepool, Belfast, and Folkestone (all doing from $\frac{3}{4}$ to $\frac{1}{4}$ million).

The naval harbours abroad are mostly all important mercantile ports.

Mercantile Marine.

About 36,000 vessels (about 8,000,000 tons steamers and about 3,000,000 tons sailing).

Personnel: 257,937 (of which 41,021 are Lascars, &c., and 40,396 of other foreign nationalities).

Principal Private Yards.

(From N. round East Coast, South Coast, to North again).

[*Note.*—By "big slip" one able to build any warship is meant].

1. ARMSTRONG-WHITWORTH (Elswick & Walker), Eight large slips, seven small. Employees, including gun works, etc., *circa* 25,000.
2. PALMER'S (Jarrow). Six slips. Employees 7000. (Has one dock, 440 × 70 × 18 feet; also patent slipway—both used by warships).
3. HAWTHORN-LESLIE (Hebburn). Seven slips up to 680 feet long. Employees 3000. (Has one dock, 450 × 68 × 21 feet). 26 feet draught at quay at low water. Engine department of 100,000 I.H.P. per annum.

Note.—There is a dock on the Tyne (Tyne Pontoons) that has taken a first-class battleship; and one to take any warship in the world completed during 1904.

4. DOXFORD (Sunderland). (Undergoing extensive alterations).
5. THAMES IRONWORKS (Canning Town). Six slips. One dry dock 475 × 65, one 335 × 46 feet. No docks for big ships in the district. Employees 3000 at Canning Town, 1000 at Greenwich and Deptford.
6. YARROW (Isle of Dogs, Poplar). Destroyer and torpedo boat yard. Employees 1500. (Removing to Belfast).
7. THORNYCROFT (Chiswick). Destroyer and torpedo boat yard. Employees 1000.
8. WHITE (Cowes). Destroyer and torpedo boat yard. Employees
9. LAIRD (Birkenhead). Two big slips, five small slips. Three medium docks able to take *County* class at a pinch; two small. Two docks able to take almost any warship existing in the Mersey (see list of big private docks). Employees 3500.
10. VICKERS-MAXIM (Barrow). Six big slips, six small slips. No docks in yard, but there is a small dock in the town 500 × 60 × 22 feet. Employees: shipbuilding, *circa* 3950; gun-mounting department, 2830; machinery, &c., 3750.
11. HARLAND & WOLFF (Belfast). Six big slips, three smaller. There are one large (825 × 80 × 26 feet) and three small docks in the district. Big liners are constructed here, the only Government work being machinery. Employees 12,000.
12. JOHN BROWN & CO., Ltd., (Clydebank). Nine big slips. Employees 7000—8000.
13. FAIRFIELD CO. (Glasgow). big slips, smaller. Employees *circa*
14. LONDON & GLASGOW CO. (Govan). Three big slips, three smaller. Employees 3000.
15. WM. BEARDMORE & CO., Ltd. (late NAPIER) (Govan). Three big slips, two smaller. Employees *circa* 3000. (Same company as Vickers Maxim).
    (Dalmuir, new yard). Six big slips, four smaller. Employees *circa* 10,000. This yard is designed for vessels up to 900 feet long. 200-ton crane. Fitting basin 28 feet at low water.

(*Note.*—In the Clyde district are two large docks which could accommodate any warship in existence *if sufficiently lightened*.

16. SCOTTS' SHIPBUILDING & ENGINEERING CO., Ltd. (Greenock). Slips for six large and four small vessels; fitting-out basin, 540 × 172 feet, equipped with 120 ton electric jib crane on one side, and a 80 ton electric travelling crane on the other; the depth of water at lowest Spring tides is 28 feet. Graving dock 369 feet long × 48 feet at the top, and 42 feet at the bottom. Men employed: Shipyard, 2,000 to 3,000; Engine Works, 1,500 to 2,000.
17. HANNA, DONALD & WILSON (Paisley). Destroyer and torpedo boat yard.
    (There are 27 other firms which do not do Government work).

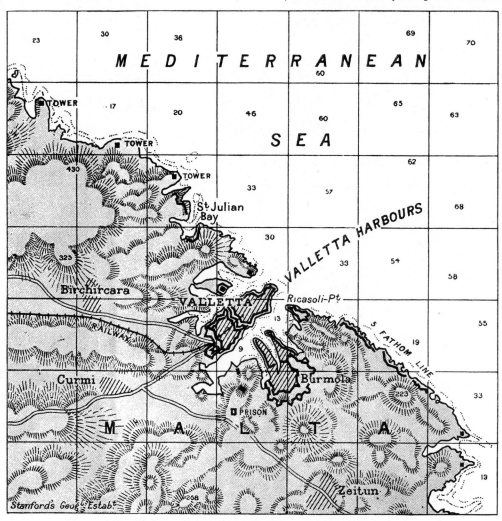

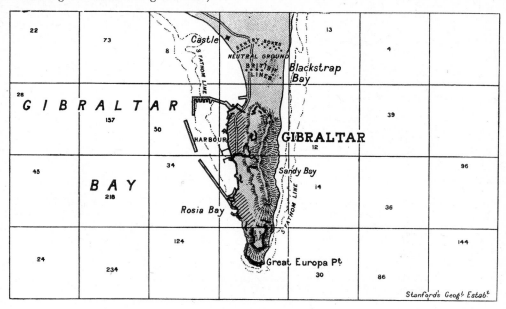

GIBRALTAR. *West Harbour*—No slips. Dry docks:—
>   No. 1 (King Edward), able to take any warship, size, 850 × 90 × 35½ feet.
>   „ 2,   „   „   „   550 × 90 × 35½ „
>   „ 3,   „   „   battleship, „   450 × 90 × 35½ „

Area of harbour, 450 acres, depth 30 feet at low water.
East Harbour (not yet built).
No. 1 dry dock, able to take any warship, size 850 × 90 × 36 feet.
Area of harbour, 400 acres.
Well fortified—guns mounted 1000 feet above water. Base for Atlantic Fleet.

MALTA. One small building slip. Dry docks (only Nos. 3 & 4 yet complete):—
>   No. 4 (Hamilton), able to take any warship, size, 520 × 94 × 35½ feet.
>   „ 3, (Somerset)   „   „   battleship, „   468 × 85 × 34   „
>   „ 2,   „   „   warship,   „   525 × 85 × 25   „
>   „ 1,   „   „   „   „   525 × 85 × 25   „
>   „ 7, (bldg.) (single)   „ any warship, „   550 × 94 × 35½ „
>   „ 5-6, „ (double)   „   „   „   750 × 94 × 35½ „

Area of war harbour, about 100 acres. *New mole in progress—new works to be completed* 1908. Well fortified. Good anchorage. Base for Mediterranean Fleet.

ALEXANDRIA. Protected by a 2-mile breakwater. Coaling. Slight forts. Direct cable communication with Malta, Gibraltar, Crete, Cyprus, Port Said, Suez and Bona. Principal commercial port of Egypt.

E

BRITISH HARBOURS, Etc.—(Indian Ocean)

(Divided into 2000 yard squares. Uniform scale. Soundings in fathoms. Heights in feet.).

ADEN. Well fortified. Coaling. Harbour 8 × 4 miles.

BOMBAY. Harbour 14 × 5 miles. Dry docks:—
Upper Duncan: 302 × 60 × 24 feet.
Lower Duncan: 316 × 60 × 24 „
Merewether: 539 × 65½ × 28¼ „
Ritchie (P. & O.): 495 × 66 × 18 „
Also seven smaller docks.

CALCUTTA. Commercial harbour 80 miles up the Hougli. 10 miles of docks. Dry docks:—
(Port Commissioners) 533 × 70 × 24½ feet; (Caledonia) 363 × 44½ × 23½ feet, and
twelve smaller.

COLOMBO (Ceylon). Fortified Coaling station. Excellent and deep harbour, sheltered by
breakwaters. Dry dock: 600 × 85 × 32 feet.

MADRAS. Commercial port. Average depth of harbour 7 fathoms. Entrance protected by
breakwaters, with entrance 173 yards wide.

MAHÉ (Seychelle Islands). Small coaling station. Commercial harbour, Good and safe
anchorage. Cable to Zanzibar.

MAURITIUS (Port Louis). Good harbour, with awkward entrance. Coaling station. Fortified.
One dry dock: 384 × 60 × 19½ feet, and two smaller.

PENANG (Straits Settlements). Good deep harbour. Coaling station. Dry dock: 343 × 46
× 14½ feet.

RANGOON (Bormah). Commercial harbour. 21 miles up the Trawaddi. 15 to 24 feet at low
water.

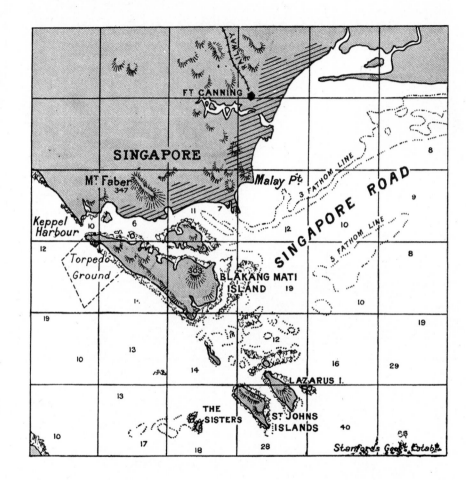

SINGAPORE. Coaling station. Good roads. Average anchorage, 10 fathoms.

SUEZ (Red Sea). Commercial harbour. Dry dock here: 406 × 73¾ × 28½ feet. (Egyptian
Government).

BRITISH HARBOURS, Etc.

(Divided into 2000 yard squares. Uniform scale. Soundings in fathoms. Heights in feet.).

China Station.

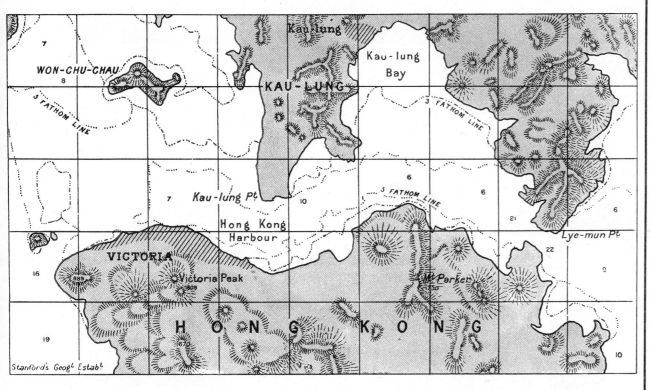

HONG KONG. Repairing yard. No slips. Dry docks :—
    No. 1, able to take any warship, size, 550 × 85 × 29 feet.
    New dock   ,,   ,,   ,,   550 × 95 × 30 ,,
    Also two small docks for small craft.
    Area of basin (tidal), 9¼ acres (bldg.)   Average depth of harbour, 40 feet.

WEI-HAI-WEI (China). Anchorage. Unfortified base. Coaling station.

ESQUIMAULT (British Columbia). Formerly dockyard. Dry dock : 450 × 65 × 26½ feet.

Cape Station.

CAPE COAST CASTLE (British Gold Coast, W. Africa). Fortified coaling station. Anchorage average, 28 feet.

PORT STANLEY (Falkland Is.) Good deep harbour. Fortified coaling station.

ST. HELENA. Fortified coaling station. 10-fathom harbour.

SIERRA LEONE (W. Africa). Fortified coaling station. Anchorage, 6-16 fathoms.

SIMON'S BAY (Cape of Good Hope). New dock, to take any warship, (bldg.) 750 × 95 × 30 feet. Tidal basin (bldg.) 28 acres, 30 feet deep. Fortified moderately. (To be completed 1907).

N. America and West Indies.

BERMUDA. Royal dockyard. Fortified. Large floating dock, 545 × 100 × 33 feet. Shallow harbour. New works in progress, to be completed 1906-7.

BRIDGETOWN (Barbadoes). Coaling. Open roadstead.

HALIFAX (Nova Scotia). Formerly Dockyard. Coaling station. Anchorage average, 13 fathoms. Dry dock : 600 × 89 × 30 feet.

Australian Station.

ADELAIDE (S. Australia). Commercial harbour, 7 miles from the town. Dry dock : 500 × 60 × 26 feet.

AUCKLAND (New Zealand). Coaling station. Excellent harbour ; average 40 feet deep. Dry dock (Calliope) : 500 × 80 × 33 feet.

BRISBANE (Queensland, Australia). 25 miles up river. Navigable for ships drawing 20 feet. Coaling station. Dry dock : 457 × 60 × 18 feet, and one small.

HOBART (Tasmania). Coaling station. Anchorage average, 10 fathoms.

KING GEORGE SOUND (W. Australia). Coaling station. Fortified.

SYDNEY (N.S.W., Australia). Fortified coaling station and base. Harbour excellent. Bar 27 feet at low water. Dry docks : (Sutherland) 638 × 84 × 32 feet, (Fitzroy) 482 × 59 × 21½ feet, and four smaller.

MELBOURNE. Commercial harbour. One dry dock : 470 × 80 × 27 feet, and three smaller. Port Philip has an area of 800 square miles.

HO   TRAFALGAR *class* (*page* 54) (2 *ships*).
(*Note funnels. Note also that they are very wide apart in these two ships, and look like two fore and aft if the ship is not seen full broadside. Nile has higher funnels than Trafalgar.*)

HR   HOOD (*page* 53).
(*Low freeboard, otherwise like Royal Sovereigns*).

HS   ROYAL SOVEREIGN *class* (*page* 52) (7 *ships*).
(*Funnels very wide apart, look like two fore and aft, if the ship is not full broadside*).

HT   CENTURION *class* (*page* 55) (2 *ships*).

I   MAJESTIC *class* (*page* 51) (9 *ships*).

IN   RENOWN (*page* 56).
(*Note maintop*).

J   QUEEN, LONDON & FORMIDABLE *classes* (*pages* 46, 47 & 48) (8 *ships*).
(*Fore funnel close to foremast*).

K   DUNCAN *class* (*page* 49) (6 *ships*).
(*Bigger funnels than Formidables*).

L   CANOPUS *class* (*page* 50) (6 *ships*).
(*Funnels close together, compare with Formidables*).

M   KING EDWARD *class* (*page* 44) (7 *ships*).

M   KING EDWARD *class* (1 *ship—Britannia*).

N   SWIFTSURE *class* (*page* 45) (2 *ships*).

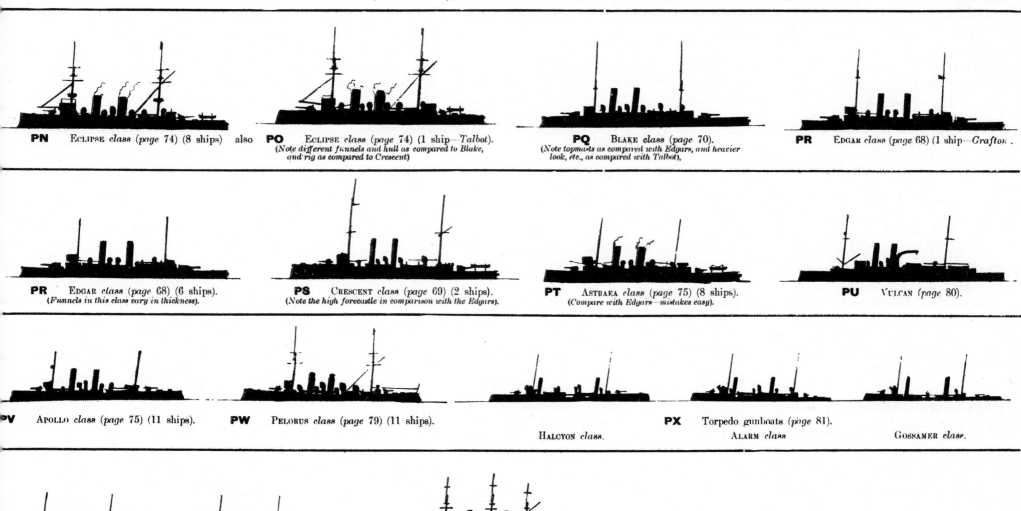

PN   ECLIPSE *class* (*page* 74) (8 ships)   also   **PO**   ECLIPSE *class* (*page* 74) (1 ship—*Talbot*).
(*Note different funnels and hull as compared to Blake, and rig as compared to Crescent*)

PQ   BLAKE *class* (*page* 70).
(*Note topmasts as compared with Edgars, and heavier look, etc., as compared with Talbot*),

PR   EDGAR *class* (*page* 68) (1 ship—*Grafton*).

PR   EDGAR *class* (*page* 68) (6 ships).
(*Funnels in this class vary in thickness*).

PS   CRESCENT *class* (*page* 69) (2 ships).
(*Note the high forecastle in comparison with the Edgars*).

PT   ASTRAEA *class* (*page* 75) (8 ships).
(*Compare with Edgars—mistakes easy*).

PU   VULCAN (*page* 80).

PV   APOLLO *class* (*page* 75) (11 ships).

PW   PELORUS *class* (*page* 79) (11 ships).

PX   Torpedo gunboats (*page* 81).

HALCYON *class*.

ALARM *class*

GOSSAMER *class*.

PX   Torpedo gunboats (*page* 81).

SEAGULL.

SHARPSHOOTER.

PZ   BARHAM (*page* 80).

R   Monmouth *class* (*page* 64).

RM   Challenger and Highflyer *class* (*page* 72 and 73).

RN   Arrogant *class* (*page* 71).
(Note fighting top on fore only).

RO   Gem *class* (*page* 76).

RP   Speedy (*page* 81).

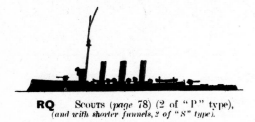

RQ   Scouts (*page* 78) (2 of " P " type),
(and with shorter funnels, 2 of " S " type).

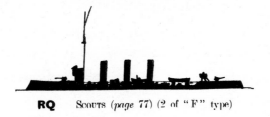

RQ   Scouts (*page* 77) (2 of " F " type)

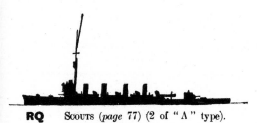

RQ Scouts (*page 77*) (2 of "A" type).

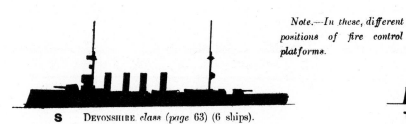

S Devonshire *class* (*page 63*) (6 ships).

Note.—In these, different positions of fire control platforms.

T Duke of Edinburgh *class* (*pages 60 and 59*) (2 + 4 ships).

V Drake *class* (*page 61*) (4 ships).
(*Note.—Only Drake is without afterbridge*).

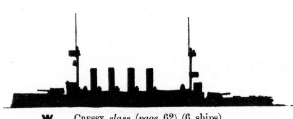

W Cressy *class* (*page 62*) (6 ships).
(*Funnels closer than in Drake class*).

WL Ariadne *class* (*page 66*) (4 ships).
(*Distinguished from Cressy class by absence of big guns forward and aft*).

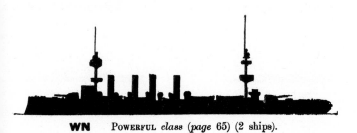

WN Powerful *class* (*page 65*) (2 ships).

WO Diadem *class* (*page 67*) (4 ships).

TWO FUNNELS.

J   Taku t. b. d.   **K**   River *class* t. b. d.   **L**   30 knot t. b. d.   **M**   27 knot t. b. d.   **N**   Modern t. b.

THREE FUNNELS.

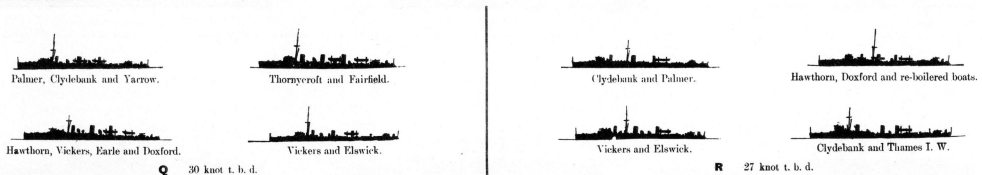

Palmer, Clydebank and Yarrow.   Thornycroft and Fairfield.   Clydebank and Palmer.   Hawthorn, Doxford and re-boilered boats.

Hawthorn, Vickers, Earle and Doxford.   Vickers and Elswick.   Vickers and Elswick.   Clydebank and Thames I. W.

Q   30 knot t. b. d.   **R**   27 knot t. b. d.

FOUR FUNNELS.

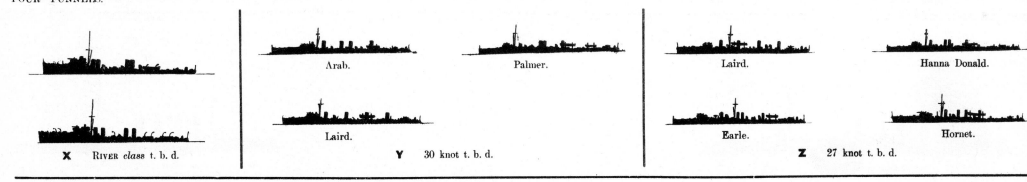

Arab.   Palmer.   Laird.   Hanna Donald.

Laird.   Earle.   Hornet.

X   River *class* t. b. d.   **Y**   30 knot t. b. d.   **Z**   27 knot t. b. d.

ROYAL NAVY.

Personnel: About 129,000 and 23,000 Fleet Reserve, and about 30,000 R. N. R. and R. N. Volunteers.

Colour of ships: Light grey all over; destroyers, black, except in hot climates.

Sea Lords of the Admiralty: Admiral of the Fleet, Sir John Fisher; Vice-Ad. Sir C. Drury, Captain Jackson (Controller), Captain Inglefield.

Chief Constructor: Sir Philip Watts.

TORPEDOES.

18 inch and 14 inch Whiteheads. All fitted with gyros.

| Name or Mark. | Pressure. | Charge. | Max. Range. | Average Speed if set for | | |
				1000	2000	4000
inch.		lbs.	yds.	kts.	kts.	kts.
18 Model '04 "Fiume III"	2150	205	4000	33	27	19
18 3 cylinder R.G.F., Mark V*	2000	205	4000	31	26	18
18 3 cylinder R.G.F., Mark V	1700	205	2000	26	24	
18 3 cylinder R.G.F., Mark IV	1700	190	2000	26	19	
14 Marks X* and XI	2000	97	2000	28	20	
14 Earlier patterns	2000	97	2000	26	16	

Uniforms.

Admiral   Vice-Admiral   Rear-Admiral   Commodore   Captain   Commander   Lieutenant   Lieutenant (over 8 years)   Lieutenant (under 8 years)   Sub-Lieutenant

Admiral of the fleet one stripe more than a full Admiral.

In relative ranks, Engineers have the same *without the curl*, and with purple between the stripes.

"	"	Doctors	"	"	"	red	"	"
"	"	Paymasters	"	"	"	white	"	"
"	"	Naval Instructors	"	"	"	blue	"	"

Engineer officers have executive titles.

Naval Guns.

| Notation. | Calibre. | Mark. | Length in calibres. | Weight of gun. | Weight of A.P. projectile. | Initial velocity. | Maximum penetration with A.P. capped at K.C. | | Danger space for average ship at | | | Average rate of fire. rounds per minute. |
							5000	3000	10,000 yards.	5000 yards.	3000 yards.	
	inches.			tons.	lbs.	f.s.	inches.	inches.	yards.	yards.	yards.	
AA	13·5	...	30	67	1250	2016	9	12	105	300	540	·4
AAAAA	12	XI.	45		850	2900 (M.D.)	17½	22				1
AAAA	12	IX.	40	50	850	2750 (M.D.)	16	20	150	540	800	1
AAA	12	VIII.	35	46	850	2367 (c.)	11½	14½	150	390	620	1
AAA	10	new	45	32½	500	2800 (M.D.)	11½	14½	150	480	720	1
B	10	old	32	29	500	2040 (c.)	5½	7½	90	270	540	·6
AAA	9·2		50	30	380	2800 (M.D.)	10	13				
AA	9·2	IX. & X.	45	27	380	2640 (c.)	8¾	11¼	147	420	630	2-3
A	9·2	VIII.	40	25	380	2347 (c.)	6¾	9¼	111	360	600	2-3
D	9·2	VII.-III.	30	24	380	2065 (c.)	4	6½				·8
A	7·5	II.	50	16	200	2800 (M.D)	6½	9¼	105	420	600	2-3
B	7·5	I.	45	14	200	2600 (c.)	5¾	7½				2-3
C	6	IX. & X.	50	7½	100	2800 (M.D.)	4	5½	75	250	475	7
D	6	VII.-VIII.	45	7½	100	2535 (c.)	3	4½	66	210	435	7
E	6	wire	40	7	100	2200 (c.)			37	150	360	8
F	4·7	wire	40	2	40	2188 (c.)			...	...	...	
F	4	wire	40	1⅓	25	2300 (c.)			...	...	...	
F	3·5	...	...		18	— (M.D).			...	...	...	
F	3	12 pdr.	28	12 cwt.	12	2200 (c.)			...	...	...	

F

DREADNOUGHT (February, 1906) & Others pro.

Displacement *about* 18,000 tons. Complement

Length (*waterline*), 520 feet. Beam, 82 feet. *Maximum* draught,   feet.

Guns :
10—12 inch, XI. (*AAAAA*).
27—12 pdrs.
Torpedo tubes :
4 *submerged* (broadside).
1 *submerged* (stern).

Armour :
11″ Belt (amidships) ... *aaa*
  ″ Belt (forward) ......
  ″ Belt (aft) ....

DREADNOUGHT after launch.

Photo, Symonds & Co.

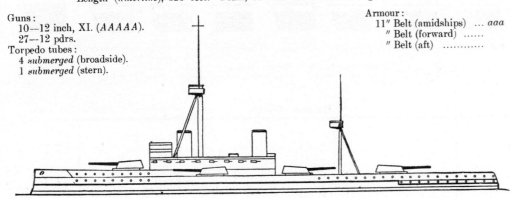

Ahead :
6—12 in.

Astern :
6—12 in.

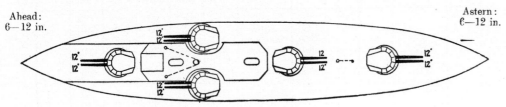

Broadside : 8—12 in.

Machinery : Parsons' Turbine. 4 screws.
Designed H.P. 23,000 = 21 kts.

Boilers : Babcock.

Note.—In accordance with Admiralty request, the usual details of armour, gun fittings, hull, etc., are omitted.

Name.	Built at	Machinery by	Laid down.	To be completed.	Trials.	Boilers.
Dreadnought	Portsmouth	Vickers	Sept., '05	1907		Babcock
A	Portsmouth		To be '06			
B	Devonport		To be '06			

General Notes.—Dreadnought, estimates 1905-6.

NEW BRITISH BATTLESHIPS (18½ knot).

(Lord Nelson Class—2 Ships).

LORD NELSON (1905), & *AGAMEMNON* (1905).

Displacement 16,600 tons.   Complement——.

Length (*p.p.*), 406½ feet.   Beam, 79 feet.   *Maximum* draught——.

Guns :
  4—12 inch, IX., (*AAAA*).
  10—9·2 inch, XI., (*AAA*).
  18—3·5 inch (*F*).
  6—3 pdr.
  6—Pompoms.
  2 Maxims.
Torpedo tubes(18in.) ('04 M) :
  4 *submerged* (broadside).
  1 *submerged* (stern).

Armour (Krupp) :
  12″ Belt (amidships) ... *aaa*
  4″ Belt (ends) ....   *d*
  2″ Deck (slopes) ....
  Protection to vitals... =*aaaa*
  14″ Barbettes (N.C.) ...*aaaa*
  8″ Turrets to these ...... =*aa*
  7″ Lower deck side ......   *a*
  7″ Secondary turrets (N.C.) *a*
  12″ Conning tower(N.C.)*aaa*

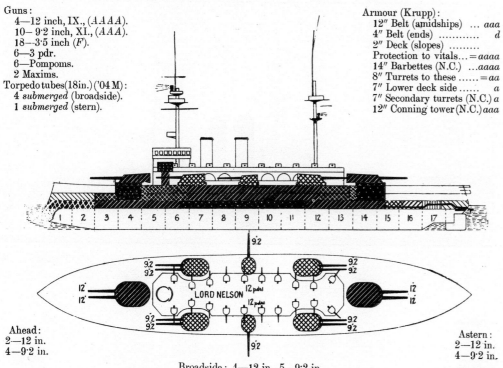

Ahead :
2—12 in.
4—9·2 in.

Astern :
2—12 in.
4—9·2 in.

Broadside : 4—12 in., 5—9·2 in.

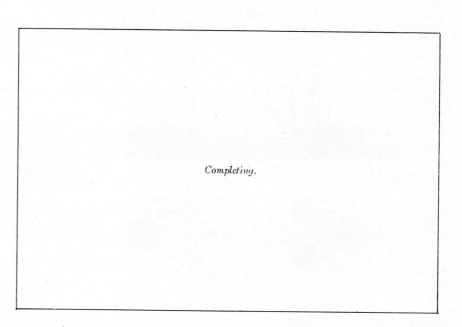

Completing.

Machinery : 2 sets 4 cylinder vertical triple expansion. 2 screws. Boilers : 15 Yarrow or Babcock. Designed H.P. 20,000 = 18·5 kts.   Coal : *normal* 900 tons ; *maximum* 2500 tons : also 400 tons oil.

Gunnery Notes.—Big guns, central pivot mountings. Hoists, electric or hand all guns. Guns manœuvred hydraulic, electric and hand gear.
  Arcs of fire : 12 inch, 240°.

Torpedo Notes.—4000 yard torpedoes. Complete electrical installation.

Engineering Notes.—

Name.	Builder	Boilers and Machinery	Laid down	To be completed			Boilers	
Lord Nelson	Beardmore	Vickers	Nov., '04	1907	...	...	Yarrow	...
Agamemnon	Palmer	Palmer	Oct., '04	1907	...	...	Babcock	...

General Notes.—Estimates 1904-05.   Estimated cost about £1,500,000 per ship.   Designed by Sir P. Watts.
  Laid down, 1904.

(KING EDWARD CLASS – 8 SHIPS).

COMMONWEALTH (May, 1903), **KING EDWARD** (July, 1903), **DOMINION** (August, 1903),
HINDUSTAN (December, 1904), **NEW ZEALAND** (February, 1904), **HIBERNIA** (June, 1905),
AFRICA (1905) and **BRITANNIA** (1905).

Displacement 16350 tons. Complement 777.

Length (*waterline*), 439 feet. Beam, 78 feet. *Mean* draught, 26¾ feet. Length *over all*, 453¾ feet.

Guns :
4—12 in. IX. (*AAAA*)
4—9·2 in., IX. (*AA*)
10—6 in., VII. (*D*)
14—12 pdr. (*F*).
14—3 pdr.
2 Maxims.
Torpedo tubes
(4000 yard.)
4 submerged
(broadside).
1 submerged (stern)

Armour (Krupp) :
9″ Belt (amidships) .... *aa*
6—2″ Belt (forward)............*a-f*
2″ Deck (slopes) ....
Protection to vitals .... = *aaa*
12″ Barbettes (N.C.) ....*aaa*
8″ Turrets to these (K.C.) = *aaa*
8″ Lower deck side .... *aa*
7″ Battery .... *a*
7″ Secondary turrets .... *a*
12″ Conning tower........... *aaa*

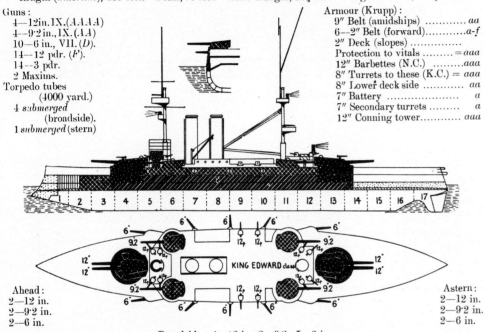

Ahead :
2—12 in.
2—9·2 in.
2—6 in.

Astern :
2—12 in.
2—9·2 in.
2—6 in.

Broadside : 4—12 in., 2—9·2., 5—6 in.

Machinery : 2 sets 4 cylinder triple expansion. 2 screws. Boilers : assorted (*see notes*). Designed H.P. 18000 = 18·5 kts. Coal : *normal* 950 tons ; *maximum* 2150 tons ; *also* 400 tons oil.
Armour Notes.—Main Belt is 7¼ feet wide by about 285 feet long ; lower edge 9″ thick amidships. Main deck 1″ thick ; upper deck ditto amidships.
Gunnery Notes.—Loading positions, big guns all round. Hoists, electric for all guns. Big guns manœuvred electric, hydraulic and hand gear.
Arcs of fire : 12 in., 240° ; 9·2 in., about 135° ; 6 in., 120°.
Torpedo Notes.—4000 yards torpedoes carried. Nearly all round net defence.
Engineering Notes.— 120 revolutions = full power.

Name.	Builder.	Machinery etc. by	Laid down	Completed	30 hours ¾ power.	8 hours full power.	Boilers.	Speed last sea trial.
Commonwealth	Fairfield	Fairfield	June '02	1905	12,769=17·9	18,538=19·01	Babcock	19·4 (*Max.*)
King Edward	Devonport	Harland & W.	Mar. '02	1905	12,884=17·5	18,138=19·04	Babcock, &c.	16·4
Dominion	Vickers	Vickers	May '02	1905	12,843=18·3	18,439=19·35	Babcock	19·3 (*Max.*)
Hindustan	Clydebank	Clydebank	Oct. '02	1905	12,926=17·7	18,521=19·08	Babcock	18·7
New Zealand	Portsmouth	Humphrys & T.	Feb. '03	1905	...	...	Niclausse	18·9
Hibernia	Devonport	Harland & W.	Jan. '04	1906-7	...	...	Babcock	...
Africa	Chatham	Clydebank	Jan. '04	1906-7	...	...	Babcock	...
Britannia	Portsmouth	Humphrys & T.	Feb. '04	1906-7	...	...	Babcock, &c.	...

Coal consumption has been heavy in ships yet tried in service, and especially in *King Edward* which has burned at the rate of about 12 tons an hour at 12,000 H.P., and nearly 18 tons at 18,000 H.P. All were light on first trials.

COMMONWEALTH.   *Photo, Symonds.*

(only flagships carry gaffs and yards on main.)

All alike except *Britannia*, which has a double top on foremast.

Differences.—

Name.	Steam pipes. Fore funnel.	After funnel.	Notes.
Africa			
Britannia			
Commonwealth			
Dominion	abaft	both sides	
Hibernia			
Hindustan			
King Edward	before	both sides	
New Zealand	before	both sides	

Class distinction.—To be recognised at once by rig and by the enormous funnels. No after-bridge.

General Notes.—Tactical diameter very small, about 340 yards at 15 knots. The ships are extremely handy. Cost per ship about £1,500,000. These are the last British battleships designed by Sir William White.

SWIFTSURE & TRIUMPH (January, 1903).

(Purchased from Chili, 1903).

Displacement 11,800 tons.   Complement 700.

Length (*waterline*), 458 feet; Beam, 71 feet; *Maximum* draught, 24⅔ feet; Length (*p.p.*) 436 feet.

Guns :
4—10 inch, 45 cal. (*AAA*).
14—7·5 inch, II., 50 cal. (*A*).
14—14 pdr. (*F*).
2—12 pdr., 8 cwt.
4—6 pdr.
4 Maxims.
Torpedo tubes (Elswick, 18 in.) :
2 *submerged*.

Armour (Krupp) :
7″ Belt (amidships)   ...   *a*
3″ Belt (ends)   ....   ϵ
10″ Bulkheads .... *aaa*
1½″ Deck (amidships) ...
Protection to vitals ......=*aa*
3″ Deck (outside citadel)
10″ Barbettes   ....   *aa*
8″—6″Turrets(K.C)=*aaa-aa*
6″ Lower deck............ *a*
7″ Battery................. *a*
7″ Casemates (4) (N.C.) *a*
10″ Conning tower ...... *aa*

(Total weight: *about* 3200 tons).

SWIFTSURE.

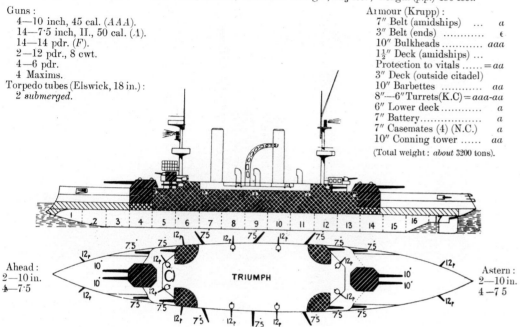

Ahead :
2—10 in.
4—7·5

TRIUMPH

Astern :
2—10 in.
4—7·5

Broadside : 4—10 in., 7—7·5 in.

Machinery : 2 sets triple expansion.   2 screws.   Boilers : 12 Yarrow large tube.   Designed H.P. 14,000=20 kts.   Coal : *normal* 800 tons ; *maximum* 2000 tons.

Armour Notes.—Belt is 15 feet wide, 7″ tapering to 3″, Citadel 260 feet long.   1″. screens in battery.   1″ main deck.   Flat sided K.C. turrets.

Gunnery Notes.—Loading positions, big guns all round, load every position.   Hoists, electric, all guns. All guns manœuvred electrically.   Few safety arrangements to guns.   Excellent sights. Ammunition carried : 10 in., 80 per gun ; 7·5 in., 150 per gun.

Torpedo Notes.—Main deck shelf for nets.   Amidship defence only.

Engineering Notes.—These ships are very fast for short spurts, but cannot maintain speed for any length of time or in any sea way.   At full power the vibration is tremendous.

Trials.—

Name.	Builders.	Engines and Boilers.	Laid down.	Completed	30 hours 3/5. 130 revs.	6 hours full. 152 revs.	Boilers.	Last sea trial.
Swiftsure	Elswick	Humphrys and T.	March, '02	1904	8700=17	14,018=20	Yarrow	19·1
Triumph	Vickers	Vickers	March, '02	1904		14,090=20·17,	Yarrow	19·3

Coal consumption averages at 10,000 H.P. 9½ tons per hour ; at 14,000 H.P. (20 kts.) 14 tons per hour or more.   Both ships tend to be "coal eaters."

General Notes.—Purchased from Chili for £949,900 each.   Poor sea boats but very fast.   Scantlings much lighter than in normal British ships.   Designed by Sir E. J. Reed.

TRIUMPH.   *Photos, Symonds.*

Fire control stations fitting as per plan.

Differences.—

SWIFTSURE.
Higher cowls.
Bow scroll.

TRIUMPH.
Low cowls.
No bow scroll.

(QUEEN CLASS—2 SHIPS).

QUEEN (March, 1902) & **PRINCE OF WALES** (March, 1902).

Displacement 15,000 tons.   Complement 750 (flagship, 789).

Length (*waterline*), 411 feet.   Beam, 75 feet.   *Maximum* draught, 29 feet.   Length over all, 430 feet.

Guns:
4—12 inch. IX., 40 cal. (*AAAA*)
12—6 inch, VII., 45 cal. (*D*).
16—12 pdr., 12 cwt. (*F*).
2—12 pdr., 8 cwt. (*F*).
6—3 pdr.
2 Maxims.
Torpedo tubes (18 inch):
4 *submerged*.
(Total weight with ammunition, 1200 tons.)

Armour (Krupp):
9″ Belt (amidships) ....*aa*
6″—2″ Belt (bow)..............*a-f*
12″ After bulkhead...........*aaa*
3″ Armour deck....................
Protection to vitals ....= *aaa*
12″ Barbettes ....*aaa*
10″—8″ Turrets (K.C) =: *aaa-aa*
6″ Casemates (12) (N.C.) ...... *b*
12″ Conning tower (N.C.) ...*aaa*
(Total weight 4295 tons).

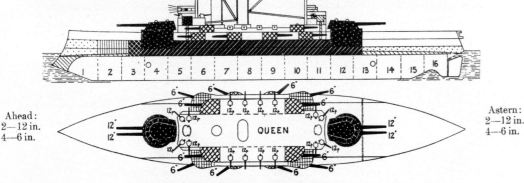

Ahead:
2—12 in.
4—6 in.

QUEEN

Astern:
2—12 in.
4—6 in.

Broadside : 4—12 in., 6—6 in.

QUEEN.   *Photo, Symonds.*

Machinery : 2 sets 3 cylinder vertical inverted triple expansion. 2 screws. Boilers : *Queen*, 20 Babcock and Wilcox, *Prince of Wales*, 20 Belleville. Designed H.P. 15,000 = 18 kts. Coal : *normal* 900 tons ; *maximum* 2100 tons.

Armour Notes.—Belt is 15 feet wide by 300 feet long, from bow. Flat-sided turrets, K.C.

Gunnery Notes.—Loading positions, big guns : all round. Hoist, for 6 inch, electric. Big guns manœuvred by hydraulic gear. Arcs of fire : Big guns, 260° ; secondary guns, 120°. Fire control fitted or fitting as plan. Ammunition carried : 12 in., 80 rounds per gun ; 6 in. 200 per gun.

Torpedo Notes.—Main deck shelf for nets. Defence almost all round. 2 torpedo launches carried. 6 searchlights.

Engineering Notes.—Pressure 300 lbs. at boilers, reduced to 250 at engines. Heating surface, 37,000 square feet.

Name.	Built at	Engines & Boilers by	Laid down	Completed	30 hours 4/5 power. 101 revs.	8 hours full power. 110 revs.	Speed last Boilers. sea trial.
Queen	Devonport	Harland & Wolff	March, '01	1904	11,670 = 16·97	15,556 = 18·39	Babcock 18·2
Prince of Wales	Chatham	Greenock Foundry	March, '01	1904	11,669 = 17·04	15,364 = 18·45	Belleville 18·6

Coal consumption in service : *Prince of Wales* averages 8¼ tons an hour at 10,000 H.P. (15 kts.), 11¾ at 15,000 H.P. (18 kts.). *Queen* averages 9 tons an hour at 10,000 H.P. (15 kts.), 14 at 15,000 H.P. (18 kts.).

General Notes.—Very handy ships. Slightly improved *Londons*. Open 12 pdr. batteries and kidney-shaped fighting tops. Cost per ship averaged just over £1,000,000. Laid down, 1901.

Differences.—*Prince of Wales* has conspicuously higher funnels than *Queen*.

Class distinctions.—Kidney-shape lower tops. Open 12 pdr. battery. Flat-sided turrets. No scuttles to lower deck forward.

46

(LONDON CLASS—3 SHIPS).

LONDON (Sept., 1899), **BULWARK** (Oct., 1899), **VENERABLE** (Nov., 1899).

Displacement 15,000 tons.   Complement 750 (flagship, 789).

Length (*waterline*), 411 feet.   Beam, 75 feet.   *Maximum* draught, 29 feet.   Length over all, 430 feet.

Guns :
4—12 inch, IX., 40 cal. (*AAAA*).
12—6 inch, VII., 45 cal. (*D*).
16—12 pdr., 12 cwt. (*F*).
2—12 pdr., 8 cwt. (*F*).
6—3 pdr.
2 Maxims.
Torpedo tubes (18 inch) :
4 *submerged*.
(Total weight with ammunition,
1200 tons).

Armour (Krupp) :
9″ Belt (amidships) .... *aa*
6″—2″ Belt (bow) .... *a-f*
12″ After bulkhead .... *aaa*
3″ Armour deck..............
Protection to vitals ....= *aaa*
12″ Barbettes.................. *aaa*
10″—8″ Turrets (K.C.) = *aaa-aa*
6″ Casemates (12) (N.C.) ... *b*
12″ Conning tower (N.C.)... *aaa*
(Total weight 4295 tons).

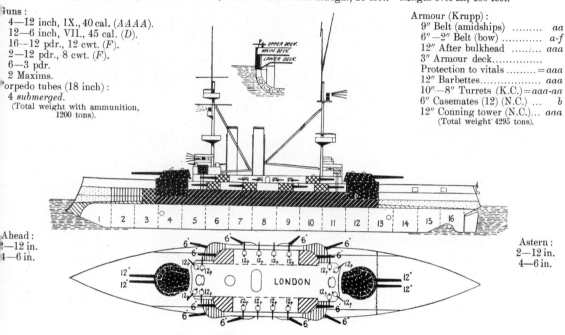

Ahead :
2—12 in.
4—6 in.

Astern :
2—12 in.
4—6 in.

Broadside : 4—12 in., 6—6 in.

Machinery : 2 sets 3 cylinder vertical inverted triple expansion.   2 screws.   Boilers : 20 Belleville.   Designed
H.P. 15,000 = 18 kts.   Coal : *normal* 900 tons ; *maximum* 2100 tons.

Armour Notes.—Belt is 15 feet wide by 300 feet long, from bow.   Flat sided K.C. turrets.

Gunnery Notes.—Loading positions, big guns : all round.   Hoist, for 6 inch, electric.   Big guns manœuvred, hydraulic
gear.   Arcs of fire : Big guns, 260° ; secondary guns, 120°.
Ammunition carried : 12 in., 80 rounds per gun ; 6 in. 200 per gun.

Torpedo Notes.—Main deck shelf for nets.   Defence almost all round.   2 torpedo launches carried.   6 searchlights.

Engineering Notes.—Pressure, 300 lbs. at boilers, reduced to 250 at engines.   Heating surface, 37,000 square feet.

Name.	Built at	*Engines of Boilers* by	Laid down	Completed	30 hours 4/5 power. 101 revs.	8 hours full power. 110 revs.	Boilers.	Speed last sea trial.
London	Portsmouth	Earle	Dec. '98	1902	11,718 = 16·4	15,264 = 18·10	Belleville	18·5
Bulwark	Devonport	Hawthorn Leslie	March, '99	1902	11,755 = 16·8	15,353 = 18·15	Belleville	18·5
Venerable	Chatham	Maudslay	Nov. '99	1902	11,364 = 16·8	15,345 = 18·40	Belleville	18·3

Coal consumption in service : Averages 8¼ tons an hour at 10,000 H.P. (15 kts.), 11¾ at 15,000 H.P. (18 kts.).

General Notes.—Very handy ships.   Cost per ship averaged just over £1,000,000.

Photo, Lieut. Reinold, R.N.

Fire control stations fitting or fitted as per plan.

Differences.—

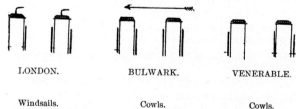

LONDON.   BULWARK.   VENERABLE.

Windsails.   Cowls.   Cowls.

BRITISH BATTLESHIPS (18 knot).

(FORMIDABLE CLASS—3 SHIPS).

FORMIDABLE (Nov. 1898), **IRRESISTIBLE** (Dec. 1898), & **IMPLACABLE** (March, 1899).

Displacement 15,000 tons.   Complement 780 (flagship 810).

Length (waterline), 411 feet.   Beam, 75 feet.   Maximum draught, 29 feet.   Length over all, 430 feet.

Guns :
4—12 in., IX., 40 cal. (AAAA)
12—6 inch, VII., 45 cal. (D.)
16—12 pdr., 12 cwt. (F.)
2—12 pdr., 8 cwt. (F.)
6—3 pdr.
2 Maxims.
Torpedo tubes (18 inch) :
4 submerged.
(Total weight with ammunition, 1200 tons).

Armour (Krupp) :
9″ Belt (amidships) .... aa
2″ Belt (bow) .... f
1½″ Belt (aft) .... f
12″ Bulkheads .... aaa
3″ Deck (on slopes) ....
Protection to vitals .... = aaa
12″ Barbettes (N.C.) .... aaa
10″—8″ Turrets (N.C.) = aaa–aa
6″ Casemates (12) (N.C.) ... b
12″ Conning tower (N.C.)... aaa
(Total weight about 4300 tons)

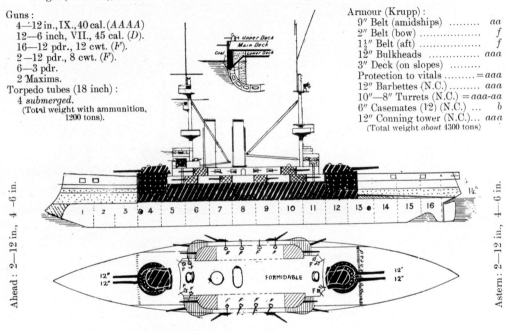

Broadside : 4—12 in., 6—6 in.

Ahead : 2—12 in., 4—6 in.   Astern : 2—12 in., 4—6 in.

Machinery : 2 sets 3 cylinder vertical inverted triple expansion.   2 screws.   Boilers : 20 Belleville.
Designed H.P. 15,000 = 18 kts.   Coal : normal 900 tons ; maximum 2200 tons.

Armour Notes.—Belt is 15 feet wide by 216 feet long ;   2″ continuation to bow ;   lower edge is normal thickness.   Curved turrets of K.N.C.

Gunnery Notes and Torpedo Notes.—As for later Formidables, previous page.

Engineering Notes.—(See also later Formidables).

Name.	Built at	Engines & Boilers by	Laid down.	Completed	30 hours 4/5 power.	8 hours full power.	Boilers.	Speed last sea trial.
Formidable	Portsmouth	Earle	March, '98	1901	11,618 = 17·15	15,511 = 18·13	Belleville	18·4
Irresistible	Chatham	Maudslay	April, '98	1902	11,626 = 17·5	15,603 = 18·20	Belleville	18·5
Implacable	Devonport	Laird	July '98	1902	11,618 = 16·81	15,244 = 18·22	Belleville	18·7

Coal consumption in service averages 8 tons an hour, at 10,000 H.P. (15 kts.), 11½ tons at 15,000 H.P. (18 kts.)

General Notes.—Very handy ships, answer the least touch of helm.   Average cost just over £1,000,000 per ship.

FORMIDABLE.

(Fire control stations to be fitted or fitting as per plan).

Differences—

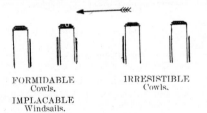

FORMIDABLE
Cowls.

IRRESISTIBLE
Cowls.

IMPLACABLE
Windsails.

Class distinctions :—

Formidable London Queen	Fore funnel close to foremast and smaller than after.	Round turrets. No scuttles lower deck ....ard. Flat-sided turrets. Open upper deck.
Duncan	Funnels as in Formidable, but equal sized and big.	Slightly smaller ship. Open upper deck.
Canopus	Funnels close together, and more amidships.	Shorter masts, closer together, ship lower in water, and generally smaller. Round turrets.

(DUNCAN CLASS—6 SHIPS.)

RUSSELL (February, 1901), **ALBEMARLE** (March, 1901), **MONTAGU** (March, 1901),
DUNCAN (March, 1901), **CORNWALLIS** (July, 1901), **EXMOUTH** (August, 1901).

Displacement 14,000 tons. Complement 750 (flagships 778).

Length (*waterline*), 418 feet. Beam, 75½ feet. *Maximum* draught, 27¼ feet. Length over all, 429 feet.

Guns :
4—12 inch, IX. (*AAAA*).
12—6 inch, VII. (*D*).
12—12 pdr. (*F*).
6—3 pdr.
2 Maxims.
Torpedo tubes (18 inch) :
4 *submerged*.

Armour (Krupp) :
7″ Belt (amidships) ......   *a*
5″—3″ Belt (bow) .... *b-c*
1½″ Belt (aft) ....
2½″ Deck (on slopes) ...
Protection to vitals ...... = *aa*
11″ Barbettes (N.C.) ...   *aa*
6″ Turrets (K.C.) .... = *aa*
6″ Casemates (12) ......   *b*
12″ Conning tower ...... *aaa*
(Total weight *about* 3500 tons).

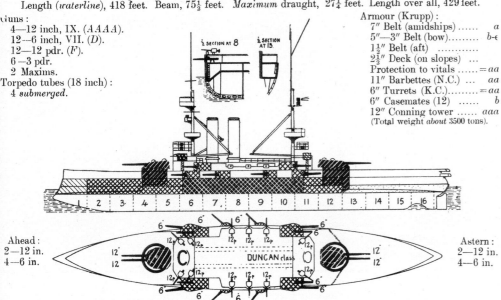

Ahead :
2—12 in.
4—6 in.

DUNCAN class

Astern :
2—12 in.
4—6 in.

Broadside : 4—12 in., 6—6 in.

Machinery : 2 sets 4 cylinder vertical inverted triple expansion. 2 screws. Boilers : 24 Belleville.
Coal : *normal* 900 tons ; *maximum* 2000 tons. Designed H.P. 18,000 = 19 kts.
Armour Notes.—Main belt is 14 feet wide by 285 feet long ; lower edge is full thickness. Flat-sided turrets (K.C.)
Gunnery Notes.—Loading positions, big guns : all round. Hoists, for 6 inch, electric and hand. Big guns manœuvred by hydraulic gear. Fire control stations fitted 1905.
Arcs of fire : 12 in., 240° ; 6 in., 120°. Fire control platforms fitted to *Russell, Albermarle,* and *Exmouth,* 1905, to others, 1906.
Engineering Notes.—Machinery, etc., weighs 1580 tons.

Name.	Builder.	Engines by	Laid down	Completed	First trials :— 30 hours at 4/5.	First trials :— 8 hours full.	Boilers.	Last recorded best speed.
Russell	Palmer	Palmer	March, '99	1903	13,695 = 17·95	18,222 = 19·3	Belleville	19·8
Duncan	Thames I.W.	Thames I.W.	July, '99	1903	13,717 = 18·1	18,232 = 19·11	Belleville	20·1
Cornwallis	Thames I.W.	Thames I.W.	July, 99	1904	13,694 = 17·94	18,238 = 18·98⊛	Belleville	19·56
Exmouth	Laird	Laird	Aug. '99	1903	13,774 = 18	18,346 = 19·03	Belleville	20·0
Albemarle	Chatham	Thames I.W.	Jan., '00	1903	13,587 = 17·2⊛	⊛18,296 = 18·6	Belleville	19·8
Montagu	Devonport	Laird	Nov., '99	1903	13,652 = 17·8	18,265 = 18·8	Belleville	19·4

⊛Run in bad weather.

Coal consumption averages 2¾ tons an hour at 10 kts. ; at 13,000 H.P. (17 kts.) about 10¾ tons an hour ; at 18,000 H.P. (19 kts.) about 15 tons an hour or less. All these ships are excellent steamers, and make or exceed their speeds in almost any weather. Boilers are of 1900 pattern.
General Notes.—The ships are proving very passable sea boats. Hull without armour weighs 9055 tons.
Cost per ship, *complete*, just over £1,000,000. Very handy. First of class laid down 1899.

RUSSELL (Present rig).   *Photo, Symonds & Co.*

Distinctions..—All identical with each other. They are to be distinguished from other battleships by their large round funnels. Open upper deck. They are lower in the water than the *Londons* and *Formidables*. No cowls.

Broad and narrow red bands on funnels as below :—

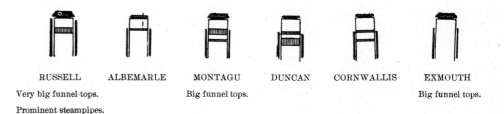

RUSSELL   ALBEMARLE   MONTAGU   DUNCAN   CORNWALLIS   EXMOUTH

Very big funnel-tops.   Big funnel tops.   Big funnel tops.

Prominent steampipes.

(CANOPUS CLASS—6 SHIPS).

CANOPUS (October, 1897), **GOLIATH** (March, 1898), **ALBION** (June, 1898),
OCEAN (July, 1898), **GLORY** (March, 1899), *also* **VENGEANCE** (July, 1899).

Displacement 12,950 tons. Complement 750 (flagship 780).
Length (*waterline*), 400 feet. Beam, 74 feet. *Maximum* draught, 26½ feet. Length over all, 418 feet.

Guns:
4—12 inch, VIII., 35 cal. (*AAA*)
12—6 inch, *wire*, 40 cal. (*E*).
10—12 pdr., 12 cwt. (*F*).
2—12 pdr., 8 cwt. boat.
6—3 pdr.
2 Maxims.
Torpedo tubes (18 inch) :
4 *submerged*.

(Total weight, with ammunition, 1000 tons).

Armour (Harvey-nickel) :
6″ Belt (amidships)   *b*
2″ Belt (bow) .... *f*
1½″ Belt (aft) .... *f*
12″ Bulkheads ...... *aaa*
2½″ Deck (on slopes).
Protection to vitals... = *a*
12″ Barbettes...... *aaa-aa*
8″ Turrets to these ... *aa*
5″ Casemates (12) ... *c*
12″ Conning tower... *aaa*

(Total weight, *about* 3600 tons.

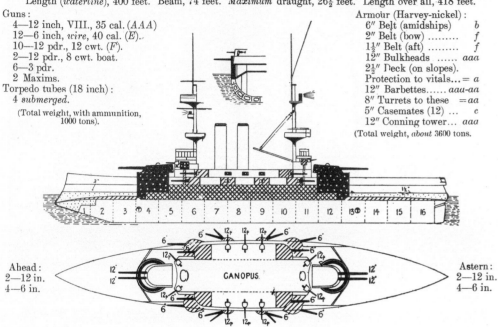

Ahead :
2—12 in.
4—6 in.

CANOPUS.

Astern :
2—12 in.
4—6 in.

Broadside : 4—12 in., 6—6 in.

Machinery : 2 sets 3 cylinder vertical inverted triple expansion. 2 screws. Boilers : 20 Belleville.
Designed H.P. 13,500 = 18·25 kts. Coal : *normal* 1000 tons ; *maximum* 2300 tons.
Armour Notes.—Belt is 14 feet wide by 210 feet long. Barbettes circular, the thickness given being the maximum. Belt is normal thickness at lower edge. Weight of side armour only, 1740 tons. Main deck 1″ steel. Barbettes 37 feet in diameter. Circular turrets (H.N.)
Gunnery Notes.—Loading positions, big guns : all round. *Vengeance's* load in any position also. Big guns manœuvred : hydraulic and hand gear, Hoists, for 6 inch, electric and hand. Fitting with fire control stations as plan.
Arcs of fire : Big guns. 260° ; casemates, 120°.
Torpedo Notes.—Net defence amidships ; stowage on shelf at main deck level. Electric machinery : 3 dynamos, 8 electric fans for ventilation.

Name	Built at	Engines and boilers by	Laid down	Com-pleted	30 hours 4/5. 99-102 revs.	8 hours full power. 107-110 revs.	Boilers.	Speed last 8 hours sea trial.
Canopus	Portsmouth	Greenock Fdy.	Jan., '97	1900	10,454 = 17·2	13,763 = 18·5	Belleville	18·6
Goliath	Chatham	Penn	Jan., '97	1900	10,413 = 17·3	13,918 = 18·4	Belleville	18·6
Albion	Thames I.W.	Maudslay	Dec., '96	1902	10,809 = 16·8⁕	13,885 = 17·8⁕	Belleville	18·7
Ocean	Devonport	Hawthorn Leslie	Feb., '97	1900	10,314 = 16·2	13,728 = 18·5	Belleville	18·8
Glory	Laird	Laird	Dec., '96	1901	10,587 = 16·8	13,745 = 18·1	Belleville	18·6
Vengeance	Vickers	Vickers	Aug.,'97	1901	10,387 = 17·2	13,852 = 18·5	Belleville	19·1

⁕ Run in a gale.

Coal consumption averages : 8 tons an hour at 10,000 H.P. (16·5 kts.), 10¼ tons at 13,500 H.P. (18·25 kts.)

Fire control stations fitting as per plan.

Differences.—

CANOPUS   ALBION

GOLIATH   OCEAN

GLORY   VENGEANCE

For identifications of class from *Formidables* and *Duncans* see page 48, *Formidable* class.

Engineering Notes.—70 revolutions = 12½ kts. Boilers : 15—9 element generators, and 5—8 element generators. Total heating surface (including economisers), 33,700 square feet. Grate area 1055 feet. Pressure, 300 lbs., reduced to 250 lbs. at engines. Distilling machinery : 2 evaporators, capacity 68 tons per 24 hours. Distillers produce 40 tons per day. Auxiliary engines : 4 air compressing, 2 boat hoists, 2 refrigerating, 2 coal hoists, 5 blowing, 2 steam fans. Funnels 11 feet in diameter. Height above furnace bars, 90 feet. Screws : 4 bladed. Diameter of cylinders 30 in., 49 in., and 80 in. Stroke 51 in.

General Notes.—Tactical diameter, extreme helm at 15 kts., 450 yards ; with the engines, 350 yards. Cost, *complete*, about £900,000 per ship.

(MAJESTIC CLASS—9 SHIPS).

MAGNIFICENT (December, 1894), **MAJESTIC** (January, 1895), **HANNIBAL** (April, 1895),
PRINCE GEORGE (August, 1895), **VICTORIOUS** (October, 1895), **JUPITER** (November, 1895),
MARS (March, 1896), *also* **CÆSAR** (September, 1896), & **ILLUSTRIOUS** (September, 1896).

Displacement 14,900 tons.   Complement 757.

Length (*waterline*), 399 feet.   Beam, 75 feet.   *Maximum* draught, 30 feet.   Length over all, 413 feet.

Guns :
- 4—12 inch, VIII., 35 cal. (*AAA*)
- 12—6 inch, *wire*, 40 cal. (*E*).
- 16—12 pdr.
- 12—3 pdr.
- 2 Maxims.
- 2—12 pdr. boat guns.

Torpedo tubes (18 inch) :
- 4 *submerged*.
- 1 *above water* (stern).

(Total weight with ammunition,
1500 tons).
(Ammunition only, 355 tons).

Armour (Harvey) :
- 9″ Belt (amidships)   *a*
- 14″ Bulkheads ......   *aa*
- 4″ Deck (on slopes)
- Protection to vitals = *aaa*
- 14″ Barbettes......... *aa*
- 10″ Turrets to these = *aa*
- 6″ Casemates (12) ...   *c*
- 14″ Conning tower   *aa*

(Total weight 4260 tons).

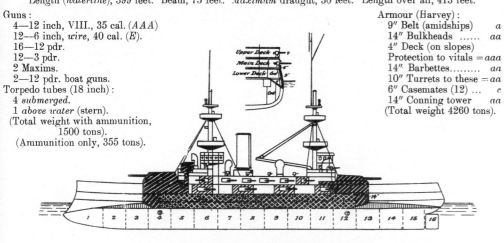

Ahead :
2—12 in.
2—6 in.

MAJESTIC class

Astern :
2—12 in.
2—6 in.

Broadside : 4—12 in. (*AAA*), 6—6 in. (*E*).

Machinery : 2 sets 3 cylinder vertical inverted triple expansion.   2 screws.   Boilers : 8 cylindrical, with 4 furnaces each.   Designed H.P. *natural* 10,000 = 16.5 kts. ; *forced* 12,000 = 17.5 kts.   Coal : *normal* 1200 tons ; *maximum* 2,000 tons (always carried).   Oil, 400 tons.

Armour Notes.—Belt is 16 feet wide by 220 feet long. *Cæsar* and *Illustrious* have circular barbettes.
Gunnery Notes.—Loading positions, big guns : all round (end on in first two and all round for a few rounds).   Hoists, electric and hand.   Big guns manœuvred, hydraulic and hand.   Arcs of fire : Big guns, 260° ; Casemates, 120°.
Torpedo Notes.—Midship net defence.   Nets stow on main deck shelf in most of the class (all are being so fitted).   Two torpedo launches.   6 searchlights.
Engineering Notes.—Machinery and boilers weigh 1,600 tons.   32 furnaces.   Heating surface, 24,400 square feet.   All fitting or fitted for oil fuel.   Screws : 17 feet in diameter, 19¼ feet pitch, 4 bladed.   Cylinders : 40, 59 and 88 ins. diameter.   Stroke : 51 ins.   Pressure : 155 lbs.

Name.	Builder.	Engines by	Laid down	Completed	First trials :— 8 hours nat.	8 hours f. d.	Speed last sea trial.
Magnificent	Chatham	Penn	Dec., '93	1895	10,301 = 16·50	12,157 = 18·4	15·9
Majestic	Portsmouth	Vickers	Feb., '94	1895	10,418 = 16·99	12,097 = 17·9	16·8
Hannibal	Pembroke	Harland & Wolff	April, '94	1897	10,357 = 16·30	12,138 = 18·0	16·2¼
Prince George	Portsmouth	Humphrys & T.	Sept., '94	1896	10,464 = 16·52	12,253 = 18·3	—
Victorious	Chatham	Hawthorn, L.	May, '94	1897	10,319 = 16·92	12,201 = 18·7	16·4
Jupiter	Clydebank	Clydebank	Oct., '94	1897	10,258 = 15·80	12,475 = 18·4	—
Mars	Laird	Laird	June, '94	1897	10,159 = 15·96	12,434 = 17·7	16·6
Cæsar	Portsmouth	Maudslay	March, '95	1897	10,630 = 16·70	12,652 = 18·7	17
Illustrious	Chatham	Penn	March, '95	1898	10,241 = 15·96	12,112 = 16·5*	16·1

*Bad weather.

PRINCE GEORGE.   *Photo, Symonds & Co.*

Differences.—

Name.	Steam pipes :— Starboard funnel. before.	abaft.	Port funnel. before.	abaft.	Notes on Peculiarities.
Majestic Magnificent	...	1	...	2	
Mars	2	...	2	...	
Victorious Jupiter Prince George	1	1	1	1	Higher masts.
Hannibal	1	2	...	2	Very high after-bridge. Chart house before mast over C. T.
Illustrious					Higher masts.
Cæsar	2	1	2	...	Higher masts. Chart house over C. T.

All the ships were *light* on trials and drawing about 2 feet less than the normal.   Sea trials run with full coal and stores aboard.

Coal consumption for the class averages :   at 8 kts., 1¼ ton an hour ;   at 8,000 H.P. (15 kts.), 8½ tons ;   at 10,000 H.P. (16·5 kts.), 10¼ tons.   The *Hannibal*, which is the most economical ship, burns somewhat less.

General Notes.—150 w. t. compartments.   208 w. t. doors.   Tactical diameter : at 15 kts., 450 yards ; with one engine, 350 yards.   Ships answer helm very well.   Cost nearly £1,000,000 per ship *complete*.

G 2

(ROYAL SOVEREIGN CLASS—7 SHIPS).

ROYAL SOVEREIGN (Feb., 1891), **EMPRESS OF INDIA** (May, 1891), **REPULSE** (Feb. 1892), **RAMILLIES** (March, 1892), **RESOLUTION** (May, 1892), **REVENGE** (Nov. 1892), and **ROYAL OAK** (Nov. 1892).

Displacement 14,100 tons. Complement 712.
Length (*waterline*), 380 feet. Beam, 75 feet. *Maximum* draught, 30 feet.

Guns :
  4—13·5 inch (*AA*).
  10—6 inch, *wire* (*E*).
  16—6 pdr.
  12—3 pdr.
  2—9 pdr. boat.
  2 Maxims.
Torpedo tubes (18 inch) :
  2 *submerged*.
  1 *above water* (stern).
  (Total weight with ammunition, 1410 tons).

Armour (compound) :
  18″ Belt (amidships) .... *aa*
  16″ Belt (bulkheads) .... *aa*
  3″ Deck (flat on belt)........
  Protection to vitals is ...... *aa*
  17″ Barbettes................. *aa*
  4″ Lower deck (redoubt) ... *ε*
  3″ Main deck (bulkheads) ... *f*
  6″ Casemates (main deck)... *d*
  5″ Casemates (upper) K.N.C. *c*
  4″ Hoists..................... *ε*
  14″ Conning tower .... *a*
  (Total weight 4600 tons).

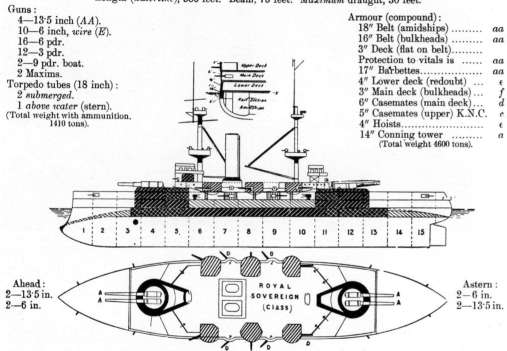

Ahead :
2—13·5 in.
2—6 in.

ROYAL SOVEREIGN (Class)

Astern :
2—6 in.
2—13·5 in.

Broadside : 4—13·5 in., 5—6 in.

Machinery : 2 sets vertical 3 cylinder triple expansion. 2 screws. Boilers : cylindrical (8 single ended with 4 furnaces each). Designed H.P. *natural*, 9,000 = 15 kts. ; *forced*, 13,000 = 17 kts. Coal : *normal* 900 tons ; *maximum* 1,400 tons (always carried).
Armour Notes.—Belt is 8⅔ feet wide by 250 feet long ; 6⅔ feet of it below waterline. Lower edge is 8″ thick. New casemates by Cammell.
Gunnery Notes.—Loading positions, big guns : end on. Electric hoists to 6 in. guns. Big guns manœuvred : hydraulic gear.
  Arcs of fire : Big guns 240° ; 6 in. 120°.
Torpedo Notes—Net defence amidships, net shelf on main deck level. 6 searchlights (25,000 candle power).
Engineering Notes.—The ships cannot now steam very fast, but they can keep station at 13 kts. as long as their coal lasts.

ROYAL OAK   *Photo, Symonds.*
(Present rig, except that gaff is now removed in some).

Differences.—Except *Royal Oak*, all have steam pipes *abaft* the funnels. Practically impossible to differentiate these other six. Striking top masts fitted 1903-05. Gaffs removed February, 1905, from all the class.

Name.	Builder.	Machinery and Boilers by	Laid down.	Completed.	Speed last 8 hour sea trial.
R. Sovereign	Portsmouth	Humphrys & T.	Sept. '99	1892	13·9
Empress of I.	Pembroke	Humphrys & T.	July '99	1893	15·1
Repulse	Pembroke	Humphrys & T.	May '89	1894	
Ramillies	Clydebank	Clydebank	Oct. '89	1893	
Resolution	Palmer	Palmer	Jan. '91	1893	
Revenge	Palmer	Palmer	Oct. '89	1895	13·8
Royal Oak	Laird	Laird	May '90	1894	14·7

Coal consumption : at 6,000 H.P. about 9 tons an hour ; at 9,000 H.P. (15 kts, nominal), 10 tons an hour.

General Notes.—Average cost per ship, *complete*, just over £900,000.

BRITISH BATTLESHIP (14 knot).

HOOD (July, 1891).

Displacement 14,200 tons.   Complement 654.   Actual displacement about 15,400 tons.

Length (*waterline*), 380 feet.   Beam, 75 feet.   *Maximum* draught, 31 feet.

Guns:
    4—13·5 inch (*AA*).
    10 —6 inch (*E*).
    10 —6 pdr.
    12—3 pdr.
    2 Maxims.
Torpedo tubes (18 inch):
    2 *submerged*.
    1 *above water* (stern).
Total weight, with ammunition,
    1410 tons).

Armour (compound):
18″—14″ Belt (amidships)…*aa-a*
17″ Bulkheads …………… *aa*
3″ Armour deck (flat on belt)
Protection to vitals is …=   *aa*
17″ Turrets……………… *aa*
17″ Turret bases ………… *aa*
4″ Lower deck (side)……… *ϵ*
6″ Casemates (4) ………… *d*
14″ Conning tower………… *aa*

(Total weight 4800 tons).

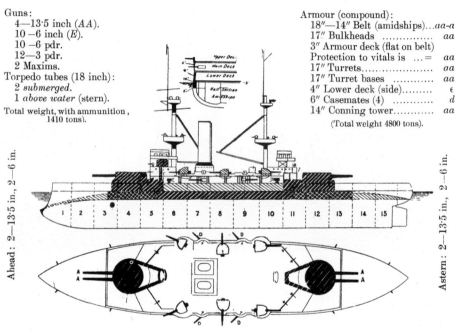

Ahead: 2 –13·5 in., 2 –6 in.

Astern: 2 –13·5 in., 2 –6 in.

Broadside: 4—13·5 in., 5—6 in.

Machinery: 2 sets vertical triple expansion.   2 screws.   Boilers: Cylindrical.   Designed H.P.
natural 9000 = 15 kts.; *forced* 13,000 = 17·5 kts.   Coal: *normal* 900 tons; *maximum* 1450 tons.

Armour Notes.—Belt is 8⅔ feet wide by 250 feet long; 6½ feet of it below waterline;   lower edge is
    8″ thick.

Gunnery Notes.—Loading positions, big guns : end on.   Big guns manœuvred hydraulically.

HOOD (Gaff now gone).   *Photo, Ellis.*

Engineering Notes.—Made her speed on first trials, but not good for much over 14 knots now.   Coal
    consumption: as for *Royal Sovereign*.

General Notes.—Laid down at Chatham.   Completed, 1893.   First cost, *complete*, about £920,000.
    Loses speed in a sea way, but can fight her bow guns in a moderately stiff sea.

(TRAFALGAR CLASS—2 SHIPS.)

TRAFALGAR (Sept., 1887), & **NILE** (March, 1888).

Displacement 11,940 tons. Complement 520.

Length (*waterline*), 345 feet. Beam, 73 feet. *Maximum* draught, 30 feet.

Guns :
4—13·5 inch (*AA*).
6—6 inch wire (*E*).
8—6 pdr.
11—3 pdr.
6 Machine.
3 Boat guns.
Torpedo tubes (14 inch) :
2 *submerged.*
2 *above water* (bow and stern).

Armour (compound) :
20″ Belt (amidships) ....*aaa*
16″ Bulkheads ....*aa*
3″ Deck (flat on belt) ....
Protection to vitals is ....*aaa*
18″ Redoubt ....*aa*
18″ Turrets ....*aa*
4″ Battery.........,..............*e*
14″ Conning tower ....*aa*
(Total weight 4230 tons).

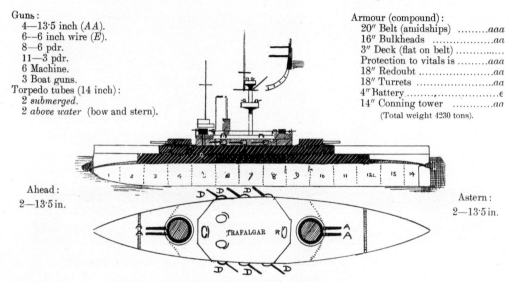

Ahead :
2—13·5 in.

Astern :
2—13·5 in.

Broadside 4—13·5 in., 3—6 in.

NILE.   *Photo, Ellis.*

Machinery : 2 sets vertical triple expansion. 2 screws. Boilers : Cylindrical. Designed H.P. *natural* 7,500 = 15·6 kts.; *forced* 12,000 = 17 kts. Coal : *normal* 900 tons; *maximum* 1,200 tons (always carried).

Armour Notes.—Belt is 8½ feet wide by 245 feet long; lower edge is 8″ thick; 2″ skin behind the backing of all armour.

Gunnery Notes.—Loading positions, big guns : end on. Big guns manœuvred, hydraulic gear.
Arcs of fire : Big guns, 260°; 6 in., 90°.
Height of guns above water : *about* 12½ feet.

Torpedo Notes.—Net defence amidships.

Engineering Notes.—

Name.	Built at	Engines & boilers by	Laid down	Completed	Max. present speed
Trafalgar	Portsmouth	Humphrys & T.	Jan., '86	1890	13·7
Nile	Pembroke	Maudslay	April, '86	1890	14·1

General Notes.—In 1905 both were modernised internally, but their low freeboard and small speed makes them of comparatively little fighting value. Protection is still very good. Cost about £900,000 each to build complete.

Differences, etc.—*Trafalgar* has shorter funnels and a shorter signal mast. *Nile's* funnels peculiar black tops. Steam pipes are before the funnels in *Nile*, abaft them in *Trafalgar*. Funnels abreast in both—very wide apart.

(CENTURION CLASS—2 SHIPS.)

BARFLEUR & CENTURION (both launched August, 1892).

Displacement (since reconstruction) about 11,000 tons.   Complement 620.

Length (*waterline*), 360 feet.   Beam, 70 feet.   *Maximum* draught, 27 feet.

Guns :
4 —10 inch, 30 cal. (*B*).
10—6 inch, VII., 45 cal. (*D*).
8 —6 pdr.
12—3 pdr.
2 —9 pdr. boat.
2 Maxims.
Torpedo tubes (18 inch) :
2 *submerged*.
1 *above water* (stern).

Armour (Compound, Harvey,
and K.N.C.) :
12″ Belt (amidships) ...... *a*
6″ Bulkheads .... *c*
2¼ Deck (flat on belt)......
Protection to vitals is ... *a*
9″ Barbettes .... *b*
6″ Hoods to these (H). ... *c*
4″ Lower deck side (H) .. *d*
5″ Casemates (10) (K.N.C.) *c*
12″ Conning tower (H).... *aa*

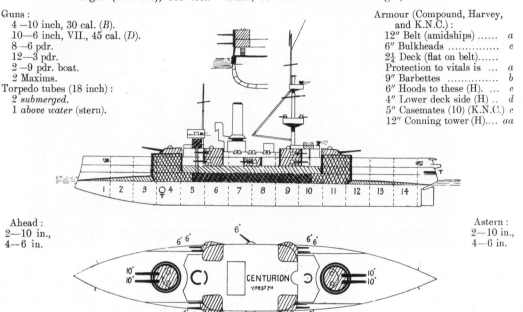

Ahead :
2—10 in.,
4—6 in.

Astern :
2—10 in.,
4—6 in.

Broadside 4—10 in., 5—6 in.

BARFLEUR (Present rig).   *Photo, Symonds.*
Centurion practically identical.

Machinery : 2 sets vertical triple expansion.   2 screws.   Boilers : Cylindrical.   Designed H.P. *natural*
draught 9000 = 17 kts ; *forced* 13000 = 18·5 kts.   Coal : *normal* 750 tons ; *maximum* 1125 tons.

Armour Notes.—Belt is 200 feet long ; lower edge is 8″ thick.

Gunnery Notes.—Loading positions, big guns : end on.   Hoists : electric to 6 in. guns.   Big guns manœuvred
by hydraulic gear.
Arcs of fire : Big guns 240°.   Casemates 120°.

Torpedo Notes.—¾ net defence.

Engineering Notes.—Used to be very fast, speed much reduced by reconstruction.

Name.	Built at	Engines and Boilers by	Laid down.	Completed.	Original max. speed.	Present max. speed.
Barfleur	Chatham	Greenock Foundry	November '90	1894	19	
Centurion	Portsmouth	Greenock Foundry	March '91	1893	18·7	16·4

Coal consumption about 10½ tons an hour at 9000 H.P.

General Notes.—Reconstructed 1903, casemates then fitted.   Original cost per ship, about £620,000.   Cost of
reconstruction about £150,000.   Very handy ships.   Top masts fitted to signal pole, 1905.

RENOWN (1895). 12,350 tons. Guns: 4—10 inch, 32 cal. (B). Armour (Harvey): 8″—6″ Belt (b—c). 10″ Barbettes. Designed H.P. 12,000 = 18 kts. Fast and economical steamer, but of little present fighting value. Formerly carried secondary armament of 10—6 inch wire, etc. First cost £746,247. At present serving as a subsidiary yacht.

COLOSSUS (1882) and EDINBURGH (1882). 9420 tons. Guns: 4—old 12 inch, 5—old 6 inch. Armour (compound): 18″—14″ Belt amidships (aa—a). 16″ Turrets. Designed H.P. 5500 = 14·2 kts. Poor steamers and of little, if any, fighting value. Used for harbour service.

RENOWN.

Note.—In deference to political agitation, the names of several other old battleships remain of the Navy List. These are ANSON, CAMPERDOWN, RODNEY and HOWE, all of the "ADMIRAL" class, carrying 4—13·5 inch and 6—old 6 inch; Also BENBOW, of the same class, 2—110 ton B.L. and 10—old 6 inch. Armour: a short 18″ compound belt amidships, under *waterline*, and 18″—11″ on barbettes. Speeds, when in service, about 15 kts. Displacement, about 10,600 tons. Also THUNDERER and DEVASTATION, sea-going monitors of about 9000 tons odd. Armament: 4—old 10 inch B.L. Armour: 14″ soft iron all over. Speeds poor.

COLOSSUS & EDINBURGH.

NEW BRITISH CRUISERS. (Laid down 1905-06.)

(INVINCIBLE CLASS—4 SHIPS).

INVINCIBLE, INFLEXIBLE & INDOMITABLE (1905-6 estimates).

Displacement 14,900. Complement —.

Length (*waterline*),   feet. Beam,   feet. *Maximum* draught   feet. Length over all,   feet.

Guns (*rumoured*):
  10 *or* 8—9·2 in., XI., 50 cal. (*AAA*).
Torpedo tubes (18 inch):
  3 *submerged.*

Armour (Krupp):
  ″ Belt (amidships) ......
  ″ Belt (bow) ... ...
  ″ Belt (aft) ... ...
  ″ Deck ....
  Protection to vitals ...... =
  ″ Lower deck redoubt
  ″ Turrets............. ....
  ″ Turret bases ....

Building.

(Cruiser editions of *Dreadnought*).

Machinery: Parsons' turbine.   screws. Boilers: Designed H.P. 35,000 = 25 kts.   Coal:
normal   tons; *maximum*   tons. Also oil fuel.

H

(MINOTAUR CLASS—3 SHIPS.)

MINOTAUR, DEFENCE, SHANNON (1904-05 Estimates).

Displacement 14,600 tons.   Complement ——.

Length (*waterline*), 520 feet.   Beam,   feet.   *Maximum* draught,   feet.   Length over all,   feet.

Guns :
4—9·2 inch, XI., 50 cal. (*AAA*).
10—7·5 inch, II., 50 cal. (*A*).
(rest not yet announced).
Torpedo tubes (18 inch) :
3 *submerged*.

Armour (Krupp) :
6″ Belt (amidships) .... *a*
4″ Belt (bow)................ *d*
3″ Belt (stern) .... *e*
″ Deck (on slopes) ......
Protection to vitals ....=
″ Barbettes ....
6″ Turrets to these (K.C.) =*aa*
″ Secondary turrets ......

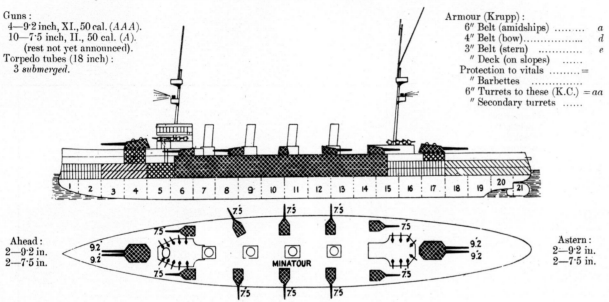

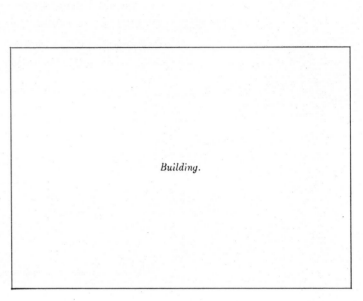

Building.

Ahead :
2—9·2 in.
2—7·5 in.

Astern :
2—9·2 in.
2—7·5 in.

Broadside : 4—9·2 in., 5—7·5 in.

Machinery : 2 sets 4 cylinder.   2 screws.   Boilers : probably Yarrow.   Designed H.P. 27,000=23 kts.   Turbines to some.

Gunnery Notes.—Loading positions, big guns : central pivot.   Hoists, electric; all guns.   All guns manœuvred electrically and by hand.

Torpedo Notes.—1904 model torpedoes.   Stern *submerged* tube.

Engineering Notes.—

Name.	Builder.	Engines and boilers by.	Laid down.	Completed.	Boilers.
Minotaur	Devonport	...	Jan., '05	...	
Defence	Pembroke	...	Jan., '05	...	
Shannon	Chatham	...	Jan., '05	...	

NEW BRITISH ARMOURED CRUISERS (22⅓ knot). (Laid down 1904.)

(WARRIOR CLASS—4 SHIPS.)

ACHILLES (——— 1905), *COCHRANE* (——— 1905), *NATAL* (Sept., 1905) & *WARRIOR* (Nov., 1905).

Displacement, 13,550 tons.

Length (*waterline*), 480 feet.   Beam, 73½ feet.   *Maximum* draught, 27½ feet.

Guns :
6—9·2 in., XI., 50 cal. (*AAA*).
4—7·5 inch, II., 50 cal. (*A*).
22—3 pdr. (semi-automatic)
8 Pompoms.
Maxims.
Torpedo tubes (18 inch) :
3 *submerged*.

Armour (Krupp) :
6″ Belt (amidships) .... *a*
4″ Belt (bow) .... *d*
3″ Belt (aft.) ....
¾″ Deck...................... *ϵ*
Protection to vitals ......= *a*
6″ Barbettes (6).............. *b*
6″ Turrets to these (K.C.)=*aa*
6″ Secondary turrets (4) ... *b*

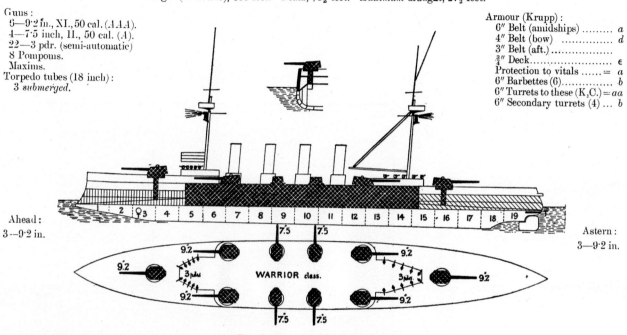

Ahead :
3—9·2 in.

Astern :
3—9·2 in.

Broadside : 4—9·2 in., 2—7·5 in.

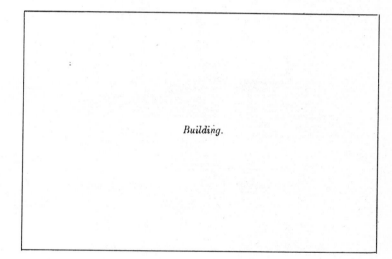

Building.

Machinery : 2 sets 4 cylinder triple expansion.   2 screws.   Boilers : 19 Yarrow large tube and 6 cylindrical.   Designed H.P. 23,500 = 22·33 kts. (but 24 kts. hoped for).   Coal, *normal* 1,000 tons ; *maximum* 2,000 tons.   Also 400 tons of oil.

Armour Notes.—Thick part of belt 300 feet long.   Armour deck made of two thicknesses of ⅜″ steel.

Gunnery Notes.—Loading positions, big guns : central pivot.   Hoists, all electric.   Big guns manœuvred, hydraulically and hand ; secondary guns, electrically and hand.

Arcs of fire : End 9·2 in.—285° ;   Broadside 9·2 in.—120° ;   7·5 in.—about 110°.

Torpedo Notes.—1904 model torpedoes.   *Submerged* stern tubes.

Engineering Notes.—Machinery all standardized.   Weight complete, 2250 tons.

Name.	Builders	Machinery and Boilers made by	Laid down.	Completed	Boilers.
					Yarrow,
Achilles	Elswick	Humphry's & T	Jan., '04	...	with 6 cylindrical
Cochrane	Fairfield	Fairfield	Feb., '04	...	″
Natal	Vickers	Vickers	Jan., '04	...	″
Warrior	Pembroke	Wallsend Co.	Nov., '04	...	″

General Notes.—Design altered since first conception.   These were originally to have been sisters to the *Duke of Edinburgh.*   Estimated cost per ship about £1,150,000.   Designer : Sir P. Watts.   Built under 1903-4 estimates.

59

H 2

(DUKE OF EDINBURGH CLASS—2 SHIPS).

DUKE OF EDINBURGH (June 1904), & **BLACK PRINCE** (November, 1904).

Displacement 13,550 tons. Complement —

Length (*waterline*), 480 feet. Beam, 73½ feet. *Maximum* draught, 27½ feet.

Guns :
6—9·2 inch, XI., 50 cal. (*AAA*).
10—6 inch, XI., 50 cal. (*C*).
22—3 pdr. (semi-automatic)
8—1¼ pdr. (pompoms).
Torpedo tubes (18 inch) :
   3 *submerged*.

Armour (Krupp) :
6″ Belt (amidships) .... *a*
4″ Belt (bow)................ *d*
3″ Belt (aft) .... *ε*
¾″ Armour deck ....
Protection to vitals :........= *a*
6″ Barbettes (6) (N.C.)...... *b*
6″ Turrets to them (K.C.) ... *aa*
6″ Battery .... *a*
7″ Conning tower (N.C.)... *a*

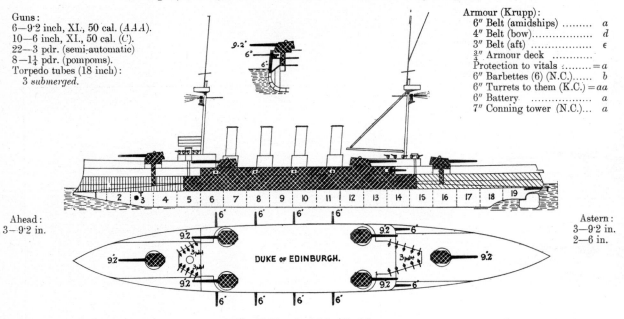

Ahead :
3—9·2 in.

Astern :
3—9·2 in.
2—6 in.

DUKE of EDINBURGH.

Broadside : 4—9·2 in., 5—6 in.

Photo, Symonds & Co.

Machinery : 2 sets 4 cylinder triple expansion. 2 screws. Boilers : 20 Babcock and Wilcox+6 cylindrical. Designed H.P. 23,500 = 22·33 kts. (24 hoped for). Coal : *normal* 1000 tons ; *maximum* 2000 tons ; also 400 tons oil :

Gunnery Notes.—Loading positions, big guns : central pivot. Hoists : hydraulic for 9·2 inch ; electric for 6 inch guns. Big guns manœuvred hydraulically and hand.
   Arcs of fire : End, 9·2, 285° ; Beam, 9·2, 120° ; Battery guns, about 120°.

Torpedo Notes.—1904 model torpedoes. *Submerged* stern tube. Nets to be fitted.

Engineering Notes.—Standardised machinery. Weight 2250 tons complete.

Trials.—

Name.	Builder.	Engines and boilers.	Laid down	Completed	Trials :— 30 hours at 4/5.	8 hours full.	Boilers.	Last recorded best speed.
Duke of Edinburgh	Pembroke	Humphrys & T.	Feb., '03	Dec., '05	16,699 = 21·6	23,939 = 23·66	Babcock	
Black Prince	Thames I.W.	Thames I.W.	June, '03	Jan., '06			Babcock	

General Notes.—Estimates, 1902-3. Cost, per ship, about £1,150,000. Designed by Sir P. Watts.

(DRAKE CLASS—4 SHIPS.)

GOOD HOPE (February, 1901), **DRAKE** (March, 1902), **LEVIATHAN** (July, 1901), & **KING ALFRED** (Oct. 1901).

Displacement 14,100 tons.   Complement 900.

Length (*waterline*), 515 feet.   Beam, 71 feet.   *Maximum* draught, 28 feet.   Length over all, 529½ feet.

Guns :
2—9·2 inch, IX., 45 cal. (*AA*)
16—6 inch, VII., 45 cal. (*D*).
14—12 pdr.
3—3 pdr.
2 Maxims.
Torpedo tubes (18 inch) :
2 *submerged*

Armour (Krupp) :
6″ Belt (amidships) ...... *a*
3 Belt (bow) .... *ϵ*
8″ Bulkheads (aft) (H.N.) *a*
3″—2″ Deck slopes ......
Protection to vitals ...=*aaa*
6″ Barbettes (N.C.) ...... *b*
5″ Turrets to these......... *c*
6″ Casemates (16) (N.C.) *b*
12″ Conning tower (H.N.) *aaa*
(Total weight *about* 2700 tons).

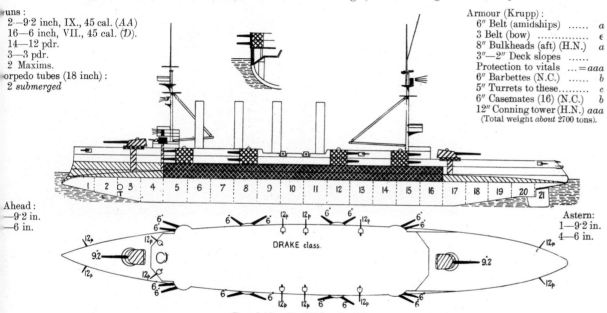

Ahead :
—9·2 in.
—6 in.

Astern :
1—9·2 in.
4—6 in.

DRAKE class.

Broadside : 2—9·2 in., 8—6 in.

KING ALFRED.

Machinery : 2 sets 4 cylinder vertical inverted triple expansion.   2 screws.   Boilers : 43 Belleville.   Designed H.P. 30,000 = 23 kts.   Coal : *normal* 1250 tons : *maximum* 2500 tons.

Armour Notes—Belt is 11½ feet wide by 400 feet long.

Gunnery Notes—Loading positions, big guns : all round.   Hoists, electric for 6 inch guns.   Big guns manœuvred by hydraulic gear. Fire control platform fitted 1905-06.

Engineering Notes—Machinery boilers with water, &c., weigh 2,500 tons.   Boiler rooms 185 feet long.   All the class are excellent steamers, the *Drake* holding the record.   They easily beat their contract speeds in service.   Heating surface 72,000 square feet.   Grate area 2313 square feet.   In 1905 Cross Atlantic Race of 2nd Cruiser Squadron the *Drake* was the first ship to reach Gibraltar.

Name.	Builder.	Engines & Boilers made by	Laid down.	Completed.	First Trials :— 30 hrs. at 4/5.	Full power.	Boilers.	Speed last sea trial.
Good Hope	Fairfield	Fairfield	Sept. '99	1902	22,703=22·7	31,071=23·05	Belleville	24·54
Drake	Pembroke	Humphrys & T.	April, '99	1902	23,103=22·08	30,849=23·05	Belleville	24·38 ('05)
King Alfred	Clydebank	Clydebank	Nov. '99	1903	22,540=21·98	30,893=23·46	Belleville	
Leviathan	Vickers	Vickers	Aug. '99	1903	22,990=21·96	31,203=23·23	Belleville	24·1

Coal consumption averages 11 tons an hour at 19 kts. ; and 19-20 tons an hour at 30,000 H.P. (24 kts).

General Notes—Tactical diameter about 750 yards, extreme helm.   The ships are a little cranky in a sea way, but not to any abnormal extent, and have proved good sea boats in regular commission.   Cost *complete* per ship averaged just over £1,000,000.

Differences :—

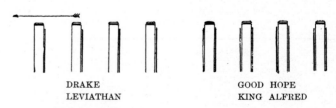

DRAKE
LEVIATHAN

GOOD HOPE
KING ALFRED

Drake has Admiral's bridge forward.   No after bridge.   Small top gallant on main.

61

(CRESSY CLASS.—6 SHIPS.)

SUTLEJ (November, 1899), **CRESSY** (December, 1899), **ABOUKIR** (May, 1900), **HOGUE** (August, 1900), **BACCHANTE** (February, 1901), & **EURYALUS** (May, 1901).

Displacement 12,000 tons.   Complement 700 (flagship 745).

Length (*waterline*), 454 feet.   Beam, 69½ feet.   *Maximum* draught, 28 feet.

Guns :
    2—9·2 inch, VIII., 45 cal. (*A*)
    12—6 inch, VII., 45 cal. (*D*).
    12—12 pdr., 12 cwt. (*F*).
    2—12 pdr., 8 cwt. (*F*).
    3—3 pdr.
    2 Maxims.

Torpedo tubes (18 inch) :
    2 *submerged.*

Armour (Krupp) :
    6″ Belt (amidships) ...... *a*
    2″ Belt (bow) (N). ...... *f*
    5″ Bulkheads .... *b*
    3″ Deck.....................
    Protection to vitals ...... = *aa*
    6″ Barbettes (H.N.) ...... *b*
    6″ Turrets to these ...... *b*
    5″ Casemates (12) (K.N.C.) *c*
    12″ Conning tower ...... *aaa*
    (Total weight 2100 tons).

CRESSY class

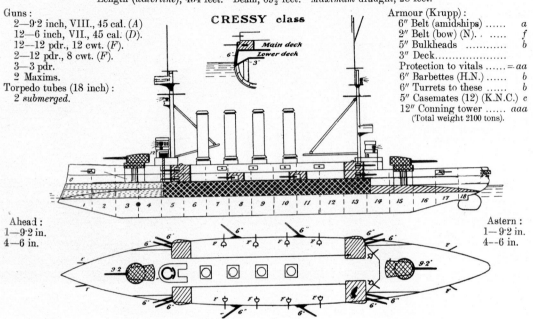

Main deck
Lower deck

Ahead :
1—9·2 in.
4—6 in.

Astern :
1—9·2 in.
4—6 in.

Broadside : 2—9·2 in., 6—6 in.

Machinery : 2 sets 4 cylinder vertical inverted triple expansion.   2 screws.   Boilers : 30 Belleville.   Designed H.P. 21,000 = 21 kts.   Coal : *normal* 800 tons ; *maximum* 1600 tons.

Armour Notes.—Belt is 11½ feet wide by 230 feet long, 5 feet of it below water.

Gunnery Notes.—Loading positions, big guns : all round (central pivot).   Hoists : Electric for 6 inch guns.   Big guns manœuvred by hydraulic gear.   Fire control platforms fitted 1905-06.

Engineering Notes.—Good steamers.   All can exceed the designed speed in service.   Machinery weighs 1800 tons.   Boiler space 130 feet.

| Name. | Builder. | Machinery and Boilers by | Laid down. | Completed | First Trials. | | Boilers. | Speed last sea trial. |
					30 hours at 4/5 114 revs.	8 hours full power 122 revs.		
Sutlej	Clydebank	Clydebank	Aug., '98	1902	16,604 = 20·62	21,261 = 21·77	Belleville	
Cressy	Fairfield	Fairfield	Oct., '98	1901	16,800 = 20·50	21,200 = 20·79	Belleville	22·5
Aboukir	Fairfield	Fairfield	Nov., '98	1902	16.274 = 20·40	21,352 = 21·6	Belleville	22·5
Hogue	Vickers	Vickers	July, '98	1902	16,456 = 20·15	22,065 = 22·1*	Belleville	22·4
Bacchante	Clydebank	Clydebank	Dec., '99	1902	16,446 = 20·60	21,520 = 21·75	Belleville	22·4
Euryalus	Vickers	Vickers	July, '99	1904		21,318 = 21·63	Belleville	21·1

* Run in bad weather.

Coal consumption : at 21,000 H.P. (22 kts.) about 16½-17 tons an hour ; at 16,000 H.P. (20 kts.) about 12¼ tons an hour.

General Note.—Tactical diameter about 700 yards.   Non-flammable wood fittings.   Hull with armour weighs 7840 tons.   Cost complete just under £800,000.   First of class laid down 1898.

Photo, Symonds & Co.

Differences. —

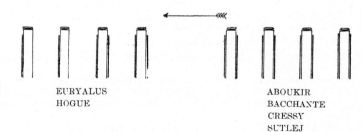

EURYALUS
HOGUE

ABOUKIR
BACCHANTE
CRESSY
SUTLEJ

62

(DEVONSHIRE CLASS—6 SHIPS.)

HAMPSHIRE (Sept., 1903). **CARNARVON** (Oct., 1903), **ANTRIM** (Oct., 1903),
ROXBURGH (Jan., 1904), **ARGYLL** (March, 1904) & **DEVONSHIRE** (April, 1904).

Displacement 10,850 tons. Complement 655.

Length (*waterline*), 450 feet. Beam, 68½ feet. *Maximum* draught., 25½ feet.

Guns :
4—7·5 inch I. (A).
6—6 inch VII. (D).
2—12 pdr.
22—3 pdr.
2 Maxims.
Torpedo tubes :
2 *submerged.*

Armour (Krupp):
6″ Belt (amidships) .... *a*
2″ Belt (ends) .... *f*
2″ Deck (reinforcing belt) ...
Protection to vitals = *aa* (barely).
6″ Bulkheads .... *a*
6″ Lower deck (side) .... *a*
6″ Barbettes .... *b*
5″ Hoods to these.............. *b*
6″ Casemates .... *b*
12″ Conning tower (fore)......*aaa*
With Hull :
Total weight 6665 tons.

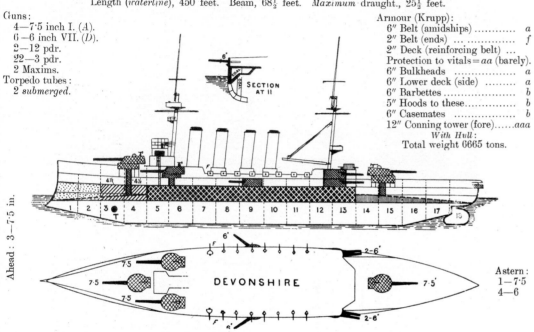

Ahead : 3—7·5 in.

Astern :
1—7·5
4—6

DEVONSHIRE

Broadside : 3—7·5 in. ; 3—6 in.

Machinery : 2 sets vertical triple expansion. 2 screws, "penny type." Boilers : ⅘ water-tube and ⅕ cylindrical. Designed H.P. 21,000 = 22·25 kts. Coal : *normal* 800 tons ; *maximum* 1,800 tons.
Armour Notes.—Belt is 10½ feet wide by 325 feet long from bow. Lower edge is full thickness.
Gunnery Notes.—Loading positions, big guns : central pivot. Hoists, electric and hand. Big guns manœuvred electrically.
Engineering Notes.—

Name.	Built at	Laid down.	Completed.	Trials :—		Boilers 4/5 in.	Last best speed.
				30 hours at 4/5.	8 hrs. full power.		
Devonshire	Chatham		1904	14,830 = 21·0	21,475 = 22·97	Niclausse	23·8
Antrim	Clydebank		1905	14 628 = 21·21	21,604 = 23·20	Yarrow	
Argyll	Greenock Foundry Co.		1905	15,108 = 20 8	21,190 = 22·28	Babcock	
Carnarvon	Beardmore		1904	15,212 = 21·43	21,489 = 23·3	Niclausse	22·4
Hampshire	Elswick		1905		=	Yarrow	
Roxburgh	London and Glasgow		1905	15,005 = 21·54	21,875 = 23·63	Dürr	

(Engines by builders, except for *Devonshire*, which are by Thames Ironworks.)
The coal consumption is heavy in all this class. Niclausse ships burn about 21 tons an hour at full speed, the others about 22 tons or so.
General Notes.—All laid down in 1902. Cost, per ship, about £850,000.

CARNARVON.

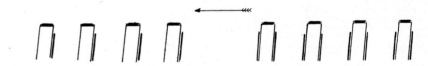

ANTRIM (*shorter than in others*).
CARNARVON

HAMPSHIRE

ROXBURGH

63

(Monmouth Class—10 Ships). ("County Class")

KENT (Mar., 1901), **ESSEX** (Aug., 1901), **BEDFORD** (Aug., 1901), **MONMOUTH** (Nov. 1901), **LANCASTER** (Mar., 1902), **BERWICK** (Sept., 1902), **DONEGAL** (Sept., 1902), **CORNWALL** (Oct., 1902), **CUMBERLAND** (Dec., 1902), & **SUFFOLK** (Jan., 1903).

Displacement 9,800 tons. Complement 678.
Length (*waterline*), 440 feet. Beam, 66 feet. *Mean* draught, 24½ feet.

Guns :
14—6 in., VII., 45 cal. (*D*).
8—12 pdr., 12 cwt. (*F*).
2—12 pdr., 8 cwt. (*F*).
3—3 pdr.
8 Pompoms.
Torpedo tubes—(18 inch) :
2 *Submerged*.

Armour—(Krupp) :
4″ Belt (amidships) ...... *d*
2″ Belt (bow) .... *f*
5″ Bulkhead (aft) .... *b*
2″ Deck (slopes) ....
Protection to vitals ...... =*c*
5″ Barbettes (H.N.) ...... *d*
5″ Turrets to these (H.N.) =*c*
4″ Casemates (10) .... *d*
10″ Conning tower ...... *aa*
(Total weight *about* 1,800 tons).

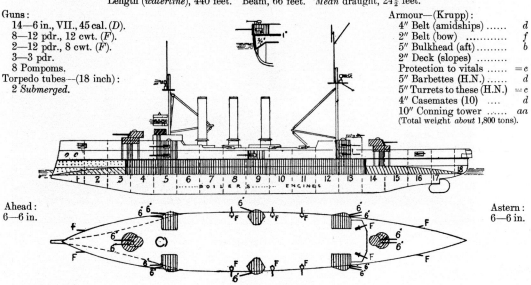

Ahead :
6—6 in.

Astern :
6—6 in.

Broadside : 9—6 in.

Machinery : 2 sets 4 cylinder vertical triple expansion. 2 screws. Boilers : Various—see Notes. Designed H.P. 22,000 = 23 kts. Coal : *normal* 800 tons ; *maximum* 1,600 tons ; also 400 tons oil.

Armour Notes.—Belt is 11½ feet wide by 330 feet long from bow ; 5 feet of it below waterline.

Gunnery Notes.—Hoists : electric. The twin turrets do not give satisfaction, and a project for replacing them with 7·5's has been mooted. Fire control stations fitting as per plan.
Arcs of fire : Turrets, 240° ; casemates, 120°.

Engineering Notes.—"Penny" screws. The trials of ships marked * below were run with ordinary propellers.

Name.	Built at	Machinery and Boilers by	Laid down.	Completed.	30 hrs. 4/5.	8 hours full power.	Boilers.	Speed last sea trial.
*Essex**	Pembroke	Clydebank	Jan., '00	1903	16,132 = 19·6	22,219 = 22·8	Belleville	24·8
*Kent**	Portsmouth	Hawthorn	Feb., '00	1903	16,209 = 20·4	22,249 = 21·7	Belleville	24·1
*Bedford**	Fairfield	Fairfield	Feb., '00	1903	16,005 = 21·2	22,457 = 22·7	Belleville	24·4
*Monmouth**	L. & Glasgow	L. & Glasgow	Aug., '99	1903	16,326 = 20·4	22,189 = 22·6	Belleville	23·9
Lancaster	Elswick	Hawthorn L.	Mar., '01	1904	16,004 = 22·0	22,881 = 24	Belleville	24·8
Berwick	Beardmore	Humphrys	Apl., '01	1903	16.554 = 21·7	22,680 = 23·7	Niclausse	24·4
Donegal	Fairfield	Fairfield	Feb., '01	1903	16,333 = 22·3	22,154 = 23·7	Belleville	24·3
Cornwall	Pembroke	Hawthorn	Mar., '01	1904	16,487 = 21·8	22,694 = 23·6	Babcock	24·0
Cumberland	L. & Glasgow	L. & Glasgow	Feb., '01	1904	16,472 = 22·1	22,784 = 23·7	Belleville	24·4
Suffolk	Portsmouth	Humphrys & T.	Mar., '02	1904	16,350 = 21·2	22,645 = 23·7	Niclausse	23·7

Coal consumption is rather high in all ships of this class. Averages in service :—
Belleville ships—17½ tons an hour at 22,000 H.P.—24 kts.
Niclausse „ 19 „ „ „ „ „
Babcock „ 19½ „ „ „ „ „

In Cross Atlantic Race, 1905 (2nd Cruiser Squadron), *Berwick* and *Cumberland* averaged well over 18 kts. for the whole trip beating *Essex* and easily beating *Cornwall*. *Bedford* got hot bearings and had to ease down, after being second ship for four days.

General Notes.—Cost about £775,000 each. First of class laid down 1900.

64

Photo, Symonds.

BEDFORD
DONEGAL

MONMOUTH (*very prominent steam pipes*)
CUMBERLAND (*high steam pipes*)

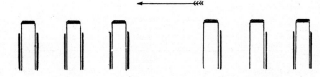

KENT
CORNWALL
LANCASTER

BERWICK
ESSEX
SUFFOLK

(POWERFUL CLASS—2 SHIPS).

POWERFUL (July, 1895), TERRIBLE (May, 1895).

Displacement 14,200 tons.   Complement 894.

Length (*waterline*), 520 feet.   Beam, 71 feet.   *Maximum* draught, 31 feet.

Guns :
2—9·2 inch, VIII, 40 cal. (*A*)
16—6 inch, wire, 40 cal. (*E*)
16—12 pdr., 12 cwt. (*F*)
2—12 pdr., 8 cwt. (*F*)
12—3 pdr.
2 Maxims.
Torpedo tubes (18 inch) :
4 *submerged*.

Armour (Harvey) :
6″ Deck (on slopes) ...... = *a*
Protection to vitals ...... = *a*
6″ Barbettes .... *c*
6″ Turrets to these ...... *c*
6″ Casemates (12 old) ... *c*
6″ Casemates (4 new) ... *b*
12″ Conning tower ...... *aa*
Total weight, 2200 tons.

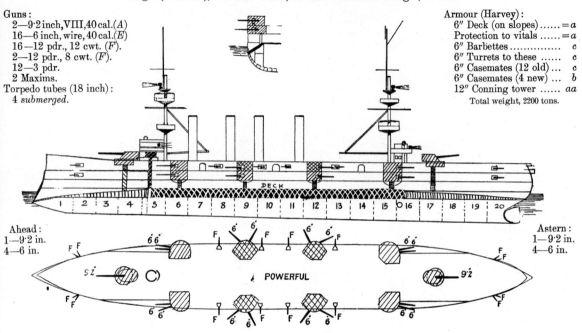

Ahead :
1—9·2 in.
4—6 in.

Astern :
1—9·2 in.
4—6 in.

POWERFUL

Broadside : 2—9·2 in., 8—6 in.

POWERFUL.   *Photo, Symonds.*

Machinery : 2 sets vertical 4 cylinder triple expansion.   2 screws.   Boilers : 48 Bellevilles, without economisers.
Designed H.P. 25,000 = 22 kts.   Coal : *normal* 1,500 tons ; *maximum* 3,000 tons.   Oil, 400 tons.

Armour Notes.—Deck is 6″ amidships, 3″—4″ at ends.

Gunnery Notes.—Loading positions, big guns : all round.   Hoists, electric.   Big guns manœuvred electrically and by hand.
Height of guns above water : 9·2 about 30 feet.

Engineering Notes.—Heating surface, 67,800 sq. feet.   Grate area, 2,200 feet.

Name.	Built and engined by	Laid down.	Completed.	First trials.—Speeds at				Boilers.	Speed last sea trial.
				5,000	18,000	22,000	25,000		
Powerful	Vickers	1894	1898	14·0	20·9	22·6	21·8	Belleville	22·2
Terrible	Clydebank	1894	1898	13·4	20·9	22·3	22·4	Belleville	22·5

Coal consumption : In the early days these ships burned for all purposes 21 tons an hour at full power (25,000 H.P.)
and *pro rata*. Present consumption is considerably lower, and *Terrible* (1904) obtained results as good as those with ships
fitted with economisers. *Normal* consumption to-day may be placed at about 18 tons an hour at 25,000 H.P.

General Notes.—Owing to the thick deck, armament and enormous size, these ships may be
regarded as equal if not superior to the Counties in many ways. They should be able
to stand a great deal of fire without serious results. Tactical diameter about 1,100
yards. Very unhandy ships. Cost about £750,000 each.

I

(LATER DIADEMS—4 SHIPS).

ARGONAUT (January, 1898), **ARIADNE** (April, 1898), **AMPHITRITE** (July, 1898), and **SPARTIATE** (October, 1898).

Displacement 11,000 tons.   Complement 677.

Length (*waterline*), 450 feet.   Beam, 69 feet.   *Maximum* draught, 27½ feet.   Length over all, 462½ feet.

Guns :
16—6 in. wire, 40 cal. (*E*).
12—12 pdr., 12 cwt. (*F*).
2—12 pdr., 8 cwt. (*F*).
12—3 pdr.
2—Maxims.
Torpedo tubes (18 inch) :
2 *submerged*.
Total weight, with ammunition, 652 tons.

Armour :
4″ in Armour deck ... = *b*
Protection to vitals ...   *b*
6″ Casemates (12)...... *c*
12″ Conning tower......*aaa*
Total weight, 1,900 tons, of which 1500 is for deck.

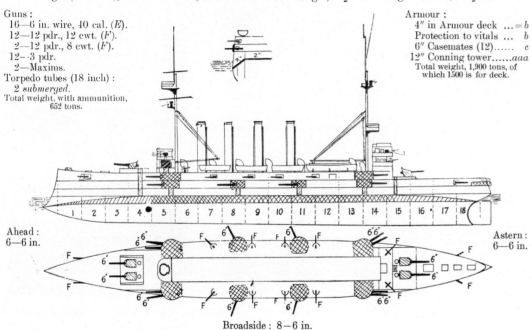

Ahead :
6—6 in.

Astern :
6—6 in.

Broadside : 8—6 in.

Machinery : 2 sets 4 cylinder vertical inverted triple expansion.   2 screws.   Boilers : 30 Bellevilles.   Coal : *normal* 1000 tons ; *maximum* 2000 tons ; 400 tons oil also to be carried.

Gunnery Notes.— Each gun has its own hoist.   Electric hoists.
Ammunition carried : 200 rounds per gun.

Engineering Notes.—Machinery weighs 1525 tons.   Boiler space 132 feet.   Heating surface 47,282 square feet.   Grate area 1390 feet.   Boilers of these ships are of an improved pattern to those in the four earlier *Diadems*.

Name.	Builders.	Machinery and Boilers by	Laid down.	Completed.	Trials :— 30 hours at 4/5.	8 hours full.	Boilers.	Speed last sea trial.
Argonaut	Fairfield	Fairfield	Nov. '96	1900	13,815 = 19·86	18,894 = 21·17	Belleville	20·9
Ariadne	Clydebank	Clydebank	Oct. '96	1900	14,046 = 20·1	19,156 = 21·50	Belleville	21·6
Amphitrite	Vickers	Vickers	Dec. '96	1900	13,695 = 19·5	18,229 = 20·78	Belleville	21·32
Spartiate	Pembroke	Maudslay	May '97	1902		18,658 = 21	Belleville	21·1

Coal consumption : about 15½-16 tons an hour at 18,000 H.P.

Spartiate was delayed in completion owing to an accident with the white metal bearings in her engines.   In 1903 she made a "war cruise" of 25,000 miles with no defects except a split condenser during manœuvres.   About 75% second class or raw stokers.

General Notes.—Built under estimates 1896-95.   Hull with armour weighs 6975 tons.   Tactical diameter about 1000 yards.   Average cost per ship, about £600,000.

Fire control platforms fitting as per plan.   *Photo, Symonds.*

Differences.—

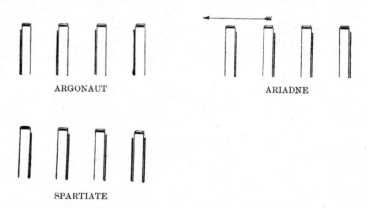

ARGONAUT   ARIADNE

SPARTIATE

Class Distinction.—From early *Diadems*, by being more built up under after-bridge (compare photographs) and having platforms for after 6 in. guns.   Also fire control stations.

From *Cressy* class by being generally "lighter" in appearance, and the absence of large fore and aft turrets.   Mistakes are easy at sea unless the last point is carefully observed.

(EARLY DIADEMS CLASS—4 SHIPS).

DIADEM (October, 1896), **NIOBE** (February, 1897), **EUROPA** (March, 1897), **ANDROMEDA** (April, 1897).

Displacement 11,000 tons. Sheathed and Coppered. Complement 677.

Length (*waterline*), 450 feet. Beam, 69 feet. *Maximum* draught, 27½ feet. Length over all, 460½ feet.

Guns :
16—6 in. wire, 40 cal. (*E*).
12—12 pdr., 12 cwt. (*F*).
2—12 pdr., 8 cwt. (*F*).
12—3 pdr.
2 Maxims.
Torpedo tubes (18 inch) :
2 *submerged*.
(Total, with ammunition, 652 tons.)

Armour (Harvey) :
4″ Armour Deck............= *b*
Protection to vitals......... *b*
6″ Casemates (12) .... *c*
12″ Conning tower ....*aaa*
(Total weight, 1,900 tons, of which 1,500 tons is deck armour.)

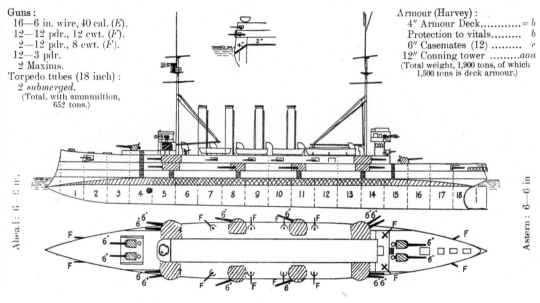

Broadside : 8—6 in.

EUROPA.   *Photo, Symonds.*

Machinery : 2 sets 4 cylindrical vertical inverted triple expansion. 2 screws. Boilers : 30 Bellevilles, with economisers added later. Designed H.P. 16,500 = 20.25 kts. Coal : *normal* 1000 tons ; *maximum* 2000 tons. 400 tons oil also to be carried.

Gunnery Notes.—Each gun has its own hoist, electric and hand.

Engineering Notes.—Machinery, etc., weighs 1,525 tons. The economisers were added after the boilers were installed. Boiler space, 132 feet long. Heating surface, 40,538 square feet. Grate area, 1450 square feet.

Name.	Builder.	Engines and boilers by	Laid down.	Completed.	First trials:—		Boilers.	Last sea trial.
					30 hours at 12,500 H.P.	8 hours at full power.		
Diadem	Fairfield	Fairfield	January, '96	1899	12,791 = 19.8	17,262 = 20.65	Belleville	20.45
Niobe	Vickers	Vickers	December, '95	1899	12,961 = 19.3	16,834 = 20.5	Belleville	
Europa	Clydebank	Clydebank	January, '96	1899	12,739 = 19.3	17,137 = 20.4	Belleville	20.7
Andromeda	Pembroke	Hawthorn L.	December, '95	1900	12,261 = 19.3	16,751 = 20.4	Belleville	21.4

Coal consumption : These ships all burn more per I.H.P. than the later *Diadems*, and at 16,500 H.P. full power, consumes 15-17 tons an hour. Less has been burned.

In 1903 *Europa* made a war cruise to China and back, followed by manœuvres. 25,000 miles without a single defect. 75% raw stokers.

General Notes.—Built under estimate, 1895-96. Hull, with armour, weighs 6,975 tons. Tactical diameter, 1000 yards. Average cost per ship, under £600,000.

Differences.—*Diadem* and *Andromeda* have no steam pipes abaft the first two funnels.

Class Distinctions.—Differ from later *Diadems* by being less built up under the after-bridge. Compare photos. No fire control stations.

I 2

(Edgar Class—7 Ships).

EDGAR (November, 1890), **HAWKE** (March, 1891), **ENDYMION** (July, 1891), **THESEUS** (September, 1891), **GRAFTON** (January, 1892), also **GIBRALTAR** (April, 1892), & **ST. GEORGE** (June, 1892).

Displacement 7350 tons (except last two which are sheathed and coppered, and displace 7700 tons).

Complement 540 (flagship 571).

Length, 360 feet. Beam, 60 feet. *Maximum* draught, about 26 feet.

Guns :
  2—9·2 inch, 30 cal. (C).
  10—6 in. VII., 40 cal. (D).
  (The 6 inch wire formerly carried now being replaced by 6 inch VII.)
  12—6 pdr.
  5—3 pdr.
  2 Maxims.
Torpedo tubes (18 inch) :
  2 *submerged*.

Armour (steel) :
  5″ Armour deck .... =c
  Protection to vitals .... =c
  7″ Hoists to big guns .... d
  6″ Casemates (4) .... d
  2″ Hoists to these ....
  12″ Conning tower .... a

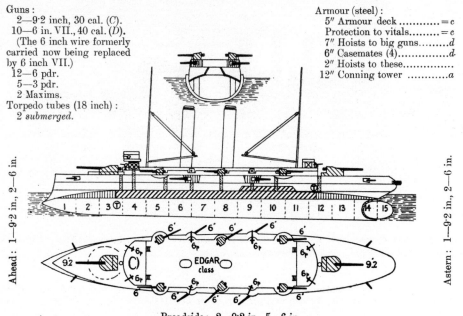

Ahead : 1—9·2 in., 2—6 in.

Astern : 1—9·2 in., 2—6 in.

Broadside : 2—9·2 in., 5—6 in.

Machinery : 2 sets vertical involved triple expansion. 2 screws. Boilers : cylindrical. Designed H.P. *natural* 10,000 = 18·5 kts, *forced* 12,000 = 19·5 kts. Coal : *normal* 850 tons ; *maximum* 1250 tons.

Engineering Notes.—Grafton and *Theseus* have 8 single-ended boilers, the other 4 double-ended, and 1 single ended. 48 furnaces. Heating surface, 24·902 sq. feet. Grate area, 812 sq. feet. All these ships steam very well, and can do 19 kts. for several hours, except in a sea way. The *f.d.* only very slightly increases speed. Engine room troubles in this class almost unknown. Coal consumption : about 11 tons an hour at 10,000 H.P. (18-19 kts.), 6¼ tons at 6000 H.P.

General Notes.—Laid down in 1889-90. Completed, 1893-94. Cost about £430,000 per ship on the average.

THESEUS.

Photo, Symonds.

Differences :—

Name.	Steampipes to fore funnel.	Notes.
Edgar Hawke Gibraltar St. George	before	
Endymion	abaft	
Theseus	abaft	Thinner funnels.
Grafton	abaft	Thinner funnels. Striking top masts.

Class distinctions :—

From *Blake* class by rig.

From *Crescent* class by forecastle being absent.

From *Hermoine* class by larger size and big guns at bow and stern, and positions of funnels—but mistakes at sea are possible.

(CRESCENT CLASS—2 SHIPS).

ROYAL ARTHUR (February, 1891) and **CRESCENT** (March, 1892).

Displacement 7700 tons. Sheathed and coppered. Complement 544 (flagship 571).

Length, 360 feet. Beam, 60¾ feet. *Maximum draught*, 26¼ feet.

Guns :
  2—9·2 inch, 30 cal. (*C*).
  12—6 inch, VII. (*D*).
    (being or to be fitted).
  12—6 pdr.
  2—9 pdr. (boat)
  5—3 pdr.
  2 Maxims.
Torpedo tubes (18 inch) :
  2 *submerged.*

Armour (steel) :
  5″ Armour deck .... = *c*
  Protection to vitals .... = *c*
  6″ Casemates (4) .... *d*
  12″ Conning Tower .... *a*

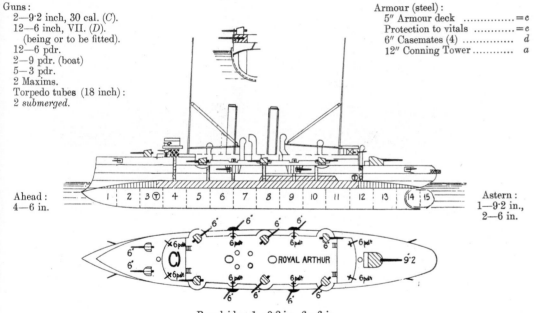

Ahead :
4—6 in.

Astern :
1—9·2 in.,
2—6 in.

Broadside : 1—9·2 in., 6—6 in.

Machinery : 2 sets vertical inverted triple expansion. 2 screws. Boilers : cylindrical (6 double-ended). Designed H.P. *natural* 10,000 = 18·5 kts. ; *forced* 12,000 = 19·5 kts. Coal : *normal* 850 tons ; *maximum* 1250 tons.

Engineering Notes.—As for *Edgar* class. Both are excellent steamers and fine sea boats.

General Notes.—Both built at Portsmouth. Cost about £420,000 each.

ROYAL ARTHUR.   *Photo, Symonds & Co.*

Differences.—

Name.	Steam pipes to fore funnel.	Notes.
Royal Arthur	abaft	Fore top mast fitted.
Crescent	before	Shorter and less conspicuous cowls.

Class distinction.—The high forecastles distinguish these ships from the *Edgars*, *Blakes* and *Astræas*.

(BLENHEIM CLASS—2 SHIPS).

BLAKE (November 1889) & **BLENHEIM** (July, 1890).

Displacement 9150 tons.   Complement 590.

Length, 375 feet.   Beam, 65 feet.   *Maximum* draught, $27\frac{1}{2}$ feet.

Guns :
2—9·2 inch, 30 cal. (C).
10—6 inch wire (E).
16—3 pdr.
2—9 pdr. boat.
7 Machine.
Torpedo tubes (14 inch) :
2 *submerged*.
2 *above water*.

Armour (steel and compound) :
6″-3″ Deck (slopes) ......= c-d
Protection to vitals........   c
8″-4″ Cylinder protection ...
7″ Big gun hoists.
6″ Casemates (4)...........   d
12″ Conning tower ....   a

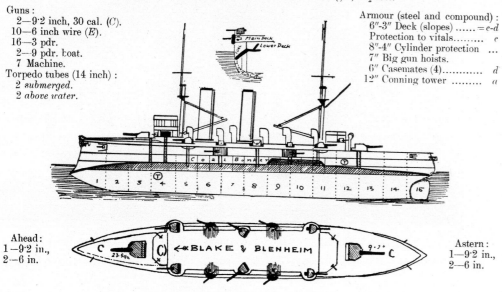

Ahead :
1—9·2 in.,
2—6 in.

Astern :
1—9·2 in.,
2—6 in.

Broadside : 2—9·2 in., 5—6 in.

Machinery : 4 sets vertical triple expansion coupled.   2 screws.   Boilers : 6 cylindrical (double ended).
Designed H.P. *natural* 13,000 = 18·5 kts ; *forced* 20,000 = 22 kts.   Coal : *normal* 1,500 tons ; *maximum* 1,800 tons.

Engineering Notes.—The ships never reached designed speeds, but were able to exceed and maintain 20 kts. for long periods. *Blenheim* is still good for 20 kts or so—but *Blake* is getting worn out, and likely soon to disappear from the effective list, as the type are not considered worth the cost of extensive repairs.

General Notes.—*Blake*, built at Chatham.   *Blenheim*, by Thames Ironworks.

BLAKE.   *Photo, H. Nye, Esq.*

Differences.—

Name.	Lower masts.	Notes.
Blake		
Blenheim	*Much shorter*	

Class Distinctions.—Easily distinguished from the *Edgar* and *Crescent* classes by their funnels and topmasts, and from the *Talbot* by general shape of hull, size, and funnels.

(ARROGANT CLASS—4 SHIPS).

ARROGANT (May, 1896), **FURIOUS** (December, 1896), **GLADIATOR** (December, 1896),

& **VINDICTIVE** (December, 1897).

Displacement 5750 tons.   Complement 480.

Length, 320 feet.   Beam, 57½ feet.   *Maximum* draught, 24 feet.

Guns :
10—6 in. VII., 45 cal. (D).
8—12 pdr., 12 cwt. (F).
1—12 pdr., 8 cwt.
3—3 pdr.
2 Maxims.
Torpedo tubes (18 inch) :
2 *submerged.*
1 *above water* (stern).

Armour :
2″ Belt (bow) .... *f*
3″ Armour deck .... = *d*
Protection to vitals ...... *d*
4″ Engine hatches .... = *b*
3″ Gun shields ....
8¾″ Conning tower......... *a*

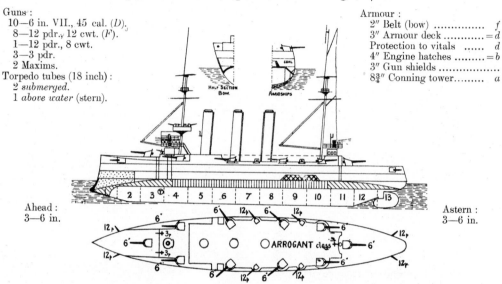

Ahead :
3—6 in.

Astern :
3—6 in.

Broadside : 6—6 in.

Machinery : 2 sets vertical triple expansion.   2 screws.   Boilers : 18 Belleville *without* economisers.
Designed H.P. 10,000 = 19 kts.   Coal : *normal* 500 tons ; *maximum* 1175 tons, and oil in *Arrogant*.

Armour Notes—The deck is in two thicknesses of hardened steel.

Gunnery Notes—Hoists, electric.

Engineering Notes :—

Name.	Builder.	Engines and Boilers by	Laid down.	Completed.	30 hours at 7000 H.P.	8 hours full.	Boilers.	Speed last sea trial.
Arrogant	Devonport	Earle	June, '95	1898	7624 = 17·8	10,290 = 19·6	Belleville	19·9
Furious	Devonport	Earle	June, '95	1896	7155 = 18·7	10,272 = 20·1	Belleville	19·7
Gladiator*	Portsmouth	Maudslay	Jan., '96	1896	7149 = 17·5	10,018 = 19·1	Belleville	20
Vindictive	Chatham	Chatham	Jan., '96	1899	7164 = 17·7	10,262 = 20·1	Belleville	19·9

* *Gladiator* had a foul bottom on trials.

Coal consumption in all this class is heavier than in any other Belleville cruisers, boilers being of an old and uneconomical pattern.   Average 9-9½ tons at 10,000 H.P. (19 kts).   All are or were excellent steamers in fine weather, but being short quickly fall off in a sea way.   *Vindictive* has kept station for 12 hours at 19 kts.   *Arrogant's* boilers re-tubed 1904.

General Notes—Tactical diameter very small indeed, about one length.   Ships were designed as " rams," and have double rudders.   Average cost per ship, just under £300,000.

FURIOUS.

Differences :—

Name.	Steam pipes to first 2 funnels.	Notes.
Arrogant	Abaft	
Furious	Abaft	
Gladiator	None	
Vindictive		

Class distinctions—Easily distinguished from *Highflyer* and *Challenger* classes by their extreme shortness, and also by absence of main fighting top.

(CHALLENGER CLASS—2 SHIPS).

CHALLENGER (May, 1902) & **ENCOUNTER** (June, 1902).

Displacement 5915 tons.   Complement 475.

Length, *p.p.* 355 feet.   Beam, 56 feet.   *Maximum* draught, 21¼ feet.

Guns :
  11—6 inch, VII., 45 cal. (*D*).
  8—12 pdr., 12 cwt. (*F*).
  1—12 pdr., 8 cwt. (*F*).
  6—3 pdr.
  2 Maxims.
Torpedo tubes (18 inch) :
  2 *submerged.*

Armour :
  3″ Deck (amidships) ...= *d*
  Protection to vitals ......= *d*
  2″ Deck forward and aft = ε
  5″ Engine hatches (K.C.) = *aa*
  6″ Conning tower........ = *b*
  (Total weight about 500 tons).

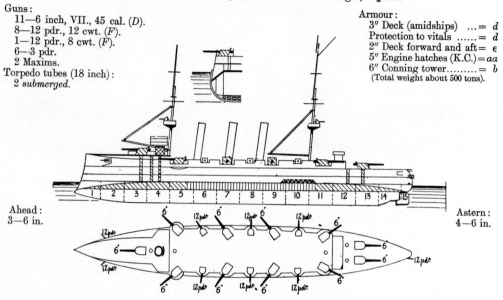

Ahead :
3—6 in.

Astern :
4—6 in.

Broadside : 6—6 in.

Machinery : 2 sets triple expansion.   2 screws.   Boilers : Babcock and Dürr (*see notes*).   Designed H.P. 12,500 = 21 knots.   Coal : *normal* 500 tons ; *maximum* 1225 tons.

Gunnery Notes.—Hoists, electric to all guns.

Engineering Notes.—*Encounter* failed on first trials.   Cylinders : 28 inch, 45 inch and 52 inch.   Stroke : 32 inch.

Differences, etc.—See next page.

Name.	Built at	Boilers and Engines.	Laid down.	Completed.	Trials :—			Boilers.	Last sea trial.
					30 hours 4/5.	8 hours full power.			
Challenger	Chatham	Wallsend Co.	December, '00	1905	=	=21·1 kts.		Babcock	19·8
Encounter	Devonport	Keyham Yard	January, '01	1905	=19 kts.	=		Dürr	...

General Notes.—Built under 1900-01 estimates.   Cost about £420,000 per ship.   Draught : forward, 19¼ feet ; aft, 21¼ feet.

(HIGHFLYER CLASS—3 SHIPS.)

HERMES (April 1898), **HIGHFLYER** (June, 1898), **HYACINTH** (October, 1898).

Displacement 5600 tons.   Complement 450.

Length, 350 feet.   Beam, 54 feet.   *Maximum* draught, 22 feet.

Guns :
  11—6 inch wire (E).
  8—12 pdr. 12 cwt. (F).
  1—12 pdr. 8 cwt. (F).
  6—3 pdr.
  2 Maxims.
Torpedo tubes (18 inch) :
  2 *submerged.*

Armour :
  3″ Armour deck ....= *d*
  Protection to vitals ...= *d*
  5″ Engine hatches ......= *a*
  6″ Conning tower ......= *b*

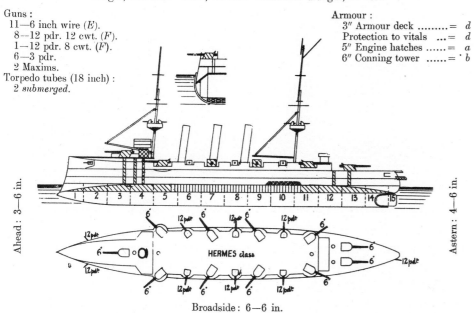

Ahead : 3—6 in.

Astern : 4—6 in.

HERMES class

Broadside : 6—6 in.

Machinery : 2 sets 4 cylinder triple expansion. 2 screws. Boilers : Belleville and Babcock (see notes). Designed H.P. 10,000 = 20 kts. Coal : *normal* 500 tons ; *maximum* 1100 tons.

Gunnery Notes.—Electric hoists.
  Ammunition carried : 200 rounds per gun.

Torpedo Notes.—7 torpedoes.

Engineering Notes.—Hermes reboilered 1902. Machinery weighs 835 tons.

Name.	Builder.	Machinery, etc., by	Laid down	Completed	30 hrs. at ¾.	8 hrs. full.	Boilers	Speed last sea trial
Hermes	Fairfield	Fairfield & Harland & W.	April, '97	1900	7713 = 18·8	10,500 = 20·5	Babcock	20·9
Highflyer	Fairfield	Fairfield	June, '97	1900	7644 = 19·4	10,334 = 20·1	Belleville	21·1
Hyacinth*	L. Glasgow	L. Glasgow	Jan., '97	1901	7718 = 17·34	10,536 = 19·4	Belleville	21

*Hyacinth had a foul bottom on trials.

Coal consumption : about 6 tons an hour at 7500 H.P., and about 8¼ tons at 10,000 H.P. *Hermes* burns 8¾ tons at 10,000 H.P.

General Notes.—Built under estimates 1896-97. Cost about £300,000 per ship. Hull with armour weighs 3120 tons.

HERMES.   (Gaff now removed in all.)   *Photo, Symonds.*

	Steam pipes to first two funnels.	Notes.
Hermes	before	
Highflyer	before	
Hyacinth	abaft	
Challenger		Kidney shape fighting tops
Encounter	none	,, ,, ,, ,,

(Eclipse Class—9 Ships.)

ECLIPSE (July, 1894), **TALBOT** (April, 1895), **MINERVA** (Sept., 1895), **VENUS** (Sept., 1895), **JUNO** (Nov., 1895), **DIANA** (Dec., 1895), **DIDO** (March, 1896), **DORIS** (March, 1896), & **ISIS** (June, 1896).

Displacement 5600 tons. Complement 450.

Length (*waterline*), 364 feet. Beam, 54 feet. *Maximum* draught, 23 feet. Length over all, 370⅓ feet.

Guns (re-armed 1902-05) :
11—6 inch, VII. (*D*).
8—12 pdr., 12 cwt.
1—12 pdr., 8 cwt.
7—3 pdr.
2 Maxims.
Torpedo tubes (18 in.) :
2 *submerged*.
1 *above water* (stern).

Armour :
2½″ Armour deck = *d*
Protection to vitals = *d*
6″ Engine hatches ...
6″ Conning tower
(Harvey) *c*

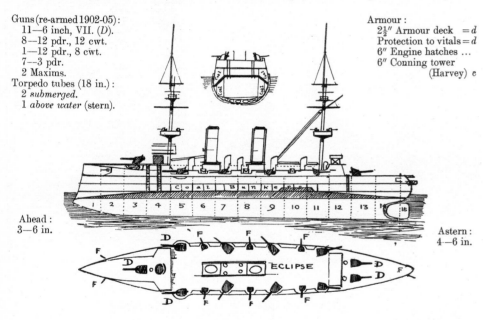

Ahead :
3—6 in.

Astern :
4—6 in.

Broadside : 6—6 in.

Machinery : 2 sets inverted triple expansion. 2 screws. Boilers : 8 single-ended cylindrical. Designed H.P. *natural* 8000 = 18·5 kts. ; *forced* 9600 = 19·5 kts. Coal : *normal* 550 tons ; *maximum* 1076 tons.

Engineering Notes.—24 furnaces. Heating surface, 19,200 square feet. Grate area, 599 square feet. Machinery, &c., weighs 938 tons. All these ships for short periods reach or exceed 19 kts. On trial *light* all touched 20 kts.

Doris and all others except *Talbot*.

TALBOT.   *Photos, Symonds.*

Differences :—*Dido, Isis, Diana, Venus, Eclipse,* have steam pipes before fore funnel ; *Doris, Juno, Minerva,* have them abaft. *Eclipse's* steam pipes are high ; those of the other ships are not. *Talbot* (see photo). (Gaffs now removed in all ships fitted with wireless).

HERMIONE.   *Photo, Symonds.*

Photo, Symonds.

Difference.—Except *Hermione* and *Flora*, all have a steam pipe before fore funnel. *Hermione*, *Astræa*, *Bonaventure*, *Fox*, have stern walks and carry an extra pair of boats aft.

(ASTRÆA CLASS—8 SHIPS.)

HERMIONE, ASTRÆA, CAMBRIAN, CHARYBDIS, FLORA, FORTE, FOX (—1893), BONAVENTURE (1892).

Displacement 4360 tons.   Complement 318.
Length 320 feet.   Beam, 49½ feet.   *Maximum* draught, 21 feet.

Guns :
2—6 inch wire (*E*).
8—4·7 inch (*F*)
8—6 pdr.
1—3 pdr.
Torpedo tubes (18 inch) :
4 *above water.*

Armour (steel) :
2″ Deck ....ϵ
5″ Engine hatches ....*c*
4½″ Gun shields ....
3″ Conning tower ....*f*

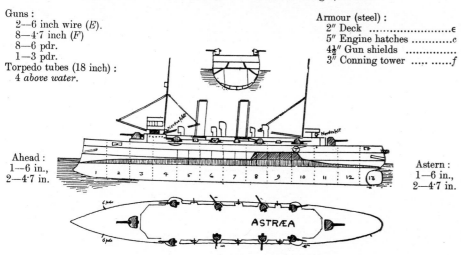

Ahead :
1—6 in.,
2—4·7 in.

Astern :
1—6 in.,
2—4·7 in.

ASTRÆA

Broadside : 2—6 in., 4—4·7 in.

Machinery : vertical triple expansion.   2 screws.   Boilers : 8 1-ended.   Designed H.P. *natural* 7,000 = 18 kts. ; *forced* 9,000 = 19·5 kts.   Coal : *normal* 400 tons ; *maximum* capacity 1000 tons.

General Notes.—Can steam at about 18½ kts. still.   Fighting value small and ships likely soon to be removed from effective list.   Built under Naval Defence Act.   Cost about £250,000 per ship.

(APOLLO CLASS—10 SHIPS.)

LATONA (1890), TERPSICHORE (1890), THETIS (1890), SAPPHO (1891), SCYLLA (1891), SIRIUS (1891), ÆOLUS (1891), BRILLIANT (1891), INDEFATIGABLE (1891) and IPHEGENIA (mining ship) (1891).

Displacement (unsheathed) 3400 tons.   Complement 273.
Length, 300 feet.   Beam, 43⅔ feet.   *Maximum* draught, 18 feet.

Guns :
2—6 inch wire (*E*).
6—4·7 inch (*F*)
8—6 pdr.
1—3 pdr.
4 Machine.
Torpedo tubes (14 inch):
4 *above water.*

Armour (steel) :
2″ Deck. ....ϵ
Protection to vitals...........ϵ
5″ Engine hatches ....*c*
4½″ Gun shields ....
3″ Conning tower ....*f*

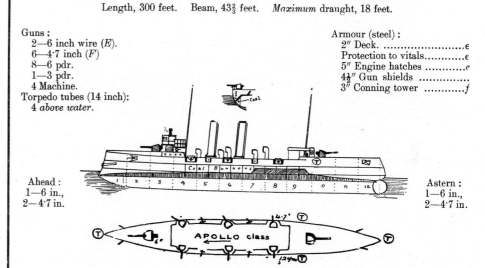

Ahead :
1—6 in.,
2—4·7 in.

Astern :
1—6 in.,
2—4·7 in.

APOLLO class

Broadside : 2—6 in., 3—4·7 in.

Machinery : 2 sets vertical triple expansion.   2 screws.   Boilers : cylindrical, 3 2-ended + 2 1-ended.   Designed H.P. *natural* 7000 = 18·5 kts. ; *forced* 9000 = 20 kts.   Coal : *normal* 400 tons ; *maximum* 535 tons.

General Notes.—17 kts. is the best speed that most of these can now make for anything but a short spurt.   Fighting value very small.   Being removed from effective list.   Built under Naval Defence Act.   Cost about £200,000 per ship.

(GEM CLASS—4 SHIPS).

TOPAZE (July, 1893), **AMETHYST** (Nov., 1903), **DIAMOND** (Jan., 1904),
& **SAPPHIRE** (March, 1904).

Displacement 3000 tons.   Complement 296.

Length, 360 feet.   Beam, 40 feet.   *Mean* draught, 14½ feet.

Guns :
    12—4 inch (*F*).
    8—3 pdr.
    2 Maxims.
Torpedo tubes (18 inch) :
    2 *above water.*

Armour (steel) :
    2″ Deck..............= *d*

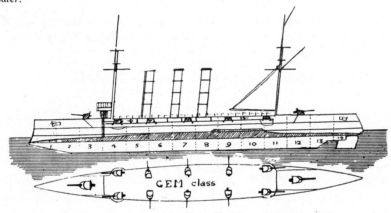

Machinery : 2 sets triple expansion except *Amethyst*, Turbine. 2 screws. Boilers : various (*see notes*).
Designed H.P. 9800 = 21·75 kts. *nominal* (23 or more expected). Coal : *normal* 300 ; *maximum* 500 tons.

Engineering Notes.—Turbine revolutions, 400 at 7000 H.P., 450 at 10,000. Reciprocating engines, 245 at 10,000. *Amethyst* has Parsons turbines with small turbines for cruising speeds (slow).

General Notes.—First two built under estimates, 1902-03, second two, estimates, 1903-4. Cost about £240,000 per ship.

Name	Built by	Engines by	Laid down	Completed	8 hours 4/5 power.	4 hours full power.	Boilers.	Speed last sea trial.
Topaze	Laird	Laird	Aug., '02	1904	... = ...	... = ...	Normand Laird	...
Sapphire	Palmer	Palmer	March, '03	1905	7281=20·6	10,200=22·3	Normand Laird	...
Amethyst	Elswick	Parsons	Jan., '03	1904	7280=20·6	13,000=23·6	Yarrow (curved)	...
Diamond	Laird	Laird	March, '03	1905	7145=19·3	9,868=22·1	Yarrow	...

Coal consumption heavy in all.

Topaze and *Sapphire* about 7½ tons an hour at 7000 H.P., and 11½ tons an hour for 9800 H.P.
Diamond   „   6½ „   „   „   „   „   10   „   „   „   „
Amethyst (turbine)   „   7 „   „   „   „   „   9   „   „   „   „

Differences :—

Name.	Notes.
Topaze	
Amethyst	
Diamond	
Sapphire	

76

Photo, Elswick,

ADVENTURE (8th September, 1904), & **ATTENTIVE** (24th November, 1904).

Displacement 2940 tons.   Length, 374 feet.   Beam, 38¼ feet.   *Maximum* draught, 13½ feet.   Complement 268.

Guns:
10—12 pdr.
8—3 pdr.
Torpedo tubes (18 inch):
  2 *submerged.*

Armour:
2″ Deck ....
¾″ Gun shields ......

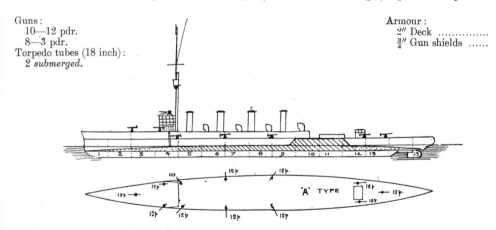

Machinery: 2 sets 6 cylinder.   2 screws.   Boilers: ⅘ Yarrow curved, 2⅕ cylindrical.   Designed H.P. 16,000 = 25 kts.   Coal: *normal*   tons; *maximum*   tons.

General Notes.—Built at Elswick.   Engined by Hawthorn, Leslie & Co.   Laid down January, 1904.   Completed October, 1905.   Average cost, £275,000.

First Trials.—Adventure, I.H.P. 15,850 = 25·42 kts.   *Attentive*, 25·6.

Distinctions.—4 funnels.

Photo, Symonds & Co.

FORWARD (29th August, 1904), & **FORESIGHT** (8th October, 1904).

Displacement 2945 tons.   Length, 360 feet.   Beam, 39 feet.   *Maximum* draught, 14 feet.   Complement 268.

Armour:
2″ Belt amidships ...
1½″—⅝″ Deck ....

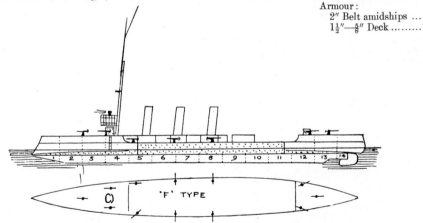

Machinery: 2 sets 6 cylinder.   2 screws.   Boilers: White-Forster (with ⅓ cylindrical).   Designed H.P. 16,500 = 25 kts.   Coal: *normal* 150 tons; *maximum* 380 tons.

General Notes.—Built and engined by Fairfield.   Laid down October, 1903.   Completed early in 1905.   Average cost, £289,000.

First Trials.—Forward, I.H.P.   *Foresight*, I.H.P. 15,800 = 25·28 kts.

Distinctions.—Poop, high funnels, no cowls.

PATHFINDER (16th July, 1904), & PATROL (13th October, 1904).

Displacement 3000 tons.   Length, 370 feet.   Beam, 38¾ feet.   *Maximum* draught, 14 feet.   Complement 268

Guns :
    10—12 pdr.
    8 Pompoms.
Torpedo tubes (18 inch) :
    2 submerged.

Armour :
    ½" Deck ....

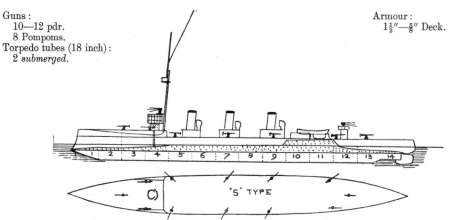

'P' TYPE

Machinery : 2 sets 4 cylinder.   2 screws.   Boilers : ⅘ Normand-Laird, ⅕ cylindrical.   Designed H.P. 16,500 = 25 kts.   Coal : *normal* 165 tons ; *maximum* 380 tons.

General Notes.—Built and engined by Laird Bros., Birkenhead.   Laid down August and October, 1903.   Completed, 1905.   Average cost, £279,000.

Trials.—*Pathfinder,* I.H.P. 14,330 = 25·22 kts.   *Patrol,* I.H.P.

Distinction.—High funnels.

Photo, Symonds & Co.

SENTINEL (19th April, 1904), & SKIRMISHER (1905).

Displacement 2940 tons.   Length, 360 feet.   Beam, 40 feet.   *Maximum* draught, 14¼ feet.   Complement 268.

Guns :
    10—12 pdr.
    8 Pompoms.
Torpedo tubes (18 inch) :
    2 submerged.

Armour :
    1½"—⅝" Deck.

'S' TYPE

Machinery : 2 sets 4 cylinder.   2 screws.   Boilers : Express.   Designed H.P. 17,500 = 25 kts.   Coal : *normal* 160 tons ; *maximum* 380 tons.

General Notes.—Built and engined by Vickers Maxim.   Laid down June, 1903 and July, 1903.   Average cost, £282,000.

Trials.—*Sentinel,* I.H.P. 17,500 = 25·25 kts. (rough sea).   *Skirmisher,* I.H.P.   =   kts.

Distinctions.—Shorter funnels than the others.   Conspicuous cowls.

(PELORUS CLASS—9 SHIPS.)

PELORUS (Feb., 1896), **PROSERPINE** (Dec., 1896), **PEGASUS** (March, 1897),
PYRAMUS (May, 1897), **PERSEUS** (July, 1897), **PSYCHE** (July, 1898),
PROMETHEUS (Oct., 1898), **PIONEER** (June, 1899), **PANDORA** (Jan., 1900).

Displacement 2,135 tons, *except* last 2, which are 2,200 tons.   Complement 224.

Length, 300 feet. Beam, 36½ feet. Draught, 17 feet.

Maximum draught of *Pandora, Pioneer,* and *Psyche* is 19½ feet.

Guns :
  8—4 inch.
  8—3 pdr.
Torpedo tubes (14 in.) :
  2 *above water.*

Armour :
  2″ Deck ....= ϵ

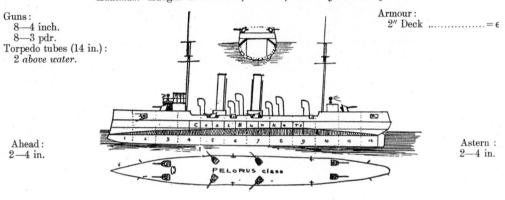

Ahead :
2—4 in.

Astern :
2—4 in.

Broadside : 4—4 in.

PELORUS.   (All alike.)   *Photo, Symonds*

Pioneer has steam pipe *before* fore funnel instead of abaft.

Machinery : inverted 3 cylinder triple expansion.   2 screws.   Boilers : various, see *Trials.*   Designed H.P. 7000 = 20·5 kts.   Coal : *normal* 250 tons.

Engineering Notes.—

Name.	Built at	Engined by	Laid down	Completed	8 hours at 5000	4 hours full p.	Boilers	Speed last sea trial.
Pelorus	Sheerness	Clydebank	May, '95	1897	5075=19·7	7028=20·7	Normand	...
Proserpine	Sheerness	Keyham	March, '96	1899	5534=19·7	7146=21	Thornycroft	...
Pegasus	Palmer	Palmer	May, '96	1899	5400=20·0	7134=21·2	Reed	...
Perseus	Earle	Earle	May, '96	1901	5239=19·1	7058=20·0	Thornycroft	...
Prometheus	Earle	Earle	June, '96	1901	5183=19·8	7274=20·8	Thornycroft	...
Pyramus	Palmer	Palmer	May, '96	1900	5424=19·9]	7303=20·7	Reed	...
Pioneer	Chatham	Fairfield	Dec., '97	1900	5265=17·7	7192=20	Thornycroft	...
Psyche	Devonport	Keyham	Nov., '97	1900	5000=19·5	7006=20·48	Thornycroft	17
Pandora	Portsmouth	Portsmouth	Jan., '98	1901	5000=18·6	7331=20·8	Thornycroft	...

About 16 kts. or less where not stated.

These ships have all lost in speed, being too small and light to stand knocking about at sea without deterioration. Boiler troubles in most are continual.

General Notes.—Built under Estimates 1895—1898.   Cost about £150,000 each.

BARHAM   *Photo, West.*

BARHAM (1889), (re-constructed 1898-99).

Displacement 1830 tons. Complement 169.

Length, 280 feet. Beam, 35 feet. *Maximum* draught, 16 feet.

Guns :
  6—4·7 inch (*F*).
  4—3 pdr.
Torpedo tubes :
  2 *above water*.

Armour (steel) :
  2″ Deck (amidships)...= є
  1″ Deck (ends) ....

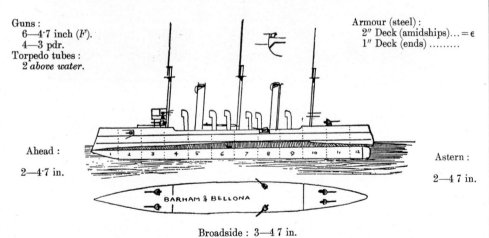

Ahead :

2—4·7 in.

Astern :

2—4·7 in.

Broadside : 3—4·7 in.

Machinery : 2 sets vertical triple expansion. 2 screws. Boilers : (1898) Thornycroft. Designed H.P. 4700 = 19 kts. Coal : 140 tons.

Notes—After re-boiling, exceeded 20 knots on trial, and can still steam well over 19 knots.

VULCAN.   *Photo, West.*

VULCAN (1889).

Displacement 6620 tons. Complement 433.
Length, 350 feet. Beam, 58 feet. *Maximum* draught 24¾ feet.

Guns :
  8—4·7 inch (*F*).
  12—3 pdr.
  12 Nordenfelts.
Torpedo tubes (14 in.) :
  2 *submerged*.
  4 *above water*.

Armour (steel) :
  5″ Deck (amidships)...= c
  6″ Conning tower...... d
  5″ Engine hatches ...= c

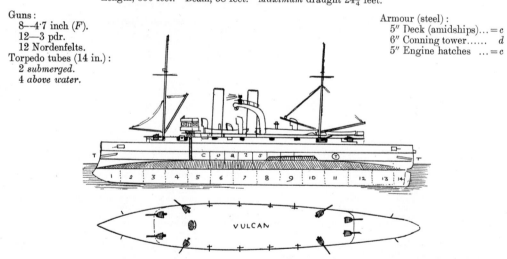

Machinery : 2 sets vertical triple expansion. 2 screws. Boilers : 4 2-ended and 1 1-ended auxiliary. Designed H.P. : *forced* 12,000 = 20 kts. Coal : *normal* 1000 tons ; *maximum* 1300 tons.

Notes—Reached her speed on first trials, but well below it now.

(Carries 6 small torpedo boats).

DRYAD CLASS.

Distinguished from others by their poops and very numerous ventilators; also by funnel positions.

ALARM CLASS.

Except the 2 specified, *Gossamer* class all the same, *except* that they show fewer cowls.

SHARPSHOOTER.

Seagull the same *except* that fore funnel is smaller.

SPEEDY.   *Photos, H. Nye, Esq.*

DRYAD, HALCYON, HARRIER, HAZARD, & HUSSAR, (all launched 1894).

Displacement 1,070 tons.   Complement 120.

Length, 250 feet.   Beam, 30½ feet.   *Maximum* draught, 13 feet.

Guns:
2—4·7 inch.
4—3 pdr.
Torpedo tubes, (18 in.):
5 *above water*.

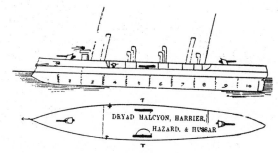

DRYAD HALCYON, HARRIER, HAZARD, & HUSSAR

Machinery: 2 sets vertical triple expansion. 2 screws. Boilers: 4 locomotive. Designed H.P. *natural* 2,500 = 17 kts.; *forced* 3,500 = 18·5. Coal: *normal* 100 tons; *maximum* 160 tons.

Note.— Most of these can do 17·5—18 kts. without trouble.

(GOSSAMER CLASS—7 SHIPS.)
GOSSAMER (1890), **GLEANER** (1890), **SEAGULL** (1889), **SHARPSHOOTER** (1888), **SKIPJACK** (1889), **SPANKER** (1889), & **SPEEDWELL** (1889).

Displacement 735 tons.   Complement 90.

Length, 230 feet.   Beam, 27 feet.   *Maximum* draught, 12 feet.

Also

(ALARM CLASS—9 SHIPS).
ALARM (1892), **CIRCE** (1892), **HEBE** (1892), **JASON** (1892), **LEDA** (1892), **NIGER** (1892), **ONYX** (1892), **RENARD** (1892), & **SPEEDY** (1893).

Displacement 810 tons.   Complement 85.

Length, 230 feet.   Beam, 27 feet.   *Maximum* draught, 12½ feet.

Guns:
2—4·7 inch.
4—3 pdr.
Torpedo tubes:
5—14 inch in 735 ton.
3—18 inch in 810 ton.

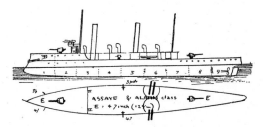

ASSAYE & ALARM class

Machinery: 2 sets vertical triple expansion. 2 screws. Boilers: 4 locomotive, except *Sharpshooter*, Belleville; *Seagull*, Niclausse: *Spanker*, Du Temple; *Gossamer*, Reed; *Speedy*, Thornycroft. Coal: *normal* 100 tons; *maximum* 160 tons.

Note.—All the water-tube boilered boats can make 18-19 kts. or more; those with locomotive boilers average about 16-15 kts. or less.

L

SUMMARY OF DESTROYERS.

There are five general types—

Built.

(a) 42 27-KT. BOATS, dating from 1893-95, averaging 260 tons; with *maximum* draught about 9 feet. Able to average about 21 kts. at sea. Coal : 60 tons. H.P. *circa* 4000.

(b) 70 30-KT. BOATS, dating from 1896-1902, averaging 300 tons. *Maximum* draught, 11 feet. Average sea speed, 24 kts. Coal : 80 tons. H.P. *circa* 6000.

(c) 34 25½ KT. BOATS, dating from 1903-05, averaging 550 tons. *Maximum* draught, 12 feet. Average sea speed, 23 kts. Coal : about 130 tons. H.P. 7000. High forecastles instead of turtle backs.

Building.

(d) *1* 36-KT. "OCEAN-GOING" (1905-06) of 800 tons. Turbine engines. H.P. about 30,000.

(e) *5* 33-KT. "OCEAN-GOING" (1905-06) of 600 tons. Turbines.

There are also "costal destroyers," practically torpedo boats. These will be found under the head of Torpedo boats (p. 87).

There is also one turbine boat (*Velox*) of 440 tons.

Of types (*a*) and (*b*) the Palmer boats are best for keeping their speed in a sea-way, losing very little. The Thornycroft boats stand hard weather better than any others, and are reliable in speed.

In the following pages the boats will be found grouped as follows :—

1—36-KT. "OCEAN-GOING." 800 tons.

5—33-KT. "OCEAN-GOING." 600 tons.

2 Elswick—*Afridi, Ghurka.*

1 Laird—*Cossack.*

1 White—*Mohawk.*

1 Thornycroft—*Tartar.*

BRITISH "RIVER CLASS" DESTROYERS.

ALL 550 TONS, 7000 H.P., AND 25½ KNOT SPEED.   ALL NOW CARRY TOP MASTS.

(Two short funnels).

6 *Hawthorn:*—**Boyne, Derwent, Doon, Kale, Waveney, Eden** *(turbine).*

2 *White:*—**Nith, Ness** (1905).

7 *Laird:*—**Arun, Blackwater, Foyle, Itchen, Liffey, Moy, Ouse.**

4 *Thornycroft:*—**Chelmer, Colne, Jed, Kennet.**

(Four funnels closely paired).

9 *Palmer:*—**Cherwell, Dee, Erne, Ettrick, Exe, Swale, Ure, Wear** (1904), **Rother** 1905).

(Four funnels openly paired, and no raised piece in the eyes).

Yarrow:—**Ribble, Teviot, Usk, Welland** (1904), **Gala, Garry** (1905).

BRITISH DESTROYERS (4 funnels).

21 4-FUNNELLED 30-KNOT DESTROYERS (1896—1903).
(All have large fore-bridges).

10 4-FUNNELLED 27-KNOT DESTROYERS (1894—95).
(All have small fore-bridges).

(Middle funnels extremely close together).

5 *Palmer*—**Kangaroo, Myrmidon, Peterel, Spiteful, Syren.** 2 *Doxford*:—**Lee, Success** (*middle funnels still closer together and without the bands which the Palmer boats have*).

(Funnels very wide apart).

13 *Laird*:—**Earnest, Griffon, Locust, Quail, Thrasher, Virago, Panther, Seal, Orwell, Lively, Sprightly,** *and, with stern somewhat depressed aft,* **Express.**

1 *Clydebank*:—**Arab.**

2 *Hanna-Donald*:—**Zephyr, Fervent.** *(With peculiar tops to funnels).*

1 *Yarrow*:—**Hornet.**

Same as 30-knot Laird boats except for position of mast).

5 *Laird*:—**Banshee, Contest, Dragon,** *and, with bow tubes,* **Ferret, Lynx.**

2 *Earle*:—**Salmon, Snapper.**

All Photos, Symonds.

BRITISH DESTROYERS (3 funnels).

36 3-FUNNELLED 30-KNOT DESTROYERS (1896—1901).
(All have big fore-bridges).

7 Palmer:—**Bat, Crane, Star, Fawn, Flying Fish, Whiting,** and (with different funnel tops, and search-light on platform abaft bridge) **Flirt.** 2 Clydebank:—**Tiger, Vigilant.** 1 Yarrow:—**Thorn.**

(High funnels).

5 Hawthorn:—**Cheerful, Mermaid, Racehorse, Roebuck, Greyhound.** 4 Vickers:—**Avon, Bittern, Leopard, Vixen.** 2 Earle:—**Dove, Bullfinch.** 2 Doxford:—**Sylvia, Violet.**

(Three equal funnels).

1 Thornycroft:—**Albatross** (both tubes abaft). 1 Hawthorn:—**Velox** (tubes as Albatross, s.l. platform abaft bridge, high mast). 6 Fairfield:—**Falcon, Fairy, Gipsy, Leven, Ostrich, Osprey** (tube between 2 and 3 funnels and abaft).

5 Clydebank:—**Brazen, Electra, Kestrel, Recruit, Vulture.**

27 3-FUNNELLED 27-KNOT DESTROYERS (1893—95).
(All have small fore-bridges).

(Small looking, short funnels and low in the water).

3 Vickers:—**Skate, Sturgeon, Starfish.** 2 Elswick:—**Spitfire, Swordfish.**

3 Hawthorn:—**Ranger, Opossum, Sunfish.** 4 Reboilered boats with bow tubes:—**Charger, Dasher, Hasty, Havock.** 2 Doxford:—**Hardy, Haughty.**

3 Palmer:—**Janus, Lightning, Porcupine.** 3 Clydebank:—**Rocket, Shark, Surly.**

(Irregular funnels)

3 Clydebank:—**Wizard, Conflict, Teaser** (very low in water, and with cut-away sterns).
1 Thames Ironworks:—**Zebra** (higher in water and stern as usual, not cut away).

2-FUNNELLED 30-KNOT DESTROYERS (1896—1901).

(Cut-away bow, big round stern, tubes both abaft funnels).

5 *Thornycroft:*—**Angler, Ariel, Desperate, Fame, Foam.**

(Cut-away bow, rudder showing (instead of Thornycroft stern), tubes both aft).

5 *Thornycroft:*—**Cygnet, Cynthia, Coquette, Mallard, Stag.**

(Two high funnels, no turtle back).

Schichau (ex-Chinese), **Taku.**

27-KNOT 2-FUNNELLED DESTROYERS (1893—95).
(All have small fore-bridges).

(Ram bow, round Thornycroft stern, small bridge, tubes both aft).

4 *Thornycroft:*—**Ardent, Boxer, Bruiser,** *and with bow tube also,* **Daring.**

(As above, but cut-away bow, rudder exposed tubes between funnel and aft).

3 *Fairfield:*—**Handy, Hart, Hunter.**

BRITISH TORPEDO BOATS.

"COSTAL DESTROYERS."

12 (laid down 1905-06). 230 tons :—

Dragonfly, Firefly, Grasshopper, Greenfly, Gadfly, Glowworm, Gnat, Cricket, Mayfly, Moth, Sandfly, Spider.

TORPEDO BOATS.

No.	Builders.	Numbers.	Launched.	Displace-ment.	H.P.	Max. speed.	Tubes.	Coal.	Comple-ment.
				tons.		kts.			
13	T. & W.	117—109	1902—03	200	2900	25	3	42	32
4	T.	98, 99, 107, 108	1901	178	2850	25	3	20	32
7	T. W. & L.	97—91	1893—94	130	2000	23·5	3	25	18
3	Y.	90—88	1894—95	112	1600	23	3	25	18
27		L = Laird.　　T = Thornycroft.　　W = White.　　Y = Yarrow.							

Note bow.　　　　No. 98.　　　　(Type 98—108).

OLD BOATS of no fighting value.

There are also old boats dating from 1885-89 as follows :—

6 " 80 class " Yarrow (87-82), 85 tons ; original speed 23 kts.　Present speed about 18 kts.

22 old Yarrow, etc., boats (80-61 and 30-33), 75 tons ; (bottle-nosed).　Present speed about 16 kts.

24 old Thornycroft (60-41 and 29-25), 60 tons.　Present speed about 16 kts.

10 old assorted.　Also 16 old boats belonging to the Colonies.

No. 92.　　　　(Type 97- 91)
(90—88 almost identical).

Photos by favour of Messrs. Thornycroft.

No.	Class.	Date. First: begun. Last: completed.	Displacement submerged.	Motive Power, above and below.	H.P.	Actual speed.	Dimensions, in feet.	Bow Tubes.	Actual Radius, Submerged.
5	"Hollands"	1901-03	120	Petrol 4 cylinder accumulators.	$\frac{190}{70}$	$\frac{8}{5}$	$63 \times 11\frac{1}{2} \times 11\frac{1}{2}$	1	3 hours.
4	"A 1—A 4"	1903-04	180	Petrol 12 cylinder accumulators.		$\frac{11}{7}$	$100 \times 11\frac{1}{2} \times 11\frac{1}{2}$	2	3 hours.
10	"A 4—A 14"	1904-05	200	Petrol 16 cylinder accumulators.			$150 \times 11\frac{1}{2} \times 11\frac{1}{2}$	2	3 hours.
2 + 14	"B 1—B 16"	1904-06	300	Petrol 12 cylinder accumulators.		$\frac{12}{8}$	$150 \times 12 \times 12$	2	3 hours.

Notes.—All the above are the single screw American type "Holland," modified.

"Hollands" have a 4 cylinder vertical petrol engine of American make, M.O. valves, long periscopes, and short conning towers. They are practically experimental boats and of very little fighting value.

The earlier "A" class had originally a 16 cylinder petrol engine, Wolseley make. 4 cylinders subsequently removed to get better firing. Short periscopes and high conning towers. These boats are much superior to the "Hollands," but only moderately satisfactory. Later "A's," 16 cylinder engines. Horizontal engine in all.

"B" class have 16 cylinder horizontal Wolseley petrol engine. They are greatly improved "A's" and superior to any other boats extant. Surface radius over 1000 miles.

Speed is controlled in all by cutting out cylinders.

"A" CLASS.

HOLLANDS.

"B" CLASS.   *Photo, West.*

UNITED STATES FLEET.

(Revised by H. Reuterdahl, A. United States Naval Institute).

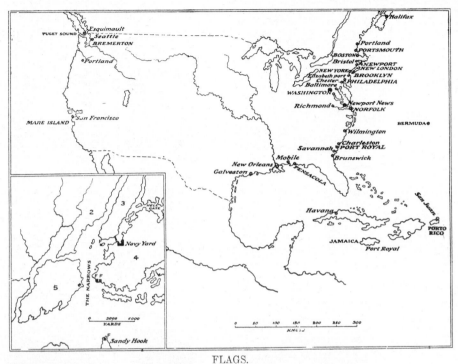

FLAGS.

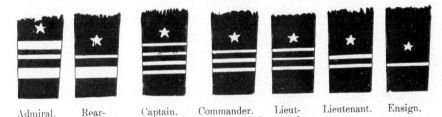

	NEW YORK.	
	to	knots
Berehaven	... ...	30
Bermuda	... ...	680
Boston (Mass.)	... ...	315
Brest	... ...	2954
Caracas	... ...	1770
Cherbourg	... ...	3066
Colon	... ...	1985
Galveston	... ...	1910
Gibraltar	... ...	3670
Havana	... ...	1320
Havre	... ...	3125
Jamaica	... ...	1495
Key West	... ...	1180
La Guayra	... ...	1840
New Orleans	... ...	1710
Norfolk Navy Yard	...	300
Pernambuco	... ...	3690
Philadelphia (Pa.)	...	240
Portsmouth Navy Yard		330
Portsmouth (England)		3060
Wilhelmshaven	...	3570

	KEY WEST	
	to	knots.
Bermuda	... ...	1100
Boston (Mass.)	... ...	1387
Galveston	... ...	730
Jamaica (Port Royal		
Harbour)	... ...	850
New York	... ...	1180
Norfolk Navy Yard	...	1000
Pensacola	... ...	235
Philadelphia	... ...	1020
Port Royal Naval Station		450
Portsmouth Navy Yard		1400

	PORT ROYAL	
	to	knots.
Bermuda	... ...	810
Norfolk Navy Yard	...	450
Key West	... ...	550
New York	... ...	650
Pensacola	... ...	785

	MARE ISLAND	
	to	knots.
Auckland (N. Zealand).		5965
Esquimault	... ...	750
Honolulu	... ...	2095
Kiao-chau	... ...	5600
Manila	... ...	7500
Panama	... ...	3424
Puget Sound	... ...	800
Yokosuka	... ...	4500

	KAVITE.	
	to	knots.
Amoy	... ...	700
Hong Kong	... ...	650
Kiao-chau	... ...	1325
Nagasaki	... ...	1300
Saigon	... ...	875
Singapore	... ...	1320
Vladivostock	... ...	2080
Yokosuka	... ...	1720
Hampton Roads	...	18,000

Uniforms.

| Admiral. | Rear-Admiral. | Captain. | Commander. | Lieut-Commander. | Lieutenant. | Ensign. |

Note.—Lieutenants, junior grade, have 1½ stripes. Midshipmen serving at sea ½ stripe. Warrant officers star without any stripe.

Engineers same as line officers (interchangeable).

All other branches have corresponding executive rank and titles without the star on sleeve.

Colour of significance (between the sleeve stripes): *Medical,* dark maroon: *Pay,* white; *Constructors,* purple; *Civil Engineers,* light blue; *Professors of Mathematics,* olive green.

Mercantile Marine.

8054 steamers (of about 3 million tons), 12,836 sailing (about 2 million tons.)

Coinage.

Dollar (100 cents)—approximately 4*s.* 2*d.* British.

Senior officer when of or below rank of captain flies a blue triangular flag. Assistant Secretary of Navy has a flag same as Secretary's with colours reversed, *i.e.,* white ground and blue anchor and stars.

M

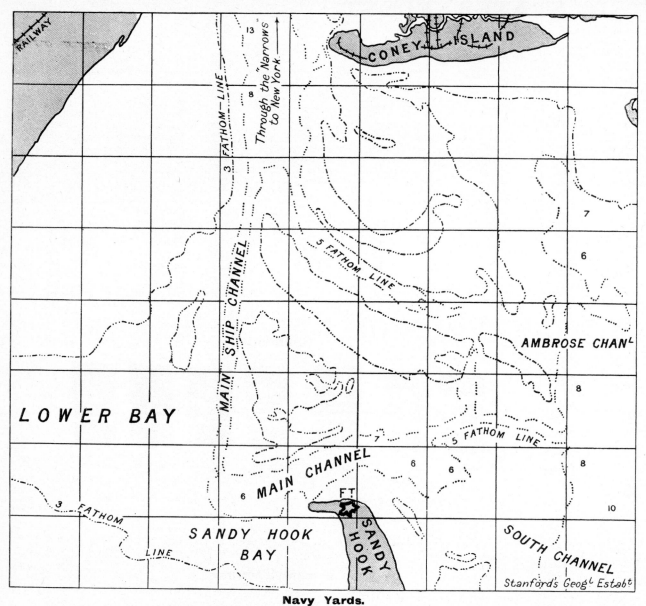

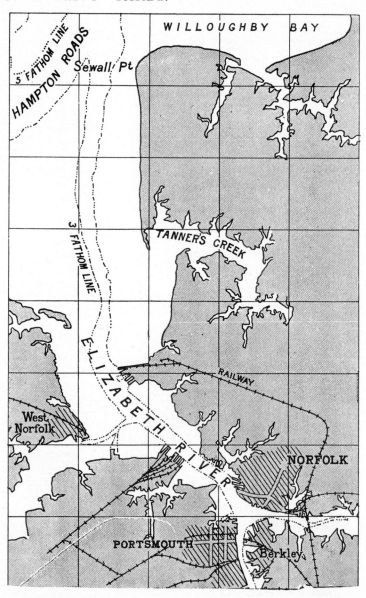

Navy Yards.

1. BROOKLYN AND NEW YORK.   Depôt and shipbuilding yard.   Two slips.   One wood dry dock able to take any warship; one concrete, 459×85×25½ feet; one granite, for third-class cruisers (338×66×25¼ feet). Naval hospital here.
(21 other docks in the city, but only one is large enough to take any cruiser—Erie Co.)

2. NORFOLK, VA.   Depôt and shipbuilding yard.   Naval hospital here.
Wood dock, 460 × 85 × 25½ feet; granite, 302 × 60 × 25 feet.

90

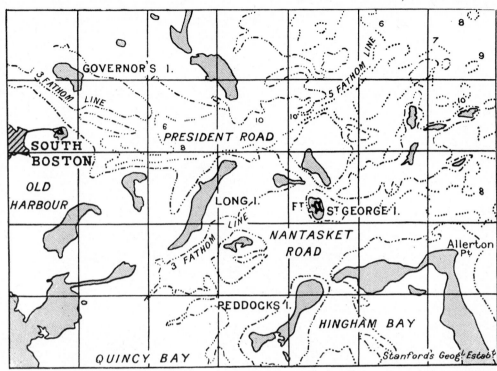

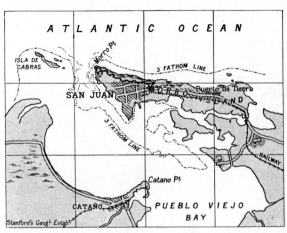

SAN JUAN, PORTO RICO.

Naval Station.—1st Class.

1. NEWPORT, R.I. Chief torpedo station. Manufactory of torpedoes, etc. Naval war college and apprentice training station. Naval hospital.

Naval Stations.—2nd Class.

1. PORT ROYAL, S.C. One wooden dock, 459 × 97 × 26 feet.
2. NEW LONDON, Conn. No docks.
3. CHARLESTON, S.C. (*Station building*).
4. KEY WEST. No docks.
5. NEW ORLEANS, SA.
6. SAN JUAN: PORTO RICO. (*Dock projected.*)
7. CULEBRA, PR.
8. GUANTANAMO CUBA (*projected*).

Private Yards (West Coast).

BATH IRONWORKS (Bath, Me.). One big slip.
CITY POINT WORKS (Boston, Mass.).
COLUMBIAN IRONWORKS (Baltimore, Md.). Five docks, all shallow.
CRAMPS (Philadelphia, Pa.). One dock, 400 × 67 × 20 feet. Two big slips.
CRESCENT SHIPYARD (Elizabethport, N.J.). One small dock.
FORE RIVER ENGINE CO. (Quincy, Mass.). Three big slips.
GAS ENGINE AND POWER CO. (Morris Heights, N.J.).
HARLAN & HOLLINGSWORTH CO. (Wilmington, Del.). One small dock.
HERRESCHOFF MANUFACTURING CO. (Bristol, R.I.).
HILLMAN SHIP AND ENGINE CO. (Philadelphia, Pa.).
LAWLEY & SONS (South Boston).
MARYLAND STEEL CO. (Baltimore, Md.).
NEAFY & LEVY (Philadelphia, Pa.).
NEWPORT NEWS COMPANY. 200 acres. Deep water alongside. Water front, 1 mile. One 140-ton crane, and two smaller. Very large modern shops. Two dry docks able to take any warship in the world. Total employees *circa* 3000. Three big slips.
ROACH (Chester, Pa.).
TRIGG & CO. (Richmond, Va.).

Mercantile Ports (West Coast).

(In order of importance, with approximate tons of shipping entering per year in brackets).

New York, N.Y. (9 million); Boston, Mass. (2½ million); Philadelphia, Pa. (2 million); New Orleans (2 million); Baltimore, Md. (1½ million); Galveston, Texas (⅔ million); Mobile, Ala. (½ million); Newport News, Va. (½ million); Portland, Me. (⅓ million); Pensacola, Fla. (½ million); Savannah, Ga. (¼ million); Key West (¼ million); and lesser ports—Brunswick, Ga.; Charleston, S.C.

The bulk of vessels entering U.S. ports are British (nearly 16 million tons). Next in order German (under 3 million) and Norwegian (about 1½ million). American trade is chiefly with Great Britain.

Navy Yards (West Coast).

3. BOSTON, Mass. Depôt. One granite dock, 367½ × 60 × 24⅝ feet. Naval hospital here.
4. LEAGUE ISLAND, PHILADELPHIA, Pa. Depôt. One wooden dock, 459 × 85 × 25½ feet; one concrete, to take any ship (*building*). Naval hospital here.
5. WASHINGTON. No docks. Yard devoted to ordnance construction. Naval hospital here.
6. PORTSMOUTH, N.H. 2nd class yard. One wooden dry dock, 350 × 90 × 25 feet; one concrete, to take any ship (*building*). Naval hospital here.
7. PENSACOLA, Fla. 2nd class yard. Floating dock, purchased from Spain. Dock able to take any warship projected at Algiers, New Orleans.

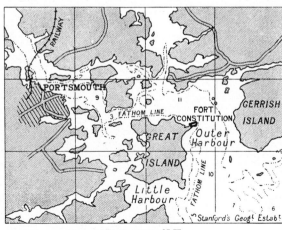

PORTSMOUTH N.H.

Navy Yard.

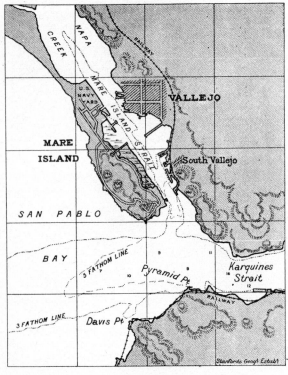

MARE ISLAND, inside the Golden Gate, S. Francisco (CALIFORNIA).
Depôt and Building Yard.

Dry Docks:

Granite	... ...	$510 \times 80\frac{1}{2} \times 27\frac{1}{2}$ feet. ⎫ Able to take any
Timber	... ...	$739 \times 103 \times 30$,, ⎬ U. S. warship.
Concrete	... ...	$500 \times 90 \times 33$,, *building.* ⎭

There is a dock $490 \times 90 \times 23$ in S. Francisco, another $446 \times 62 \times 19\frac{1}{4}$, and four small floating docks suitable for torpedo craft.

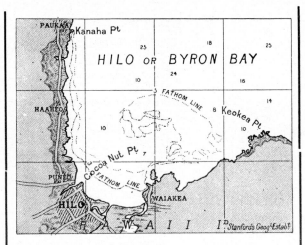

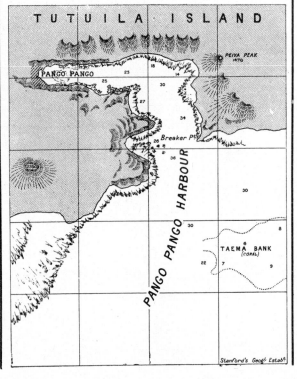

Naval Stations.—2ND CLASS, PACIFIC.

1. BREMERTON (Puget Sound). One dry dock, $640 \times 92 \times 30$ feet.
2. HILO (HAWAII).
3. TUTUILA (SAMOA).
4. KAVITE (P.I.)
5. OLONGAPO (P.I.) Floating dock to take any U.S. ship.

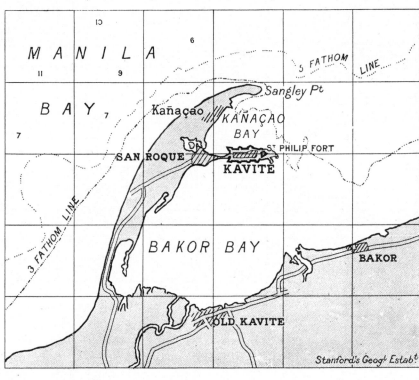

KAVITE PI.

Private Yards.—PACIFIC COAST.

MORAN BROS. & CO. (SEATTLE, PUGET SOUND). One big slip.
UNION IRONWORKS (SAN FRANCISCO).
WOLFF & ZWICKER (PORTLAND, ORE). (*West Coast.*)

Mercantile Ports.

(With tons of shipping cleared annually.)

PUGET SOUND ($1\frac{1}{4}$ million); SAN FRANCISCO (1 million).

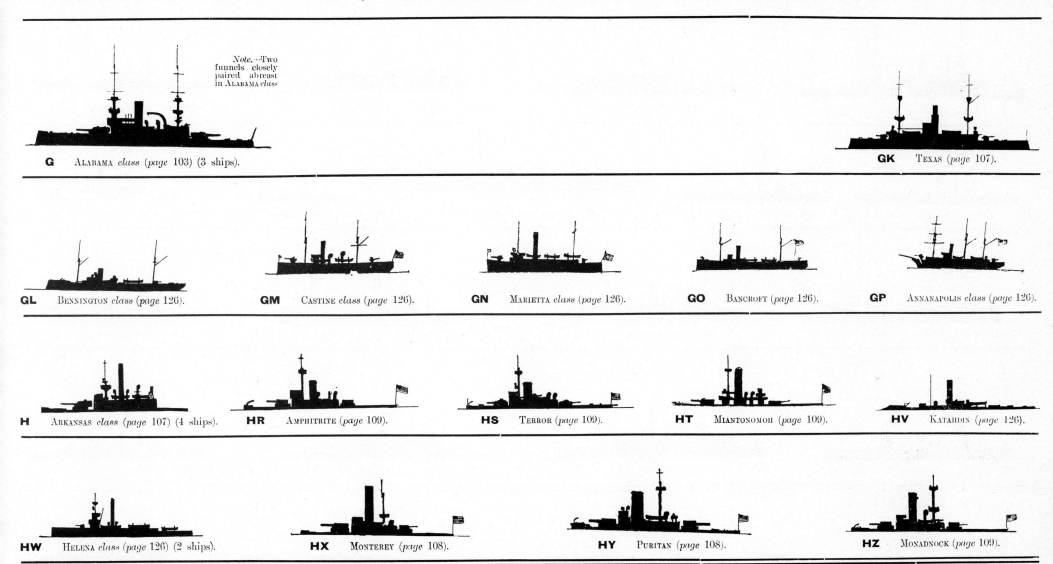

Note.—Two funnels closely paired abreast in ALABAMA class

G   ALABAMA *class* (*page* 103) (3 ships).

GK   TEXAS (*page* 107).

GL   BENNINGTON *class* (*page* 126).

GM   CASTINE *class* (*page* 126).

GN   MARIETTA *class* (*page* 126).

GO   BANCROFT (*page* 126).

GP   ANNANAPOLIS *class* (*page* 126).

H   ARKANSAS *class* (*page* 107) (4 ships).

HR   AMPHITRITE (*page* 109).

HS   TERROR (*page* 109).

HT   MIANTONOMOH (*page* 109).

HV   KATAHDIN (*page* 126).

HW   HELENA *class* (*page* 126) (2 ships).

HX   MONTEREY (*page* 108).

HY   PURITAN (*page* 108).

HZ   MONADNOCK (*page* 109).

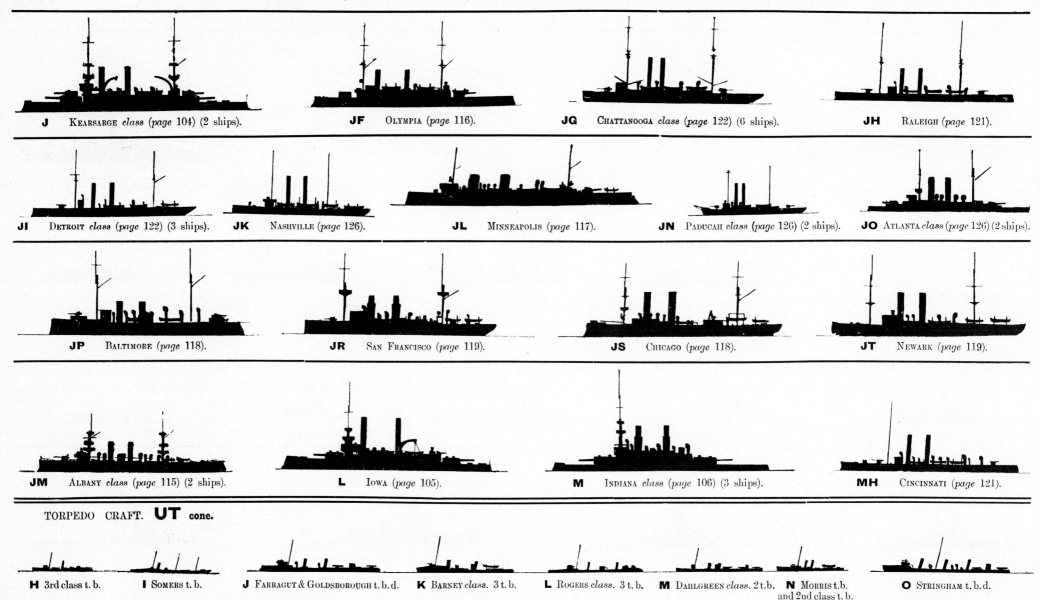

J　Kearsarge *class* (*page* 104) (2 ships).　　**JF**　Olympia (*page* 116).　　**JG**　Chattanooga *class* (*page* 122) (6 ships).　　**JH**　Raleigh (*page* 121).

JI　Detroit *class* (*page* 122) (3 ships).　　**JK**　Nashville (*page* 126).　　**JL**　Minneapolis (*page* 117).　　**JN**　Paducah *class* (*page* 126) (2 ships).　　**JO**　Atlanta *class* (*page* 126) (2 ships).

JP　Baltimore (*page* 118).　　**JR**　San Francisco (*page* 119).　　**JS**　Chicago (*page* 118).　　**JT**　Newark (*page* 119).

JM　Albany *class* (*page* 115) (2 ships).　　**L**　Iowa (*page* 105).　　**M**　Indiana *class* (*page* 106) (3 ships).　　**MH**　Cincinnati (*page* 121).

TORPEDO CRAFT. **UT** cone.

H 3rd class t. b.　　**I** Somers t. b.　　**J** Farragut & Goldsborough t. b. d.　　**K** Barney *class.* 3 t. b.　　**L** Rogers *class.* 3 t. b.　　**M** Dahlgreen *class.* 2 t. b.　　**N** Morris t. b. and 2nd class t. b.　　**O** Stringham t. b. d.

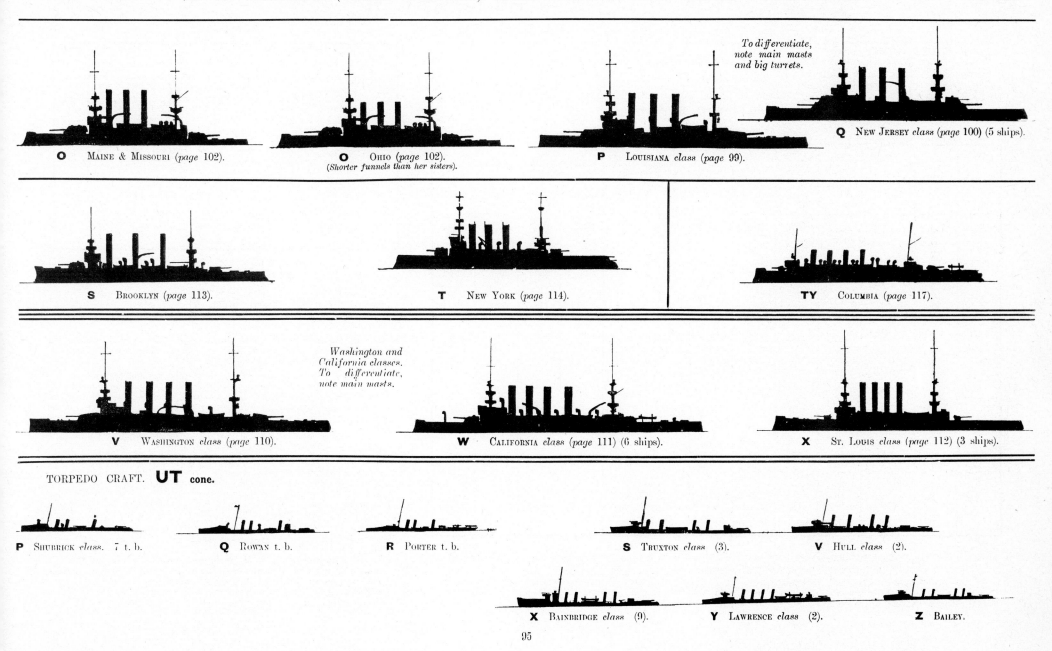

O   MAINE & MISSOURI *(page 102)*.

O   OHIO *(page 102)*.
(Shorter funnels than her sisters).

P   LOUISIANA *class (page 99)*.

To differentiate, note main masts and big turrets.

Q   NEW JERSEY *class (page 100)* (5 ships).

S   BROOKLYN *(page 113)*.

T   NEW YORK *(page 114)*.

TY   COLUMBIA *(page 117)*.

Washington and California classes. To differentiate, note main masts.

V   WASHINGTON *class (page 110)*.

W   CALIFORNIA *class (page 111)* (6 ships).

X   ST. LOUIS *class (page 112)* (3 ships).

TORPEDO CRAFT.   **UT** cone.

P   SHUBRICK *class*. 7 t. b.

Q   ROWAN t. b.

R   PORTER t. b.

S   TRUXTON *class* (3).

V   HULL *class* (2).

X   BAINBRIDGE *class* (9).

Y   LAWRENCE *class* (2).

Z   BAILEY.

Oversea Possessions: Philippines, Hawaian Islands (Hilo coaling station), Porto Rico, Guam.
Personnel: About 35,000 all ranks.
Colour of Ships: White hulls, yellow ochre upper works, masts and funnels. Torpedo craft: bottle green.
Secretary of the Navy: Charles Bonaparte.
Chief Constructor: Washington Lee Capps.

Guns in the U. S. Fleet.

(With present *service* velocities).

Notation.	Nominal Calibre.	Mark or Model.	Length in Calibres.	Weight of Gun.	Weight of A.P. Shot.	Service Initial Velocity.	Maximum penetration firing capped A.P. direct impact against K.C. armour.		Approximate Dangerous Space average ship, at			Service Rounds per minute.
							5000	3000	10,000 yards.	5000 yards.	3000 yards.	
	inches.			tons.	lbs.	ft. secs.	inches.	inches.	yards.	yards.	yards.	
AAA	13	I. & III.	35	60½	1099	2100	11	13	110	310	550	·3
AAAAA	12	IV. ('02)	45	50	850	2700	16½	20	...	...	...	...
AAAA	12	III. ('99)	40	45	850	2700	15	19	...	...	800	1·1
AA	12	I.	35	52	850	2100	9¾	12½	100	390	580	·5
AAA	10	III. ('99)	40	33½	500	2700	11¾	14½	140	460	700	1·25
B	10	I. & II.	35	28	500	2000	5	7½	90	270	540	slow
D	10	I. of	30	25¾	500	2000	4	6½	90	270	540	slow
A	8	V. ('99)	45	18	250	2700	7¼	10	125	420	615	1
C	8	III.	40	15	250	2100	4½	7	45	...	...	1
E	8	III.	35	13	250	2100	3	4¾	45	...	...	·8
F	8	I. & II.	30	13	250	2100	2½	4½	45	...	...	·8
B	7	I. ('99)	50	13⅓	165	2700	5½	7¾	95	385	580	2
C	6	VI. ('99)	50	8⅓	100	2800	4½	6	75	250	470	6
*F**	6	III.—VII.	40	6	100	2150	...	3	35	150	355	4
*E**	5	V. ('99)	50	4½	60	2800	...	4¼	...	...	...	5
*F**	5	Q.F.	40	3	50	2300	...	2¾	...	...	...	...
F	5	I.	30	2¾	60	2000	...	2	...	...	...	...
*F**	4	VII. ('99)	50	2½	32	2800	...	...	...	...	...	7—8
*F**	4	I.—VI.	40	1½	33	2000	...	2½	...	...	...	...
*F**	3	I. ('99)	50	⅘	14	2700	...	...	...	...	...	15

Gunnery Notes.—A capped A.P. high-explosive shell exists for all guns. A few old 6 inch of 35 and 30 calibres, converted into Q.F., exist in all ships, but all are in process of being replaced.

All guns use smokeless powder. * = brass cartridge cases. Model 1899 and later guns have Vickers breech, etc., and use nitro-cellulose, as also do the older guns. The Model 1902, Mark IV., 12 inch, is substantially the same as Mark III. in all particulars except for the five foot addition to the muzzle.

Torpedoes.

Size.	Name or Mark.	Air Pressure.	Charge.	Max. Range.	Average speed if set for		
					1000	2000	4000
inches.		lbs.	lbs.	yds.	kts.	kts.	kts.
21	Bliss Leavitt M. '05		300	4000	36	33	27
18	Bliss Leavitt M. '05		200	4000	36	33	27
18	Whitehead long II	2000	200	2000	28	22	
18	„ „ I	1850	200	2000	26	20	
18	Whitehead short	1850	200		26	19	
17	Howell		174	1000	27		
14	Howell M. '94	2000	100		26	16	

Notes on Personnel.

Till the last year or so the U. S. Navy was of a very moderate order. It is at present (except in gunnery) still inferior to several other navies in general efficiency, but it is very markedly on the up-grade.

In *Gunnery* vast strides have been made, and the general system of training is as good or better than can be found anywhere. Very marked care is expended on gun sights.

Torpedo is more backward; destroyers are chiefly used as despatch vessels, and the torpedo regarded as an altogether inferior arm. This owing to the geographical situation of the U. S.—is probably quite logical.

Submarine efficiency is moderate.

Engineering efficiency is, with some exceptions, quite moderate, there being a dearth of capable officers.

General Notes.—U. S. naval *officers* are, as a rule, promoted too late to give their best work. A movement for earlier promotion is now afoot. *Men* have a strong tendency to desert and to be less amendable to discipline than in European navies, but, on the other hand, have plenty of initiative, and are to be relied upon in case of need. Efforts are being made to remedy the weak points.

General Note.

It is proposed at any early date to remove from the effective list a great many protected cruisers of little if any fighting value (as has been done in the British Navy), and all battleships below the *Maines* will be relegated to coast service so soon as the ships now in hand can be completed.

(S. Carolina Class—2 Ships).

SOUTH CAROLINA & MICHIGAN (authorised 1905).

Normal displacement 16,000 tons.   Complement 869.

Length (*waterline*), 450 feet.   Beam, 80⅕ feet.   *Mean* draught, 24½ feet.   Length over all, — feet.

Guns :
  8—12 inch, 45 cal. (*A A A A A*).
  32—14 pdr.
  2 —3 pdr. (semi-automatic)
  8—1 pdr. (semi-automatic).
  4 -·30 (automatic).
  2 Field guns (3 inch).
Torpedo tubes (21 inch).
  2 *submerged*.

Armour (Krupp) :
  12"—10" Belt (amidships).........*aaa*
  4" Belt (ends) ....   *d*
  " Armour deck (slopes)
  Protection to vitals.................. ⸗
  12"—8" Turrets(N.C.) ....*aaa-a*
  10"—8" Turret bases (N.C.) ......*aa*
  10"—8" Lower deck, redoubt *aaa-aa*
  12" Conning tower (N.C.).........*aaa*
  9" tube .... *aa*

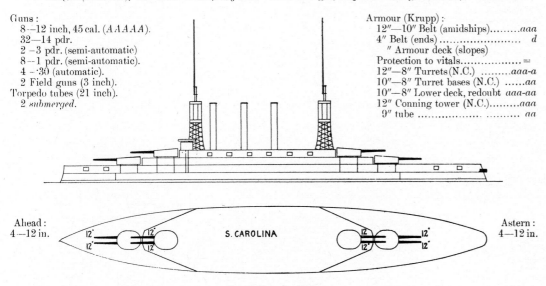

Ahead :
4—12 in.

Astern :
4—12 in.

Broadside : 8—12 in.

Machinery : 2 sets vertical 4 cylinder triple expansion.   2 screws (outward turning).   Boilers : 12 Babcock in 3 compartments.   Designed H.P. 16,500 = 18-20 kts.   Coal : *normal* 900 tons ; *maximum* 2200 tons.

Armour Notes.—Belt is 8 feet wide ; 6¾ feet of it below waterline ; lower edge is about 15% thinner than upper. Redoubt belt about 20% thinner at upper edge than at lower.   Low turrets with small bases.   Fronts of turrets, 12", sides, 8".

Gunnery Notes.—Loading positions, big guns : all round.   Special sights.   Hoists, electric.   Big guns manœuvred electrically.   Arcs of fire, 270° each turret.   Twelve hoists for 14 pdr.

General Notes.—To be laid down 1906.   These ships will have a new special type of skeleton mast, as indicated in plan.

A 19,000 ton battleship, armament 12—12 inch, authorised 1906.   No plan yet passed.

Contracts given out 23rd July, 1906.

Note.—The plan given last year has been finally abandoned in favour of the one here shewn.

N

(KANSAS CLASS—4 SHIPS).

KANSAS (Sept., 1905), *VERMONT* (Aug., 1905), *MINNESOTA* (April, 1905), & *NEW HAMPSHIRE*—*(Building)*.

Normal displacement 16,000 tons. *Full load* displacement, 17,650 tons. Complement 916 (as flagship).

Length (*waterline*), 450 feet. Beam, 76⅝ feet. *Maximum* draught, 26¾ feet.

Guns :
4—12 inch, 45 cal. (*AAAAA*).
8—8 inch, 45 cal. (*A*).
12—7 inch, 50 cal. (*B*).
20—14 pdr. (*F*).
12—3 pdr. S.A.
4—1 pdr. S.A.
2 machine ·30.
2 Automatic ·30.
2 Field guns, 3 inch.
Torpedo tubes (21 inch) :
4 *submerged*.
(Total weight with ⅔ ammunition 1468½ tons).
(Armament only, 1063 tons).

Armour (Krupp) :
9″ Belt (amidships) .... *aa*
4″ Belt (ends) .... *d*
3″ Deck (slopes)..............
Protection to vitals .... =*aaa*
7″ Lower deck side .... *a*
10″ Barbettes .... *aa*
12-8″ Turrets to these ......*aaa-a*
7″ Battery .... *a*
2″ Casemates (for 14 pdrs.).
6″-4″ Small turrets .... *b-d*
9″ Conning tower .... *aa*
5″ after C.T. 6″ tube .... *c*
5″ Director station (near C.T.). *c*
(Total weight 3920¼ tons).

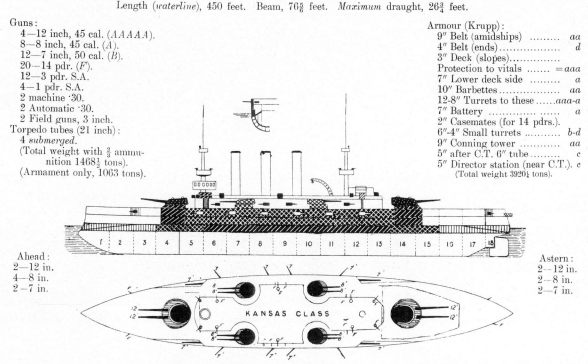

Ahead :
2—12 in.
4—8 in.
2—7 in.

Astern :
2—12 in.
2—8 in.
2—7 in.

KANSAS CLASS

Broadside : 4—12 in., 4—8 in., 6—7 in.

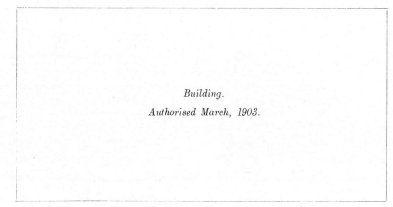

Building.

Authorised March, 1903.

Machinery : 2 sets vertical 4 cylinder triple expansion. 2 screws (outward turning). Boilers : 12 Babcock. Designed H.P. 16,500 = 18 kts. Coal : *normal* 900 tons ; *maximum* 2314 tons.

Armour Notes.—Main belt is 9½ feet wide, thick part 285 feet long, gradually thinning to 4″ armour 8 feet wide at ends ; lower edge always 25% less thick than waterline. Belt is K.C. up to sills of main deck gun ports, above that H.N. or K.N.C.

Gunnery Notes.—Loading positions, big guns : all round. Hoists, electric all guns. Big guns manœuvred electrically. Secondary turrets electric control.
Arcs of fire : Big guns, 270° ; Secondary turrets, 135° ; 7 inch guns, 110°.
Ammunition carried : *normal* 12 inch, 40 rounds per gun ; 8 inch, 100 per gun ; 7 inch, 100 per gun ; full supply ⅛ more.

Engineering Notes.—Machinery weighs 1500 tons ; ⅔ stores 26½ tons ; reserve water 66 tons. Heating surface 46,750 sq. feet. Grate area 1100 sq. ft. Working pressure, 265lbs. Funnels 100 feet high. Water carried 17,000 gallons. 33 Blowers for forced ventilation.

Name.	Builders	Laid down	Completed	Trials		Boilers
Kansas	Camden N.S.	'04	Jan '07	...	...	Babcock
Vermont	Fore River Co.	'04	May '07	...	...	Babcock
Minnesota	Newport News.	'04	Dec. '06	...	...	Babcock
New Hampshire	Moran Bros.	'05	Feb. '08	...	...	...

General Notes.—Boats etc. weigh 51½ tons. Masts and spars 31 tons. ⅔ Miscellaneous stores 81½ tons. ⅜ Small stores, provisions, etc. 144½ tons. Crew etc. 110 tons. 35 Sliding water-tight doors, and 6 armoured hatches. Freeboard 20½ feet.

(LOUISIANA CLASS.—2 SHIPS).

LOUISIANA (August, 1904) & **CONNECTICUT** (September, 1904).

Normal displacement 16,000 tons.   *Full load* 17,770 tons.   Complement 916 (as flagship).

Length (*waterline*), 450 feet.   Beam, 76⅝ feet.   *Maximum* draught, 26¾ feet.   Length over all, 456¼ feet.

Guns :
- 4—12 inch, 45 cal. (*AAAAA*)
- 8—8 inch, 45 cal. (*A*).
- 12—7 inch, 50 cal. (*B*).
- 20—14 pdr.
- 12—3 pdr.
- 4—1 pdr. S.A.
- 2—·30 (automatic).
- 2—·30 (machine).
- 2—Field guns, 3 inch.

Torpedo tubes (21 in.) :
- 4 *submerged*.

(Total weight with ⅜ ammunition, 1536 tons).

Armour (Krupp) :
11″ Belt (amidships)	*aaa*
4″ Belt (ends)	*d*
3″ Deck (flat on belt)	
Protection to vitals is	*aaa*
10″—8″ Turrets (N.S.)... =	*aaa-a*
12″ Turret bases (N.C.) ...	*aaa*
7″ Lower deck redoubt ...	*a*
2″ Battery	*a*
7″ Casemates (14 pdr.).... ..	*f*
6″ Secondary turrets (N.C.)	*b*
9″ Conning tower	*aa*
5″ Signal tower..............	*c*

(Total weight 3992 tons.)

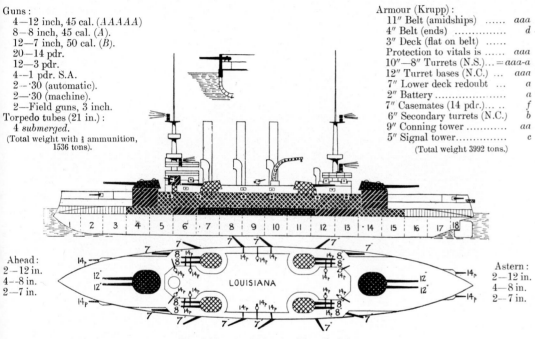

Ahead :
2—12 in.
4—8 in.
2—7 in.

Astern :
2—12 in.
4—8 in.
2—7 in.

Broadside : 4—12 in., 4—8 in., 6—7 in.

Machinery : 2 sets 4 cylinder triple expansion.   2 screws.   Boilers : 12 Babcock and Wilcox.   Designed H.P. 16,500 = 18 kts.   Coal : *normal* 900 tons ; *maximum* 2200 tons.

Notes.—All notes to *Kansas* class apply to these which differ only in disposition of the armour deck and belt thickness

	Name.	Builder.	Laid down.	Completed.	Trials.	Boilers.
Authorized	Louisiana	Newport News	Feb., '03	June '06		Babcock
1902	Connecticut	New York Yard	April, '03	June '06		Babcock

(NEW JERSEY CLASS—5 SHIPS).

VIRGINIA (April, 1904), **NEW JERSEY** (November, 1904), **GEORGIA** (October, 1904),
NEBRASKA (October, 1904), **RHODE ISLAND** (May, 1904).

Normal displacement 14,948 tons. *Full load* displacement 16,094 tons. Complement 703.

Length (*waterline*), 435 feet. Beam, 76⅛ feet. *Maximum* draught, 26 feet. Length *over all* 441 feet.

Photo by favour of H. Reuterdahl, Esq.

Guns—(Model, '99) :
4—12 inch, 40 cal. (*AAAA*).
8—8 inch, 45 cal. (*A*).
12—6 inch, 50 cal. (*C*).
20—14 pdr.
12—3 pdr.
4—1 pdr. (automatic).
4—1 pdr. (R.F.)
8 Colts.
Torpedo tubes (21 inch) :
4 *submerged*.
(Total weight without ammunition, 805 tons).
(Two-thirds ammunition 408 tons).

Armour—(Krupp and H N.) :
11″ Belt (amidships) ... *aaa*
4″ Belt (ends) .... *d*
3″ Deck (flat on belt amidships)
Protection to vitals ...... *aaa*
10″—7″ Barbettes (H.N.) *aaa*
12″—8″ Turrets (H.N.) ...*aaa*
6″ Secondary turrets ... *b*
6″ Lower deck side (H.N.) *b*
6″ Battery (H.N.) .... *b*
2″ on 14 pdr. guns ...... *f*
9″ Conning tower (K.N.C.) *aa*
(Total weight 3,690 tons).

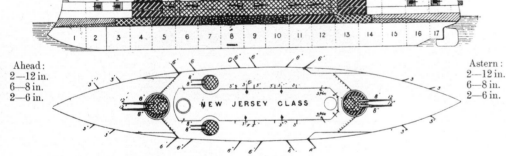

Ahead :
2—12 in.
6—8 in.
2—6 in.

NEW JERSEY CLASS

Astern :
2—12 in.
6—8 in.
2—6 in.

Broadside : 4—12 in., 6—8 in., 6—6 in.

Machinery : 2 sets 4 cylinder vertical inverted triple expansion. 2 screws. Boilers : Babcock and Wilcox. Designed H.P. 19,000 = 19 kts. Coal : *normal* 900 tons ; *maximum* 1,700 tons.

Armour Notes.—Belt is 8 feet wide, 7 feet of it below waterline (at *maximum* draught) ; lower edge is 25% thinner than at waterline, except at bow and stern. Protective deck flat on belt amidships, but reinforces sides at ends.

Gunnery Notes.—Loading positions, big guns : all round. Hoists : electric, to all guns : serve : 12 in., 1 in 30 seconds ; 8 in., 1 in 20 seconds ; 6 in., 3 per minute. Big guns manœuvred electrically. Secondary turrets electrically.

Arcs of fire : 12 in., 270° ; superposed 8 in., 270° ; beam 8 in., 180° ; battery 6 in., 110° (55° before and abaft).

Ammunition carried : 12 in., 60 per gun ; 8 in., 125 per gun ; 6 in., 200 per gun (only ⅔ normally carried).

Height of guns above water : 12 in., 26½ feet ; axial, 8 in., 32 feet ; side 8 in., 26 feet ; battery guns, 12 feet.

Engineering Notes.—Machinery weighs 1,730 tons + 100 tons reserve water.

Name.	Builders.	Laid down	Completed	Trials	Boilers.
New Jersey	Fore River Co.	April, '02	Mar. '06	=	Babcock
Georgia	Bath Ironworks	April, '02	Mar. '06	=	Babcock
Nebraska	Moran Bros.	July, '02	Sept. '06	=	Babcock
Rhode Island	Fore River Co.	May, '02	Feb. '06	± 19 4 (Max).	Babcock
Virginia	Newport News	May, '02	Feb. '06	=	Babcock

General Notes.—Stores carried : 970 tons. Cost, *complete*, per ship, estimated at £1,300,000 or more.

(IDAHO CLASS—2 SHIPS.)

IDAHO (1905) & *MISSISSIPPI* (September, 1905).

Normal displacement 13,000 tons. *Full load* displacement 14,465 tons. Complement 720.

Length (*waterline*), 375 feet. Beam, 77 feet. *Mean* draught, 24½ feet. Length *over all*, 382 feet.

Guns :
4—12 inch, 45 cal. (*AAAAA*).
8—8 inch, 45 cal. (*A*).
8—7 inch, 45 cal. (*B*).
20—14 pdr.
6—3 pdr.
4—1 pdr.
6—·30 (automatic).
2—·30 (machine).
2 Field guns.
Torpedo tubes (21 inch) :
2 *submerged*.

Armour (Krupp) :
9″—7″ Belt (amidships) *aa-a*
4″ Belt (ends) .... *d*
3″ Armour deck ....
Protection to vitals ... = *aaa*
12″—8″ Turrets ...... = *aaa-a*
10″—7½″ T'ret bases (NC) *aa-a*
6″ Secondary turrets (N.C.) *b*
7″ Lower deck (redoubt) ... *a*
7″ Battery (redoubt) ... *a*
9″ Conning tower ...... *aa*
(Total weight 3377 tons).

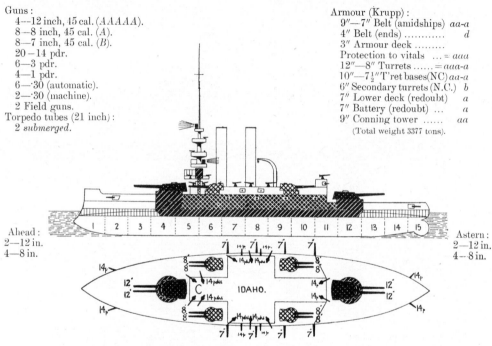

Ahead :
2—12 in.
4—8 in.

IDAHO.

Astern :
2—12 in.
4—8 in.

Broadside : 4—12 in., 4—8 in., 4—7 in.

Machinery : 2 sets vertical 4 cylinder triple expansion. 2 screws. Boilers : Niclausse. Designed H.P. 10,000 = 17 kts. Coal : *normal*, 750 tons ; *maximum*, 1750 tons.

Armour Notes.—Main belt is 9¼ feet wide by 244 feet long ; lower edge is 7″ amidships, 5″ at turret bases. Turret bases only 10″ where exposed ; only faces of turrets are 12″. 3″ tubes to 8″ turrets.

Gunnery Notes.—Loading positions, big guns : all round. Hoists, electric all guns. Big guns manœuvred electrically ; secondary guns, electric and hand gear.
Arcs of fire : 12 in., 270° ; 8 in., 135° ; 7 in., 110°.
Ammunition carried : 12 in., 60 rounds per gun ; 8 in. and 7 in., 125 per gun. (Only ⅔ of this carried normally.)
Heights of guns above water : Bow turret, 26½ feet ; after turret, 19 feet ; 8 inch guns, 26 feet ; 7 in. guns, 11 feet.

Torpedo Notes.—Whitehead torpedoes ; tubes may be 21 in. instead of 18 in.

Name.	Builder.	Laid down.	To be Completed.	Trials.	Boilers.
Idaho	Cramp's	1904	May '07	—	Niclausse
Mississippi	Cramp's	1904	March '07	—	Niclausse

General Notes : Estimated cost *complete*, about £900,000 per ship. Authorised, 1903.

(MAINE CLASS.—3 SHIPS).

OHIO (May, 1901), **MAINE** (July, 1901), **MISSOURI** (December, 1901).

Normal displacement 12,500 tons.   *Full load* displacement 13,500 tons.   Complement 551.
Length (*waterline*), 388 feet ; *Beam*, 72¼ feet ; *Mean draught*, 24 feet ; *Length over all*, 394 feet.

Guns (**M. '99**) :
4—12 inch, III. (*AAAA*).
16—6 inch, VI., 50 cal. (*C*).
6—14 pdr.
8—3 pdr.
6—1 pdr. (automatic)
2—1 pdr. (R.F.)
2 Colts.
4 Machine.
Torpedo tubes (18 inch) :
2 *submerged.*
(Total weight with ammunition, 1058 tons).

Armour (Krupp) :
11″ Belt (amidships) ... *aaa*
4″ Belt (bow) .... *d*
10″ Bulkhead (aft) ...... *aaa*
2½″ Deck (on slopes) ...
Protection to vitals = *aaaa*
4″ Deck (aft) ....
12″ Turrets (H.N.)...... *aaa*
12″—8″ Turret bases...*aaa-a*
6″ Lower deck side ... *a*
6″ Battery (*see notes*)... *a-b*
6″ Casemates (forward) *b*
10″ Conning tower...... *aa*
(Total weight 3053 tons).

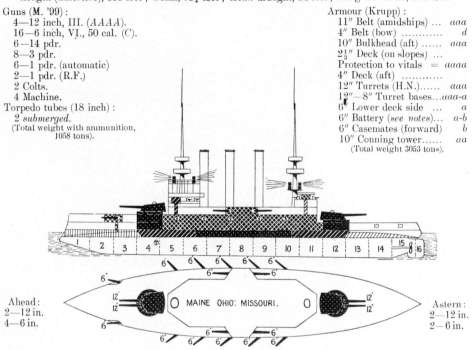

Ahead :
2—12 in.
4—6 in.

MAINE OHIO: MISSOURI.

Astern :
2—12 in.
2—6 in.

Broadside : 4—12 in., 8—6 in.

Machinery : 2 sets vertical inverted triple expansion 3 cylinder, except *Missouri* which is 4 cylinder.
2 screws. Boilers : 24 Thornycroft, except *Maine*, 24 Niclausse. Designed H.P. 16,000 = 18 kts.
Coal : *normal* 1,000 tons ; *maximum* 2,000 tons.
Armour Notes.—Belt is 7½ feet wide by 300 feet long from bow. Lower edge is 7½ in. amidships at
1 foot below water. Armour without deck weighs 2453 tons. Deck 600 tons. Cornpith belt
along water line. Battery K.C. to sills of ports ; above that K.N.C. (*b*).
Gunnery Notes.—Loading positions, big guns : all round. Hoists : electric for all guns. Big guns
manœuvred electrically.
Arcs of fire : Big guns 270° ; 6 in. 110°.
Ammunition carried : 12 in., 60 rounds per gun ; 6 in., 200 per gun (only ⅔ of this normally carried).
Height of guns above water : Bow turret 26½ feet ; After turret guns 19 feet ; Conning tower 34½ feet.
Engineering Notes.—Machinery, &c. (with water) weighs 1396 tons.   *Trials :—*

Name.	Where built.	Laid down.	Completed.	Mean speeds : 33 kt. sea trial, 123 revolutions.	Boilers.
Maine	Cramp's	Feb. '99	1902	16,000 = 18·3 (*max.* 18.9.)	Niclausse
Missouri	Newport News	Feb. '00	1903	= 18·22 (*max,* 18·75).	Thornycroft
Ohio	Union Works, Frisco	April '99	Sept. '04	16,498 = 17·82	Thornycroft

Coal consumption at 10,000 H.P. about 9¾ tons per hour ; at 16,000 H.P. about 16¾ tons per hour (18 kts.)
General Notes : Hull weighs 4836 tons ; stores 677. Displacement with full stores, coal and ammunition
is 13,500 tons. All joiners work fireproof wood. Pneumatic w.t. doors fitted.

MISSOURI.   *Photo by favour of H. Reuterdahl, Esq.*

Maine has a white after turret ; *Missouri* a buff one.

OHIO   *Photo by favour of S. Ballou, Esq.*

Differences :

Name.	Funnels.	Steam pipes, fore funnel.	
Maine	Very high	Very conspicuous	Big hawse pipes.
Missouri	Very high	Not conspicuous	2 very high ventilators aft, small and high hawse pipes.
Ohio	Much shorter	Not conspicuous	Small hawse pipes.

(ALABAMA CLASS—3 SHIPS).

ALABAMA (May, 1898), **ILLINOIS** (October, 1898), **WISCONSIN** (November, 1898).

Normal displacement 11,552 tons. *Full load* displacement 12,150 tons. Complement 490.

Length (*waterline*), 368 feet. Beam, 72 feet. *Mean* draught, 23½ feet.

ALABAMA.   *Photo, copyright, W. Rau.*

Guns :
4—13 inch, 35 cal. (*AAA*).
14—6 inch, 40 cal. (*F*).
6—6 pdr.
6—6 pdr. (semi-automatic).
4—1 pdr.
4—1 pdr. (automatic).
4 Colts.
2 Field guns (3 inch).
Torpedo tubes (18 inch) :
4 *above water* (armoured).
(Removed in *Illinois*).

Armour (Harvey-nickel) :
16½—14″ Belt .... *aaaa-aaa*
4″ Belt (bow) .... *d*
4″ Deck (slopes) ....
12″ Bulkhead .... *aaa*
Protection to vitals......=*aaaaa*
14″ Turrets .... *aaaa*
15″—10″ Turret bases ...*aaaaa*
5¼″ Lower deck .... *c*
5¼″ Battery .... *c*
6″ Casemates .... *b*
10″ Conning tower .... *aa*
(Total *circa* 3,300 tons).

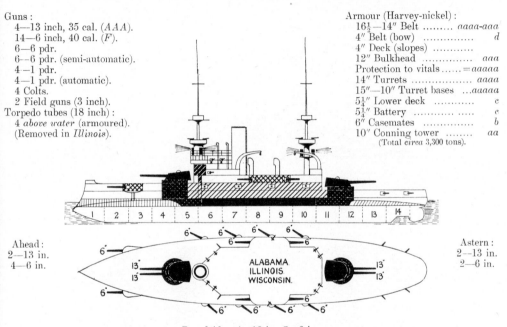

Ahead :
2—13 in.
4—6 in.

ALABAMA.
ILLINOIS.
WISCONSIN.

Astern :
2—13 in.
2—6 in.

Broadside : 4—13 in., 7—6 in.

Machinery : 2 sets vertical triple expansion. 3 cylinders. 2 screws. Boilers : Cylindrical ; 8 single ended. Designed H.P. *forced* 10,000 = 16 kts. Coal : *normal* 850 tons ; *maximum* 1,450 tons.

Armour Notes.—Main belt is 7½ feet wide by about 178 feet long, continued to bow with 4″ plates ; lower edge is 9¼″ thick, and only top strake is full thickness. Armour, without deck, weighs 2800 tons. 3 feet cofferdam behind waterline belt. 1½″ screens in battery.

Gunnery Notes.—Loading positions, big guns : all round. Big guns manœuvred, electric gear.
Arcs of fire : Big guns, 270° ; casemate guns, 135° ; battery guns, 110°.

Engineering Notes.—

Name.	Built at	Laid down	Completed	Full power on 33 kt. course.
Alabama	Cramp's	December, '96	1900	=17·45
Illinois	Newport News	February, '97	1901	11,920=16·20
Wisconsin	Union Works, 'Frisco	February, '97	1901	12,322=17·17

Wisconsin also did a 48 hours trial, I.H.P. 7,700 = 15·8 kts. *mean.* Coal consumption : somewhat large.

Cost, *complete,* per ship about £950,000.

WISCONSIN.   *Photo, S. Ballou, Esq.*

Differences.—

Name.	Cranes.	Lower part of fore mast.	Yards per mast.	Shields to 6 pdrs. on bridges.
Alabama	4	stout	1	...
Illinois	2	slight	1	...
Wisconsin	2	stout	2	none

(KEARSAGE CLASS.—2 SHIPS).

KEARSAGE & KENTUCKY (both March, 1898).

Normal displacement 11,500 tons.   *Full load* displacement 12,320 tons.   Complement 520 (586 as flag ship).
Length (*waterline*), 368 feet ; Beam, 72 feet ; *Mean* draught, 23½ feet ; Length over all, 376 feet.

Guns :
4—13 inch, II. (*AAA*).
4—8 inch, III., 40 cal. (*D*).
14—5 inch, 40 cal. (*F*).
20—6 pdr.
4—1 pdr. (R.F.).
4—1 pdr., (automatic).
4 Colts.
2 Field guns (3 inch).
Torpedo tubes (18 inch) :
  had 4 above water (removed).
  (Total weight with ammunition,
    1077 tons).

Armour (Harvey-nickel) :
16½″ Belt (amidships)   *aaaa*
4″ Belt (bow) ....   *d*
2½″ Deck (flat or belt)
10″ Fore bulkhead......   *aa*
12″ After bulkhead ...   *aaa*
Protection to vitals is   *aaaa*
4″ Deck (aft) ....
17″-15″Turrets(for13in.) *aaaa*
15″-12½″T'ret bases *aaaa-aaa*
9″ Turrets (for 8 inch)   *a*
5¼″ Lower deck side ...   *c*
5½″ Battery ....   *c*
2″ Battery (bulkheads)   *f*
10″ Conning tower......   *aa*
  (Total weight 3419 tons).

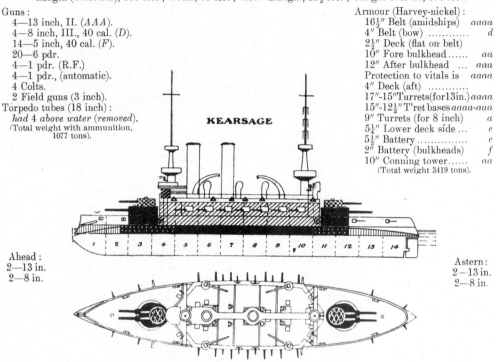

KEARSAGE

Ahead :
2—13 in.
2—8 in.

Astern :
2—13 in.
2—8 in.

Broadside : 4—13 in., 4—8 in., 7—5 in.

Machinery : 2 sets vertical triple expansion 3 cylinder. 2 screws. Boilers : cylindrical (6 double ended and 4 single ended). Designed H.P. 10,500 = 16 kts. Coal : *normal* 410 tons ; *maximum* 1210 tons.

Armour Notes.—Belt is 7½ feet wide by 290 feet long from bow. Lower edge is 9½″ thick amidships. Upper belt (lower deck side), 190 feet long. 2″ screens in battery.
Gunnery Notes.—Loading positions, big guns : all round. Hoists : electric for all guns. Big guns manœuvred electrically.
  Arcs of fire : 13 in. and 8 in. guns 255° ; battery guns 100°.
  Ammunition carried : 13 in., 60 rounds per gun ; 8 in., 150 per gun
  Height of guns above water : Big guns 18 feet ; 8 in. 25 feet, 5 in. 11 feet.
Torpedo Notes.—Whiteheads.
Engineering Notes.—Machinery, &c., weight 1100 tons.

Name.	Builders.	Laid down.	Completed.	40 hours n.d.	4 hours forced.
Kearsage	Newport News	June '96	1900	=14·1	=16·84
Kentucky	Newport News	June '96	1900	=14·9	=16·89

  Kentucky at full displacement (12996 tons), made a four hours forced trial and reached 16·33 kts.
  Coal consumption ; 12 tons an hour, at 10,500 H.P. (16 kts.) ; 9 tons an hour at 8,000 H.P. (15 kts.)
General Notes.—Cost *complete*, about £900,000.
  Differences :—

Name.	After bridge.
Kearsage	2 bridges
Kentucky	Only 1

KEARSAGE (taken 1903).   *Photo, Symonds.*

KENTUCKY turrets (port side)   *Photo, Loeffler.*

U. S. BATTLESHIP (16 knot).

IOWA (1896).

Displacement 11,410 tons.   Complement 486.

Length (*waterline*), 360 feet.   Beam, 72 feet.   *Maximum* draught, 28 feet.

Guns :
 4—12 inch, L., 35 cal. (*A*).
 8—8 inch, 30 cal. (*F*).
 4—4 inch, (*F*).
 22—6 pdr.
 4—1 pdr.
 4 Colts.
 2 Field guns (3 inch.)
Torpedo tubes (18 inch) :
 3 above water (now removed).

Armour (Harvey) :
 14"—11" Belt (amidships) *aa-a*
 12" Bulkheads .... *aa*
 3" Deck (flat on belt).
 Protection to vitals is ... *aa*
 14" Turrets .... *aa*
 5" Turret bases .... *d*
 5" Lower deck side ...... *d*
 6" Secondary turrets ... *c*
 8" Barbettes to these ... *b*
 10" Conning tower ...... *a*

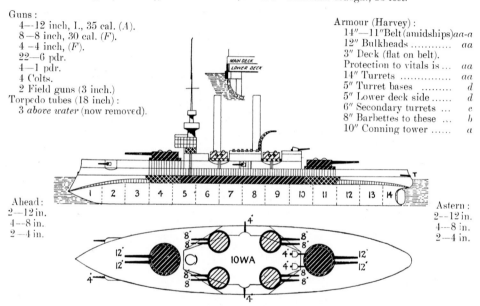

Ahead :
2—12 in.
4—8 in.
2—4 in.

Astern :
2—12 in.
4—8 in.
2—4 in.

Broadside : 4—12 in., 4—8 in., 2—4 in.

Machinery : 2 sets vertical inverted triple expansion. 2 screws. Boilers : cylindrical. Designed H.P. *forced* 11,000 = 16·5 kts. Coal : *normal* 625 tons ; *maximum* 1780 tons.

Armour Notes : Belt is 7½ feet wide by 200 feet long ; 5 feet of it below waterline ; lower edge is 9½" thick amidships. Main belt is reinforced by coal bunkers 10 feet thick.

Gunnery Notes : Loading positions, big guns : all round. Big guns manœuvred, hydraulic gear ; secondary turrets, steam.
 Arcs of fire : Big guns, 265° ; 8 in., 135° from axial line.
 Ammunition carried : 12 in., 60 rounds per gun ; 8 in., 125 rounds per gun.

Torpedo Notes : Howell torpedoes ; broadside tubes, section 8.

Engineering notes : Designed speed reached on trial.

General notes : Laid down at Cramp's, August, 1893 ; completed 1897. Cost *complete*, nearly £1,000,000.

(INDIANA CLASS—3 SHIPS.)

INDIANA (February, 1893), **MASSACHUSETTS** (June, 1893), **OREGON** (October, 1893).

Displacement 10288 tons.   Complement 470.

Length (*waterline*), 358 feet.   Beam, 69⅓ feet.   *Maximum* draught, 28 feet.

Guns :
4—13 inch, I, (*AAA*).
8—8 inch, 30 cal. (*F*).
4—6 inch, 40 cal. (*F*).
20—6 pdr.
6—1 pdr.
4 Colts.
Torpedo tubes :
removed.

Armour (Harvey) :
18"-15" Belt (amidships)
           aaaa-aaa
17" Bulkheads .... *aaaa*
3" Deck (flat on belt).
Protection to vitals is *aaaa*
17" Barbettes .... *aaaa*
8½" Turrets .... *a*
5" Turret bases .... *d*
5" Lower deck side ... *d*
6" Secondary turrets ... *c*
8" Barbettes to these ... *b*
3" Hoist .... *e*
5" Sponsons to 6" guns *d*
10" Conning tower...... *a*

Ahead :
2—13 in.
4—8 in.

Astern :
2—13 in.
4—8 in.

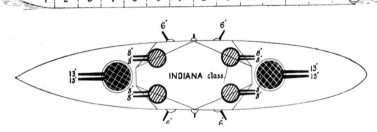

INDIANA class

Broadside : 4—13 in., 4—8 in., 2—6 in.

    Machinery : 2 sets vertical inverted triple expansion 3 cylinder. 2 screws. Boilers : *Indiana*, Babcock, others, Cylindrical, 4 horizontal return tube, 2 single ended. Designed H. P. *natural* 8000=15 kts., *forced* 9500=17 kts. Coal : *normal* 400 tons ; *maximum* 1800 tons.

Armour Notes.—Belt is 7½ feet wide by 200 feet long.

Gunnery Notes.—Loading positions, big guns : end on. Electric hoists. Arcs of fire : Big guns, 265° ; secondary turrets, 135°.

Torpedo Notes.—Whitehead torpedoes. Tubes being removed or reduced in number. Complete electric installation.

Engineering Notes.—

Name.	Builder.	Laid down.	Completed.	Mean of 62 kt. trial 1895-96.
Indiana	Cramp	May, '91	1895	9700=15·61
Massachusetts	Cramp	June, '91	1895	=16·15
Oregon	Union Co., 'Frisco	Nov., '91	1896	=16·78

Consumption : At 11 kts. 3¹⁄₁₀ tons per hour. At 9500 H.P. (15-16 kts.), 10¼ tons per hour.

Differences :—

Name.	Steampipes.	At after bridge.
Indiana	Both sides of funnels	Big cowl
Massachusetts	Both sides of funnels	Ensign staff
Oregon	Abaft funnel only	No cowl and no staff

    The *Oregon* is also distinguished from the other two by 2 searchlights aft, shields to all the 6 pdr. guns, and by the U.S. flag on her bow instead of the usual scroll-work ornament.

OLD U. S. BATTLESHIP (13 knot).

Signal letter: GK.

TEXAS (June, 1892).

Displacement 6300 tons. Complement 380.

Length (*waterline*), 301 feet. Beam, 64 feet. *Maximum* draught, 24 feet.

Guns:
- 2—12 inch, I., 35 cal. (A).
- 6—6 inch, 35 cal. RF (F).
- 12—6 pdr.
- 10—1 pdr.
- 2 Colts.
- 1 Field gun.

Torpedo tubes:
2 *above water*
   (bow & stern).

Armour (compound):
- 12" Belt .... a
- 3" Deck .... = d
  [Deck flat on belt.]
- Protection to vitals......... = a
- 12" Bulkheads (under deck) a
- 12" Redoubt.................. a
- 12" Turrets (2).............. a
- 6" Hoists to redoubt (2) ... d
- 12" Conning tower .... a

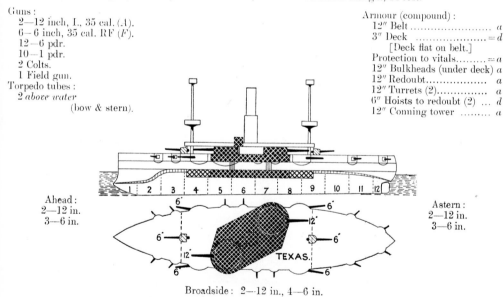

Ahead:
2—12 in.
3—6 in.

Astern:
2—12 in.
3—6 in.

Broadside: 2—12 in., 4—6 in.

Machinery: 2 sets vertical inverted direct acting triple expansion. 2 screws. Boilers: cylindrical (4 double ended). Designed H.P. 8000 *f.d.* = 17 kts. Coal: *normal* 500 tons; *maximum* 950 tons.

General Notes.—Changes have been made in the 12 in. gun mountings; they can now fire every two minutes. Laid down at Norfolk Navy Yard, June, 1889. Completed 1895. Burns a great deal of coal and is a poor steamer.

U. S. MONITORS (12 knot).

Signal letter for class: H.
   Photo by favour of F. Cresson Schell, Esq.

ARKANSAS (November, 1900), **NEVADA** (November, 1900), **FLORIDA** (November, 1901), **WYOMING** (September, 1900).

Displacement 3235 tons. Complement 130.

Length (*waterline*), 252 feet. Beam 50 feet. *Maximum* draught, 12½ feet.

Guns (M. '99):
- 2—12 inch, III, 40 cal. (AAAA).
- 4—4 inch, VII., 50 cal. (E).
- 3—6 pdr. automatic.
- 4—1 pdr. automatic.
- 4—1 pdr. R.F.
- 2 Colts.

Torpedo tubes (18 inch):
2 *above water.*

Armour (Krupp):
- 11" Belt (amidships) ..... aaa
- 5" Belt (ends) c
- 1½" Deck (reinforcing belt)
- Protection to vitals ...= aaaa
- 11" Barbettes .... aaa
- 11" Hood to this........... aaa
- 8" Conning tower........... a

Ahead:
2—12 in.
2—4 in.

Astern:
2—4 in.

Broadside: 2—12 in., 2—4 in.

Machinery: 2 sets vertical inverted 3 cylinder triple expansion. 2 screws. Boilers: *Arkansas*, 4 Thornycroft; *Nevada*, 4 Niclausse; *Florida*, 4 Normand; *Wyoming*, 4 Babcock & Wilcox. Designed H.P. 2400 = 12 kts. Coal: *normal* tons; *maximum* 400 tons.

Name.	Builders.	Laid down.	Completed.	Differences.
Arkansas	Newport News	Nov., '99	1902	As photo
Nevada	Bath Ironworks	April, '99	1903	Topmast abaft
Florida	Elizabeth Port	Jan., '99	1903	Smaller s. l. platform
Wyoming	Union I. W. 'Frisco	April, '99	1903	

24 pneumatic watertight doors.

MONTEREY (April, 1891).

Displacement 4084 tons. Complement 203.

Length, 256 feet. Beam, 59 feet. *Maximum* draught, 17 feet.

Guns :
2—12 inch, 35 cal. (A).
2—10 inch, 35 cal. (B).
6—6 pdr.
4—1 pdr.
2 Colts.
Torpedo tubes :
none.

Armour (Harvey) :
13″ Belt (amidships) .... *aa*
6″ Belt (ends) .... *c*
2″ Deck (flat) ....
Protection to vitals ....= *aa*
14″ Fore barbette (A)......... *aa*
11½″ After barbette (B) ...... *aa*
8″ Hoods to both .... *b*
10″ Conning tower .... *a*

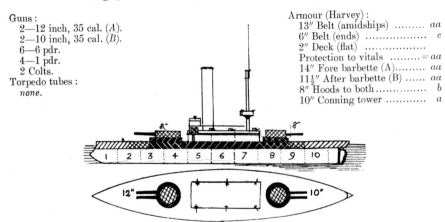

Machinery : 2 sets vertical inverted triple expansion. 2 screws. Boilers (1904) : Babcock and Wilcox. Designed H.P. 5400 = 13·6 kts. (exceeded on *trial* under favourable circumstances). Coal : *normal* 200 tons.

PURITAN (1882).

Displacement 6060 tons. Complement 230.

Length, 289 feet. Beam, 60 feet. *Maximum* draught, 20 feet.

Guns :
4—12 inch, 35 cal. (A).
6—4 inch, 40 cal. (F).
4—3 pdr.
4—1 pdr.
4 Gatlings.
Torpedo tubes :
none.

Armour (Harvey) :
14″ Belt (amidships) .... *aa*
6″ Belt (ends) .... *c*
2″ Deck (flat) ....
Protection to vitals is .... *aa*
14″ Barbettes .... *aa*
8″ Turrets to these .... *b*
8″ Conning tower.............. *b*

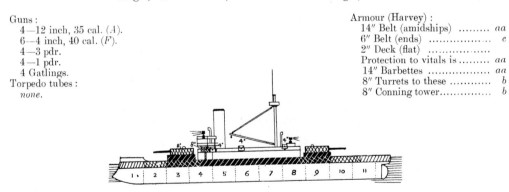

Machinery : 2 sets horizontal compound. 2 screws. Boilers : 8 cylindrical. Designed H.P. *natural* 3700 = 12·4 kts. Coal : *normal* 400 tons ; *maximum* 580 tons.

Notes.—Puritan was not completed till 1895 or thereabouts. See notes to *Terror*, all of which apply to *Puritan.*

TERROR.   *Photos, copyright, William H. Rau.*

MONADNOCK.   *Photo, copyright, Taber.*

MIANTONOMOH.

AMPHITRITE.   *Photo, copyright, Rau.*

TERROR, MIANTONOMOH, MONADNOCK, AMPHITRITE. 3990 tons. Guns: 4—10 inch, 35 cal. (*B*) in *Terror*, 30 cal. (*D*) in others. Last two also carry a couple of 4 inch. Belts (iron): 7″ in first two, with 11½″ steel low turrets; in second two 9″ iron belts, with 11½″ steel barbettes and 7½″ turrets. Nominal speeds: 10—12 knots. Coal: 330 tons *maximum*.

109

(WASHINGTON CLASS.—4 SHIPS).

WASHINGTON (1904), **TENNESSEE** (1904), *NORTH CAROLINA* (*building*) & *MONTANA* (*building*).

Normal Displacement 14,500 tons.   Complement 858 (as flagship).

Length (*waterline*), 502 feet.   Beam, 73 feet.   *Maximum* draught, 26½ feet.   Length over all, 504½ feet.

Guns (M. '99):
4—10 inch, 40 cal. (*AAA*).
16—6 inch, 50 cal. (*C*).
23—14 pdr.
12—3 pdr., semi aut.
2—1 pdr., aut.
2—1 pdr., R. F.
2 machine.
2 colt.s
2 field guns, 12 pdr.
Torpedo tubes (18 inch):
4 *submerged*.

Armour (Krupp):
5″—3″ Belt	*b*-ϵ
3″ Deck (ends)	
Protection to vitals	*a*
5″ Lower deck side	*b*
4″ Lower deck bulkheads	*d*
7″ Barbettes (N.C.)	*a*
9″—5″ Turrets ...... = *aaa-b*
5″ Battery	*b*
2″ Upper deck battery...	*f*
9″ Conning tower (fore)	*aa*
5″ After C. T. (N.C.) ...	*c*

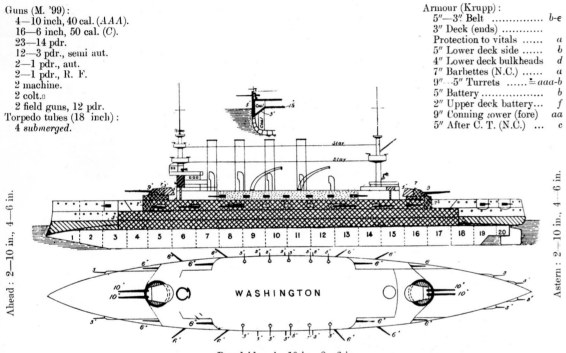

Ahead : 2—10 in., 4—6 in.

Astern : 2—10 in., 4—6 in.

WASHINGTON

Broadside : 4—10 in., 8—6 in.

Photo by favour of Collier's Weekly.

Machinery : 2 sets 4 cylinder triple expansion.   2 screws.   Boilers : 16 Babcock & Wilcox, or 32 Niclausse.   Designed H.P. 25,000 = 22 kts.   Coal : *normal* 900 tons ; *maximum* 2000 tons.

Armour Notes.—Belt is 7½ feet wide, and of uniform thickness.   It reaches to 5 feet below *normal* waterline.   2½″ N.S. tops to turrets.   1½″ screens in battery ; 2″ bulkheads.   Prot. deck amidships, 2½″ on slopes.

Gunnery Notes.—Turrets electrically manœuvred.   Electric and hand hoists.   All round loading positions to big guns.

Engineering Notes :—

Name.	Builder.	Laid down.	To be completed.	Boilers.
Washington	New York Ship-building Co.	1903	1906	Babcock
Tennesse	Cramps	1903	1906	Niclausse
N. Carolina		1905	1908	......
Montana		1905	1908	......

General Notes.—The first two authorised July, 1902.   Freeboard forward, 24 feet ; amidships, 18 feet.   Full displacement, 15,950 tons.   First of class laid down 1903.

(CALIFORNIA CLASS—6 SHIPS)

WEST VIRGINIA (April, 1903), **COLORADO** (April, 1903), **PENNSYLVANIA** (Aug., 1903),
MARYLAND (Sept., 1903), **CALIFORNIA** (April, 1904) & **SOUTH DAKOTA** (1904).

13,400 tons.   Complement 822.

Length, 502 feet.   Beam, 70 feet.   *Maximum* draught, 26½ feet at normal displacement.

Photo, copyright,
by favour of E. Scholl, Esq.

Guns––(model 1899):
4—8 inch, 45 cal. (A).
14—6 inch, 50 cal. (C).
18—14 pdr., 50 cal. (F).
12—3 pdr.
8—1 pdr.
8 Colts, etc.
2 Field guns, 3 in.
Torpedo tubes (18 in.):
2 submerged.

(700 tons with two-thirds ammunition).

Armour (Krupp):
6″ Belt........................ a
3½″ Belt (ends) .... dϵ
4″ Deck (on slopes) .. ...
Protection to vitals ......= aa
5″ Upper belt.............. b
4″ Bulkheads .... d
6″ Turrets (N.C.) .... b
6½″ fronts to these........ b
4″ Hoists to these .... d
5″ Battery .... b
2½″ Screens in battery ...
6″ Casemates (N.C.)....... b
9″ Conning tower (N.C.)... aa
5″ Signal tower (aft) c

(Total 2219 tons).

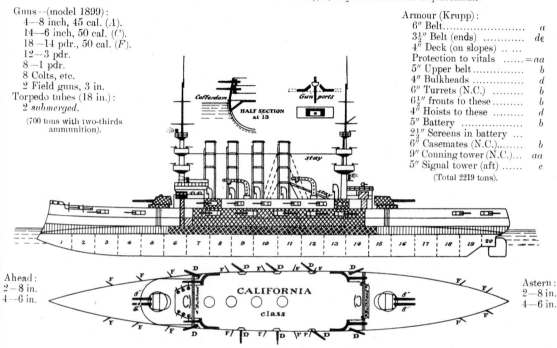

CALIFORNIA class

Ahead:
2—8 in.
4—6 in.

Astern:
2—8 in.
4—6 in.

Broadside : 4—8 in., 7—6 in.

Machinery : 2 sets 4 cylinder triple expansion.   2 screws.   Boilers : 30 Babcock or 32 Niclausse.

Designed H.P. 23,000 = 22 kts.   Coal : *normal* 900 tons ; *maximum* 2000 tons.

Gunnery Notes.—8 inch manœuvred electrically and by hand ; electric hoists supply 1 round per 50 seconds.
6 „ „ by hand ; „ „ „ „ 3 „ „ minute.
Rounds per gun : 8 inch, 125 ; 6 inch, 200 ; 14 pdr., 250 ; lesser guns, 500 per gun.
(*At normal displacement only two-thirds of this ammunition is on board*).
Arcs of fire : 8 inch, 270° ; casemate and angles of battery, 6 inch, 150° ; remaining *starboard*, 6 inch,
75° before the beam and 55° abaft ; remaining *port* guns, 55° before only, and 75° abaft ; 14 pdrs., all
about 135°.

Armour Notes.—Main belt amidships 244 feet long by 7½ feet wide, 6½ feet below water, 1 foot above.   Lowest
strake of it is 5″ thick.   Deck behind belt amidships is only about 2½″ on slopes.   Cellulose belt.   Upper
belt, 232 feet long and 7½ feet wide, forming redoubt with 4″ bulkheads.

Engineering Notes.—Grate area 1,600 square feet.   Heating surface 68,000 square feet.   Weight of machinery
and boilers, with water, 2,100 tons.

Class distinction.—Rig of main mast and big cowl abaft fore mast.

Distinctions between the ships.—

Name.	Where built	Laid down.	Completed.	4 hours full power trial.		Boilers.
				I.H.P.	Kts.	
California ...	Union Ironworks	7/5/02	1906	—	= —	Babcock
Pennsylvania	Cramp's	7/8/01	1905	29,843	= 22·48	Niclausse
West Virginia	Newport News	16/9/01	1905	—	= 22·14	Babcock
Colorado ...	Cramp's	25/4/01	1905	—	= 22·24	Niclausse
Maryland ...	Newport News	24/10/01	1906	—	= —	Babcock
South Dakota	Union Ironworks	7/5/02	1906	—	= —	Babcock

Average consumption :—Niclausse boilered ships burn about 22½ tons an hour at full speed.

Babcock boilered ships about 30 tons an hour.

General Notes.—Authorised 1899 and 1900.   Average cost, *complete*, about £1,200,000 per ship.

U. S. ARMOURED CRUISERS (21½ knot).

(St. Louis Class.—3 Ships.)

CHARLESTON (1904), **MILWAUKEE** (1904), **ST. LOUIS** (1905).

Sheathed and coppered.

Displacement 9700 tons.   Complement 564.

Length, 423 feet.   Beam, 65 feet.   *Maximum* draught, 23¼ feet.

Guns :
- 14—6 inch, 50 cal. (C).
- 18—14 pdr. (F).
- 12—3 pdr.
- 12—1 pdr.
- 8—Colts.

Torpedo tubes (18 inch) :
- *2 submerged*

Armour (Krupp) :
- 4″ Belt .. .. *d*
- 3″ Deck ... .
- Protection to vitals... = *b*
- 4″ Lower deck redoubt *d*
- 4″ Battery .... *d*
- 4″ Casemates .... *d*
- 5″ Conning tower ...... *d*
- 3″ Tube ....
- (Total 854 tons, including cellulose..)

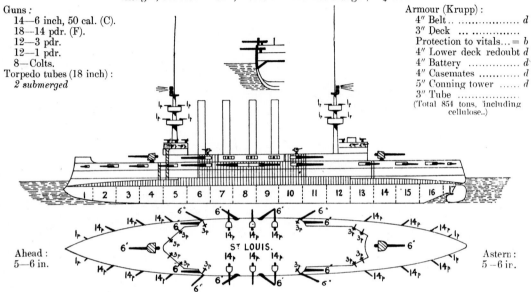

Ahead :
5—6 in.

Astern :
5—6 in.

Broadside fire : 8—6 in.

Machinery : 2 sets vertical 4 cylinder triple expansion.   2 screws.   Boilers : 16 Babcock and Wilcox. Designed H.P. 21,000 = 21·5 kts.   Coal : *normal* 650 tons ; *maximum* 1500 tons.

Armour Notes—The belt is partial ; 197 feet long, by 7½ feet wide.   Armour weighs 854 tons.

Gunnery Notes—All guns fitted with electric hoists, which will serve 6 rounds per minute to 6 inch guns, and 15 per minute to the 3 inch 14-pounder guns.

Arcs of fire : Fore and aft 6 inch, 270° ; upper casemate guns 145° from axial line ; end guns main deck 130° (85° ahead and 55° astern for fore ones, *vice versâ* for after) : other guns 110°.

Weight of ammunition *normal* 519 tons.

Engineering Notes.—

Name.	Builders.	Laid down.	Completed.	Trials.	4 hrs. f.p. at 143 revs.	Boilers
Charleston	Newport News	Jan., 1902	1905	=	= 22·03	Babcock
Milwaukee	Union I.W., 'Frisco	1903	1906	=	=	Babcock
St. Louis	Neafie & Levy	1903	1906	=	=	Babcock

General Notes—Hull and armour deck weigh 5346 tons.   These ships which are officially known as "semi-armoured" have comparatively small fighting value, being inferior even to the British *County* class.

112

St. Louis.

Photo by favour of H. Reuterdahl, Esq.

BROOKLYN (1895).

Displacement 9215 tons.   Complement 500.

Length, 400 feet.   Beam, 65 feet.   *Maximum* draught, 28 feet.

Guns :
  8—8 inch, 35 cal. (*E*).
  12—5 inch, old (*F*).
  12—6 pdr.
  4—1 pdr.
  4—Gatlings.
Torpedo tubes (Howell) :
  5 *above water* (bow and
    broadside).

Armour (Harvey) :
  3″ Belt.................... ϵ
  6″ Deck (amidships) = *aa*
  3″ Deck (ends)............
  [Cofferdam and cellulose
    belt.]
  Protection to vitals = *aa*
  8″ Barbettes .... *b*
  8″ Hoods to barbettes... *b*
  6″ Hoists .... *c*
  4″Shields(fixed) 5″ guns ϵ
  7½″ Conning tower...... *b*

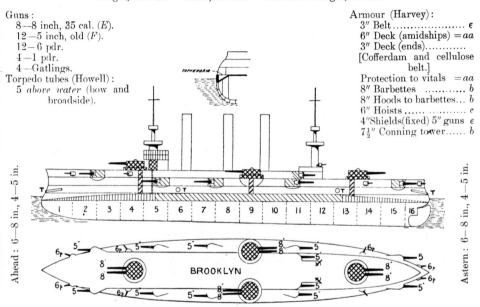

Ahead : 6—8 in., 4—5 in.

Astern : 6—8 in., 4—5 in.

Broadside : 6—8 in., 6—5 in.

Photo, Rau.

Machinery : 4 sets vertical triple expansion.   2 screws.   Boilers : cylindrical ; 20 2-ended and 8 1-ended.   Designed H.P. *forced* 18,000 = 21 kts.   Coal : *normal* 900 tons ; *maximum* 1650 tons.

Armour Notes.—The belt is 8 feet wide, and 267 feet long.   There are no bulkheads.

Engineering Notes.—On first *trial* (4 hours) she made *mean* I.H.P. 18,769 = 21·9 knots (138-140 revolutions).   She was very light, and has not since equalled this performance.   At Santiago, however, she made 16 knots without her forward engines.

NEW YORK (December, 1891).

Displacement 8200 tons.   Complement 566.

Length (*waterline*), 380 feet.   Beam, 64 feet.   *Maximum* draught, 28 feet.

Guns (Old Models):
  6—8 inch, 35 cal. (*E*).
  12—4 inch, 40 cal. (*F*).
  8—6 pdr.
  4—1 pdr.
  4 Colts.
Torpedo tubes:
  4 *above water* (broadside).
  1 *above water* (bow).

Armour (Harvey):
  4″ Belt .... *d*
  6″ Deck (amidships)
  [Cofferdam and cellulose.]
  Protection to vitals... = *a*
  10″ Barbettes .... *a*
  7″ Turrets (2) .... *b*
  5″ Hoists.............. *d*
  4″ on 4″ guns......... *d*
  7″ Conning tower ... *b*

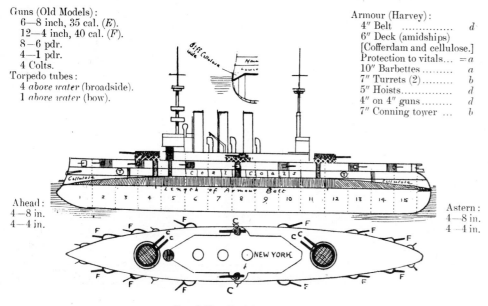

Ahead:
4—8 in.
4—4 in.

Astern:
4—8 in.
4—4 in.

Broadside: 5—8 in., 6—4 in.

Photo, copyright 1900, W. H. Rau.

Machinery: 4 sets vertical triple expansion. 2 screws. Boilers: cylindrical; 6 double-ended, 2 single-ended; 50 furnaces. Designed H.P. *forced* 16,500 = 21 kts. Coal: *normal* 750 tons; *maximum* 1150 tons.

Armour Notes.—Belt is 200 feet long.

Gunnery Notes.—The 8 inch turrets are electrically manœuvred with electric hoists. Amidship 8 inch guns, hand gear only. One electric hoist at each end of battery for the 4 inch guns. Ammunition goes to individual guns by manual power only.

Engineering Notes.—On first trials she made 21 kts. with I.H.P. 17,400. She has always been a good steamer.

General Notes.—Good sea boat. Laid down at Philadelphia, September, 1890. Completed 1893

NEW ORLEANS (Dec., 1896) & **ALBANY** (Jan., 1899).

Displacement 3450 tons.   Complement 300.

Length, 330 feet.   Beam, 43¾ feet.   *Maximum* draught, 17½ feet.

Guns :
6—6 inch, 50 cal. (*C*)
4—5 inch, 50 cal. (*E*).
10—6 pdr.
4—1 pdr.
4 Colts.
Torpedo tubes :
2 *above water.*

Armour (Harvey-nickel) :
3½″ Deck .... = *c*
[Cofferdam amidships].
4½″ Fronts to gun shields,
sides 2″.

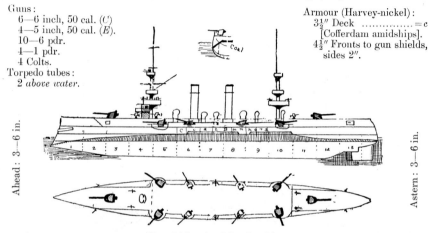

Ahead : 3—6 in.

Astern : 3—6 in.

Broadside : 4—6 in., 2—5 in.

Machinery : 2 sets 4 cylinder triple expansion. 2 screws. Boilers : 4 2-ended Scotch.
Designed H.P. *forced* 7500 = 20·25 kts.   Coal : *normal* 450 tons ; *maximum* 700 tons.

Engineering Notes.—Can do about 19½ kts. at present, *f. d.*

Trials : New Orleans, *natural* draught = 19·8 kts. ; 4 hours *forced* = 21 kts. *Albany, natural*
draught, 19·1 kts. ; 4 hours *forced* = 20·5 kts.

General Notes.—Laid down at Elswick (for Brazil) and purchased by U. S. just before war
with Spain. Re-armed with U. S. guns, 1903 ; the 6 in. may be replaced by 5 in. shortly.

Differences :—

Name	Cowls.	Notes.
Albany	High	
New Orleans	Low	

ALBANY.

NEW ORLEANS.   *Photo, S. Ballou, Esq.*

OLYMPIA (November, 1892).

Displacement 5870 tons.   Complement 466.

Length, 325 feet.   Beam 53 feet.   *Maximum* draught, 25 feet.

Guns :
    4—8 inch, 35 cal. *(E).*
    10—5 inch, 40 cal. *(F).*
    14—6 pdr.
    6—1 pdr.
    4—Colts.
Torpedo tubes :
    (had originally 6 *above*
    water.)

Armour (Harvey) :
    $4\frac{3}{4}''$ Deck (amidships)... $= b$
    2″ Deck (ends) .... $= c$
    4″ Barbettes and turrets d
    4″ Sponsons to 5″ guns... d
    5″ C.Ts. (fore and aft) ... d

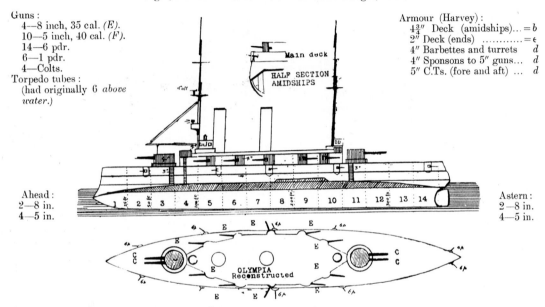

Ahead :
2—8 in.
4—5 in.

Astern :
2—8 in.
4—5 in.

Broadside : 4—8 in., 5—5 in.

Machinery : 2 sets vertical inverted triple expansion.   2 screws.   Boilers : cylindrical ; 4 2-ended and 2 1-ended. 40 furnaces.   Designed I.H.P. *forced* 17,000 = 21 kts.   Coal : *normal* 500 tons ; *maximum* 1300 tons.

Armour Notes.—Complete cellulose belt 8½ feet wide by 33″ thick.

General Notes.—Laid down at San Francisco, June 1891.   Completed 1895.   Cost, *complete*, about £550,000.   Flagship Admiral Dewey at battle of Kavite.   Reconstructed partially 1901-03.

116

U. S. COMMERCE DESTROYERS.

COLUMBIA (July, 1892), & **MINNEAPOLIS** (August, 1893).

Displacement 7,450 tons.   Complement 524.

Length (*waterline*), 412 feet.   Beam, 58 feet.   *Maximum* draught, 25½ feet.

Guns :
1—8 inch, 35 cal. (*E*).
2—6 inch, 40 cal. (*F*).
8—4 inch (*F*).
12—6 pdr.
4—1 pdr.
4 Colts.
Torpedo tubes (18 in) :
4 *above water*.

Armour (Harvey) :
4″ Armour deck ...... = *b*
Protection to vitals ... = *b*
4″ Sponsons .... *d*
3″ Hoists .... *e*
5″ Conning tower...... *d*

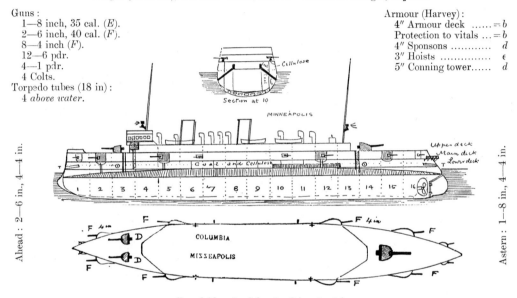

Ahead : 2—6 in., 4—4 in.

Astern : 1—8 in., 4—4 in.

Broadside : 1—8 in., 1—6 in., 4—4 in.

Machinery : 3 sets vertical inverted triple expansion.   3 screws.   Boilers : cylindrical.   Designed H.P. *forced* 21,500 = 23 kts.   Coal : *normal* 750 tons ; *maximum* 2400 tons.

Engineering Notes—On 4 hours *forced draught trial* (light) *Columbia* made 22·8 knots with 18,500 I.H.P., and *Minneapolis* 23 knots with 20,800 I.H.P.   The *Columbia* crossed the Atlantic in 7 days at a *mean* of 18·4 knots.   For 6 days the speed exceeded this considerably, but forced draught could not be used on the last day.   The sea speed for ordinary purposes is nearly 20 knots.   During the war with Spain these ships were much worked, and proved entirely successful in steaming and sea-keeping qualities.

General Notes—Tactical diameter of these ships is 800 yards.   On *trial* they turned 16 points in 2 minutes 50 seconds (5½ lengths).

Photo, Levin.

CHICAGO (1885).
Displacement, 5,000 tons.   Complement 459.
Length, 328 feet.   Beam, 48 feet.   *Maximum* draught, 23 feet.

Guns :
4—8 inch, 35 cal. (*E*).
14—5 inch, 40 cal. (*F*).
9—6 pdr.
4 small.
Torpedo tubes :
Nil.

Armour :
1½″ Deck … = *f*

BALTIMORE (1888).
Displacement 4,600 tons.   Complement 395.
Length, 325 feet.   Beam, 48½ feet.   *Maximum* draught, 23½ feet.

Guns—(M. '01) :
12—6 inch, 40 cal. (*F*).
6—14 pdr. (*F*).
4—6 pdr.
2—3 pdr.
6—1 pdr.
2 Colts.
Torpedo tubes :
5 *above water* (stern and in sections 1 and 10).

Armour (steel) :
4″ Deck.................. = *d*
3″ Conning tower...... *f*
[Cofferdam and cellulose belt.]

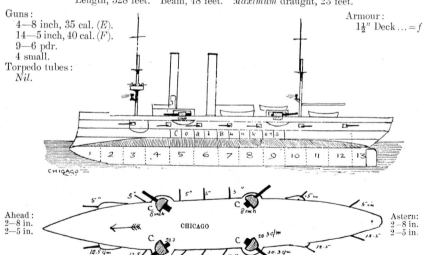

Ahead :
2—8 in.
2—5 in.

Astern :
2—8 in.
2—5 in.

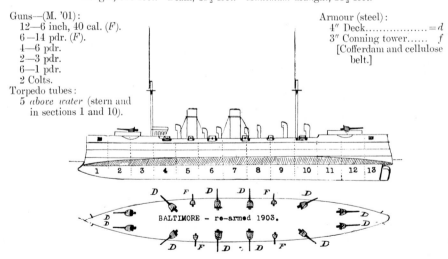

Machinery : 2 sets triple expansion. 2 screws. Boilers : 6 Babcock + 4 cylindrical.
Coal : *maximum* 940 tons. H.P. 10,000 = 19 kts.
The *Chicago* is fitted with automatic water-tight doors. She burns enormous quantities of coal, and cannot steam at much over 16 kts. Re-armed and reconstructed 1897-99.

Machinery : 2 sets horizontal triple expansion. 2 screws. Boilers : 4 2-ended Scotch ; 32 furnaces. Designed H.P. *forced* 10,000 = 20 kts. Coal : *normal* 400 tons ; *maximum* 900 tons.
Present speed about 16-17 kts. Re-armed and partially reconstructed, 1901.

Photo, Loeffler,

SAN FRANCISCO (1889).

Displacement 4098 tons.   Complement 393.

Length, 311½ feet.   Beam, 49 feet.   *Maximum* draught, 23¼ feet.

Guns:
12 —6 inch, 40 cal. (*F*).
4— 6 pdr.
4—1 pdr.
2 Colts.
Torpedo tubes:
None.

Armour (steel):
3″ Deck .... = *d*
2″ Gun shields ....

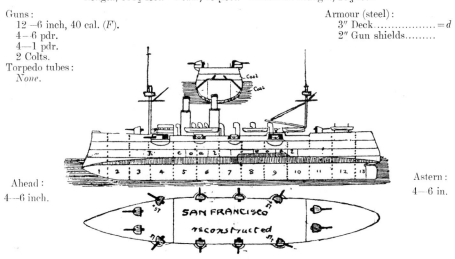

Ahead:
4—6 inch.

Astern:
4—6 in.

Broadside: 6—6 in.

Machinery: 2 sets horizontal triple expansion.   2 screws.   Boilers: 4 2-ended Scotch. Designed H.P. 8500 = 19 kts. (exceeded on first *trials*).   Coal: *normal* 400 tons; *maximum* 809 tons. *Notes.*—The guns which are carried on forecastle and poop of *San Francisco*, are, in *Newark*, below at same level as other guns.   Reconstructed 1899.   Can now steam 17 kts.

Photo, H. Reuterdahl, Esq.

NEWARK (1890).

Displacement 4098 tons.   Complement 393.

Length, 311½ feet.   Beam, 49 feet.   *Maximum* draught, 23⅓ feet.

Guns:
12—6in. 40 cal. (*F*).
4—6 pdr.
4—1 pdr.
2 Colts.
Torpedo tubes:
Nil.

Armour (steel):
3″ Deck .... = *d*
2″ Gun shields ...

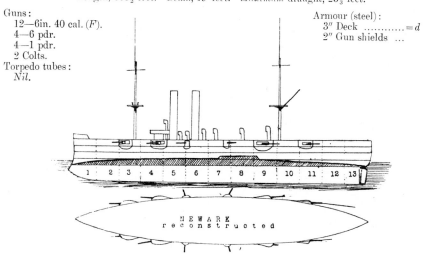

Machinery: 2 sets horizontal triple expansion.   2 screws.   Boilers: 4 2-ended Scotch.   Designed H.P. 8500 = 19 kts. (exceeded on first *trials*).   Coal: *normal* 400 tons; *maximum* 809 tons. *Notes.*—Partially reconstructed 1902.   Can steam about 17 kts.

Scouts—(3 Ships).

SALEM, BIRMINGHAM, CHESTER.

Full Displacement 4000 tons.   Complement 384.

Length (*waterline*), 424 feet.   Beam, 45 feet.   *Maximum* draught,   feet.

Guns :
    12—14 pdr. (*F*).
    Torpedo tube (21 inch).
        2 submerged

Armour :
    2″ Belt (amidships)...... *f*
    1″ Bulkheads .... *f*
    1½″ Armour deck ......= ε
    Protection to vitals ...= ε
    2″–1″ Steering gear
        protection............ *f*
    No conning tower.

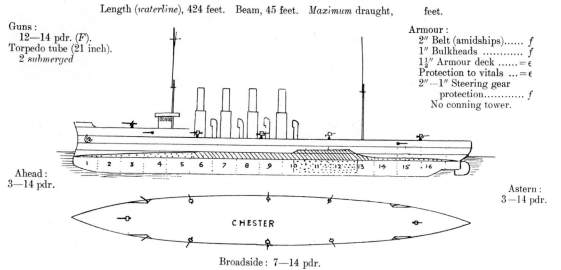

CHESTER

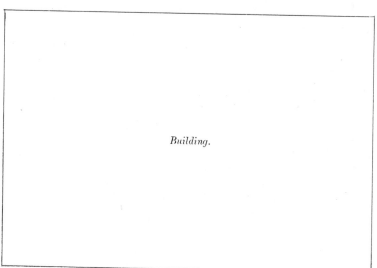

Building.

Ahead :
3—14 pdr.

Astern :
3 —14 pdr.

Broadside : 7—14 pdr.

    Machinery : Not yet settled.   2 screws.   Boilers : Not yet settled.   Designed H.P. 16,000 = 24 kts.
Coal : *normal*   tons ; *maximum* 1000 tons.

Armour Notes.—A species of box covers the entire machinery space.

Gunnery Notes.—Hoists, electric, 4.
    Arcs of fire :
    Ammunition carried : 3000 rounds for 14 pdrs.

Torpedo Notes.—Eight 21 inch torpedoes carried.   Range, 4000 yards.

Engineering Notes.— One or more will have turbines probably.

    Authorised 1904,

(CINCINNATI CLASS—2 SHIPS).

RALEIGH (March, 1892), & **CINCINNATI** (November, 1892).

Displacement 3213 tons.   Complement 339.

Length, 300 feet.   Beam, 42 feet.   *Maximum* draught, 20¼ feet.

Guns (M. '99)
11—5 inch
8—6 pdr.
4—1 pdr.
Torpedo tubes :
Nil.

Armour (steel) :
2½″ Armour deck......= ε
Protection to vitals ...= ε
2″ Conning tower.........

CINCINNATI.   *Photo, Loeffler.*

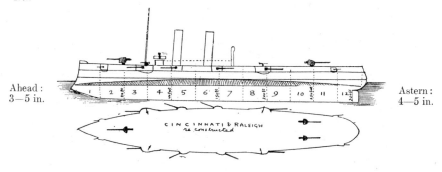

Ahead :
3—5 in.

Astern :
4—5 in.

Broadside : 6—5 in.

Machinery : 2 sets 4 cylinder vertical triple expansion (new 1900-2). 2 screws. Boilers : Babcock and Wilcox. Designed H.P. 10,000 = 19 kts. Coal : *normal* 396 tons ; *maximum* 556 tons.

Gunnery Notes.—Re-armed 1902-3. Hoists, electric.

Torpedo Notes.—No torpedo tubes.

Engineering Notes.—

Name.	Built at	Laid down	Completed	Recon-structed.	Full power trial.	Boilers.	Last recorded full speed.
Raleigh	Norfolk	Dec., '89	1894	1901	8500=	Babcock	...
Cincinnati	Brooklyn	Jan., '90	1894	1902	8490=	Babcock	18

RALEIGH..   *Photo, H. Ballou, Esq.*

Differences.—Easily differentiated by rig.

Class distinction.—*Raleigh* easily distinguished from *Detroit* class by stern (see *Detroit*).

Q

TACOMA. *Photo by favour of "New York Herald."*

CHATTANOOGA (March, 1903), **CLEVELAND** (September, 1901), **DENVER** (June, 1902),
DESMOINES (September, 1902), **GALVESTON** (July, 1903), & **TACOMA** (June, 1903).

(Wood sheathed and coppered). Displacement 3,200 tons. Complement 293.

Length, 292 feet. Beam, 44 feet. *Maximum* draught, 17¼ feet.

Guns (model 1899):
10—5 inch, 50 cals. (E).
8—6 pdr.
2—1 pdr.
2 Colts.
Torpedo tubes:
Nil.

Armour (Harvey-nickel):
2″ Deck (on engines) ...... = ε
½″ elsewhere. ....

Ahead:
5—5 in.

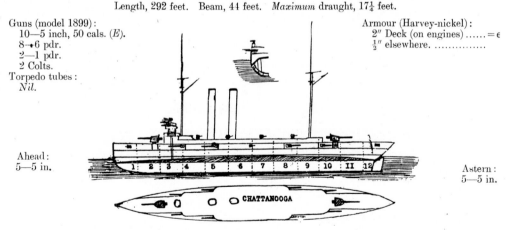

Astern:
5—5 in.

Broadside: 6—5 in.

Machinery: 2 sets 4 cylinder triple expansion. 2 screws. Boilers: 6 Babcock & Wilcox. Designed H.P 4,500 = 16·5 kts. Coal: *normal* 467 tons; *maximum* 700 tons = 7,000 miles at 10 kts.

Notes.—Speeds exceeded on *trial*, but these ships have practically no fighting value.

(All 3 alike). *Photo, Symonds.*

DETROIT (October, 1891), **MONTGOMERY** (December, 1891),
MARBLEHEAD (August, 1892).

Displacement 2,000 tons. Complement, 250.

Length, 257 feet. Beam, 37 feet. *Maximum* draught, 16½ feet.

Guns:
9—5 inch, 40 cal. (F).
6—6 pdr.
2—1 pdr.
2 Gatlings.
Torpedo tubes:
4 *above water.*

Armour (steel):
½″ Deck.................
[Cellulose belt.]
2″ Conning tower.

Ahead:
3—5 in.

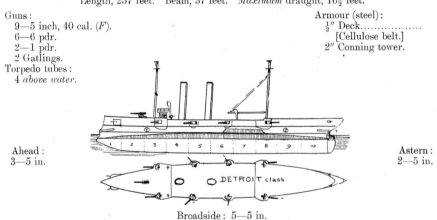

Astern:
2—5 in.

Broadside: 5—5 in.

Machinery: 2 sets vertical 3 cylinder triple expansion. 2 screws. Boilers: 2 2-ended and 1 1-ended horizontal return-tabular. Designed H.P. 5,400 = 17 kts. Coal: *normal* 200 tons; *maximum* 435 tons.

Note.—On *trial* (1896) *Detroit natural* I.H.P. 2,588 = 16·4 kts.; *forced* 4,096 = 19·2 kts., and the others have done something similar, but all were light at the time. Present speeds well below this.

All photos by or by favour of H. Reuterdahl, Esq.

1 **Farragut** (1898). 273 tons. I.H P. 5600 = 31·76 kts. Armament: 6 6 pdr. 2 tubes (aft). Coal: 44 tons.

2 *Lawrence class:*—**Lawrence** (1889), **Macdonough** (1900). 400 tons. H.P. 8400 = 30 kts. Armament: 1—14 pdr. (aft), 7—6 pdr. 2 tubes.

3 *Truxton class:*—**Truxton, Whipple, Worden** (all 1900). 433 tons. H.P. 8300 = 30 kts. Armament: 2—14 pdr. (fore and aft), 5—6 pdr. 2 tubes.

(4 funnels in pairs).

9 *Bainbridge class:*—**Barry, Bainbridge, Chauncey, Dale, Decatur, Paul Jones, Perry, Preble,** and **Stewart** (—all 1900). 420 tons. H.P. 8000 = 29 kts. Armament: 2—14 pdr., 5—6 pdr. 2 tubes (amidships and aft) Coal: 139 tons. Complement 64. *Actual endurance:* 2700 miles at 8 kts. Excellent sea boats.

(4 funnels—like Truxton's, but higher).

2 *Hull class:*—**Hopkins** and **Hull** (1900). 408 tons. H.P. 7200 = 29 kts. Armament: 2—14 pdr., 5—6 pdrs. 2 tubes (amidships and aft). Coal: 150 tons. Complement 64.

1 **Bailey** (1899) (small edition of above). 235 tons. H.P. 5600 = 30 kts. Armament: 4—6 pdrs. 2 tubes (amidships and aft).

There are two other destroyers, launched 1899, which, having failed to reach contract speed, are not yet accepted into the Navy, but will probably be accepted ultimately as they are.

These are:—**Stringham** (3 funnels). 340 tons. Designed H.P. 7200 = 30 kts. Armament: 7—6 pdrs. 2 tubes (aft); **Goldsborough.** 247 tons. (2 funnels, very like *Farragut*). Designed H.P. 5600 = 30 kts. Armament: 4—6 pdr. 2 tubes (aft).

BARNEY, BAGLEY, BIDDLE CLASS.

SHUBRICK CLASS.

PORTER CLASS.

DAHLGREEN CLASS.

Torpedo Boats.

FIRST CLASS (3 tubes.)

No.			tons.	Max. speed
3	Barney, Bagley, Biddle	'00	167	28
7	Shubrick, Thornton, Wilkes, Tingey, Stockton, De Long, Blakely	'00	165	26
2	Nicholson, O'Brien	'00	174	26
2	Porter, Dupont	'97	175	27
2	Dahlgreen, Craven	'98	147	27
3	Foote, Winslow, Rodgers	'95	143	24
1	Rowan	'98	143	26
1	Ericsson	'91	120	23
2	Davis, Fox	'98	110	23
1	Morris	'98	103	23
1	Cushing	'90	105	22
25				

SECOND CLASS (2 tubes).

2	McKee, Mackenzie	'98	65	21

THIRD CLASS (2 tubes).

2	Gwyn, Talbot	'98	46	21

There are also three old boats including *Somers* purchased 1898, too slow to be of any fighting value.

All first class boats carry 3—1 pdr. Nicholson class have however, 5—1 pdr., and Porter class 4—1 pdr. The lesser craft, 1—1 pdr.

RODGERS CLASS.

ROWAN.

MORRIS.

GWYN.

124

U. S. SUBMARINES.

No.	Type.	Date.	Tons.	Motive Power.	Horse power.	Speed kts.	Dimensions in feet.	Endurance hours.	Petrol carried.
									gallons.
1	*Holland* ...	'96	74	Petrol, 4 cyl. accumulators.	$\frac{45}{160}$	$\frac{8}{5}$	$54 \times 10\frac{3}{4} \times 10\frac{1}{2}$	$\frac{18}{3}$	1050
7	*Adder*	'96-'02	120	Petrol, 4 cyl. accumulators.		$\frac{8}{5}$	$63\frac{1}{2} \times 11\frac{3}{4} \times 12$	$\frac{20}{3}$	850
4	*N 9 — 12*	'05-'06	—						

The 7 *Adder class* are named **Adder, Shark, Grampus, Porpoise, Moccasin, Pike, Plunger.**

NOTES.

All the above are elementary Holland type boats, with high periscopes, but two are stated to be fitted to each--one large and one small one.

The petrol engine is a 4 cylinder vertical, cylinders in pairs.   Slow running engine.   Control by spark (igniter) and by cutting out cylinders.   Submersion by horizontal rudders.

The *Holland* originally carried a dynamite gun, but this was removed long ago.   She carries 3 torpedoes. The *Adder* class carry 5, 18 in. short in each case.   One tube.

A Lake type submarine, *Protector*, was experimented with, but not purchased.   This boat, being able to lie submerged and stationary, embodied features considerably superior to any possessed by the *Holland* type. *See Russian Navy*).

Photo by favour of H. Reuterdahl, Esq.

125

HELENA & WILMINGTON. *Photo, copyright, Rau.*

KATAHDIN.

NASHVILLE. *Photo, copyright, Rau.*

Ram.

KATAHDIN (1893). 2155 tons. Armament: 4—6 pdrs. No torpedoes. Covered with 6″—2½″ Harvey armour. 18″ Conning tower. Designed speed: 16 kts. Actual speed: much less.

Gunboats, etc.

ATLANTA & BOSTON (1884). 3100 tons. Armament: 2—8″, 35 cal., 6—6″ (old), 6—6 pdr., 2—3 pdr., 4—1 pdr., 2 machine. Partial 1½″ deck. Original speed: 15·5 kts. Boilers: Babcock and cylindrical.

NASHVILLE (1895), WILMINGTON (1895) & HELENA (1896), all of 1370—1392 tons. Armament: 8—4″, and some small Q.F. Armour, 2½″ deck and 2″ on guns. Speed: under 14 kts.

CASTINE, MACHIAS (1891-92), MARIETTA, WHEELING, ANNAPOLIS, VICKSBURG, NEWPORT, PRINCETON, (1896-97), DUBUQUE & PADUCAH (1905), all of *circa* 1000 tons. Armament: 6—4″, 4—6 pdr., 2—1 pdr. Speeds: about 12 kts. or less.

BENNINGTON, CONCORD, YORKTOWN (1888-90). 1700 tons. Armament: 6—old 6″, 2—6 pdr., 2—3 pdr., 2—1 pdr. Deck: ⅓″ steel. 2″ Conning tower. Original speeds: 17 kts.

Other Craft.

There are also *Bancroft* (1892), 840 tons, 4—4″, originally 14 kts.; *Petrel* (1888), 800 tons, 4 old 6″, originally 13·5 kts.; *Dolphin* (1884), 1485 tons, 2—4″, originally 15·5 kts.; *Isla de Cuba* and *Isla de Luzon* (—1886), (ex Spanish), 4—4″, 2½″ deck, originally 15·9 kts.; *Topeka* (1883), 1880 tons, 6—4″, originally 16 kts.; *Don Juan d' Austria* and *General Alvada, circa* 1300 tons, and twenty-two small gunboats, mostly captured from the Spaniards, of from 300 to 40 tons, armed with small Q.F.; five old iron steamers and twelve wood ditto used for training purposes; six wooden sailing ships, thirty-nine tugs, seventeen hulks, and six "auxiliary cruisers"—*Buffalo*, 14·5 kts. (2—5″, 4—4″), *Dixie*, 16 kts. (8—5″), *Prairie*, 14·5 kts. (6—5″, 2—4″), *Yankee*, 12·5 kts. (no guns), *Yosemite*, 16 kts. (10—5″), all *circa* 6000 tons, and *Panther*, 13 kts. (6—5″, 2—4″), of 4260 tons. This carries 475 tons of coal; the others 1000-1300 tons. Also twenty-three converted yachts, speeds 17·85-11 kts.; sixteen colliers, 12-3·5 kts., average capacity 3000 tons, mostly carrying one or two Hotchkiss guns (6 pdr.); and eleven miscellaneous ships.

Old cruiser *Philadelphia* converting into a receiving ship.

BENNINGTON CLASS.

FRENCH FLEET.

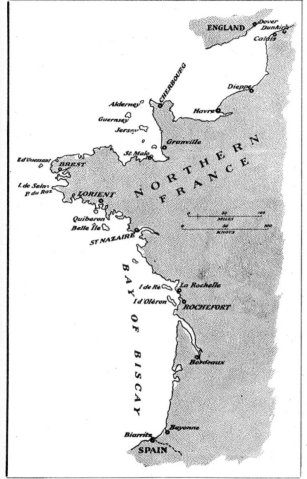

CHERBOURG

	to			knots.
Bermuda	...	...	...	2933
Brest	...	...	...	210
Copenhagen	...	...	...	834
Devonport	...	...	...	111
Dunkirk	...	...	...	180
Lorient	...	...	...	300
Kronstadt	...	...	...	1500
Portsmouth	...	...	...	72
Rochefort	...	...	...	410
Stockholm	...	...	...	1258
Toulon	...	...	...	1817
Wilhelmshaven	...	...	...	476

TOULON

	to			knots.
Aden	...	...	...	2882
Ajaccio	...	...	...	160
Algiers	...	...	...	405
Bizerta	...	...	...	450
Brest	...	...	...	1659
Constantinople	...	...	...	1356
Genoa	...	...	...	164
Gibraltar	...	...	...	713
Kronstadt	...	...	...	3289
Lorient	...	...	...	1656
Port Mahon	...	...	...	207
Malta	...	...	...	612
Naples	...	...	...	407
Oran	...	...	...	542
Port Said	...	...	...	1485
Portsmouth	...	...	...	1864
Saigon	...	...	...	7150
Sevastopol	...	...	...	1654
Spezia	...	...	...	195
Tangiers	...	...	...	738
Taranto	...	...	...	766

BREST.

	to			knots.
Algiers	...	...	...	1360
Bermuda	...	...	...	2811
Cherbourg	...	...	...	210
Devonport	...	...	...	139
Gibraltar	...	...	...	953
Liverpool	...	...	...	407
Malta	...	...	...	1934
Kronstadt	...	...	...	1672
New York	...	...	...	2954
Oran	...	...	...	1876
Portsmouth	...	...	...	226
Rio de Janeiro	...	...	...	4837
Rochefort	...	...	...	260
Toulon	...	...	...	1659
Wilhelmshaven	...	...	...	686

ORAN (Torpedo Station).

	to		knots.
Algiers	...	...	400
Bizerta	...	...	650
Gibraltar	...	...	225
Toulon	...	...	542

BIZERTA.

	to			knots.
Algiers	...	...	...	400
Gibraltar	...	...	...	875
Malta	...	...	...	240
Oran	...	...	...	650
Spezia	...	...	...	430
Toulon	...	...	...	450

SAIGON.

	to		knots.
Hong Kong	...	...	930
Manila	...	...	875
Port Arthur	...	...	2065
Singapore	...	...	640

MERCHANT FLEET: 1,300 steamers and 1,400 sailers.

COINAGE: 1 franc (100 centimes) = 9½d. British, 19 cents American.

TRADE PORTS (in order of importance): Marseilles, Havre, Paris, Dunkirk, Bordeaux, Boulogne, Calais, Dieppe, Rouen, Belfort, Jeumont, Tourcoing.

OVERSEA POSSESSIONS: Corsica, Algeria, Tunis, Senegal, etc. Madagascar, Guiana, Martinique, S. Pierre, New Caledonia, Pondicherry, Annam, Cochin China, Tonquin.

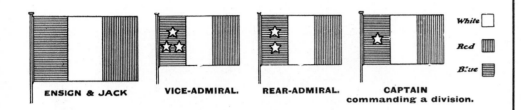

| ENSIGN & JACK | VICE-ADMIRAL. | REAR-ADMIRAL. | CAPTAIN commanding a division. |

White □ Red ▥ Blue ▦

French Flags.

Note.—A vice-admiral wears his flag at the fore, rear-admiral at the main.

French Uniform.

INSIGNIA OF RANK ON SLEEVES—EXECUTIVE OFFICERS.

Corresponding British or U.S. Navies.

Vice-Amiral.	Contre-Amiral.	Capitaine de vaisseau.	Capitaine de fregate.	Lieutenant de vaisseau.	Enseigne.	Aspirant 1 and 2 class.
„	Rear-Ad.	Captain.	Commander.	Lieut. (senior).	Lieut. (junior).	Sub-Lieut. and Midshipman. (U.S. Ensign.

Only one of the capitaine de fregate's upper stripes is gold: the other is white.

Epaulettes with parade uniform are of the usual sort, *except* that—

A Vice-Admiral's epaulettes have the usual anchor and 3 stars.

A Rear-Admiral's „ „ „ „ 2 „

Caps are the usual shape, but have gold bands round. The cocked hat carries the tri-colour.

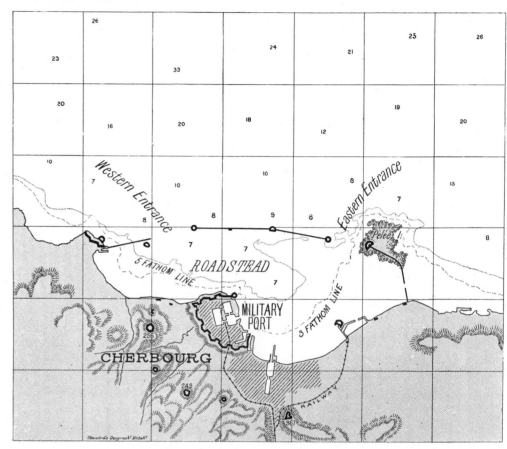

CHERBOURG. Protected by a breakwater about two miles long. Heavily fortified.

Dry Docks.

					Able to take up to :
No. 1	360 ×	94 ×	29½ feet.	Baudin	Friant
„ 2	393 ×	94 ×	29½ „	Charlemagne	Pothuau
„ 3	390 ×	94 ×	29½ „	Charlemagne	Pothuau
„ 4	360 ×	94 ×	29½ „	Baudin	Friant
„ 5	499 ×	118 ×	36½ „	République	Michelet
„ 6	513 ×	108 ×	26 „	République	Michelet
„ 7	265 ×	81 ×	17½ „	———	Avisos
„ 8	257 ×	79 ×	17½ „	———	Avisos

128

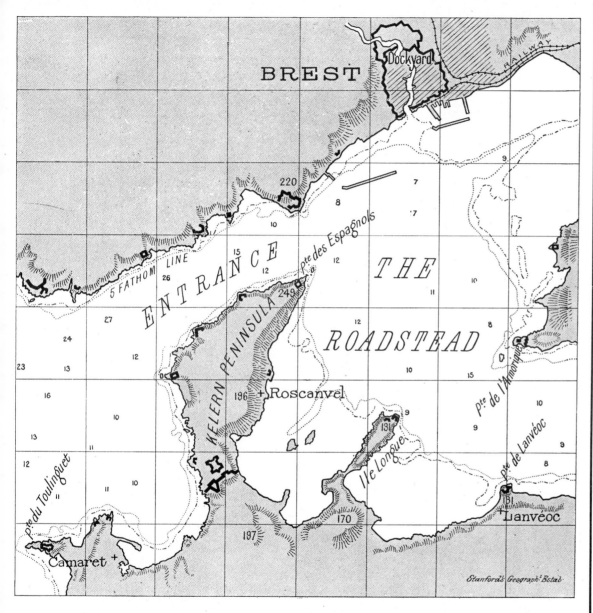

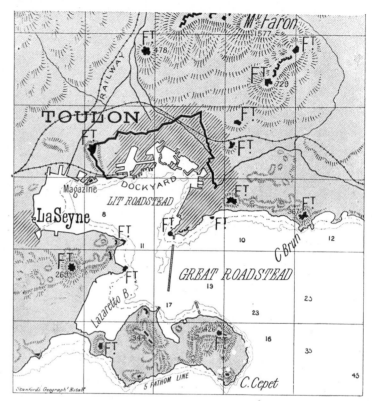

TOULON. Very strongly fortified.

Dry Docks.

Taking ships up to:

MISSIESSY.	No. 1	427 × 92 × 32½	*Suffren*	*D'Entrecasteaux*
,,	,, 2	427 × 92 × 32½	*Suffren*	*D'Entrecasteaux*
,,	,, 3	492 × 92 × 32½	*République*	*Gambetta*
,,	,, 4	*Building.*		
CASTIGNEAU.	,, 1	325 × 71 × 25½	*Bouvines*	*D'Estrées*
,,	,, 2	385 × 72 × 27½	*Jaureguiberry*	*Pothuau*
,,	,, 3	535 × 72 × 27½	*République*	*Renan*
ARSENAL.	,, 1	325 × 60 × 21½	———	*D'Estrées*
,,	,, 2	245 × 60 × 22½	———	*Avisos*
,,	,, 3	292 × 71 × 25¼	———	*Avisos*

LORIENT. One dock able to take any French warship; one for second-class cruisers.

ROCHEFORT. The three docks here cannot accommodate modern big ships. The majority of submarines are built here.

BREST. There is only one dock able to take big modern warships. There are eight smaller docks unable to take any modern warship of importance. Forts, very numerous and powerful.

FRENCH HARBOURS.

(Divided into 2000 yard squares. Soundings in fathoms. Heights in feet).

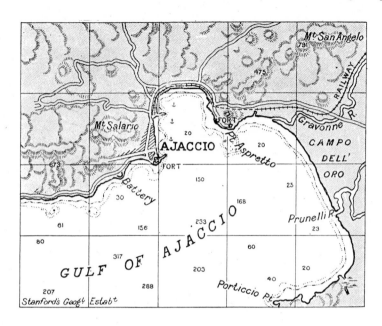

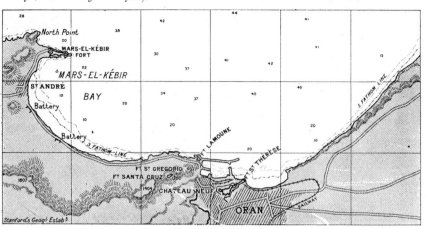

Naval Harbours.

DUNKIRK. Fine harbour. Breakwater. Torpedo base. There are five private docks here—one able to take any warship, another little smaller, and three lesser size.

AJACCIO. }
BONIFACIO. } Fortified harbours used by the French fleet. No docks.

ALGIERS. Coaling Station. Two dry docks (No. 1) 455 × 86 × 33 feet; (No. 2) 248 × 73 × 25½ feet. Average depth of harbour, 8 fathoms.

ORAN. Torpedo base. Excellent harbour, with an average depth of five fathoms. Two breakwaters. Fortified. New works in progress.

BIZERTA. New naval base still completing. Lies inside a narrow channel. One large dock suitable for any warship, one small one.

SAIGON. Situated 42 miles up the Donnoi River. Anchorage average, 9 fathoms. One large dry dock 508 × 75 × 25 feet, and two small ones.

Private Yards.

LA SEYNE. FORGES ET CHANTIERS DE LA MEDITERRANEAN. Near Toulon. Able to build any kind of warship.

GRANVILLE. } At both these all kinds of warships can be built. St. Nazaire has a dry
ST. NAZAIRE. } dock able to take any French warship.

HAVRE. The Schneider-Canet firm has an establishment here, also M. Normand has a torpedo-boat building yard. There is a dock able to take any French warship at Havre.

BORDEAUX. Shipbuilding yard.

Torpedo craft have also been built at ROUEN, NANTES, and ST. DENIS.

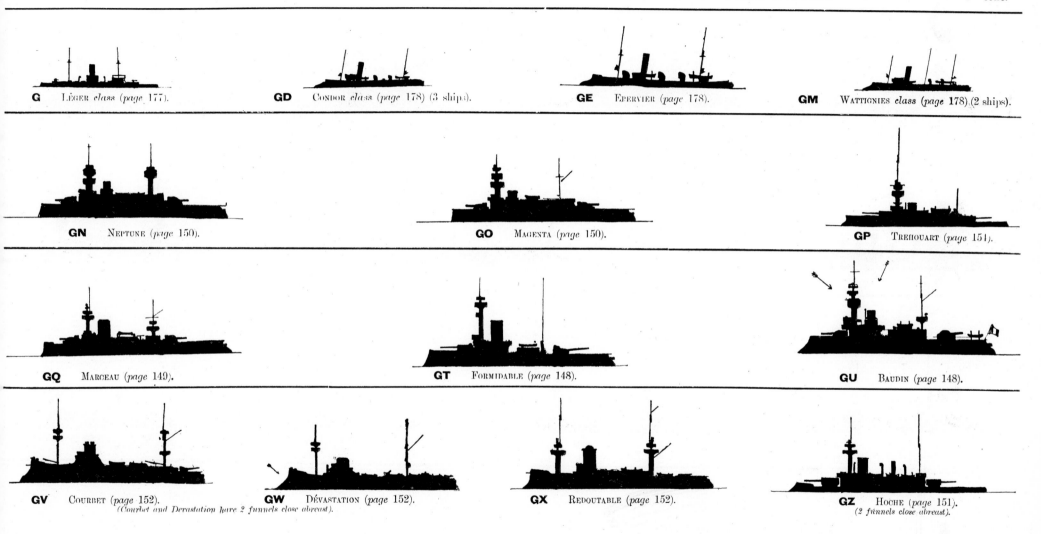

G Léger class (page 177).

GD Condor class (page 178) (3 ships).

GE Epervier (page 178).

GM Wattignies class (page 178) (2 ships).

GN Neptune (page 150).

GO Magenta (page 150).

GP Trehouart (page 151).

GQ Marceau (page 149).

GT Formidable (page 148).

GU Baudin (page 148).

GV Courbet (page 152).
(Courbet and Devastation have 2 funnels close abreast).

GW Dévastation (page 152).

GX Redoutable (page 152).

GZ Hoche (page 151).
(2 funnels close abreast).

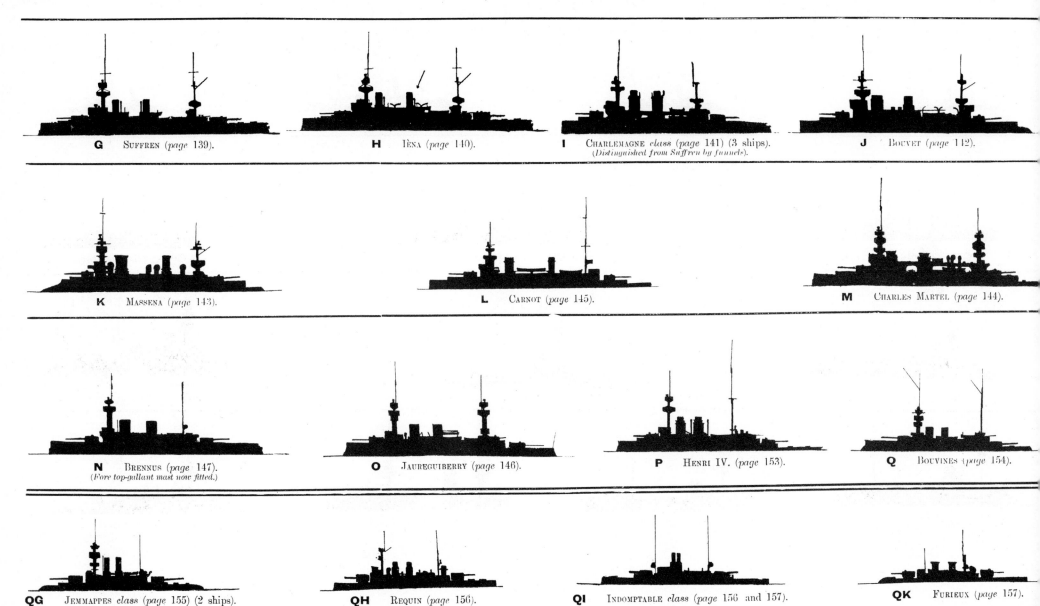

G　Suffren (*page* 139).

H　Iéna (*page* 140).

I　Charlemagne *class* (*page* 141) (3 ships).
(*Distinguished from Suffren by funnels*).

J　Bouvet (*page* 142).

K　Massena (*page* 143).

L　Carnot (*page* 145).

M　Charles Martel (*page* 144).

N　Brennus (*page* 147).
(*Fore top-gallant mast now fitted.*)

O　Jaureguiberry (*page* 146).

P　Henri IV. (*page* 153).

Q　Bouvines (*page* 154).

QG　Jemmappes *class* (*page* 155) (2 ships).

QH　Requin (*page* 156).

QI　Indomptable *class* (*page* 156 *and* 157).

QK　Furieux (*page* 157).

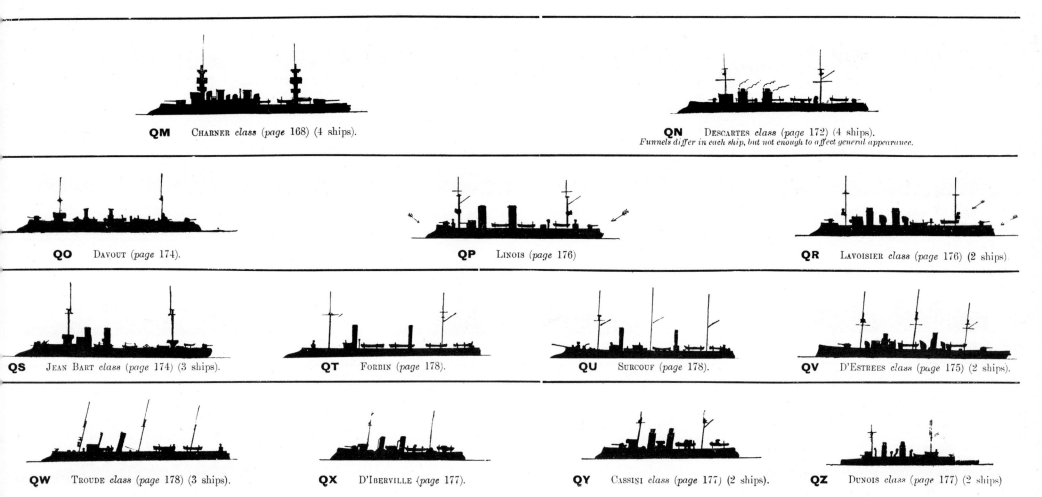

QM   CHARNER *class* (*page* 168) (4 ships).

QN   DESCARTES *class* (*page* 172) (4 ships).
Funnels differ in each ship, but not enough to affect general appearance.

QO   DAVOUT (*page* 174).

QP   LINOIS (*page* 176)

QR   LAVOISIER *class* (*page* 176) (2 ships).

QS   JEAN BART *class* (*page* 174) (3 ships).

QT   FORBIN (*page* 178).

QU   SURCOUF (*page* 178).

QV   D'ESTREES *class* (*page* 175) (2 ships).

QW   TROUDE *class* (*page* 178) (3 ships).

QX   D'IBERVILLE (*page* 177).

QY   CASSINI *class* (*page* 177) (2 ships).

QZ   DUNOIS *class* (*page* 177) (2 ships)

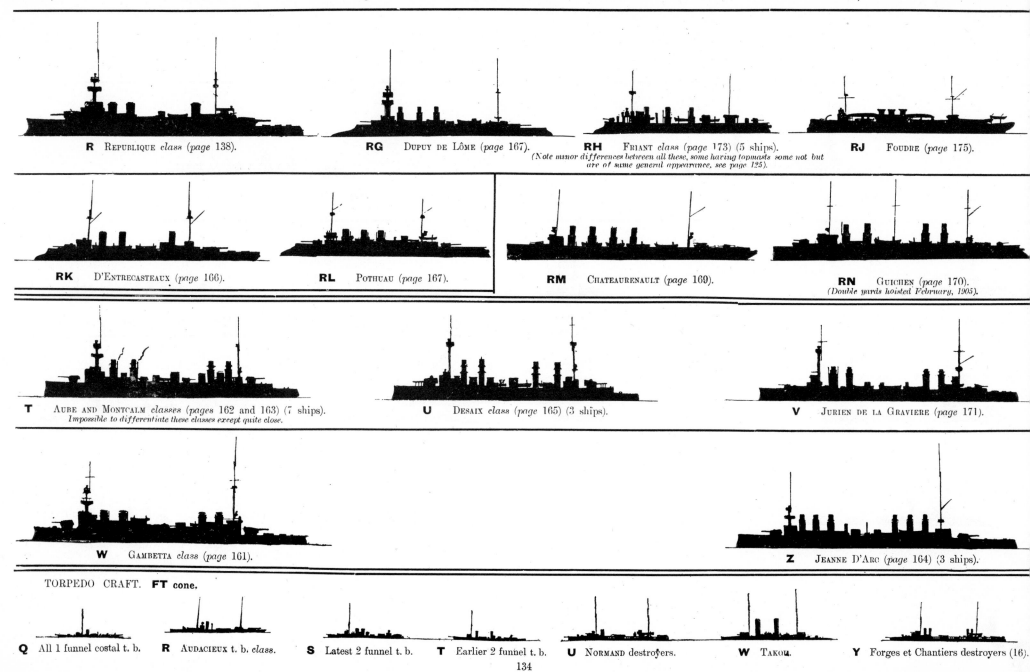

R Republique *class (page 138).*　　**RG** Dupuy de Lôme *(page 167).*　　**RH** Friant *class (page 173) (5 ships).*　　**RJ** Foudre *(page 175).*

(Note minor differences between all these, some having topmasts some not but are of same general appearance, see page 125).

RK D'Entrecasteaux *(page 166).*　　**RL** Pothuau *(page 167).*　　**RM** Chateaurenault *(page 169).*　　**RN** Guichen *(page 170).*

(Double yards hoisted February, 1905).

T Aube and Montcalm *classes (pages 162 and 163) (7 ships).*
Impossible to differentiate these classes except quite close.

U Desaix *class (page 165) (3 ships).*

V Jurien de la Graviere *(page 171).*

W Gambetta *class (page 161).*

Z Jeanne D'Arc *(page 164) (3 ships).*

TORPEDO CRAFT. **FT** cone.

Q All 1 funnel costal t. b.　　**R** Audacieux t. b. *class.*　　**S** Latest 2 funnel t. b.　　**T** Earlier 2 funnel t. b.　　**U** Normand destroyers.　　**W** Takou.　　**Y** Forges et Chantiers destroyers (16).

Guns (Schneider-Canet type).

Notation.	Calibre. French m/m.	Calibre. In inches.	Length. cals.	Model.	Weight of gun. tons.	Weight of A.P. shot. lbs.	Initial velocity. f.s.	Maximum penetration using *capped* A.P. against K.C. armour. At 5000. inches.	At 3000. inches.	Approximate Danger Space for *average ship* at 10,000 yards.	5000 yards.	3000 yards.	Usual rounds per minute.
AAA	340	13·4	35	1893	77	882	2625	12	16				0·2
AAAA	340	13·4	42 & 40	1887	61½	926	2625	12	16	150	555	1080	0·5†
AA	340	13·4	30	1884	52	926	1969	8¼	10	120	360	870	0·2
A	370	14·5	28	1879	76½	1235	2133	6	7½	120	360	870	0·2
AAAAA	305	12	50	1902	50	731	3000	18	22½				
AAAA	305	12	45	1896	46½	644	2870	14½	18	150	570	1080	1·5
AAA	305	12	40 & 45	'93, '91, '87	46½	644	2700	11	14½	150	510	1050	1
AAA	274	10·8	45	1896	35½	476	2870	12	14½	150	540	1020	0·7
AA	274	10·8	45 & 40	1893	35	476	2625	8	11¼				1
A	274	10·8	45 & 40	'87 & '84	35	476	1969	6	9				0·5
AAA	240	9·4	50	1902	24	375	2969	11½	14¼				0·4
AA	240	9·4	40 or 45	1896	23½	317½	2870	10½	13	150	570	1080	1·2
A	240	9·4	40	1893	22¾	317½	2625	7½	9¾	144	540	1080	1·2
B	240	9·4	42	1887	21½	317½	1969	5	7½				0·5
A	194	7·6	45	1902	15	185	3117	7	10	144	...	...	2-3
A	194	7·6	40	1896	12½	185	2870	6	9½	120	525	1080	2-3
B	194	7·6	40 & 45	'93 & '87	10½	165	2625	5½	7	96	435	1020	1
B	164	6·4	45	1902	9¼	114½	3002	5¼	7		330	750	4-5
C	164	6·4	45	1896	9	114½	2870	4½	6		285	630	4-5
D	164	6·4	45	1891	7	99¼	2625	3	4½	...	240	585	4-5
E	164	6·4	45	1887	6½	99¼	2297	...	3	...	150	360	3
F	138	5·5	45	'93-'87	4½	66	2526	...	3		120	300	5-6
F	100	4	55	'92 & '93	2¼	31	2494	...	2	...	...	...	9
F	100	4	45	1891	1½	31	2428	...	2	...	...	...	9
F	100	4	50	1889	2	31	2494	...	2	...	...	...	8

† With new loading mechanism. Old rate was 1 round in 8 minutes.

NOTES ON GUNS.

Powder.—1902 model fire a species of M.D. cordite; 1896 and earlier models, a nitro cellulose.

Projectiles.—Capped A.P. for all calibres. Melenite shell for guns up to 9·4.

Small pieces.—65 m/m (9 pdr.), 57 m/m (6 pdr.), 47 m/m (3 pdr.), and a 37 m/m (1 pdr.), revolver guns. Also Maxims, rifle calibre. The 1 pdr. rev. is being abolished. A 12 pounder (75 m/m) is being introduced.

Rifle.—Lebel (magazine 9 rounds) ·315 calibre sighted up to 2187 yards (2000 metres).

Torpedoes.

Whitehead pattern. Made at Fiume and at Toulon Torpedo Factory.

French Designation.	Diameter. inches.	Length. feet.	Charge. lbs.	Pressure in chamber. lbs. per sq. in.	Maximum range.
1904 model	18	19½	2198	2150	Usually set for 2600
45 c/m *long*	18	16½	198	1270	2000
45 c/m *short*	18	13¾	185	1000	1500
38 c/m *long*	15	18¾	100		1000
38 c/m *short*	15	16½	85		1000
356 m/m *long*	14	16½	79		600
356 m/m *short*	14	15	60		600

Notes.—All fitted with gyros.

The 1904 model is fitting to all battleships from and after *Patrie*, all cruisers from and after *Jules Ferry*, all t.b.d. of and after 1901 date, and all submarines after Q 47.

Submerged tubes mostly bear 20°-15° *before* the beam. Pattern very similar to the British—same sort of bar.

General Notes.

Colour of Ships.

Big ships.—Hulls, black. *Upper work*, white or canvas colour. Black tops to funnels.

Destroyers, etc.—Light grey.

Submarines.—Sea green.

Personnel.

About 53,000 all ranks and 120,000 reserve.

Officers.—Torpedo are very dashing. Gunnery, excellent in theory. Engineers, mostly very good. Navigation branch, moderate. Submarine branch, clever and efficient.

Men.—Said to have been greatly impaired by M. Pelletan, discipline being now very poor. The French fleet may not be efficient in this respect for another year probably. Stokers apt to be unreliable.

Minister of Marine.—M. Thomson (replaced M. Pelletan).

Chief Constructor.—M. Bertin (all designs by him, unless otherwise stated).

New Construction Programme for 1906-07.

3 battleships, 18,000 tons.

10 destroyers, of 431 tons.

20 submarines.

(DANTON CLASS—6 SHIPS).

DANTON, MIRABEAU, DIDEROT, CONDORCET, VERGNIAUD & VOLTAIRE (in hand).

Displacement 18,000 tons.   Complement 681 (as flagship 753).

Length (*p.p.*), 475¾ feet.   Beam, 84 feet.   *Maximum* draught, 27½ feet.   Length over all   feet.

Guns (M '02):
4—12 inch, 50 cal. (*AAAAA*)
12—9·4 inch, 50 cal. (*AAA*).
16—12 pdr.
8—3 pdr.
Torpedo tubes (M '04, 18 inch).
2 *submerged*.
3 *above water*.

Armour :
10″ Belt (amidships) ....*aaa*
6″ Belt (ends) ....*a*
3″ Deck (flat on belt) ....
3″ Deck (below belt) ....
Protection to vitals......=*aaaaa*
10″—5″ Lower deck side...*aaa-b*
3″ Upper belt (bow)..............*ε*
12″ Turrets (big guns) (N.C) *aaa*
9″ Turret bases (N.C) ....*aa*
8¾″ Secondary turrets (6) (N.C) *aa*
13″ Conning tower (N.C) ...*aaa*
Total weight about 4300 tons.

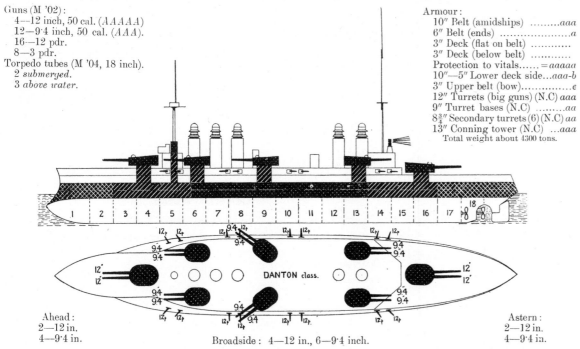

DANTON class.

Ahead :
2—12 in.
4—9·4 in.

Astern :
2—12 in.
4—9·4 in.

Broadside : 4—12 in., 6—9·4 inch.

Machinery : 3 sets vertical inverted 4 cylinder triple expansion. 3 screws. Boilers: Belleville and Niclausse.   Designed H.P. 22,500=19 kts.   Coal : *normal* 925 tons : *maximum* 2010 tons.

Armour Notes.—Main belt is about 7½ feet wide, about 4½ feet of it below waterline.   Lower edge is 4¾″ thick.   There is a deck on top of the main belt as well as below it, also lateral armoured bulkheads extend from the lower armoured deck to the bilge keels.

Arcs of fire : Big guns, 260°.   Secondary guns about 140° or more.

General Notes.—These ships belong to the 1906-7 programme.   16—11 inch have been suggested.

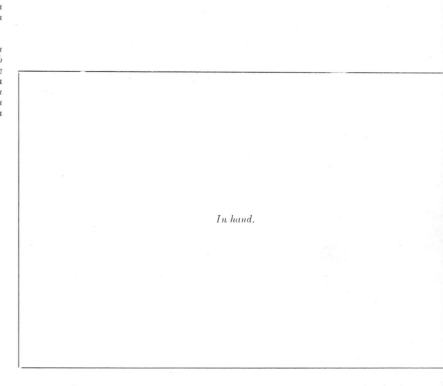

In hand.

Est. cost.	Name.	Built at.	Laid down.	To be completed.	Trials.	Boilers.
£1,600,000	Danton	Lorient	1906	1910		
	Mirabeau	Brest	1906	1910		
	Diderot		1906	1910		
£1,825,000	Condorcet	contract	1906	1910		
	Vergniaud		1906	1910		
	Voltaire		1906	1910		

NEW FRENCH BATTLESHIPS (18 knot).

(Liberté Class—4 Ships).
DÉMOCRATIE (April, 1904), *JUSTICE* (1904), *LIBERTÉ* (1905), *VÉRITÉ* (1906).
Displacement 14,865 tons.   Complement 793.
Length (*waterline*), 439 feet.   Beam, 79½ feet.   *Maximum* draught, 27½ feet.   Length over all, 452 feet.

Guns—(M. '02) :
  4—12 inch, 50 cal. (*AAAAA*).
  10—7·6 inch, 45 cal. (*AA*).
  8—4 inch (*E*).
  24—3 pdr.
Torpedo tubes (1904 pattern) :
  2 *submerged*.
  3 *above water* (broadside and
    stern).

Armour (Krupp) :
11″ Belt (amidships)	*aaa*
7″ Belt (ends)	*a*
3″ Deck (flat below belt)...	
Protection to vitals...... =	*aaaaa*
10″ Upper belt (amidships)	*aaa*
5″ Upper belt (ends)	*b*
3″ Top of belt (forward) ...	*є*
13″ Main turrets (N.C.) ...	*aaa*
9″ Turret bases	*a*
6″ Casemates (4)	*b*
6″ Secondary turrets (6) ...	*b*
13″ Conning tower	*aaa*

(Total weight *about* 4100 tons).

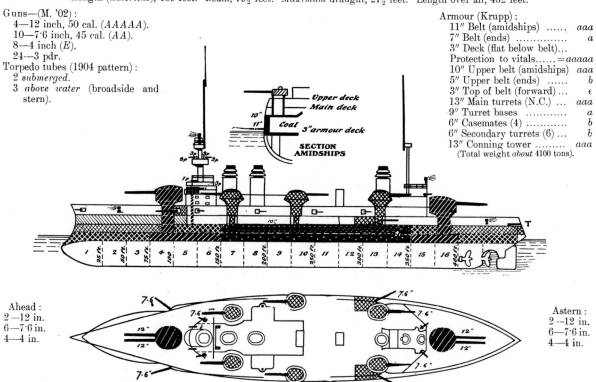

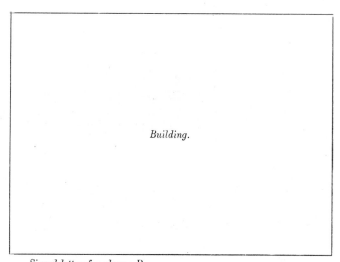

Building.

Signal letter for class : R

Ahead :
2 —12 in.
6—7·6 in.
4—4 in.

Astern :
2 —12 in.
6—7·6 in.
4—4 in.

Broadside : 4—12 in., 5—7·6 in., 4—4 in.

Machinery : 3 sets vertical inverted triple expansion, four cylinder. 3 screws. Boilers : Belleville and Niclausse.
Designed H.P. 18,000 = 18 kts.   Coal : *normal* 900 tons ; *maximum* 1850 tons.
Armour Notes.—Each belt is about 7½ feet wide, 7 feet of lower belt below waterline. Lower edge is 4¾″ thick. Back
  of casemates 4″.
Gunnery Notes.—Loading positions, big guns : all round. Balanced turrets. Hoists, electrical for all guns. All guns
  manœuvred electrically. Big guns fire three rounds in two minutes.
  Arcs of fire : Big guns 260° ; Secondary turrets 180° ; Casemates 130° from axial line.
  Height of guns above water : Bow turret, 30 feet ; after turret, 22½ feet ; secondary turret, 29 feet.
Torpedo Notes.—Submerged and above water, broadside tubes all about base of fore turret. Stern tube on main deck aft.
  1904 pattern torpedoes.
Engineering Notes :—

Name.	Built at	Laid down.	Completed.	Boilers (29)
Liberté	St. Nazaire	1903	...	Belleville
Justice	La Seyne	1903	...	...
Democratie	Brest	1903	...	...
Vérité	Bordeaux	1903	...	...

General Notes.—Estimated cost, about £1,425,000 per ship.

(REPUBLIQUE CLASS—2 SHIPS).

REPUBLIQUE (Sept., 1902), & **PATRIE** (Dec., 1903).

Displacement 14,865 tons.   Complement 793.

Length (*waterline*), 439 feet ; Beam, 79½ feet ; *Maximum* draught, 27½ feet ; Length over all, 452 feet.

Guns—(M. 1896) :
   4—12 inch, 45 cal. (*AAAA*).
   18—6·4 inch, 45 cal. (*C*).
   26—3 pdr.
   2—1 pdr.
Torpedo tubes (18 inch) :
   2 *submerged*.
   3 *above water*.

Armour (Krupp) :
   11″ Belt (amidships)...   *aaa*
   7″ Belt (ends)............   *a*
   3″ Deck (flat below belt)
   Protection to vitals ...*aaaaa*
   10″—5″Lower deck side *aaa-b*
   3″ Upper belt (forward)   ϵ
   13″ Turrets ....   *aaa*
   9″ Turret (bases) ......   *a*
   6″ Casements ....   *b*
   6″ Small turrets ....   *b*
   13″ Conning tower ...   *aaa*
      (Total weight 4100 tons).

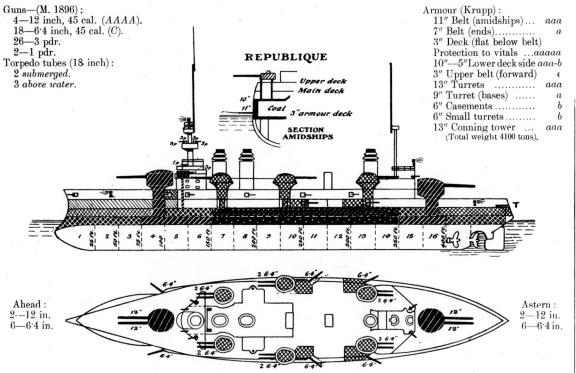

REPUBLIQUE

Upper deck
Main deck

10″
11″   Coal   3″armour deck

SECTION
AMIDSHIPS

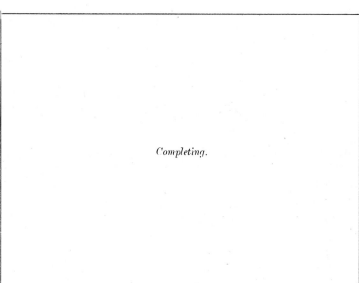

Completing.

Ahead :
2—12 in.
6—6·4 in.

Astern :
2—12 in.
6—6·4 in.

Broadside : 4—12 in., 10—6·4 in.

Machinery : 3 sets vertical inverted triple expansion. 3 screws. Boilers : Niclausse and Belleville. Designed H.P. 17,500=18 kts. Coal : *normal* 900 tons ; *maximum* 1850 tons.

Armour Notes.—See *Liberté* class, previous page. *Patrie* has 1904 model torpedoes.

Gunnery Notes.—Loading positions, big guns : all round. Balanced turrets. Hoists, electric to all guns. Big guns manœuvred, electrically. Secondary turrets, electric and hand. *Patrie's* big guns fire 3 rounds in 2 minutes ; those of *Republique* are slower.
   Arcs of fire : Amidship casemates 90° ; other guns as for *Liberté*.
   Height of guns above water : see *Liberté*.

Engineering Notes :—

Name.	Built at	Laid down.	Completed.	Boilers (22).
Republique	Brest	Dec. '01	1906	Niclausse
Patrie	La Seyne	1902	1906	Belleville

General Notes.—Cost about £1,420,000 per ship, *complete*.

FRENCH BATTLESHIP (18 knot.)

SUFFREN (July, 1899).

Displacement 12,750 tons.   Complement 730.

Length (*waterline*), 410 feet.   Beam, 70 feet.   *Maximum* draught, 28¼ feet.   Length over all, 422½ feet

Guns (M. '96):
4—12 inch, 45 cal. (*AAAA*).
10—6·4 inch, 45 cal. (*C*).
8—4 inch (*E*).
22—3 pdr.

Torpedo tubes (18 inch):
2 *submerged*.
2 *above water* (section 4).

Armour (Krupp):
12″ Belt (amidships)	*aaa*
9″ Belt (ends).................	*aa*
3″ Deck (flat below belt) ...	
1⅔″ Deck on top of main belt	
Protection to vitals...... =	*aaaaa*
13″ Turrets (N.C.) nearly...	*aaaa*
10″ Turret bases	*aa*
8″ Turret hoists..............	*a*
5¼″—3½″ Lower deck (side)	*b-c*
5¼″ Battery (redoubt, N.C.)	*c*
5¼″ Small turrets (N.C.) ...	*c*
12″—10″ Conning tower ...	*aaa*
6″ Tube to it	*b*

(Total weight *about* 4100 tons).

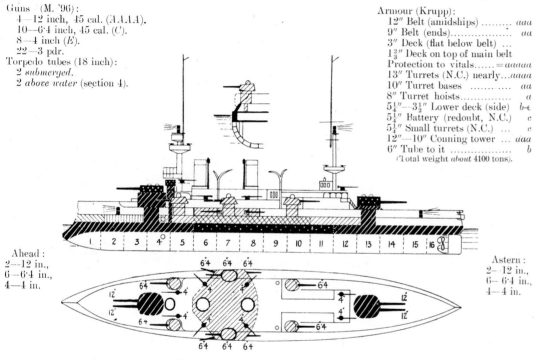

Ahead :
2—12 in.,
6—6·4 in.,
4—4 in.

Astern :
2—12 in.,
6—6·4 in.,
4—4 in.

Broadside 4—12 in., 5—6·4 in., 4—4 in.

Machinery : 3 sets vertical triple expansion.   3 screws.   Boilers : Niclausse.   Designed H.P. 16,200 = 18 kts.
Coal : *normal* 820 tons ; *Maximum* 1150 tons ; also 60 tons of oil.

Armour Notes.—Belt is 8¼ feet wide, 5 feet of it below waterline ; lower edge averages 6″ thick.

Gunnery Notes.—Loading positions, big guns : all round.   Balanced turrets.   Hoists, electric for all guns.   Big guns manœuvred electrically and hydraulic.   Secondary turrets, electrically.
Arcs of fire : big guns 260° ; midship secondary turrets 180° ; other 6·4 in. guns 135° from axial line.
Ammunition carried : 12 in., 90 rounds per gun ; 6·4 in., 150 rounds per gun.
Height of guns above water : bow turret 30 feet.

Engineering Notes.—Coal consumption about 10½ tons an hour at 12,000 H.P., and about 16 tons at 16,000 H.P.— 18 kts.

General Notes.—Laid down at Brest, January, 1899.   Completed 1903.   Cost, *complete*, £1,200,000.   Conning tower in two compartments.

SUFFREN.   *Photo, Geiser.*

Note.
To be distinguished from *Iéna* at sea only by steam pipe (very conspicuous) before instead of abaft after funnel.   Nearer view— note secondary turrets and forebridge, etc., which are very different.

Details of conning tower, etc.   Starboard side.

IÉNA (September, 1898).

Displacement 12100 tons.   Complement 630.

Length (*waterline*), 400¾ feet.   Beam, 68 feet.   *Maximum* draught, 27½ feet.

Guns :
4—12 inch (M. '93—'96) (A.A.A.A.).
8—6·4 inch (M. '91) (D).
8—4 inch (E).
24—3 pdr.
Torpedo tubes (18 inch) :
 2 *Submerged*.
 2 *above water* (section 4).

Armour (Harvey) :
 12¾″ Belt (amidships)...... aa
 9″ Belt (ends) .... a
 1½″ Deck (flat on belt)......
 3¼″ Deck (flat below belt)...
 Protection to vitals ......= aaaca
 4¾″—3″ Upper belt .... c-c
 11¾″ Turrets .... aa
 8″ Turret hoists (H.M.) ... a
 6″ Battery (H.N.) .... b
 3½″ Battery bulkhead ...... d
 4¾″ Side under battery ... c
 11¾″ Conning tower ...... aa
 (Total weight *about* 4000 tons)

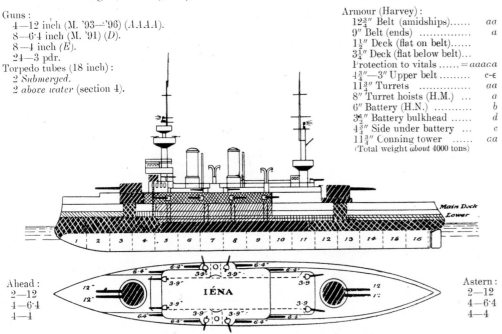

Ahead :
2—12
4—6·4
4—4

IÉNA

Astern :
2—12
4—6·4
4—4

Broadside : 4—12 in., 4—6·4 in., 4—4 in.

Photo, Bar.

Difference with *Suffren*.—Both funnels have steam pipes abaft—the absence of small turrets is difficult to pick up at sea.   Distinguished from *Charlemagne* class by different funnel casings.

Machinery : 3 sets 4 cylinder triple expansion. 3 screws. Boilers : 20 Belleville (4 groups). Designed H.P. 15500 = 18 kts. Coal : *normal* 820 tons ; *maximum* 1100 tons (including oil and briquettes).

Armour Notes.—Main belt is 7 feet wide, 4 feet below water line ; lower edge is 8″ thick amidship. 1½″ screens in battery.

Gunnery Notes.—Loading positions, big guns all round. Balanced turrets. Hoists, electric all guns. Big guns manœuvred electrically. 4 in. shields to all secondary guns. 3 pdrs. carried, 6 in battery, 4 on forebridge, 2 in stern walk, 4 on topsides and 4 in each fighting top.
Arcs of fire : Big guns, 250° ; secondary guns, 110°.
Ammunition carried : Big guns, 70 per gun. 6·4 in., 200 per gun. 4 in., 250 per gun.

Engineering Notes.—90 revolutions = 14 kts. ; 120 revolutions = 17½ kts. ; 125 = 18 kts. Owing to vibration at high speed and overheating in machinery, trials were delayed. She made 24 hours, 9830 = 16·3 *mean*, and 4 hours *full power* 16500 = 18·2 kts. Coal consumption about 12¼ tons an hour at 16500 H.P., 7 tons an hour at 10,000 H.P.

General Notes.—Laid down at Brest, Jan., 1898. Completed 1901. Cost about £1,300,000. No wood used in construction.

(CHARLEMAGNE CLASS—3 SHIPS).

CHARLEMAGNE (October, 1895), **ST. LOUIS** (September, 1896), **GAULOIS** (October, 1896).

Displacement 11,260 tons.   Complement 631.

Length (*waterline*), $380\frac{3}{4}$ feet.   Beam, $67\frac{1}{2}$ feet.   *Maximum* draught, 28 feet.   Length over all, $387\frac{1}{2}$ feet.

Guns (M. '93) :
4—12 inch (*AAA*).
10—5·5 inch (*E*).
8—4 inch (*E*).
20— 3 pdr.
Torpedo tubes (18 inch) :
4 *submerged.*

Armour (Harvey Nickel) :
14″ Belt (amidships) ......*aaa*
10″ Belt (ends) ....*aa*
$2\frac{3}{4}$″ Armour deck (flat on belt).
$1\frac{1}{2}$″ Low deck (flat below belt).
Protection to vitals ...=*aaaa*
11″ Fore turret ....*aa*
13″ After turrets ....*aaa*
8″ Turret hoists ....*a*
4-3″ Lower deck side ....*d-e*
4″ Battery ....*d*
5″ Battery bulkheads ....*c*
2″ Screens in battery ....
12″ Conning tower ....*aaa*
(Total weight, *about* 4,000 tons.)

ST. LOUIS.   *Photo, Bar.*

All have a fore top gallant mast now fitted.

Differences.	Steam pipes.	Notes.
Charlemagne Gaulois	Not at all conspicuous.	
St. Louis	One protruding from after funnel, all conspicuous.	

Class distinctions.—Peculiar funnels.

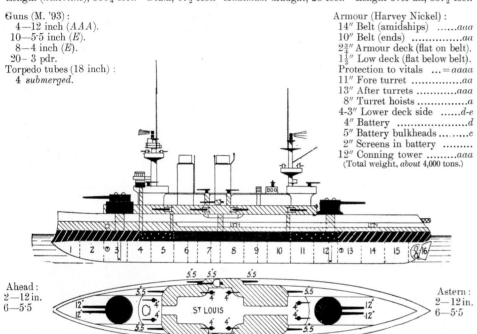

Ahead :
2—12 in.
6—5·5

Astern :
2—12 in.
6—5·5

Broadside : 4—12 in., 5—5·5 in.

Machinery : 3 sets 4 cylinder triple expansion, 2 screws. Boilers : 20 Belleville. Designed H.P. 14,500=18 kts.   Coal : *normal* 680 tons ; *maximum* 1100 tons, also 200 tons oil.

Armour Notes.—Belt is $6\frac{1}{4}$ feet wide, $4\frac{3}{4}$ feet of it below waterline ; lower edge is 6″ thick amidships. Cofferdam $3\frac{1}{2}$ feet high along waterline.

Gunnery Notes.— Loading positions big guns : all round. Balanced turrets. Hoists, electric all guns. Big guns manœuvred electrically and hand.
     Arcs of fire : Big guns, 250° ; secondary guns, 110°, but top side 5·5 can train 180°.
     Ammunition carried : Big guns, 70 per gun ; secondary guns, 200 per gun.

Torpedo Notes.—6 *above water* tubes removed during construction.
Engineering Notes.—96 revolutions=$14\frac{1}{2}$ kts ; 110 revolutions=16 kts. ; 120 revolutions=$17\frac{1}{4}$ kts. approximately.

Name.	Built at	Laid down	Completed	24 hrs. at	4 hours full power	Boilers	Present best speed
Charlemagne	Brest	July, '94	1899	9123=16·15	15,294=18·1	Belleville	...
St. Louis	Lorient	March, '95	1900	=16·2	=18·31	Belleville	18·47
Gaulois	Brest	January, '96	1899	13,400=17·7	14,963=18·2	Belleville	...

Coal consumption averages $9\frac{3}{4}$ tons an hour at 14,500 H.P. (18 kts.), and $6\frac{1}{4}$ tons at 9000 H.P. Very economical steamers.
General Notes.—Cost nearly £1,100,000 per ship.

Port side forward.

Port side amidships.

BOUVET (April, 1896).

Displacement 12,205 tons.   Complement 630.

Length (*waterline*) 397 feet.   Beam 70⅙ feet.   *Maximum* draught, 28⅓ feet.   Length over all, 401¼ feet.

Guns (M. '93, big guns;
  M. '91, secondary pieces):
  2—12 inch, 40 cal, (*AAA*).
  2—10·8 inch, 40 cal, (*AA*).
  8—5·5 inch, 45 cal. (*E*).
  8—4 inch (*E*).
  10—3 pdr.
  20—1 pdr.
Torpedo tubes (18 inch):
  2 *submerged*.
  2 *above water*.

Armour (*acier special durci*):
  16″ Belt (amidships) ... *aaa*
  12″ Belt (low) .... *aa*
  10″ Belt (aft).............. *a*
  3½″ Deck (reinforcing) ...
  1⅔″ Lower deck (topping
    main belt) ....
  Protection to vitals = *aaaaa*
  14¾″ Turrets (4) .... *aa*
  8″ Turret bases........... *b*
  4″ Lower deck side
    (amidships) .... *d*
  4″ Small turrets (8) ...... *d*
  10″ Conning tower ...... *a*
    (Total weight 2800 tons).

Ahead
1—12 in.
2—10·8 in.
4—5·5 in.
2—4 in.

Astern:
1—12 in.
2—10·8 in.
4—5·5 in.
2—4 in.

Broadside: 2—12 in., 1—10·8 in., 4—5·5 in., 4—4 in.

Machinery : 3 sets vertical triple expansion 3 cylinder. 3 screws. Boilers : 24 Belleville (1894 model), in 3 groups. Designed H.P. 14,000 = 17 kts. Coal : *normal* 620 tons ; *maximum* 800 tons.

Armour Notes.—Belt is about 7¼ feet wide ; 4 feet of it below waterline ; lower edge is 8″ and 5″ aft.

Gunnery Notes.—Loading positions, big guns : all round. Balanced turrets. Hoists, electric for all guns.
  Big guns manoeuvred electrically ; secondary turrets electrically.
  Arcs of fire : 12 inch guns, 270° ; 10·8 in., 180° ; 5·5 in., about 140° from axial line.
  Height of guns above water : Bow turret, about 28 feet ; other big turrets about 21 feet.

Torpedo Notes.—Submerged tubes *probably* in or about section 7, at an angle of 20° abaft the beam ; above water ones on main deck, section 10.

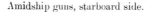

Amidship guns, starboard side.

Forward, starboard side.

Engineering Notes.—She is an excellent steamer and has kept station at 17 kts. for 24 hours.   On her *trials* (1898) she did this for 24 hours also, and made 18·8 kts. mean for four hours in dirty weather. 93 revolutions = 14 kts. (economical speed). Coal consumption, about 11 tons an hour at 14,000 H.P. (18 kts).

General Notes.—Laid down at Lorient, January, 1893. Completed 1898. Cost about £1,200,000.

MASSENA (July, 1895).

Displacement 11,924 tons. Complement 617.

Length (*waterline*), 380½ feet. Beam 66¼ feet. *Maximum* draught, 27 feet. Length over all, 384 feet.

Guns—(M. 1893):
2—12 inch, 40 cal. (*AAA*).
2—10·8 inch, 40 cal. (*AA*).
8—5·5 inch (*E*)
8—4 inch (*E*).
12—3 pdr.
2—9 pdr. boat.

Torpedo tubes (18 inch):
2 *submerged.*
2 *above water.*

Armour (Harvey):
17¾″ Belt (amidships) *aaaa*
10″ Belt (ends) ....*a*
9½″ Bulkhead (aft) ......*a*
3½″ Armour deck (slopes)
1½″ Splinter deck below this
Protection to vitals = *aaaaa*
16″—12″ Turrets.. *aaa-aa*
8½″ Turret hoists ....*a*
4″ Lower deck side ......*d*
4″ Small turrets, 2 hoists *d*
13¾″ Conning tower ...*aa*
(Total weight *about* 3800 tons).

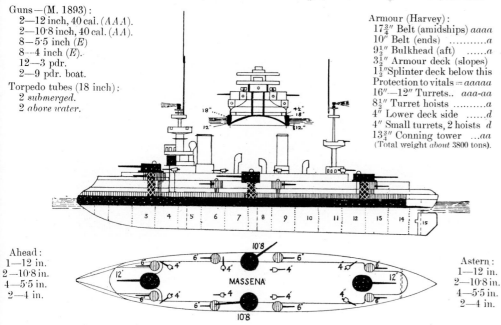

Ahead:
1—12 in.
2—10·8 in.
4—5·5 in.
2—4 in.

MASSENA

Astern:
1—12 in.
2—10·8 in.
4—5·5 in.
2—4 in.

Broadside: 2—12 in., 1—10·8 in., 4—5·5 in., 4—4 in.

Machinery: 3 sets vertical triple expansion. 3 screws. Boilers: 24 Lagrafel D'Allest. Designed H.P. 13,500 = 18 kts. Coal: *normal* 635 tons; *maximum* 800 tons, including oil.

Armour Notes.—Belt is 7½ feet wide by 350 feet long. 5 feet of it below waterline; lower edge is 13¾″ thick amidships. 4¾″ funnel bases, 3″ shields to 4 inch guns. The lower protection deck is 2⅓ feet below the chief protection deck.

Gunnery Notes.—Loading positions, big guns: all round. Hoists, electric all guns. Big guns manœuvred electrically and hand. Balanced turrets, Secondary turrets, electrically and hand. Arcs of fire: 12 in. guns 250°; 10·8 in., 180°. Secondary guns 150°.

Engineering Notes.—The ship failed to make her speed on trial by a knot, but did 17 knots in 24 hours' trial. Not good for more than that at the outside now. Burns about 12¾ tons an hour at 13,500 H.P.

General Notes.—Laid down at St. Nazaire, 1892. Completed 1898. Cost, *complete*, over £1,100,000.

Photo, Bar.

Distinction.—To be recognized anywhere by her snout bow.

CHARLES MARTEL (August, 1893).

Displacement 11,882 tons.   Complement

Length (*waterline*), 390 feet.   Beam, 70½ feet.   *Maximum* draught, 27¾ feet.

Guns—(M. '87):
  2—12 inch, 45 cal. (*AAA*).
  2—10·8 inch, 40 cal. (*A*).
  8—5·5 inch, 45 cal. (*E*).
  4—9 pdr. (*F*).
  20—3 pdr.
Torpedo tubes (18 inch):
  2 *submerged*.
  4 *above water*.

Armour (Creusot steel):
  17¾″ Belt (amidships) ......*aa*
  13¾″ Belt (bow) ....*a*
  11″ Belt (aft) ....*b*
  2¾″ Armour deck (flat on belt) ....
  1¼″ Splinter deck (flat below belt) .
  Protection to vitals ....= *aaa*
  4″ Upper belt ....*d*
   ″ Barbettes ....
  14¾″ Turrets ....*a*
  6″ Turret bases....................*d*
  4″ Small turrets ....*ε*
  4″ Hoists to these................*ε*
  9¼″ Conning tower.................*b*
  (Total weight, *about* 3,700 tons.)

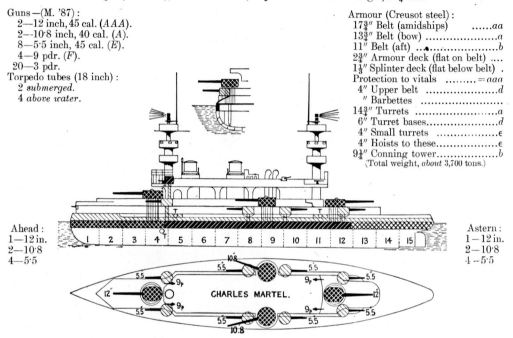

Ahead:
1—12 in.
2—10·8
4—5·5

Astern:
1—12 in.
2—10·8
4—5·5

CHARLES MARTEL.

Broadside: 2—12 in., 1—10·8 in., 4—5·5 in.

Machinery: 2 sets vertical triple expansion.   2 screws.   Boilers: 24 Lagrafel d'Allest (welded tubes) (3 groups).   Designed H.P. 14,500 = 18 kts.   Coal: *normal* 600 tons; *maximum* 1000 tons, including oil.

Armour Notes.—Belt is 7½ feet wide, and 5¾ feet of it below waterline; lower edge is 10″ thick amidships and forward, and 6¾″ aft.

Gunnery Notes.—Loading positions, big guns: all round.   Balanced turrets.   Hoists, electric, all guns, also hand.   Big guns manœuvred hydraulically.   Secondary turrets, electrically.
  Arcs of fire : 12 in., 250°; 10·8 in., 180°; secondary turrets, about 150°.

  Height of guns above water: Bow 12 in., 28 feet; after 12 in., 22 feet; 10·8 in., 22½ feet.   3 pdrs. carried, 10 on top side; 9 pdrs. on top side.

Engineering Notes.—On 24 hour first trial, at 12,000 H.P., made 17·8 kts.; at full power I.H.P., 14,996 = 18·13 kts.   She is still good for 17½ kts.   Keeps station at 17 kts.   An excellent steamer.   Coal consumption : 15⅙ tons an hour at 14,500 H.P.   *Actual* radius at full speed, about 1200 miles with full bunkers.

General Notes.—Laid down at Brest, Aug., 1891.   Completed 1896.   Cost £1,000,000 approximately.

Conning tower.—Port Side.

CARNOT (July, 1894).

Displacement, 12,150 tons.   Complement 621.

Length (*waterline*), 380½ feet.   Beam, 70½ feet.   *Maximum* draught, 28 feet.

Guns (M. '91):
2—12 inch, 45 cal. (*AAA*).
2—10·8 inch, 45 cal. (*A*).
8—5·5 inch, 45 cal. (*E*).
4—9 pdr. (*F*).
18—3 pdr.
Torpedo tubes (18 inch):
2 *submerged*.
2 *above water*.

Armour (Creusot):
17¾″ Belt (amidships) ... .   *a*
14″ Belt (low) ....   *a*
10″ Belt (aft.) ....   *b*
2¾″ Deck (slopes)...........
Protection to vitals ... =*aaaaa*
13¾″ Turrets (4) ....   *aa*
6″ Turret points ....   *d*
4″ Upper belt ....   *d*
4″ Small turrets (8) ....   *ε*
6″ Conning tower ....   *d*
Total weight, *about* 3,800 tons.

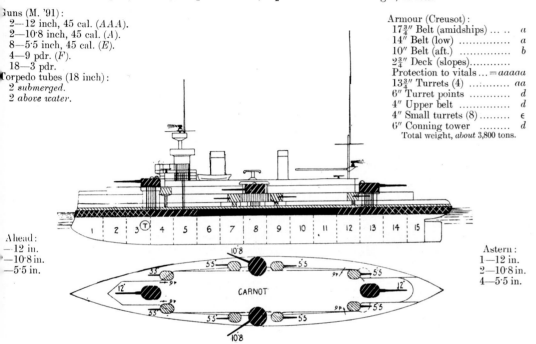

Ahead:
—12 in.
—10·8 in.
—5·5 in.

Astern:
1—12 in.
2—10·8 in.
4—5·5 in.

CARNOT

Broadside: 2—12 in., 1—10·8 in., 4—5·5 in.

Machinery: 2 sets vertical triple expansion. 2 screws. Boilers: 12 Lagrafel d'Allest (welded tube).
Designed H.P. 15,000 = 18 kts. Coal: *normal* 500 tons : maximum 700 tons.

Armour Notes.—Belt is 7½ feet wide ; 1¾ feet of it above, and 5¾ feet of it below waterline ; lower edge is 10″ thick amidships, and forward 6½″ aft.

Gunnery Notes.—Loading positions, big guns: all round.   All guns manœuvred hydraulically and by hand.
Secondary turrets : electrically manœuvred.
Arcs of fire : 12 inch.
Ammunition carried : 60 rounds per big gun.
Height of guns above water : Fore 12 in., 27½ feet ; after 12 in., 21½ feet ; 10·8 inch, 15 feet ; 5·5 in., about 14 feet.

Torpedo Notes.—6 searchlights.

Engineering Notes.—Her trial result was a *mean* of 17·8 kts. for 4 hours and 17·5 for 24 hours at 11,500 H.P.
She can keep station at 16½ kts. while coal lasts. Consumption, about 15 tons an hour at full power.
Actual radius about 580-600 miles at full speed.

General Notes.—Laid down at Toulon, August, 1891.   Completed, 1896.   Cost £1,000,000.

Starboard side amidships.
Showing turrets.

Starboard side.   Conning tower.

T

JAURÉGUIBERRY (October, 1893).

Displacement 11,900 tons.   Complement 607.

Length (*waterline*), 364 feet.   Beam, 72½ feet.   *Maximum* draught, 29 feet.

Guns :
2—12 in. (M. '91) (*AAA*)
2—10·8 inch (M.'87) (*A*).
8—5·5 inch, 45 cal. (*E*)
4—9 pdr. (*F*).
16—3 pdr.
Torpedo tubes
(18 inch) :
2 *submerged*.
4 *above water* (2 bow,
2 stern).

Armour (Creusot steel) :
17¾″ Belt (amidships) ...*aa*
9¾″ Belt (ends) ....*b*
2¾″ Deck (flat on belt) ...
1⅓″ Deck (flat below belt)
Protection to vitals ...*aaa*
4″ Side above belt ......*ϵ*
14½″ Turrets...............*aa*
?″ Turret bases ....
4″ Small turrets ....*ϵ*
4″ Bases to these ....*ϵ*
9″ Conning tower.........*b*
(Total, *about* 3,600 tons.)

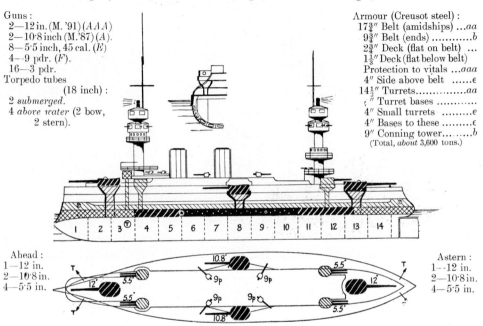

Photo, Symonds.

Ahead :
1—12 in.
2—10·8 in.
4—5·5 in.

Astern :
1—12 in.
2—10·8 in.
4—5·5 in.

Broadside : 2—12 in., 1—10·8 in., 4—5·5 in.

Machinery : 2 sets vertical triple expansion.   2 screws.   Boilers : 22 Lagrafel d'Allest in 6 groups.
Designed H.P. 14,300 = 17·8 kts.   Coal : *normal* 750 tons ; *maximum* 1100 tons, including oil, etc.

Armour Notes.—Belt is 7¾ feet wide, 6 feet of it below waterline ; lower edge is 10″ thick amidships, only 4″ forward, and 6″ aft.   Splinter deck just below the armour deck (2 feet below).

Gunnery Notes.—Loading positions, big guns : all round.   Balanced turrets.   Hoists : electric all guns. All guns manœuvred electrically and by hand.
Arcs of fire : 12 in., 250° ; 10·8 in., 180° ; secondary turrets, 160°.   Hoists are of a design peculiar to this ship, the curved base may be noted.

Torpedo Notes.—6 searchlights.

Engineering Notes.—On a 2 hour trial I.H.P. 15,931 = 18·10 *maximum* ; *mean* 13,819 = 17·7.   Is good for about 17 kts. to-day.

General Notes.—Laid down at La Seyne, April 1891.   Completed, 1895-96.   Cost just over £1,000,000.

Conning tower and port side forward.

BRENNUS (October, 1891).

Displacement 11,395 tons.   Complement 696.

Length (*waterline*), 375 feet.   Beam, 65½ feet.   *Maximum* draught, 27½ feet.   Length over all, 375 feet.

Guns (M '87):
3—13·4 inch, 42 cal. (*A A A A*).
10—6·4 inch, 45 cal. (*E*).
4—9 pdr.
14—3 pdr.
2 Maxims.
Torpedo tubes:
6 *above* water.

Armour (Creusot steel):
18″ Belt (amidships) ... *aaa*
12″ Belt (ends) .... *a*
3″ Deck reinforcing belt ...
Protection to vitals ......*aaaa*
18″ Turrets .... *aaa*
8″ Turret bases .... *c*
4½″ Lower deck side ..... *d*
4½″ Battery redoubt...... *d*
4¾″ Small turrets .... *d*
4¾″ Conning tower .... *d*
(Total weight *about* 4000 tons).

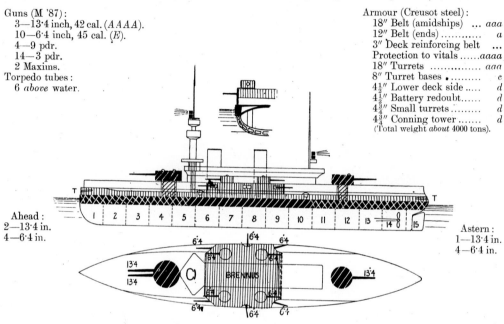

Ahead:
2—13·4 in.
4—6·4 in.

Astern:
1—13·4 in.
4—6·4 in.

Broadside: 3—13·4 in., 5—6·4 in.

Machinery: 2 sets vertical triple expansion.   2 screws.   Boilers: 32 Bellevilles, *without* economisers.
Designed H.P. 13,600 = 17·5 kts.   Coal: *normal* 550 tons; *maximum* 800 tons.

Armour Notes.— Belt is 5½ feet wide, 5½ feet of it below waterline; lower edge is 11½″ thick amidships, and 9¾″ at ends.   The backs of the turrets are 8″ thick only.

Gunnery Notes.—Loading positions, big guns: end on.   Hoists, electric.   Big guns manœuvred electrically and hand.   These guns are very powerful, but fire very slowly.
Arcs of fire: Big guns, 200°; secondary turrets, 135°; battery guns about 110°.

Engineering Notes.—The first large ship to be fitted with Bellevilles.   These are of an elementary type.   She gave considerable trouble on trials, and for a long time could not make her speed.   Afterwards she steamed well and reached 18kts., but is not good for that now.   Coal consumption: about 13 tons an hour or more at 13,600 H.P. (full speed).

General Notes.—First battleship to be built without a ram.   Laid down January, 1889.   Completed 1895.   Cost about £995,000.

AMIRAL BAUDIN (June, 1883) & **FORMIDABLE** (April, 1885).

(Reconstructed 1897-1901).

Displacement 12,150 tons.   Complement 625-650.

Length 321 feet.   Beam, 69 feet.   *Maximum* draught, 29 feet.

Guns :
2—14·5 in., old 28 cal. (*A*).
(replaced by 10·8 inch in *Formidable*).
4—6·4 in. (M. '93). (*D*).
8—5·5 in. (*E*).
18—3 pdr.
Torpedo tubes (17·7 in.) :
6 *above water*.

Armour (steel) :
16″ Belt (amidships) ... *a*
10″ Belt (bow) .... *c*
6″ Belt (aft)............. *e*
4″—3″ Deck (flat on belt)
Protection to vitals is... *a*
16″ Barbettes .... *a*
8″ Hoists .... *d*
12¾ Big gun shields ...*aa*
4½″ Battery redoubt ... *c*
(Total, *about* 4300 tons).

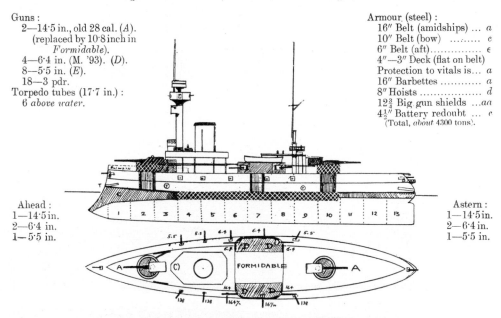

Ahead :
1—14·5 in.
2—6·4 in.
1—5·5 in.

Astern :
1—14·5 in.
2—6·4 in.
1—5·5 in.

Broadside : 2—14·5 in., 4—6·4 in., 3—5·5 in.

Machinery : 2 sets 3 cylinder compound.   2 screws.   Boilers : 12 cylindrical.   Designed H.P. *natural* 5000 = 14 kts. ; *forced* 9700 = 16 kts.   Coal : *maximum* 800 tons, also liquid fuel.

Armour Notes.—Belt is 7 feet wide (all under water).

Gunnery Notes.—Loading positions, big guns : end on.
Arcs of fire : big guns about 210°. *Formidable* now carries 2—10·8 in. (*AAA*). instead of the 14·5″

Engineering Notes.—Reboilered about 1896-97.   *Baudin* made 14·5 kts. ; *Formidable* 16·2 kts. on 24 hours trial.   Boilers of both are now nearly worn out again, especially *Formidable's*.

General Notes.—It is doubtful whether any further reconstruction will take place.   The ships cannot steer at full speed.

AMIRAL BAUDIN.   *Photo, Bar.*

FORMIDABLE.

Difference in funnels and masts.

148

OLD FRENCH BATTLESHIP (15 knot).

(MARCEAU CLASS—1 SHIP).

MARCEAU (May, 1887).

Displacement 10,900. Complement 640.

Length (*waterline*), 330 feet. Beam, 65½ feet. *Maximum* draught, 29 feet. Length over all, 347 feet.

Guns:
4—13·4 inch, 30 cal. (*B*).
15—5·5 inch, 45 cal. (*E*).
16—3 pdr.
Torpedo tubes (17·7 inch):
4 *above water* (broadside).
1 „   „   (stern).

Armour (steel):
17¾″ Belt (amidships) ... *aa*
12″ Belt (bow) .... *b*
17″ Belt (aft)............ *aa*
4″ Armour deck ....
Protection to vitals ... = *aaa*
14″ Barbettes .... *a*
2″ Turrets................. *f*
8″ Turret bases .... *c*
2″ Screens in battery ...
14″ Conning tower ...... *a*

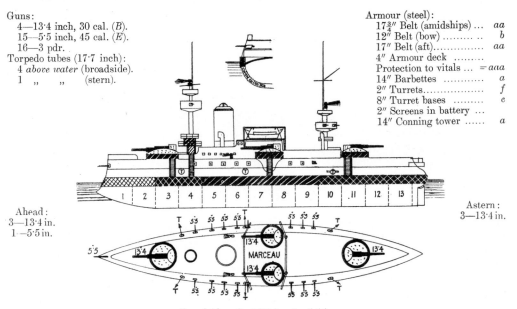

Ahead:
3—13·4 in.
1—5·5 in.

Astern:
3—13·4 in.

Broadside: 3—13·4 in., 7—5·5 in.

Photo, Bar.

Machinery: 4 sets 3 cylinder vertical compound. 2 screws. Boilers: Niclausse. Designed H.P. 12,000 = 16 kts. Coal: *normal* 600 tons; *maximum* 800 tons.

Armour Notes: Belt is 7½ feet wide; 6 feet of it below waterline; lower edge is 14″ thick amidships, 8″ at ends.

Gunnery Notes: Loading positions, big guns: end on. Big guns manœuvred, hydraulically.

Arcs of fire: Bow and stern guns, 250°; amidship big guns, 180° from axial line.

Engineering Notes: Re-boilered and engines 'modernised,' 1901—02.

General Notes: Laid down at La Seyne, 1882. Completed, 1890. Partially reconstructed, 1901—1903. First cost, £760,000.

(MARCEAU CLASS—2 SHIPS).

MAGENTA (April, 1890), & **NEPTUNE** (May, 1887).

Displacement 10,900 tons. Complement 640.

Length (*waterline*), 336 feet. Beam, 65½ feet. *Maximum* draught, 29 feet. Length over all, 347 feet.

Guns:
    4—13·4 inch, 30 cal. (*B*).
    17—5·5 inch, 45 cal. (*E*).
    16—3 pdr.
Torpedo tubes (18 inch):
    4 *above water* (broadside).
    1   ,,   ,,   (stern).

Armour (steel):
    17¾″ Belt (amidships) ... *aa*
    12″ Belt (bow) .... *b*
    17″ Belt (aft) .... *aa*
    4″ Armour deck ....
    Protection to vitals... =*aaa*
    14″ Barbettes .... *a*
    2″ Turrets................. *f*
    8″ Turret bases .... *c*
    2″ Screens in battery ...
    14″ Conning tower ...... *a*

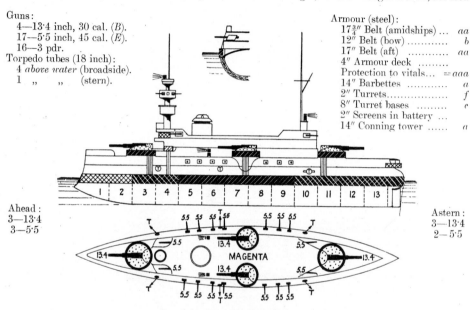

Ahead:
3—13·4
3—5·5

Astern:
3—13·4
2—5·5

Broadside: 3—13·4 in., 8—5·5 in.

Machinery: 4 sets 3 cylinder vertical compound. 2 screws. Boilers: Belleville. Designed H.P. 12,000 = 16 kts. Coal: *normal* 600 tons; *maximum* 800 tons.

Armour Notes.—Belt is 7½ feet wide, 6 feet of it below waterline; lower edge is 14″ thick amidships: 8″ at ends.

Gunnery Notes.—Loading positions, big guns: end on.
    Arcs of fire: as for *Marceau*.
    Height of guns above water: Big guns *about* 22 feet.

Engineering Notes.—Re-boilered and engines modernised 1902-03. Steam well, and can do 15 kts. or 10 kts. for any length of time.

General Notes.—*Magenta* laid down at Toulon, 1883. Completed 1893. *Neptune* laid down at Brest, 1882. Completed 1892. First cost of each over £760,000.

MAGENTA.

NEPTUNE.

Photos, Bar.

OLD FRENCH BATTLESHIP (15 knot).

HOCHE (Sept., 1886).

Displacement 11,000.   Complement 611.

Length (*waterline*), 337 feet.   Beam, 65½ feet.   *Maximum* draught, 29¼ feet.   Length over all, 347½ feet.

Guns (M. '81):
2—13·4 inch, 26 cal. (*B*).
2—10·8 inch, 28 cal. (*C*).
12—5·5 inch, 30 cal. (*F*).
4—9 pdr.
12—3 pdr.
Torpedo tubes (17·7 inch):
4 *above water* (section 2 & 6).
1 „   „   (stern).

Armour (steel):
17¾″ Belt (amidships) ...   *aa*
12″ Belt (bow) ....   *b*
15″ Belt (aft)..............   *a*
Protection to vitals ...=*aaa*
3″ Bow armour............   *f*
16″ Turrets and barbettes   *a*
6″ Bases to these ....   *d*

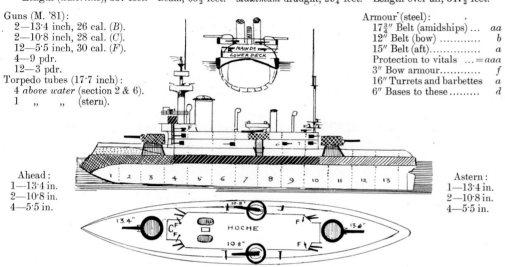

Ahead:
1—13·4 in.
2—10·8 in.
4—5·5 in.

Astern:
1—13·4 in.
2—10·8 in.
4—5·5 in.

Broadside: 2—13·4 in., 1—10·8 in., 6—5·5 in.

Photo, Bougault.

Machinery: 2 sets 3 cylinder vertical compound. 2 screws. Boilers: 18 Belleville. Designed H.P. 11,300 = 16 kts. Coal: *normal*, 600 tons ; *maximum*, 800 tons.

Armour Notes: Belt, 7½ feet wide ; 6½ feet of it below waterline ; lower edge, 14″ thick amidships, 8″ at ends.

Gunnery Notes: Loading positions, big guns : end on.
Arcs of fire : Bow and stern guns, 260° ; amidships big guns, 180° from axial line.
Height of guns above water : 13·4 in., 15 feet ; 10·8 in., 21½ feet.

Engineering Notes: Re-boilered with Bellevilles, 1899.

Trials: In 1899 her designed H.P. gave 15·9 kts. mean for 6 hours.

General Notes: Laid down at Lorient, 1881. Completed, 1889. First cost, *complete*, about £700,000.
Partially reconstructed, 1899.

COURBET (1882), & **DÉVASTATION** (1879).

Also (of no fighting value), REDOUBTABLE (1879).

All reconstructed 1898—1902.

Displacement *circa* 10,000 tons.   Complement 689.

Length, 318¼ feet.   Beam, 69 feet.   *Maximum draught,* 28¼ feet.

Guns (M '92) :

Courbet.	Devastation.	Redoubtable.
4—10·8 (AA).	4—10·8 (AA)	4—10·8 (AA).
3—9·4 (A).	2—9·4 (A).	4—9·4 (A).
1—6·4		
10—4 in.	11—4in.	
	4—9 pdr.	
14—3 pdr.	12—3 pdr.	14—3 pdr.
17—1 pdr.	20—1 pdr.	10—1 pdr.

Armour (iron) :
15″ Belt (amidships) ......*b*
8¾″ Belt (ends) ....*d*
8¾″ Bulkhead aft ....*d*
3¼″ Deck (flat on belt)   ...
Protection to vitals is   ...*b*
9½″ Battery   ....*d*
3″ Conning tower.........*f*

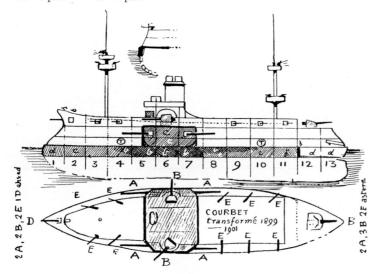

Machinery : 2 sets 3 cylinder compound. 2 screws. Boilers : *Courbet* and *Devastation* (Belleville in 1899-1900), *Redoubtable*, cylindrical. Designed H.P. 8100 = 15·1 kts. Coal : *normal* 900 tons.

Gunnery Notes.—*Devastation* is the most successful, having a more reasonable armament for her size. The arcs of fire for battery guns are trifling—90° at the outside and probably much less.

Engineering Notes.—The first two can steam well, and reached 15 kts. easily on trial after reconstruction. *Redoubtable* is worn out, also unseaworthy, and is to be dismantled at Saigon where she is used for coast defence purposes only.

COURBET.   *Photo, Bar.*

DÉVASTATION.

HENRI IV. (Aug., 1899).

Displacement 8948 tons.   Complement 460.

Length (*waterline*), 350 feet.   Beam, 73 feet.   *Maximum* draught, 24¾ feet.   Length over all, 354½ feet.

Guns—(M. '93—'96):
2—10·8 inch, 45 cal.(*AAA*)
7—5·5 inch, 45 cal. (*E*).
12—3 pdr.
2—1 pdr.
Torpedo tubes : (17·7 inch).
  2 *submerged*.
    (20° before beam).

Armour (Harvey-nickel):
  11″ Belt (amidships) ... *aa*
  8″ Belt (ends) .... *a*
  5″—3″ Armour deck, flat
    (*see notes*).
  Protection to vitals = *aaaaa*
  10″ Turrets .... *aa*
  11½″ Turret bases .... *aa*
  4½″ Lower deck side ... *c*
  4½″ Battery (redoubt) ... *c*
  4½″ Small turret (aft) ... *c*
  8″ Conning tower......... *a*
  (Total weight *about* 3500 tons.)

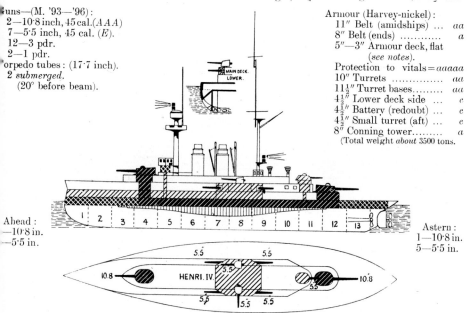

Ahead :
—10·8 in.
—5·5 in.

Astern :
1—10·8 in.
5—5·5 in.

Broadside : 2—10·8 in., 4—5·5 in.

Machinery : 3 sets vertical triple expansion. 3 screws. Boilers : Niclausse. Designed H.P. 11,500 = 17·5 knots.   Coal : *normal* 820 tons ; *maximum* 1100 tons.

Armour Notes.—Belt is 7½ feet wide, 4 feet of it below waterline.   Lower edge is 8″ thick.   This ship has under water armour protection against torpedoes.   There are flat decks both above and below main belt.   In addition lateral armoured bulkheads extends downward from the lower armoured deck to the bilge keel line, and the side below the belt is armoured amidships.   She is supposed to need three torpedoes to sink her.

Gunnery Notes.—Loading positions, big guns : all round.   Balanced turrets.   Hoists, electric.   Big guns manœuvred electrically and hydraulic.   Secondary turret, electrically.
  Arcs of fire : Big guns, 260° ; lower battery, 110° from axial line ; upper deck guns, 180° ;   after turret, 275°.
  Height of guns above water : Bow turret, 28 feet ; after turret, 16 feet ; aft, 5·5 in. turret, 21 feet ; battery guns, 15 feet.

Torpedo Notes.—6 searchlights.

Engineering Notes.—Coal consumption about 11 tons an hour at 11,500 H.P. (17 kts.)

General Notes.—Laid down at Cherbourg, July, 1897.   Completed 1903.   Cost about £810,000.   She is an excellent seaboat, being steady in the worst seas.

(Bouvines Class—2 Ships.)

BOUVINES (March, 1892), & TRÉHOUART (May, 1893).

Displacement 6535 tons. Complement 335.

Length (*waterline*), 292 feet. Beam, 59 feet. *Maximum* draught, 24½ feet.

Guns (M '87) :
  2—12 inch, 45 cal. (*AAA*).
  8—4 inch, 45 cal. (*E*).
  4—3 pdr.
  10—Small.
Torpedo tubes (17·7 inch) :
  2 *above water.*

Armour (Creusot) :
  18″ Belt (amidships)...*ag*
  12″ Belt (ends).............*a*
  4″ Deck (slopes) ....
  Protection to vitals...*aaaa*
  14½″ Turrets ....*aa*
  12″ Turret bases..........*a*
  12″ Conning tower ......*a*
  (Total *about* 2000 tons)

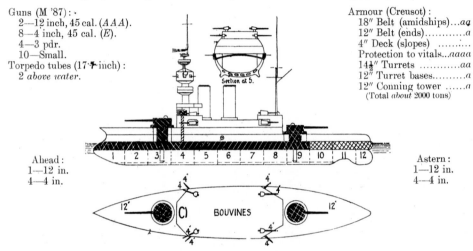

Section at 5.

BOUVINES

Ahead :
1—12 in.
4—4 in.

Astern :
1—12 in.
4—4 in.

Broadside : 2—12 in., 4—4 in.

Machinery : 2 sets inclined triple expansion. 2 screws. Boilers : *Bouvines*, Lagrafel d'Albert, *Trehouart*, Belleville *without* economisers. Designed H.P. 8900 = 16·2 kts. Coal : *normal* 300 tons ; *maximum* 337 tons.

Armour Notes.—Belt is 7 feet wide ; lower edge is 10″ thick amidships.

Gunnery Notes.—Loading positions, big guns : all round. Hoists, electric. Big guns manœuvred electrically. Turret guns fitted for high angle fire.

Engineering Notes.—Trehouart is said to have worked up to 9250 H.P. and 17·5 kts. speed, and Bouvines to 17kts., but these are fancy results and 16 kts. their usual speed. They can keep station at 14 kts. easily.

General Notes.—Bouvines built at La Seyne, *Tréhouart* at Lorient. Laid down 1890. Cost about £575,000 per ship.

BOUVINES.

TRÉHOUART.

Photos, Bar.

(JEMMAPPES CLASS—2 SHIPS).

JEMMAPPES (April 1892), & VALMY (May, 1892).

Displacement 6487 tons. Complement 334.

Length (*waterline*), 283⅔ feet. Beam, 57⅓ feet. *Maximum* draught, 24½ feet..

Guns—(M. '87):
2—13·4 inch, 40 cal. (*AAAA*).
4—4 inch (*F*).
6—3 pdr.
8—1 pdr.
Torpedo tubes (17·7 inch):
2 *above water.*

Armour (Creusot):
18″ Belt (amidships) ...... *aa*
12″ Belt (ends) .... *a*
4″ Armour deck (on slopes)
Protection to vitals ......=*aaaa*
14½″ Turrets .... *aa*
12″ Turret bases .... *a*
12″ Conning tower .... *a*

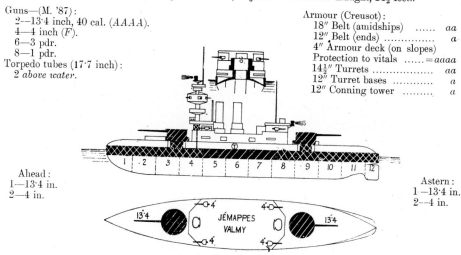

Ahead:
1—13·4 in.
2—4 in.

Astern:
1—13·4 in.
2—4 in.

Broadside: 2—13·4 in., 2—4 in.

JÉMMAPPES.   *Photo, Symonds.*

(*Valmy* is identical).

Machinery: 2 sets horizontal 3 cylinder compound. 2 screws. Boilers: 16 Lagrafel d'Allest. Designed H.P. 8400=17 kts. Coal: *normal* 300 tons; *maximum* 337 tons=actual radius of 650 kts. at full speed.

Armour Notes.—Belt is 7 feet wide; lower edge is 10″ thick amidships.

Gunnery Notes.—Loading positions, big guns modified 1901: end on. Can fire 1 round a minute. Big guns manœuvred electrically. Hoists are electric and hand. Ports specially fitted for high angle fire.
Arcs of fire: Big guns about 250°.

Engineering Notes.—On first *trials Jemmappes* reached 16·7 kts. and *Valmy* 15·9. Present speed is about 15·4 (last recorded for *Valmy*), but they lose speed badly in a sea way. Coal consumption in service, 4½ tons per hour at 5000 H.P., and 7¾ tons at 8400 H.P. (full speed).

General Notes.—Laid down at St. Nazaire, *circa* 1889. Completed 1894-95. Cost, per ship, about £550,000.

INDOMPTABLE (September, 1883), **CAIMAN** (May, 1885), **REQUIN** (June, 1885).

Displacement about 7000 tons.   Complement 381.

Length (*waterline*), 278 feet.   Beam, 59 feet.   *Maximum* draught, 25 feet.   Length over all, 294 feet.

Guns (M. '93):
2—10·8 inch, 45 cal. (AA).
6—4 inch (E).
10—3 pdr.
Torpedo tubes:
none.

Armour (compound):
19½" Belt (amidships) ...*aaa*
11¾" Belt (ends)............ *aa*
4" Deck (flat on belt)......
Protection to vitals is ...*aaa*
10" Turrets (H.N.)......... *aa*
7½" Turret bases (H.N.)   *a*
12" Conning tower (steel)

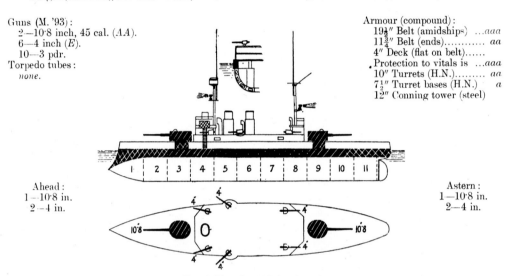

Ahead:
1—10·8 in.
2—4 in.

Astern:
1—10·8 in.
2—4 in.

Broadside: 2—10·8 in., 3—4 in.

Machinery: 2 sets 3 cylinder vertical compound.   2 screws (4 bladed).   Boilers: *Requin*, 12 Niclausse, others, cylindrical.   Designed H.P. 6000 = 14·5 kts.   Coal: *normal* 400 tons; *maximum* 800 tons.

Armour Notes.—Belt is 7½ feet wide, 5 feet of it below waterline; lower edge is 11" thick amidships.

Gunnery Notes.—Loading positions, big guns: all round.   Hoists, electric.   Big guns manœuvred electrically.
Arcs of fire: Big guns. 200°.
Ammunition carried: 10·8 in., 60 rounds per gun.   4 in., 250 per gun.
Height of guns above water: 10·8 in., 13½ feet.

Torpedo Notes.—Tubes removed.

Engineering Notes.—*Requin* on trial made I.H.P. 6230 = 15·1 kts.   Others are slower than *Requin* by at least 1 knot, and probably more.   Coal consumption heavy in all—about 6¼ tons an hour at full power (6000 H.P.)

General Notes.—All reconstructed, 1901-03, and greatly modernised.

Class distinction.—*Requin* has 2 funnels fore and aft; the other 2 and *Terrible*, 4 funnels in groups of 2 abreast.

TERRIBLE (1881).

Displacement 7500 tons.   Complement 405.

Length *(waterline)*, 278 feet.   Beam, 59 feet.   *Maximum* draught, 26½ feet.

Guns :
  Being re-armed with—
  2—13·4 inch (M '87) (*AAA*).
  4—4 inch (*E*)
  10—3 pdr.
Torpedo tubes:
  2 *above water*
  Old armament 2—16·5 inch,
    19 cal. (M '79).

Armour (compound) :
  19½″ Belt (amidships) ....*aaa*
  11¾″ Belt (ends) .... *a*
  4″ Deck (flat on belt) ....
  Protection to vitals is ....*aaa*
  17″ Barbettes (steel)........... *aa*
  8″ Hoists to these.............. *d*

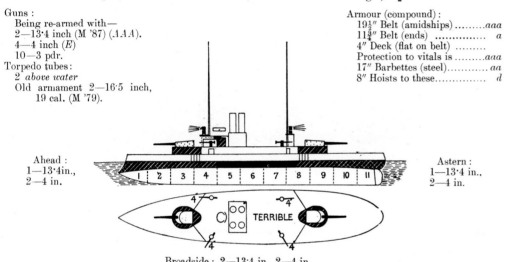

Ahead :
1—13·4in.,
2—4 in.

Astern :
1—13·4 in.,
2—4 in.

Broadside : 2—13·4 in., 2—4 in.

Photo, Barr.

Machinery : 2 sets vertical compound.   2 screws (4 bladed).   Boilers : 12 cylindrical.   Designed H.P.
6000 = 14·5 kts.   Coal : *normal* 400 tons ; *maximum* 800 tons.

Armour Notes.—Belt is 7½ feet wide all of it below waterline.

Engineering Notes.—Burns about 7½ tons of coal an hour at 6000 H.P.

General Notes.—To be re-armed, but not otherwise modernised unless reboilered,

FURIEUX (1883).

Displacememt 6000 tons.   Complement 250.

Length (*waterline*), 249 feet.   Beam, 58¾ feet.   *Maximum* draught, 25 feet.

Guns (M. '96) :
  2—9·4 inches (A.A)
  4—9 pdr.
  8—3 pdr.
Torpedo tubes :
  2 *above water*

Armour (compound) :
  19½″ Belt (amidships) .... *aa*
  13¼″ Belt (ends) .... *a*
  3½″ Deck (flat on belt)........
  Protection to vitals is......... *aa*
  9″ Turrets (KNC) .... *aa*
  6″ Hoists to these .... *b*
  10″ Conning tower (KNC)... *aa*

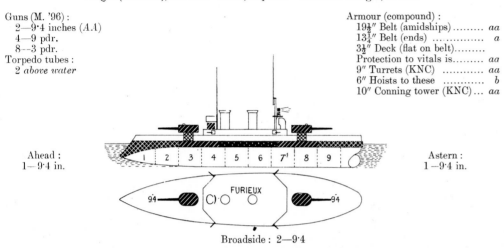

Ahead :
1—9·4 in.

Astern :
1—9·4 in.

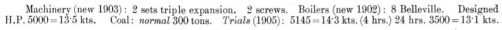

Broadside : 2—9·4

Machinery (new 1903): 2 sets triple expansion.   2 screws.   Boilers (new 1902): 8 Belleville.   Designed H.P. 5000 = 13·5 kts.   Coal: *normal* 300 tons.   *Trials* (1905): 5145 = 14·3 kts. (4 hrs.) 24 hrs. 3500 = 13·1 kts.

General Notes.—Completely reconstructed and modernised (1902-1905).

The French Navy also contains an old battleship AMIRAL DUPERRÉ, launched in 1879 with a 21½″ iron belt, and 3 old monitors, TEMPÊTE, TONNERE and FULMINANT used as torpedo bases and local defence.   Antique guns in all and none of any fighting value whatever.

158

ERNEST-RENAN, EDGARD-QUINET, WALDECK ROUSSEAU (all building).

Displacement 13,644 tons.   Complement 750.

Length *(waterline)*, 515 feet.   Beam, 72 feet.   *Mean* draught, 27 feet.

Guns—(M. '02):
4—7·6 inch, 45 cal. (*AA*).⎱ Proposed 1906 to substitute a single 7·6
16—6·4 inch. 50 cal. (*B*). ⎰   for each pair of 6·4 in turrets.
8—9 pdr.
24—3 pdr.
Torpedo tubes (18 inch):
2 *submerged.*

Armour (Krupp):
6¾″ Belt (amidship)...... *a*
3″ Belt (ends) .... *ε*
6″ Bulkhead (aft)......... *a*
2½ Deck (slopes) ....
Protection to vitals...... = *aa*
8″ Turrets .... *a*
8″ Turret bases .... *a*
5½″ Casemates (4) ...... *b*
5½″ Small turrets (8) ... *b*
8″ Conning tower ...... *a*
(Total weight 3400 tons).

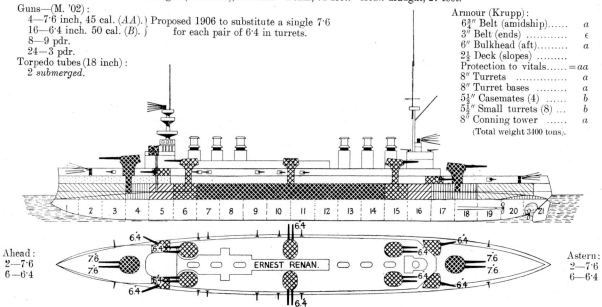

Broadside: 4—7·6 in., 8—6·4 in.

Ahead:
2—7·6
6—6·4

Astern:
2—7·6
6—6·4

Building.

Design several times changed, and may be altered again.

Machinery: 3 sets vertical triple expansion.   3 screws.   Boilers: *See Notes.*   Designed H.P. 37,000 = 23 knots.   Coal:
normal 1,400 tons; *maximum* 2,300 tons.   *Nominal endurance:* 10,000 miles at 10 kts.

Armour Notes.—Belt is 12¼ feet wide.   4¾ feet below waterline.   Upper and lower edges 5″ thick.

Gunnery Notes.—Loading positions, big guns: all round.   Hoists: electric to all guns.   All guns manœuvred electrically and hand.
Arcs of fire : Big turrets 240°; secondary turrets 150°; casemates 110°.
Height of guns above water: Bow and secondary turrets, 29½ feet; after turret, 22 feet.   Forward casemates, 20 feet;
after casemates, 12 feet.

Torpedo Notes.—1904 model torpedo.

Engineering Notes.—

Est. cost.	Name.	Built at	Laid down.	To be completed.	Trials.	Boilers.	Best recent speed.
£1,444,431	E. Renan	St. Nazaire	'03	1908		Niclausse	
£1,247,035	E. Quinet	Brest Yard	'05	1908		Guyot	
£1,226,593	W. Rousseau	Lorient Yard	'06	1909		Belleville	

159

NEW FRENCH ARMOURED CRUISER (22 knots).

JULES MICHELET (1905).

Displacement 12,600 tons.   Complement 724

Length (*waterline*): 485 feet.   Beam, 70 feet.   *Mean* draught, 27 feet.   Length over all, 493 feet.

Guns—(M. '02):
4—7·6 inch, 45 cal. (*AA*).
12—6·4 inch, 50 cal. (*B*).
24—3 pdr.
Torpedo tubes (18 inch):
2 *submerged*.
2 *above water*.

Armour (Krupp):
6¾″ Belt (amidship)...... *a*
3″ Belt (ends) .... ϵ
6″ Bulkhead (aft) ...... *a*
2½″ Deck (slopes) ....
Protection to vitals...... = *aa*
8″ Turrets .... *a*
8″ Turret bases .... *a*
5½″ Casemates (4) ...... *b*
5½″ Small turrets (8)... *b*
8″ Conning tower ...... *a*
(Total weight 3400 tons).

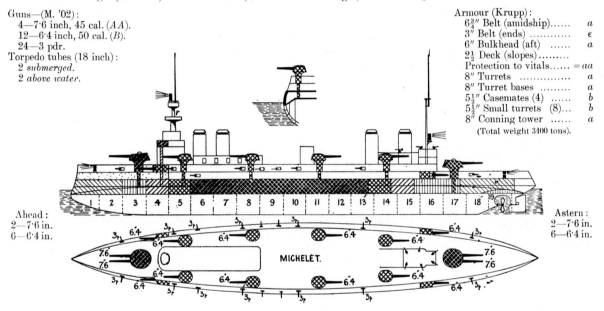

Ahead:
2—7·6 in.
6—6·4 in.

Astern:
2—7·6 in.
6—6·4 in.

Broadside: 4—7·6 in., 6—6·4 in.

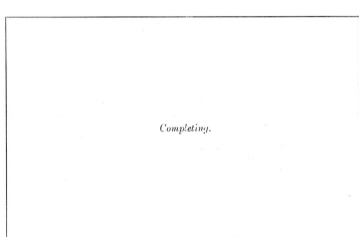

Completing.

Machinery: 3 sets vertical triple expansion.   3 screws.   Boilers: Du Temple-Guyot.   Designed H.P. 29,000 = 22 knots.
Coal: *normal* 1400 tons; *maximum* 2300 tons.

Armour Notes.—Belt is 12¼ feet wide.   4¾ feet below waterline.   Upper and lower edges 5″ thick.

Gunnery Notes.—Loading positions, big guns: all round.   Hoists: electric to all guns.   All guns manœuvred **electrically** and hand.
Arcs of fire: Big turrets, 240°; secondary turrets, 150°; casemates, 110°.
Height of guns above water: Bow and secondary turrets, 29 feet; after turret 22 feet.

Torpedo Notes.—1904 model torpedo.

Engineering Notes.—

General Notes.—Laid down at Lorient, 1902.   To be completed 1907.   Estimated cost £1,233,709.

(GAMBETTA CLASS—3 SHIPS.)

ON GAMBETTA (October, 1901), **JULES FERRY** (August, 1903), & **VICTOR HUGO** (March, 1904).
Displacement 12,416 tons. Complement 710.
Length (*waterline*), 476 feet. Beam, 71 feet. *Mean* draught, $26\frac{1}{4}$ feet.

s (M. '96) :
—7·6 inch, 45 cal. (A).
—6·4 inch, 45 cal. (C).
—3 pdr.
edo tubes (18 inch) :
submerged.
above water.

Armour (Krupp) :

$6\frac{3}{4}''$ Belt (amidships)	a
$3''$ Belt (ends)	ε
$6''$ Bulkhead (aft) ...	a
$2\frac{1}{2}''$ Deck (slopes) ...	
Protection to vitals	= aa
$8''$ Turrets	a
$8''$ Turret bases	a
$4''$ Casemates (4) ...	d
$5\frac{1}{2}''$ Small turrets ...	b
$8''$ Conning tower ...	a

(Total weight 3800 tons).

ead :
7·6 in.
6·4 in.

Astern :
2—7·6 in.
6—6·4 in.

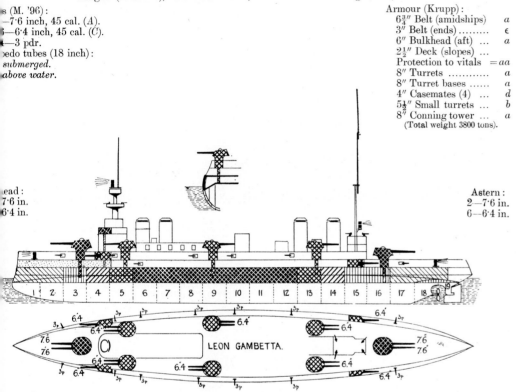

LEON GAMBETTA.

Broadside : 4—7·6 in., 8—6·4 in.

LÉON GAMBETTA.　　　　　*Photo, Symonds.*

Machinery : 3 sets vertical 4 cylinder triple expansion. 3 screws. Boilers : Belleville and Niclausse.
Designed H.P. 27,500 = 22 kts. Coal : *normal* 1320 tons ; *maximum* 2100 tons and oil.
Armour Notes.—Belt is $12\frac{1}{4}$ feet wide, $4\frac{3}{4}$ feet of it below waterline ; upper and lower edges amidships $5''$ thick. There is $1\frac{1}{4}''$ main deck.
Gunnery Notes.—Loading positions, big guns : all round. Hoists, electric all guns. All guns manœuvred electrically and by hand. Very clear gun decks.
Arcs of fire : Big turrets, 250° ; Secondary turrets, 160° ; Casemates, 110°.
Height of guns above water : Bow and secondary turrets, 29 feet ; after turret, 22 feet.
Torpedo Notes.—*Victor Hugo* 1904 model torpedoes.
Engineering Notes.—Engines and boilers weigh 1808 tons.

Name.	Built at	Engines by	Laid down	Completed			Boilers	
on Gambetta	Brest	St. Nazaire	Jan., '01	1903	...	...	Niclausse	...
les Ferry	Cherbourg	Indret	Oct., '01	1906	...	...	Belleville	...
ctor Hugo	Lorient	Indret	April, '03	1906	...	...	Belleville	...

General Notes.—Cost : *Gambetta*, £1,177,667 ; *J. Ferry*, £1,155,915 ; *V. Hugo*, £1,209,487.

161　　x

(AUBE CLASS.—4 SHIPS).

GLOIRE (June, 1900), **MARSEILLAISE** (July, 1900), **CONDÉ** (March, 1902), & **AMIRAL AUBE** (May, 1902).

Displacement 10,000 tons.

Length (*waterline*), 452¾ feet. Beam, 63½ feet. *Maximum* draught, 26½ feet. Length over all, 460 feet.

Guns (M. '96):
- 2—7·6 inch, 40 cal. (*A*)
- 8—6·4 inch. 45 cal. (*C*)
- 6—4 inch (*E*).
- 18—3 pdr.
- 2 boat guns, 9 pdr.

Torpedo tubes (18 in.)
- 2 *submerged* (section 7)
- 2 *above water* (section 3)
- 1 *above water* (stern).

Armour (Krupp):
6¾″ Belt (amidships)	*a*
4″ Belt (ends)	*d*
4″ Bulkheads	*d*
2½″ Deck (slopes) ...	
Protection to vitals	=*aa*
8″ Turrets (N.C.)	*a*
4″ Turret bases	*d*
5″ Lower deck side	*b*
2¼″ Bow	*e*
4¾″ Casemates (4) ...	*c*
4¾″ Small turrets (4)	*c*
3¾″ Bases to these ...	*d*
8″ Conning tower ...	*a*

(Total *about* 2300 tons).

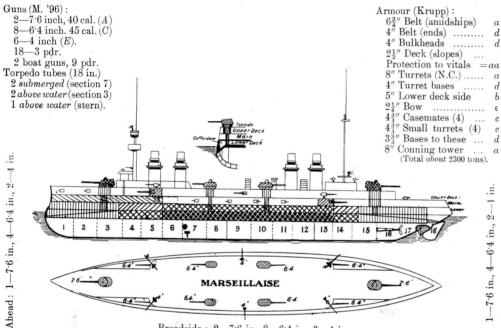

Ahead: 1—7·6 in., 4—6·4 in., 2—4 in.

Astern: 1—7·6 in., 4—6·4 in., 2—4 in.

MARSEILLAISE

Broadside: 2—7·6 in., 8—6·4 in., 3—4 in.

Machinery: 3 sets vertical triple expansion. 3 screws. Boilers: Belleville and Niclausse. Designed H.P. 20,500 = 21 knots. Coal: *normal* 970 tons; *maximum* 1590 tons.

Armour Notes.—Belt is 6½ feet wide, 3¼ feet of it below waterline. Lower edge amidships is 3¼″ thick.

Gunnery Notes.—Loading positions, big guns: all round. Hoists, electric all guns. Big guns manœuvred electrically and hand. All machinery inside hoists.

Arcs of fire: 7·6 in. about 250°; Secondary turrets 150°; Casemates 110°.

Engineering Notes :—

Name.	Built at	Engines, &c.	Laid down.	Completed.	24 hours at 10,000.	3 hours full power.	Boilers.	Last recorded full speed.
Gloire	Lorient	Lorient	Sept., '99	1904	10,788= ...	... =21·58	Niclausse	21·3
Marseillaise	Brest	Ch. d. la Loire	Jan., '00	1903	10,658=18·5	21,820=21·64	Belleville	21·6
Condé	Lorient	Lorient	March, '01	1904	10,500= ...	22,175=21·35	Niclausse	21·7
A. Aube	St. Nazaire	St. Nazaire	Aug., '00	1904	10,800=18·6	22,258=21·87	Belleville	22

Coal consumption : Belleville ships at 10,000 H.P. (18—18·5 kts.), about 7⅓ tons an hour ; at 20,500 H.P. 16¼ tons. Niclausse ships a little more, but not much. *Aube* on trials burned only 1·29 lbs. per I.H.P., at 10,000 H.P. All these ships steam well.

General Notes.—Cost on the average £875,000 per ship. A fifth ship (*Sully*) lost February, 1905.

Photo, Bougault.

Differences :—

Name.		Notes.
Marseillaise	Large ventilators between funnels	
Gloire	Triatic wireless cable high up	Steam pipes abaft first two funnels
Condé	Triatic wireless just above tops	Steam pipes abaft first two funnels
A. Aube	Main topmast before instead of abaft	

(See Montcalm class.)

(MONTCALM CLASS—3 SHIPS).

GUEYDON (September, 1899), **MONTCALM** (March 1900), **DUPETIT THOUARS** (July, 1901).

Displacement 9517 tons.   Complement 612.

Length (*waterline*), $452\frac{3}{4}$ feet.   Beam, $63\frac{2}{3}$ feet.   *Mean* draught, $24\frac{1}{2}$ feet.   Length over all, 460 feet.

Guns :
2—7·6 inch, M. '93 (B).
8—6·4 inch, M. '91 (D).
4—4 inch (F).
16—3 pdr.
Torpedo tubes (18 inch)
  2 submerged.

Armour (Harvey Nickel) :
$6\frac{3}{4}''$ Belt (amidships)	...	a
4″ Belt (ends)		d
3″ Forecastle		ϵ
2″ Deck (on slopes)		
Protection to vitals		=aa
$3\frac{3}{4}''$—$2\frac{1}{4}''$ Lower deck side		d-ϵ
8″ Turrets		a
5″ Turret bases		d
4″ Casemates (8)		d
6″ Conning tower		b

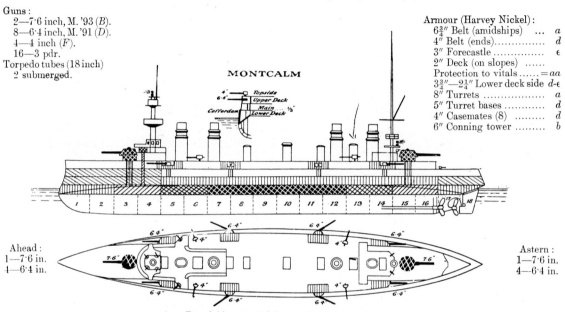

MONTCALM

Ahead :
1—7·6 in.
4—6·4 in.

Astern :
1—7·6 in.
4—6·4 in.

Broadside : 2—7·6 in., 4—6·4 in., 2—4 in.

MONTCALM.   *Photo, Bar.*

Machinery : 3 sets vertical triple expansion. 3 screws. Boilers : various (*see notes*). Designed H.P. 19,600 = 21 kts.
Coal : *normal* 1,000 tons ; *maximum* 1,600 tons, including oil.

Armour Notes : Belt is $7\frac{1}{2}$ feet wide ; $4\frac{1}{2}$ feet of it below waterline.

Gunnery Notes : Loading positions big guns : all round. Hoists : electric, all guns. Big guns manœuvred : electrically and by hand. All machinery inside hoists.

  Arcs of fire : Big guns, 240° ; Casemates, 120°.

  Ammunition carried : 7·6 in., 100 rounds per gun ; 6·4 in., 200 per gun ; 4 in., 250 per gun.

Name	Built at	Laid down	Completed	24 hours at 10,000	3 hours full power.	Boilers.	Best speed recently recorded.
Gueydon	Lorient	May, '97	1902	... =	19,664 = 20·3	Niclausse	20·9
Montcalm	La Seyne	Jan., '98	1902	... =	... = 21	Normand	21·1
D. Thouars	Toulon	April, '99	1903	10,977 = 17·92	20,382 = 21·38	Belleville	21·3

  Coal consumption : On trial *D. Thouars* burned the record consumption of only 1·21 lbs. per I.H.P. at full power. In service, all are economical ships, and *D. Thouars* (1904), for all purposes burned about $5\frac{3}{4}$ tons an hour at 10,000 H.P., and $11\frac{1}{2}$ tons at 19,600 H.P. (21 kts.), but average for the class is higher than this.

General Notes : Cost per ship averaged about £875,000.

Differences.	Steampipes. First 2 funnels.	Mainmast.	'Collerettes,' to funnels	Notes.
Gueydon	2 very prominent abaft	Topmast	Conspicuous	
Montcalm	...	High pole		
D. Thouars	...	Topmast	Conspicuous	

Class distinctions : These ships at sea cannot well be distinguished from *Aube* class ; there are distinctions, but it is difficult to pick them up. Note that *Aube* class have a thicker foremast.

  All the *Aubes* have turrets on the upper deck ; their funnels are a trifle larger, and hence look shorter. Tops on foremasts of the *Montcalms* are a little further apart than in the *Aube* class. (Compare also *Desaix* class).

x 2

JEANNE D'ARC (June, 1899).

Displacement 11,270 tons.   Complement 626.

Length (*waterline*), 475⅔ feet.   Beam, 70 feet.   *Maximum* draught, 27 feet.

Guns :
  2—7·6 inch, 45 cal. (*A*).
  14—5·5 inch, 45 cal. (*E*).
  12—3 pdr.
  8—1 pdr.
Torpedo tubes (18 inch) :
  2 *submerged*.

Armour (Harvey model) :
  6″ Belt (amidships) .... *b*
  4″ Belt (bow) .... *d*
  3″ Belt (aft) .... *ε*
  2¼″ Deck (on slopes) ....
  Protection to vitals .... *a*
  7¾″ Turrets .... *a*
  4″ Turret bases .... *d*
  3″ Lower deck (side and bow) *ε*
  5″ Casemates (8) .... *c*
  6″ Conning tower .... *b*
    (Total weight 2500 tons).

Photo, Bar.

Ahead :
  1—7·6 in.
  6—5·5 in.

Astern :
  1—7·6 in.
  6—5·5 in.

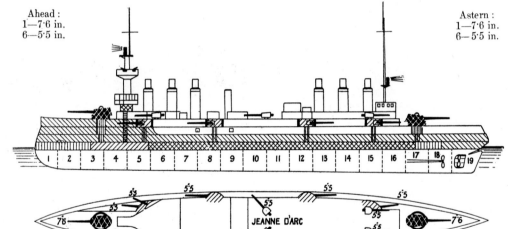

Broadside : 2—7·6 in. 7—5·5 in.

Machinery : 3 sets vertical inverted triple expansion. 3 screws. Boilers : Du Temple (small tube).
Designed H.P. 28,500 = 23 kts. Coal : *normal* 1400 tons ; *maximum* 2100 tons and liquid fuel.

Armour Notes—Belt is 7¼ feet wide ; 5 feet of it below waterline ; lower edge is 4″ thick.

Gunnery Notes—Loading positions, big guns : all round. Balanced turrets. Hoists : electric for all guns
  (separate). Big guns manœuvred electrically. Hoists pass through engine rooms.
  Arcs of fire : Big guns 270°.
  Height of guns above water : bow turret, 29 feet ; after turret *about* 21 feet.

Engineering Notes—Can only make her speed with great difficulty—great trouble on trials. Lines of ship
  are bad. Coal consumption : about 27 tons an hour at full power (28,500 H.P.)

General Notes—Laid down at Toulon, October, 1896. Completed 1903. Cost : over £900,000 spent on her
  before completion.

Stern.

Bow.

DUPLEIX (April, 1900), **DESAIX** (March, 1901), & **KLÈBER** (September, 1902).

Displacement 7,700 tons.

Length (*waterline*), 426½ feet.　Beam, 58½ feet.　*Mean* draught, 24¼ feet.

Guns—(M. '96):
　8 —6·4 inch, 45 cal. (*C*)
　4—4 inch (*E*).
　10—3 pdr.
Torpedo tubes (18 in.):
　2 *above water*
　　　(section 3).

Armour (Krupp):
　4″ Belt (amidships) *d*
　3¼″ Belt (bow) ...... *e*
　2¾″ Armour deck...
　Protection to vitals *b*
　4″ Turrets..:......... *d*
　4″ Turret bases ... *d*
　6″ Conning tower *b*
　(Total weight 1300 tons).

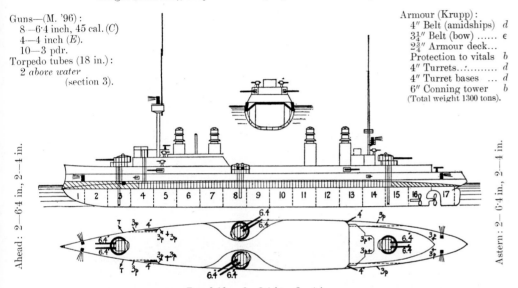

Ahead: 2—6·4 in., 2—4 in.

Astern: 2—6·4 in., 2—4 in.

Broadside: 6—6·4 in., 2—4 in..

DUPLEIX.　　　　　　　　　Photo, Bougault.

Machinery: 3 sets 3 cylinder vertical triple expansion.　3 screws.　Boilers: 20 Belleville or Niclausse.
Designed H.P. 17,000 = 21 knots.　Coal: *normal* 880 tons; *maximum* 1200 tons, *including oil*.

Armour Notes—Belt is 7¼ feet wide by 330 feet long; 3¼ feet of it below waterline.

Gunnery Notes—Loading positions: all round.　Hoists, electric.　Turrets electrically manœuvred.　All
　machinery inside hoists.
　Arcs of fire: Bow and stern turrets 270°; Amidship turrets 135°.
　Ammunition carried: 200 rounds per 6·4 in.

Engineering Notes :—

Name.	Built at	Laid down.	Completed.	24 hours at 10,000.	3 hours at 17,000.	Boilers.	Best recent speed.
Dupleix	Rochefort	1899	1903	10,022 = 18·5	17,715 = 20·9	Belleville	21·35
Desaix	St. Nazaire	1899	1904	10,196 = 18·6	17,979 = 20·61	Belleville	21·1
Kleber	Bordeaux	1899	1903	10,310 = 18·9	17,730 = 21·25	Niclausse	21·27

All burn a good deal of coal,

General Notes—Cost about £750,000 each,

Differences :—

Name.	Steam pipes:—		Notes.
	first funnel.	second funnel.	
Dupleix	Portside and before	Port and starboard	Fore top gallant mast
Desaix	Only portside	Port side only	No afterbridge.　Top low on main
Klèber	Big between 1 and 2 funnels.		Topmast well abaft fore top, main top gallant

D'ENTRECASTEAUX (June, 1896).

Displacement 8,114 tons.   Complement 521.

Length (*waterline*), 393½ feet.   Beam, 58½ feet.   *Maximum* draught, 26 feet.

Guns—(M. '92):
   2—9·4 inch, 40 cal. (*A*).
   12—5·5 inch, 45 cal. (*E*).
   12—3 pdr.
   4 Maxims.
Torpedo tubes (18 inch):
   2 *submerged*.
   4 *above water*.

Armour (Harvey):
   3¼″ Armour deck .... =c
   Protection to vitals ...... =c
   8″ Turrets .... b
   4″ Turret bases .... d
   3″ Casemates (8) .... ϵ
   10″ Conning tower ...... a
   (Total weight: 644 tons).

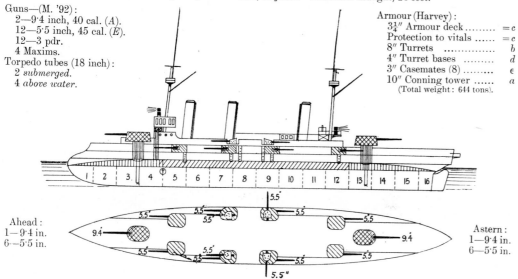

Ahead:
1—9·4 in.
6—5·5 in.

Astern:
1—9·4 in.
6—5·5 in.

Broadside: 2—9·4 in., 6—5·5 in.

Photo, Bar.

Machinery: 2 sets triple expansion.   2 screws.   Boilers: Cylindrical (5 double ended).   Designed H.P. 13,500 = 19·5 kts.   Coal: *normal*, 650 tons; *maximum*, 1,000 tons.   *Also* oil.

Gunnery Notes.—Electric hoists to each gun.   Big gun turrets, electrically manœuvred.
   Ammunition carried: 9·4 in., 75 rounds; 5·5 in., 200 rounds per gun.

Engineering Notes.—The ship has never made her designed speed—19·2 being her *maximum* on a 4 hours trial, and her present speed is not over 18 knots, if as much.   Coal consumption: about 15½ tons an hour, at 13,500 H.P. and *pro rata*.

General Notes.—Laid down at La Seyne, June, 1894, and completed 1898.   Cost, about £670,000.

Photo, Le Yacht.

DUPUY DE LÔME (October, 1890).

Displacement 6400 tons. Complement 521.
Length (*waterline*), 374 feet. Beam, 51½ feet. *Maximum* draught, 26⅙ feet.

Guns (M. '87) :
2—7·6 inch (*B*).
6—6·4 inch (*E*).
6—9 pdr.
8—3 pdr.
Torpedo tubes (17·7 in) :
4 *above water*
(behind armour).

Armour (steel) :
4¾″ Belt (amidships)... = *c-d*
Belt ends ....
2½″ Deck (slopes)........
Protection to vitals ...... = *b*
4″ Turrets................ ε
4″ Turret bases .... ε
4″ Secondary turrets .... ε
4¾″ Conning tower ...... *d*
(Total weight *about* 1400 tons).

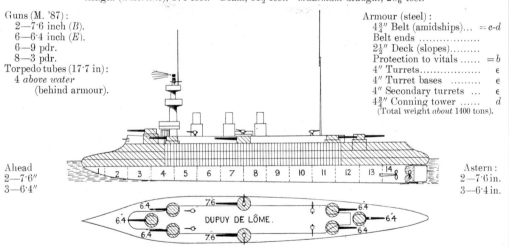

Ahead :
2—7·6″
3—6·4″

Astern :
2—7·6 in.
3—6·4 in.

Broadside : 1—7·6 in., 4—6·4 in.

Machinery : Being re-engined. 3 screws. Boilers : (1904) Normand Sigaudy. Designed H.P. new = 22 kts.
Armour Notes—Belt is 17½ feet wide, 4½ feet of it below waterline. Cellulose belt at waterline.
Gunnery Notes—All guns manœuvred hydraulically and hand.
Arcs of fire : 7·6 in., 180° ; bow and stern 6·4 in., 200° ; other 6 in., 150°.
Ammunition carried : 160 rounds per 7·6 in. gun ; 200 per 6·4 in.
Engineering Notes—Being re-engined. Original designed speed 20 kts., which she could easily reach.
General Notes—Laid down at Brest in 1889. Completed in 1893. Cost £416,000.

Photo, W. Nye, Esq.

POTHUAU (1895).

Displacement 5,360 tons. Complement 463.

Length (*waterline*), 370¾ feet. Beam, 50 feet. *Maximum* draught, 22½ feet.

Guns :
2—7·6 inch (*B*).
10—5·5 inch (*E*).
10—3 pdr.
Torpedo tubes :
4 *above water*.

Armour (*acier special durci*) :
2⅜″ Belt (amidships) ...... ε
1¼″ Belt (ends) .... *f*
3⅜″ Deck (reinforcing belt)
Protection to vitals ...... = *c*
7″ Turrets .... *b*
3″ Hoists to these .... ε
2″ Casemates .... *f*
2″ Hoists to these .... *f*
9½″ Conning tower ...... *aa*

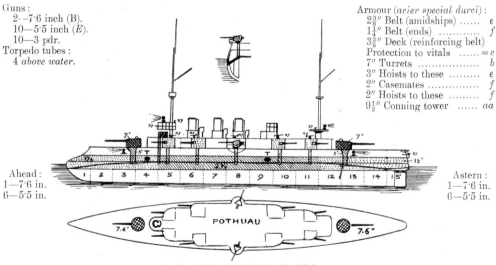

Ahead :
1—7·6 in.
6—5·5 in.

Astern :
1—7·6 in.
6—5·5 in.

Broadside : 2—7·6 in., 5—5·5 in.

Machinery : 2 sets horizontal triple expansion. 2 screws. Boilers : 16 Belleville (old type). Designed H.P. 10,000 = 19 kts. Coal : *normal* 538 tons ; *maximum* 638 tons.
On first *Trials*, I.H.P. 10,200 = 19·2 kts. She can still touch 19 knots.
Notes—The belt is carried up to the main deck, and the ship is generally a reduced copy of the *Dupuy de Lôme*, or an enlarged *Charner*. All guns have electric appliances, and the machinery of all is entirely protected by the turrets and hoists. The ship is a good sea boat. Laid down at Graville, 1893. Completed, 1896. Cost £384,000.

(CHARNER CLASS—4 SHIPS).

LATOUCHE TRÉVILLE (October, 1892), **AMIRAL CHARNER** (March, 1893), **CHANZY** (January, 1894), and **BRUIX** (August, 1894).

Displacement 4750 tons.   Complement 370.

Length (*waterline*), 361 feet.   Beam, 46 feet.   *Maximum* draught, 19¾ feet.

Guns (M. '87).
2—7·6 inch, 45 cal. (*B*).
6—5·5 inch, 45 cal. (*E*).
6—9 pdr.
4—3 pdr.
Torpedo tubes (17·7 inch).
   4 above water.

Armour (Creusot steel).
3⅝″ Belt (amidships)... ϵ
2¾″ Belt (ends) .... *f*
3″ Deck (slopes)
   Protection to vitals... = *c*
4″ Turrets .... ϵ
4¼″ Turret bases......... ϵ
4″ Secondary turrets ... ϵ
3⅝″ Conning tower ... ϵ
   (Total *about* 850 tons).

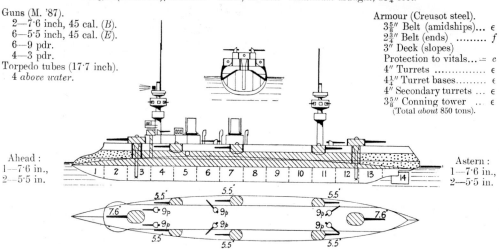

Ahead :
1—7·6 in.,
2—5·5 in.

Astern :
1—7·6 in.,
2—5·5 in.

Broadside : 2—7·6 in., 3—5·5 in.

CHANZY.   *Photo, Symonds.*

Machinery : 2 sets horizontal triple expansion.   2 screws.   Boilers : Belleville *without* economisers. Designed H.P. 8300 = 18·5 kts.   Coal : *normal* 406 tons.

Armour Notes.—Belt is 12 feet wide, 4 feet of it below waterline ; lower edge is 2″ thick ; cofferdam at waterline.

Gunnery Notes.—Big guns manœuvred, electrically in *L. Treville* ; hydraulic in others.
   Arcs of fire : 7·6 in., 270° ; 5·5 in., 150°.
   Ammunition carried : 7·6 in., 106 per gun ; 5·5 in., 200 **per gun.**

Engineering Notes.—

Name.	Built at	Laid down.	Completed.	First trials.	Boilers.	Best recorded present speed.
L. Treville	Havre	1890	1893	8310 = 18·1		18·4
A. Charner	Rochefort	1889	1895	9148 = 18·4	In all	...
Chanzy	Bordeaux	1890	1896	8537 = 17·8	Belleville (Old type)	...
Bruix	Rochefort	1891	1896	8800 = 19·0		18·9

Coal consumption high.   *Bruix* steams excellently ; others passably only.   Ships getting worn out.

General Notes.—Cost about £350,000 per ship.

Differences.—Only in rig and these alter continually.   *Bruix* has a very high foretopmast, but the others have topgallants and so look much like her.

CHATEAURENAULT (May, 1898).

Displacement 8018 tons.   Complement 600.

Length (*waterline*), 443 feet.   Beam, 56 feet.   *Mean* draught, 22½ feet.   Length over all, 457 feet.

Guns—(M. '91):
  2—6.4 inch, 45 cal. (D).
  6—5.5 inch, 45 cal. (E).
  10—3 pdrs.
Torpedo Tubes :
  None.

Armour :
  3″ deck ....= d
  [cellulose belt.]
  1½″ Casemates ...f

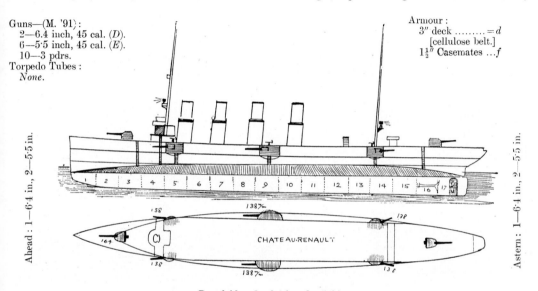

Ahead : 1—6.4 in., 2—5.5 in.

Astern: 1—6.4 in., 2—5.5 in.

Broadside : 3—6.4 in., 2—5.5 in.

Machinery : Vertical triple expansion. 3 screws. Boilers : Niclausse. Designed H.P. 23,000 = 23 kts. Coal : *normal* 1400 + liquid fuel ; *maximum* 2100 tons.

Engineering Notes.—*Chateaurenault* is an excellent steamer, far better than *Guichen*. Burns a good deal of coal.

Trials (1900-01): 24 hours, 108 revolutions, I.H.P. 14,000 = 21 kts.
  2 ,, 120 ,, ,, 18,000 = 22·69 kts.
  8 ,, ? ,, ,, 23,500 = 24·1 kts.
  1 ,, ,, ,, 24,964 = 24·545 kts.

General Notes.—Laid down at La Seyne, May, 1896. Completed 1902. Cost about £610,000.

Photo, Bar.

Note.—This ship was designed for commerce destruction, and to be mistaken by her victims as an Atlantic liner. There is, however, no liner to which she bears any particular resemblance. The forecastle gun is generally very obvious : the funnels are characteristic and the absence of promenade decks noticeable. She can, however, be mistaken for a "liner unknown" at about 6 miles off.

GUICHEN (May, 1898).

Displacement 8,277 tons (sheathed). Complement 625.

Length (*waterline*), 436⅓ feet; Beam, 55 feet; *Maximum* draught, 27 feet.

Guns—(M. '91):
2—6·4 inch, 45 cal. (*D*).
6—5·5 inch, 45 cal. (*E*).
10—3 pdr.
5—1 pdr.
Torpedo tubes:
2 *above water*.

Armour (Harveyed):
2½″ Deck .... = *d*
[Cellulose belt].
Protection to vitals ... = *d*
1½″ Casemates .... *c*
2″ Gun shields ....
6¼″ Conning tower (fore) *c*

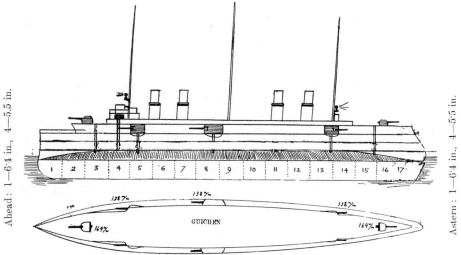

Ahead: 1—6·4 in., 4—5·5 in.

Astern: 1—6·4 in., 4—5·5 in.

Broadside: 2—6·4 in., 3—5·5 in.

Machinery: 3 sets 4 cylinder triple expansion. 3 screws. Boilers: 36 Lagrafel d'Allest. Designed H.P. 24,000 = 23 kts. Coal: *normal* 1,460 tons; *maximum* 2,000 tons and liquid fuel.

Notes.—The *Guichen*, like the *Chateau-Renault*, is primarily a commerce destroyer, and carries a very small armament for her size. The armour deck rises amidships to 4½ feet above the waterline.

On *trial* she made:

24 hours *natural* draught I.H.P. 18,500 = 20 knots.
4 ,, *forced* draught I.H.P. 25,455 = 23·55 knots.

Originally *Guichen* had but two masts—the third (a main) was added in 1900 to facilitate coaling operations. It is designed to carry a couple of Temperley transporters.

Laid down at St. Nazaire, 1895. Completed 1902. Cost about £650,000.

Photo, Bar.

Note.—Has now an extra yard on each mast just above the one shown on photo.

JURIEN DE LA GRAVÌERE (July, 1899).

Displacement 5685 tons.   Complement 511.

Length (*waterline*), 440 feet.   Beam, 48⅔ feet.   *Mean* draught, 22 feet.

Guns :
  8—6·4, 45 cal. (*C*).
  10—3 pdr.
Torpedo tubes :
  2 *above water.*

Armour (Harvey Nickel) :
  3″ Deck.................... = *e*
  (Cellulose belt).
  6½″ Conning tower ...... *a*

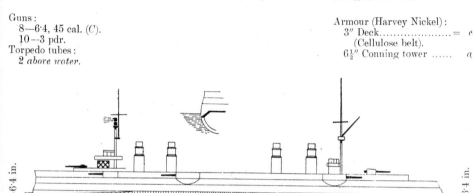

Broadside : 5—6·4 in.

JURIEN DE LA GRAVÌERE.   *Photo, Kuhn.*

Distinctions.—Differs in appearance from *Montcalm* and *Aube* classes in foremast, and generally smaller look. Lower in the water.

Machinery : 3 sets vertical triple expansion.   3 screws.   Boilers : Guyot.   Designed H.P. *full power* 17,000 = 23 kts. (not yet made).   Coal : *normal* 600 tons ; *maximum* 900 tons.

Engineering Notes.—No trial yet has produced more than 14,000 H.P. = 21·7 kts., and it is doubtful whether she can keep up 21 kts. for an hour or less.   She is a complete failure in steaming.

Laid down at Lorient, Nov., 1897.   Completed 1901   Cost about £476,000.

(DESCARTES CLASS—4 SHIPS).

DESCARTES (September, 1894), **PASCAL** (September, 1895),

Length (*waterline*), 316 feet. Beam, $42\frac{1}{3}$ feet.

CATINAT (October, 1896), & **PROTET** (July, 1898).

Displacement *about* 4000 tons. Complement 378.

Length (*waterline*), 332 feet. Beam, $44\frac{1}{2}$ feet. *Maximum* draught, $21\frac{1}{4}$ feet.

Guns—(M. '93) :
4—6·4 inch, 45 cal. (*D*).
10—4 inch (*E*).
10—3 pdr.
4—1 pdr.
Torpedo tubes (17·7 in.) :
  2 *above water* (section 8).

Armour (steel) :
  2″ Armour deck ......= ϵ
  Protection to vitals ...= ϵ
  2″ Casemates (to 6·4)   *f*
  ″ Conning tower......

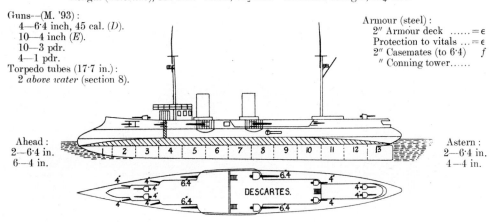

Ahead :
2—6·4 in.
6—4 in.

Astern :
2—6·4 in.
4—4 in.

Broadside ; 2—6·4 in., 5—4 in.

Machinery : 2 sets vertical triple expansion. 2 screws. Boilers : 16 Bellevilles *without* economisers. Designed H.P. 8500 = 19·5 kts. Coal : *normal* 550 tons ; *maximum* 750 tons.

Arcs of fire : 6·4 in., 110° from axial line ; 4 in. about the same.

Ammunition carried : 6·4 in., 200 rounds per gun ; 4 in., 250 rounds per gun.

Name.	Built at	Laid down	Completed.	24 hours at 5500.	4 hours full.	Boilers.	Present best speed.
Descartes	St. Nazaire	Jan. '93	1896	5802 = 17·5	8870 = 19·6*		...
Pascal	Toulon	Dec. '93	1897	6170 = 17·5	8720 = 19·7	Old type	...
Catinat	Granville	Nov. '94	1897	6455 = 17·5	9936 = 19·6	Belleville in all.	19·8
Protet	Bordeaux	Sept. '95	1900	... = ...	9304 = 20·2		20·0

* For 24 hours instead of 4 hours.

Coal consumption : about $4\frac{3}{4}$ tons an hour at 5500 H.P., and 8 tons an hour at full power.

General Notes—Cost about £350,000 per ship.

Differences :

Name.	Funnels.	Steam pipes	Notes.
Descartes	Casings $\frac{4}{5}$ way up	Very conspicuous	
Pascal		Hardly show	No rake
Catinat	Slighter	Do not show	Small bridge
Protet	Higher. Covers	Short ; conspicuous	Small bridge

(Friant Class—5 Ships.)

DU CHAYLA (November, 1895), **D'ASSAS** (March, 1896), & **CASSARD** (May, 1896).

Displacement 4,000 tons.   Complement 393.

Length (*waterline*), 325½ feet.   Beam, 45 feet.   *Maximum* draught, 23 feet.

FRIANT (April, 1893), & **CHASSELOUP-LAUBAT** (April, 1893).

Displacement 3,772 tons.   Complement 358.

Length, 308 feet.   Beam, 43 feet.   *Maximum* draught, 22 feet.

Guns—(M. '91) :
 6—6·4 inch. (*D*)
 4—4 inch. (*E*)
 4—3 pdr.
 11—1 pdr.
Torpedo tubes :
 2 *above water*.

Armour :
 3" Deck....................*d*
 [Cellulose belt.]
 2" Sponsons to 6·4 in.
  guns.

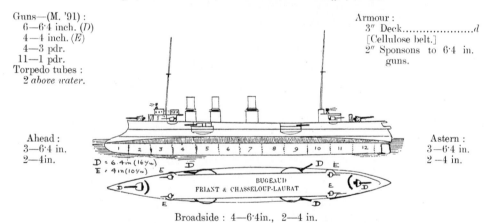

Ahead :
3—6·4 in.
2—4in.

Astern :
3—6·4 in.
2—4 in.

Broadside : 4—6·4in., 2—4 in.

Machinery : 2 sets vertical triple expansion.   2 screws.   Boilers : various (*see notes*).   Designed H.P. 9500 = 19 kts.   Coal: *normal*   ; *maximum* (*first 3*), 624 tons; (*others*), 587 tons.

Name.	Built at	Laid Down.	Completed	4 hrs. full p.	Boilers.	Present best speed.
Du Chayla	Cherbourg	March, '93	1897	10,009 = 20·2	L. d'Allest	17·8
D'Assas	St. Nazaire	January, '95	1898	9,500 = 19·8	L. d'Allest	—
Cassard	Cherbourg	October, '93	1898	10,143 = 19·8	L. d'Allest	17·0
Friant	Brest	December, '91	1894	— = 18·1	Niclausse	17·6
C. Laubat	Cherbourg	October, '91	1894	9,678 = 19·2	L. d'Allest	18·3

Differences :

Name.	Foremast.	Mainmast.	Steam pipes:— 1st funn.	2nd funn.	3rd funn.	Notes.
Du Chayla Cassard	Topmast	Pole	1 before	2 before	1 before.	Searchlight low on foremast.
Friant	Pole	Pole	1 before	1 before	2 before	Bridge abaft foremast. Big afterbridge.
D'Assas	Pole	Pole	1 abaft	4 round fun.	before abaft	Bridge abaft. Big ventilator before mainmast. No afterbridge.
C. Laubat	Topmast	Topmast	1 abaft	2 high before	1 abaft	Chart house abaft foremast.

Coal consumption : All are very economical.

General Notes. In all the ventilation is defective, and they are very unhealthy in hot climates. Stability poor, and some have had to have sand as ballast in the double bottom. Cost about £300,000 per ship. A sixth ship, *Bugeaud*, sold out of service. The others likely to go soon.

DAVOUT (November, 1889).
Displacement 3027 tons. Complement 336.
Length (*waterline*), 289 feet. Beam, 40 feet. *Maximum* draught, 20½ feet.

Guns—(M. '84) :
6—6·4 inch, 30 cal. (F).
4—9 pdr.
8—3 pdr.
Torpedo tubes :
4 *above water*.

Armour :
3¼″ Deck ....= d
[Cellulose belt.]
1½″ Conning tower ......f

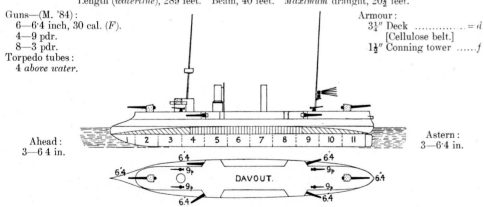

Ahead :
3—6·4 in.

Astern :
3—6·4 in.

Broadside : 4—6·4 in.

Machinery : 2 horizontal triple expansion. 2 screws. Boilers : (1901) Niclausse. Designed H.P. 9000 = 20·5 kts.

Notes.—Laid down at Toulon, March, 1887. Partially reconstructed 1901. Steams moderately well (last record 18·4 kts.) but has little—if any—fighting value. Original cost, £222,000. A larger sister (*Suchet*) sold out of service.

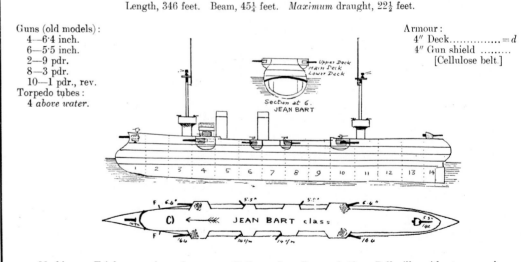

ALGER (1889), JEAN BART (1889), & ISLY (1891).
Displacement 4200 tons. Complement 407.

Length, 346 feet. Beam, 45¼ feet. *Maximum* draught, 22½ feet.

Guns (old models) :
4—6·4 inch.
6—5·5 inch.
2—9 pdr.
8—3 pdr.
10—1 pdr., rev.
Torpedo tubes :
4 *above water*.

Armour :
4″ Deck...............= d
4″ Gun shield ....
[Cellulose belt.]

Machinery : Triple expansion. 2 screws. Boilers : *Jean Bart* and *Alger*, Belleville, without economisers ; *Isly*, cylindrical. Designed H.P. 8000 = 19 kts. The *Jean Bart* after re-boilering, 1892, made I.H.P 8127 = 19·6 kts., and the other two are passable steamers, though of no fighting value worth mention.

FOUDRE (October, 1895).

Displacement 6,086 tons.   Complement 410.

Length, 374½ feet.   Beam, 51¾ feet.   *Maximum* draught, 25 feet.

Guns :
  8—4 in., 45 cal.
  4—9 pdr.
  5—1 pdr.
Torpedo tubes :
  none.

Armour (steel) :
  3½″ Deck... = d

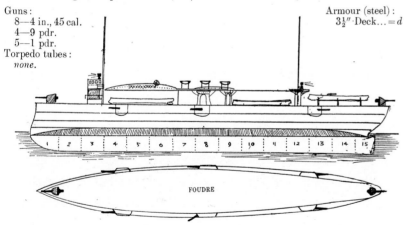

FOUDRE

Machinery : 2 sets triple expansion.   2 screws.   Boilers : 24 Lagrafel d'Allest.
Designed I.H.P. 8000 = 17 kts. ; *full power* 11,400 = 19·9 kts.   Coal : *normal* 845 tons ; *maximum* 1000 tons.

  Trials (1897) : I.H.P. 11,930 = 19·57 kts.

General Notes—Carries 8 torpedo boats and 4 torpedo launches.   Laid down at Bordeaux 1892.   Completed 1897.   Cost about £410,000.

D'Estrées. (Both alike.)   *Photo, M. Desrez.*

D'ESTRÉES (October, 1897) & **INFERNET** (September, 1899).

Displacement 2460 tons.   Complement 234.

Length (*waterline*), 312 feet.   Beam, 39⅓ feet.   *Mean* draught, 16 feet.

Guns—(M '93 and '91) :
  2—5·5 in., 45 cal. (E).
  4—4 in., 45 cal. (E).
  8—3 pdr.
Torpedo tubes :
  3 *above water.*

Armour (hard steel) :
  1½″ Deck............ = ε
  [Cellulose belt.]

Ahead :
  1—5·5 in.
  2—4 in.

Astern :
  1—5·5 in.
  2—4 in.

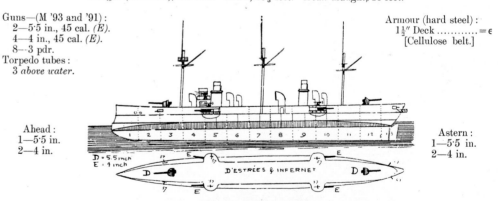

D = 5·5 inch
E = 4 inch

D'ESTRÉES & INFERNET

Broadside : 2—5·5 in., 2—4 in.

Machinery : 2 sets triple expansion.   2 screws.   Boilers : *D'Estrees*, Lagrafel D'Allest ; *Infernet*, Normand.   Designed H.P. 8500 = 21 kts.   Coal : *normal* 345 tons ; *maximum* 480 tons.

General Notes.—*D'Estrees* built at Rochefort ; *Infernet* at Bordeaux.   Cost about £210,000 per ship.

175

LINOIS (January, 1894), **GALILÉE** (April, 1896), & **LAVOISIER** (April, 1897).

Displacement *about* 2,350 tons. Complement 248.

Length (*waterline*), 330 feet. Beam, 34½ feet. *Maximum* draught, 19 feet.

Guns—(M. '91):
  4—5·5 inch, 45 cal. (*E*).
  2—4 inch, 45 cal. (*E*).
  8—3 pdr.
Torpedo tubes:
  2 *above water*.

Armour—(steel):
  1½″ Deck .... = *f*
  2″ Sponsons ......
  2″ Gun shields ...
  4″ Conning tower   *d*

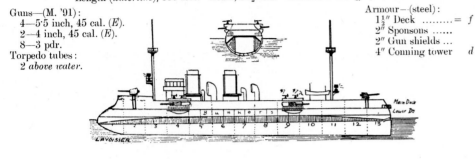

Ahead:
2—5·5 in.
1—4 in.

Astern:
2—5·5 in.
1—4 in.

Broadside: 2—5·5 in., 2—4 in.

Machinery: 2 sets vertical triple expansion. 2 screws. Boilers: Cylindrical and Belleville.
Designed H.P. 7,000 = 20 knots. Coal: *normal* 200 tons; *maximum* 380 tons.

Engineering Notes.—

Name.	Built at	Laid down	Completed	24 hours at 4,500.	4 hours full power.	Boilers.	Present best speed.
Linois	La Seyne	January, 1893	1895	=	6,600 =	Cylindrical	18·3
Lavoisier	Rochefort	December, 1893	1899	4560 = 18·6	7,400 = 21·5	Belleville	21·7
Galilée	Rochefort	December, 1893	,1897	=	6,900 = 20	Belleville	20

General Notes.—Linois originally built for Turkey, and purchased by France. Cost per ship, about £200,000.

LINOIS.

LAVOISIER (GALILÉE very similar).   *Photos, Bar.*

GALILÉE.

Differences.—

Name.	Rig.	Funnels.	Notes.
Linois	See photo	Big and high	Raised forecastle.
Lavoisier	See photo	Smaller	Searchlight on main.
Galilée	See photo	Smaller	Light on deck abaft main mast. Big ventilator abaft after funnel.

DUNOIS (*La Hire* identical).   *Photo. Bar.*

DUNOIS CLASS—2 SHIPS).

DUNOIS (1896), & LA HIRE (1898).

Displacement 900 tons. Complement 128.

Length, 256 feet. Beam, 28 feet. *Maximum* draught, 12¾ feet.

Guns :
6—9 pdr.
6—3 pdr.
Torpedo tubes :
Nil.

Armour :
Nil.

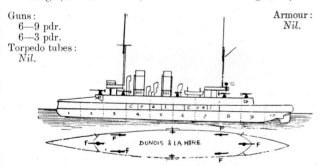

Machinery : 2 sets vertical triple expansion. 2 screws. Boilers : Normand. Designed H.P. 6400 = 23 kts. Coal : *normal* 137 tons.

Trials : Dunois (1898-1899) 4 hours, 7500 = 21·7 kts.
La Hire (1899) 4 ,, 7100 = 22·11 kts.

Notes.—These ships have never made the designed speed ; they are, however, always good for 20 kts.

D'IBERVILLE.   *Photo, J. Geiser.*

(*Casabianca* & *Cassini* have bigger funnels.)

(D'IBERVILLE CLASS— 3 SHIPS).

CASABIANCA (1895), & CASSINI (1894).

Displacement 960 tons. Complement 139.

Length, 269 feet. Beam, 27½ feet. *Maximum* draught, 12 feet.

Also **D'IBERVILLE** (1892).

Displacement 925 tons. Complement 140.

Length, 262½ feet. Beam 26¼ feet. *Maximum* draught, 11¾ feet.

Guns :
1—4 inch (bow)
3—9 pdr.
7—3 pdr.

Armour (steel) :
⅗″ Deck (amidships).
Cellulose belt.

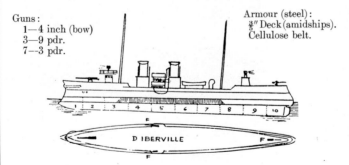

Machinery : 2 tandem triple expansion. 2 screws. Boilers : Lagrafel d'Allest. Designed H.P. 5000 = 21 kts. (21·5 in *D'Iberville*). Coal : *normal* 117 tons ; *maximum* 135 tons.

Notes.—On 4 hours trials each just exceeded designed H.P. and speed.

LÉVRIER.   *Photo, copyright, Geiser.*

(LEGER CLASS—2 SHIPS).

LÉGER (1891), & LÉVRIER (1891).

Displacement 444 tons. Complement 80.

Length, 197 feet. Beam, 23 feet. *Maximum* draught, 12 feet.

Guns :
1—9 pdr.
3—3 pdr.
Torpedo tubes :
3 *above water.*

Armour :
Nil.

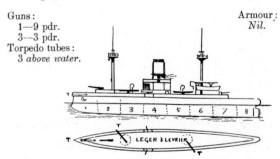

Machinery : 2 sets horizontal triple expansion. 2 screws. Boilers : Belleville. Designed H.P. *full power* 2200 = 18·5 kts. Coal : 130 tons.

Note.—Both slightly exceeded designed speed on trials.

OLD FRENCH "AVISOS."

(ALL FITTED FOR DROPPING BLOCKADE MINES).

LALANDE (all 3 identical).

COSMAO (1889), & LALANDE (1889), & TROUDE (1888).

Displacement 1877 tons.   Complement 220.

Guns: (old) 4—5·5 inch, 7—3 pdr., 7—1 pdr., 5 Torpedo tubes (14 inch).   1½″ deck amidships.   Designed H.P. *forced* 6300 = 20·5 kts. Present speed: Poor.   Coal: *maximum* 330 tons.

BOMBE *class.*

BOMBE, COULEUVRINE, DAGUE, FLÈCHE, SAINTE-BARBE (—1885), LANCE, SALVE (—1886), & DRAGONNE (1885).

Displacement 395 tons.   Complement 63.

Guns: 4—3 pdr., 3—1 pdr., 2 Torpedo tubes (14 inch).   Designed H.P. 2000 = 18 kts.   *Lance & Salve* had Normand boilers fitted 1899 and can still do about 17-16 kts.: the others are perfectly useless.

Dragonne used for experimental purposes has no foremast.

SURCOUF.

FORBIN & COËTLOGON.

SURCOUF (1889), COËTLOGON (1888, & FORBIN (1888).

Displacement 1932 tons.   Complement 210.

Guns: (old) 4—5·5 inch, 45 cal., 7—3 pdr., 4—1 pdr.   4 Torpedo tubes (14 inch).   Designed H.P. 6000 = 20 kts.   Present speeds about 15 kts.

VAUTOUR, CONDOR & FAUCON; *also (with topmasts)* ÉPERVIER.

WATTIGNIES & FLEURUS.

CONDOR (1885), ÉPERVIER, (1886), FAUCON (1887). VAUTOUR (1889).

Displacement 1240 tons.   Complement 134; also

WATTIGNIES (1891), & FLEURUS (1893).

Displacement 1310 tons.   Complement 175.

Guns: 5—4 inch, 6—3 pdr., 4—1 pdr.   5 Torpedo tubes (14 inch).   1½″ deck.   Designed H.P. 3500-4000 = 18-20 kts.   Present speeds very poor indeed.

37 of Model 1900.

French destroyers, except the ex-Chinese *Takou*, are all of a general type.

There are 37 boats (1900-1904) Normand and Forges et Chantiers build, of 303 tons average displacement with Normand boilers. Dimensions: $180 \times 21 \times 10$ feet. The average speed is 27 kts., but many of the more recent boats have made nearly 30 kts. on trial. Each may be relied on for at least 26 kts. in almost any weather. Two screws. About 38 tons of coal. Complement 45-48. Armament 1—9 pdr. forward, and 6—3 pdr. 2 Torpedo tubes (15 inch). Without gyros. One spare torpedo carried.

The chief peculiarity of this type of boat is the flying deck, which runs nearly all the length of the boat at a height of some 3 feet above the hull proper. The hull has a great tumble home, and is very strongly built. Tubes carried one between funnels and one right aft. The boats are excellent sea boats.

4 of Model 1905.
10 pro. for 1906.

Identical with above in general features but of 431 tons. Dimensions $190\frac{1}{2} \times 20\frac{1}{2} \times 9\frac{3}{4}$ feet. Armament as above except that tubes are 17·7 inch, and the 1904 model torpedo will be carried.

1 Schichau.

The *Takou* (ex-Chinese is 250 tons displacement, a trifle longer than the French boats and drawing about $9\frac{1}{2}$ feet *maximum*. Speed originally 32 kts. Armament 6—3 pdr. 2 Tubes (18 inch), one between funnels and one just abaft them. Schulz-Thornycroft boilers.

28 *Normand*:—**Arbelete, Arquebuse, Arc, Bélier, Baliste, Carabine, Carquois, Catapulte, Dard, Durandal, Escopette, Épieu, Flamberge, Fronde, Francisque, Hallebarde, Harpon, Javelaine, Mousqueton, Mousquet, Pistolet, Pertuisane, Rapière, Sagaie, Sarabacane, Sabre, Tromblou, Trident.**

Photo, Bar.

9 *Forges et Chantiers*:—**Coutelas, Claymore, Épée, Mortier, Obusier, Pierrier, Pique, Stylet** and **Yatagan.**

27 Torpilleurs de haute mer.

2 screws. 15 inch torpedoes.

All armed with 2—3 pdr. Boilers: Normand, Thornycroft, and Du Temple.

Totals.	Type.	Date.	Displacement.	I.H.P.	Max. Speed.	Coal.	Complement.	Tubes.	Max. Draught.
					kts.	tons.			feet.
6	*Audacieux*	1900-1	185	1200	26	25	18	3	9
6	*Forban*	'95 & '98	140	3200	31·2	15	...	2	7½
1	*Mangini*	1896	129	2100	27·5	17	34	2	7
1	*Chevalier*	1893	134	2700	27·2	17	32	2	7
1	*Corsaire*	1892	171	2500	25·2	15	32	2	5½
5	*Dragon*	'92-'93	129	1400	25·21	15½	26	2	8½
1	*Mousquetaire*	1893	150	2100	24·7	18	32	2	6½
6	*Argonaute*	'93-'99	120	2000	26·17	16	34	2	9½
2	*Veloce*	1890	133	1750	24	20	27	2	5
5	*Éclair*	1891	128	1100	21·5	17	26	2	7½

(The *Forban* (Normand type) all considerably exceeded 31 knots on *trial*).

Audacieux type are armoured with ¾″ steel amidships. Named **Audacieux, Mistral, Simoun, Sirocco Trombe, Typhon.**

Forban type named **Forban, Cyclone, Tramontane, Borée, Bourrasque, Rafale.**

Dragon type, **Dragon, Grenadier, Lancier, Turco, Zouave.**

Argonaute type, **Argonaute, Aquilon, Filibustier, Averne, Dauphin, Tourmente.**

Véloce type, **Véloce** and **Grondeur.**

OLD BOATS.

12 old torpilleurs de haute mer dating from 1887-1891, as follows:—

1 *Agile*—121 tons, originally 21½ knots. 1 *Coureur*—120 tons, originally 23 knots. 5 *Éclair*—128 tons, originally 21½ knots. 4 *Défi*—Originally 21 knots, and 1 *Archer*—130 tons, originally 20½ knots.

Haute-mer boats. AUDACIEUX type.

227 + 20 Torpilleurs de Defence Mobile (Armed with 2—1 pdrs. and 14 inch torpedoes).

Totals.	Numbers.	Begun.	Completed.	Displacement.	I.H.P.	Max. Speed.	Coal.	Complement.	Tubes.	Max. Draught.
				tons.		kts.	tons.			
20	389—370	'05	'07	} 97½	2000	26		23	3	10
52	369—318	'04	'06							
24	317—294	'03	'06	} 90	1800	24	10	23	2	9
30	293—264	'02	'04							
8	263—256	'03	'04							
20	255—236	'03	'04							
20	235—216	'99	'01	86	1500	23	10	23	2	9
4	215—212	'98	'99	88	1800	27	10	23	2	9
30	211—182	'94	—'98	84	1450	24	12	21	2	9
39	181—126	'89	—'93	84	1000	21	10	21	2	9

No. 293 has Parsons turbines, 294 Bréquet turbines.

"SECOND CLASS."

All armed with 2—1 pdr. and tubes (14 inch). Average draught, 7 feet.
74 boats with 2 tubes, *maximum* speeds under 20 knots, displacements from 66 to 12 tons.

Defence mobile boats.

Haute-mer boats.   *Photo, Bar.*

Forban. Very similar are *Chevalier, Mangini, Corsaire, Dragon* type, *Argonaute* type. The later *Forbans* have the funnels closer together forward.

FRENCH "SUBMERSIBLES" (Sea-going Submarines).

No. in Class.	Type and Designation.	Displacement, above and below.	Begun.	Completed.	Motive Power, above and below.	Surface H.P.	Max. Speed, above and below.	Length × Beam × Diameter in feet.	Draught when on surface.	Torpedo Tubes.	Actual endurance, above and below.	Complement.	First Submerges, in minutes.
1	*Narval* (Q 4)	$\frac{106}{200}$	1898	'00	Steam accumulators.	250	$\frac{12}{8}$	111½×12×	5⅓	4 slings	100 miles at 12 kts. 500 at 8 kts. / 6 hours, 30 miles at 5 kts.	13	18
2	*Triton* (Q 5-6)	$\frac{106}{200}$	1900	'02	Steam accumulators.	250	$\frac{12}{8}$	111½×12×9	5⅓	4 slings	ditto	12	9
2	*Silure* (Q 13-14)	$\frac{106}{200}$	1901	'03	Steam accumulators.	250	$\frac{12}{8}$	118×9¼×9¼	5⅓	1 tube	ditto	12	7
2	*Aigrette* (Q 38-39)	$\frac{172}{\quad}$	1903	'05	Steam accumulators.	200	$\frac{10·5}{8}$	118×12¾×	8⅓	1 tube	125 miles at 12 kts., 600 at 8 kts. / 8 hours.	20	4
1	*X* (Q 35)	$\frac{168}{\quad}$	1902	'05	Petrol 8 cylinder accumulators.	220	$\frac{10·5}{8}$	123×10×10	7½	2 tubes	400 miles *nominal* / ? hours	15	
1	*Z* (Q 36)	$\frac{202}{\quad}$	1902	'05	Paraffin accumulators.	190	$\frac{11}{8}$	136×10×10	7½	2 tubes	500 miles *nominal* / ? hours	20	
1	*Y* (Q 37)	$\frac{213}{\quad}$	1903	'05	Compressed air.	250	$\frac{11}{8}$	143⅔×9×10		2 tubes	400 miles *nominal* / ? hours	15	
1	*Omega* (Q 40)	$\frac{301}{375}$	1903	'05	Steam accumulators.	330	$\frac{11}{8}$	136×9×		2 tubes	600 miles *nominal* / ? hours	20	
6	*Émeraude* (Q 41-46)	$\frac{309}{442}$	1903	'06	Petrol 8 cylinder accumulators.	600	$\frac{12}{8}$	147×13×12		2 tubes 4 slings	1000 miles *nominal* / ? hours	22	
8	Q 53-60	$\frac{375}{500}$	1905	'08	Petrol 12 cylinder accumulators.	600		160½×		ditto			
20	Q 61-81		1906	'09									

NARVAL, TRITON & SILURE types.

AIGRETTE type.

SPECIAL NOTES.

(LAUBEUF DESIGN).

Narval. Surface motor is a triple expansion steam engine, fired with heavy petroleum. Flash boiler. Fulmen accumulators. Can nominally do 70 miles submerged at 5 kts., but cannot really keep under so long. The boat is built like a torpedo boat with a double skin, and is submerged by the admission of water into the space between the skins.

Triton type named **Triton** & **Sirène**.

Silure type, **Silure** & **Espadon**.

Aigrette type, **Aigrette** & **Cigogne**.

These six are merely *Narvals* with improved submerging powers. Defects of all is that the steam engine, should they submerge in the time stated, gives out a great deal of extremely inconvenient heat, and the actual time of submerging is rarely under 12 minutes in the latest of them.

(BERTIN DESIGN—TWIN SCREW).

Emeraude class, named **Émeraude, Opale, Rubis, Saphir, Turquoise,** and **Topaze.** These six, with the experimental **Y** and **Omega,** are official developments of the Laubeuf type. In the *Emeraudes,* improved *Omegas,* a petrol motor is introduced. There is a vertical petrol motor, low tension magneto ignition, M.O. inlet valves with variable lift, scynchronised ignition, and automatic lubrication. A Krebs type carburetter is fitted. These boats will run on the throttle and not on the spark as in American type. The **Y** type is a failure. **X,** a twin screw boat designed by Romazotti, is an experimental boat, a *Morse* type modified into a submersible. **Z,** single screw, designed by Mangas, is of very similar type. Neither of these boats promise well.

GENERAL NOTES.

Up to Q 46 all carry the long 45 c/m (17·7 inch) torpedo. Later boats, the 1904 model.

All when running on surface are fitted to re-charge their accumulators.

FRENCH SUBMARINES (Harbour Defence Boats).

No. in Class	Type and Designation.	Displ'cement.	Begun.	Completed.	Motive Power, above and below.	H.P.	Max. Speed, above and below.	Length × Beam × Depth, in feet.	Torpedo Tubes.	Actual endurance, above and below.	Complement.	First Submerges, in minutes.
		tons.										
1	*Gymnote* (Q 1)	30	1886	1889	Accumulators. / Accumulators.	55	$\frac{6}{3}$	$56\frac{1}{2} \times 6 \times 6$	2 slings.	About 6 miles (2 hrs.)	4	about 20.
1	*Gustave Zédé* (Q 2) ...	270	1890	1893	Accumulators. / Accumulators.	220	$\frac{10}{5}$	$160 \times 10\frac{3}{4} \times 12$	1 tube.	48 miles at 6 kts. / 48 miles at 6 kts. (8 hrs.)	8	10
1	*Morse* (Q 3) & (Q 11-12)	146	'97-'99	'00-'02	Accumulators. / Accumulators.	360	$\frac{12}{6}$	$118 \times 9 \times 9\frac{3}{4}$	1 tube.	80 miles at 10 kts. / 64 miles at 8 kts. (8 hrs.)	9	5 — 2
4	*Farfadet* (Q 7-10)	185	1899	1902	Accumulators. / Accumulators.		$\frac{12}{8}$	$134\frac{1}{2} \times 9\frac{3}{4} \times 9\frac{3}{4}$	1 tube, 2 slings.	30 miles at 12 kts. 140 at 7. / 30 miles at 8 kts. (10 hrs.)	9	5 — 2
20	*Perle* (Q 15-34)	68	1901	'04-'05	Benzol Motor / Accumulators.	60	$\frac{8}{4\frac{1}{2}}$	$76 \times 7\frac{1}{2} \times 8$	1 tube.		5	3—1 (expected).
6	*Guêpe* (Q 47-52)	44	1904	*1907*	Petrol / Accumulators.	50	$\frac{9}{5}$	70	2 slings (?).	*small.*	4	2 (expected).

SPECIAL NOTES.

Gymnote is now a purely experimental boat. Designed by Gustave Zédé. Laurent Cely accumulators. No armament at present fitted. Originally carried 14 in. torpedoes.

(ROMAZOTTI TYPE.—1 SCREW).

Gustave Zédé was the first of these.

Morse class, named **Morse, Francais,** and **Algérian.**

Perle class, named **Alose, Anguille, Bouite, Castor, Dorade, Estergeon, Grondin, Ludion, Loutre, Lynx, Méduse, Naïade, Oursin, Otarie, Phoque, Protée, Perle, Souffleur, Thon, Truite.**

All these are based of *Gustave Zédé*, with minor improvements. They submerge by vertical rudders and the admission of water. A heavy lead keel is fitted to ensure stability when submerged. They steer and manœuvre excellently on the surface, but are extremely lively, and at times erratic, when submerged. Laurent Cely accumulators.

(MANGAS TYPE.—1 SCREW).

Farfadet class, named **Farfadet, Gnome, Korrigan** and **Lutin,** are essentially adaptations of the Romozotti type, and differ from them only in minor details.

Guêpe class are very small reductions of the *Farfadet* class.

GUSTAVE ZÉDÉ awash.

FARFADET *class.*

PERLE *class.*

PERLE *class.*

FRENCH SHIPS OF NO FIGHTING VALUE.

GUNBOATS (Armoured).

ACHERON, COCYTE, PHLEGETON, STYX (1885-1891). 1720-1790 tons, drawing about 12 feet. Normal speed, 13 kts. Guns (old): 1—10·6 inch and from 1 to 3 smaller. Armour: Belt 9½″, Turret 8″ compound.

FLAMME, FUSÉE, GRENADE, MITRAILLE (1884-88). 1046-1150 tons, drawing 10½ feet. Nominal speed, 13 kts. Guns (old): 1—9·4 inch, 1—3·5 inch. Armour: Belt 9½″, Gun 8″ compound.

CRUISERS AVISOS (4).

KERSAINT (1897) 1243 tons. Guns: 1—5·5 inch, 5—4 inch, 7 small. No torpedoes. Designed H.P. 2,200＝15 kts. Coal: 200 tons.

CHIMÈRE (1881); also IBIS (1883) and MOUETTE (1879). 227 and 254 tons. Draught, 8 feet. Guns: IBIS, 2—9 pdrs; others, 2—1 pdr. 1 screw.

CHAMOIS (bldg.). 431 tons. Designed H.P. 600＝12 kts.

AVISOS-TRANSPORTS (8).

AUBE (1885), BOUGAINVILLE (1878), DURANCE (1887), MANCHE (1890), MEURTHE (1885), RANCE (1888), VAUCLUSE (1901). Guns: 4—5·5 inch and two to four 12 or 9 pdrs. Speed, nominally 11-10 kts. Draught, about 18 feet.

SCREW GUNBOATS.

ASPIC (1880), CAPRICORNE (1882), DÉCIDÉE (1899), SCORPION (1884), SURPRISE (1895), VIPÈRE (1881), ZÉLÉE (1899). All of from 640-450 tons. The first two and VIPÈRE carry 2 old 5·5 inch, 2—4 inch; SCORPION, 2—5·5 inch; DÉCIDÉE, SURPRISE, and ZÉLÉE carry 2—4 inch, 45 cal., 4—9 pdr., 4—1 pdr. Draught, about 12 feet. Nominal speeds, 13 kts. for newer and 10 kts. for older boats.

CHALOUPES-CANONNIÈRES À HÉLICE (6) (Twin Screw.)

AVALANCHE, BAÏONNETTE, BOUCLIER, CARONADE, CASSE-TÊTE, CIMETERRE. 140 tons. Guns: 2—3·5 inch and 3 revolvers. Speed, nominal, 9 kts. Draught, about 4 feet (maximum).

FOURNIR (1897) 225 tons. No guns. Speed, 9 kts.

JAVELOT (1866). 89 tons. 1—5·5 inch gun. Speed 5·7 kts.

CHALOUPES-CANONNIÈRES DE RIVIÈRE. (Screw.)

OLRY (1893). Of about 10 kts. nominal speed. Guns: 2 to 6 revolvers or 1 pdrs. (In China.)

ARGUS and VIGILANTE (1900). 123 tons. Speed, 13 kts. Guns: 2—3·5 inch, 4—1 pdr. (In China.)

TRANSPORTS (13).

BIEN HOA (1880), GIRONDE (1884), MYTHO (1879), NIVE (1883), SHAMROCK (1878), VINH-LONG (1881). All of about 5,700 tons. Guns: 2—5·5 inch, 3—3·5 inch, 5 revolvers. Speeds, nominal, 13—13·9 kts. Draughts, about 22 feet.

MAGELLAN (1884). About 3,900 tons. Guns: 2—5·5 inch and 4 revolvers. Nominal speed, 11·2 and 9·3 kts.

CHARENTE, DROME, ISERE, LOIRET, VIENNE. All old, and of about 2,000 tons. Speeds, about 8 kts. One old gun in some.

There are also 9 school-ships, 9 paddlers, 3 sailing ships, and 1 cutter.

JAPANESE FLEET.

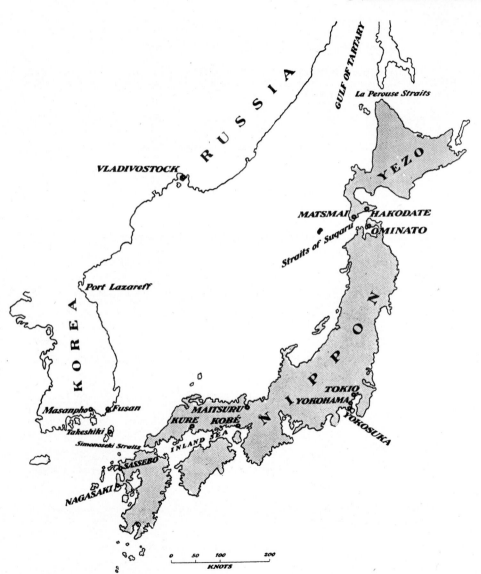

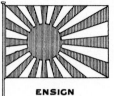
ENSIGN

JACK & MERCANTILE ENSIGN

IMPERIAL STANDARD

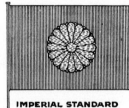
TRANSPORT

SHIP REQUIRES REPAIR

Red | White | Gold | Blue

SENIOR OFFICER

ADMIRAL

VICE ADMIRAL

REAR ADMIRAL

COMMODORE

OFFICER COMMANDING TORPEDO DIVISION

YOKOSUKA

to	knots.
Hakodate	450
Hong Kong	1580
Honolulu	3400
Kobe	300
Kure	400
Manila	1720
Nagasaki	760
Port Arthur	1350
Saigon	2400
Shanghai	1050

NAGASAKI

to	knots.
Chemulpo	446
Foo-chau	650
Hong Kong	1067
Kelung (Formosa)	630
Kiao-chau	450
Kure	240
Kobe	340
Maitsuru	400
Manila	1300
Masampho	170
Matsmai	750
Pescadores	820
Port Arthur	585
Takeshiki	120
Saigon	1990
Shanghai	330
Vladivostock	620
Wei-hai-wei	480

TAKESHIKI

to	knots.
Kiao-chau	420
Maitsuru	340
Masampho	70
Matsmai	600
Nagasaki	120
Port Arthur	500
Vladivostock	525
Wei-hai-wei	430

MATSMAI

to	knots.
Maitsuru	440
Nagasaki	750
Port Arthur	1150
Takeshiki	600
Vladivostock	380
Yokosuka	560
Nearest Russian coast (150 English miles N.E. by E. of Vladivostock)	250

MAITSURU

to	knots.
Matsmai	440
Nagasaki	400
Ominato	465
Takeshiki	340
Vladivostock	620

PORT ARTHUR

to	knots.
Hong Kong	1275
Kiao-chau	280
Nagasaki	585
Vladivostock	1170
Wei-hai-wei	100

JAPANESE DOCKYARDS.

Divided into 2000 yard squares.   Uniform scale.   Soundings in fathoms.   Heights in feet.

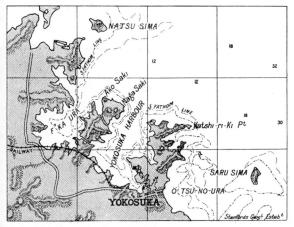

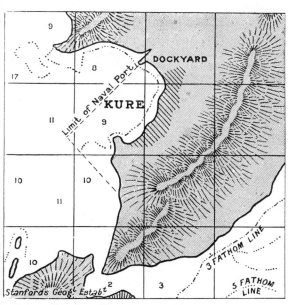

YOKOSUKA (in Sagami). One slip. One dock (No. 2) able to take any warship; two others: No. 1, 392 × 82 × 22½ feet; No. 3, 308 × 45¼ × 17¼ feet. There are also two small docks at Tokio.

KURE (in Aki). One slip. One dock able to take *Takasago* class. New armour plate factory here.

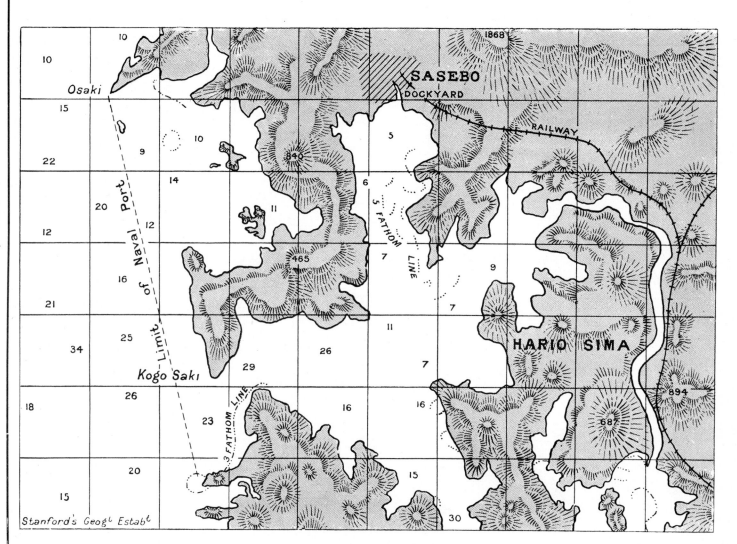

SASSEBO (in Hizen).   No docks or slips.

JAPANESE DOCKYARDS.

Divided into 2000 yard squares.   Uniform scale.   Soundings in fathoms.   Heights in feet

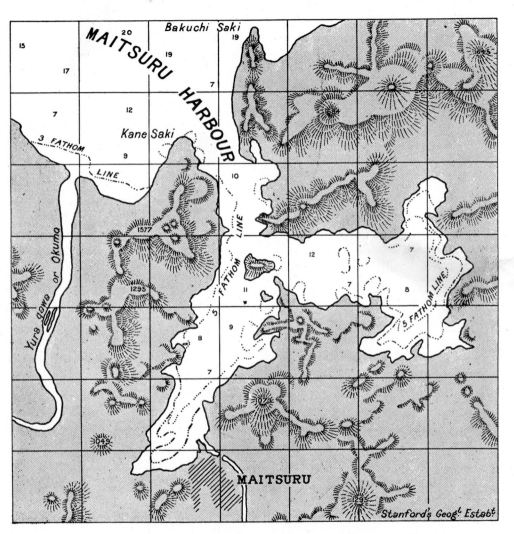

MAITSURU (or MAIZURU) (in Tango).   New dockyard.

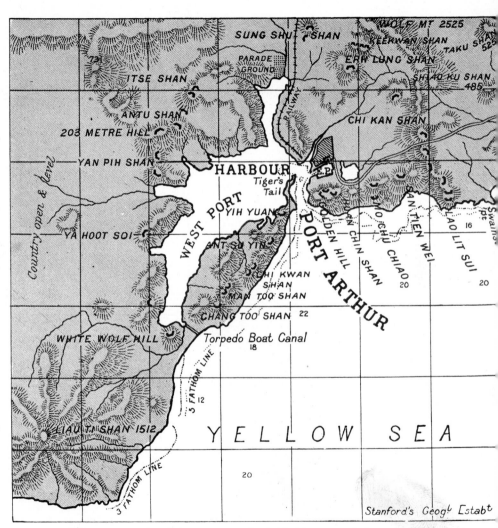

PORT ARTHUR.   One dry dock too narrow for battleships; two docks partly built, and now probably in ruins.

Divided into 2000 yard squares.   Uniform scale.   Soundings in fathoms.   Heights in feet.

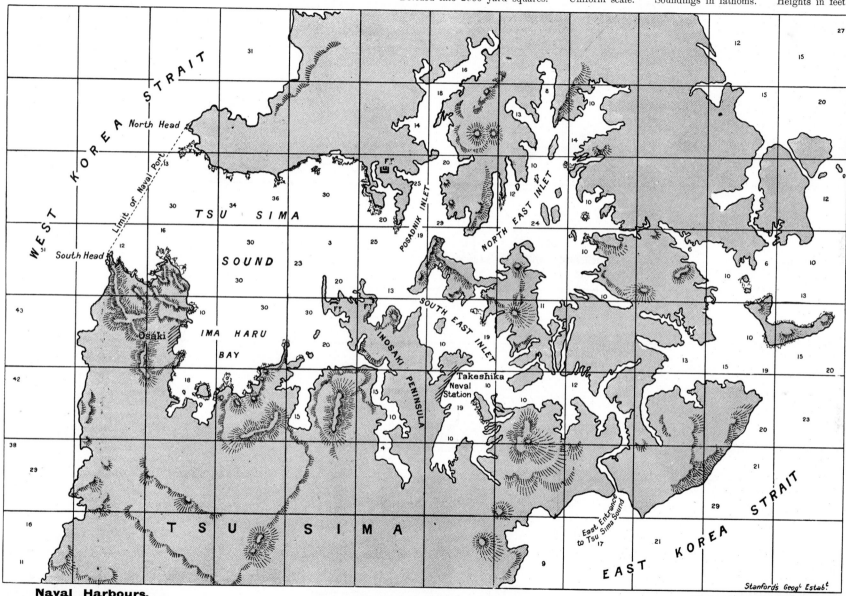

Stanford's Geogᵗ Estabᵗ

Naval Harbours.

NAGASAKI. Two long and one 371 foot docks here, all too shallow
to take any warship larger than *Takasago*.
TAKESHIKI. Coaling station. Strongly fortified advance base.
OMINATO. Torpedo base.
MATSMAI.
KOBÉ. Torpedo boat building yard here.
MASANPO (Korea).

Principal Mercantile Ports.

Yokohama, Hakodate, Nagasaki.

Mercantile Marine.

Total tonnage about 1,205,000. Contains 1309 steamers (882,092
tons) (including large liners), 3564 sailing ships (323,328 tons, and
over 900 junks, &c., for coast trade.

Coinage.

1 Yen (100 sen) = 2s. 0½d. British, $0.50 U.S.A., *about*.

2 A 2

JAPANESE WARSHIPS (ONE FUNNEL) IDENTIFICATION AND SIGNAL SILHOUETTES.

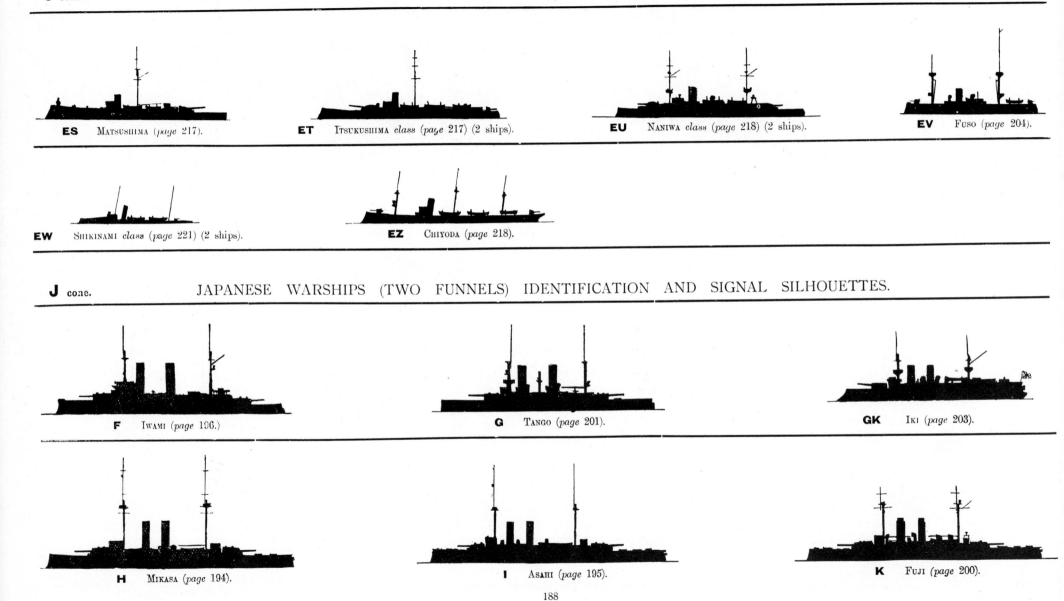

ES   Matsushima (*page* 217).

ET   Itsukushima *class* (*page* 217) (2 ships).

EU   Naniwa *class* (*page* 218) (2 ships).

EV   Fuso (*page* 204).

EW   Shikinami *class* (*page* 221) (2 ships).

EZ   Chiyoda (*page* 218).

JAPANESE WARSHIPS (TWO FUNNELS) IDENTIFICATION AND SIGNAL SILHOUETTES.

F   Iwami (*page* 196.)

G   Tango (*page* 201).

GK   Iki (*page* 203).

H   Mikasa (*page* 194).

I   Asahi (*page* 195).

K   Fuji (*page* 200).

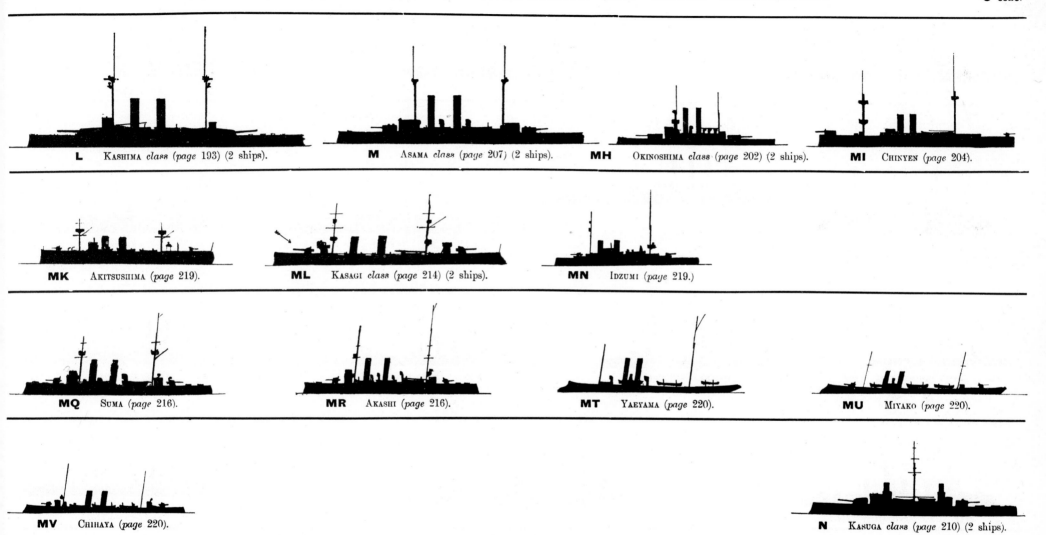

L KASHIMA *class* (*page* 193) (2 ships).

M ASAMA *class* (*page* 207) (2 ships).

MH OKINOSHIMA *class* (*page* 202) (2 ships).

MI CHINYEN (*page* 204).

MK AKITSUSHIMA (*page* 219).

ML KASAGI *class* (*page* 214) (2 ships).

MN IDZUMI (*page* 219.)

MQ SUMA (*page* 216).

MR AKASHI (*page* 216).

MT YAEYAMA (*page* 220).

MU MIYAKO (*page* 220).

MV CHIHAYA (*page* 220).

N KASUGA *class* (*page* 210) (2 ships).

JAPANESE WARSHIPS (THREE FUNNELS) IDENTIFICATION AND SIGNAL SILHOUETTES.

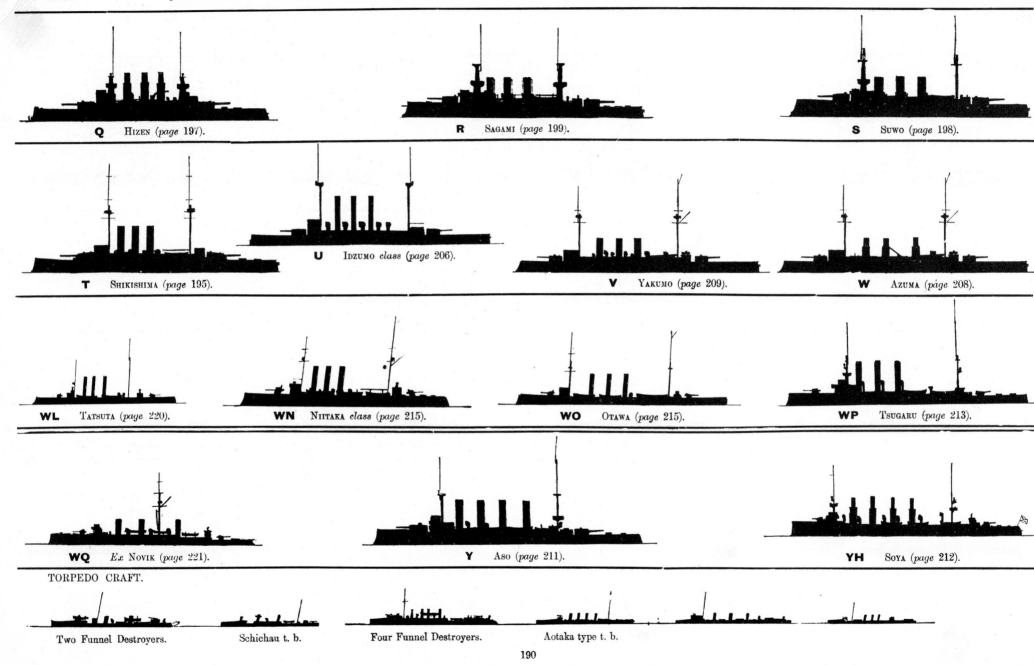

Q Hizen (*page 197*).

R Sagami (*page 199*).

S Suwo (*page 198*).

T Shikishima (*page 195*).

U Idzumo *class* (*page 206*).

V Yakumo (*page 209*).

W Azuma (*page 208*).

WL Tatsuta (*page 220*).

WN Niitaka *class* (*page 215*).

WO Otawa (*page 215*).

WP Tsugaru (*page 213*).

WQ Ex Novik (*page 221*).

Y Aso (*page 211*).

YH Soya (*page 212*).

TORPEDO CRAFT.

Two Funnel Destroyers.   Schichau t. b.   Four Funnel Destroyers.   Aotaka type t. b.

Naval Guns.

*=Q.F. with brass cartridge case.

Notation.	Calibre.	Length in calibres.	Model.	Weight of Gun.	Weight of A.P. shot.	*Maximum* Initial Velocity.	*Maximum* penetration firing A.P. capped at K.C. 5000 yards.	*Maximum* penetration firing A.P. capped at K.C. 3000 yards.	Danger space against average ship, at 10,000 yards.	Danger space against average ship, at 5000 yards.	Danger space against average ship, at 3000 yards.	*Service* rate of Fire. Rounds per minute.
	inches.			tons.	lbs.	F. S.	inches.	inches.				
AAA	12·5	40	C	66	990	2306	12	15	...	...	...	0·2
AAAAA	12	45	E ('04)	58½	850	2800	16	20	...	...	...	...
AAAA	12	40	O	59	724	2600	14	18	150	460	750	...
AAA	12	40	E	49	850	2423	12	15½	120	450	720	1
D	12	20	K	35½	725	1755	4	6	...	...	...	0·3
AAA	10	45	E	32½	500	2710	10½	13½	150	480	720	3
AAA	10	45	O	32	490	2500	9¾	12½	130	450	700	...
B	9	35		19½	268	2400	5½	7¼	...	...	...	...
*A**	8	45	O	15½	188	2800	7½	10½	105	430	625	1
A	8	45	E	17⅓	250	2740	7	10	110	425	600	1·2
*B**	8	40	E	15½	250	2580	5½	7½	100	400	580	1·2
C	6	45	E ('04)	8½	100	3000	4½	6½	75	250	475	...
C	6	50	V	8	100	3000	4½	6½	75	250	475	6
D	6	45	O	7½	89	2900	4	6	60	250	485	...
D	6	45	O	7	89	2600	3¼	5	50	200	430	...
*E**	6	40	E	6½	100	2500	3	4½	65	210	435	7
*E**	6	40	E	6	100	2220	2½	4	35	150	360	8
*F**	4·7	40	E	2	45	2150	...	2½	...	...	...	8
*F**	4·7	32	E	1⅔	36	1938	...	...	...	...	...	8-6
*F**	3	...	V	...	14	...	...	...	...	...	...	...
*F**	3	40	E	2	12	2200	...	...	...	...	...	...

In the Model column C = Schneider-Canet; E, Elswick; O, Obuchoff (Russian); K, Krupp; V, Vickers.

Notes.—8 inch, 6 inch, and 4·7 inch Japanese guns are now made on the latest Elswick and Vickers model, with the same ballistics. All guns fire H.E. shell, loaded with a Japanese compound (practically lyddite).

All guns of 40 calibres and over use smokeless powder—a nitro-cellulose of Japanese invention. There are a few old Krupp and Armstrong guns not noted in the table.

Ballistics of Obuchoff guns as for Russian nitro-cellulose.

Torpedo.

Whiteheads of the usual models. *Submerged tubes.* Elswick pattern.

Personnel: About 35,000 all ranks.
Minister of Marine: Admiral Saito.
Chief Constructor:

Cap.

The cap is the same as the British, *except that it has a gold band.* Peak as British.

Cap Badge.

A chrysanthemum and anchor.

INSIGNIA OF RANK—EXECUTIVE OFFICERS—SLEEVES.

Executive Branch:	Tai-sho.	Tchu-sho.	Tcho-sho.	Tai-sa.	Tchu-sa	Tcho-sa.	Tai-i.	Tchu-i.	Tcho-i
Corresponding British or U.S.:	*Admiral.*	*Vice-Ad.*	*Rear-Ad.*	*Captain.*	*Commander.*	2½ *Lieut. Lieut. Com.*	*Lieutenant.*	*Sub-Lieut.*	*Acting Sub-Lieut.* and Tcho-i Ko-hoshei., *Midshipman.*
							Tai-kikansh. Guini-tai.		

Band between stripes. Same insignia without the curl.

(Branches, with but after Executive).
- Purple — Kikan-o (*Engineer*) (with executive rank).
- Red — Gui-ni (*Doctor*).
- White — Shukei (*Paymaster*).
- Blue — Zosin (*Constructor*).

The senior officer of any branch on board the ship always carries the affix "*tcho.*" Thus: Ho-dju-tcho (*Gunnery*), Sui-ri-tcho (*Torpedo*), Ko-ki-tcho (*Navigator*)—these three having always Tcho-sa rank.—Kikan-tcho (*Chief Engineer*), Gui-ni-tcho (*Senior Doctor*), Shukei-tcho (*Senior Paymaster*).

Undress is a military tunic (dark blue) with the sleeve insignia of rank in black braid only, with curl for executives, without curl for other branches, which cannot be distinguished from each other in this tunic.

(AKI CLASS—2 SHIPS).

KURAMA (1906) & *AKI* (*building*).

Displacement about 19,000 tons.   Complement

Length (*waterline*),   feet. Beam   feet.   *Maximum* draught,   feet.   Length over all,   feet.

Guns (Elswick **M** '04):
   4—12 inch, 45 cal. (*AAAAA*)
   12—10 inch, 45 cal. (*AAA*).
   12—4·7 inch, 45 cal. (*E*).
Torpedo tubes (18 inch):
   4 *submerged*) broadside).
   1 *submerged* (stern).

Armour (Krupp):
   9″ Belt (amidships) ......*aaa*
   6½″ Belt (ends) ....*a*
   ″ Deck ....
   Protection to vitals ....

Ahead:
2·—12 in.
4—10 in.
2—4·7 in.

[These ships are practically copies of the British *Lord Nelson* with two guns instead of one in the amidship turrets].

Astern:
2—12 in.
4—10 in.
2—4·7 in.

Reported to be designed to carry auxiliary sail.

Broadside: 4—12 in., 6—10 in., 6—4·7 in.

Machinery: 2 sets 4 cylinder quadruple expansion.   2 screws.

General Notes.—First of class laid down 1905.

(KASHIMA CLASS—2 SHIPS).

KASHIMA ましか (1905) & **KATORI** りさか (1905).

Displacement 16,400 tons.   Complement

Length (*waterline*), 455 feet.   Beam, 78⅙ feet.   *Mean* draught, 26⅗ feet.

Guns (Elswick M. '04.):
  4—12 inch, 45 cal. (*AAAAA*).
  4—10 inch, 45 cal. (*AAA*).
  12—6 in, 45 cal. (*C*).
  12—12 pdr. (*F*).
  3—3 pdr.
  6—Pompoms.
Torpedo tubes (18 inch):
  5 *submerged*.

Armour (Krupp):
  9″ Belt (amidships) ...... *aa*
  6½″ Belt (ends)............. *a*
  3″ Deck on slopes ......
  Protection to vitals ... =*aaa*
  9″ Turrets (N.C.)......... *aa*
  9″—5″ Turret bases......*aa-b*
  8″—6″ Secondary Turrets (N.C.).......... *a-b*
  6″ Lower deck (side) ... *a*
  6″ Battery................. *a*
  9″ Conning tower ...... *aa*
  4″ Upper deck battery... *d*

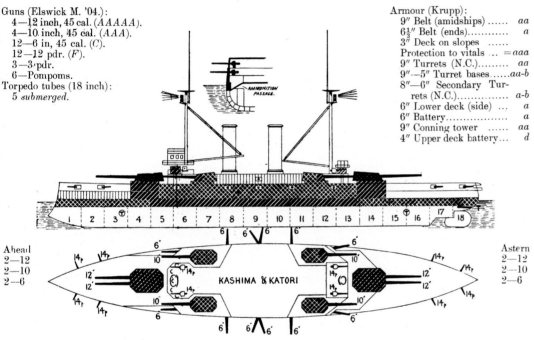

KASHIMA & KATORI

Ahead
2—12
2—10
2—6

Astern
2—12
2—10
2—6

Broadside : 4—12 in., 2—10 in., 6—6 in.

Machinery : 2 sets 4 cylinder vertical quadruple expansion.   2 screws.   Boilers : Niclausse. Designed H.P. 17,000=18·5 kts.   Coal : *normal*, 1,200 tons ; *maximum*, 2,000 tons.

Armour Notes.—Belt is 7½ feet wide, 5 feet of it below waterline.   Deck at ends is 2½″ all over.   Screens between 6inch guns in battery.   Special protection to magazines.

Gunnery Notes.—Loading positions all round.   Hoists : electric, semi-automatic.   Big guns manœuvred by electric, hydraulic and hand gear.   15 H.P. motors for big guns. Arcs of fire : 12 in., 270° (train round in 60 seconds) ; 10 in., 120° from axial line ; battery, 120°. Height of guns above water : 12 in., 26 feet ; 10 in., 22 feet ; main deck guns, 14½ feet.

KATORI.   *Photo by favour of Messrs. Vickers Maxim.*

Torpedo Notes.—Net defence nearly all round.   2 fast 56 feet torpedo launches carried.   Stern submerged tube.   6 searchlights (automatic).

Engineering Notes.—

Name.	Built by	Machinery,	24 hours at 4/5.	Full power.		Boilers.
				Miles.		
Kashima	Elswick	Humphrys	13,000=18 kts.	17,280=19·24 (*mean*)		Niclausse
Katori	Vickers	Vickers	=17·8 kts. (at ⅘ths.)	=20·22 (*maximum*)		Niclausse

General Notes.—2 electric derricks.   Steam boat hoists and after capstan.   10 boats carried. Laid down, 1904.

MIKASA (November, 1900).

Displacement 15,200 tons. Complement

Length (*waterline*), 415 feet. Beam, 75½ feet. *Maximum* draught, 27½ feet. Length over all, 432 feet.

Guns:
4—12 inch, 40 cal. (*AAA*).
14—6 inch, 40 cal. (*E*).
20—12 pdr. (*F*)
8—3 pdr.
4—2½ pdr.
8 Maxims, etc.
Torpedo tubes (18 inch):
4 *submerged.*

Armour (Krupp).
9″ Belt (amidships) .... *aa*
4″ Belt (ends) .... *d*
12 Bulkheads .... *aaa*
3″ Deck (slopes) ....
Protection to vitals .... *aaa*
14″—10″ Barbettes ......*aaaa-aa*
10— 8″ Turrets to these = *aaa-aa*
6″ Lower deck redoubt ...... *a*
6″ Battery .... *a*

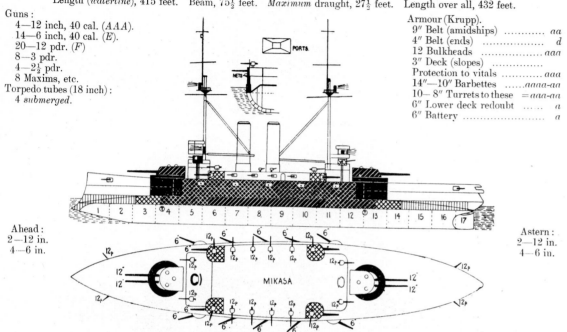

Ahead:
2—12 in.
4—6 in.

Astern:
2—12 in.
4—6 in.

Broadside: 4—12 in., 7—6 in.

Machinery: 2 sets 3 cylinder vertical triple expansion. 2 screws. Boilers: 25 Belleville. Designed H.P. 15,000 = 18 kts. Coal: *normal* 700 tons; *maximum* 1690 tons.

Armour Notes.—Thickest part of belt is 7¾ feet wide by 156½ feet long; 5¼ feet of it below waterline. Lower deck redoubt is 156 feet long. Battery has 2″ screens enclosing each gun and forming casemates. Deck: 3″ amidships; 4″ at barbettes; 2½″ at ends. Main deck, 1″.

Gunnery Notes.—Loading positions, big guns: all round. Hoists: electric, steam and hand. Big guns manœuvred hydraulic, steam and hand gear.

Arcs of fire: Big guns, 240°; secondary guns, about 120°.

Ammunition carried: Big guns, 60 rounds per gun; 6 inch, 200 per gun.

Height of guns above water: Big guns, 25 feet.

Torpedo Notes.—Nets carried at main deck level. 6 searchlights (automatic).

Engineering Notes.—Machinery, 1355 tons. Grate area, 1276 feet. Heating surface, 37,452 feet.

Trials.—6 hours, 12,236 = 17·3 kts. (Consumption, 1·53 lbs). *Full power*, 16,400 = 18·6 kts. Can steam 18 kts. easily. Coal consumption averages 12 tons an hour at *full power*.

General Notes.—Built and engined by Vickers. Laid down 1899. Completed 1902. Blown up, September, 1905, but since raised and repairing. Fighting tops removed, 1905.

さかみ

Mikasa.

Class distinctions.—Easily differentiated from *Asahi*, because her funnels are much more amidships.

SHIKISHIMA (November, 1898) & ASAHI (March, 1899).

Displacement about 15,000 tons.   Complement 741.

Length (*waterline*), 415 feet.   Beam, 76 feet.   *Maximum* draught, 28¼ feet.   Length over all, 425 feet.

Guns:
4 —12 inch, 40 cal. (*AAA*).
14—6 inch, 41 cal. (*E*).
20 —12 pdr. (*F*).
8—3 pdr.
6—2½ pdr.
Torpedo tubes (18 inch) :
4 *submerged.*
Shikishima has also
1 *above water.*

Armour (Harvey Nickel) :
9″ Belt (amidships) .... *aa*
4″ Belt (ends) .... *d*
11″ Bulkheads ....*aaa*
3″ Deck (amidships slopes)
   Protection to vitals .... =*aaa*
11″—10″ Barbettes ......*aaa—aa*
10″—8″ Turrets to these =*aaa—a*
6″ Lower deck redoubt......... *b*
6″ Casemates (14) .... *b*
14″ Conning tower ....*aaa*
4″ After tower .... *d*
(Total weight *about* 4500 tons.)

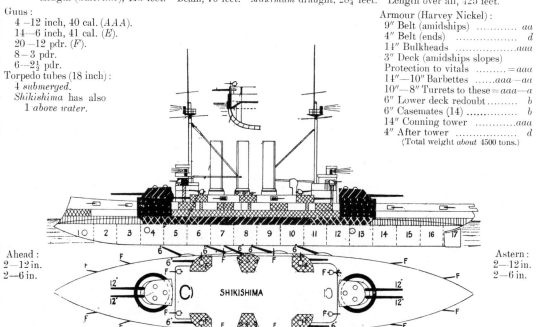

Ahead :
2 —12 in.
2—6 in.

SHIKISHIMA

Astern :
2—12 in.
2—6 in.

Broadside : 4—12 in., 7—6 in.

Machinery : 2 sets vertical triple expansion. 2 screws. Boilers : 25 Belleville. Designed H.P. 14,500 = 18 kts. Coal : *normal* 700 tons ; *maximum* 1400 tons.

Armour Notes.—Main belt is 8⅙ feet wide ; 6 feet of it below waterline. Upper belt is 250 feet long. Barbettes about main deck are *probably* only 10″ thick (*aa*). Deck slopes 3″ behind belt amidships, 4″ at barbettes, 2″ at ends.

Gunnery Notes.—Loading positions, big guns all round. Load any elevation in *Asahi*. Big guns manœuvred, steam and hydraulically. Electric, steam and hand hoists.

Arcs of fire : Big guns, 240° ; casemates, about 120°.

Ammunition carried : 12 inch, 60 per gun ; 6 inch, 200 per gun.

Height of guns above water : Turret guns, about 25 feet (high barbettes).

Torpedo Notes.—Nets carried upper deck level. Partial defence only. 2 torpedo boats carried. *Shikishima* only has a bow tube (armour protected).

Engineering Notes.—

Name.	Builder.	Engines and Boilers.	Laid down.	Completed.	At 12,500 H.P.	Full Power	Boilers.	Present Best Speed.
Shikishima	Thames I. W.	Humphrys & T	Jan., '97	1900	12,874 = 17·0	16,907 = 18·78	Belleville	18·5
Asahi	Clydebank	Clydebank	July, '97	1901	12,957 = 17·5	16,360 = 18·3	Belleville	18·6

Coal consumption : *Asahi* was once a coal eater, but is now economical. They average about 12¼ tons an hour at full power. Weight of machinery, etc., 1335 tons. Heating surface, 37,936 square feet.

General Notes.—*Shikishima*'s barbette guns have sunk, owing to having been trained while ship was in dry dock.

The *Asahi* somewhat injured her frame by grounding on Southsea Beach on her way out. Fighting tops removed, 1905.

ましき志
SHIKISHIMA.

ひさあ
ASAHI.

Differences.—*Shikishima* has an extra funnel.

Class distinction.—*Asahi* is something like *Mikasa*, but easily distinguished from her because her fore funnel is much nearer fore mast than *Mikasa's.*

2 B 2

IWAMI (July, 1902).

Displacement 13,566 tons.   Complement 750.

Length (*waterline*), 376½ feet.   Beam, 76 feet.   *Mean* draught, 26 feet.   Length over all, 397 feet.

Guns (Russian):
4—12 in., 40 cal. (*AAAA*)
12—6 inch, 45 cal. (*D*).
20—3 inch, 60 cal. (*F*).
20—3 pdr.
8—1 pdr.
Torpedo tubes (18 inch):
2 *submerged* (broadside).
1 *above water* (bow).
1 *above water* (stern).

Armour (Krupp):
10″ Belt (amidships)...... *aaa*
4″ Belt (ends) .... *d*
4″ Armour deck
(flat below belt)
Protection to vitals = *aäaaaaa*
11″ Turrets .... *aaa*
8″ Turret bases (NC)...... *a*
6″—2½″ Lower deck side *a—f*
7″ Small turrets (N.C.)... *a*
6″ bases to these .... *c*
10″ Conning tower......... *aa*
(Total weight, 4000 tons).

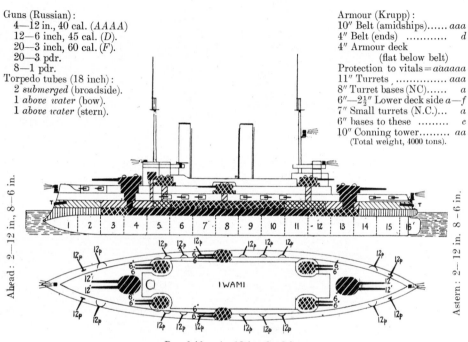

Ahead: 2—12 in., 8—6 in.

Astern: 2—12 in. 8—6 in.

Broadside: 4—12 in., 6—6 in.

みはひ

IWAMI.

(Fighting tops now removed).

Machinery: 2 sets vertical 4 cylinder triple expansion. 2 screws. Boilers: 20 Belleville. Designed I.H.P. 16500 = 18 kts. Coal: *normal* 750 tons; *maximum* 1250 tons.

Armour Notes.—Belt is 6¾ feet wide, 5 feet of it below waterline; lower edge is 7″ thick amidships; upper belt 5¾ feet wide.

Gunnery Notes.—Loading positions big guns: all round. Hoists, electric and hand.
Big guns manœuvred electrically; secondary turrets electrically. Arcs of fire: Big guns 240° (nominal only); 6 in., amidships, 180° (actual); other 6 in., 150° from axial line.

Torpedo Notes—18 torpedoes carried. 6 searchlights (automatically controlled).

Engineering Notes.—Boilers placed fore and aft.

General Notes.—Formerly the Russian *Orel*. Captured after Tsushima, 1905. Laid down at Galernii Island, June, 1900. Completed for sea, September, 1904.

196

HIZEN (October, 1900).

Displacement, 12,700 tons. Complement 750.

Length (*waterline*), 376 feet. Beam 72 feet. *Maximum* draught, 28¼ feet.

Guns (Russian):
4—12 inch, 40 cal. (*AAAA*).
12—6 inch, 45 cal. (*D*).
20—12 pdr.
20—3 pdr.
6—1 pdr.
Torpedo tubes (18 inch):
2 *submerged* (25° abaft).
2 *above water* (bow & stern).

Armour (Krupp):
9″ Belt (amidships) ....*aa*
4″ Belt (bow) ....:*d*
9″ Bulkhead...................*aa*
3″ Deck (slopes)..............
Protection to vitals..... =*aaa*
6″ Lower deck redoubt ......*a*
10″ Turrets (*N.C*) ... .*aa*
9″ Turret bases (*N.C*)......*aa*
5″ Battery redoubt (*N.C*) ...*c*
5″ Casemates (4)..............*c*
10″ Conning tower (*N.C*)...*aa*

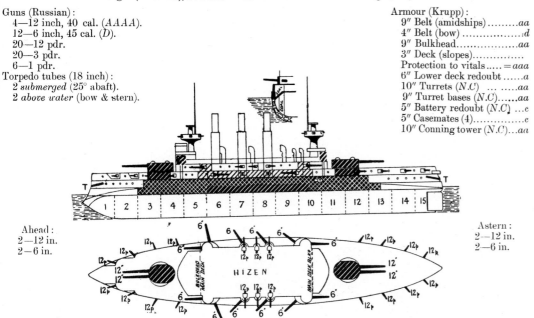

Ahead:
2—12 in.
2—6 in.

Astern:
2—12 in.
2—6 in.

HIZEN

Broadside: 4—12 in., 6—6 in.

んせひ

HIZEN.   (Tops to be removed).

Machinery: 2 sets, 3 cylinder triple expansion. 2 screws. Boilers: 24 Niclausse. Designed H.P. 16,000 = 18 kts. Coal: *normal* 1016 tons; *maximum* 2000 tons.

Armour Notes.—Main belt is 7½ feet wide by about 250 feet long; 6 feet of it below waterline. Lower edge is about 5″ thick. The main belt has 9″ bulkheads. It is continued with thin armour to the bow.

Gunnery Notes.—Loading positions, big guns: all round. Hoists: electric, hydraulic, and hand. Big guns manœuvred electrically. Russian turrets to big guns.

Arcs of fire: Big guns 225°. The upper casemates about 120° from axial line. The end battery guns have no axial training. The battery wall stands well back from the side of the ship, the ports being sponsoned out. Arcs about 110° per gun.

Torpedo Notes.—Broadside *above water* tubes were originally fitted (section 10-11) but removed before completion.

Engineering Notes.—On first *trials* she made 17·75 kts. at 122 revolutions with a dirty bottom. On 12 hours *trial* mean I.H.P. 16,121 = 18·8 kts.

General Notes.—Formerly the Russian *Retvizan*. Torpedoed at Port Arthur 9/2/04. Subsequently repaired and greatly damaged in the Battle of Round Island. Scuttled at Port Arthur and raised September, 1905. Laid down at Cramp's Yard, Philadelphia, U.S.A. in 1898. Completed for sea, 1902. Cost about £1,000,000. Tactical diameter *circa* 550 yards.

SUWO (May, 1900).

Displacement 12,674 tons. Complement 732.

Length (*waterline*) 424 feet. Beam, 71½ feet. *Maximum* draught, 27¼ feet. Length over all, 435 feet.

Guns:
  4—10 inch, 45 cal. (*AAA*).
  11—6 inch, 45 cal. (*E*).
  20—12 pdrs. (*F*).
  26—Smaller Q.F. and
        machine.
Torpedo tubes (18 inch):
  2 *submerged* (at 20° abaft).
  2 *above water* (bow & stern).

Armour (Krupp):
  9″—6″ Belt .... *aa-a*
  4″ Belt ends .... *d*
  2¾″ Deck (on slopes) ...
  Protection to vitals ...... = *aa*
  10″ Turrets (K.N.C.) ... *aa*
  8″ Turret bases (K.N.C.) *a*
  5″ Lower deck side ..... *b*
  5″ Casemates (10) .... *b*
  10″ Conning tower (K.N.C.) *aa*

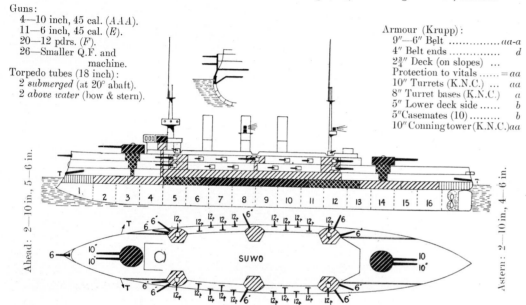

よす
Suwo.

Machinery: 3 sets vertical 3 cylinder triple expansion. 3 screws. Boilers: 30 Bellevilles, placed fore and aft. Designed H.P. 14,500 = 19 kts. Coal: *normal* 1063 tons; *maximum* 2058 tons. Also liquid fuel.

Armour Notes.—Main belt is 7½ feet wide; 5 feet of it below waterline; lower edge is 9″ thick amidships.

Gunnery Notes.—Loading positions, big guns: all round. Hoists: electric all guns. Big guns manœuvred electrically.
  Arcs of fire: Big guns, 280°; secondary guns, 130°.
  Ammunition carried: 10 in., 75 rounds per gun; 6 in., 200 rounds per gun. Height of guns above water: Bow turret, 30 feet; after turret, 22½ feet.

Torpedo Notes.—*Submerged* tubes 20° abaft the beam. Very unreliable at high speed.

Engineering Notes.—Boiler pressure is only 165 lbs.

General Notes.—Formerly the Russian *Pobieda*. Laid down at New Admiralty, St. Petersburg, August, 1898. Completed 1902. Total cost, nearly £1,000,000. Tactical diameter, about 650 yards. Scuttled at Port Arthur, 1904. Raised, September, 1905.

SAGAMI (May, 1898).

Displacement 12,674 tons.   Complement 732.

Length (*waterline*) 424 feet.   Beam, 71½ feet.   *Maximum* draught, 27¼ feet.   Length over all, 435 feet.

Guns :
4—10 inch, 45 cal. (*AAA*)
11—6 inch, 45 cal. (*E*).
20—12 pdrs. (*F*).
26—Smaller Q.F. and
           machine.
Torpedo tubes (18 inch) :
2 *submerged* (at 20° abaft).
2 *above water* (bow & stern)

Armour (Harvey) :
9″—6″ Belt (amidships) *a-c*
9″ Bulkheads .... *a*
2¾″ Deck (on slopes) ...
Protection to vitals ...... =*aa*
10″ Turrets (K.N.C.) ... *aa*
8″ Turret bases (K.N.C.) *a*
5″ Lower deck side (H). *c*
5″ Casemates (10) ...... *c*
10″ Conning tower (K.N.C.)*aa*

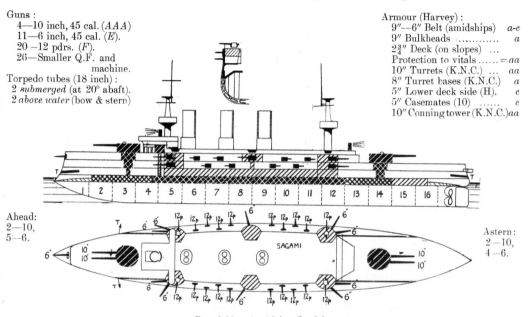

Ahead:
2—10,
5—6.

Astern:
2—10,
4—6.

SAGAMI

Broadside : 4—10 in., 5—6 in.

みかさ

SAGAMI.

Machinery : 3 sets vertical 3 cylinder triple expansion.   3 screws.   Boilers : 30 Bellevilles.   Designed H.P. 14,500 = 19 kts.   Coal : *normal* 1063 tons ; *maximum* 2058 tons.   Also liquid fuel.

Armour Notes.—Belt is 7½ feet wide by about 360 feet long ; 5 feet of it below waterline ; lower edge is 9″ thick amidships.

Gunnery Notes.—Loading positions, big guns : all round.   Hoists, electric all guns.   Big guns manœuvred electrically.
Arcs of fire : Big guns, 280° ; secondary guns, 130°.
Ammunition carried : 10 in., 75 rounds per gun ; 6 in., 200 rounds per gun.   Height of guns above water : Bow turret, 30 feet ; after turret, 22½ feet.

Torpedo Notes.—*Submerged* tubes 20° abaft the beam.   Very unreliable at high speed.

Engineering Notes.—Boiler pressure is only 165 lbs.

Trials.—15,000 H.P. trial.   15,053 = 18·33 kts. (104 revolutions).

General Notes.—Originally the Russian *Peresviet*.   Laid down at New Admiralty, St. Petersburg, November, 1895.   Completed 1901.   Total cost, nearly £1,000,000.   Tactical diameter, about 650 yards.   Scuttled at Port Arthur, 1904.   Salved 1905 and re-named *Segami*.

FUJI (March, 1896).

Displacement 12,300 tons.   Complement 600.

Length (*waterline*), 390 feet.   Beam, 73¾ feet.   *Maximum* draught, 29 feet.   Length over all, 412 feet.
Length (*p.p.*), 374 feet.

Guns :
4 — 12 inch, 40 cal. (*A A A*).
10 — 6 inch, 40 cal. (*E*).
16 — 12 pdr. (*F*).
4 — 2½ pdr.
Torpedo tubes (18 inch) :
4 *submerged*.
1 *above water* (bow).

Armour (Harvey) :
18″ Belt (amidships) ....*aaaa*
14″ Bulkheads .... *aa*
2½″ Deck (flat on belt)...........
Protection to vitals is ....*aaaa*
4″ Lower deck redoubt .... *d*
14″ Barbettes .... *aa*
6″ Turrets to these ....=*a-c*
6″ Casemates (4) .... *c*
14″ Conning tower .... *aa*

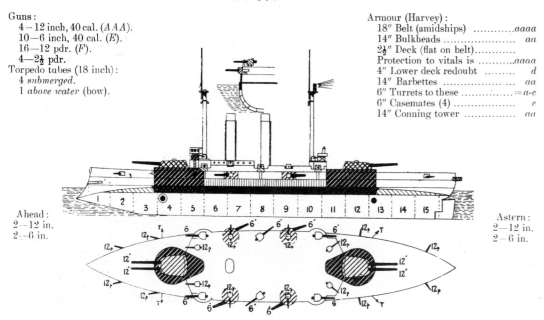

Ahead :
2 — 12 in.
2 — 6 in.

Astern :
2 — 12 in.
2 — 6 in.

Broadside : 4 — 12 in., 5 — 6 in.

Fuji.

Machinery : 2 sets 4 cylinder vertical triple expansion. 2 screws. Boilers : Cylindrical. Designed H.P. *forced* 13,690 = 18 kts.   Coal : *normal* 700 tons ; *maximum* 1300 tons.

Armour Notes.—Belt is 7½ feet wide by 230 feet long ; 5½ feet of it below waterline ; lower edge is 8″ thick.

Gunnery Notes.—Loading positions, big guns : end on (but can load very slowly in other positions). Big guns manœuvred ; hydraulic and steam.
Arcs of fire : Big guns, 250°.
Height of guns above water : Big guns above 21½ feet.

Torpedo Notes.—Tubes early pattern Elswick.   Cannot deliver at speeds above 14 kts.

Engineering Notes.— On first trial *Fuji* made 14,100 = 18·5, and *Yashima* reached 19 kts., but present speed does not exceed 15 kts. to any extent.

General Notes.—Fuji built at Thames Iron Works, *Yashima*, a sister, at Elswick.   Both laid down in 1894.
Yashima is at present sunk, having struck a mine, May, 1904, and foundered off Sassebo on her way back thither.

Class Distinctions : Funnels.   Can be mistaken for *Asama* class but has a different rig.   Much shorter masts and thinner funnels than *Mikasa* and *Asahi*.

TANGO (November, 1894).

Displacement 11,000 tons.   Complement, 750.

Length, 367 feet.   Beam, 69 feet.   *Maximum* draught, 28 feet.

Guns (Russian):
 4—12 inch, 35 cal. (*AA*).
 12—6 in., 45 cal. M '90 (*E*)
 1—9 pdr. Baronovsky
 16—3 pdr.
 12—1 pdr.
 8 various.
Torpedo tubes (18 inch):
 4 *above water*.

Armour (compound):
 15″ Belt (comp.) ....*a*
 3½″ Deck ....
  (Deck flat on belt)
 Protection to vitals is ...*a*
 9″ Bulkheads ....*c*
 4″ Redoubt ....*e*
 10″ Big turrets (steel) ...*b*
 5″ Turret bases (steel)...*e*
 5″ Small turrets ....*e*
 5″ Bases to these ....*e*
 5″ Casemates (4) ....*e*
 12″ Conning tower ......*a*
  (Total weight, 2700 tons).

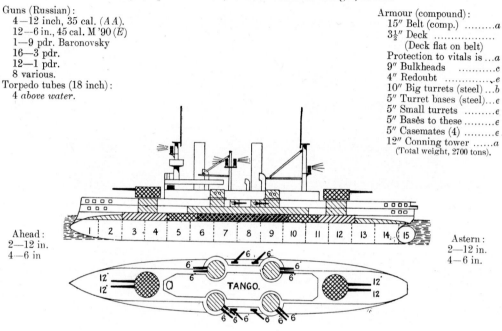

Ahead:
2—12 in.
4—6 in

Astern:
2—12 in.
4—6 in.

TANGO.

Broadside: 2—12 in., 6—6 in.

こんた (TANGO.) (Pole masts to be fitted).

Machinery: 2 sets vertical triple expansion.   2 screws.   Boilers: 16 cylindrical.   Designed H.P. *natural* 9000 = 16 kts.; *forced* 10,600 = 17 kts.   Coal: *normal* 700 tons; *maximum* 1050 tons.

Armour Notes.—Belt is 280 feet long by 7 feet wide, 6 feet of it under water ($\frac{1}{6}$).   Big turrets, which are very nearly circular, run on the deck without protection to the lower edges.   Small turrets have protecting rims.

Gunnery Notes.—Big guns electrically controlled.   All round loading positions.   Electric hoists to all guns.

Engineering Notes.—Machinery by Humphrys & Tennant.   When new this ship steamed excellently and with *n d.* made on a twelve hour *trial* I.H.P. 11,200 = 16·5 kts.   As the contract was exceeded with *n.d.*, *f.d.* was not tried.   At the present time, however, the boilers are quite worn out, and steaming capacity very poor.   Coal consumption averages 1 ton per 1000 H.P. per hour.

General Notes.—Formerly the Russian *Poltava*.   Sunk at Port Arthur in the Russo-Japanese War, 1904, and subsequently salved (1905).   Laid down at St. Petersburg, 1892.   Completed for sea, 1898.   Cost *complete* about £1,100,000.   Two sisters, *Petropavlovsk*, and *Sevastopol*, sunk at Port Arthur, have not been salved so far.

MINOSHIMA (August, 1894). まゐのみ

Displacement, 4200 tons. Complement 406.

Length, 277½ feet. Beam, 52 feet. *Maximum* draught, 17½ feet.

Guns :
    4—9 inch, 45 cal. (*AA*).
    4—4·7 inch (*F*).
    10—3 pdr.
    12—1 pdr.
Torpedo tubes (18 inch) :
    4 *above water.*

Armour (compound) :
    10″—8″ Belt (amidships) *b—c*
    3″ Deck (flat on belt) .... *c*
    Protection to vitals is ...... *a*
    8″ Turrets .... *c*
    6″ Hoists to these .... *d*
    8″ Conning tower .... *c*

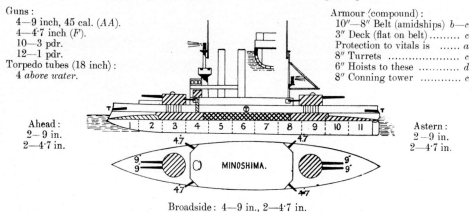

Ahead :
  2—9 in.
  2—4·7 in.

Astern :
  2—9 in.
  2—4·7 in.

Broadside : 4—9 in., 2—4·7 in.

Machinery : 2 sets triple expansion. 2 screws. Boilers : 8 cylindrical. Designed H.P. *forced,* 5700 = 16 kts.

Name.	Built at	Engined by	Laid down.	Completed.	12 hours nat. d.	Boilers.	Present BestSpeed.
Minoshima	New Admiralty	Humphrys & T.	Sept., '93		5758 = 16·2	Cylindrical	15

Formerly the Russian *Admiral Seniavin.* Captured after Tsushima, 1905.

OKINOSHIMA (May 1896). まゐのきち

Displacement, 4200 tons. Complement 404.

Length, 277½ feet. Beam, 51½ feet. *Maximum* draught, 17½ feet.

Guns :
    3—10 inch, 45 cal. (*AAA*).
    4—4·7 inch, (*F*).
    10—3 pdr.
    12—1 pdr.
Torpedo tubes :
    4 *above water.*

Armour (Harvey) :
    10″—8″ Belt (amidships) *a—b*
    3″ Deck (flat on belt) .....
    8″—6″ Bulkheads ....*b—c*
    8″ Turrets .... *b*
    6″ Hoists to these .... *c*
    8″ Conning tower .... *b*

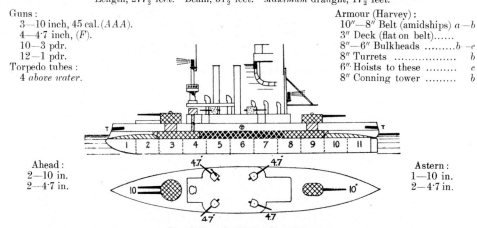

Ahead :
  2—10 in.
  2—4·7 in.

Astern :
  1—10 in.
  2—4·7 in.

Broadside : 3—10 in., 2—4·7 in.

Machinery : 2 sets triple expansion. 2 screws. Boilers : 8 cylindrical. Designed H.P. *forced* 5700 = 16 kts.

Notes.—Engined at the Baltic Works. Just made her speed on *trial* with 5757 I.H.P. (7 hours). Laid down, August, 1895. Completed, 1900. Belt in all three ships of this class is 6 feet wide by 176 feet long ; lower edge of it 6″ thick amidships. Deck flat on belt. Guns have all round loading positions, electric hoists, etc.
Differences.—Minoshima has steam pipe *abaft* the fore funnel ; the *Okinoshima* has it before. *Okinoshima* carries secondary guns on the upper deck.

Formerly the Russian *General Admiral Graf Apraksin.* Captured after Tsushima, 1905.

IKI (Oct., 1889).

Displacement about 9900 tons.   Sheathed.   Complement 604.

Length, 326½ feet.   Beam, 67 feet.   *Maximum* draught, 27 feet.

Guns (Russian) :
 2—12 inch, 30 cal. (*C*).
 12—6 inch, 45 cal. (*D*).
 16—3 pdr.
 4—1 pdr.
 (Some 12 pdrs. may also
   be carried).
Torpedo tubes :
 6 *above water*.

Armour (compound) :
 14″ Belt (amidships) ... *a*
 6″ Belt (ends) .... *d*
 3″ Deck (flat on belt) ...
 Protection to vitals is ... *a*
 10″ Turret .... *b*
 6″ Battery bulkhead...... *d*
 6″ Conning tower......... *d*

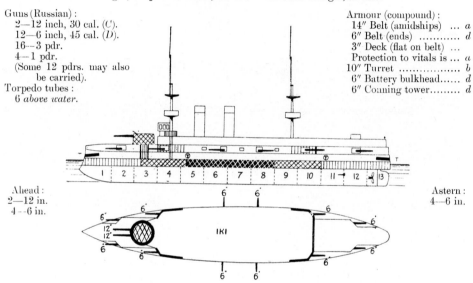

Ahead :
2—12 in.
4—6 in.

Astern :
4—6 in.

Broadside : 2—12 in., 6—6 in.

   Machinery (new about 1900) : 2 sets vertical triple expansion. 2 screws. Boilers : 16 Belleville.
Designed H.P. 8000 = 15·9 kts.   Coal : *normal*   ; *maximum* 1200 tons ; also oil.

Armour Notes.—Belt is 8 feet wide.

Gunnery Notes.—Re-armed hastily in 1904-5.

Engineering Notes.—Re-engined and re-boilered, 1900-02.

General Notes.—Formerly the Russian *Imperator Nikolai I.*   Surrendered after Battle of Tsushima

Photo, *C. de Grave Sells, Esq.*

きあ
IKI.

Now carries high top-gallant masts.

CHIN YEN (1882).
Displacement 7350 tons.   Complement 400.
Length, 308 feet.   Beam, 59 feet.   *Maximum* draught, 23 feet.

Guns :
4—12 inch, 20 cal., (Krupp).
4—6 inch, 40 cal., (Elswick).
10—3 pdr.
2—1 pdr.
Torpedo tubes :
3 *above water* (one on
stern).

Armour (compound) :
14″ Belt (amidships) ...   *a*
10″ Belt (ends) ....   *b*
14″ Bulkheads ....   *a*
3″ Deck (flat on belt)...
Protection to vitals is   *a*
12″ Lower deck redoubt   *a*
12″ Barbettes ....   *a*
3″ Hoods to these ......   *f*
2″ Bow turret ....
8″ Conning tower ......   *d*

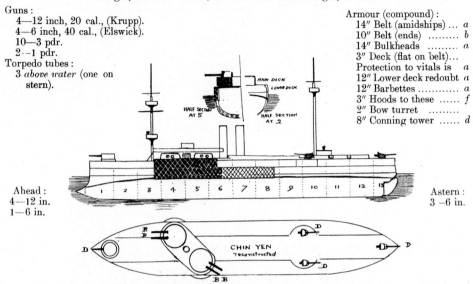

Ahead :
4—12 in.
1—6 in.

Astern :
3 —6 in.

Broadside : 4—12 in., 3—6 in.

Machinery : 2 sets 3 cylinder horizontal compound.   2 screws.   Boilers : cylindrical.   Designed
H.P. *natural* 6200=14·5 kts. ; present speed *circa* 11 kts.   Coal : *normal* 650 tons ; *maximum*
1000 tons.

Notes—The belt is about 10 feet wide.   The ship was formerly the Chinese *Chen Yuen*.   She was
captured at Wei-hai-Wei 12/2/1895.   She subsequently underwent considerable reconstruction and
a partial re-armament.   The conning tower is between the big guns.

んゑんち (CHIN YEN.)

Photo, Captain Takarabe, I.J.N.

FUSO (1877).

Old battleship of 3800 tons.   Complement 377.

Armament : 2—6 inch, 40 cal., 4—4·7 inch, 40 cal., 11—3 pdrs.   3 *above water* tubes.

Armour : 9″ iron belt and 8″ battery in which the two 6″ are.   Used for coast purposes during the
war with Russia.

うさふ (FUSO.)

Photo, Captain Takarabe, I.J.N.

Now carries a fore top-gallant mast for wireless.

204

NEW JAPANESE ARMOURED CRUISERS (? knot). (First of class laid down 1905.)

TSUKUBA (Dec., 1905), *IKOMA* (1906), *IBUKI* (pro.), & *SATSUMA* (pro.)

Displacement 13,750 tons.   Complement

Length, 440 feet. Beam, 75 feet. *Mean* draught, 26 feet.

Guns: (*believed to be*)

Either
- 2—12 inch, 45 cal. (*AAAAA*).
- 4—10 inch, 45 cal. (*AAA*).
- 10—8 inch, 45 cal. (*A*).
- 14—4·7 inch, 50 cal. (*E*).

Armour (Krupp):
Belt (amidships) ...

Ahead:
- 1—12 in.
- 2—10 in.
- 2—8 in.

(No further details available).

Ahead:
- 1—12 in.
- 2—10 in.
- 2—8 in.

Building in Japan.

Broadside: 2—12 in., (4—10 in.), 5—8 in.

Machinery: 2 screws. Boilers: Miyabara
Designed H.P. 20,500 =   kts. Coal: *normal*   tons ; *maximum*   tons.

Note.—Details of secondary armament doubtful.

Name.	Built at	Laid down.	Completed.	Trials.	Boilers.	Last recorded best speed.
Tsukuba	Kure	Jan., 1905				
Ikoma	Kure	Jan., 1905				
Ibuki	...	...				
Satsuma	...	...				

(IWATE CLASS—2 SHIPS.)

IDZUMO (September, 1899) & **IWATE** (March, 1900).

Displacement 9800 tons.   Complement 483.

Length (*waterline*), 400 feet.   Beam, 68½ feet.   *Maximum* draught, 24¼ feet.

Guns
  4—8 inch, 40 cal., (*B*).
  14—6 inch, 40 cal., (*E*).
  12—12 pdr., (*F*).
  8—2½ pdr.
  4 small.
Torpedo tubes :
  4 *Submerged.*

Armour (Krupp) :
  7″ Belt (amidship) ...... *a*
  3½″ Belt (ends) .... ϵ
  2½″ Deck (slopes) ......
  Protection to vitals... = *aa*
  5″ Lower deck (redoubt) *b*
  6″ Turrets and bases... *b*
  6″ Casemates .... *b*
  14″ Conning tower ......
      (Total 2100 tons).

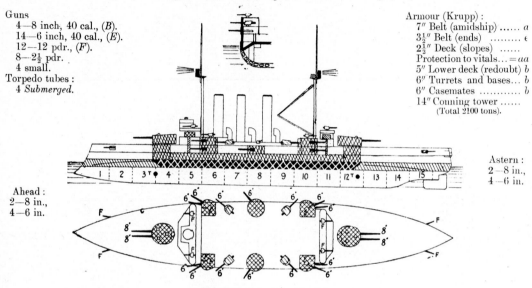

Ahead :
  2—8 in.,
  4—6 in.

Astern :
  2—8 in.,
  4—6 in.

Broadside : 4—8 in., 7—6 in.

もつい   こはい
IDZUMO.   IWATE.

Machinery : 2 sets 4 cylinder triple expansion. 2 screws. Boilers : Belleville. Designed H.P. 14,500 = 20·75 kts. Coal : *normal* 550 tons ; *maximum* 1400 tons.

Armour Notes.—The belt is about 7 feet wide and thick part of it shortened to allow of K.C. instead of H.N. ; 260 feet long.   Upper belt 200 feet long.   Deck 2½″ instead of 2″ as in *Asama.*

Gunnery Notes.—Guns load at any elevation or direction.   Electric and hand gear and hoists.

Engineering Notes.—Both ships are excellent steamers.   Machinery by Humphrys & Tennant.   4 hours *trials* :
  Idzumo, I.H.P. 15,739 = 22·04 kts ; *Iwate*, I.H.P.   = 21·8 kts.   Coal consumption is low in both, especially in the *Idzumo*.   Averages 10½ tons an hour at 15,000 H.P., and 8 tons at 10,000 H.P.

General Notes.—Both built at Elswick.

Differences.—Practically none.

Class distinction.—Funnels are quite different to those of the other 3-funnel cruisers.   Can be mistaken for *Shikishima*, though very much lighter looking and with a different rig.

(ASAMA CLASS—2 SHIPS).

ASAMA (March, 1898) & **TOKIWA** (July, 1898).

Displacement 9750 tons. Complement 500.

Length (*waterline*), 408 feet. Beam, 67 feet. *Maximum* draught, 24¼ feet.

Guns :
  4—8 inch, 40 cal. (*B*).
  14—6 inch, 40 cal. (*E*).
  12—12 pdr. (*F*).
  7—2½ pdr.
Torpedo tubes (18 inch) :
  1 *above water* (bow).
  4 *submerged*.

Armour (Harvey-nickel) :
  7″ Belt (amidships) .... *a*
  3½″ Belt (ends) .... *e*
  2″ Deck (slopes) ....
  Protection to vitals .... = *aa*
  5″ Upper belt (amidships) ... *c*
  3½″ Bulkheads to it .... *d*
  6″ Turrets and bases .... *b*
  6″ Casemates (10) .... *b*
  14″ Conning tower .... *aaa*
      (Total 2100 tons).

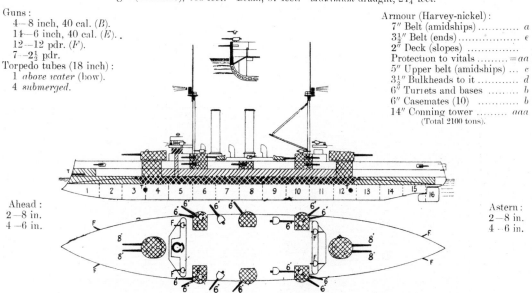

Ahead :
  2—8 in.
  4—6 in.

Astern :
  2—8 in.
  4—6 in.

Broadside: 4—8 in.. 7—6 in.

まさあ ASAMA.

はきと (TOKIWA) is almost identical, but has the standard compass on a platform.

Machinery : 2 sets 4 cylinder triple expansion. 2 screws. Boilers : cylindrical. Designed H.P. *forced* 18,000 = 21½ kts. Coal : *normal* 550 tons ; *maximum* 1300 tons.

Armour Notes.—Belt 7 feet wide ; thick part of it is 280 feet long. Upper belt is 7 feet wide by 260 feet long. 3″ hoists to casemate guns.

Gunnery Notes.—8 in. guns load at any elevation or direction. Electric hoists. Big guns electrically manœuvred.

Engineering Notes.—Machinery by Humphrys & Tennant. *Asama* on *trial* reached 23 kts. (22 kt. *mean*): *Tokiwa*, a mean of 23 kts. Neither ship can touch this now, and the utmost made by *Asama* in the war was 19 kts., and that rarely. Requires re-boilering. Coal consumption : about 10¼ tons an hour at 10,000 H.P. about 20 tons at *full power*.

General Notes.—Both built at Elswick. Very ' handy ' ships.

AZUMA (1899).

Displacement 9456 tons. Complement 482.

Length (*waterline*), 430 feet. Beam, 59 feet. *Maximum* draught, 25 feet.

Guns (Elswick) :
  4—8 inch, 40 cal. (*B*).
  12—6 inch, 40 cal. (*E*).
  12—12 pdr. (*F*).
  12—3 pdr.
Torpedo tubes :
  4 *submerged*.
  1 *above water* (bow).

Armour (Krupp mostly) :
  7″ Belt (amidships) ...   *a*
  3½″ Belt (ends) .... ϵ
  2½″ Deck (on slopes)...
  Protection to vitals   = *aa*
  6″ Turrets and bases
    (H.N.) ....   *b*
  6″ Casemates(H.N.) ...   *b*
  5″ side above belt ......   *b*
  (Total weight 2000 tons).

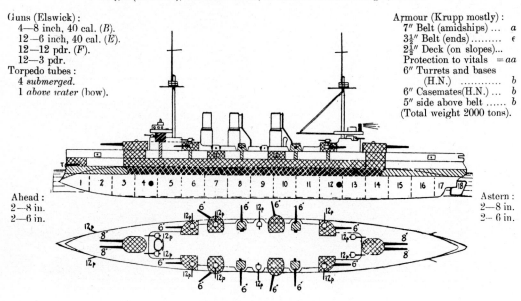

Ahead :
2—8 in.
2—6 in.

Astern :
2—8 in.
2—6 in.

Broadside : 4—8 in., 6—6 in.

まつあ
AZUMA.

Machinery : 2 sets vertical triple expansion.   2 screws.   Boilers : Belleville.   Designed H.P. 17000 =20 kts.

Armour Notes.—Main belt is 7 feet wide by 210 feet long with 6″ bulkheads.

Gunnery Notes.—As for *Asama*, etc.

Engineering Notes.—Made on *trial* 18,000 I.H.P.=21 kts.

General Notes.—This ship generally resembles the *Yakumo*, but the upper deck guns are disposed somewhat differently.   Built at St. Nazaire.   Generally erroneously called *Adzuma*.

JAPANESE ARMOURED CRUISER (20 knot).

YAKUMO (1899).

Displacement 9,850 tons.

Length (*waterline*), 390 feet.   Beam, 65½ feet.   *Mean* draught, 23¾ feet.   Length over all, 407 feet.

Guns :
4—8 inch, 40 cal. (*B*).
12—6 inch, 40 cal. (*E*).
12—12 pdr. (*F*).
7—2½ pdr.
Torpedo tubes (18 inch) :
4 *submerged.*
1 *above water* (bow).

Armour (Krupp) :
7″ Belt (amidships)   *a*
3½″ Belt (ends)......   *d*ε
2½″ Deck (slopes)...
Protection to vitals   = *aa*
6″ Turrets (N.C.)....   *b*
6″ Turret bases (N.C.)   *b*
5″ Lower deck side   *c*
6″ Casemates (8) ...   *b*
10″ Conning tower   *aa*
(Total weight 2040 tons).

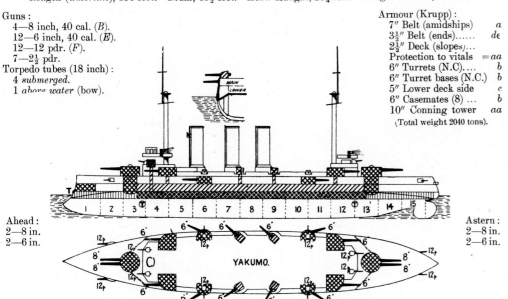

YAKUMO.

Ahead :
2—8 in.
2—6 in.

Astern :
2—8 in.
2—6 in.

Broadside : 4—8 in., 6—6 in.

やくも
YAKUMO.

Machinery : 2 sets vertical triple expansion.   2 screws.   Boilers : Belleville.   Designed H.P. 15,000 = 20 kts.   Coal : *normal* 550 tons ; *maximum* 1,300 tons.

Armour Notes : Belt is 7 feet wide.

Gunnery Notes : Hoists, electric for all guns.   Big guns manœuvred, electric and hand gear.
Arcs of fire : Big guns, 250° ; secondary guns about 110°.
Ammunition carried : 8 in., 80 rounds per gun ; 6 in., 150 per gun.

Engineering Notes : On trial I.H.P. 15,500 = 20·7 kts.   Coal consumption very moderate (less than any other ship built in Germany) ; About 5 tons an hour at 7,000 H.P., and about 12¼ tons an hour at 15,000 H.P. (20 kts.)

General notes : Laid down at Vulkan Co., Stettin, September 1897 ; completed 1901.

209

2 D

(KASUGA CLASS—2 SHIPS).

KASUGA (1902) & NISSHIN (1903).

Displacement 7,700 tons. Complement 525.

Length (*waterline*), 357 feet. Beam, 61½ feet. *Maximum* draught, 25¼ feet.

Guns—(in *Kasuga*):
  1—10 inch, 45 cal. (*AAA*).
  2 – 8 inch, 45 cal. (*A*).
In *Nisshin*:
  4—8 inch, 45 cal. (*A*).
With, in both:
  14—6 inch, 45 cal. (*D*).
  10—12 pdr. (*F*).
  2 Maxims.
  2 Field guns.
Torpedo tubes:
  4 *above water* (in casemates).

Armour (Terni):
6″ Belt (amidships) .... *a*
4½″ Belt (ends) .... *c*
1½″ Deck (on slopes) ......
Protection to vitals .... *a*
5½″ Turrets .... *b*
5½″ Turret bases .... *b*
6″ Lower deck side .... *a*
4½″ Lower deck (bulkheads) *c*
6″ Battery................... *a*
4½″ Battery (bulkheads) ... *c*
4¾″ Conning tower .... *c*

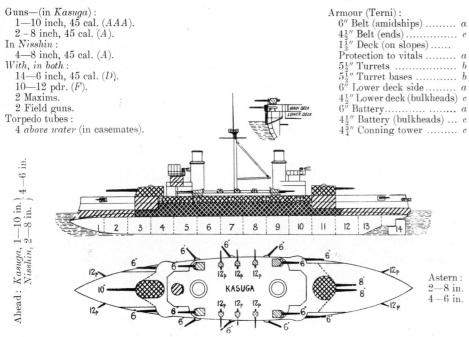

Ahead: *Kasuga*, 1—10 in. } 4—6 in.
Nisshin, 2—8 in. }

Astern:
2—8 in.
4—6 in.

Broadside: *Kasuga*, 1—10 in., 2—8 in., 7—6 in.; *Nisshin*, 4—8 in., 7—6 in.

   Machinery: 2 sets 3 cylinder vertical triple expansion. 2 screws. Boilers: 4 double ended, 4 single ended. Designed H.P. 13,500 = 20 kts. Coal: *normal*, 650 tons; *maximum* 1,100 tons.

Gunnery Notes.—Loading positions, big guns: all round. Hoists, electric. Big guns manœuvred electrically.
   Height of turret guns above water: about 17 feet.

Torpedo Notes.—Torpedo tubes in casemates.

Engineering Notes.—Boilers are placed on either side of engine rooms. Coal consumption: large; nearly 14 tons an hour at 13,500 H.P. (20 kts).

General Notes.—Laid down at Ansaldo's Sestri Ponente for Argentina in 1902. Completed early in 1904. Purchased end of 1903 by Japan for £760,000 each. Reported to be very lightly built.

Distinctions.—Trifling. Practically none, save shape of bow turret.

かすか (KASUGA).

んしひに (NISSHIN).   *Photos by favour of C. de Grave Sells, Esq.*

ASO (1900).

Displacement 7800 tons. Complement

Length (*waterline*), 443 feet. Beam 55¾ feet. *Mean* draught, 22 feet.

Guns (Russian):
 2—8 inch, 45 cal. (*A*).
 8—6 inch, 45 cal. (*D*).
 20—12 pdr. (*F*).
 7—3 pdr.
Torpedo tubes (at 20° abaft).
 2 *submerged*.

Armour (Krupp):
 8″ Belt (amidships) ...*aa*
 4″ Belt (forward) ... .*d*
 8″ Bulkhead (aft) ......*aa*
 2″ Deck (*see notes*) ......
 Protection to vitals = *aaa*
 3¼″—2½″ Upper belt *e*—*f*
 7″ Big gun turrets ......*a*
 Hoists, &c...............
 3¼″ Battery redoubts ...*e*
 6½″ Conning tower ......*a*
 (Total about 1500 tons).

BAYAN

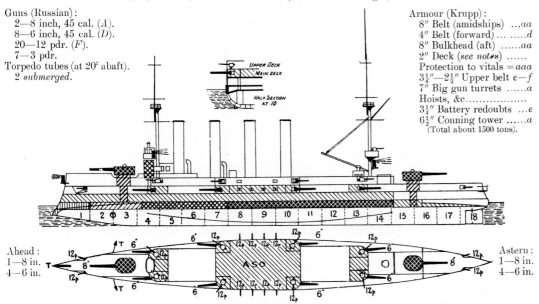

Ahead:
1—8 in.
4—6 in.

Astern:
1—8 in.
4—6 in.

Broadside: 2—8 in., 4—6 in.

うあ

Aso.

Machinery: 2 sets vertical cylinder triple expansion. 2 screws. Boilers: 26 Belleville in 4 groups. Designed H.P. 17,000 = 21 kts. Coal: *normal* 750 tons; *maximum* 1100 tons.

Armour Notes.—Main belt is 6½ feet wide, 4½ feet of it below water $\left(\frac{2}{4\frac{1}{2}}\right)$ There are two 2″ armour decks, the upper flat on main belt, the lower inclined. Coal between these decks and above them amidships.

Gunnery Notes.—Loading positions, big guns: all round. Hoists, electric and hand. Big guns manœuvred electrically and hand. Rate of fire, about 1 round per minute. Bow turret gun 28 feet above water; after-turret gun 24¾ feet. Arcs of fire, 270°. Each 6 inch gun is mounted in a complete circular shield behind the battery wall. Arcs of fire about 110° from axial line. Rounds carried: 8 inch, 100 per gun; 6 inch, 150 per gun; 12 pdr., 250 per gun; 3 pdr., 500 per gun.

Torpedo Notes.—Submerged tubes bear 20° abaft the beam.

Engineering Notes.—This ship steamed excellently when new, exceeding the contract by a knot (I.H.P 17,400 = 22 kts.). It is difficult to maintain high speed for very long in service, as the coal is not easy to get at. *Trial* consumption 1·4 lb. per I.H.P. per hour. In service, burned about 14 tons per hour at full power. Grate area, 1378 square feet. Heating surface, 43,050 square feet.

General Notes.—Formerly the Russian *Bayan*. Laid down for Russia at La Seyne, March, 1899. Completed for sea, February 1903. Electric ventilation. No wood. Steel boats. Solid bulkheads reaching to main deck. Fighting positions in both turrets as well as in conning tower. Designed by M. Lagane, of La Seyne. Sunk at Port Arthur during the Russo-Japanese War. Subsequently raised by the Japanese.

Details of Fore Part.

2 D 2

SOYA (1899).

Displacement 6500 tons.   Complement 571.

Length (*waterline*), 416 feet.   Beam, 52 feet.   *Maximum* draught, 21 feet.

Guns (Russian):
3 12—6 inch, 45 cal. (*D*).
12—12 pdr.
6—3 pdr.
Torpedo tubes (18 inch):
  2 *submerged* (at 20° abaft)
  2 *above water*.

Armour:
  3″ Deck.................... = *d*
  Engine hatches
  6″ Conning tower (H) ...*c*

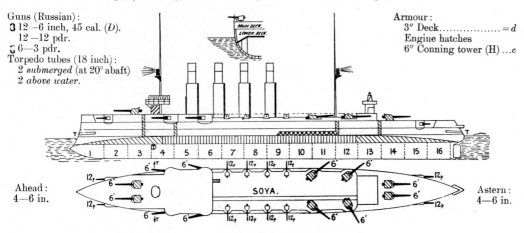

Ahead:
4—6 in.

Astern:
4—6 in.

Broadside: 6—6 in.

Machinery: 2 sets 4 cylinder vertical inverted triple expansion.   2 screws.   Boilers: 30 Niclausse.
Designed H.P. 20,000 = 23 kts.   Coal: *normal* 770 tons; *maximum* 1250 tons.

Engineering Notes.—Funnels 90 feet high above bars.   Heating surface, 62,229 square feet.
  First *trials*:   100 revs. = 16 kts.   120 revs. = 19 kts.   140 revs. = 22 kts.   154 = 23 kts.
        12 hours, 149 revs. I.H.P. 16,270 = 23·25 kts.
        8 hours, 160 „   „   20,000 = 24·6 kts.

Coal consumption: 2¾ tons an hour at 10 kts., and 31 tons an hour at 24 = 23 kts. (full power).   Actual
radius about 950 miles at full speed; 4500 miles at 10 kts.

General Notes.—Formerly the Russian *Variag*.   Sunk at Chemulpo during the Russo-Japanese War,
  February, 1904.   Salved, August, 1905.   Laid down at Cramp's, Philadelphia, 1898.   Completed for
  sea early in 1901.

やう (Fighting tops to be removed).

Photo, Rau.

TSUGARU (1900).

Displacement 6630 tons. Complement 570.

Length (*waterline*), 410 feet. Beam, 55 feet. *Maximum* draught, $21\frac{1}{4}$ feet.

Guns (Russian) :
 8—6 inch, 45 cal. (D).
 22—12 pdr. (F).
 8—Small Q.F.
Torpedo tubes :
 4 *above water*.

Armour :
 $2\frac{1}{2}''$ Deck .... $= \epsilon d$
 4″ Hoists ....
 2″ Funnels between decks
 6″ C. T. (Harvey) c
 $4\frac{1}{2}''$ Engine hatches ... = b

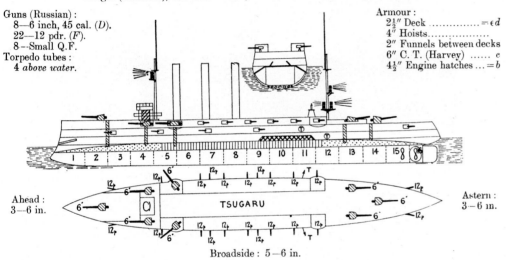

Ahead :
3—6 in.

TSUGARU

Astern :
3—6 in.

Broadside : 5—6 in.

Machinery : 3 sets horizontal 3 cylinder triple expansion. 3 screws. Boilers : 24 Belleville. Designed H.P. 11,600 = 20 kts. Coal : *normal* 900 tons ; *maximum* 1430 tons + liquid fuel.

Gunnery Notes.—Electric hoists to all guns.

Engineering Notes.—On first *trials* (1901) in measured mile runs, the *mean* of 6 runs was I.H.P. 13,100 = 19·2 kts.

General Notes.—Formerly the Russian *Pallada*. Sunk at Port Arthur and subsequently salved. Tactical diameter *circa* 750 yards. No wood used in construction. Laid down at Galernii Island, 1896. Completed 1902.

うくつ (Fighting top to be removed).

KASAGI (January, 1898), & **CHITOSE** (January, 1898).

Displacement 4760 tons.   Complement 405.

Length (*waterline*), 396 feet.   Beam, 48 feet.   *Maximum* draught, 24½ feet.   Length over all, 405 feet.

Guns :
2—8 inch, 40 cal. (*B*).
10—4·7 inch (*F*).
12—12 pdr. (*F*).
6—2½ pdr.
Torpedo tubes :
4 *above water.*

Armour :
4½″ Deck.................. = *b*
Hoists .... = *ε*
Cofferdam and bunkers
amidships ....
Protection to vitals ...... = *b*

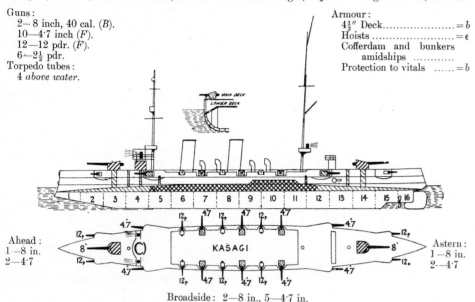

KASAGI

Ahead :
1—8 in.
2—4·7

Astern :
1—8 in.
2—4·7

Broadside : 2—8 in., 5—4·7 in.

Machinery : 2 sets vertical triple expansion.   2 screws.   Boilers : 8 cylindrical.   Designed H.P. *forced* 15,000 = 22·5 kts.   Coal : *normal* 350 tons ; *maximum capacity* 1000 tons.

Armour Notes.—Very little of the deck is 4½″ thick, most of it is half that thickness.

Gunnery Notes.—The 8 in. guns have only small shields to them, 4½ in. thick on faces.   The guns stand on stout armoured supports rising from protection deck.   Electric hoists.

Torpedo Notes.—25 torpedoes carried.   A bow tube has been suppressed.   Folding tubes.   Automatic searchlights.

Engineering Notes.—On *trials* both exceeded slightly the designed speed, but they were very light. They cannot touch 22 kts. at the present day.   Working pressure, 165 lbs.

General Notes.—These ships roll very much and are not very seaworthy.   2 similar ships *Takasago* and *Yoshino*, built at Elswick, lost in the war.   *Kasagi* built by Cramp's, U.S.A.; *Chitose* at San Francisco.

きさか (KASAGI).   *Photo by C. O. Travers, Esq.*

せさち (CHITOSE).

No photo yet procurable.

No photo yet procurable.

かたいに

NIITAKA.

ましつ

TSUSHIMA.

OTAWA (1903) & *TONE* (building).

Displacement 3050 tons. Complement 312.

Length, 351 feet. Beam, 41 feet. *Maximum* draught, 16¼ feet.

Guns (Japanese):
  2—6 inch, 50 cal. (C).
  6—4.7 inch.
  4—12 pdr.
  2—1 pdr.
Torpedo tubes (18 inch):
  2 *above water.*

Armour :
  3″ Deck (amidships) = d
  2″ Deck (ends) .... = ϵ
  1½″ Gunshields ......
  4″ Conning tower (K.N.C.)

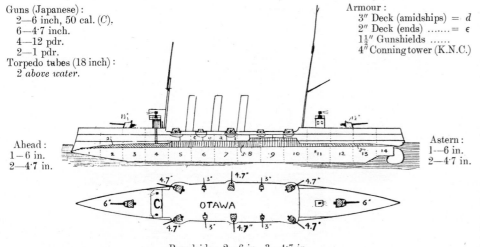

Ahead :
1—6 in.
2—4.7 in.

Astern :
1—6 in.
2—4.7 in.

Broadside : 2—6 in., 3—4.7 in.

Machinery : 2 sets triple expansion. 2 screws. Boilers : Miyabara. Designed H.P. 10,000 = 21 kts. Coal : *normal* 600 tons ; *maximum* 850 tons.

NIITAKA & **TSUSHIMA** (1902).

Displacement 3420 tons. Complement 320.

Length, 334½ feet. Beam, 44 feet. *Maximum* draught, 16½ feet.

Guns (Elswick):
  6—6 inch, 40 cal. (E).
  10—12 pdr.
  4—2½ pdr.
Torpedo tubes :
  None.

Armour (steel) :
  2½″ Deck ....= d
  [Cellulose belt.]
  4″ Conning tower (K.N.C.) d

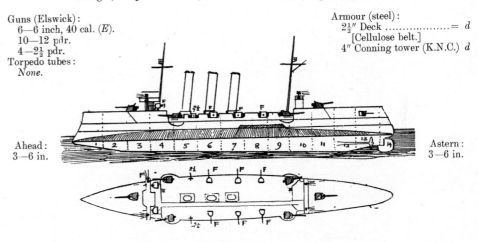

Ahead :
3—6 in.

Astern :
3—6 in.

Broadside : 4—6 in.

Machinery : 2 sets triple expansion. 2 screws. Boilers : Niclausse. Designed H.P. 9500 = 20 kts. Coal : *normal*   tons ; *maximum* 600 tons.

ます (SUMA)　　*Photo, Captain Takarabe, I.J.N.*

SUMA (1895).

Displacement 2700 tons.　Complement 275.

Length, 305 feet.　Beam, 41 feet.　*Maximum* draught, $16\frac{1}{3}$ feet.

Guns (Elswick):
2—6 inch, 40 cal. (*E*).
6—4·7 inch, 40 cal. (*F*).
12—3 pdr.
Torpedo tubes:
2 above water.

Armour:
2″ Deck ....= ε
$4\frac{1}{2}$″ Shields to 6 inch guns

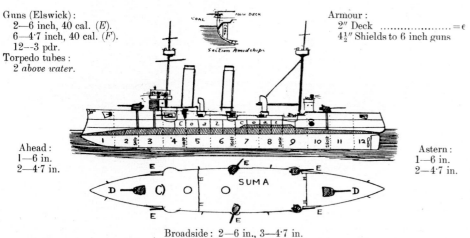

Ahead:
1—6 in.
2—4·7 in.

Astern:
1—6 in.
2—4·7 in.

Broadside: 2—6 in., 3—4·7 in.

Machinery: 2 sets vertical triple expansion.　2 screws.　Boilers: 8 cylindrical.　Designed H.P.
forced draught 8500 = 20 kts.　Coal: *normal* 200 tons; *maximum* 600 tons.

しかあ
(AKASHI).

AKASHI (1897).

Displacement 2700 tons.　Complement 275.

Length, 305 feet.　Beam, 41 feet.　*Maximum* draught, $16\frac{1}{3}$ feet.

Guns (Elswick):
2—6 inch, 40 cal. (*E*).
6—4·7 inch, 40 cal. (*F*).
12—3 pdr.
4 Nordenfelts.
Torpedo tubes:
2 above water.

Armour:
2″ Deck ....= ε
$4\frac{1}{2}$″ Shields to 6 inch guns

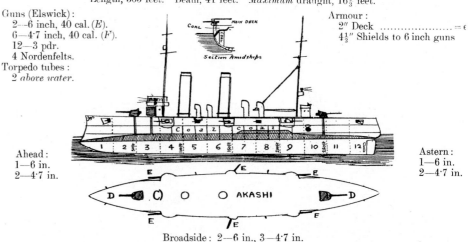

Ahead:
1—6 in.
2—4·7 in.

Astern:
1—6 in.
2—4·7 in.

Broadside: 2—6 in., 3—4·7 in.

Machinery: 2 sets vertical triple expansion.　2 screws.　Boilers: 8 cylindrical.　Designed H.P.
8500 = 20 kts.　Coal: *normal* 200 tons; *maximum* 600 tons.

Notes.—Both ships designed and built in Japan.　They were intended to have been sisters, but the
Suma proving very wet, the *Akashi* was built up amidships and other modifications introduced.

ましつま
MATSUSHIMA.

Fighting tops removed, 1903.

MATSUSHIMA (1890).

Displacement 4277 tons.   Complement 360.

Length, 295 feet.   Beam, 50½ feet.   *Maximum* draught, 21¼ feet.

Guns :
  1—12·6 inch, Canet, (*AAA*).
  12 —4·7 inch, 40 cal., Elswick, (*E*).
  6—12 pdr.
  4—3 pdr.
  6—1 pdr.
Torpedo tubes :
  4 *above water* (bow, stern, and
    quarter).

Armour (steel) :
  1½″ Deck .... = ε
    [Cellulose belt].
  5″ Engine hatches ...... = *a*
  12″ Barbette .... *a*
  4″ Hood to it .... ε
  12″ Hoists .... *a*
    Conning tower.

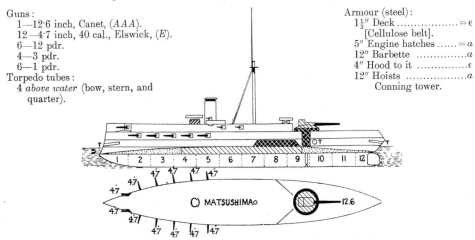

Machinery : 2 sets triple expansion. 2 screws. Boilers : Belleville (1902). Designed H.P.
natural 3400 = 15·7 kts. ; *forced* 5400 = 16·7 kts.   Coal : 405.

Note.—Matsushima is an improved *Itsukushima*.   Built at La Seyne.   During war with Russia this ship
proved the best steamer of the three.

てたしは・　ましくつい
HASHIDATE.　　ITSUKUSHIMA.

Almost identical, but the 4·7 inch are without the small sponsons in *Itsukushima*.
Fighting tops removed, 1903.

ITSUKUSHIMA (1889), & HASHIDATE (1891).

Displacement 4277 tons.   Complement 360.

Length, 295 feet.   Beam, 50½ feet.   *Maximum* draught, 21¼ feet.

Guns :
  1—12·6 inch (*AAA*).
  11—4·7 inch, 40 cal. (*F*).
  5—12 pdr.
  11—3 pdr.
  2 Machine.
Torpedo tubes :
  4 *above water* (bow, stern, and
    section 2).

Armour (steel) :
  1½″ Deck .... = ε
    [Cellulose belt].
  5″ Engine hatches ...... = *a*
  12″ Barbette .... *a*
  4″ Hood to it .... ε
  12″ Hoist .... *a*
    Conning tower.

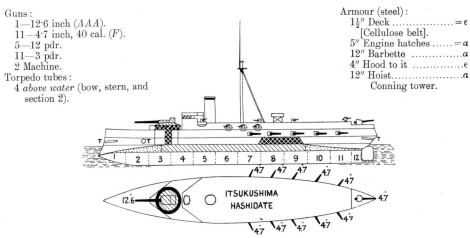

Machinery : 2 sets triple expansion. 2 screws. Boilers : *Hashidate*, Miyabara (1903);
Itsukushima, Belleville (1900-01).   Designed H.P. 5400 = 16·7 kts.   Coal : 405 tons.

Note.—Itsukushima built at La Seyne. *Hashidate* put together in Japan from imported material.
Designed by M. Bertin, 1887.

2 E

たよち
CHIYODA.

(Fighting tops now removed).   *Official Photo.*

はにな　ほちか多
NANIWA.　　　TAKACHIHO.

Official photo.

(*Takachiho* exactly like her, but has only one yard on main mast.)

CHIYODA (June, 1890).

Displacement 2450 tons.　Complement 350.

Length, 308 feet.　Beam, 43 feet.　*Maximum* draught, 17 feet.

Guns (Elswick) :
　10—4·7 inch, 40 cal.
　15—3 pdr.
　3 Gatlings.
Torpedo tubes :
　3 *above water.*

Armour (chrome steel) :
　4½″ Belt ....   *d*
　1″ Deck at ends ....
　　[Deck flat on belt.]
　Protection to vitals is ...   *d*
　　[Cellulose belt.]

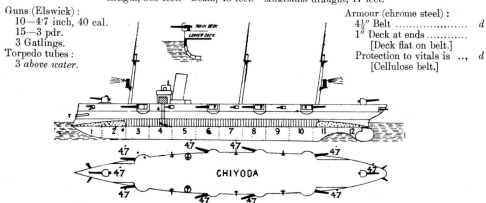

CHIYODA

Machinery : 2 sets triple expansion.　2 screws.　Boilers (1898) : Belleville without economisers.
Designed H.P. 5500 = 19 kts.　Coal : *normal* 330 tons ; *maximum* 420 tons.
Notes.—Built at Clydebank.　Originally had locomotive boilers, and was given Bellevilles as the old
boilers choked up with Japanese coal.　Burns about 4¼ tons an hour at full speed.

NANIWA (1885) & TAKACHIHO (1885).

Displacement 3700 tons.　Complement 357.

Length, 300 feet.　Beam, 46 feet.　*Maximum* draught, 20 feet.

Guns :
　2—10·2 inch, old Krupp.
　6—6 inch, 40 cal., Elswick.
　2—6 pdr.
　10—1 inch Nordenfelts.
　4 Gatlings.
Torpedo tubes :
　4 *above water.*

Armour (steel) :
　3″ Deck .... = ε
　3″ Engine hatches .... = ε
　1½″ Hoods to big guns ... *f*
　1½″ Conning tower ....

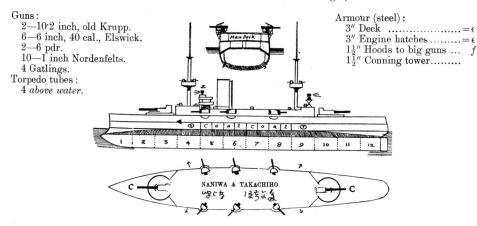

NANIWA & TAKACHIHO
ばじち　ほちよ多

Machinery : 2 sets horizontal compound.　2 screws.　Boilers : cylindrical.　Designed H.P. 7000
= 18·5 kts.　On first *trial* both made about 7120 = 18·7 kts.　After refit (1900), *Naniwa* made 17·8 kts.
mean natural draught.　Coal : *normal* 350 tons ; *maximum* 800 tons.

Note.—Built at Elswick from designs of Sir William White.　Secondary armament new in 1900.

218

Official Photo.

まじつきあ

AKITSUSHIMA (1892).

Displacement 3150 tons.　Complement 330.

Length, 302 feet.　Beam, 43 feet.　*Maximum* draught, 18½ feet.

Guns (Elswick):
　4—6 inch, 40 cal. (E).
　6—4·7 inch, 40 cal. (F)
　10—3 pdr.
Torpedo tubes:
　4 *above water.*

Armour (steel):
　3″ Deck .... = d

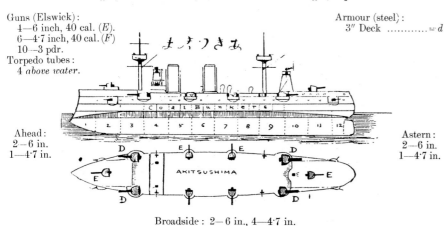

Ahead:
2—6 in.
1—4·7 in.

Astern:
2—6 in.
1—4·7 in.

Broadside : 2—6 in., 4—4·7 in.

Machinery : 2 sets vertical triple expansion.　2 screws.　Boilers : cylindrical.　Designed
H.P. *natural*　　= 16 kts.; *forced* 8400 = 19 kts.　Coal : *normal* 500 tons.

Notes.—This ship is a reduced copy of the United States *Baltimore* and *Philadelphia*.　She was
　　built and engined in Japan, but most of her material imported.　She is not a satisfactory
　　steamer, and rolls a great deal.

みつい

IDZUMI (1884).

Reconstructed 1901.

Displacement 3000 tons.　Complement 300.

Length, 270 feet.　Beam, 40 feet.　*Maximum* draught, 18½ feet.

Guns (Japanese):
　2—6 inch, 40 cal. (E).
　6—4·7 inch, 40 cal. (F)
　1—6 pdr.
　6—3 pdr.
Torpedo tubes:
　nil.

Armour (steel):
　1″ Deck ....

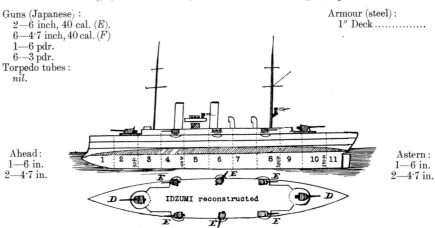

Ahead:
1—6 in.
2—4·7 in.

Astern:
1—6 in.
2—4·7 in.

Broadside : 2—6 in., 3—4·7 in.

Machinery : 2 sets　　　　　　　.　2 screws.　Boilers : Niclausse.　Designed
H.P. 6000 = 18 kts.　Coal : *normal* 400 tons ; *maximum* 600 tons.

Notes.—The first protected cruiser ever built, formerly the *Esmeralda*.　She was purchased from
　　Chili, 1895, and found unseaworthy.　Originally carried two 10-inch Krupp and six 6 inch
　　ditto.　Battery changed 1899.　6 inch substituted for big guns, 1901.　Is now a fairly good
　　sea boat.

やはち **CHIHAYA** (1901) & *YODO* (1906).

Displacement 850 tons.   Complement 125.

Guns (Japanese):
  2—4·7 inch, 40 cal.
  4—12 pdr.
Torpedo tubes:
  3 *above water.*

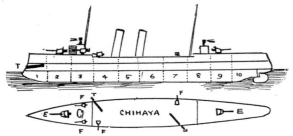

Machinery: 2 screws.   Designed H.P. 6000 = 21 kts.   Coal 250 tons.

TATSUTA (1893).

Displacement 875 tons.   Complement 100.

Guns (Elswick):
  2—4·7 inch, 40 cal.
  4—3 pdr.
Torpedo tubes (14 inch):
  5 *above water.*

Machinery: 2 sets vertical triple expansion. 2 screws. Boilers: Miyabara.   Designed H.P. *forced* 5500 = 21 kts.   Coal: 188 tons.

まや屋を **YAYEYAMA** (1889).

Displacement 1600 tons.   Complement 200.

Guns (Krupp):   Armour (steel):
  3—4·7 inch, 35 cal.   ½″ Deck over engines.
Torpedo tubes:
  2 *above water.*

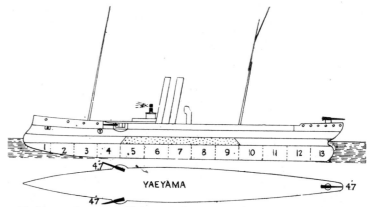

Machinery: 2 screws.   Niclausse boilers.   Designed H.P. 5500 = 20 kts.
Note.—Sunk last year, but since raised.

こやみ **MIYAKO** (1897).

Displacement 1800 tons.   Complement 220.

Guns (Japanese):
  2—4·7 inch, 40 cal.
  8—3 pdr.

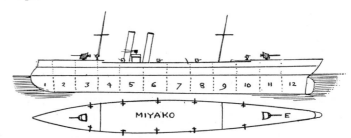

Machinery: 2 sets triple expansion.   2 screws.   Boilers: cylindrical.   De-signed H.P. 6130 = 20 kts.   Coal: 400 tons.

Note.—Built in Japan.   Sunk during the war at Dalny, but since reported raised.

MAKIGUMO (1893) & **SHIKINAMI** (1893).

Displacement 411 tons.   Complement 61.

Length, 190 feet.   Beam, 24 feet.   *Maximum* draught, 9 feet.

Guns :
  3—3 pdr.
  3—1 pdr.

Coal protection to engines
and boilers.

Machinery : 2 sets triple expansion.   2 screws.   Designed H.P. 3400 = 21 kts.
(Present speed about 16-17 kts. or less).   Coal : 90 tons.

Built by Schichau.   Formerly the Russian *Vsadnik* and *Gaidamak*.

The *Novik* and *Boyarin*, *ex* Russian ships, sunk during the war, are being salved.   Armament: 6—4·7 inch.   Displacement: about 3000 tons.   Speeds: 25-23 knots.   Indifferent coal supply.

Miscellaneous Vessels.

An old merchant ship, TOYOHASCHI, of 4200 tons, has been converted into a torpedo depôt ship.

There are 5 gunboats, AKAGI, TAKAO, MAYA, CHIOKAI, and TSUKUSHI, of slow speed and no fighting value.   Also 2 old wooden ships, AMAGI and TENRIU, 3 old wooden gunboats, also 6 Rendel gunboats captured from China (1895) and several other minor craft.

5 *Thornycroft.* **Kagero, Murakumo, Usugumo, Shinonome, Shiranui** (1898-99). 275 tons.
Armament: 1—12 pdr. (aft), 5—6 pdr.. 2—18″ tubes. H.P. 5400=30 kts. Coal: 81 tons. Complement 54
Maximum draught: feet.

18 *Yarrow.* **Akebono, Ikadsuchi, Inazuma, Oboro, Sazanami** (1898-99). 306 tons. Armament:
1—12 pdr. (aft), 5—6 pdr., 2—18″ tubes. H.P. 6000=31 kts. Coal: 95 tons. Complement 55. *Maximum* draught:
8½ feet; also **Akatsuki, Kasumi, Hayatori, Murasame** (1901), **Fubuki, Arare, Ariake, Ushio,
Hatsushimo, Kamikaze, Yayoi, Nenohi, Kisaragi** (1905). 380 tons. Other particulars as above,
except draught increased to 9 feet.

New Destroyers, *in hand* :—*Hibiki, Makaba, Hatsuyuki, Yuguri, Yudachi, Mikadzuke, Newake,
Yunagi, Quite, Shiratsuyu, Shirayuki, Matsukase, Shiretaye, Asakase, Harukase, Schigure, Asatsuyu,
Ayakase.*

4 *Thornycroft.* **Asashiho, Shirakumo, Asagiri, Harusame** (1901). 365 tons. Armament: 1—12 pdr. (aft),
5—6 pdr. 2—18″ tubes. H.P. 6000=31 kts. Coal: 90 tons. Complement 60. *Maximum* draught: 9 feet,

3 *Ex* Russian destroyers. *Yarrow* type. **Satsuki** (*ex Bdevoi*), 350 tons; **Fumitzuki** (*ex Silny*), 220 tons;
and one *Normand* type, (*ex Rechitelni*), (All three have four funnels),

Torpedo Boats.

No.	Type.	Date.	Displacement.	Maximum Speed.	Coal.	Complement.	Tubes.
				kts.	tons.		
45	*Projected* ...*pro. bldg.*		150	27	...	...	3
10	Aotaka	'03-'05	120	27	...	...	3
19	Normand ...	'98-'01	150	29	26	...	3
10	Yarrow	'00-'01	110	27	24	...	3
2	Schichau ...	'99-'00	130	28	30	...	3
5	Yarrow	'98	135	27	...	...	3
1	Krupp	'95	128	19	...	...	6
12	*various*	'00-'04	80	23	...	...	3
3	Schichau ...	'91	85	23	24	22	3
2	Normand ...	'91	80	23	10	21	3

There are also 1 old Yarrow boat (*Kotaka*) launched in 1886, and 20 old boats of 56-53 tons, original speeds 20 kts. or less, and 4 old Yarrow boats, very old, of 40 tons.

The *Aotaka* class are named **Aotaka, Hato, Hibari, Kari, Kiji, Tsubame, Sagi, Uzuri, Kainone, Hashitaka,** and **Otori,** all built in Japan.

Normand boats are the **Hayabusa** type.

5 + 7 **Submarines.**

5 *Holland* type (1904), 120 tons displacement. Dimensions, $65 \times 11\frac{3}{4} \times 12\frac{1}{4}$ feet. Motive power: $\dfrac{\text{Petrol, 160 H.P.} = 8 \text{ kts.}}{\text{Accumulators, 70 H.P.} = 7 \text{ kts.}}$ 4 cylinder vertical petrol engine. Control by ignition and cutting-out cylinders. Petrol carried: 850 gallons. Armament: 1—18″ tube (short torpedoes). Double periscope (one small scale, one large). Built by the Holland Co.

7 new boats, *building.*

———

There is also a small Russian boat, Peter Kotchka type, captured at Port Arthur, but this is reported to have been rendered useless before the surrender.

GERMAN FLEET.

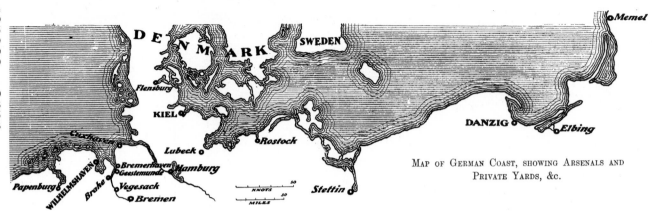

WILHELMSHAVEN to		knots.	KIEL to			knots.
	Cherbourg	510		Copenhagen		160
	Dover	330		Danzig		345
	Gibraltar...	1565		Libau		710
	Havre	450		Memel		660
	Hull	330		Kronstadt...		800
	Kiao-chau...	11100				
	Malta...	2555				
	New York...	3570	DANZIG to	Libau...		160
	Port Said	3530		Memel		113
	Portsmouth	440		Kiel		345
	Rio de Janeiro	5470		Kronstadt...		558
	Rosyth	450				
	Sheerness	280				

Wilhelmshaven to Kiel, 80 miles (by canal much of the way).

MAP OF GERMAN COAST, SHOWING ARSENALS AND PRIVATE YARDS, &c.

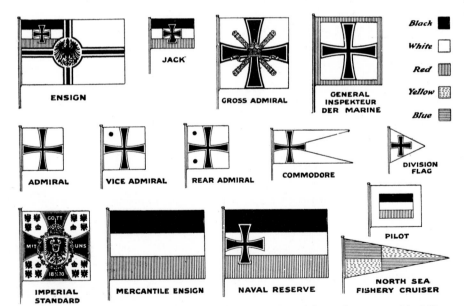

Imperial standard : Square ; yellow, with black cross ; Imperial arms in centre and in field.

Mercantile Marine (excluding fishing craft, &c.).

1464 steamers (418 over 2000 tons, 271 of 2000-1000 tons), total tonnage about 1,500,000.
2500 sailing (58 over 2000 tons, about 2000 *under* 1000 tons), ,, ,, ,, 590,000.
Total crews for these ships *circa* 60,000 men.

Principal Trade Ports (with approximate annual clearance).

Hamburg and Cuxhaven ($8\frac{1}{4}$ million tons), Bremen district ($2\frac{1}{4}$ million), Stettin ($1\frac{1}{2}$ million), Danzig (Neufahrwasser) ($\frac{3}{4}$ million), and Kiel, Lubeck, and Kônigsberg (near Memel) all about $\frac{1}{2}$ million).

Coinage.

Mark (100 pfennige) = $11\frac{3}{4}d$. British, 24 cents U.S.A.

Colour of Ships.

Big ships : light grey all over ; red distinguishing bands on funnels.
Torpedo craft : not settled ; varies from black to dull brown.

Naval *Personnel.*

About 33,000 all ranks.
Minister of Marine : Admiral von Tirpitz.
Commander-in-Chief : Admiral von Knorr.

The German *personnel* is very efficient, both above and below. More attention is paid to smartness of appearance in men and ships than in any other navy (except, perhaps, the American). Discipline, good. Shooting, moderately fair. Torpedo craft are usually extremely well handled.

INSIGNIA OF RANK ON SLEEVES FOR EXECUTIVES (See Offizierkorps).

| Admiral. | Vizeadmiral. (Vice-Ad.) | Kontreadmiral. (Rear-Ad.) | Kommodore (Captain acting as Commodore). | Kapitän z. See. and Fregatten-Kapitän (Captain). | Korvetten-Kapitän. (Commander). | Kapitän-Leutnant. (Senior Lieut.) | Oberleut z. See. (Junior Lieut.) | Leutenant z. See (Sub-Lieut.) |

Note.—Torpedo officers are without the crown on sleeve, as also are all civilian branches.

Torpedo officers have between the gold stripes, *brown.*
Engineer   ,,   ,,   ,,   *black.*
Doctors   ,,   ,,   ,,   *blue.*
Paymasters   ,,   ,,   ,,   *light blue.*
Constructors ,,   ,,   ,,   *black.*

(The colour of the branch is also worn on the epaulettes, full dress, and worked into the shoulder straps).

Paymasters and constructors have silver instead of gold epaulette fringes, and cloth instead of velvet between the stripes.

Torpedoes.

All of Schwartzkopf type. Phosphor bronze. Fitted with gyroscopes. Very similar to the Whitehead. These torpedoes find and keep the set depth very well.

Name or Mark.	Air Pressure.	Charge.	Max. Range.	Average speed if set for		
				1000	2000	4000
inch.	*about*	lbs.		kts.	kts.	kts.
17·7	2000	246½	2000	30	26	
13·7	2000	100	2000	28	20	

Submerged tubes are bow, broadside, and 45° abaft the beam. Type of early model tube somewhat similar to the Elswick, but portions of the bar permanently project outside the hull. The 1904 model, submerged tube, is a training one on a ball and socket arrangement.

Naval Guns (Krupp).   ❋ = Brass Cartridge case.

Notation.	Calibre.	Designation.	Length in cals.	Date of Model.	Weight of Gun.	Weight of A.P. shot.	Initial Velocity.	Maximum penetration direct impact against K.C at 5000 yards.	3000 yards.	Dangerous space against average ships at 10,000	5000	3000	Maximum rounds per minute.
	inches.	c/m.			tons.	lbs.	F.S.	inches.	inches.	yards.	yards.	yards.	
AAAAA	11	28	{45 or 50	'04					22				
AAA	11	28	40	'01	34	595	2854	12	15	150	450	740	1
A	11	28	40		44	474	2296	6	8½	120	320	600	1¼
B	11	28	35		43½	474	2231	5	7½	...	...	600	1¼
AA	9·4	24	40	'99	21	309	2900	8½	11¼	...	...	...	1½
A*	9·4	24	40		21	309	2500	7½	10¼	110	350	620	1½
B	9·4	24	35		22	252	2300	5½	8	...	...	...	2
A	8·2	21	40		16	242½	2526	6½	9	...	...	...	3
B	6·7	17	40	'01	8	132	2887	5¼	6¾	80	240	460	5
E*	6	15	40		5	88	2460	3½	5·	...	140	350	7
F*	6	15	35		5½	88	2230	...	2½	...	...	200	7
F*	4·1	10	40		1½	38	2300	...	2	...	...	...	8
F*	4·1	10	35		1¼	38	2000	...	...	...	...	...	8
F*	3·4	8·8	35		1¼	24	2788	...	...	...	...	...	10
F*	3·4	8·8	30		¾	15½	2165	...	...	...	...	...	10
F*	2	5				6	2165	...	...	...	...	...	12

❋ = Brass cartridge case.

Mitrailleuse : Maxims and Nordenfelt.   *Rifle :* Mauser (1898) magazine, 7 rounds.

Powder : Nitro-cellulose.

Projectiles : A.P. shot, A.P. shell, semi-A.P. shell (H.E. burster), common steel pointed (H.E. burster), common (H.E. burster). Only high velocity guns use caps, and these may be abolished.

Most "Q.F.'s" have the Krupp horizontal breech, but some have the Welin breech mechanism—The 1899 and later models have the recoil utilized to return the gun to firing position for pieces over 6-in. In 6-in. compressed air is employed.

GERMAN DOCKYARDS.

(Divided into 2000 yard squares. Uniform scale. Soundings in fathoms. Height in feet).

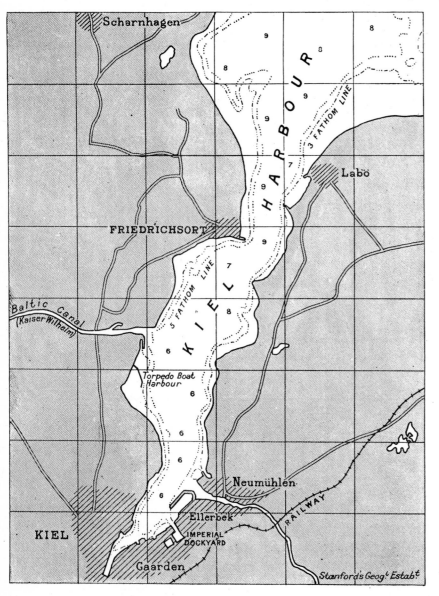

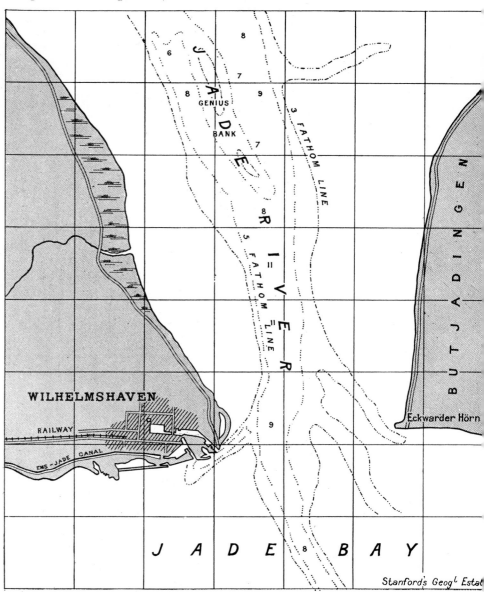

1. KIEL. Two large basins.

Docks :

(1) $423 \times 71 \times 28$

Can just take *Wittelsbach* or *Bismark*.

(2) $382 \times 70 \times 25\frac{1}{2}$

Can just take *Brandenburg*.

(3) $362 \times 64\frac{1}{2} \times 22\frac{1}{2}$

For *Bremen* or coast defence ships.

(4) $344 \times 67 \times 16$

(5) and (6) taking any ship.

Also one floating dock able to take any warship, and a second floating for destroyers or gun boats.

Three building slips.

Men employed, about 7300.

2. WILHELMSHAVEN. Two large basins. Harbour for torpedo craft inside yard.

Docks :

(1) $438 \times 72 \times 27\frac{1}{2}$
(2) $438 \times 72 \times 27$
(3) $370 \times 61\frac{1}{2} \times 22$

Two floating docks for small torpedo boats.

Two docks able to take any ship *building*.

Two building slips.

Men employed, about 3500.

GERMAN ARSENALS, Etc.

(Divided into squares of 2000 yards. Uniform scale. Soundings in fathoms. Heights in feet).

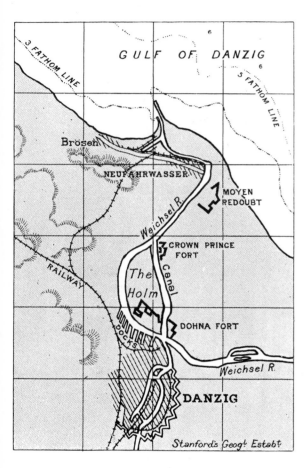

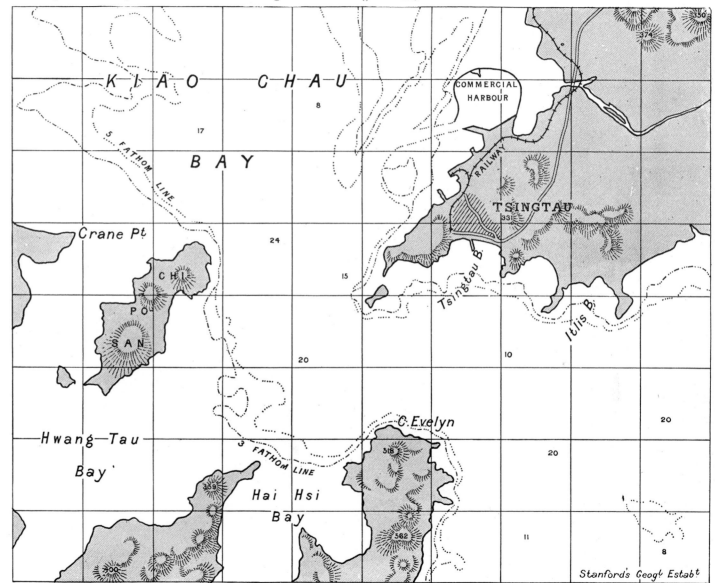

DANZIG. Two small floating docks and three patent slips. All for torpedo craft. New dock to take any ship (*to be built*).

One large building slip, one small one.

Men employed, about 3500.

KIAO-CHAU (China). Fortified base for Far Eastern Squadron. No docks.

GERMAN HARBOURS.

(Divided into 2000 yard squares.   Uniform scale.   Soundings in fathoms.   Heights in feet).

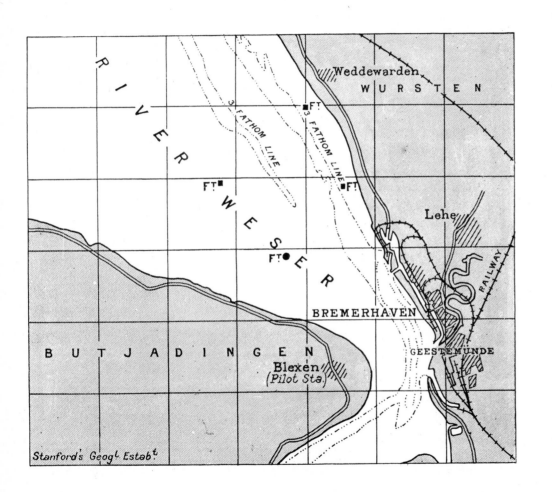

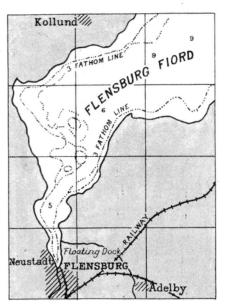

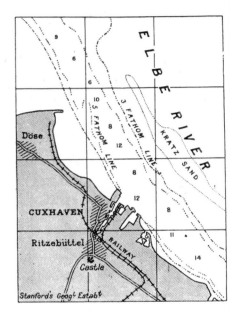

Principal German Harbours.

BREMERHAVEN (for Bremen, etc.)
CUXHAVEN.
FLENSBURG.
SWINEMUNDE (for Stettin).

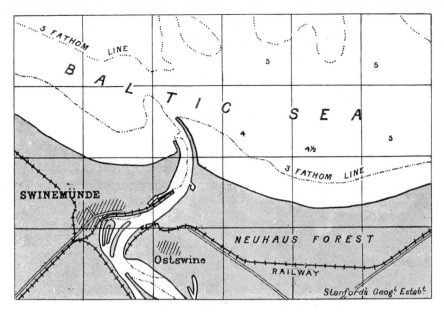

Private Yards.

(Building slips over 320 feet long are called big here.)

			Big slips.	Small slips.	Docks.	Employees circa.
KIEL	... ...	Howaldt*	8	4	3	3200
„	... ...	Germania (Krupp)* ...		ten	—	3000
HAMBURG	... ...	Blohm & Voss*	6	—	4	5100
„	... ...	H. Brandenburg	—	6	2	650
„	... ...	Jansen Act. Ges.	—	7	1	300
„	... ...	Reiherstieg A. G. ...	2	—	2	1700
„	... ...	Stülcken Sohn	—	6	3	420
DANZIG	... ...	Johannsen & Co.	—	2	1	280
„	... ...	Klawitter & Co.	—	4	3	500
„	... ...	Schichau*	7	—	—	2400
GEESTEMÜNDE	...	Rickmers A. G.	1	2	—	420
„		Seebeck A. G.	1	6	5	1280
„	...	Tecklenbourg	6	1	3	1800
ELBING	... ...	Schichau*	—	8	2	5000
BREMEN	...	Weser*	4	4	3	2200
FLENSBURG	...	Flensburg S. G.	8	1	1	2600
VEGESACK	...	Bremer Vulkan	9	—	—	2650
LUBECK	... ...	H. Koch	—	3	2	830
PAPENBURG	...	S. L. Meyer	—	3		450
ROSTOCK	... ...	Neptune A. G. ...	2	2	1	1550

Those marked * have built for the Navy. Except at Geestemünde the docks are floating or patent slips.

GERMAN WARSHIPS (ONE FUNNEL) IDENTIFICATION AND SIGNAL SILHOUETTES.

G cone.

HD   GEIER.   HF   BUSSARD.   HJ   FALKE.

(All page 253).

HK   SEE ADLER class (page 253) (3 ships).   HM   HELA (page 251).

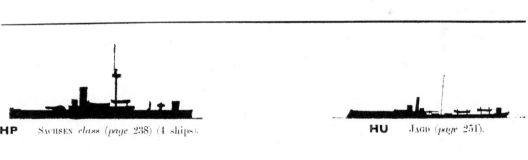

HP   SACHSEN class (page 238) (4 ships).   HU   JAGD (page 251).

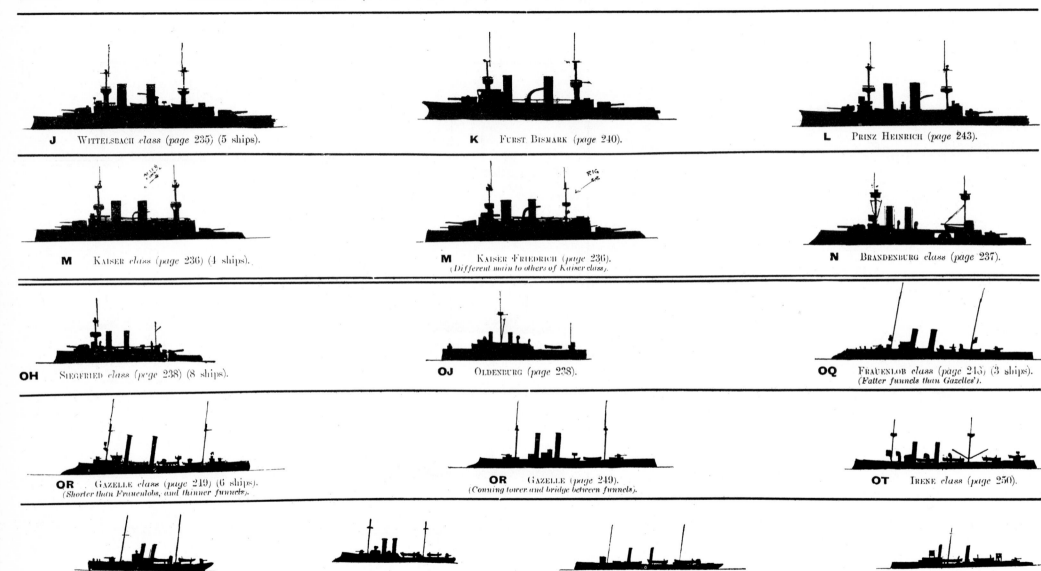

J   WITTELSBACH *class (page 235) (5 ships).*

K   FURST BISMARK *(page 240).*

L   PRINZ HEINRICH *(page 243).*

M   KAISER *class (page 236) (4 ships).*

M   KAISER FRIEDRICH *(page 236).*
(Different main to others of Kaiser class).

N   BRANDENBURG *class (page 237).*

OH   SIEGFRIED *class (page 238) (8 ships).*

OJ   OLDENBURG *(page 238).*

OQ   FRAUENLOB *class (page 245) (3 ships).*
(Fatter funnels than Gazelles').

QR   GAZELLE *class (page 249) (6 ships).*
(Shorter than Frauenlobs, and thinner funnels).

OR   GAZELLE *(page 249).*
(Conning tower and bridge between funnels).

OT   IRENE *class (page 250).*

OV   LUCHS *class (page 253) (4 ships).*

OW   JAGUAR *class (page 253) (2 ships).*

OX   BLITZ *class (page 251) (2 ships).*

OZ   COMET *(page 251)*

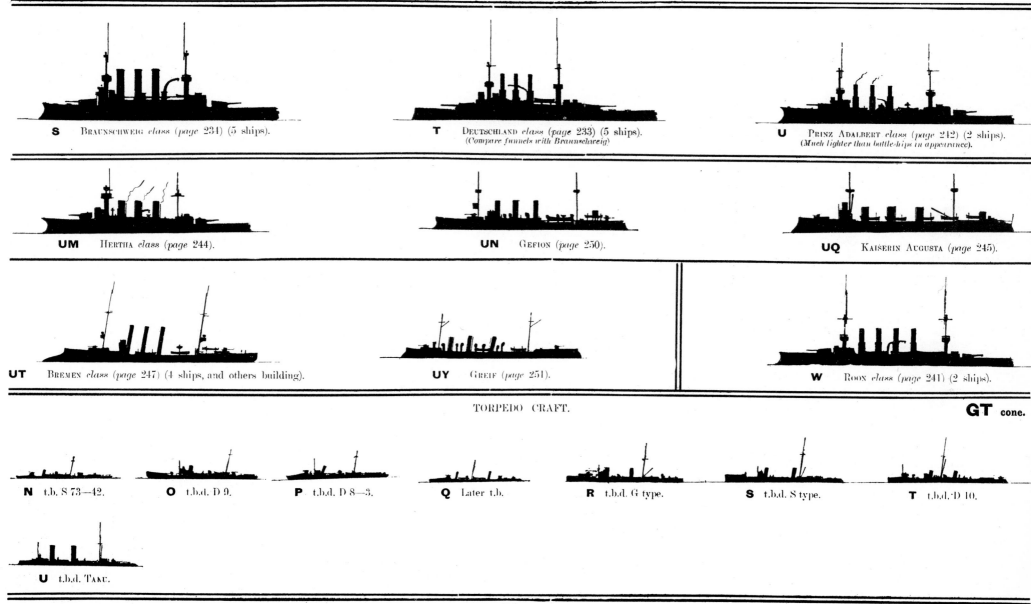

S BRAUNSCHWEIG *class (page 234) (5 ships).*

T DEUTSCHLAND *class (page 233) (5 ships).*
(Compare funnels with Braunschweig)

U PRINZ ADALBERT *class (page 242) (2 ships).*
(Much lighter than battleships in appearance).

UM HERTHA *class (page 244).*

UN GEFION *(page 250).*

UQ KAISERIN AUGUSTA *(page 245).*

UT BREMEN *class (page 247) (4 ships, and others building).*

UY GREIF *(page 251).*

W ROON *class (page 241) (2 ships).*

TORPEDO CRAFT. **GT** cone.

N t.b. S 73—42.

O t.b.d. D 9.

P t.b.d. D 8—3.

Q Later t.b.

R t.b.d. G type.

S t.b.d. S type.

T t.b.d. D 10.

U t.b.d. TAKU.

LATEST GERMAN BATTLESHIPS (19.5 kts).

ERSATZ-SACHSEN & ERSATZ-BAIERN (to be laid down, 1906-7).

Displacement about 19,000 tons. Complement —

Length (*waterline*),   feet. Beam,   feet. *Maximum* draught,   feet. Length over all,   feet.

Guns (M '04) : (*probably*)
  14 –11 in., 50 cal. (ΛΛΛΛΛ).
  22—24 pdrs.
Torpedo tubes (18 inch) :
  6 *submerged* (bow, stern, and
    broadside training).

Armour (Krupp) :
  " Belt (amidships) ...*aaa*
  " Belt (ends) ....*d*
  " Deck on slopes.........
  Protection to vitals = *aaaa*
  " Barbettes ....*aaa*
  " Turrets to these ...*aaa*
  " Lower deck redoubt *aa*
  " Battery ....*a*
  " Conning tower ...*aaa*
  (Total weight : — tons).

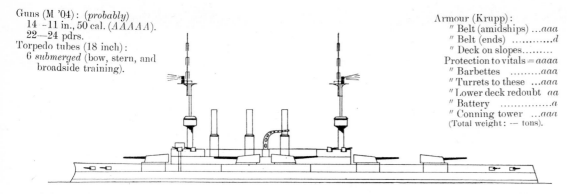

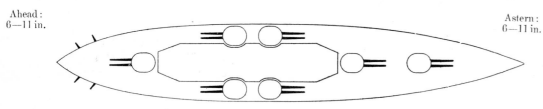

Ahead :
6—11 in.

Astern :
6—11 in.

Broadside : 10—11 in.

To be laid down.

These ships were to have been of 16,000 tons and armed with 8—11 in.,
12—7·6 in., but design has since been completely changed.

SKETCH PLAN REPRESENTS WHAT THE PRESENT DESIGN
IS *BELIEVED* TO BE.

Machinery :   screws. Boilers : Schulz Thornycroft. Designed
H.P.   =19·5 kts. Coal : *normal*   tons ; *maximum*   tons.

Armour Notes.—Underwater lateral bulkheads, 2″ thick amidships.

Gunnery Notes.—All round loading positions to big guns. Electric, hydraulic and hand gear. Electric
  hoists to all guns.

Torpedo Notes.—Training submerged tubes.

(DEUTSCHLAND CLASS—5 SHIPS.)

DEUTSCHLAND (Nov., 1904), *HANNOVER* (Sept., 1905), *POMMERN* (Dec., 1905), "*Q*," & "*R*."

Displacement 13,200 tons.   Complement 729.

Length (*waterline*), 410 feet.   *Beam*, 72 feet.   *Mean* draught, 25 feet.   Length over all, 430 feet.

Guns (M. '01):
  4—11 inch, 40 cal. (*AAA*).
  14—6·7 inch, 40 cal. (*B*).
  20—24 pdr. (*F*).
  4—1 pdr.
  4 Machine.
Torpedo tubes (17·7 inch):
  6 *submerged* (bow, stern, and
    broadside—training).

Armour (Krupp):
  9¾″ Belt (amidships) ... *aaa*
  4″ Belt (ends) .... *d*
  3″ Deck on slopes ...... ·
  Protection to vitals... = *aaaa*
  11″ Barbettes .... *aaa*
  11″ Turrets to these...... *aaa*
  8″ Lower deck (side) ... *aa*
  6¾″ Battery .... *a*
  6¾″ Casemates (4) ...... *a*
  12″ Conning tower (fore) *aaa*
  5½″ After C.T. .... *b*

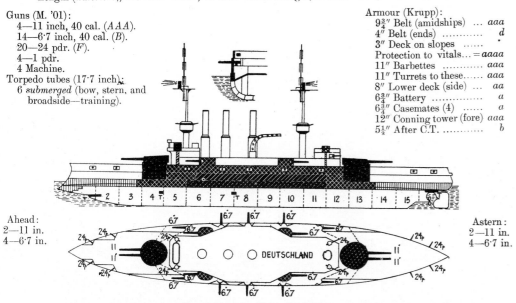

Ahead:
2—11 in.
4—6·7 in.

Astern:
2—11 in.
4—6·7 in.

Broadside: 4—11 in., 7—6·7 in.

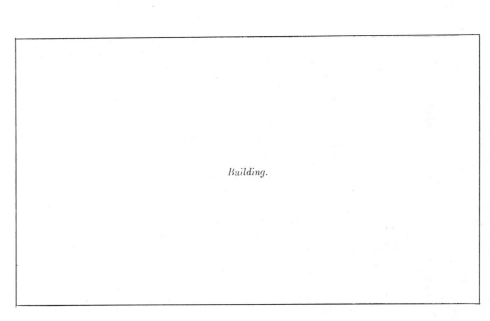

Building.

Machinery: 3 sets 3 cylinder vertical triple expansion.   3 screws.   Boilers: 12 Schulz Thornycroft.   Designed H.P. 16,000 = 18 kts.   Coal: *normal* 700 tons; *maximum* 1800 tons.   Also liquid fuel (in double bottom).

Gunnery Notes.—Loading positions, big guns: all round.   Hoists: electric, all guns.   Big guns manœuvred by electric and hand gear; secondary guns, electric and hand gear.
  Arcs of fire: Big guns, 270°; casemates and end battery guns 135° from axial line; other battery guns, 110°.

Torpedo Notes.—First ships to be fitted with the training submerged tube, 1904 pattern.   Stern submerged tube.

Engineering Notes.

Name.	Builder.	Laid down.	Completed
Deutschland	Krupp	June, '03	To be 1906
Hannover	Wilhelmshaven	April, '04	„ 1907
Pommern	Vulkan Co.	April, '04	„ 1907
"Q"	Schichau	November, '04	„ 1908
"R"	Krupp	November, '04	„ 1908

General Notes.—Estimated cost per ship complete about £1,200,000.   First of class laid down June, 1903.

2 d

(BRAUNSCHWEIG CLASS—5 SHIPS.)

BRAUNSCHWEIG (1902), **ELSASS** (1903), **LOTHRINGEN** (1904),
HESSEN (1903), & **PREUSSEN** (1903).

Displacement 13,200 tons. Complement 691.

Length (*waterline*), 410 feet. Beam, 72 feet. *Mean* draught, $25\frac{3}{4}$ feet. Length over all, 430 feet.

Guns—(M. '01.):
  4—11 inch, 40 cal, (*AAA*)
  14—6·7 inch, 40 cal. (*B*).
  12—24 pdr. (*F*).
  12—1 pdr.
  8 Machine.
Torpedo tubes (17·7 inch):
  5 *submerged*
    (bow and broadside).
  1 *above water* (stern).

Armour (Krupp):
  9″ Belt (amidships) ...... *aa*
  4″ Belt (ends) .... *d*
  3″ Deck on slopes ......
  Protection to vitals ... =*aaa*
  11″ Barbettes to these... *aaa*
  11″ Turrets (side) ...... *aaa*
  5″ Lower deck .... *b*
  6″ Battery .... *a*
  $6\frac{3}{4}$″ Small turrets ...... *a*
  12″ Conning tower ... .. *aaa*
  $5\frac{1}{2}$″ ,, ,, (aft)... *b*
    (Total weight 4200 tons).

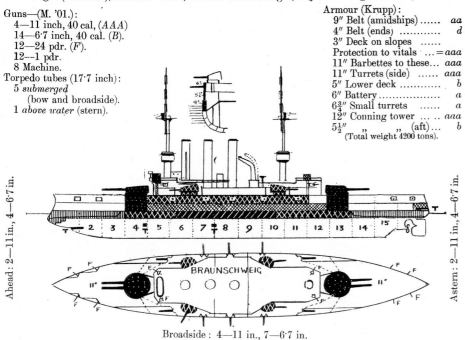

Ahead: 2—11 in., 4—6·7 in.

Astern: 2—11 in., 4—6·7 in.

Broadside: 4—11 in., 7—6·7 in.

BRAUNSCHWEIG

Photo, Renard.

Machinery: 3 sets 3 cylinder vertical inverted triple expansion. 3 screws. Boilers: 8 Schulz-Thornycroft+6 cylindrical. Designed H.P. 16,000=18 kts. Coal: *normal* 700 tons; *maximum* 1600 tons. Also 200 tons of oil (in double bottom).

Armour Notes—Belt is 7 feet wide, $4\frac{1}{4}$ feet of it below waterline; lower edge is about 7″ thick amidships.

Gunnery Notes—Loading positions, big guns all round. Hoists, electric for all guns. Big guns manœuvred, electric, hydraulic, and hand gear; secondary guns, electric and hand gear.
  Arcs of fire: Big guns 250°; small turrets 150° from axial line; end battery guns 135°; other battery guns 110°.
  Height of guns above water: Big turrets about 23 feet.

Engineering Notes—116 revolutions=full speed; 97=16·4 kts.; 67=12 kts.; 45=8·2 kts. *about.*

Name.	Built by	Laid down.	Completed.	Full power trials.
Braunschweig	Krupp	Oct., '01	June, '04	= kts.
Hessen	Krupp	April, '02	To be '05	= kts.
Preussen	Vulkan Co.	June, '02	April, '05	18,374 = 18.69 kts.
Elsass	Schichau	Sept., '01	Oct., '04	= kts.
Lothringen	Schichau	Dec., '02	To be '06	= kts.

General Notes—Average cost *complete*, £1,160,000.

(Wittelsbach Class—5 Ships.)

WITTELSBACH (1900), **WETTIN** (1901), **ZÄHRINGEN** (1901), **MECKLENBURG** (1901),
SCHWABEN (1901).

Displacement 11,830 tons. Complement 650.
Length (*waterline*) 400 feet. Beam 67 feet. *Maximum* draught, 28 feet. Length over all, $416\frac{1}{2}$ feet.

Guns—(M. '99):
  4—9·4 inch, 40 cal. (*AA*).
  18—6 inch, 40 cal. (*E*).
  12—$15\frac{1}{2}$ pdr. (*F*).
  12—1 pdr., revolver.
  8 Machine.
Torpedo tubes (17·7 inch):
  5 *submerged*
    (bow and broadside).
  1 *above water* (stern).

Armour (Krupp):
  9″ Belt (amidships) ...... *aa*
  4″ Belt (ends) .... *d*
  3″ Deck on slopes ......
  Protection to vitals ... =*aaa*
  10″ Barbettes .... *aa*
  10″ Turrets to them...... *aa*
  $5\frac{1}{2}$″ Lower deck (redoubt) *b*
  $5\frac{1}{2}$″ Battery .... *b*
  6″ Casemates (4 bow) ... *b*
  6″ Small turrets .... *b*
  10″ Conning tower ...... *aa*
    (Total weight 4000 tons.)

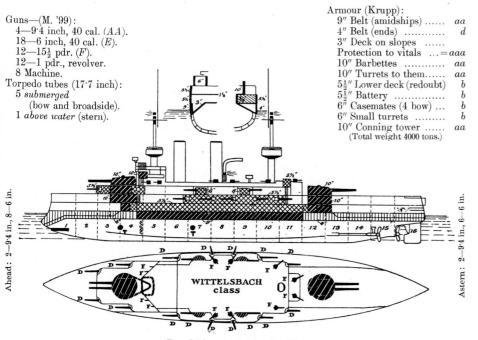

Ahead: 2—9·4 in., 8—6 in.

Astern: 2—9·4 in., 6—6 in.

WITTELSBACH class

Broadside: 4—9·4 in., 9—6 in.

Machinery: 3 sets vertical triple expansion. 3 screws. Boilers: 6 Schulz-Thornycroft and 6
cylindrical. Designed H.P. 15,000 kts. Coal: *normal* 653 tons; *maximum* 1,400 tons, also 200 tons
liquid fuel.
Armour Notes.—Belt is $7\frac{1}{2}$ feet wide by 180 feet long (thick part); 5 feet of it below waterline; lower edge is 7″ thick
  amidships; $1\frac{3}{4}$″ deck over citadel.
Gunnery Notes.—Loading positions, big guns: all round. Hoists, electric for all guns. Big guns manœuvred, electric,
  hydraulic and hand gear.
  Arcs of fire: Big guns, 240°; small turrets, 150° from actual line; end guns of battery, 135°; other guns, 110°.
  Height of guns above water: Bow turret, 30 feet; after turret, 23 feet.
Trials:

Name.	Built by	Laid down	Completed	At 10,000 H.P. (95 revs.)	Full power (104 revs.)
Wittelsbach	Wilhelmshaven	Sept. '98	1902	10,000=16 kts.	14,483=18 kts.
Wettin	Schichau	Oct. '99	1902	10,300=16·3 ,,	14,500=18 ,,
Zähringen	Germania	Nov. '99	1902	= ,,	=
Mecklenburg	Vulcan Co.	May, '00	1903	= ,,	=
Schwaben	Wilhelmshaven	Nov. '00	1903	= ,,	=

  Coal consumption averages $9\frac{1}{4}$ tons an hour at 10,000 H.P. (16 kts.); 14 tons an hour at 15,000 H.P. (18 kts)
    about $3\frac{1}{4}$ tons an hour at 10 kts.
General Notes.—Average cost per ship, *complete*, £1,100,000.

Photo, Renard.

Differences.—All five ships are practically identical, distinguishable by funnel bands (red), in squadron. Also *Wittelsbach, Schwaben,*
  and *Mecklenburg* have steam pipes abaft funnels, while the other two show none.

Name.—*Wittelsbach, Wettin, Zaehringen, Mecklenburg, Schwaben.*

(KAISER CLASS—5 SHIPS).

KAISER FRIEDRICH III. (1896), K. WILHELM II. (1897), K. WILHELM DER GROSSE (1899), K. KARL DER GROSSE (1899), and K. BARBAROSSA (1900).

Displacement 11,150 tons. Complement 660.

Length (*waterline*), 384 feet. Beam, 65½ feet. *Maximum* draught, 27½ feet.

Guns—(M. '95):
4—9·4 inch, 40 cal. (A).
18—6 inch, 40 cal. (E).
12—15½ pdr.
12—1 pdr.
8 Machine.
Torpedo tubes (17·7 inch):
5 *submerged*
(bow and broadside).
1 *above water* (stern).

Armour (Krupp):
12″ Belt (amidships) ... *aaa*
4″ Belt (bow) .... *d*
8″ Bulkheads (aft) ...... *aa*
3″ Deck (flat on belt) ...
Protection to vitals is... *aaa*
10″ Barbettes .... *aa*
10″ Turrets to these ... *aa*
6″ Casemates (12) ...... *b*
6″ Small turrets (6) ... *b*
10″ Conning tower (N.C.) *aa*
(Total weight 3,800 tons).

K. FRIEDRICH III — *Photo, Symonds.*

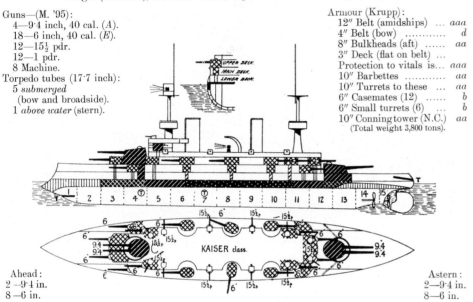

KAISER class.

Ahead:
2—9·4 in.
8—6 in.

Astern:
2—9·4 in.
8—6 in.

Broadside: 4—9·4 in., 9—6 in.

Machinery: 3 sets vertical 3 cylinder triple expansion. 3 screws. Boilers: (in first 3) 8 cylindrical, 4 Schultz; (in other 2) 6. Designed H.P. 14,000 = 18 knots. Coal: *normal* 650 tons; *maximum* 1,050 tons; also 100 tons liquid fuel (double bottom).

Armour Notes.—Belt is 6¼ feet wide by 294 feet long; 3½ feet of it below waterline; lower edge is 6″ thick. 4/5″ splinter deck below armour deck.

Gunnery Notes.—Loading positions, big guns end on. Hoists, electric. Big guns manœuvred by hand and hydraulical gear. Hoists for 15½ pdrs. badly placed; it is hard to serve these guns. Big guns fire very slowly in practice.
Arcs of fire: Big guns, 270°; small turrets, about 135°; casemates, 110°.
Height of guns above water: Bow turret, 30 feet.

Engineering Notes.—The ships all steam well, but are "coal-eaters." Coal consumption: at 10,000 H.P., is about 11 tons an hour; at 14,000, 16 tons.

Trials.—On first trials all reached about 13,850 H.P. and made 18 kts.

General Notes.—

Name.	Built by	Laid down	Completed
K. Friedrich III.	Wilhelmshaven	May, '95	September, '98
K. Wilhelm II.	Wilhelmshaven	July, '96	March, '00
K. Wilhelm der Grosse	Krupp	January, '98	April, '01
K. Karl der Grosse	Blohm & Voss	August, '98	December, '01
K. Barbarossa	Schichau	September, '98	April, '01

Average cost, *complete*, £962,500.

OTHER FOUR "KAISERS." — *Photo, Renard.*

Differences.—K. F. III., different rig to others (note main mast). K. W. II. has unequal funnels (after one smaller). Other 3 have equal sized round funnels. Steam pipes: K. F. III. and K. W. II. before and abaft both funnels. K. Karl none before after funnel. K. W. der Grosse, none before either funnel. K. Barbarossa, none at all.

(BRANDENBURG CLASS—4 SHIPS).

BRANDENBURG (1891), WEISSENBÜRG (1891), WÖRTH (1892), and KURFÜRST FRIEDRIĆH WILHELM (1891)

Displacement 10,060 tons.   Complement 568.

Length (waterline) 354¼ feet.   Beam, 64 feet.   Maximum draught, 26 feet.   Length over all, 380½ feet.

Guns—(old models) :
  4—11 inch, 40 cal. (B).
  2—11 inch, 35 cal. (C).
  8—4·1 inch, 30 cal. (F).
  8—15½ pdr. (F).
  12—1 pdr.
  4 Machine.
Torpedo tubes (17·7 inch) :
  2 submerged.
  1 above water (stern).

Armour (compound) :
  15″ Belt (amidships) ... aa
  12″ Belt (ends)............ a
  2½″ Deck (flat on belt)...
  Protection to vitals is... aa
  12″ Barbettes .... a
  5″ Turrets (may be less) d
  3″ Battery   ,, ε
  12″ Conning tower ...... a
    (Total weight 2800 tons).

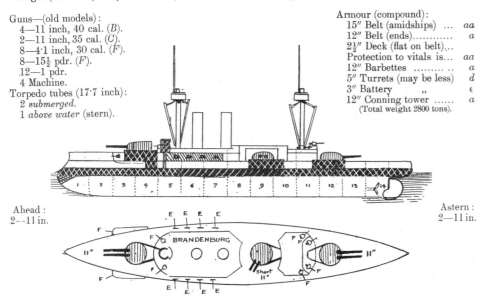

Ahead :
2—11 in.

Astern :
2—11 in.

BRANDENBURG

Broadside : 4—11 in., 2—11 in., 4—4·1 in.

Machinery : 2 sets vertical triple expansion.   2 screws.   Boilers : 12 cylindrical, return flame.
Designed H.P. forced 10,000 = 17 kts.   Coal : normal 600 tons ; maximum 1050 tons.

Armour Notes.—Belt is 6½ feet wide, 3¾ feet of it below waterline.   Lower edge is about 8″ thick.
  Screens in battery.   Two of the 4·1″ guns added 1902-04.

Gunnery Notes.—Loading positions, big guns : end on.   Big guns manœuvred : hydraulic and hand
  gear.
  Arcs of fire : Long 11 in. guns 250° ; amidship 11 in., about 90° either side ; Battery guns about 80°.

Torpedo Notes.—Submerged tubes fitted 1902-04 (section 3).

Engineering Notes.—Ships cannot reach designed speed now, though re-boilered since 1900.   They burn
  about 11 tons an hour at full power.   Bunker capacity increased 1902-04.

General Notes.—All laid down in the spring of 1890, and completed 1893-94.   Cost complete about
  £750,000.

WÖERTH.   Photo, Renard.

Differences.—All four practically identical.

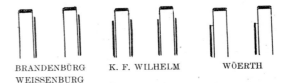

BRANDENBÜRG   K. F. WILHELM   WÖERTH
WEISSENBURG

GERMAN COAST SERVICE BATTLESHIPS (15 knot).

HAGEN.   *Photo, Renard.*

Differences.—All identical in appearance.

(SIEGFRIED CLASS.—8 SHIPS).

SIEGFRIED (1889), BEOWULF (1890), FRITHJOF (1891), HEIMDALL (1892), HILDEBRAND (1892), HAGEN (1893), ODIN (1894), & ÆGIR (1895).

Displacement 4150 tons.   Complement 297.
Length (*waterline*), 254 feet.   Beam, 49 feet.   *Maximum* draught, 18¼ feet.

Guns:
3—9·4 inch, 35 cal. (C).
10—15½ pdr.
6—1 pdr.
4 Machine.
Torpedo tubes (17·7 inch):
3 *submerged*
(bow and broadside).
1 *above water* (stern).

Armour (compound in first four, nickel steel in last four. (See notes.)
9½″ Belt (amidships) .... *b*
6″ Belt (ends) .... *d*
″ Deck (flat on belt).........
Protection to vitals is ...... *b*
8″ Barbettes .... *c*
5½″ Cupolas .... *d*
3¼″ Hoists .... *f*
3¾″ Funnel bases ....
7″ Conning tower (K.N.C.) *a*
6″ on stern tube.............. *b*

Ahead :
2—9·4 in.

Astern :
1—9·4 in.

Broadside : 3—9·4 in.

Machinery : 2 sets vertical triple expansion. 2 screws, Boilers : 8 Schulz-Thornycroft. Designed H.P. 5100=15·5 kts.
Coal : *normal*   tons ; *maximum* 580 tons. Also 100 tons oil.
Armour Notes.—Belt is 7½ feet wide (in *Aegir* and *Odin* 150 feet long). The later ships have slightly thinner armour.
Gunnery Notes.—Loading positions, big guns : end on. Hoists : electric.
Torpedo Notes.—New tubes fitted 1899-1903.
Engineering Notes.—Since reconstruction these ships steam well. 142 revs.=15.1 kts. 136 give 4800 H.P.
General Notes.—Laid down between 1888 and 1892. Completed 1890-97. Reconstructed 1899-1903. Ships were lengthened 15 feet. Tactical diameter, 432 yards at 12 kts.

OBSOLETE GERMAN BATTLESHIPS OF NO FIGHTING VALUE.

(All alike)   *Photo, A. Renard.*

(SACHSEN CLASS.—4 SHIPS).

SACHSEN (1877), BAYERN (1878), WÜRTTEMBERG (1878), & BADEN (1880). 7370 tons.

Guns : 6 old 10·2 in. (E) ; 8—15½ pdr. ; 4 *submerged* tubes. Armour : 16″ iron belt, amidships only (*b*) ; 10″ compound battery (*c*). Speeds about 15½ kts. (steam well).

Photo, Renard.

OLDENBURG (1884).   Displacement 5200 tons.

Guns : 8 old 9·4 in. (E) ; 2—15½ pdr. ; 1 *submerged* tube. Armour : 12″—10″ compound belt, complete (*a-b*) ; 8″ Battery (*c*). Speed very poor ; under 12 kts.

NEW GERMAN ARMOURED CRUISERS (22½ knot).

(C) *VON BÜLOW* (*building*), "D" (*building*).

Displacement 11,500 tons.   Complement 650.

Length (*waterline*), 429¾ feet.   Beam, 67 feet.   *Mean* draught, 25 feet.   Length over all,   feet.

Guns :
8—8·2 inch, 40 cal. (*A*).
6—6 inch, 40 cal. (*E*).
20—24 pdr., 35 cals.
14—1 pdr.
4 machine.
Torpedo tubes :
4 *submerged* (bow, stern, and broadside).

Armour (Krupp) :
6″ Belt (amidships) ...... *a*
4″ Belt (ends) .... *d*
2″ Armour deck ....
Protection to vitals ...= *aa*
6″ Barbettes .... *b*
6¾″ Turret hoods ...... *a*
″ Lower deck side ......
6″ Battery (K.C.)......... *a*
5″ Battery bulkheads (K.C.) *b*
8″ Conning tower........

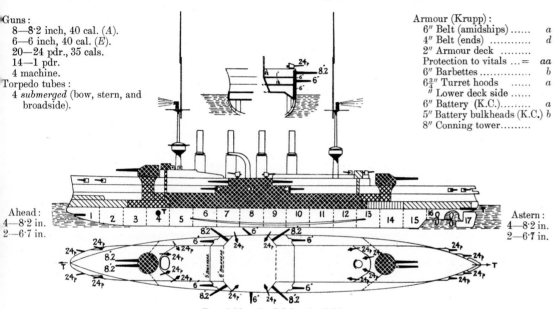

Ahead :
4—8·2 in.
2—6·7 in.

Astern :
4—8·2 in.
2—6·7 in.

Broadside : 6—8·2 in., 3—6·7 in.

Machinery : 3 sets   expansion   cylinder. 3 screws. Boilers : 18 Schulz-Thornycroft.
Designed H.P. 26,000 = 22·5 kts.   Coal : *normal* 800 tons ; *maximum* 2000 tons (also 200 tons oil).

Armour Notes.—

Gunnery Notes.—

Torpedo Notes.—All *submerged*.   Training tubes on broadside.

Engineering Notes.—

General Notes.—First of class laid down, 1904.

Name.	Boilers.	Laid down.	To be completed	Trials.	Boilers.
"C"	Weser, Bremen.	June, '04	Oct., '07		Schulz Thornycroft.
"D"	Blohm & Voss, Hamburg	'05	Dec., '07		Schulz Thornycroft.

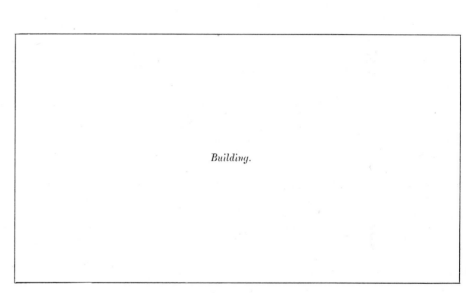

Building.

NEW CRUISERS (to be built).

About 15,000 tons. *Probable* armament : 6 *or* 8—11 inch, several 8·2 inch.

FÜRST BISMARK (1897).

Displacement 10,700 tons (Sheathed).   Complement 529.

Length (*waterline*), 399 feet.   Beam, 65½ feet.   *Maximum* draught, 27 feet.   Length over all, 410 feet.

Guns (M. 99) :
4—9·4 inch, 40 cal. (*AA*).
12—6 inch, 40 cal. (*E*).
10—15½ pdr.
10—1 pdr.
Torpedo tubes (17·7 inch) :
5 *submerged* (bow and broadside).
1 *above water* (stern).

Armour (Krupp) :
8″ Belt (amidships) ...... *aa*
4″ Belt (ends) .... *d*
2″ Deck (flat on belt amidships) ....
Protection to vitals is ... *aa*
8″ Barbettes (N.C.) ...... *a*
8″ Turrets to these (N.C.) *a*
4″ Battery .... *d*
4″ Casemates (2) .... *d*
4″ Small turrets (6) ...... *d*
8″ Conning tower .... *a*
(Total weight about 3400 tons).

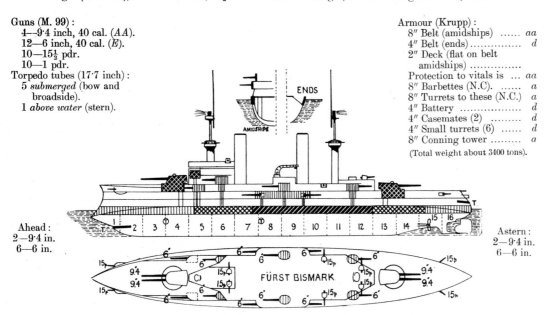

Ahead :
2—9·4 in.
6—6 in.

Astern :
2—9·4 in.
6—6 in.

Broadside : 4—9·4 in., 6—6 in.

Machinery : 3 sets vertical triple expansion. 3 screws. Boilers : 8 Schulz Thornycroft and 8 cylindrical. Designed H.P. 13,600 = 19 kts.   Coal : *normal* 1000 tons ; *maximum* 1200 tons.

Armour Notes.—Belt is 7½ feet wide.   Deck reinforces belt fore and aft.

Arcs of fire : Big guns, 270° ; 'midship secondary turrets, 180° ; other small turrets, 135° ; casemates, 110°.

Engineering Notes.—On her first *trials*, I.H.P. 13,500 gave 18·7 kts., and 12,676 = 18·5 kts.   She rarely exceeds 18 kts. in service.   Coal consumption : about 4 tons an hour at 8 kts. ; about 13 tons an hour at 13,500 H.P. (18-19 kts.)

General Notes.—Laid down at Kiel Dockyard, June 1896.   Completed in 1900.   Cost complete about £900,000.

Photo, Renard.

Note.—Can be distinguished from *P Heinrich* (q.v.) by noting how much she is built up around fore-mast ; also by lower masts.   Can be confounded with *Wittelsbach* at a long distance, but can be picked out by noting :—(1) Slighter funnels, and after funnel nearer to the mainmast than in *Wittelsbach* class.   (2) More squat appearance of bow turret.   (3) *Bismark's* cranes are between the funnels, while those of the *Wittelsbachs* are more abaft the funnels.

(ROON CLASS.—2 SHIPS).

ROON (June, 1903) & **YORCK** (May, 1904).

Displacement 9050 tons. Complement 557.

Length (*waterline*), 403¼ feet. Beam, 65½ feet. *Maximum* draught, 25¾ feet.

Guns :
4—8·2 inch, 40 cal. (*A*).
10—6 inch, 40 cal. (*E*).
12—24 pdr.
10—1 pdr.
4 machine.
Torpedo tubes :
4 *submerged*
  (bow, stern, and broadside).

Armour (Krupp) :
4″ Belt (amidships) .... *d*
3″ Belt (ends) .... ϵ
2¾″ Deck (slopes)..............
Protection to vitals .... =c
6″ Turrets...................... *b*
4″ Turret bases .... *d*
4″ Lower deck redoubt ...... *d*
4″ Battery..................... *d*
4″ Small turrets .... *d*
6″ Conning tower (fore) ...... *b*
3″   „   „   (aft) ...... ϵ

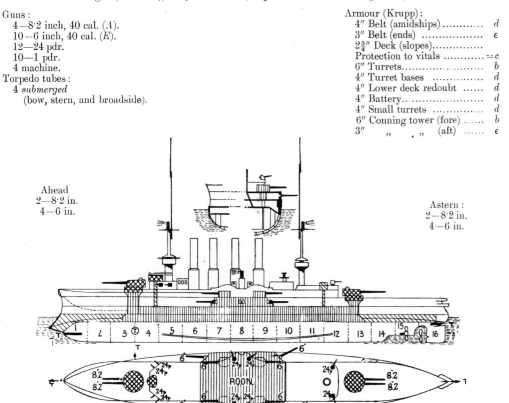

Ahead :
2—8·2 in.
4—6 in.

Astern :
2—8·2 in.
4—6 in.

ROON.

Broadside : 4—8·2 in., 5—6 in.

YORCK.   (Both alike).   *Photo, Karl Speck.*

Machinery : 3 sets vertical triple expansion. 3 screws. Boilers : 16 Dürr. Designed H.P. 19,000 = 21 kts. Coal : *normal* 750 tons ; *maximum* 1600 tons ; also 200 tons of oil.

General Notes.—Except for some minor details and slightly increased H.P., these ships are identical with the *P. Adalbert* class (*q.v.*)

				Trials.		
Name.	Built at	Laid down.	Completed.	24 hours.		Boilers.
Yorck	Blohm & Voss	April, '03	May, '06	13,711 = 19 kts.	20,295 = 21·4 kts.	Dürr
Roon	Kiel Dockyard	Aug., '02	Oct., '05			Dürr

(PRINZ ADALBERT CLASS—2 SHIPS.)

PRINZ ADALBERT (June, 1901) & **FRIEDRICH KARL** (June, 1902).

Displacement 9050 tons.   Complement 557.

Length (*waterline*) 394 feet.   Beam, 65 feet.   *Maximum* draught, 25¾ feet.

Guns :
4—8·2 inch, 40 cal. (A).
10—6 inch, 40 cal. (E).
10—15½ pdr. (F).
10—1 pdr.
4 Maxims.
Torpedo tubes (17·7 inch) :
1 *submerged* (bow).
2 *submerged* (broadside).
1 *above water*
          (stern, armoured.)

Armour (Krupp) :
4″ Belt (amidships) .... d
3″ Belt (ends) .... ϵ
2″ Deck on slopes ....
Protection to vitals ...... $= c$
6″ Turrets .... b
4″ Turret bases .... d
4″ Lower deck redoubt ... d
4″ Battery .... d
4″ Small turrets .... d
6″ Conning tower........... b

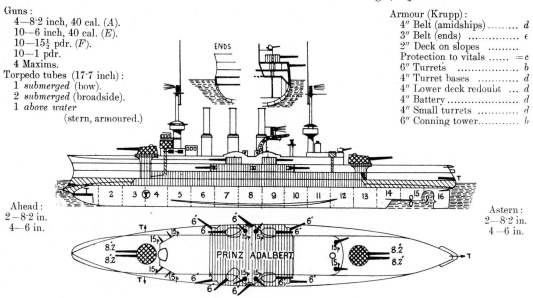

Ahead :
2—8·2 in.
4—6 in.

Astern :
2—8·2 in.
4—6 in.

Broadside : 4—8·2 in., 5—6 in.

FRIEDRICH KARL.   *Photo, Sergeant Cleaves, R.G.A*

Machinery : 3 sets 4 cylinder vertical inverted triple expansion.   3 screws.   Boilers : 14 Dürr.   Designed H.P. 18500 = 21 kts.   Coal : *normal* 750 tons ; *maximum* 1500 tons ; 200 tons of liquid fuel.

Armour Notes—Belt is about 7 feet wide by 194 feet long, 5 feet of it below waterline.   1″—2″ steel lower deck at end.   Armoured floor to main deck battery.

Gunnery Notes.—Loading positions, big guns : all round.   Hoists : electric for all guns.   Big guns manœuvred electrically and by hand.   Secondary turrets, electrically and hand.
Arcs of fire : Main turrets 270°. ; Small turrets 150° from axial line ; other guns about 135°.

Torpedo Notes.—Fixed tube aft armoured.

Engineering Notes.—Coal consumption has reached 19 tons an hour at 18,000 H.P. (21 kts.) but is usually well under this.   Both ships are good steamers.   F. Karl made 20·5 in a gale of wind, force 9.

General Notes.—P. Adalbert laid down Kiel Dockyard, April 1900 ; completed Autumn of 1903.
      F Karl   „   „   Blohm & Voss, August 1901 ;   „   „   „   1903.
Cost of each ship *complete*, nearly £900,000.   Workmanship in them is excellent, but the design mediocre.
Grouping of guns does not assist fire control and the protection is very poor.

Differences.—None.

Class Distinction.—It is possible to mistake these at sea for the *Braunschweig* class, though they are easily differentiated by the funnels, and are of course much lighter looking.

GERMAN ARMOURED CRUISER (20 knot).

PRINZ HEINRICH (1900).

Displacement 8930 tons.   Complement 501.

Length (waterline), 394 feet.   Beam, 65 feet.   Maximum draught, 25½ feet.

Guns—(M. '99) :
2—9·4 inch, 40 cal. (AA).
10—6 inch, 40 cal. (E).
12—15½ pdr. (F).
10—1 pdr.
Torpedo tubes (17·7 inch).
  1 submerged (bow).
  2 submerged (broadside).
  1 above water (stern).

Armour (Krupp) :
4″ Belt (amidships) ....d
2″ Belt (ends) ....e
2″ Deck (inclined) ....
Protection to vitals c
6″ Turrets (N.C.) ....b
4″ Turret bases (N.C.) ......d
4″ Lower deck side ....d
4″ Battery ....d
4″ Small turrets ....d
6″ Conning tower (N.C.) ...b

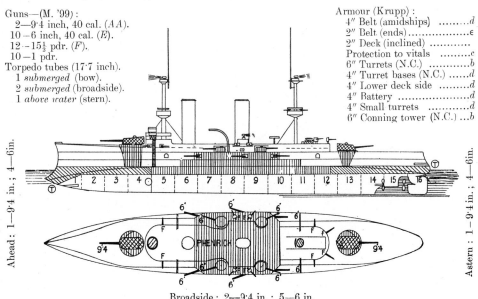

Ahead : 1—9·4 in. ; 4—6 in.

Astern : 1—9·4 in. ; 4—6 in.

Broadside : 2—9·4 in. ; 5—6 in.

Photo, Renard.

Machinery : 3 sets triple expansion four cylinder.   3 screws.   Boilers : 14 Dürr.   Designed H.P. 15,700 = 20 kts.   Coal : *normal* 750 tons ; *maximum* 1,500 tons.   Also 200 tons liquid fuel.

Armour Notes.—4″ part of belt is 7 feet wide by 194 feet long ; 5 feet of it below waterline ; ¾″ steel lower deck.

Gunnery Notes.—Loading positions, big guns : all round.   Hoists : electric and hand.   Big guns manœuvred electrically.   Secondary turret hoists, 1·2 in. steel, go down through battery.

Arcs of fire : 9·4 in., 260°.   Small turrets, 150° from axial line.   Battery 6 in., about 135°.   The big guns are too powerful for the ship's size, and shake her up considerably.

Torpedo Notes.—Fixed tube aft has some armour about it.

Engineering Notes.—Coal consumption is about 16 tons an hour at 15,000 H.P. (20 kts.).   She made her speed on trial, but did not exceed it.   The oil is carried in the double bottom under engines.

General Notes.—Laid down at Kiel Yard, December, 1898.   Completed early in 1902.   Total cost about £750,000.

Class Distinction.—A long way off at sea it is possible to mistake this ship with the *Wittelsbach* class or the *Bismark*.   Observe *Heinrich's* slight masts and small fighting tops.

243

(HERTHA CLASS — 5 SHIPS).

FREYA (1897), **HERTHA** (1897), **VICTORIA LUISE** (1897), **HANSA** (1898),

and **VINETA** (1897).

Displacement 5880 tons.   Complement 465.

Length (*waterline*), 344½ feet.   Beam, 57 feet.   *Maximum* draught, 23 feet.

VINETA

Guns :
2—8·2 inch, 40 cal. (*B*).
8—6 inch, 40 cal. (*E*).
10—15½ pdr. (*F*).
10—1 pdr.
4 Machine.
Torpedo tubes (17·7 inch) :
3 *submerged* (1 in bow).

Armour (Krupp) :
4″ Deck...................... = *c*
Cork belt amidships ......
Protection to vitals... ...= *c*
4″ Turrets and casemates   *d*
5″ Glacis to funnels.........
3¼″ Hoists...................
8″ Fore C.T.................*ba*

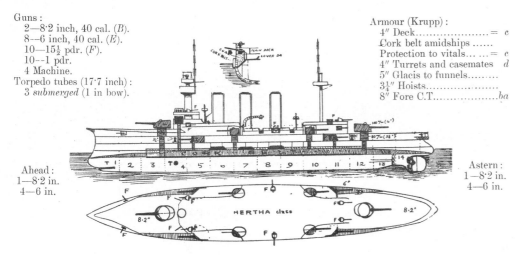

Ahead :
1—8·2 in.
4—6 in.

Astern :
1—8·2 in.
4—6 in.

HERTHA class

Broadside :   2—8·2 in. (*B*), 4—6 in. (*E*).

Machinery : 3 sets 4 cylinder triple expansion. 3 screws. Boilers: *Freya*, 12 Niclausse ; *Hertha*, 12 Belleville ; *Victoria Luise*, Dürr ; *Hansa*, 18 Belleville ; *Vineta*, 12 Dürr. Designed H.P. 10,500 = 19 kts. Coal : *normal* 900 tons ; *maximum* 1,000 tons.

Notes.—*Trials* rarely reached the designed H.P. in most cases. None are very good steamers, except the *Hansa*, which is the only one that reaches the designed speed in service. Laid down, 1895—96, and completed 1898—99.   Cost about £500,000 each.

Differences in funnels and steam pipes as noted.

Vineta   Victoria Luise only has funnels like this.   Hertha & Hansa

HERTHA class

GERMAN PROTECTED CRUISER (18 knot).

KAISERIN AUGUSTA (1892).

Displacement 6,300 tons. Complement 436.

Length, 338 feet. Beam, 49 feet. *Maximum* draught, 25½ feet.

Guns :
  12—6 inch, 35 cal. (F).
  8—15½ pdr. (F).
  8 Machine.
Torpedo tubes :
  1 *submerged* (bow).
  4 *above water* (broadside).

Armour :
  3½″ Deck ....= d
  This thickness is only amidships (between sections 5 and 11); at the ends it is a good deal less. There is a water-tight splinter deck below protective deck.
  Protection to vitals ....= c

Ahead :
2—6 in.

Astern :
4—6 in.

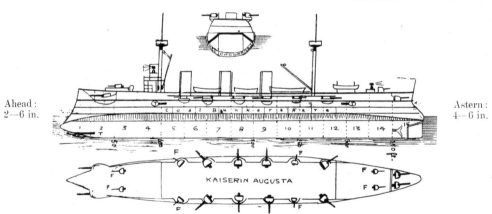

Broadside : 6—6 in.

Photo, Renard.

Machinery : 3 sets vertical triple expansion. 3 screws. Boilers : 8 2-ended cylindrical. Designed H.P. *forced* draught 12,000 = 20·7 kts. Coal : 900 tons = *circa* 4,000 miles at 10 kts.

Engineering Notes.—On a short first *trial* with I.H.P. 12,000 she made 22·5 kts. The sea speed is *circa* 18·5—19 kts.

General Notes.—Tactical diameter *circa* 750 yards. Laid down at Krupp's Germania yard in the spring of 1890. Completed 1892.

NEW SMALL GERMAN CRUISERS (23·5 knot),

("O" CLASS—5 SHIPS).

"O" (building), ERSATZ WACHT (building) & ERSATZ BLITZ (building),
& 2 others (to be laid down).

Displacement 3420 tons.   Complement 295.

Length (*waterline*), 354¼ feet.   Beam, 43 feet.   *Maximum* draught, 17½ feet.   Length over all,   feet.

Guns :
   10—4·1 inch, 40 cal.
   8—3 pdr., 55 cal.
   4 Machine.
Torpedo tubes (17·7 inch) :
   2 *submerged*.

Armour (Krupp) :
   2″ Deck.................... $= \epsilon$
   ¾″ Deck (at ends)......... $= f$
   4″ Conning tower .... d
   Protection to vitals ...... $= \epsilon$

Building.

Ahead :
4—4·1 in.

[Practically the same as *Bremen* class].

Astern :
4—4·1 in.

Broadside : 5—4·1 in.

Machinery : 2 sets 4 cylinder triple expansion.   2 screws.   *E. Wacht*, turbine.   Boilers : Schulz-Thornycroft.   Designed H.P. 13,200 = 23·5 kts.   Coal : *normal* 400 tons; *maximum* 850 tons.   *Nominal* radius 5500 knots.

Name	Where built.	Laid down.	Completed.	Trial on sea course of 170 miles.
"O"	Danzig Yard	1905	*for 1908*	=
Ersatz Wacht	Vulkan, Stettin	1905	*for 1908*	=
Ersatz Blitz	Kiel Yard	1905	*for 1908*	=

NEW SMALL GERMAN CRUISERS (23 knot).

(BREMEN CLASS—8 SHIPS).

BREMEN (1903), **HAMBURG** (1903), **BERLIN** (1903), **LUEBECK** (1904),
MUENCHEN (1904), *LEIPZIG* (March, 1905), *ERSATZ METEOR* (1905) & *DANTZIG* (1905).

Displacement 3250 tons.   Complement 280.

Length (*waterline*), 341 feet.   Beam, 40 feet.   *Maximum* draught, 17½ feet.

Guns :
  10—4·1 inch, (*F*).
  10—1 pdr.
  4 Machine.
Torpedo tubes (17·7 inch) :
  2 *submerged*.

Armour (Krupp) :
  2″ Deck.................... = ϵ
  ¾″ Deck (at ends)......... = *f*
  4″ Conning tower .... *d*
  Protection to vitals ...... = ϵ

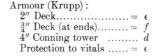

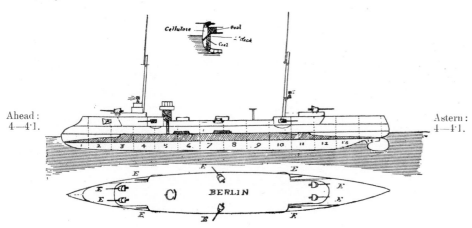

Ahead :
4—4·1.

Astern :
4—4·1.

Broadside : 5—4·1 in.

HAMBURG. (All identical).   *Photo, Speck.*

Machinery : 2 sets 4 cylinder triple expansion. 2 screws. *Luebeck*, turbine. Boilers : 10 Schulz-Thornycroft. Designed H.P. 11,000 = 23 kts. Coal : *normal* 400 tons ; *maximum* 800 tons. *Nominal* radius 5000 knots.

Name.	Where built.	Laid down.	Completed	Trial on sea course of 170 miles.
Bremen	Weser, Bremen	August, '02	May, '04	= 23·2
Hamburg	Vulkan, Stettin	April, '02	May, '04	11,000 = 23·1
Berlin	Danzig Dockyard	April, '02	October, '04	= 23·2
Lubeck (turbine)	Vulkan, Stettin	May, '03	December, '04	11,580 = 23·5
München	Weser, Bremen	August, '03	April, 05	= 23·4
Ersatz Meteor	Kiel Dockyard	June, '04	for 1907	=
Dantzig	Danzig Dockyard	June, '04	for 1907	=
Leipzig	Weser, Bremen	May, '04	for 1907	=

SMALL GERMAN CRUISERS (21½ knot).

FRAUENLOB (1902), **ARCONA** (1902), & **UNDINE** (1902).

Displacement 2,715 tons.   Complement 259.

Length, 328 feet.   Beam, 40 feet.   *Maximum* draught, 17¼ feet.

Guns :
 10—4·1 inch, (F).
 10—1 pdr.
 4 Machine.
Torpedo tubes (17·7 inch) :
 2 *submerged*.

Armour (Krupp) :
 2″ Deck.................... = ϵ
 4″ Conning tower........... d
 Protection to vitals ......= ϵ

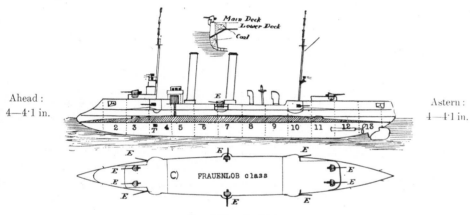

Ahead :
4—4·1 in.

Astern :
4—4·1 in.

Broadside : 5—4·1 in.

(All alike).

Differ from *Gazelle* class in having a larger fore funnel and searchlight platform on main mast.

Machinery : 2 sets 4 cylinder triple expansion.   2 screws.   Designed H.P. 8,000 = 21·5 kts.
Coal : *normal* 450 tons; *maximum* 700 tons.   Boilers : Schulz-Thornycroft.

Name.	Where built.	Laid down.	Completed.	Trials.
Frauenlob	Weser Bremen	June, '00	April, '03	= 21·7 kts.
Arcona	Weser Bremen	June, '00	May, '03	= 21·5 kts.
Undine	Howalt, Kiel	December, '01	December, '03	= kts.

Coal consumption : about 8¼ tons an hour, at 8,000 H.P. (21·5 kts.).

248

(GAZELLE CLASS—7 SHIPS).

GAZELLE (1898), **NYMPHE** (1899), **NIOBE** (1899), **THETIS** (1900), **ARIADNE** (1900), **AMAZONE** (1900), & **MEDUSA** (1900).

(Sheathed and Muntz metalled).

Displacement 2,650 tons.   Complement 249.

Length (*waterline*), 328 feet.   Beam, 39 feet.   *Maximum* draught, $17\frac{1}{4}$ feet.

Guns :
10—4·1 inch (*F*).
14—1 pdr.
4 Machine.
Torpedo tubes (17·7 inch) :
2 *submerged*,
but *Gazelle* has
1 *submerged* (bow).
2 *above water* (broadside).

Armour (Krupp) :
2″ Deck (amidships)......= є
1″ Deck (at ends).........= *f*
Protection to vitals ......= є
$3\frac{1}{2}″$ Glacis to hatches, &c.
3″ Conning tower ....*d*
Cofferdam and cellulose
amidships.

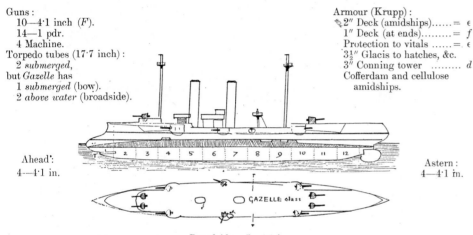

Ahead :
4—4·1 in.

Astern :
4—4·1 in.

Broadside : 5—4·1 in.

Machinery : 2 sets 4 cylinder triple expansion.   2 screws.   Boilers : *See Notes.*   Designed H.P. 8500 = 21 kts.   Coal : *normal* 300 tons ; *maximum* 560 tons (always carried).

Engineering Notes.—In these ships, as a rule, 79 revolutions = 11 kts. ; 87 = 12 kts. ; 127 = 17 kts. ; 140 = 19·5 kts. ; 166 = 21·6 kts.

Name.	Built by	Laid down.	Completed.	Trials.	Boilers.
Gazelle	Krupp	April, '97	1898	6,400 = 19·5	8 Niclausse
Niobe	Weser	June, '98	1899	8,113 = 21·6	5 Thornycroft
Nymphe	Krupp	Oct., '98	1901	9,000 = 22·3	4 Thornycroft
Thetis	Danzig Yard	Dec., '99	July, '01	8,888 = 21·75	9 Schulz, Th.
Ariadne	Weser	Dec., '99	April, '01	8,827 = 21·18	9 Schulz, Th.
Amazone	Krupp	Dec., '99	July, '01	8,850 = 21·5	9 Schulz. Th.
Medusa	Weser	Jan., '00	July, '01	8,927 = 22·0	9 Schülz, Th.

General Notes.—The deck is made of three thicknesses, each about 0·6 of an inch thick.   The cofferdam is filled with cork and gelatine.

(All except *Gazelle*.)   Photo, *Symonds.*

Gazelle has chart house between the funnels, and no searchlight on fore, otherwise identical.

Photo, Symonds.

GEFION (1893).

Displacement 3,770 tons.   Complement 302.

Length (*waterline*), 325 feet.   Beam, 42½ feet.   *Maximum* draught, 21½ feet.   Length over all, 334 feet.

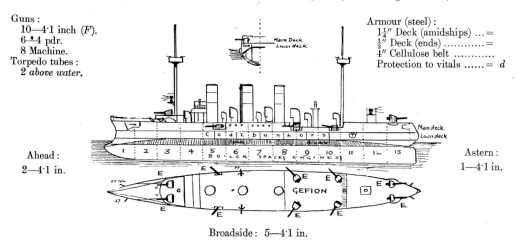

Guns :
  10—4·1 inch (*F*).
  6—4 pdr.
  8 Machine.
Torpedo tubes :
  2 *above water.*

Armour (steel) :
  1¼″ Deck (amidships) ... =
  ½″ Deck (ends) .... =
  4″ Cellulose belt ....
  Protection to vitals ..... = *d*

Ahead :
  2—4·1 in.

Astern :
  1—4·1 in.

Broadside : 5—4·1 in.

Machinery : 2 sets triple expansion. 2 screws. Boilers : 6 2-ended cylindrical. Designed H.P. *forced* 9,000 = 20 kts. Coal : *maximum* 750 tons.

Engineering Notes.—4 hours *forced* draught, I.H.P. 9,828 = 20·5 kts. Coal consumption : about 2½ tons an hour at 10 kts. ; 9 tons at 9,000 H.P. = 20 kts.

(Bulwarks now cut down amidships).

PRINZESS WILHELM (1887), & IRENE (1888).

Displacement, 4,300.   Complement 365.

Length (*waterline*), 225 feet.   Beam, 42½ feet.   *Maximum* draught, 21½ feet.   Length over all, 334 feet.

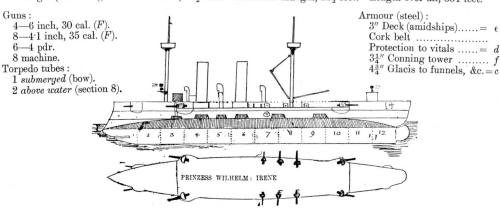

Guns :
  4—6 inch, 30 cal. (*F*).
  8—4·1 inch, 35 cal. (*F*).
  6—4 pdr.
  8 machine.
Torpedo tubes :
  1 *submerged* (bow).
  2 *above water* (section 8).

Armour (steel) :
  3″ Deck (amidships) ...... = ε
  Cork belt ....
  Protection to vitals ...... = *d*
  3¼″ Conning tower .... *f*
  4¾″ Glacis to funnels, &c. = *c*

Machinery : 2 sets 4 cylinder horizontal compound.   2 screws.   Boilers : 4 2-ended.   Designed H.P. 8,000 = 18 kts.   (On first *trials* nearly 20 kts. was made).   Coal : *normal* 540 tons ; *maximum* 750 tons.

Notes.—The armament of these ships has been once or twice shifted. It is now proposed to mount only 4·1 inch. In appearance the two ships are practically identical, but if they are together the *P. Wilhelm* may be distinguished by the fact that her ventilator cowls are a trifle shorter and larger than those of the *Irene*. Both ships are peculiar in that they have very long sterns, the mainmast being an unusually long way forward.

HELA.   *Photos, Renard.*   COMET.

HELA (1895).

Displacement 2040 tons.   Complement 178.

Length, 328 feet.   Beam, 36 feet.   *Maximum* draught, 15¾ feet.

Guns :
 4—15½ pdr., 30 cal.
 6—6 pdr.
 2 machine.
Torpedo tubes (18 inch) :
 1 *submerged* (bow).
 2 *above water* (section 10)

Armour (steel) :
 1″ Deck ....
 1⅔″ Engine hatches ......
 1¼″ Conning tower........
 1¼″ Funnel base............

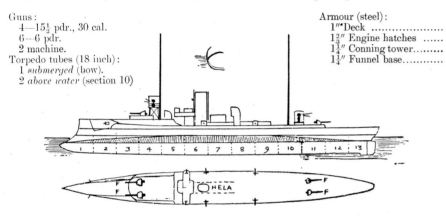

Machinery : 2 sets vertical triple expansion.   2 screws.   Boilers : 6 locomotive.   Designed H.P. 6000 = 22 kts. (*trial* gave 21 kts. nearly).   Coal : 330 tons.

Other torpedo gunboats of no fighting value are :—

JAGD (1888).   1250 tons.   Guns : 4—15½ pdrs.   Torpedo tubes : 1 *submerged*, 2 *above water*.   1¾″ armour deck.   Designed H.P. 400 = 19 kts.   Coal : 230 tons.

GREIF (1886).   2060 tons.   Guns : 8—15½ pdrs.   No tubes.   No armour deck.   Designed H.P. 5400 = 18 kts.   Coal : 350 tons.

BLITZ & PFEIL (1882).   1390 tons.   Guns : 6—15½ pdrs.   Torpedo tubes : 1 *submerged* and 2 *above water*.   No armour deck.   Designed H.P. 2700 = 15·5 kts.   Coal : 180 tons.

(These ships were amongst the first torpedo gunboats ever built.)

JAGD.

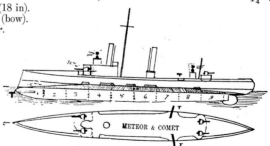

BLITZ and PFEIL.

COMET (1892).

Displacement 960 tons.   Complement 115.

Length, 233 feet.   Beam, 31½ feet.   *Maximum* draught, 13⅕ feet.

Guns :
 4—15½ pdr., 40 cal.
 2 Machine.
Torpedo tubes (18 in).
 1 *submerged* (bow).
 2 *above water.*

Armour :
 1″ Deck ....
 1¼″ Conning tower.

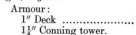

Machinery : 2 sets horizontal triple expansion.   2 screws.   Boilers : 4 locomotive. Designed H.P. 4500 = 19 kts.   Coal : 120 tons.
Note.—Boilers give considerable trouble now and again.   Present speed poor.

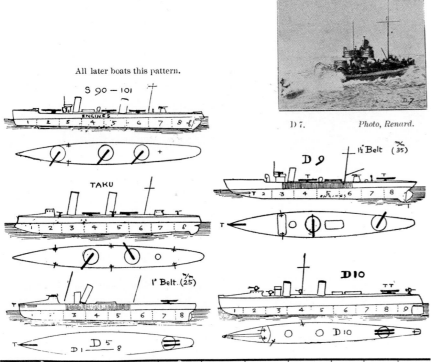

All later boats this pattern.

S 90 — 101

TAKU

D 9

1½ Belt (35)

1" Belt (25)

D 1   D 5   8

D 10

D 7.   Photo, Renard.

D 10 (*Thornycroft boat*).

"G" (*Germania*) type of destroyers.   "S" (*Schichau*) are practically identical.

No. of Boats.	Name.	Date.	Displacement.	I.H.P.	Max. Speed.	Torpedo Tubes.	Coal.	Complement
			tons.		Kts.		tons.	
40	*New boats*	1906-07						
6	S 132—137	1905-06						
18	S 114—131	1902-05	420	6500	30	3	100	49
6	G 108—113	1901-02	400	6500	30	3	100	49
6	S 102—107	1900-01	400	5400	27	3	100	49
12	S 90—101	1899-00	400	5400	26·5	3	100	49
1	*Taku*	1898	280	6000	30	2	67	50
1	D 10 (Thornycroft)	1898	355	5500	27·75	3	80	49
1	D 9	1894	380	4043	24·5	3	80	40
2	D 7 & 8...............	1890-91	350	4000	26	3	80	40
2	D 5 & 6...............	1888&89	320	3600	23	3	60	40
2	D 3 & 4...............	1888	300	2500	21	3	—	35
2	D 2 & 1...............	1887	230	2000	11	3	—	30
53+46								

All except *Taku* (which carries 6—3 pdrs.) are armed with 1—4 pdr. Tubes in G and S before, between and abaft funnels. In D 10, D 8—1 they are paired aft and in bow. D 9 has one bow tube, one abaft funnel, and one right aft. All bow tubes in the D's are submerged.

Note.—40 more destroyers will be laid down early in 1907.

Note.—These "G" and "S" destroyers are excellent sea boats, strongly constructed, and, in every case, tested by acceptance trials in really bad weather in order to guarantee against leaking or straining. They are in no sense the fragile craft that destroyers are popularly supposed to be, and all of them are able to make or exceed their contract speeds. It should also be remembered that they are manned by very competent officers and crews, possessing that appreciation of the work which is essential to the effective handling of torpedo craft.

German Torpedo Boats.

(Single screw. All armed with 1-4 pdr. gun, and draw about 7½ feet.)

Totals.	Name or Number.	Date.	Displace-ment.	I.H.P	Max. Speed.	Torpedo Tubes.	Coal.	Comple-ment.
			tons.		kts.		tons.	
6	*building*	1905	155	1800	25	3	37	24
2	G 88 & 89	1898	155	1800	25	3	37	24
6	S 87—82	1898	155	1800	25	3	37	24
7	S 81—76, 74......	1895	153	1800	25	4	53	24
1	S 75	1892	145	1800	26	4	40	20
8	S 73—76	1890	170	1800	22	3	—	24
8	S 65—58	1889	153	1800	22	3	53	24
9	S 57—49	1887	130	1500	22	3	—	24
6	S 47—42	1887	145	1350	22	3	40	24

47+6

German Submarines.

(All built at Kiel).

No.	Class.	Date.	Displace-ment.	Motive Power, above and below.	H.P.	Max. Speed.	Dimensions, in feet.	Tubes.	Actual Radius, above and below.	Comp-lement.
1	Holland No. 1	1902	120	Petrol 4 cylinder / accumulators.	160 / 70	$\frac{7}{5}$	$63\frac{1}{3} \times 11\frac{3}{4} \times 12$	1	about 3-6 hours.	5
3	—	1903-06	180	Petrol 8 cylinder / accumulators.	250 / 100	$\frac{12}{9}$	$128 \times 9 \times —$	2	—	9
1	"Howalt"	1901	85	Accumulators only.		$\frac{7}{6}$	$49\frac{1}{4} \times 6\frac{1}{2} \times 6\frac{1}{2}$	1	very small.	3

German Gunboats, etc.

CRUISERS:
GEIER (1894), CONDOR (1892), COROMORAN (1892), SEEADLER (1892), FALKE (1891) & BUSSARD (1890).
All of 1630—1570 tons. Guns: 8—4·1 in., 35 cal., 5—1 pdr. 2 torpedo tubes. Speeds, 16—15 kts.
SPERBER (1888), & SCHWALBE (1887).
1,120 tons.
Guns: 8—4·1 in., 5—1 pdr. 2 torpedo tubes. Speeds about 13 kts. or less.

GUNBOATS.
EBER (1903), PANTHER (1901), LUCHS (1899), TIGER (1899). 977 tons. Guns: 2—4·1 in., 40 cal., and 6—1 pdr. Nominal speed, 13·5 kts. (*One other building*).
JAGUAR (1898), & ILTIS (1898). 900 tons. Guns: 4—15½ pdr., 6—1 pdr. Nominal speed, 13 kts.
RIVER GUNBOATS (for China).
VATERLAND (1903), TSINGTAU (1903), VORWÄRTS (1899). 168 tons. 1—15½ pdr., 1- 4 pdr. Bullet-proof belt on waterline, ⅓ in. nickel steel. ½ in. conning tower. Speeds, 13—11 kts. (*Another building*.)
There are 11 old armoured gunboats (MÜCKE class), 1,100 tons, carrying one old 12 in. gun of 22 cals.,—no fighting value.

SCHWALBE.　　　*Photo, Renard.*

TIGER & LUCHS.　　　*Photo, Renard.*

ILTIS & JAGUAR.　　　*Photo, Renard.*

RUSSIAN FLEET.

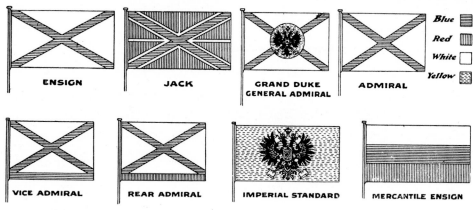

ENSIGN	JACK	GRAND DUKE GENERAL ADMIRAL
ADMIRAL		
VICE ADMIRAL	REAR ADMIRAL	IMPERIAL STANDARD
MERCANTILE ENSIGN		

Blue
Red
White
Yellow

The *Ensign* is white, with a blue St. Andrew's cross; the *Jack* red, with a blue St. Andrew's cross.
Admiral's Flag: ensign made square; Vice-Admiral ditto, with a blue line at bottom; Rear-Admiral the same, with a red line. Port Admirals have a central rectangle in flag, with blue crossed anchors.
Mercantile Ensign: white, blue and red, in lines.
Imperial Standard: yellow, with black two-headed eagle, &c., in centre.

SEVASTOPOL to	knots.
Batûm	400
Biserta	1300
Constantinople	298
Gibraltar	2000
Kertch	175
Malta	1000
Nikolaieff	200
Novorossisk	200
Odessa	165
Piræus	660
Salonika	643
Toulon	1654

LIBAU to	knots.
Brest	1430
Cherbourg	1220
Copenhagen	465
Danzig	360
Gibraltar	2330
Kiel	550
Memel	230
Revel	50
St. Margaret's Hope ...	1010
Vladivostock	12,405
Windau...	50

KRONSTADT to	knots.
Abo	250
Bornholm	627
Brest	1680
Cherbourg	1470
Copenhagen	715
Danzig	558
Gibraltar	2580
Helsingfors	150
Kiel	800
Libau	250
Memel	480
Revel	150
St. Margaret's Hope ...	1345
St. Petersburg	21
(By sea canal)	
Vladivostock... ...	12,655
Windau...	200

VLADIVOSTOCK to	knots.
Hong Kong	1740
Kiao-chau	1150
Maitsuru	470
Manila	2080
Matsmai...	380
Nagasaki	620
Port Arthur	1170
Sassebo...	600
Wei-hai-wei	950

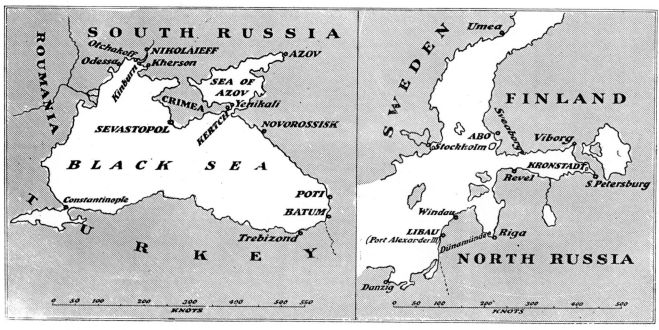

FULL DRESS, EPAULETTES. *(Gold for executives, silver for non-executive branches.)*

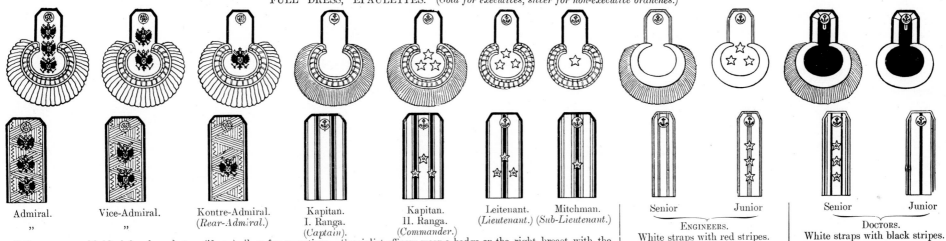

Admiral.	Vice-Admiral.	Kontre-Admiral. *(Rear-Admiral.)*	Kapitan. I. Ranga. *(Captain).*	Kapitan. II. Ranga. *(Commander.)*	Leitenant. *(Lieutenant.)*	Mitchman. *(Sub-Lieutenant.)*	Senior	Junior	Senior	Junior
„	„						ENGINEERS. White straps with red stripes.		DOCTORS. White straps with black stripes.	

Yellow straps, with black bands and stars (if any) silver for executives. Specialist officers wear a badge on the right breast with the usual insignia for gunnery, torpedo, and navigation. The uniforms are: Full dress parade with epaulettes and cocked hats; Undress, blue reefer coat of the usual sort with shoulder straps; white (duty) undress coat with shoulder straps as before and white cap. Dirks are worn instead of swords.

Modern Naval Guns (Obuchoff).

Nota- tion.	Desig- nation.	Length in Calibres.	Weight of Guns.	Weight of A.P. Shot.	Initial Velocity (approxi- mate).	Maximum Penetration with A.P. Capped Shell against K.C. Armour.		Danger Space against average warship, at			Usual Rounds per minute.
						5000 yards.	3000 yards.	10,000 yards.	5000 yards.	3000 yards.	
	inches.	calibres.	tons.	lbs.	f. s.	inches.	inches.	yards.	yards.	yards.	
AAAA	12	40	59	724	2600	14	18	150	460	750	0·30
AA	12	35	56	731	2200	8	11	120	380	580	0·25
AAA	10	45	32	490	2500	$10\frac{1}{2}$	13	130	450	700	0·45
AA	9	45	26	403	2500	$8\frac{1}{2}$	11	...	...	...	0·80
B	9	35	$19\frac{1}{2}$	268	2400	$5\frac{1}{2}$	$7\frac{1}{4}$	...	...	...	0·50
A*	8	45	$15\frac{1}{2}$	188	2800	$7\frac{1}{2}$	$10\frac{1}{2}$	105	430	625	1
DC*	6	45	$7\frac{1}{2}$	89	2900	$4\frac{1}{4}$	6	60	250	485	3
E*	6	45	7	89	2600	$3\frac{1}{4}$	5	50	200	430	3
E*	5·5	45	$4\frac{1}{2}$	66	2460	...	3	...	...	...	3
F*	4·7	45	$2\frac{1}{4}$	46	2600	...	...	...	...	...	about 4
F*	3	60	14 cwt.	$13\frac{1}{5}$	2700	...	...	...	...	...	...
F*	3	35	12 „	$13\frac{1}{5}$	2600	...	...	...	...	...	...

* = Brass cartridge cases.

Gunnery Notes.

All modern Obuchoff guns have Canet breech rifling system and mounting, and are practically equivalent to, and identical with Schneider-Canet guns.

The 10 inch and 8 inch of 45 calibres are both excellent guns. The 12 inch, 40 cal. is also a pretty good gun of fine range.

There are still a few old guns afloat in one or two obsolete ships of other and inferior models to the above, but practically all Russian ships have been re-armed with the above guns.

Russian guns use nitro-cellulose propellant, and fire Capped A.P. shell and steel pointed Common.

Torpedo Notes.

Submerged tubes are mostly of a very elementary type, and quite unreliable. Some of the latest ships are, however, believed to be fitted with the Canet submerged tube, which is very similar to the Elswick one.

The principal torpedoes (Whiteheads, mostly made in Russia) are:—

Size.	Model.	Air Pressure.	Charge g.c.	Max. Range.	Average Speed.			
					1000 yards.	2000 yards.	3000 yards.	4000 yards.
inches.			lbs.	yds.	yards.	yards.	yards.	yards.
18	'04	2150	205	4000	33	27	23	19
18	'97	2000	200	2000	30	25	—	—
18	'95	1500	200	—	25	—	—	—
14	?	1700	97	?	25	?	—	—

Very few of the '04 model are in service. Gyros to all torpedoes.

Merchant Fleet.

This, exclusive of vessels on the Caspian, consists of about 500 steamers and 1750 sailing.

Chief Trade Ports.

Riga, Odessa, Vladivostok, Helsingfors.

COINAGE : 1 rouble (100 kopecks) = 2s. 1½d. British, half-a-dollar American (*approx.*).

Colour of Ships.

Foreign Service : Grey.

Home Service : black hulls ; light cream funnels with black tops ; black or white masts.

Personnel.

About 60,000 all ranks (exact number at present very uncertain).

As a result of the war the *personnel* of the Russian Navy is in a chaotic condition.

Oversea Possessions : None.

General Admiral : H.I.H. the Grand Duke Alexis.

Minister of Marine : Vice-Admiral Birileff.

Naval Arsenals, Etc.

1. KRONSTADT. Fitting out and repairing yard for Baltic Fleet. No slips. Four large dry docks ; (*a*) Alexander, able to take any ship ; (*b*) Constantine, ditto up to 490 feet ; (*c*) Nikolai ; (*d*) Peter, smaller, but both able to take all Russian ships except the big cruisers.

Kronstadt is fed from the shipbuilding yards at St. Petersburg, the New Admiralty (2 slips), Galernii Ostrov (3 slips), Baltic works (3 slips), and torpedo-boat yards at Ijora (on the Neva) and Abo (Finland). The channel above Kronstadt is only 22 feet deep ; no completed big ships can therefore ascend to the capital.

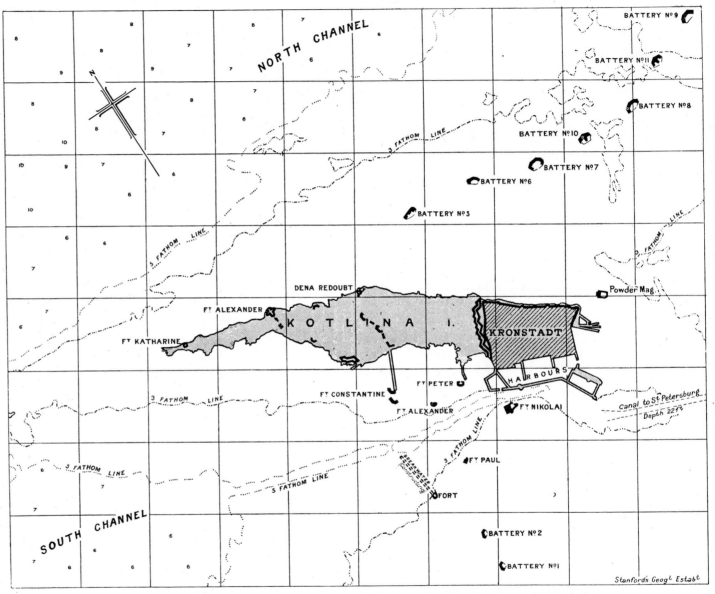

This and the other maps are all divided into squares of 2000 yards. Soundings in fathoms. Heights in feet.

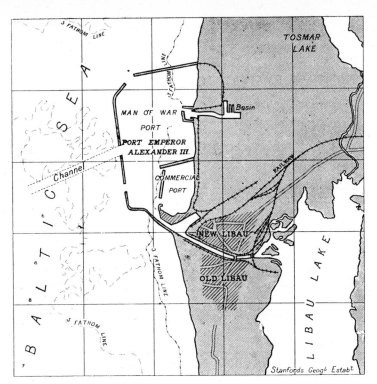

Divided into 2000 yard squares on the uniform scale. Soundings in fathoms. Heights in feet.

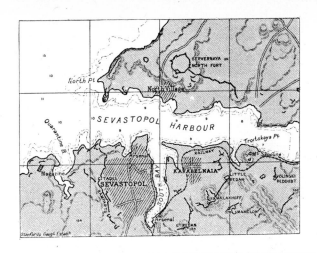

2. PORT ALEXANDER III. (Libau). New ice-free base down the Baltic coast. Two big basins; two docks able to take any ships afloat.

Other fortified Baltic bases, without docks, etc., are: Dünamünde, Viborg, Sveaborg, Revel, Riga, Windau.
    Commercial harbours at Libau, Revel (old State yard), Riga, Kronstadt, St. Petersburg, Helsingfors (with a dock 314 × 56 × 18½ feet).

(*In the Black Sea*).

SEVASTOPOL. Two slips. Two large docks able to take any ship in Black Sea Fleet. One basin.

NIKOLAIEFF. Building yard only. Strongly fortified approaches. Too shallow water for use as a base. A private yard exists here.

Other fortified black Sea bases without yards or docks; Batûm, Kinburn, Ochakoff, Azov, Kertch, Yenikali, Poti (all well fortified).

    Commercial harbours at Odessa, Batûm.

(*In the Pacific*).

VLADIVOSTOK. Small dockyard. One dock able to take any warship in the world. One small floating dock 300 feet long. Two small basins. Some repairing shops. Water shallow. Good *tideless* protected harbour. Strongly fortified (high-site batteries with 10 in. disappearing guns).
    Commercial harbours: Vladivostok, Nikolaievitch.

2 k

BLACK SEA.

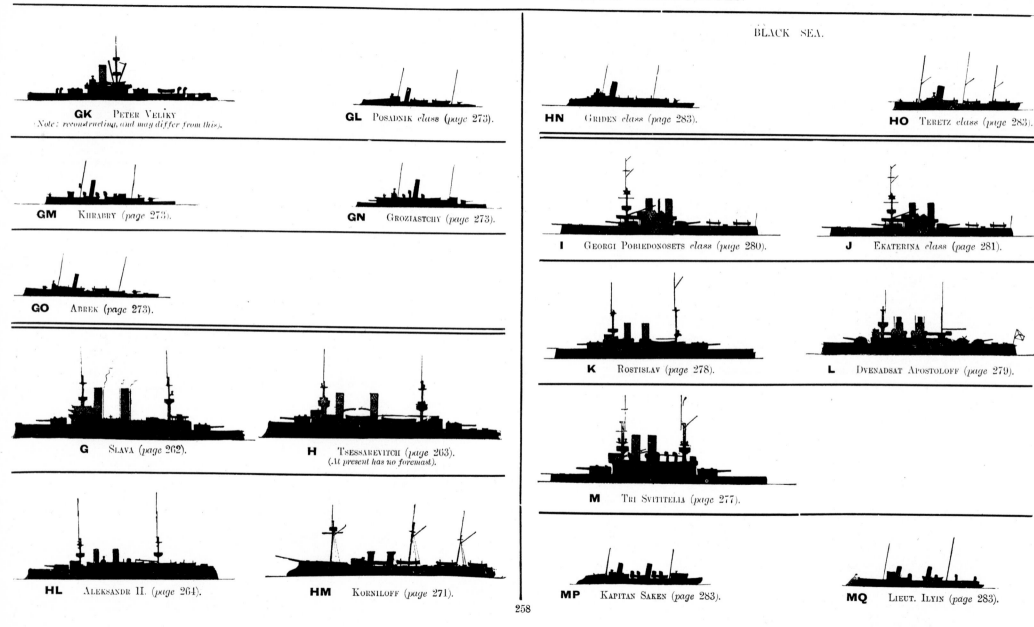

GK PETER VELIKY
(Note: reconstructing, and may differ from this).

GL POSADNIK class (page 273).

HN GRIDEN class (page 283).

HO TERETZ class (page 283).

GM KHRABRY (page 273).

GN GROZIASTCHY (page 273).

I GEORGI POBIEDONOSETS class (page 280).

J EKATERINA class (page 281).

GO ABREK (page 273).

K ROSTISLAV (page 278).

L DVENADSAT APOSTOLOFF (page 279).

G SLAVA (page 262).

H TSESSAREVITCH (page 263).
(At present has no foremast).

M TRI SVITITELIA (page 277).

HL ALEKSANDR II. (page 264).

HM KORNILOFF (page 271).

MP KAPITAN SAKEN (page 283).

MQ LIEUT. ILYIN (page 283).

BALTIC, ETC.

BLACK SEA.

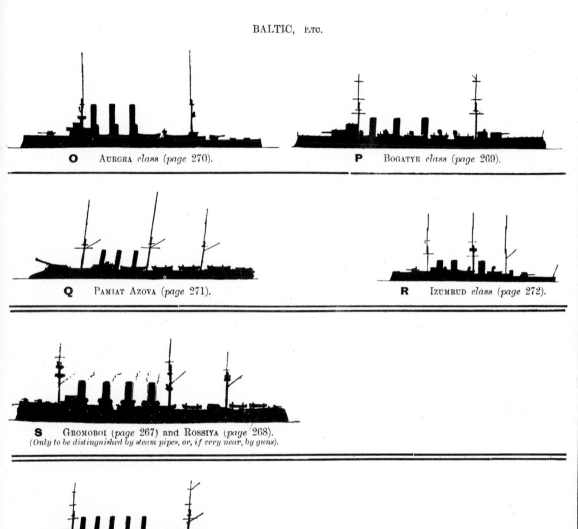

O AURORA *class* (*page 270*).

P BOGATYR *class* (*page 269*).

Q PAMIAT AZOVA (*page 271*).

R IZUMRUD *class* (*page 272*).

S GROMOBOI (*page 267*) and ROSSIYA (*page 268*).
(*Only to be distinguished by steam pipes, or, if very near, by guns*).

V ASKOLD (*page 270*).

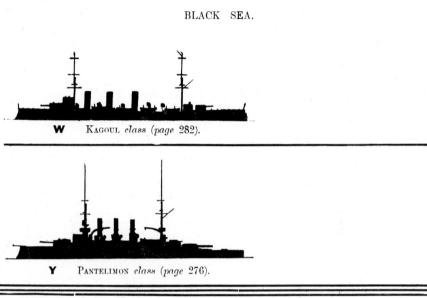

W KAGOUL *class* (*page 282*).

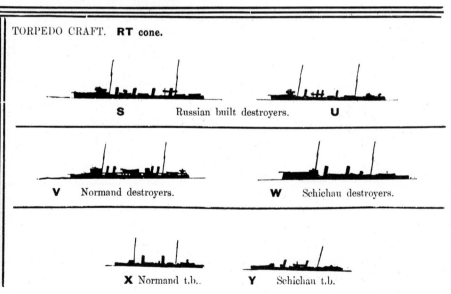

Y PANTELIMON *class* (*page 276*).

TORPEDO CRAFT. **RT** cone.

S   Russian built destroyers.   **U**

V   Normand destroyers.

W   Schichau destroyers.

X Normand t.b..   **Y** Schichau t.b.

2 K 2

LATEST RUSSIAN BATTLESHIPS.

"A" (building) and others projected.

Displacement 16,500 tons.   Complement

Length (waterline),   feet.   Beam,   feet.   Maximum draught,   feet.   Length over all,   feet.

Guns (probably):
 4—12 ins., 45 cal. (AAAA).
 4—10 ins., 45 cal. (AAA).
 14—8 ins., 45 cal. (A).
 20—12 pdrs. (F).
 20 smaller.
Torpedo tubes:
 2 submerged.
 2 above water (bow and stern).

Armour (Krupp):
 11″ Belt (amidships)...   aaa
 6″ Belt (ends) ....   a
 3″ Armour deck.
 Protection to vitals ... aaaaa
 12″ Main turrets (N.C.)   aaa
 10″ Turret bases (N.C.)   aaa
 7″ Secondary turrets   a
 7″ Lower deck side...   a
 7″ Battery ....   a
 12″ Conning tower ...   aaa

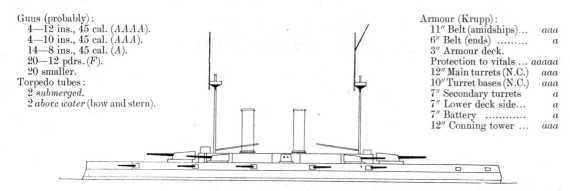

Ahead:
2—12 in.
2—10 in.
6—8 in.

Astern:
2—12 in.
2—10 in.
6—8 in.

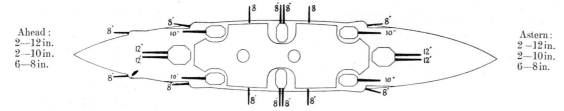

Broadside : 4—12 in., 4—10 in., 7—8 in.

Machinery : 2 sets vertical triple expansion. 2 screws. Boilers: Belleville. Designed H.P. 19,750 =
Coal : normal   tons ; maximum 3000 tons.

General Notes.—

Name.	Builder.	Machinery by	Laid down.	To be completed.		Boilers.	
"A"			1905	1907		Belleville	

(Building and projected.)

"A" is believed to be of this type.

New battleships projected. 18,000 tons.

Armament : 4—12 inch, 12—10 inch.

NEW RUSSIAN BATTLESHIPS (18 knot).

(IMPERATOR PAVEL CLASS—2 SHIPS).

IMPERATOR PAVEL (1905), & *ANDREI PERVOSWANNI* (1905).

Displacement 16,630 tons. Complement ——

Length (*waterline*), 425 feet. Beam, 78 feet. *Mean* draught, 27 feet.

Guns:
4—12 inch, 40 cal. (A.A.A.A).
12—8 inch, 45 cal. (A).
20—12 pdr. (F).
20—3 pdr.
Torpedo tubes:
2 *submerged*.
2 *above water* (bow and stern).

Armour (Krupp):
11″ Belt (amidships) . ... *aaa*
6″ Belt (ends)................. *a*
3″ Deck (flat below belt) ...
1½″ Splinter deck above it
Protection to vitals....:. = *aaaaa*
″Barbettes....................
12″ Turrets (N.C.) .... *aaa*
10″ Turret bases .... *aa*
6—4½″ Upper belt........... *a-e*
7″ Small turrets.............. *a*
12″ Conning tower............. *aaa*
(Total weight 4400 tons).

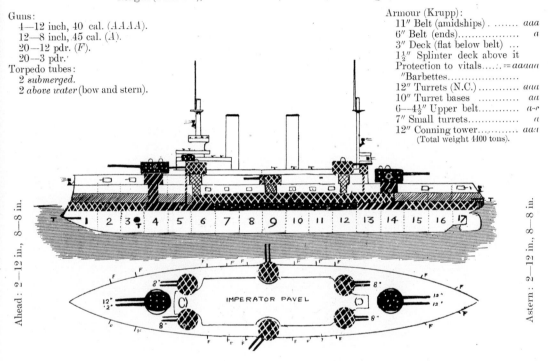

Ahead: 2—12 in., 8—8 in.

Astern: 2—12 in., 8—8 in.

IMPERATOR PAVEL

Broadside: 4—12 in., 6—8 in.

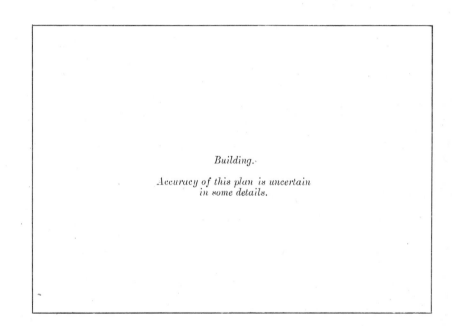

Building.

Accuracy of this plan is uncertain in some details.

Machinery: 2 sets triple expansion. 2 screws. Boilers: Belleville. Designed H.P. 17,600 = 18 kts
Coal: *normal* 1,500 tons; *maximum* 3,000 tons.

Armour Notes.—Belt is 7½ feet wide, 5 feet of it below waterline; lower edge is 7″ thick.

Gunnery Notes.—Loading positions, big guns: all round. Hoists: electric. Big guns manœuvred electrically and hydraulically; secondary turrets, electrically.
Arcs of fire: Big guns, 270°; secondary turrets (amidships) 180°, (others) 150°.

Torpedo Notes.—6 searchlights.

Engineering Notes.—

General Notes.—Laid down at St. Petersburg, September, 1903. Estimated total cost, £1,500,000. To be completed in 1906.

SLAVA (August, (1903).

Displacement 13,566 tons.   Complement 750.

Length (*waterline*), 376½ feet.   Beam, 76 feet.   *Mean* draught, 26 feet.   Length over all, 397 feet.

Guns :
4—12 in., 40 cal. (*AAAA*)
12—6 inch, 45 cal. (*D*).
20—3 inch, 60 cal. (*F*).
20—3 pdr.
8—1 pdr.
Torpedo tubes (18-inch) :
2 *submerged* (broadside).
1 *above water* (bow).
1 *above water* (stern).

Armour (Krupp) :
10″ Belt (amidships).... .*aaa*
4″ Belt (ends) .... *d*
4″ Armour deck
(flat below belt)
Protection to vitals = *aaaaaa*
11″ Turrets ....*aaa*
8″ Turret bases (N.C.)... *a*
6″—2½″ Lower deck side *a-f*
7″ Small turrets (N.C.)... *a*
6″ bases to these .... *c*
10″ Conning tower ...... *aa*
(Total weight, 4000 tons.)

Ahead : 2—12 in., 8—6 in.

Astern : 2—12 in., 8—6 in.

Broadside : 4—12 in., 6—6 in.

Distinction.—Easily recognised from *Tsessarevitch* by the rig.

Machinery : 2 sets vertical 4 cylinder triple expansion. 2 screws. Boilers : 20 Belleville. Designed I.H.P. 16,500 = 18 kts. Coal : *normal* 750 tons ; *maximum* 1250 tons.

Armour Notes.—Belt is 6¾ feet wide, 5 feet of it below waterline ; lower edge is 7″ thick amidships ; upper belt is 5¾ feet wide.

Gunnery Notes.—Loading positions big guns : all round. Hoists, electric and hand.
Big guns manœuvred electrically : secondary turrets, electrically. Arcs of fire : Big guns 240° (nominal only) ; 6 in., amidships, 180° (actual) ; other 6 in., 150° from axial line.

Torpedo Notes.—18 torpedoes carried. 6 searchlights (automatically controlled).

General Notes.—Laid down at the New Admiralty, October, 1902. Completed March, 1905. Total cost about £1,500,000. Three sisters, *Borodino, Imperator Aleksandr III.*, and *Kniaz Suvaroff*, sunk at Battle of Tsushima, 1905, and a fourth sister, *Orel*, now the Japanese *Iwami*.

TSESSAREVITCH (February, 1901).

Displacement 13,380 tons.

Length (*waterline*), 388¾ feet. Beam, 75½ feet. *Maximum* draught, 28¼ feet. Length over all, 401 feet.

Guns :
4—12 inch, 40 cal. (*AAAA*).
12—6 inch, 45 cal. (*C*).
20—12 pdr. (*F*).
2—9 pdr. Baronovski.
20—3 pdr.
6—1 pdr.
Torpedo tubes (18 inch) :
2 *submerged*.
2 *above water* (bow and stern).

Armour (Krupp) :
4″ Belt (ends) .... *d*
10″ Belt (amidships)......*aaa*
4″ Deck (slopes)...........
Protection to vitals ...*aaaaa*
6″—2½″ Lower deck side *a—f*
2″ Main deck ....
11″ Turrets (NC) .....*...aaa*
10—8″ Turret bases (NC) *aa*
7″ Small turrets (6)......... *b*
5″ Bases to these........... *c*
10″ Conning tower (NC)...*aa*
5″ Tube to it ....
(Total weight 4000 tons.)

Photo, Bar.

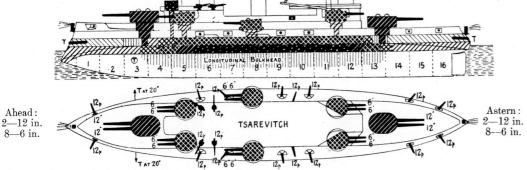

Ahead :
2—12 in.
8—6 in.

Astern :
2—12 in.
8—6 in.

Broadside : 4—12 in., 6—6 in.

Machinery : 2 sets triple expansion. 2 screws. Boilers : 20 Belleville. Designed H.P. 16,300 = 18 kts.

Coal : *normal* 800 tons ; *maximum* 1350 tons.

Armour Notes.—Main belt is 6½ feet wide ; 5 feet of it below waterline ; lower edge is 7″ thick amidships.

Gunnery Notes.—Loading positions, big guns : all round. Hoists : electric, all guns. Big guns manœuvred electrically, hydraulic, and hand ; secondary guns, electrically and hand.

Arcs of fire : Big guns, 270° ; secondary guns, 150° ; and amidship turrets, 180°.

Ammunition carried : 12 inch, 70 rounds per gun ; 6 inch, 200 per gun.

Height of guns above water : Bow guns, 30 feet ; after, 23 feet ; secondary turret, 29½ and 23 feet.

Torpedo Notes.—6 searchlights (automatic). Special defence against torpedoes in 1⅔ in. lateral bulkheads running length of ship amidships. 2 second class torpedo boats carried. 18 torpedoes for ship use.

Engineering Notes.—*Tsessarevitch* on *trial* made 16,500 I.H.P. = 18·78 mean. 19·4 kts. subsequently reached with about 17,000 H.P. At 12½ kts., burned only 1·3 lbs. per H.P. ; average sea consumption at 16,300 H.P. (18 kts.) is about 12 tons an hour or less.

General Notes.—Laid down at La Seyne, May 1899. Completed 1904. The ship is remarkably handy, answering the least touch of the wheel. Considerable heel in turning. Freeboard, 26 feet. Torpedoed at Port Arthur, February, 1904. Interned at Kiao Chau, August, 1904.

Present Rig.   *Photo by favour of H. W. Wilson, Esq.*

IMPERATOR ALEKSANDR II. (July, 1887).

Displacement about 9900 tons.   Sheathed.   Complement

Length, 326½ feet.   Beam, 67 feet.   *Maximum* draught, 27 feet.

Guns (1905 armament) :
  2—12 inch, 30 cal. (*C*).
  12—6 inch, 45 cal. (*D*).
  16—3 pdr.
  4—1 pdr.
  (Some 12 pdrs. may also
    be carried).
Torpedo tubes :
  6 *above water*.

Armour (compound) :
  14″ Belt (amidships) ... *a*
  6″ Belt (ends) .... *d*
  3″ Deck (flat on belt) ...
  Protection to vitals is ... *a*
  12″ Barbette.............. *a*
  6″ Battery bulkhead   ... *d*
  6″ Conning tower......... *d*

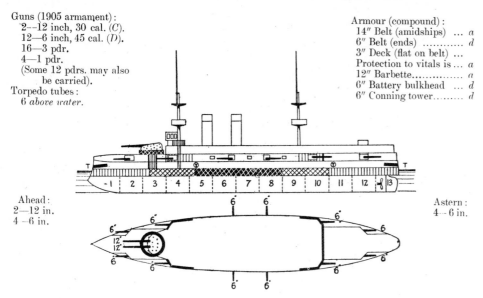

Ahead :
2—12 in.
4—6 in.

Astern :
4—6 in.

Broadside : 2—12 in., 6—6 in.

Machinery (new about 1900) : 2 sets vertical triple expansion.   2 screws.   Boilers (1905) : 16 Belleville.   Designed H.P. 8000 = 15·9 kts.   Coal : *normal*   ; *maximum* 1200 tons ; also oil.

Armour Notes.—Belt is 8 feet wide.

Gunnery Notes.—Re-armed hastily in 1904-5.

Engineering Notes.—In 1905 she had her old cylindrical boilers replaced by Bellevilles taken out of the Imperial Yacht.

The Russian Navy also contains *Petr Veliky*, an old turret ship some thirty years old, which is reconstructing at present.

NEW RUSSIAN ARMOURED CRUISERS (21 knot).

RURIK (building) and 2 others pro.

Displacement 15,000 tons.   Complement 800.

Length (*waterline*), 490 feet.   Beam, 75 feet.   *Mean* draught, 26 feet.   Length over all, — feet.

Guns:
4—10 inch (*A A A*)
8—8 inch (*A*)
20—·4·7 inch.
14 smaller.
Torpedo tubes (18 inch):
2 *submerged.*

(Total weight, with ammunition
tons).

Armour: (Krupp)
6″ Belt (amidships)   *a*
4″ Belt (bow) ....   *d*
3″ Belt (stern) ......   *ε*
1½″ Armour deck ...
Protection to vitals   =*aa*
8″ Turrets (K.C.) ...   *aa*
″ Turret bases ......
7″ Secondary turrets   *a*
3″ Redoubt ....   *ε*
3″ Battery ....   *ε*
″ Conning tower ....
(Total weight   tons).

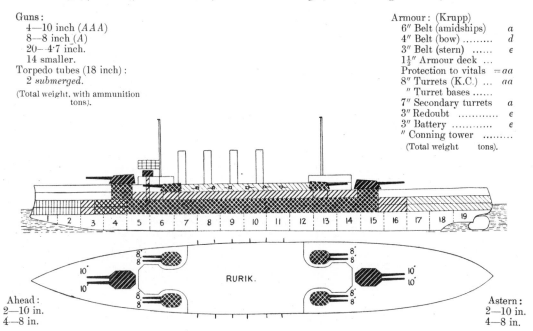

Ahead:
2—10 in.
4—8 in.

RURIK.

Astern:
2—10 in.
4—8 in.

Broadside: 4—10 in., 4—8 in., 10—4·7 in.

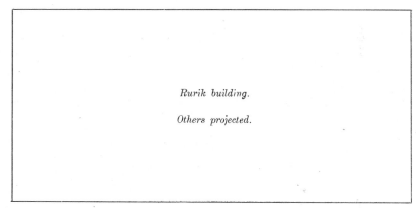

Rurik building.

Others projected.

Machinery: 2 sets 4 cylinder quadruple expansion. 2 screws. Boilers: Belleville.
Designed H.P. 19,700 = 21 kts. Coal: *normal* 1200 tons; *maximum* 2000 tons.

Name.	Builder.	Machinery and Boilers by	Laid down.	To be completed.	Trials.	Boilers.
Rurik A B	Vickers	Vickers	1905	1907		Belleville

Note.—Enormous increase of weight of defensive material has been introduced into this ship in view of the lessons learned from the Russo-Japanese War.

NEW RUSSIAN ARMOURED CRUISERS (22 knot).

(MAKAROFF CLASS—3 SHIPS *and 3 others*).

ADMIRAL MAKAROFF (May, 1906), *PALLADA (building), BAYAN (building), & 3 others projected.*

Displacement about 8,000 tons.   Complement —.

Length (*waterline*), 443 feet.   Beam, 55 feet.   *Maximum* draught,   feet.   Length over all,   feet.

Guns :
  2—8 inch, 45 cal. (*A*).
  8—6 inch, 45 cal. (*D*).
  20—12 pdr.
  7—3 pdr.
Torpedo tubes :
  2 *submerged*.

Armour (Krupp) :
  8″ Belt amidships) ... *aa*
  4″ Belt (forward) ...... *d*
  2″ Armour deck ......
  Protection to vitals = *aaa*
  3¼″-2½″ Upper belt ... *e-f*
  7″ Turrets.............. *a*
  ″ Turret bases .....
  3¼″ Battery .... *e*
  6½″ Conning tower ... *a*

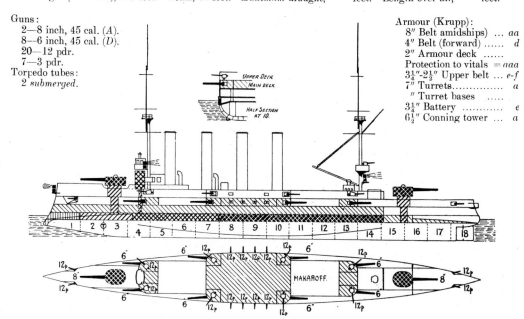

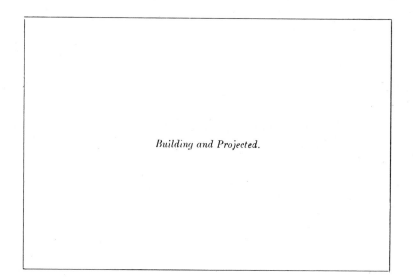

Building and Projected.

Machinery : 2 sets vertical triple expansion. 2 screws. Boilers : Belleville. Designed H.P.   =22 kts.
Coal : *normal*   tons ; *maximum*   tons.

Armour Notes.—Belt is 6½ feet wide by 350 feet long ; 4½ feet of it below waterline. Lower edge is 4″ thick.

General Notes.—

Name.	Built at	Laid down.	Completed.	Trials.	Boilers.	Present best speed.
Ad. Makaroff	La Seyne	1905			Belleville	
Pallada	Galernii	1905			Belleville	
Bayan	New Admiralty	1905			Belleville	
"A"						
"B"						
"C"						

GROMOBOI (May, 1899).

Displacement 12,367 tons. Wood sheathed and coppered. Complement 800.

Length (*waterline*), 472¼ feet. Beam, 68 feet. *Maximum* draught, 29 feet.

Guns :
 4—8 inch, 45 cal. (*A*).
 16—6 inch, 45 cals. (*E*)
 20—12 pdr. (*F*)
 16—3 pdr.
 8—1 pdr.
Torpedo tubes :
 2 *submerged*.
 2 *above water*. (training).

Armour (Harvey-nickel) :
 6″ Belt .... *b*
 2″ Deck .... = *d*
 Protection to vitals... = *aa'*
 6″ Bulkheads .... *b*
 4″ Lower deck (amidships) *d*
 6″ Casemates (14) ...... *b*
 2″ Hoists .... *ε*
 10″ Conning tower ...... *aa*
 (Total *about* 2100 tons.)

Громобой. (GROMOBOI). *Photo, Renard.*

For *distinctions* from *Rossiya* :

 Note.—She has no steampipes before the funnels ; also guns differently arranged.

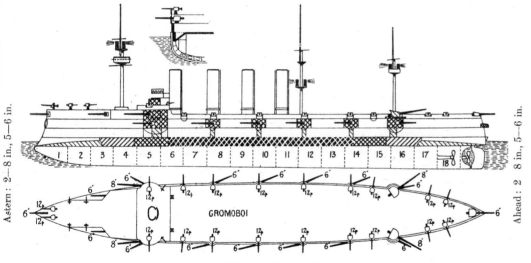

Astern : 2—8 in., 5—6 in.

GROMOBOI

Ahead : 2—8 in., 5—6 in.

Broadside : 2—8 in., 7—6 in.

Details abaft foremast, port side.

Machinery : 3 sets triple expansion. 3 screws. Boilers : 30 Belleville. Designed H.P. 18,000 = 20 kts.
Coal : *normal* 800 tons ; *maximum* 2500 tons and liquid fuel.

Armour Notes.—Belt is 7 feet wide by about 330 feet long. Lower deck side armoured for 100 feet in wake of
 engines.

Gunnery Notes. Hoists badly arranged. 8 inch guns electrically manœuvred, and all hoists electric.

Engineering Notes.—The ship steams well, and did over 18 kts. after the battle of Tsushima Straits, Aug. 1904.

General Notes.—Laid down at the Baltic Works, St. Petersburg, May, 1898, and completed for sea early in 1901.
 Cost complete, over £900,000. Tactical diameter, 1000 yards.

ROSSIYA. (1896).

Displacement 12,500 tons (sheathed and coppered).   Complement 735.

Length (*waterline*), 472 feet.   Beam, 68 feet.   *Maximum* draught, 29 feet.   Length over all, 480 feet.

Guns :
4—8 inch, 45 cal. (*A*)
16—5·5 in, 45 cal. (*E*)
12—12 pdr. (*F*)
36 smaller QF.
Torpedo tubes :
6 *above water* (bow,
  stern and broadside
  all unprotected).

Armour (Harvey) :
10″-5″ Belt ......*a-d*
2½″ Deck ....= *d*
[Deck flat on belt.]
6″ Bulkheads ......*c*
Prot. to vitals = *a*
4″ Lower deck
    (amidships) *d*
6″ B't'ry b'lkh'ds *c*
2″ Casemates (to 8″)
2″ Screens in battery

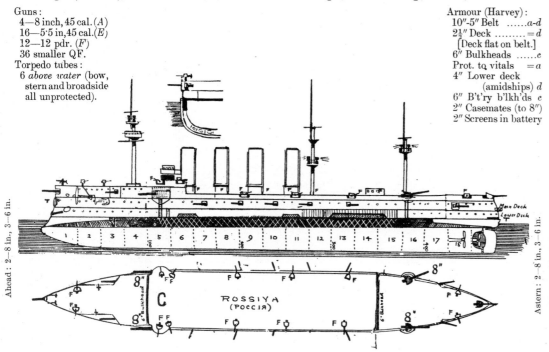

Ahead : 2—8 in, 3—6 in.

Astern : 2—8 in, 3—6 in.

ROSSIYA
(POCCIЯ)

Broadside ; 2—8 in , 7—6 in.

Россія (ROSSIYA).   *Photo, H. Nye, Esq.*

To be distinguished from *Gromoboi* by having more steam pipes and the different arrangement of the battery amidships.

Machinery : 3 sets vertical triple expansion.   3 screws.   Boilers : 32 Belleville (without economisers) in 4 groups.   Designed H.P. 18,000 = 20 kts.   Present sea speed : *circa* 18½ kts.   Coal : *normal* 1000 tons ; *maximum capacity* 2500 tons and liquid fuel.

Armour Notes.—Belt is nearly complete, but comparatively little of it is the maximum thickness.   It is *about* 7 feet wide.

Gunnery Notes.—Electric hoists to all guns.   Hoists at end of battery and full service difficult.   The big guns are 45 cal. :—the first four guns of this model to be made.   They are powerful guns of high velocity.   The bow and stern guns will not train on the broadside.

Torpedo Notes.—Net defence.

Engineering Notes.—On her first *trials* she made I.H.P. 18,446 = 20·25 in a run on the measured mile.   After battle of Tsushima Straits steamed at 18 kts. or more with damaged funnels, and may be regarded as an excellent steamer.   Burns about 18 tons an hour at 20,000 H.P. (20 kts.).

General Notes.—Laid down at the Baltic Works, St. Petersburg, in 1893.   Completed 1898.   Said to have cost over £900,000 to build.—Four small torpedo boats carried.

(BOGATYR TYPE—2 SHIPS,)   (*See also Black Sea Fleet.*)

BOGATYR (January, 1901), **OLEG** (August, 1903), *VITIAZ* (*building—burned while building*).

Displacement 6550 tons.   Complement 573.

Length (*waterline*), 437 feet.   Beam, 52¼ feet.   *Maximum* draught, 24¾ feet.

Guns (M. '99):
- 12—6 inch, 45 cal. (*D*).
- 12—12 pdr. (*F*).
- 8—3 pdr.
- 2—1 pdr.

Torpedo tubes :
- 2 *submerged* (20° abaft).
- 1 *above water* (bow).
- 1 *above water* (stern).
- 2 *above water* (training).

Armour (Krupp) :
- 3″ Deck (on slopes) ... = *d*
- Protection to vitals ... = *d*
- 3″ Turrets .... ϵ
- 3″ Casemates........... ϵ
- 2″ Hoists ....
- 6″ Conning tower...... *b*
- 2″ Funnel bases ......= ϵ

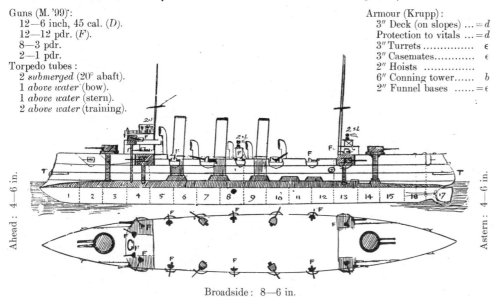

Ahead : 4—6 in.   Astern : 4—6 in.

Broadside : 8—6 in.

Богатырь (BOGATYR).   *Photo, Geiser.*

Machinery : 2 screws.   Boilers : Normand-Sigaudy.   Designed H.P. 19,500 = 23 kts.   Coal : *normal* 700 tons ; *maximum* 1000 tons.

Gunnery Notes.—Electric hoists to all guns.   Turrets electrically manœuvred.

Engineering Notes. –

Name.	Builders.	Laid down.	Completed.	8 hours full power trial.	Boilers.
Bogatyr	Vulkan Co.	May, '98	1902	20,000 = 23·45 kts.	Normand
Oleg	New Admiralty	Nov., '01	Aug., '04	20,176 = 23·47 kts.	Normand
Vitiaz*	Galernii Ostrov	May, '01			

* Uncertain whether the *Vitiaz* is being proceeded with.

Coal consumption about 19 tons an hour at 19,500 H.P. (23 kts.)   Boilers need considerable cleaning to give efficient work.   Ships steam very well.

General Notes.—Tactical diameter about 850 yards.

Distinctions :

Name.	Funnels.	Masts.
Bogatyr	Not very high, and stout	High
Oleg	Thinner funnels	Very high indeed

Аскольдъ.

ASKOLD (March, 1900).

Displacement 6500 tons.   Complement 580.

Length (*waterline*), 444 feet.   Beam, 49 feet.   *Maximum* draught, $20\frac{3}{4}$ feet.

Guns (Obuchoff):
- 12—6 inch, 45 cal. (C)
- 12—12 pdr. (F).
- 8—3 pdr.
- 2—1 pdr.

Torpedo tubes:
- 2 *submerged*
- 4 *above water.*
- (bow and stern and section 10).

Armour (Krupp):
- 3″ Deck .... = d
- Protection to vitals = ε
- 1½″ Hoists ....
- 4″ Funnel bases ... d
- 6″ Conning tower ... b
- 2⅓″ Torpedo tubes

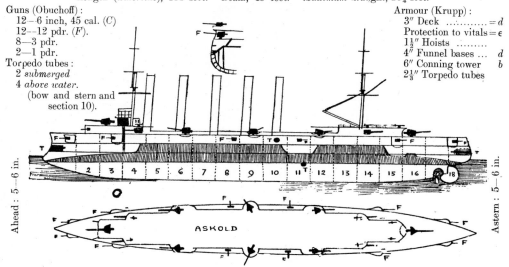

Ahead: 5—6 in.   Astern: 5—6 in.

ASKOLD

Broadside: 7—6 in.

Machinery: 3 sets triple expansion. 3 screws. Boilers: 18 Schulz-Thornycroft. Designed H.P. 19,500 = 23 kts. Coal: *normal* 720 tons; *maximum* 11,000 tons.

Gunnery Notes.—Electric hoists to all guns.

Torpedo Notes.—Net defence fitted amidships.

Engineering Notes.—On a 6 hours trial *maximum* recorded was I.H.P. 23,600 = 24·5 kts., at Round Island 23 kts.

General Notes.—Laid down at Krupp's Germania Yard, March, 1899. Completed 1901.

(Діана: Аурора.)   *Photo by favour of H.I.H. Grand Duke Alexander of Russia.*

DIANA (October, 1899), & **AURORA** (May, 1900).

Displacement 6630 tons.   Complement 570.

Length (*waterline*), 410 feet.   Beam, 55 feet.   *Maximum* draught, $21\frac{1}{4}$ feet.

Guns:
- 8—6 inch, 45 cal. (D).
- 22—12 pdr. (F).
- 8—Small Q.F.

Torpedo tubes:
- 4 *above water.*

Armour:
- 2½″ Deck .... = d
- 4″ Hoists .... d
- 2″ Funnels between decks
- 6″ C.T. (Harvey) c
- 4½″ Engine hatches... = b

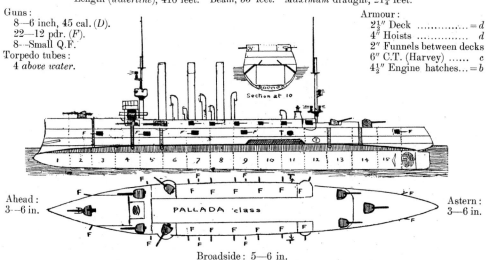

Section at 10

Ahead: 3—6 in.   Astern: 3—6 in.

PALLADA class

Broadside: 5—6 in.

Machinery: 3 sets horizontal 3 cylinder triple expansion. Designed H.P. 11,600 = 20 kts. Contract sea speed: 19 kts. 3 screws. Boilers: 24 Belleville. Coal: *normal* 900 tons; *maximum* 1430 tons + liquid fuel.

Gunnery Notes.—Electric hoists to all guns.

General Notes.—Tactical diameter *circa* 750 yards. No wood used in construction. Laid down at Galernii Island, 1896. Completed 1902.

(Souvenir of the *Azov*).

PAMIAT-AZOVA (1888).
Displacement 6,700 tons.   Complement 525.
Length, 378 feet.   Beam, 50 feet.   *Maximum* draught, 25 feet.

Guns (new in 1901):
  14—6 inch, 45 cal., (*D*)
Torpedo tubes:
  2 *above water.*

Armour (compound):
  10″-8″ Belt (amidships) *b-c*
  2¾″ Deck (flat on belt)
  Protection to vitals ... = *b*
  2¼″ Deck (at ends) ... = ϵ
  8″ Bulkheads .... *c*
  8″ Barbettes (2) ...... *c*
  2″ Hoods to these...... *f*
  1½″ Conning tower ...

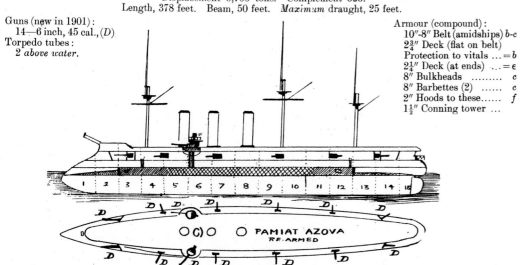

Machinery (new in 1902): 2 sets vertical triple expansion. 2 screws. Boilers: Belleville. Designed H.P. 11,000 = 18·8 kts. Coal: *normal* 550 tons; *maximum* 1000 tons.
Notes.—The belt is 8⅙ feet wide, by 259 feet long. It reaches 1⅔ feet above the water-line.

Адмиралъ Корниловъ.
ADMIRAL KORNILOFF (April, 1887).
Displacement 5,800 tons.   Complement 478.

Guns:
  14—6 inch, 45 cal. (*E*).
  6—3 pdr.
  6—1 pdr.
  5—4 pdr. boat.
Torpedo tubes:
  6 *above water.*

Armour:
  2½″ Deck (on slopes) = *d*ϵ

Ahead:
  2—6 in.

Astern:
  2—6 in.

Broadside: 7—6 in.

Machinery: 2 sets horizontal triple expansion. 2 screws. Boilers: 8 cylindrical (new in 1895-96). Designed H.P. *natural* 7500 = 17·5 kts.; *forced* 9000 = 18·5 kts. Coal: *normal* 700 tons; *maximum* (always carried) 1100 tons. The ship burns a great deal of coal. Electric hoists have been fitted to some guns, but the battery is not well supplied. Built at La Seyne.

JEMTCHUG (1903).

Displacement 3050 tons.   Complement 334.

Length (*waterline*) 345 feet.   Beam 49 feet.   *Mean* draught, 16 feet.

Guns (M. '00) :
  6—4·7 inch., 45 cal. (*E*).
  6—3 pdr.
  2—1 pdr.
Torpedo tubes :
  1 *above water* (stern).
  4 *above water* (broadside).

Armour (Krupp) :
  2″ Deck.................. = є
  3″ Conning tower...... є

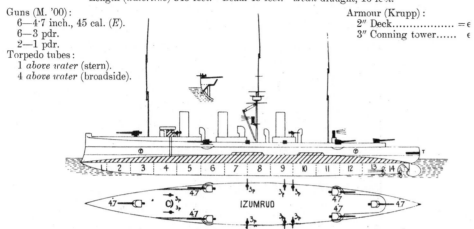

Machinery : 2 sets 4 cylinder triple expansion.   2 screws.   Boilers : 16 Yarrow in 3 compartments.
Designed H.P. 19,000 = 24 kts.   Coal : *normal* 500 tons ; *maximum* 600 tons.

ALMAZ (1903).

Displacement 3300 tons.   Complement 275.

Guns : 4—12 pdr.   Armour deck 3″.   Designed H.P. 7500 = 19 kts.   Boilers : 16 Belleville (without economisers).   This vessel is an armed yacht.

RUSSIAN SMALL CRAFT.

KHRABRY (1895).

Displacement *circa* 1700 tons.   Complement 135.

Length, 223 feet.   Beam, $41\frac{2}{3}$ feet.   *Maximum* draught, $13\frac{1}{3}$ feet.

Guns (Obuchoff) :
2—8 inch, 45 cal. (*A*).
1—6 inch, 45 cal. (*D*).
10 small Q.F.
Torpedo tubes :
1 *above water* (bow).

Armour (Harvey) :
5″ Belt.................... *d*
1″ Deck (flat on it) ...
$1\frac{1}{2}$″ Deck (end)......... = *f*
$3\frac{1}{2}$″ Bulkhead .... ϵ
[Cellulose belt].

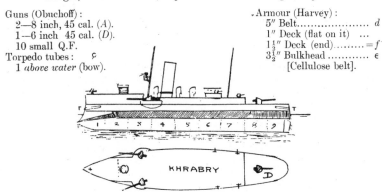

Храбрый (KHRABRY).

Machinery : 2 sets vertical triple expansion. 2 screws. Boilers : 8 Niclausse.
Designed H.P. *forced* 2640 = 16 kts. (= 14·5 kts. on *trial*). Coal : *normal* 100
tons ; *maximum* 130 tons.

Грозящія (GROZIASTCHY).

Photos, Symonds.

GROZIASTCHY (1890-92).

Displacement *circa* 1500 tons.   Complement 120.

Length, 223 feet.   Beam, $41\frac{2}{3}$ feet.   *Maximum* draught, $13\frac{1}{3}$ feet.

Guns :
1—9 inch, 35 cal. (*B*).
1—6 inch, 45 cal. (*D*).
16 small Q.F.
Torpedo tubes :
1 *above water*.

Armour (compound) :
5″ Belt................. ϵ
1″ Deck (flat on it) ...
$1\frac{1}{2}$″ Deck (forward) ... = *f*
$3\frac{1}{2}$″ Bulkhead ....

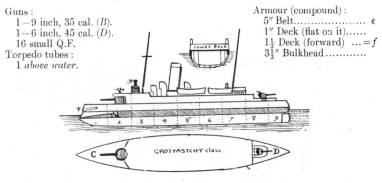

Machinery : 2 sets vertical triple expansion. 2 screws. Boilers : 6 Belleville.
Designed H.P. 2000 = 15 kts. Coal : *normal* 100 tons ; *maximum* 130 tons.

Torpedo Gunboats.

ABREK (1896).

Displacement 534 tons.   Complement 109.

Length, 212 feet.   Beam, 25 feet.   *Maximum* draught, 13 feet.

Guns :
2—4·7 inch (*E*).
4—3 pdr.
2—1 pdr.
Torpedo tubes :
2 *above water*.

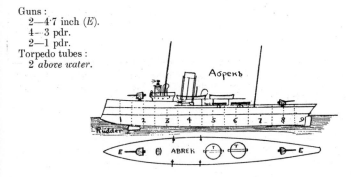

Абрекъ (ABREK).   *Photo, Steinitz, Kiel.*

Machinery : 2 sets vertical triple expansion.   2 screws.   Boilers : Normand.
Designed H.P. 4500 = 21 kts. (exceeded on *trial*). 2 rudders.

(Of no fighting value).

POSADNIK (1892) & VOEVODA (1893).

Displacement 411 tons.   Complement 61.

Guns :
3—3 pdr.
3—1 pdr.

Coal protection to engines
and boilers.

Machinery : 2 sets triple expansion.   2 screws.   Designed H.P.
3400 = 21 kts. (Present speed about 16-17 kts. or less). Coal : 90 tons.
Built by Schichau.

Посадникъ (POSADNIK).

2 м

All Yarrow type more or less like this.

Summary of Russian Destroyers.

No.	Type.	Displacement.	Date.	H.P.	Max. Speed.	Coal.	Complement.	Tubes.	Max. Draught.
8	Kondeatenko	625	'05–'06	6800	28	...	...	3	9
5	Emir Bucharski	580	'04–'06	6500	28	...	89	3	$8\frac{1}{2}$
9	Finn (Y)	508	'04–'06	5200	26	...	75	2	...
29	*New* Boyevoi (F & Y)	356	'04–'06	5700	26	80	62	3	7
6	Bravi (Y)	356	'02–'04	5700	26	80	62	3	7
3	Bestraschni (S)..............	352	'00–'01	6000	27	60	60	3	$8\frac{1}{2}$
2	Grosovoi (F).................	312	'00–'01	4750	26	80	53	2	8
2	Grosovoi (F).................	305	'04–'05	5500	27	80	53	2	7
13	Smyeli (Y)	245	'01–'03	5700	27	53	53	2	9
5	Prütky (Y)	220	'95–'00	3800	28	60	51	2	8
82									

The above all carry 18 inch torpedoes. Boats of 500 tons and over carry 2—12 pdr., 5—6 pdr.; those of over 300 tons, 1—12 pdr., 5—3 pdr.; those of under 300 tons, 1—12 pdr., 3—3 pdr. (Y = Yarrow type. F = French type. S = Schichau.)

All French Type.

Schichau type much like German "G" class destroyers, but fitted with two masts as a rule.

Torpedo Boats.

No.	Type.	Date.	Tons.	Coal.	Tubes.	H.P.	Max. speed.
				Tons.			kts.
1	Yarrow	'03-'04	...	...	...	...	...
15	Normand	'94-'04	120	30	3	2000	24·0
7	Schichau	'93-'02	130	40	3	2400	27·5
12	Schichau	1897	120	60	2	2000	21·0
11	Schichau	'93-'95	100	—	3	1250	21
9	Normand	'94-'97	85	16	3	1200	21
55							

Also about 100 old boats of various sizes, slow and of no fighting value at all.

The *Yarrow* boat has turbines, and named **Latoschka** (ex *Caroline*).

LAKE TYPE.

OSSETYR (*ex Protector*).

No. of boats.	Class or Type.	Date.	Displacement.	Motive Power, above and below.	H.P.	Max. speed above & below.	Dimensions in feet.	Tubes.	Radius
						kts.			
9	Lake	'02-'05		petrol / accumulators.		9 / 7		2	
7	Holland type ("Bubnoff.")	'03-'05	175	petrol / accumulators.	...	7 / 5	77 × ×	1	
4	Poukaloff	'04-'06	20	accumulators / accumulators.	...	10 / 5	50 × 14 × 10	2 slings	
1	Drzewiecki	(?)	(?)	? ?	...	10 / 5	80 ×	2 tubes	
6	French type	'05-'07							

The "*Holland*" type are known as the "*Bubnoff*" type, and named **Feld Marshall-Graf-Scheremetyeff, Okuny, Sig, Piotwa, Pescar, Kefal, Akula.**

"*Lake*" boats purchased in America, 1904-05, named **Ossetyr, Schtschuka, Kassatka, Skat, Sterliad, Forel, Losos, Byeluga, Lom.**

"*Ponkaloff*" boats named **Makryei, Bytschok, Nalim, Käta.** The *Drzewiecki* boat is named **Paltus.**

"*Kondeatenko type*" named **Kondratenko, Amuretz, Sibersky-Strelok, Ochotnik, Pogzanitschisk, Ussurietz,** and 2 *unnamed.*

"*Emir Bucharski*" type named **Emir Bucharski, Dobrovoletz, Gaidamak, Vsadnik, Moskwityanin.**

"*Finn*" type named **Finn, Donskoï-Kassack, Kasanets, Steregouchi, Strashni, Stavropolski-Truchmenets, Ukraïna, Voïskovoi,** *unnamed.*

New 356 ton named **Boyevoi, Bditelni, Burni, Leit. Bourakoff, Djelni, Dostoini, Dejatelni, Iskussni, Ispoinitelni, Krepki, Mjetki, Liet. Sergeloff, Molodetzki, Moschstchinni, Kapitan-Jurassowski, Insch. Mechswereff, Insch. Mech. Dmitrieff,** also **Legki, Letutschi, Lowki, Lichoi, Silni, Stroini, Storeschevoi, Vnimatelni, Vnuschitelni, Vinoslivi, Rasyaschtschi, Rastoropni.** (Of these the last 12 are of French type; the others may be Yarrow type).

"*Bravi*" type named **Bravi, Boiki, Bodry, Grosni, Gomyastchi, Vidni.**

"*Bestrachni*" type named **Bestrachni, Besposchtschadni, Beschumni** (Schichau boats with 2 funnels).

"*Grosovoi*" type named **Grosovoi, Vlastni, Leit. Malejeff, Insch. Mech. Anastassoff.**

"*Smyeli*" class named **Smyeli, Serdity, Statni, Skori, Retivi, Ryaswi, Ryani, Posluschi Pülki, Prosorlivi, Twerdi, Totschni, Trevoschni.**

"*Prütki*" type named **Prütki** (ex *Sokol*), **Protschni, Podwischni, Pransitelni, Porajuschtschi.**

(TAVRITCHESKY CLASS—3 SHIPS).

PANTELIMON (Ex. K. P. Tavritchesky) (1900), *IEVSTAFI* (building), & *IOANN ZLATOUST* (building).

Displacement 12,600 tons.   Complement 731.

Length (*waterline*), 371 feet.   Beam, 72⅓ feet.   *Maximum* draught, 28 feet.

Guns :
- 4—12 in., 40 cal. (*AAAA*)
- 16—6 in., 45 cal. (*D*).
  (*Last two 4—8 in. and 12—6 in.*)
- 14—12 pdr. (*F*).
- 2—2½ Baronovsky.
- 6—3 pdr.
- 6—1 pdr.

Torpedo tubes :
- 1 *submerged* (bow).
- 2 *submerged* (broadside).
- 1 *above water* (stern).

Armour (Krupp) :
- 9″—7″ Belt (amidships) ... *aa-a*
- 2″ Belt (bow) .... *f*
- 2¼″ Armour deck (behind belt)
- Protection to vitals ....=*aaa*
- 3″ Deck (forward and aft).
- 12″ Turrets (N.C.) .... *aaa*
- 10″ Turret bases .... *aa*
- 6″ Lower deck side .... *a*
- 5″ Battery .... *b*
- 10″ Conning tower .... *aa*
- 5″ Tube to it.

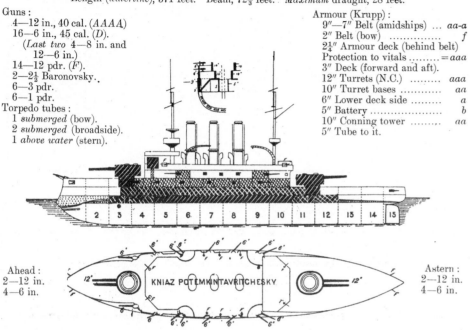

Ahead :
2—12 in.
4—6 in.

Astern :
2—12 in.
4—6 in.

Broadside : 4—12 in., 8—6 in.

Machinery : 2 sets vertical triple expansion. Designed H.P. 10,600=18 kts. 2 screws. Boilers : 22 Belleville in groups, placed longitudinally. Coal : *normal* 670 tons and 580 tons of naphtha ; double bottom fitted to take 200 extra tons of coal.

Armour Notes.—Belt is 7½ feet wide by 237 feet long, 4½ feet of it below waterline. Lower edge is 5″ thick.

Gunnery Notes.—Loading positions, big guns : all round. Hoists, electric. Big guns manœuvred electrically. Balanced turrets.

Arcs of fire : Fore 12 in. turret, 200° ; after turret 240° ; fore and aft 6 in. guns, 135° ; broadside 6 in., 115° ; 12 pdr. in battery, 90° ; those at ends of superstructure, 100° ; those at bow and stern, 120°.

Torpedo, &c., Notes.—Bow tube somewhat uncertain. 6 searchlights.

Engineering Notes.—The first boiler group burns petroleum fuel, the other two coal and naphtha. Machinery, &c., made by Société Anonyme des Chantiers Navals de Nikolaieff.

Trials (1904) (made for H.P. only), *Pantelimon.*

    8 hours, 22 boilers, 10,300 I.H.P., 83 revs (coal and oil).
    8 „ 14 „   7,200   „   75 „ (coal only).
    8 „ 22 „ 11,300   „   (coal and oil).

General Notes.—*Kniaz Potemkin Tavritchesky*, re-named *Pantelimon*, laid down at Nikolaieff, 1898. Completed 1903. Cost about £1,000,000. *Ievstafi* laid down at Nikolaieff, 1903 (*building*). *Ioann Zlatoust* laid down at Nikolaieff, 1904 (*building*).

Signal letter : Y.

Пантелimoнъ (PANTELIMON).

TRISVITITELIA (1893).

Displacement 12,540 tons.   Complement 731.

Length (*waterline*), 377½ feet.   Beam, 72⅓ feet.   *Maximum* draught, 29 feet.

Guns :
4—12 inch 35 cal. (*AA*).
8—6 inch, 45 cal. (*E*).
4—4·7 inch, (*F*).
10—3 pdr.
40—1 pdr. and machine.
Torpedo tubes (18 inch) :
2 *above water* (bow and stern).

Armour (Creusot special) :
16″ Belt (amidships)......... *aaa*
3″ Armour deck (flat on belt).
Protection to vitals is ...... *aaa*
12″ Bulkheads (waterline).   *aa*
16″ Turrets .... *aaa*
12″ Turret bases .... *aa*
16″ Lower deck (redoubt)... *aaa*
5″ Battery (redoubt) .... *d*
12″ Conning tower .... *aa*
(Total weight 4100 tons).

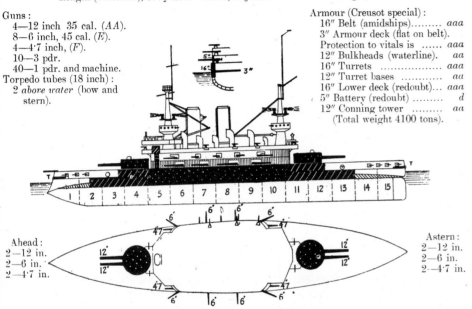

Ahead :
2—12 in.
2—6 in.
2—4·7 in.

Astern :
2—12 in.
2—6 in.
2—4·7 in.

Broadside : 4—12 in., 4—6 in., 2—4·7 in.

Machinery : 2 sets triple expansion.   2 screws.   Boilers : cylindrical.   Designed H.P. 10,600 = 18 kts.   Coal : *normal* 750 tons ; *maximum* 1,000 tons.

Armour Notes.—Main belt 8 feet wide by 288 feet long, 6 feet of it below waterline ; lower edge is about 11″ thick.   2″ screens between guns in battery.

Gunnery Notes.—Loading position, big guns : end on.   Hoists, electric.   Big guns manœuvred, electrically and hydraulic.
Arcs of fire : Big guns, 270° ; amidships 6 in, 100° ; end ones, 140° from axial line.
Height of guns above water : *about* 13 feet.

Torpedo Notes.—Above water training tubes used to be before and abaft the turrets (unprotected) now removed.   4 searchlights.

Engineering Notes.—Engined by Humphrys and Tennant.

Trials.—On a 12 hour *normal* draught trial she made I.H.P. 11,400 = 17 kts. ; *Full* draught not tried.

General Notes.—Built at Nikolaieff at a total cost of about £1,200,000.   Laid down August, 1891, and completed 1897-98.

Три Святителя (Three Saints).   *Photo by favour of H.I.H. Grand Duke Alexander of Russia.*

Signal letter : M.

ROSTISLAV (Sept., 1896).

Displacement 9000 tons.   Complement 631.

Length (*waterline*), 341 feet.   Beam, 69 feet.   *Mean* draught, 25 feet.   Length over all, 348 feet.

Guns :
   4—10 inch, 45 cal. (*AAA*).
   8—6 inch, 45 cal. (*E*).
   12—3 pdr.
   4—1 pdr.
Torpedo tubes (18 inch) :
   4 *above water* (broadside).
   2   ,,   ,,   (bow and stern).

Armour (Harvey) :
   15″—8″ Belt (amidships)...*aaa-b*
   3″ Deck (flat on belt)..............
   Protection to vitals is ....*aaa*
   12″ Fire turret ....*a*
   9″ After turret .... *a*
   6″ Turret bases ....*c*
   6″ Lower deck redoubt..........*c*
   6″ Small turrets ....*c*
   5″ Small turret bases ....*d*
   10″ Conning tower ....*a*
   (Total weight 2400 tons).

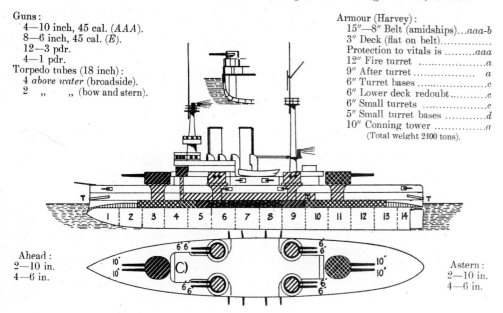

Ahead :
2—10 in.
4—6 in.

Astern :
2—10 in.
4—6 in.

Broadside : 4—10 in., 4—6 in.

Machinery : 2 sets vertical triple expansion. 2 screws. Boilers : 16 cylindrical. Designed H.P. 8500 = 16 kts. Liquid fuel also carried. Coal : *normal* 500 tons ; *maximum* 800 tons.

Armour Notes.—Belt is 7 feet wide by 274 feet long ; 5 feet of it below waterline ; lower edge is 8″ thick amidships. Redoubt 130 feet long.

Gunnery Notes.—Loading positions, big guns : all round. Hoists, electric and hand. Big guns manœuvred electrically. Secondary turrets, electric and hand.

Arcs of fire : Big guns, 240° ; small turrets, 110° (perhaps less).

Engineering Notes.—On trial burning petroleum she made 18 kts. Coal consumption heavy.

General Notes.—Laid down at Nikolaieff, 1895, and completed for sea 1898. Cost about £850,000.

Ростиславъ (Rostislav).

Signal letter : K.

Photo by favour of H.I.H. Grand Duke Alexander of Russia.

Note.—Now carries a bowsprit and conspicuous wireless gaff.

DVIENADTSAT APOSTOLOV (1890).

Displacement 8560 tons.   Complement 601.

Length (*waterline*), 330 feet.   Beam, 60 feet.   *Maximum* draught, 26 feet.

Guns :
4—12 inch, 35 cal. (*AA*).
4—6 inch, 35 cal. (*F*).
10—3 pdr.
15 smaller Q.F.
Torpedo tubes :
6 *above water* (some removed).

Armour (compound) :
14—10″ Belt (amidships) ... *a-b*
12″ Bulkheads .... *a*
2½″ Deck (flat on belt) ......
Protection to vitals is ...... *a*
10″ Barbettes .... *b*
3″ Turrets .... *ϵ*
10—6″ Lower deck side ... *b-d*
5″ Battery (redoubt) .... *ϵ*
12″ Conning tower........... *a*

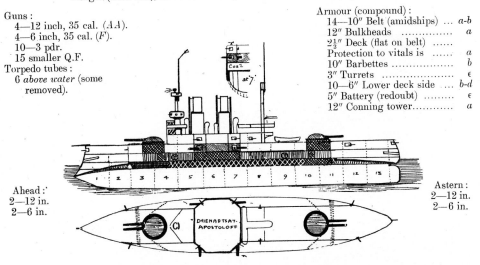

Ahead :
2—12 in.
2—6 in.

Astern :
2—12 in.
2—6 in.

Broadside : 4—12 in., 2—6 in.

Machinery : 2 sets vertical triple expansion.   2 screws.   Boilers : cylindrical, 4 2-ended and 4 1-ended.   Designed H.P. 11,600 = 16·5 kts.   Coal : *normal* 500 tons ; *maximum* 800 tons.

Armour Notes.—Belt is 5½ feet wide by 213 feet long ; 4¼ feet of it below waterline ; lower edge is 6″ thick.

Gunnery Notes.—Loading positions, big guns : end on only.   Very slow in firing.   Obsolete mountings.
Big Guns manœuvred by steam.
Arcs of fire : Big guns, 270° ; secondary guns, 100° from axial line.
Height of guns above water : Big guns, 17 feet ; secondary guns, 9½ feet.

Engineering Notes.—Made her speed on trial (1894) and still steams fairly well.   Burns a great deal of coal.

General Notes.—Laid down at Nikolaieff, 1888.   Completed 1892.   Cost complete about £750,000.

Signal letter : L.   Двѣнадцать Апостоловъ.   (Twelve Apostles).

Signal letter : I.   **Синопъ** (Sinop).

(Sinop Class.—2 Ships).

GEORGI POBIEDONOSETS (1892), **SINOP** (1887).

Displacement 10,250.   Complement 560.

Length, 339 feet.   Beam, 69 feet.   *Maximum* draught, 29 feet.

Guns (Obuchoff) :
 6—12 inch, 35 cal. (*AA*).
 7—6 inch, 35 cal. (*F*).
 8—12 pdr. (*F*).
 18—1 pdr.
Torpedo tubes (T) :
 7 *above water*.

Armour (compound) :
 16″ Belt (amidships) .... *aa*
 10″ Belt (bow) .... *b*
 9″ Belt (aft) .... *c*
 2½″ Deck (flat on belt)........
 Protection to vitals .... *aa*
 12″ Lower deck redoubt ...... *a*
 12″ Barbette redoubt .... *a*
 2″ Hoods to big guns .... *f*
 16″ Conning tower (*see notes*) *aa*

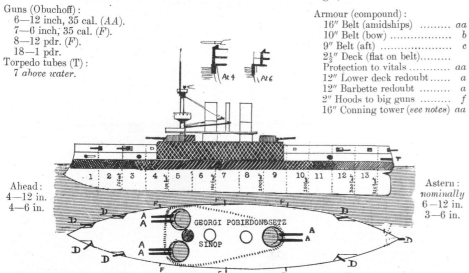

Ahead :
4—12 in.
4—6 in.

Astern :
nominally
6—12 in.
3—6 in.

Machinery : 2 sets vertical triple expansion.   2 screws.   Boilers : 16 cylindrical.   Designed H.P. *natural* 10,600＝15 kts ; *forced* 13,000＝16·5 kts.   Coal : *normal* 700 tons ; *maximum* 870 tons.

Armour Notes—The belt is a comparatively narrow one, soon diminishing from its maximum thickness.   The redoubt (lower and main decks) rises from it, and has a 1″ steel floor.   The conning tower is between the forward big guns, and the view from it is poor.   Some of the *Georgi Pobiedonosets'* belt is Creusot steel, and a little superior to the compound belt of the *Sinop*.

General Notes.—It is difficult or impossible to fire all six heavy guns astern.

Георгій Побѣдоносецъ (George the Victorious).

The only distinction between the two is that the small auxiliary funnel of *Georgi Pobiedonosets* has steam pipes to it, and her funnels are a trifle smaller.

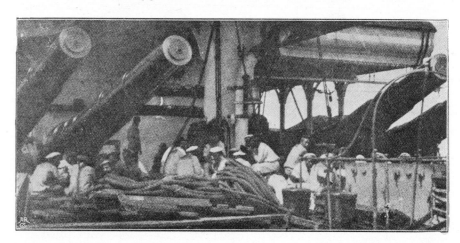

Georgi Pobiedonosets.   *All photos C. de Grave Sells, Esq.*
Fore part of Battery and Conning tower.

Engineering Notes—*Sinop* was the first ship ever fitted with triple expansion engines.   *Georgi Pobiedonosets* has electric hoists, and was one of the first ships to be so fitted.   The machinery of both ships is of British manufacture—*Georgi Pobiedonosets* being by Maudslay, and *Sinop's* by Napier, of Glasgow.   On 12 hours' trial, *Georgi Pobiedonosets* with 13,468 *natural draught* made 16·5 kts. easily ; *Sinop*, with about the same I.H.P. *forced*, made over 17 kts. *maximum*.

EKATERINA II. (1886), *TCHESMA* (1886) (reconstructing).

Displacement 10,250 tons.   Complement 530.

Ekaterina reconstructed 1900-02.

Length, 339 feet.   Beam, 69 feet.   *Maximum* draught, 28¾ feet.

Guns :
  6—12 inch, 30 cal. (C)
  7—6 inch, 45 cal.
  8—3 pdr.
  4—1 pdr.
  6 Maxims.
Torpedo tubes :
  7 above water

Armour (compound) :
  18″ Belt (amidships) ...... *aa*
  10″ Belt (ends) .... *b*
  2″ Deck (flat on belt).
  Protection to vitals ...... =*aa*
  12″ Lower deck (redoubt) *a*
  12″ Barbette (redoubt)...... *a*
  2″ Hoods on big guns......
  16″ Conning tower (fore) *aa*

Екатерина II. (Ekaterina II.)

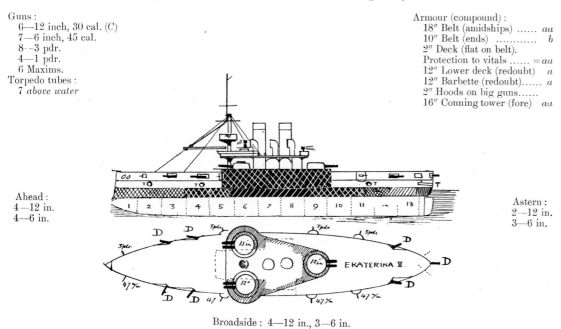

Ahead :
4—12 in.
4—6 in.

Astern :
2—12 in.
3—6 in.

Broadside : 4—12 in., 3—6 in.

Чесма (Tchesma) (before reconstruction).

Machinery : 2 sets compound vertical 3 cylinder.   2 screws.   Boilers : Belleville, fitted *Ekaterina II* (1900), *Tchesma* (1903).   Designed H.P. 11,000 = 16 kts.   Coal : *normal* 700 tons ; *maximum* 870 tons.

Notes.—All description of the *Sinop* applies to these ships, which are early and inferior editions of *Sinop*.   The armour is without any backing.   The big guns are on disappearing mountings in these two ships.   Those of *Tchesma* are Krupp's ; had the muzzles cut off, so are scarcely 30 calibres long.   They will be replaced when the ship is taken in hand for reconstruction and re-boiling.   In both these ships the barbettes form big sponsons.   They have armoured floors like *Sinop*.

FAST RUSSIAN BLACK SEA CRUISERS (23 knot).

(BOGATYR CLASS—2 SHIPS).

OTCHAKOV (October, 1902) and **KAGOUL** (June, 1903).

Displacement 6750 tons.   Complement 573.

Length, 436 feet.   Beam, 54 feet.   *Mean* draught, 20½ feet.

Guns—(M. '00) :
    12—6 in., 45 cal. (C).
    12—12 pdr., 50 cal. (F).
    6—3 pdr.
    1—1 pdr.
    2—Field guns.
Torpedo tubes (18 inch).
    2 *submerged* (at 20° abaft).
    2 *above* (bow and stern).

Armour :
    3″ Deck.............................= d
    Armoured funnel bases ......
    Protection to vitals............= d
    5″ Turrets (KNC) (2) c
    5″ Casemates (4) c
    5¼″ Conning tower c

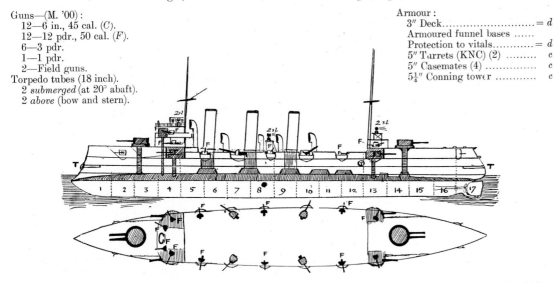

Machinery : 2 sets 4 cylinder triple expansion.   2 screws.   Boilers : Belleville.   Designed H.P. 19500 = 23 kts.
Coal : *normal* 700 tons ; *maximum* 1100 tons.

Gunnery Notes.—Electrically manœuvred turrets.   Electric hoists to all guns.
    Ammunition carried : 200 rounds per 6 in. guns.

Torpedo Notes.—*Submerged* tubes amidships.   Two extra above water tubes on broadside are apparently not being
    fitted.   6 automatic searchlights.

Engineering Notes.—

Name.	Built at	Laid down.	Completed.	...	hours full power.	Boilers.	Best present speed.
Otchakov	Sevastopol	March '01	1905	...	...	Belleville	...
Kagoul	Nikolaieff	Sept. '01	1906	...	...	Belleville	...

KAPITAN SAKEN (1889).   Displacement 600 tons.   Complement 120.
Length, 210 feet.   Beam, 24 feet.   *Maximum* draught, 11 feet.

Guns :
 4—3 pdr.
 2—1 pdr.
 4 Machine.
Torpedo tubes :
 4 *above water*.

Armour :
 ¾″ Deck (amidships).
 [Cellulose belt and
 cofferdam.]

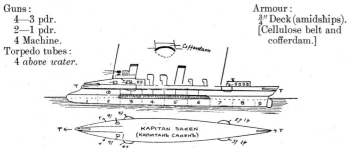

Machinery : 2 screws.   Boilers : Yarrow.   Designed H.P. 3400 = 18·5 kts.

LIEUTENANT ILYIN (1886).   Displacement 600 tons.
Complement 109.
Length, 227 feet.   Beam, 24 feet.   *Maximum* draught, 11 feet.

Guns :
 7—3 pdr.
 10 Machine.
Torpedo tubes :
 7 *above water*.

Armour (steel) :
 ¾″ Deck.
 [Cofferdam and
 cellulose above it].

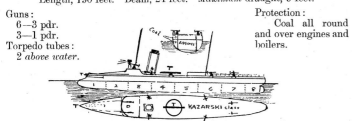

Machinery : 2 sets triple expansion.   2 screws.   Boilers (?) : Yarrow or
Locomotive.   Designed H.P. *forced* 3550 = 20 kts. (20·5 made on *trial*).
Coal : 97 tons.

KAPITAN-LIEUTENANT KASARSKI (1890). & **GRIDEN** (1893).
Displacement 411 tons.   Complement 61.
Length, 190 feet.   Beam, 24 feet.   *Maximum* draught, 9 feet.

Guns :
 6—3 pdr.
 3—1 pdr.
Torpedo tubes :
 2 *above water*.

Protection :
 Coal all round
 and over engines and
 boilers.

Machinery : 2 sets triple expansion.   2 screws.   Boilers : Locomotive.
Designed H.P. 3400 = 21 kts.   Coal : 90 tons.

Лейтенантъ Ильинъ (Ilyin).

Капитанъ Сакенъ (Kapitan Saken).

Kasarski.

There are also 6 gunboats of 1200 tons carrying 2—8 inch, 35 cal. and 1—6 inch, 35 cal. DONETS, URALETS,
TERETS, TSCHEROMOROETS, KOUBANETS, and ZAPOROROSETS,—launched 1887, but recently reboilered
with Bellevilles.

RUSSIAN BLACK SEA TORPEDO FLOTILLA.

Destroyers.

9 boats (Laird type). **Savitny, Savetny, Shivoi, Shivulka, Shutki, Sarky, Swonky, Sadorny** (1903). 350 tons. H.P. 5500=27 kts. Boilers: Normand. Carry 80 tons, oil fuel. Armament: 1—12 pdr., 5—3 pdr., 2 tubes (18 inch). *Maximum* draught: 8½ feet.

---

4 funnels
The amidship ones rather near together.

4 boats (early Yarrow type). **Strogy, Smetlivy, Stremiteliny, Svirepy** (1901). 240 tons. H.P. 3800=26 kts. Boilers: Yarrow. Carry 60 tons, coal or oil. Armament: 1—12 pdr., 3—3 pdr., 2 tubes (18 inch). *Maximum* draught: 8 feet.

Torpedo Boats.

No.		Laid down.	Tons.	Max. Speed.	Tubes.	Max. Draught.	Coal.
1	*Adler* (Schichau)	1890	130	27·4	3	feet. 8½	tons. 40
4	New	1904-'05	120	24	3	8½	17
2	*Schichau* type....	1903	85	22	2	7	17
5	*Anapa* type.........	1901-'03	81	21	2		
3	*Nikolaieff*	1898					

There are also somewhere between 10 and 60 old boats of about 20 tons dating from the early eighties used for various local purposes, which have no kind of fighting value.

Submarines.

No.	Class or Type.	Date.	Displacement.	Motive Power, above and below.	H.P.	Max. Speed, above and below.	Dimensions in feet.	Tubes.	Actual Radius.	Designer or Type.
1	*Petr Kotchka*	1902	20	accumulators. accumulators	small	$\frac{6}{3\frac{1}{2}}$	50 × 14 × 10	2	20 miles	Kuteinkoff

ITALIAN FLEET.

Chief Torpedo Stations.

Genoa, Spezia, Maddalena, Gaeta, Messina, Taranto, Venice,

MADDALENA

to	knots.
Ajaccio ...	60
Bonafacio ...	20
Naples ...	310

SPEZIA

to	knots.
Ajaccio ...	160
Bizerta ...	430
Genoa ...	50
Leghorn ...	40
Maddalena ...	175
Malta ...	580
Naples ...	290
Taranto ...	630
Toulon ...	195
Venice ...	1000

NAPLES

to	knots.
Ajaccio ...	265
Bizerta ...	315
Bonafacio ...	225
Maddalena ...	210

VENICE

to	knots.
Pola ...	75
Taranto ...	575
Toulon ...	1197

TARANTO

to	knots.
Bizerta ...	550
Malta ...	310
Messina ...	220
Naples ...	380
Venice ...	575

ENSIGN

JACK

ADMIRAL

VICE ADMIRAL

REAR ADMIRAL

COMMODORE

ROYAL STANDARD

MERCANTILE ENSIGN

SUBVENTED LINER

SENIOR NAVAL OFFICER

Red

Blue

Green

Yellow

Naval Arsenals.

SPEZIA. One dock able to take any warship in the world; one nearly able to (508 × 90 × 33 feet); two able to take any Italian warship (430 × 77 × 30 feet); two smaller (358 × 71 × 30 feet. Two large slips. Total employees 6,100.

NAPLES (NAPOLI). One small dock, 247 × 62 × 19½ feet. One small slip. Total employees 3,270.

VENICE (VENEZIA). One dock (*pro.*) able to take any warship; one dock for long cruisers 525 × 59 × 28½ feet); one small dock for third-class cruisers (295 × 59 × 19½ feet). Two large slips, one small slip. Employees 3,150.

CASTELLAMARE. No docks. Building yard. Two large slips, two small. Total employees 1,920

TARANTO. One dock able to take any warship in the world. One large slip. Total employees 1,800.

MADDALENA. No docks. Total employees 110.

ONE FUNNEL.

GH   Castelfidardo *class (page 297)*.

GK   Calabria *(page 304)*.

TWO FUNNELS.

H   Ammiraglio di St. Bon *class (page 293)*.
(E. Filiberto has higher funnels)

J   G. Garibaldi *class (page 299)*.

K   Sardegna *class (page 294)*.
(Note.—Two funnels forward closely paired).
(Funnels vary in shape).

L   Ruggiero di Lauria *class (page 295)*.

M   Duilio *(page 297)*.

N   Dandolo *(page 297)*.

P   Carlo Alberto *class (page 301)*.

K   Benedetto Brin *class (page 292)*.
(Note.—Two funnels forward, closely paired).
(Brin has much shorter funnels. Margherita funnels as here)

QL   Affondatore *(page 297)*.

QM   Marco Polo *(page 301)*.

QN   Piemonte *(page 304)*.

TWO FUNNELS—Continued.

 **QO** STROMBOLI *class (page 303).*

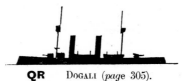 **Q P** GIOVANNI BAUSAN *(page 303).*

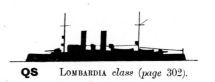 **QR** DOGALI *(page 305).*

 **QS** LOMBARDIA *class (page 302).*

QT GOITO *(page 305)*

 **QU** AGORDAT *class (page 305).*

 **QV** CAPRERA *(page 305).*

 **QW** PARTENOPE *class (page 306).*

 **QX** TRIPOLI *(page 305).*

THREE FUNNELS.

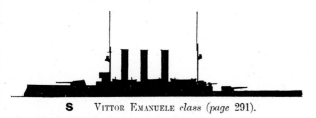 **S** VITTOR EMANUELE *class (page 291).*

 **SM** MONTEBELLO *(page 305).*

FOUR FUNNELS.

 **L** LEPANTO *(page 296).*

(Reconstructing. Will be like *Lepanto*,
but have two pole masts.)

M ITALIA *(page 296).*

287

ITALIAN FLEET.

Uniforms.

COCKED HAT.
Gold laced for admirals,
Purple „ for captains,
Grey „ junior officers.

CAP.
Gold bands,
as per sleeves.

Admirals. Captains. Lieutenants, &c. Doctor. Constructor.

SHOULDER STRAPS.

(*Note.*—A five pointed silver star is worn on lappel of coat).

INSIGNIA OF RANK ON SLEEVES.   *NOTE*—STAFF OFFICERS HAVE NO CURL.

Ammiraglio.	Vice-Ammiraglio.	Contr'-Ammiraglio.	Capitano di vascello.	Capitano di fregata.	Capitano di corvetta.	Tenente di vascello.	Sotto tenente di vascello.
Admiral.	*V.-Admiral.*	*R. Admiral.*	*Captain.*	*Commander.*	*Lieut.(senior).*	*Lieut.(junior).*	*Sub-Lieut.*

Lesser ranks are Guardia marina (*Midshipman*) and Allievo di marina (*Naval Cadet*).

Other branches : Macchinista (*Engineer*), Ingegnere (*Constructor*) Commissario (*Paymaster*), Medico (*Doctor*)—with relative rank with the executives, without curl.

Colours : *Engineers*, black ; *Constructors*, dark crimson ; *Paymasters*, red ; *Doctors*, blue.

EXECUTIVES ENGINEER

PAYMASTER DOCTOR CONSTRUCTOR

CAP BADGES.

Note—An undress military tunic has been introduced. It has braided insignia on sleeve and shoulder straps. All officers under arms on duty wear a blue sash over right shoulder, ending in a blue knot at left hip ; worn with belt. Officers on staff duty wear it on opposite shoulder, and without belt.

Dockyards.

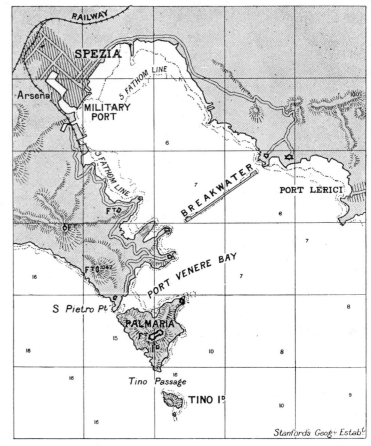

In 2000 yard squares.   Soundings in fathoms.   Heights in feet.

SPEZIA. One dock able to take any warship in the world ; one nearly able to (508 × 90 × 33 feet) ; two able to take any Italian warship (430 × 77 × 30 feet) ; two smaller (358 × 71 × 30 feet). Two large slips. Total employees 6,100.

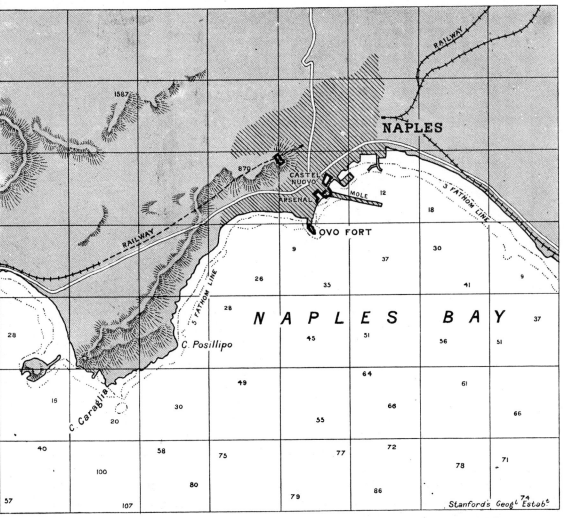

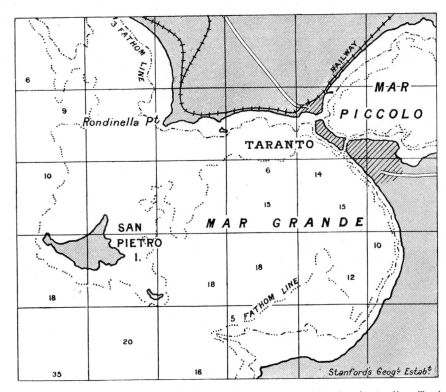

NAPLES (Napoli). One small dock, $347 \times 62 \times 19\frac{1}{2}$ feet. One small slip. Total employees 3,270.

CASTELLAMARE. No docks. Building yard Two large slips, two small. Total employees 1,920.

TARANTO. One dock able to take any warship in the world. One large slip. Total employees 1,800.

VENICE (Venezia). One dock (pro.) able to take any warship; one dock for long cruisers ($525 \times 59 \times 28\frac{1}{2}$ feet); one small dock for third-class cruisers ($295 \times 59 \times 19\frac{1}{2}$ feet). Two large slips, one small slip. Employees 3,150.

MADDALENA. No docks. Total employees 110.

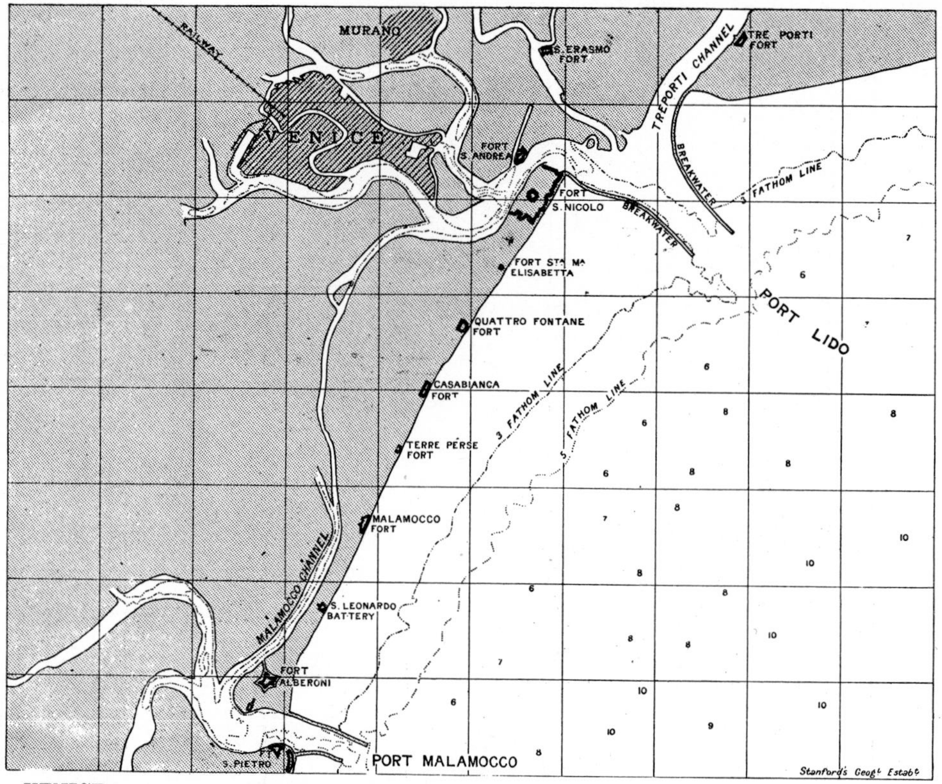

VENICE. In 2000 yard squares—ON SPECIAL SCALE.

Private Yards.

(All do Government work).

1. ANSALDO—ARMSTRONG (GENOA and SESTRI PONENTE). Total employees 4,000.
   At Genoa there is a dock able to take any warship, and three able to take smaller cruisers (*Garibaldi* type).
2. ORLANDO (LEGHORN). Total employees 2,800.
   At Leghorn there is a dock 443 × 65 × $23\frac{1}{4}$ feet.
3. PATTISON (NAPLES). Total employees Destroyers built here.
4. ODERO (SESTRI PONENTE, near GENOA). Total employees Cruisers built.

Principal Mercantile Ports.

Genoa (*Genova*), Naples (*Napoli*), Leghorn (*Livorno*), Messina, Palermo, Venice (*Venezia*).

Mercantile Marine (945,000 tons).

446 steamers (45 over 2,000 tons, 134 of 2,000-1,000 tons, and 137 under 100 tons).
5,511 sailing (115 over 1,000 tons, but 4,186 under 50 tons).

Coinage.

Lira (100 centesimi) = 10*d.* British, about 20 cents U.S.A. Value varies.

ITALIAN FLEET.

Personnel: About 26,000 all ranks.
Colour of Ships: Dark grey.
Minister of Marine: Rear-Admiral Carlo Mirabello.
Chief Constructor: Colonel V.U. Cuniberti.

Principal Naval Guns. (* = brass cartridge case.)

Notation.	Nominal Calibre.		Model.	Length in Calibres.	Weight of Gun.	Weight of A.P. Shot.	Initial Velocity (*service*).	*Maximum* penetration using *capped* A.P. against K.C. armour (*direct impact*)		Danger Space against average warship, at			Average Rounds per minute.
								At 5000	At 3000	10,000	5000	3000	
	c/m.	in.		cals.	tons.	lbs.	ft. secs.	inches.	inches.	yards.	yards.	yards.	secs.
AAA	*43*	17	'84	29	105	2000	1988	11	13	...	...	...	0·2
AA	*43*	17	'83	27	102	2000	1929	10	$12\frac{1}{2}$	...	...	...	0·2
AA	*43*	17	'82	26	100	2000	1685	10	12	...	...	...	0·2
AA	*34*	13·5	...	30	67	1250	2014	10	12	105	300	540	0·3
AAAA	*30·5*	12	'00	40	49	850	2750	15	19	160	480	725	1·2
AAA	*25·4*	10	...	45	$32\frac{1}{2}$	500	2700	11	14	140	460	700	1·8
AA	*25·4*	10	...	40	30	500	2460	$8\frac{1}{2}$	$10\frac{3}{4}$	...	...	...	1·25
A	*203*	8	...	50 or 45	?	210	2800	$7\frac{1}{2}$	$10\frac{1}{2}$	...	...	...	2—3
*A**	*203*	8	...	45	18	210	2600	$6\frac{1}{4}$	$8\frac{1}{2}$	...	...	...	2—3
*E**	*152*	6	...	40	$6\frac{3}{5}$	100	2600	$2\frac{3}{4}$	$4\frac{1}{4}$	60	200	430	3—4
*E**	*152*	6	...	40	$6\frac{1}{2}$	100	2297	...	$3\frac{3}{4}$	40	165	380	3—4
*F**	*152*	6	...	40	$5\frac{3}{4}$	100	2149	...	3	35	130	320	4
*F**	*120*	4·7	...	40	$2\frac{1}{5}$	44	2180	...	...	...	...	...	6—8
*F**	*100*	4	...	46	2	31	2600	...	...	...	...	...	8—10
*F**	*76*	3	...	40	$\frac{3}{5}$	...	2600	...	...	...	...	...	12

All Italian guns are of Elswick model, and differ little from British pieces. A few old guns are omitted.

All Italian ships since and including *G. Garibaldi* have Terni armour, the figure of merit of which, even for thin plates, average 2·7. (See 1901 Edition of this book.)

Torpedoes.

Whiteheads of the usual models (18 inch, 15 inch, and 14 inch).

NEW ITALIAN BATTLESHIPS.

(V. Emanuele Class—4 Ships).

VITTORIO EMANUELE (1905), *REGINA ELENA* (1905), *NAPOLI* (1905),

ROMA (1906), & *another projected.*

Displacement 12,625 tons (metric).   Complement

Length (*p.p.*), 435 feet, Beam, 73½ feet. *Maximum* draught, 25⅝ feet. Length over all, 475 feet.

Guns :
  2—12 in. 40 cal. (*AAAA*).
  12—8 inch 45 cal. (*A*).
  12—12 pdr. (*F*)
  12—3 pdr.
  4 Maxims.
Torpedo tubes (18 in.) :
  4 *submerged.*

Armour (Terni) :
  10″ Belt .... *aaa*
  4″ Belt (ends)................. *d*
  4″ Deck (reinforcing).........
  Protection to vitals...... =*aaaa*
  8″ Bulkheads .... *aa*
  8″ Barbettes (N.C.) .... *a*
  6″ Hoods to barbettes ...... *b*
  8″ Lower deck side .... *aa*
  6″ Secondary turrets (6) ... *a*
  10″ Conning tower (N.C.)... *aa*
  3¼″ Tertiary battery ...... *e*
  3¼″ Lower deck (bow)......... *e*

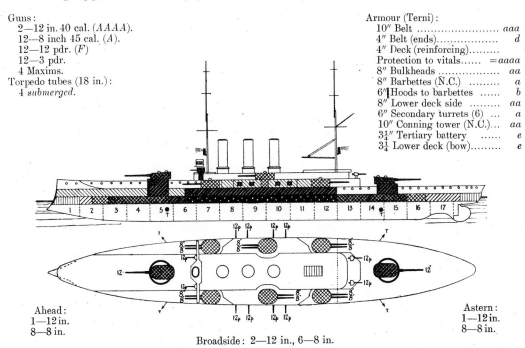

Ahead :
1—12 in.
8—8 in.

Astern :
1—12 in.
8—8 in.

Broadside : 2—12 in., 6—8 in.

Machinery : 2 sets 4 cylinder vertical inverted triple expansion. Designed H.P. 20,000 = 22 kts. 2 screws. Boilers : *V. Emanuele* and *R. Elena*, 28 Belleville ; *Napoli* and *Roma*, Babcock & Wilcox. Coal : *normal* 1000 tons ; *maximum* 2800 tons.

Gunnery Notes.—Central pivot mountings. All guns electric control. Electric hoists. The arcs of fire are very large : 12 inch, 300° ; amidships, 8 inch, 180° ; end, 8 inch, 135° from axial line. 12 pdrs. about 100°.

Torpedo Notes.—Elswick '04 pattern submerged tubes.

Armour Notes.—Note that in these and other Terni armoured ships that their Terni plates are slightly superior to K.C. in value, and armour notated *d* is nearly *c*, according to proving ground results.

V. Emanuele & R. Elena, building.   *Photos by favour of C. de Grave Sells, Esq.*

Engineering Notes.—Over 22 knots is expected from the tank trials of the models.

Name.	Built at		Boilers.
V. Emanuele	Castellamare	...	Belleville.
R. Elena	Spezia	...	Belleville.
Napoli	Castellamare	...	Babcock.
Roma	Spezia	...	Babcock.

General Notes.—Designed by Colonel Cuniberti. Excellent ships for the Italian Navy and its requirements. The slight heavy gun armament makes them battleship-cruisers rather than battleships. They represent the ideal armoured cruiser. Note the excellent protection to vitals. First of class laid down September, 1901. To be completed 1907. Average cost per ship, *complete*, £1,000,000 (*estimated*).

(BRIN CLASS—2 SHIPS).

BENEDETTO BRIN (1901), & REGINA MARGHERITA (1901)

Displacement 13,427 tons.   Complement 720.

Length (*waterline*), 426½ feet. Beam, 78 feet. *Mean* draught, 27¼ feet. Length over all, 430 feet.

Guns :
4—12 in., 40 cal. (*AAAA*).
4—8 inch (*A*).
12—6 inch (*E*).
16—12 pdr. (*F*).
8—6 pdr.
2—1 pdr.
2 Maxims.
Torpedo tubes (18 inch) :
4 *submerged.*
(With ammunition 1473 tons.)

Armour (Terni) :
6″ Belt .... *a*
2″ Belt (at ends) .... *f*
3″ Armour deck (reinforcing)
  Protection to vitals ...... =*aa*
8″ Barbettes and bulk-
  heads.................... *aa*
8″ Hoods to big guns (N.C.) *a*
6″ Casemates (N.C.)...... *b*
6″ Battery (N.C.) .... *b*
12″ Conning tower (N.C.) *aaa*
(Total 3155 tons.)

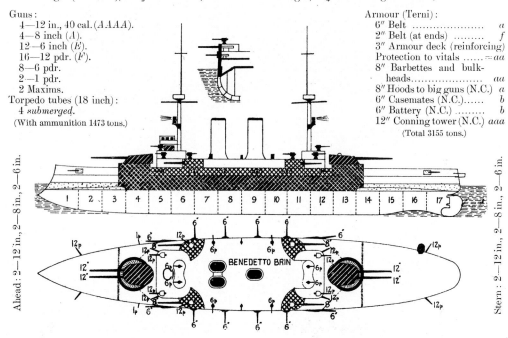

Ahead: 2—12 in., 2—8 in., 2—6 in.

Stern: 2—12 in., 2—8 in., 2—6 in.

BENEDETTO BRIN

Broadside : 4—12 in., 2—8 in., 6—6 in.

Machinery : About 1,600 tons. 2 sets 4 cylinder triple expansion. 2 screws. Boilers: *Brin*, Belleville ; *Margherita*, Niclausse. Designed H.P. *natural* draught 14,000 = 18 kts. ; *forced* 19,000 = 20 kts. (26).   Coal: *normal* 1,000 tons + petroleum ; *maximum* 2,000 tons.

Gunnery Notes. —Big guns : central pivot mountings, load at any elevation.
  Arcs of fire : Big guns 240°, 8 in. and end 6 in. 135° from axial line ; other 6 in. 125°

Armour Notes. —The main belt is 10⅓ feet wide. Armoured main deck 1⅜″ extends whole length of ship.

Engineering Notes.—

Name.	Where built.	Machinery, etc., by	Boilers.	⅘ power.	Full power, 120 revs.
Brin ....Castellamare		Hawthorn Leslie	Belleville	15,600 = 18 kts.	20,400 = kts.
R. Margherita...Spezia		Ansaldo	Niclausse	17,600 = 18·5 kts.	19,556 = 20·2 kts.

General Notes. —Freeboard, 21 feet forward. Weight of hull, 6195 tons.   First of class laid down November, 1898. Completed 1904. Average cost per ship, *complete*, £1,150,000.

After part of battery —*Benedetto Brin* class.

BENEDETTO BRIN.   *Photo by favour of C. de Grave Sells, Esq.*

REGINA MARGHERITA.   *Photo, Bougault, Toulon.*
Difference. —*Brin* has much shorter funnels than *Margherita.*

OLD ITALIAN BATTLESHIPS.

(St. Bon Class—2 Ships).

AMMIRAGLIO DI St. BON (1897), & EMANUELE FILIBERTO (1897).

Displacement 9800 tons.   Complement 542.

Length (*waterline*), 344½ feet.   Beam, 69 feet.   *Maximum* draught, 26 feet.

Guns :
4—10 in., 40 cal. (*AA*).
8—6 in., 40 cal. (*E*).
8—4·7 in. (*F*).
St. Bon.   Filiberto.
8—6 pdrs.   6—12 pdrs. (*F*).
12—1 pdr.   6—3 pdrs.
Torpedo tubes (18 in.) :
4 *submerged*.
(Total with ammunition, 1052 tons).

Armour (Harvey nickel) :
9¾″ Belt (amidships) ...... *aa*
4″ Belt (ends) .... *d*
3″ Deck (reinforcing)......
Protection to vitals ...= *aaa*
6″ Bulkheads .... *b*
6″ Lower deck side ...... *b*
9¾″ Barbettes.............. *aa*
6″ Hoods to these (fronts)= *aa*
6″   „   „   (sides) *b*
6″ Battery .... *b*
6″ Conning tower .... *b*
(Total 2355 tons).

E. Filiberto.   *Photo, Geoffrey Parratt, Esq.*

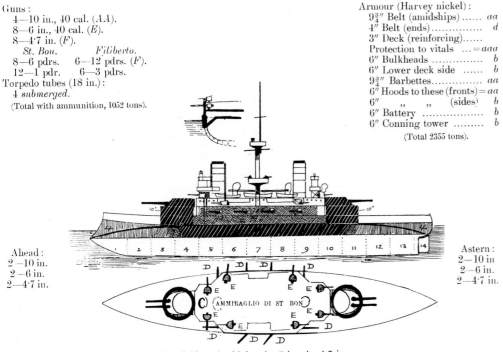

Ahead :
2 —10 in.
2 —6 in.
2 —4·7 in.

Astern :
2—10 in
2—6 in.
2—4·7 in.

Broadside : 4—10 in., 4—6 in., 4—4·7 in.

Machinery : 1300 tons. 2 sets 3 cylinder triple expansion. 2 screws. Boilers : 12 cylindrical, 36 furnaces.
Designed H.P. *natural* 9000 = 16 kts., *forced* 13,500 = 18 kts.   Coal : *normal* 600 tons and petroleum : *maximum* 1000 tons.

Gunnery Notes.—Observe differences in tertiary armaments.   Bow guns 22 feet above water.

Armour Notes.—2″ floor to main deck battery.   Cofferdam behind belt.

Engineering Notes.—Machinery made in Italy from British designs (Maudslay).

First Trials :—

Name.	Built at	6 hours natural (94 revs.)	1½ hours forced (101 revs.)
St. Bon	Venice	10,459 = 17·54 kts.	14,406 = 18·3 kts.
Filiberto	Castellamare	9959 = 16·79 kts.	13,630 = 18·0 kts.

Coal consumption about 9 tons an hour at 9000 H.P. (16 kts.), 14½ tons an hour at 13,500 H.P. (18 kts.).
Pressure at full speed, 150 lbs.

General Notes.—Freeboard forward 14½ feet ; aft 10 feet.   Both laid down, 1895.   Completed, 1901.   Average
cost per ship complete, about £700,000.

St. Bon.   *Photo by favour of C. de Grave Sells, Esq.*

Difference.—Easily distinguished by the different height of funnels.

ITALIAN BATTLESHIPS.

(SARDEGNA TYPE—3 SHIPS).

RE UMBERTO (1887). 13,251 tons. Complement 794.
SARDEGNA (1890). 13,860 tons. Complement 794.
SICILIA (1891). 13,375 tons. Complement 794.

Length (first two), 400¼ feet. Beam, 75½ feet. *Maximum* draught, 29 feet.
„ (*Sardegna*), 410 feet. „ 77 feet. „ „ 29¼ feet.

Guns :
    4—13·5 inch (*AA*).
    8—6 inch, 40 cal., old (*F*).
    16—4·7 in. (*F*).
    20—6 pdr. (*Re Umberto* only)
        15—6 pdr.)
    10—1 pdr.
Torpedo tubes (18 inch) :
    2 *submerged* (old pattern).
    3 *above water*.

Armour (steel) :
    4⅓″ Belt (amidships) ...... ϵ
    4½″ Deck .... =d
    Protection to vitals, with
        coal=d, nearly.
    2¾″ Bulkheads ....
    4″ Lower deck side ...... ϵ
    14″ Barbettes (at 23°)...=aaa
    1″ Hoods to these........
    12″ Hoists .... b
    12″ Conning tower ...... b

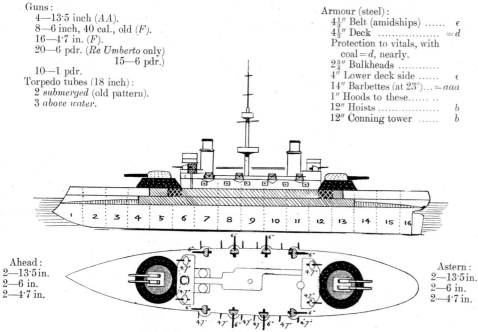

Ahead :
2—13·5 in.
2—6 in.
2—4·7 in.

Astern :
2—13·5 in.
2—6 in.
2—4·7 in.

Broadside : 4—13·5 in., 4—6 in., 4—4·7 in.

Machinery : 2,022 tons. 4 sets (in *Sardegna* 3 cylinder triple expansion ; in other ships,
vertical compound 2 cylinder). 2 screws. Boilers : 18 cylindrical (return tube), 72 furnaces.
Designed H.P., *natural* 15,200=19 kts. ; *forced* 19,500=20 kts. ; (in *Sardegna* 22,800=21·2 kts.)
Coal : *normal* 1,200 tons + petroleum ; *maximum* 3,000 tons.

Gunnery Notes.—Central pivot mountings for big guns. First guns to be so mounted on ship-
    board. Big guns about 25 feet above water.

Armour Notes.—Belt is 249¼ feet long by 12½ feet wide. It extends from 3 feet below water to
    the main deck. Very thick coal bunkers behind it.

Torpedo Notes.—Wireless fitted.

Engineering Notes.—Machinery designed by Maudslay. All these ships can still steam at very
    good speeds. The coal consumption is very high, over 20 tons an hour at 19,500 H.P.
    (*nominal* 20 kts.)

Differences.—*Re Umberto* only has a searchlight platform above the upper fighting top. Funnels
    differ in each ship.

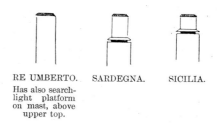

RE UMBERTO.   SARDEGNA.   SICILIA.

Has also search-
light platform
on mast, above
upper top.

First trials.—Name.	Built at	Natural (3-6 hours).	Forced (2 hours).
Sardegna (1894)...........	Spezia	14,190=19·06 kts.	19,650=20·11 kts.
Sicilia (1895)	Venice	15,974=19·2 kts.	19,131=20·3 kts.
Re Umberto (1893)	Castellamare	(*assisted*)	17,000=18·2 kts.

General Notes.—Triple bottoms. Tactical diameter nearly 1,000 yds. First of class laid down 1885.
    Completed 1893. Average cost per ship, *complete*, £1,050,000.·

OLD ITALIAN BATTLESHIPS.

(Lauria Class—3 Ships).

RUGGIERO DI LAURIA (1884), ANDREA DORIA, FRANCESCO MOROSINI (1885).

Displacement about 11,200 tons.   Complement 526.

Length (*waterline*), 328 feet.   Beam, 65⅓ feet.   *Maximum* draught, 30 feet.

Guns (old models) :
4—17 in., 27 cal., 105 ton (*AAA*).
2—6 in., 26 cal. (*F*).
4—4·7 in., (*F*).
2—12 pdr. (*F*).
10—6 pdr.
17—1 pdr.
2 machine.

Torpedo tubes (old pattern) :
2 *submerged.*
1 *above water.*

Armour (compound) :
17¾″ Belt (amidships) ... *aa*
3″ Deck (at ends) .... = *de*
Protection to vitals is ... *aa*
17¾″ Redoubt (amidships) *aa*
14″ Bulkheads .... *a*
1″ Hoods to big guns......
17¾″ Conning tower ...... *aa*

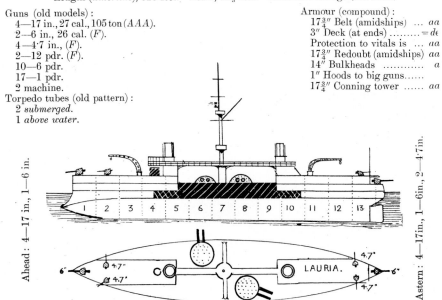

Ahead: 4—17 in., 1—6 in.

Astern : 4—17in., 1—6in., 2—4·7in.

Broadside: 4—17 in., 2—6 in., 2—4·7 in.

Machinery : 2 sets vertical compound 3 cylinder (made in England).   Boilers : 8 cylindrical, 48 furnaces.   Designed H.P., *natural* 7,500 = 15 kts., *forced* 10,000 = 16·5 kts.   Coal : *normal* 850 tons + petroleum.

Gunnery Notes.   The big guns being of old model have a high trajectory, but as the projectile weighs about a ton the smashing power is great.

Engineering Notes.—Lauria re-boilered 1902.   Coal consumption is heavy, being about 15 tons an hour at 10,000 H.P.

General Notes.—First of class laid down 1882.   Completed 1887.   Average cost per ship, *complete*, £780,000.

FRANCESCO MOROSINI.   *Photo, Conti Vecchi.*

Distinctions.—*Doria* has a shifting topmast, no searchlight platform, steam-pipes each side of each funnel. *Lauria* has a crane aft.   Steam-pipes as *Doria.*   No shifting topmast.

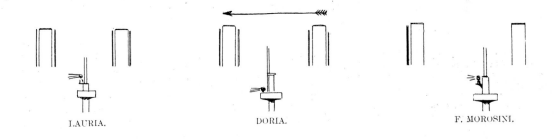

LAURIA.   DORIA.   F. MOROSINI.

ITALIAN BATTLESHIPS.

(ITALIA CLASS—2 SHIPS).

ITALIA (1880).   Displacement 15,654 tons.   Complement 675.

LEPANTO (1883).   Displacement 15,900 tons.   Complement 700.

Length (*waterline*), 400¼ feet.   Beam, 75½ feet.   *Maximum* draught, 33 feet.

Guns :
4—100 ton *Italia*, 102 ton in *Lepanto* (*AA*).
8—old 6 in., 26 cal., converted to QF. (*F*).
4—old 4·7 in., 23 cal., converted (*F*).
12—6 pdr.
22—1 pdr.
Lepanto carries 34—1 pdr.
Torpedo tubes :
4 *above water*.
(removed or removing).

Armour (compound) :
3″ Deck..................................... = *de*
Very thick coal bunkers.
Protection to vitals .... = *e*
16″ Funnel bases, slanting.............. =*aaa*
19″ Redoubt for A guns (inclined) ...=*aaaaa*
18″ Big Hoist (amidships), steel .... *aa*

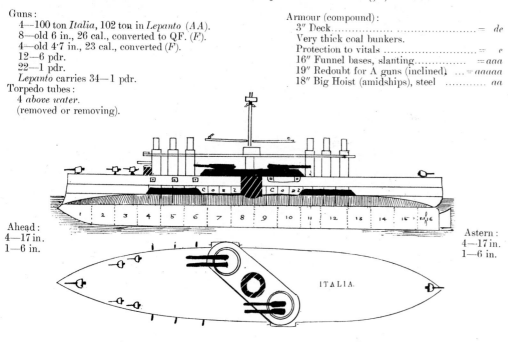

Ahead :
4—17 in.
1—6 in.

Astern :
4—17 in.
1—6 in.

ITALIA.

Broadside : 4—17 in., 5—6 in., 2—4·7 in.

Machinery : 4 sets vertical 3 cylinder compound. 2 screws. Boilers : *Italia*, 15 locomotive and 8 cylindrical ; *Lepanto*, 16 locomotive and 8 oval. Designed H.P. : *Italia*, 11,900 =17·5 kts.; *Lepanto*, 16,000 =18·5 kts. Coal : *normal* 1,650 tons ; *maximum* up to 3,000 tons or more.

Gunnery Notes.—The secondary guns cannot be fought when the big guns are firing. Mountings of big guns are very antiquated, and the rate of fire extremely slow.

General Notes.—*Italia* is reconstructing. The old armament will be retained. A special extra shell is being built, so as to enlarge the coal protection by 3 feet each side. Average cost per ship, *complete*, £1,200,000. *Italia* laid down 1878. Completed 1884. Rig (new) will be 2 pole masts and 4 funnels.

ITALIA (before reconstruction).   *Photo, Conti Vecchi.*

LEPANTO.   *Photo, West.*

DANDOLO (1878).

Displacement 12,265 tons (after reconstruction). Complement 506 tons.
Length (*waterline*), 341 feet. Beam, 65½ feet. *Maximum* draught, 30 feet.

Guns :
4—10 in., 40 cals. (A).
7—6 in., 32 cals. (F).
5—4·7 in., 35 cals. (F).
16—6 pdr.
8—1 pdr.
4 machine.
Torpedo tubes :
4 *above water*.

Armour (steel) :
21½" Belt (amidships) *aa*
3" Deck (at ends) ... = *ed*
[Deck flat on belt].
Protection to vitals is *aa*
16" Bulkheads .... *a*
17" Redoubt........... *a*
10" Turrets (Harvey) = *aa*
2" Screens, on forecastle abaft E guns, and on main deck before D guns.

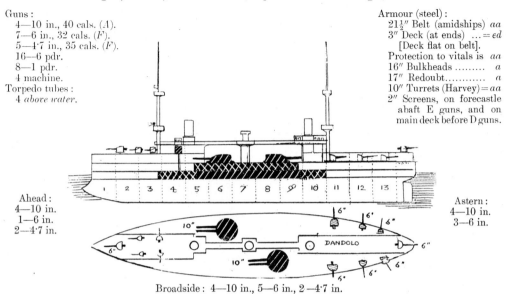

Ahead :
4—10 in.
1—6 in.
2—4·7 in.

Astern :
4—10 in.
3—6 in.

Broadside : 4—10 in., 5—6 in., 2—4·7 in.

Photo, Conti Vecchi.

Machinery : 2 sets vertical compound (new 1898). 2 screws. Boilers : oval (new 1898). Designed H.P. *natural* draft 7,500 = 15 kts. Coal : *normal* 732 tons ; *maximum* 1,000 tons.

Gunnery Notes.—Big guns on central pivot mountings. Hoists: electric. One dredger hoist for group of 7 guns aft; one ditto forward group.

Engineering Notes.—On *trial* (1898-99) she made during 8 hours a *mean* I.H.P. 8,045.

General Notes.—Average original cost, about £860,000. Reconstruction, about £350,000.

OBSOLETE BATTLESHIPS (of no fighting value).

DUILIO (Sister to *Dandolo*), 11,138 tons.

Guns : 4 C (old 100 tons M.L.) and 3 F (4·7 old). Armour : belt as *Dandolo*, with 18 in. steel turrets.

Speed : about 8 knots.

There are 3 old armoured ships—CASTELFIDARDO, MARIA PIA (broadside), and AFFONDATORE (turret ship), of no fighting value, used as torpedo depôts in harbours.

CASTELFIDARDO & MARIA PIA.

AFFONDATORE. *Photos, Conti Vecchi.*

DUILIO. *Photo, Conti Vecchi.*

2 P

ST. GIORGIO (building) & S. MARCO (building) & two others (pro.)

Displacement 9830 tons.   Complement   —

Length *(over all)*, 429½ feet.   Beam, 69 feet.   *Mean* draught, 23 feet.

Guns:
  4—10 inch, 45 cal. (*AAA*).
  8—8 inch, 45 cal. (*A*).
  Many smaller.

Torpedo tubes:
  3 *submerged*.

Armour (Terni):
  8″ Belt (amidships) ......*aa*
  3¼″ Belt (ends) .... *ε*
  Deck ....
  Protection to vitals ....
  7″ Lower deck redoubt *aa-a*
  6½″ Main barbettes ...... *a*
  6½″ Turrets to these...... *a*
  7″ Citadel ... . *a*
  7″ Secondary turrets ... *a*
  7″ Conning towers (4)... *a*

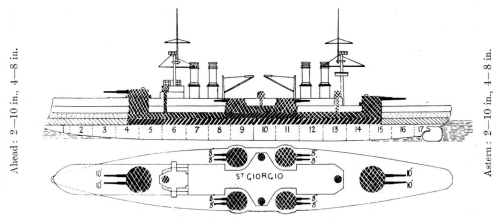

Ahead : 2—10 in., 4—8 in.

Astern : 2—10 in., 4—8 in.

Broadside : 4—10 in., 4—8 in.

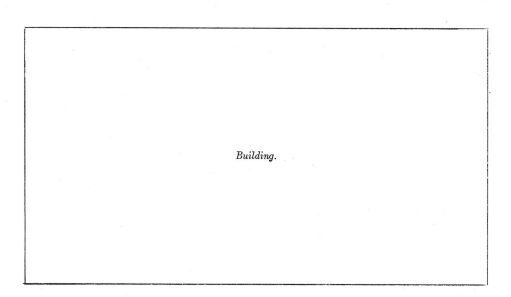

Building.

Machinery : 2 sets 4 cylinder triple expansion.   2 screws.   Boilers :   Designed H.P. 18,000
= 22·5 kts.   Coal : *normal*   ; *maximum*

Gunnery Notes.—All guns electrically controlled.   Central pivot mountings.

Engineering Notes.—

Name.	Built at	Laid down.	To be completed.	Trials :—	Boilers.	Best speed last recorded.
St. Giorgio S. Marco "C" "D"	Castellamare Venice	July, '04 Nov., '05				

ITALIAN ARMOURED CRUISERS (20 knot).

(New Garibaldi Class— 3 Ships.)

GUISEPPE GARIBALDI (1899), **VARESE** (1899),

& **FRANCESCO FERRUCIO** (1902).

Displacement 7400 tons. Complement 517.

Length (*waterline*), 344 feet. Beam, 59 feet. *Maximum* draught, *about* 25 feet.

Guns:
  1—10 inch, 45 cal. (*AAA*).
  2—8 inch, 45 cal. (*A*).
  14—6 inch, 40 cal. (*E*).
  10—12 pdr. (*F*).
  6—3 pdr.
  2—1 pdr.
Torpedo tubes (18 inch):
  4 *above water*, in 6 inch casemates.

Armour (Terni):
  6″ Belt (amidships)...   *a*
  3″ Belt (ends)........   *ε*
  1½″ Deck ....
  Protection to vitals... = *aa*
  6″ Lower deck (redoubt) *a*
  6″ Barbettes (N.C.)...   *b*
  6″ Hoods to these (N.C.) *b*
  6″ Battery (N.C.) ...... *b*
  4¾″ Battery bulkheads   *c*
  6″ Conning tower (N.C.) *b*
  1100 tons, without deck.

G. GARIBALDI.

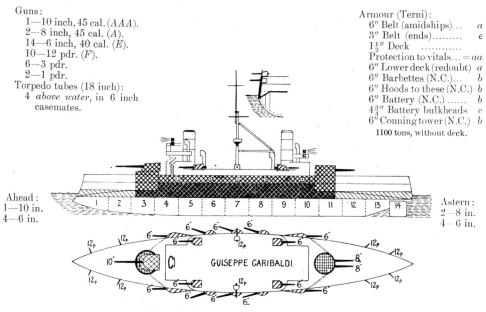

Ahead:
1—10 in.
4—6 in.

Astern:
2—8 in.
4—6 in.

Broadside: 1—10 in., 2—8 in., 7—6 in.

Machinery: 2 sets triple expansion. 2 screws. Boilers: *Varese*, 24 Belleville; *G. Garibaldi* and *Ferrucio*, Niclausse. Designed H.P. 13,500 = 20 kts. Coal: *normal* 650 tons; *maximum* 1200 tons.

Armour Notes.—2″ screens in battery, one fore and aft, one athwartships, between sections 6 and 7.

Gunnery Notes.—Big guns: central pivot mountings. Electric hoists to all guns.

Torpedo Notes.—Tubes are in casemates, with 2 in. sides and backs.

Engineering Notes.—

First trials—Name.	Builder.	Boilers.	6 hours at 3/5 power.	1½ hours full power.
G. Garibaldi (1901)	Ansaldo	Niclausse	9948 = 17·9 kts.	14,713 = 19·66 kts.
Varese (1901)	Leghorn	Belleville	9479 = 18·36 kts.	13,835 = 20·2 kts.
F. Ferrucio	Venice	Niclausse	=	=

Coal consumption: *Varese* burns 11¾-12 tons an hour at full power (20 kts.); *G. Garibaldi*, 12½ tons.

General Notes.—Average cost per ship, *complete*, about £600,000.

VARESE.   *Photos, Bar.*

Differences.—*Varese* has a much larger fighting-top than *Garibaldi*.

ITALIAN ARMOURED BLOCKADE-MINE SHIP (25 knot).

" *C* " (blockade ship) *(building).*

Displacement *between* 5500 & 6000 tons.   Complement   —

Length 413 feet.   Beam 54 feet.   *Mean* draught   feet.

Guns :
   4—8 inch, 45 cal.
   Many smaller.

Armour (Terni) :
   6″ Belt ....*a*
   4¾″ Battery.................

Machinery :   screws.   Boilers :
Designed H.P.   =25 kts.   Coal :

General Notes.—This ship is specially designed for mine laying, and to be unsinkable.   It is the
   vessel described in Col. Cuniberti's article in Part III of the 1905 edition.

C. ALBERTO.   *Photo, Conti Vecchi.*

V. Pisani almost identical, slightly different about the funnel tops.

(C. ALBERTO CLASS.—2 SHIPS).
CARLO ALBERTO (1896), **VETTOR PISANI** (1895).
Displacement 6500 tons. Complement 500.
Length (*waterline*), 324¾ feet. Beam, 59 feet. *Maximum* draught, 24¼ feet.

Guns :	Armour (Harvey) :	
12—6 inch, 40 cal. (*E*).	6″ Belt (amidships) ...	*c*
6—4·7 inch, 40 cal. (*F*).	4½″ Belt (ends)..........	*d*
14—6 pdr.	1½″ Deck (flat on belt)	
6—1 pdr.	Protection to vitals ...	=*c*
Torpedo tubes :	Lower deck (redoubt)	*c*
4 submerged.	Battery (redoubt)......	*c*
	2″ Screen in battery...	
	4½″ Gun shields	
	6″ Conning tower (fore)	*c*

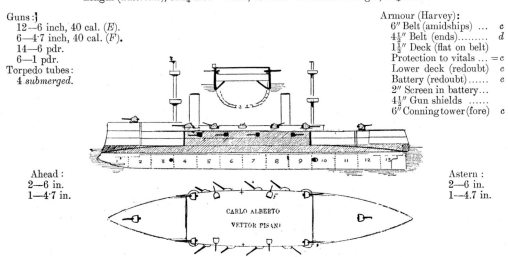

Ahead :
2—6 in.
1—4·7 in.

Astern :
2—6 in.
1—4·7 in.

Broadside : 6 in., 3—4·7 in.

Machinery : 2 sets 3 cylinder triple expansion. 2 screws. Boilers : 8 cylindrical. Designed H.P. *natural* 8600 = 1 7 kts ; *forced* 13,000 = 19 kts. Coal : *normal* 600 tons ; *maximum* 1000 tons and fuel.
Armour Notes—Battery is 137 feet long, screens as in *G. Garibaldi* class. Deck over main deck battery, 2″ thick.
Engineering Notes :—

Trials :	Name.	Completed.	6 hours natural.	1½ hours forced.
	C. Alberto	1898	8821 = 17·7	13,116 = 19·11
	V. Pisani	1899	8290 = 17·5	

General Notes.—*V. Pisani* laid down at Castellamare, December, 1892. Completed 1899.
    C. Alberto   „   Spezia in 1893.   „   1898.

Photo, Conti Vecchi.

MARCO POLO (1892).
Displacement 4583 tons. Complement 394.
Length (*waterline*), 327 feet. Beam, 48¼ feet. *Maximum* draught, 21½ feet.

Guns :	Armour (steel) :	
6—6 inch, 40 cal., *old* (*F*).	4″ Belt................	є
10—4·7 inch *old* (*F*).	1″ Deck (flat on belt)	
9—6 pdr.	Protection to vitals is	є
4—1 pdr.	4″ Bulkheads	є
2 machine.	Conning tower	
Torpedo tubes :		
4 above water.		

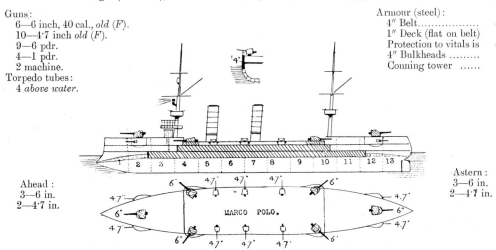

Ahead :
3—6 in.
2—4·7 in.

Astern :
3—6 in.
2—4·7 in.

Broadside : 4—6 in., 5—4·7 in.

Machinery : 2 sets vertical triple expansion. 2 screws. Boilers : 4 cylindrical. Coal : 600 tons. Designed H.P. *forced* 10,600 = 19 kts.

Armour Notes—Belt is 214 feet long.

Engineering Notes—This ship has never reached her designed speed by at least a knot. On first *trials* 7047 I.H.P. = 16.86 knots, and 10,664 = 17·8 kts. Machinery, Maudslay design.

General Notes—Laid down at Castellamare, 1890. Completed 1895. Total cost about £400,000.

(LOMBARDIA CLASS—6 SHIPS.)

PUGLIA (1898).

Displacement 2538 tons. Complement 274.
Length (*waterline*), 273 feet. Beam, $40\frac{3}{4}$ feet. *Maximum* draught, $16\frac{1}{4}$ feet.

ELBA (1893).

Displacement 2730 tons. Complement 247.
Length (*waterline*), $272\frac{1}{3}$ feet. Beam, $42\frac{2}{3}$ feet. *Maximum* draught, 18 feet.

also

LOMBARDIA (1890), ETRURIA (1891), UMBRIA (1891), LIGURIA (1893).

Displacement 2280 tons. Complement 246.
Length (*waterline*), $262\frac{1}{2}$ feet. Beam, $39\frac{1}{3}$ feet. *Maximum* draught, 17 feet.

Guns (as re-armed) :
2—6 in., 32 cal. *aft* (F).
8—4·7 in., 40 cal. (F).
8—6 pdr.
8—1 pdr.
Torpedo tubes :
3 *above water*.

Armour (steel) :
1″ Deck................. f

Photo by favour of C. de Grave Sells, Esq.

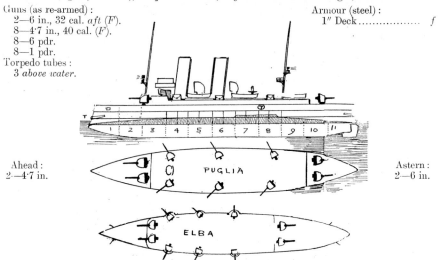

Ahead :
2—4·7 in.

Astern :
2—6 in.

Broadside : 1—6 in., 4—4·7 in.

Machinery : 2 sets horizontal triple expansion. 2 screws. Boilers : 4—2 ended.
Designed H.P. 7500 = 18·5 kts. Coal : 430 tons ; 500 tons in *Elba*.

Gunnery Notes.—Originally carried 2—6 in. forward.

Engineering Notes.—

Name.	Built at	6 hours natural draught.	3 hours forced draught.
Lombardia	Castellamare	3028 = 15·07 kts.	6813 = 17·00 kts.
Etruria	Orlando, Leghorn	4296 = 16·9 ,,	7585 = 19·81 ,,
Umbria	Orlando, Leghorn	4487 = 17·4 ,,	7104 = 18·83 ,,
Liguria	Ansaldo, S. Ponente	4319 = 17·05 ,,	7677 = 19·6 ,,
Elba	Castellamare	4928 = 15·9 ,,	7471 = 17·9 ,,
Puglia	Taranto	4900 = 17·6 ,,	7000 = 19·00 ,,

Liguria did 10 instead of 6 hours *natural draught* trial. *Elba*, only $1\frac{1}{2}$ hours *forced draught*.

General Notes.—The first of the class was laid down in 1888, and with slight modifications the design has followed up to *Puglia*. Average cost per ship, £200,000.

ELBA.

LOMBARDIA, ETRURIA, UMBRIA, & LIGURIA. (All 4 alike.) *Photos, Conti Vecchi.*

Slight differences in appearance.

Lombardia group have	2 platforms on foremast and very high funnels.		
Elba	has 1	,,	,,	low funnel casings.
Puglia	has 1	,,	,,	shorter funnels.

SMALL ITALIAN CRUISERS (about 16 knot).

(Bausan Type.—5 Ships).

FIERAMOSCA (1888). 3600 tons. Complement 308.
Length (*waterline*), 290 feet. Beam, 46 feet. *Maximum* draught, 20 feet.

VESUVIO (1886). 3427 tons. Complement 308.
Length (*waterline*), 283½ feet. Beam, 42½ feet. *Maximum* draught, 18¾ feet.

STROMBOLI (1886). 3898 tons. Complement 308.
Length (*waterline*), 283½ feet. Beam, 42½ feet. *Maximum* draught, 20½ feet.

ETNA (1885). 3530 tons. Complement 308.
Length (*waterline*), 283½ feet. Beam, 42½ feet. *Maximum* draught, 20 feet.

GIOVANNI BAUSAN (Elswick, 1883). 3330 tons. Complement 295.
Length (*waterline*), 278 feet. Beam, 42 feet. *Maximum* draught, 19 feet.

Guns :
  Present armament of 2 very old 10 inch, and 6 old 6 inch, being replaced by :—
  8—6 inch, 45 cal. (D).
    (only 6 in *Bausan*).
  5—6 pdr. (4 only in *Bausan*).
  8—1 pdr.
Torpedo tubes :
  1 *submerged* (bow).
  3 *above water.* except *Fieramosca*, 2 submerged.
  2 above water.

Armour (steel) :
  2″ Deck in all except *Bausan*, which has 1½″ only).
  1″ Conning tower (except *Bausan*, 2″).
  Cork and Cellulose waterline belt.

STROMBOLI. *Photo, West.*
(*Fieramosca, Etna, Vesuvio* and *Stromboli* all just like her).

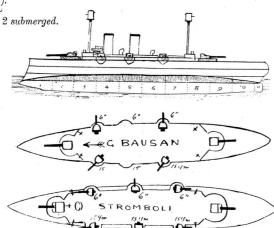

Machinery : 2 sets triple expansion (*Fieramosca* has horizontal compound). 2 screws. Boilers : 10 cylindrical. Designed I.H.P. *forced*, *Fieramosca* 7700 = 17·5 kts. ; *Etna* 7480 = 17·8 kts. ; *Stromboli* and *Vesuvio* 6252 = 17 kts. ; *Bausan* 6550 = 17·5 kts. Coal : *normal* 600 tons.

Gunnery Notes.—Re-armed ships will have electric hoists.

General Notes.—The *Bausan* was designed and built at Elswick, the others in Italy ; adoptions of the same design. Average first cost per ship, £225,000.

G. BAUSAN. *Photo, Conti Vecchi.*

PIEMONTE (1888).

Displacement 2650 tons.   Complement 325.
Length (*waterline*), 305 feet.   Beam, 38 feet.   *Maximum* draught, 16 feet.

Guns :
 6—6in. 40 cal., *old type* (F).
 6—4·7 in., 40 cal., „ (F).
 10—6 pdr.
 6—1 pdr.
 4 Maxims.
Torpedo tubes :
 3 *above water* (one in bow).

Armour (steel) :
 3″ Deck (amidships) ......=·ϵ
 1″ Deck (ends). ....=*f*
 3″ Conning tower ....*f*

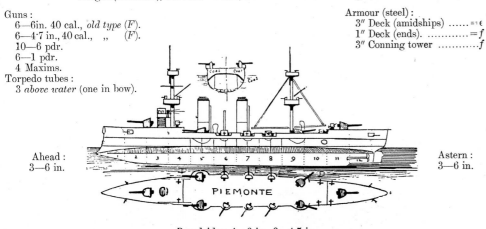

Ahead :
 3—6 in.

Astern :
 3—6 in.

Broadside : 4—6 in., 3—4·7 in.

Machinery : 2 sets vertical 4 cylinder triple expansion. 2 screws. Boilers : 4 2-ended. H.P. 7000 = 20 kts ; *forced* 12,000 = 23 kts.   Coal : *normal* 200 tons ; *maximum* 560 tons.

Engineering Notes.—Trials : natural 7040 = 20·4 kts. (mile) ; *forced* 12,980 = 22·3 kts.

General Notes.—This ship is one of the earliest examples of the Elswick cruisers, and is the most heavily armed vessel in proportion to displacement in the world. Built at Elswick. Cost about £220,000.

CALABRIA (1894).

2492 tons.   Sheathed and zinced.   Complement 254.
Length (*waterline*), 249 feet.   Beam, 42⅔ feet.   *Maximum* draught, 17¼ feet.

Guns :
 4—6 in., 40 cal. (E).
 6—4·7 in. (F).
 8—6 pdr.
 8—1 pdr.
 2 machine.
Torpedo tubes :
 2 *submerged*.

Armour (steel) :
 2″ Deck (amidships)...=ϵ
 1″ Deck (ends) ....=*f*

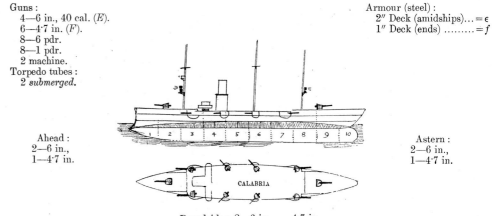

Ahead :
 2—6 in.,
 1—4·7 in.

Astern :
 2—6 in.,
 1—4·7 in.

Broadside : 2—6 in., 4·7 in.

Machinery : 2 sets triple expansion. 2 screws. Boilers : 4 cylindrical. Designed H.P. *forced* 4000 = 16 kts. Coal : *maximum* 500 tons, and liquid fuel.

Engineering Notes.—Trials (1897) : 6 hours *natural draught* 2439 = 14·5 kts. ; 1½ hours *forced* 4094 = 16·4 kts.

Gunnery Notes.—The 4·7½ are on poop, forecastle and amidships.

General Notes.—Built for foreign service ; too slow to have much fighting value. Built at Spezia. Cost about £185,000.

ITALIAN SMALL CRAFT.

OLD CRUISERS AND GUNBOATS.

DOGALI (launched at Elswick, 1888), 2088 tons. Complement 246. Guns: 2 old 6 in., 9—6 pdr., 2—1 pdr., and 2 machine. Torpedo tubes: 2 *above water*. Armour: 2½″ deck (over machinery). Designed H.P. 7000=20 kts. Cannot make anything like this now. Coal: *normal* 160 tons; *maximum* 430 tons.

FLAVIO GIOIA (1881) and AMERIGO VESPUCCI (1882). 3050 tons. Complement 280. Guns: *Gioia*, 6—4·7 in.; *Vespucci*, 6—6 in.; and in both 4—6 pdr. and 8—1 pdr. Torpedo tubes: 2 *above water*. Armour (steel): 1½″ deck (over machinery only). Cellulose belt. H.P. *circa* 4000. Speed 12-11 kts. 1 screw. Coal: 500 tons.

CRISTOFORO COLOMBO (1875) (1892). 2780 tons. Complement 210. Guns: 6—4·7 in., 4—6 pdr., 4—1 pdr. Torpedo tubes: 0. H.P. 3780=*nominal* 15 kts. Coal: 460 tons.

VOLTURNO (1887) and CURTATONE (1888) 1155 tons, and GOVERNOLO (1894) 1255 tons. Guns: 4—4·7 in., 4—6 pdr., 2—1 pdr. Torpedo tubes: 0. Designed H.P. 1100=15 kts. in *Governolo*, 11·7 kts. in the other two.

DOGALI.

AGORDAT (1899) & **COATIT** (1899). Displacement 1313 tons. Complement 154.
Length (*waterline*), 287½ feet. Beam, 30½ feet. *Maximum* draught, 10¼ feet.

Guns :
  12—12 pdr. (F).

Torpedo tubes :
  2 *above water*.

Armour (steel) :
  ¾″ Deck............

Machinery : 2 screws. Designed H.P. 8000=23 kts. Coal : *normal* 160 tons, and liquid fuel.

Trials—	Name.	6 hours.	f.d. 3 hours.
	Coatit	5080=20·6 kts.	—
	Agordat	—	8200=23·1 kts.

AGORDAT & COATIT.   *Photo, Bar.*

CAPRERA (1894). Displacement 853 tons. Complement 118.
Length, 230 feet. Beam, 27 feet. *Maximum* draught, 11 feet.

Guns :
  2—4·7 in. (F)
  4—6 pdr.
  2—1 pdr.

Torpedo tubes :
  5 *above water*.

Armour (steel)
  1½″ Deck = f

CAPRERA.

Machinery : 2 sets vertical triple expansion. 2 screws. Boilers : cylindrical. Designed H.P. *forced* 4250=19·8 kts. (made on *trial*). Coal : *normal* 120 tons ; *maximum* 180 tons.

(PARTENOPE CLASS.)

PARTENOPE (1889), ARETUSA (1891), EURIDICE (1891), IRIDE (1891), CALATAFIMA (1892), URANIA (1891), & MINERVA (1892).

Circa 850 tons. Complement 118.

Guns:
1—4·7 inch (F).
6—6 pdr.
3—1 pdr.
Torpedo tubes:
6 *above water.*

Armour (steel):
1½″ Deck.........= f

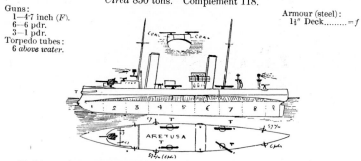

Machinery: 2 sets vertical 3 cylinder. 2 screws. Boilers: 4 locomotive, except *Minerva*, which has water-tube boilers (1900-01). Designed H.P. 4100-4400 = 19-20·5 kts. Actual speeds *circa* 16-17 kts. Coal: *normal* 120 tons; *maximum* 180 tons.

MONTEBELLO (1887), GOITO (1887), TRIPOLI (1886)

860 tons. Complement 105.

Guns (*Goito & Tripoli*):
6—6 pdr.
Montebello.
4—6 pdr., amidships.
Torpedo tubes:
3 *above water.*

Armour (steel):
1½″ Deck.........= f
(Cofferdam also).

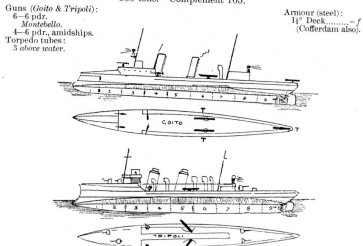

Tripoli reconstructed 1897-98.

Machinery: *Montebello*, triple expansion; other 3, 2 cylinder compound. 3 screws. Boilers: 6 locomotive, except *Montebello*, which has an assortment of water-tube boilers for training purposes. Designed H.P. *natural* 1900 = 17 kts.; *forced* 3600 = 20 kts. (The only one that can approach this is *Tripoli*, which burns petroleum). Coal: *normal* 100 tons; *maximum* 130 tons.

General Notes.—Average first cost. £70,000 each.

MINERVA

GOITO

ARETUSA.

TRIPOLI.

MONTEBELLO.

PARTENOPE.

MINERVA PARTENOPE URANIA ARETUSA EURIDICE CATALAFIMI IRIDE
funnels

PARTENOPE *class.*

ITALIAN TORPEDO FLOTILLA.

Destroyers (13 + 14).

DARDO, FRECCIA, etc.

6 Schichau boats:—**Lampo, Freccia** (1899), **Dardo, Strale, Euro** (1900), **Ostro** (1901). 320 tons. H.P. 6000=30 kts. Boilers: 3 Thornycroft. Coal: 80 tons. Armament: 1—12 pdr., 5—6 pdr. 2 tubes, twin (18 inch). *Maximum* draught 8⅔ feet.

FULMINE

1 Ansaldo boat:—**Fulmine** (1898). 298 tons. H.P. 4800=28 kts. Boilers: Bleychenden. Carries 60 tons of oil fuel. Armament: 5—6 pdrs., 3 single tubes (18 inch), 2 tubes aft conning tower, one right aft. *Maximum* draught, 9 feet.

(Thornycroft type).

6 Pattison (Naples) boats:—**Nembo, Turbine** (1901), **Aquilone** (1902), **Borea** (1903), **Zeffiro, Espero** (1904), and 4 *building* (1905). 330-350 tons. H.P. 6000=30 kts. Boilers: 3 Thornycroft. Coal: 80 tons. Armament: 6—6 pdr., 2 tubes (18 inch). *Maximum* draught, 7¾ feet.

(Some carry 1—12 pdr. in place of one of the 6 pdr.).

10 new boats (1906). 380 tons.

Torpedo School Ship.

Pegasa (1905). 208 tons. Speed, 25·8 kts. 3 tubes.

Torpedo Boats. (All carry 3—3 pdr.).

No.	Class.	Launched	Displacement.	Max. Speed.	Tubes.	Max. Draug't	Coal.
			tons.			feet.	tons.
15 + 27	Airone	...	215	30	2	...	...
1	Pellicano ...	'98	147	27	2	4¾	40
1	Condore ...	'98	136	27	2	5	40
2	78 & 79.	'95	110	25	3	5¼	30
43	112—153	'90-'95	79	22	2	7	17

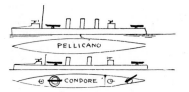

PELLICANO

CONDORE

OLD BOATS (No fighting value).

5 Schichau (1888), 130 tons. Originally 26 kts.   2 Yarrow (1887), 110 tons. Originally 25 tons.
40 *various* (1889-86), 79 „   „ 22 „   38 *various* (1882-88), 44 „   „ 22 „

Submarine Flotilla

(All built at Venice).

No.	Class.	Date.	Displ'ce'nt above and below.	Motive Power, above and below.	H.P.	Max. Speed.	Dimensions, in feet.	Tubes.	Actual radius, above & below.	Designer or Type.
5	Submersibles. Glauco	1903-05	...	Petrol 12 cyl. accumulators.	500 ...	$\frac{12}{8}$	× ×	1 tr	2000 kts. *nom.* small.	Laurente
1	Submarines. Delfino	1895	$\frac{95}{107}$	Accumulators. Accumulators.	150 ...	$\frac{9}{5}$	78½ × 10½ × 10½	1	very moderate	Pullino
2	pro.	1906	...	Petrol 4 cyl. Accumulators.						Holland

Glauco class, named *Glauco, Squalo, Narvalo, Trichero, Otario.*

AUSTRO-HUNGARIAN FLEET.

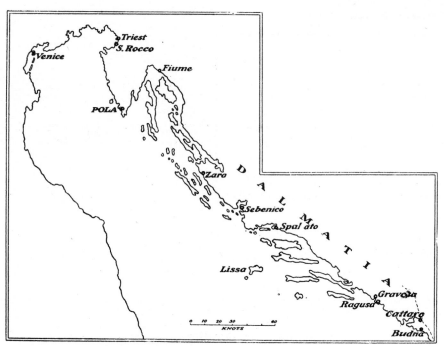

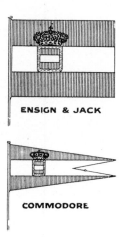

ENSIGN & JACK

COMMODORE

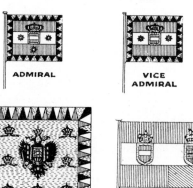

ADMIRAL

VICE ADMIRAL

REAR ADMIRAL

IMPERIAL STANDARD

MERCANTILE ENSIGN

Black ■
White □
Yellow
Red
Green

Private Yards.

SAN ROCCO (TRIEST). STABILIMENTO TECNICO. One dock, 382×73×20. Some warships have been built here.

FIUME. WHITEHEAD torpedo factory.

Arsenals.

POLA. Two dry docks able to take any Austrian warship also one small floating dock. Employés vary from 2000 to 4000. 2 slips. Naval hospital.

TRIEST. No Government docks. 1 slip. (Austrian Loyds have a dock here 382×73×20 feet; and there is a dock at San Rocco, across the bay.)

Torpedo Stations.

ZARA, BUDNA, CATTARO, RAGUSA, SEBENICO, SPALATO, CASTELNUOVO.

Coaling Stations.

LISSA, GRAVOSA (Ragusa)

FIUME is also a naval harbour, and has the Naval Academy.

Mercantile Marine.

Austrian.—215 steamers of 226,713 tons, about 1,500 sailing ships (mostly coasters), and 11,000 fishing boats, etc.

Hungarian.—79 steamers of 63,000 tons, about 100 sailing ships, and 200 fishing boats.

Principal Mercantile Ports.

TRIEST, FIUME.

Coinage (new).

One krone (100 fillér) = { 10d. British. { 20 cents U.S.A.

The old coinage piece the *kreuzer* = 2 fillér (heller), and the florin = 10 kronen. Gold coins are the 20 kronen (= 16/8 British, 4 dollars U.S.A.), the 10 kronen, and the ducat (9/4¾ English).

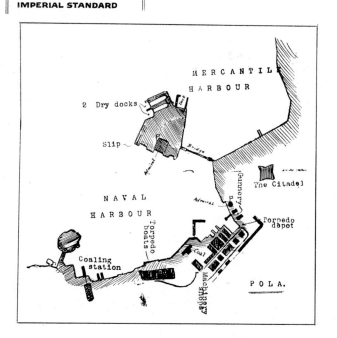

AUSTRO-HUNGARIAN NAVY.

CAPS.

Admirals, etc., have 3 gold bands.
Commanders, Lieuts, have 2 gold bands.
Sub-Lieutenants have 1 gold band.
Cadets have none.

EPAULETTES.

Admirals, with   other
stars to denote rank.

| Admiral. | Vice-Admiral. | Kontre-Admiral. | | Linienschiff Capitän. | Fregatten Capitän. | Corvetten Capitän. | Linienschiff Lieutenant. | Linienschiff Fahnrich. | See Cadet. |

Corresponding British or U.S. — Rear-Admiral. ... Captain. Commander. Lieutenant Sub-Lieutenant.

The men wear a French style of cap, with *K. ü K. Kriegs Marine* on the ribbon.

Naval Guns. (Krupp Model.)

Notation.	Designaton.		Length in Calibres.	Model.	Weight.	Weight, A.P. Shot.	Initial Velocity	Maximum penetration A.P. capped against K.C. air at impact.		First mounted in	Rounds per minute.
								at 5000 yards.	at 3000 yards.		
	c/m.	in.			tons.	lbs.	ft. secs.	inches.	inches.		
A	30·5	12	35	1880	...	1,000	1970	8	10	Stephanie .	·4
A A	24	9·4	40-45	1901	25	...	2441	9	11¾	A.B.C. . .	2
A	24	9·4	40	1894	28	474	2264	7½	10¼	Wien . .	2
B	24	9·4	35	1886	27	474	2100	5	7½	Teggethoff	·6
A	19	7·6	40	1901	...	...	2500	5¾	8¼	Erz. Karl .	3-4
E	15	6	40	1901	...	...	2500	2½	4	Erz. Karl .	...
F	15	6	40	1894	4½	100	2297	2	3	Wien . .	5-8
F	15	6	35	1886c	5	112	1960	1¼	2½	Old cruisers	...
FF	12	4·7	40	...	...	...	2297	...	...	...	7
	7·5	2·9	...	...	...	12	2379	...	...	...	...

A new buster " Ammonal " (made from aluminium), is to be used for all shell.

Personnel : 12,770 all ranks (conscript).
Colour of Ships : Sea green.
Torpedo used : Whitehead.
Chief Constructor : Herr Popper.

309

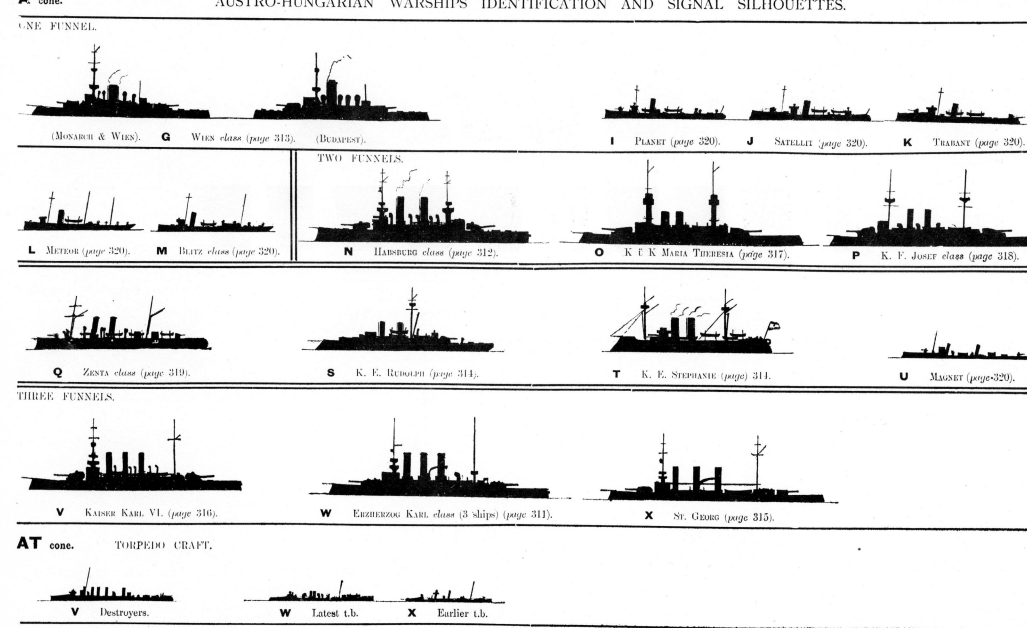

ONE FUNNEL.

(MONARCH & WIEN). **G** WIEN *class (page 313).* (BUDAPEST). **I** PLANET *(page 320).* **J** SATELLIT *(page 320).* **K** TRABANT *(page 320).*

L METEOR *(page 320).* **M** BLITZ *class (page 320).*

TWO FUNNELS.

N HABSBURG *class (page 312).* **O** K ü K MARIA THERESIA *(page 317).* **P** K. F. JOSEF *class (page 318).*

Q ZENTA *class (page 319).* **S** K. E. RUDOLPH *(page 314).* **T** K. E. STEPHANIE *(page) 314.* **U** MAGNET *(page 320).*

THREE FUNNELS.

V KAISER KARL VI. *(page 316).* **W** ERZHERZOG KARL *class (3 ships) (page 311).* **X** ST. GEORG *(page 315).*

AT cone. TORPEDO CRAFT.

V Destroyers. **W** Latest t.b. **X** Earlier t.b.

ERZHERZOG KARL (1903), **ERZHERZOG FRIEDRICH** (1904), and
ERZHERZOG-FERDINAND MAX (1905).

Displacement 10,600 tons.

Length (*waterline*), 390½ feet.   Beam, 72 feet.   *Mean* draught, 24½ feet.

Guns :
4—9·4 inch, 40 cal. (*AA*).
12—7·6 inch, 42 cal. (*A*).
14—12 pdr. (*F*).
12—1 pdr.
4 Maxims.
Torpedo tubes (17·7 inch) :
2 *submerged*.

Armour (Krupp) :
8¼″—6″ Belt (amidships) ...*aa-a*
9″ Bulkheads .... *aa*
2″ Belt (bow) .... *f*
2″ Deck (flat on belt).........
2¾″ Deck (at ends)............ =ϵ
Protection to vitals is ...... *aa*
9½″ Barbettes .... *aa*
9½″ Turrets.................... *aa*
9½″ Turret bases .... *aa*
5″ Lower deck (side) .... *b*
6¾″   „   „   (bulkhead)... *a*
6″ Battery .... *a*
6″ Small turrets (N.C.) ...... *b*
8½″ Conning tower...........

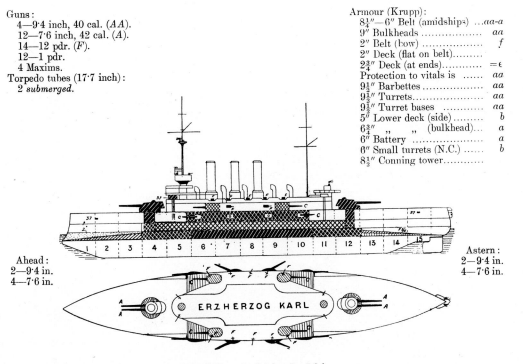

Ahead :
2—9·4 in.
4—7·6 in.

Astern :
2—9·4 in.
4—7·6 in.

Broadside : 4—9·4 in., 6—7·6 in.

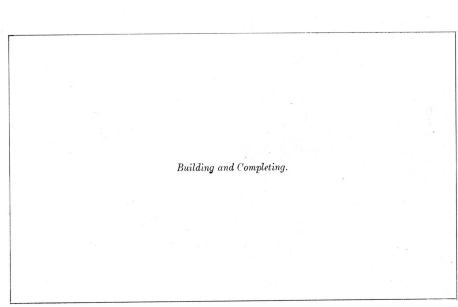

Building and Completing.

Machinery : 2 sets 4 cylinder triple expansion. 2 screws. Boilers : 12 Yarrow. Designed H.P. 14,000 = 19·25 kts. Coal : *normal* 550 tons ; *maximum* 1315 tons.

Armour Notes.—Belt is 8¼ feet wide by 225 feet long ; 3½ feet of it below waterline ; lower edge is about 6″ thick.

Gunnery Notes.—Loading positions, big guns : all round. Hoists, electric. Big guns manœuvred electrically and hydraulic ; secondary guns electrically. Big guns with 20° elevation have a range of 17,000 yards.
Arcs of fire : Big guns, 260°.
Height of guns above water : Bow turret, 20½ feet. After turret, 20 feet. Main deck battery, 13 feet.

Torpedo Notes.—7 searchlights.

General Notes.—The double bottom extends 240 feet amidships only. *E. Karl* laid down at Triest, 1901. Completed, 1905. *E. Friedrich* laid down at Triest, 1902 ; completed, 1906. *E. Ferdinand Max* laid down at Triest, 1903 ; to be completed, 1907. Average cost per ship, anticipated, £912,500.

Trials :—

E. *Karl*		=19·3 kts. (*max.*)
E. *Friedrich*	18,340	=20·3 kts. (*max.*)
E. *Ferdinand Max*		

(HABSBURG CLASS—3 SHIPS.)

HABSBURG (1900), **ARPAD** (1901), **BABENBURG** (1902).

Displacement 8340 tons. Complement —

Length (*waterline*), 354⅓ feet. Beam, 65½ feet. *Maximum* draught, 25 feet.

Guns :
3—9·4 inch, 40 cal. (*A*).
12—6 inch, 40 cal. (*E*).
10—12 pdr. (*F*).
16 Maxims, machine, &c.
Torpedo tubes (18 inch.) :
2 *submerged*.

Armour (Krupp) :
8¾″ Belt (amidships)... *aa*
2″ Belt (bow) (N.C.) ... *f*
2½″ Armour deck (flat amidships)
8″ Bulkheads ... ... *aa*
Protection to vitals is... *aa*
8½″ Barbettes (N.C.)... *aa*
8½″ Turrets to these (NC) ... ... *aa*
7″ Barbette bases (N.C.) *a*
4″ Lower deck side ... *d*
5″ Casemates (12) (N.C.) *c*
8″ Conning tower (N.C.) *a*
4″ C. tower, aft ... ... *d*
(Total weight 2250 tons).

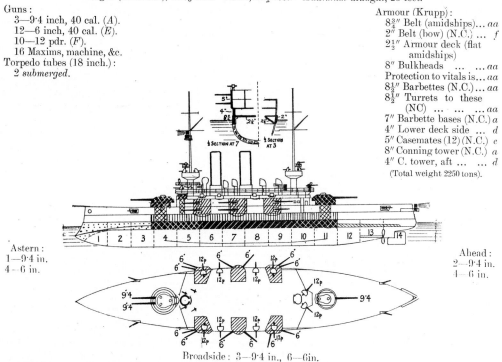

Astern :
1—9·4 in.
4—6 in.

Ahead :
2—9·4 in.
4—6 in.

Broadside : 3—9·4 in., 6—6in.

Machinery : 2 sets triple expansion. 4 cylinder. 2 screws. Boilers : 16 Belleville (model, 1900).
Designed H.P. 11,900 = 18·5 kts. Coal : *normal* 500 tons, *maximum* 840 tons.

Armour Notes.—Main belt is 8 feet wide by 223 feet long, 4½ feet of it below waterline, lower edge is 6 ins. thick.

Gunnery Notes.—Big guns, central pivot mountings. Hoists (electric), serve 3 rounds a minute to each big gun and 8 to each 6-inch gun. Big guns manœuvred electrically and by hand.
Arcs of fire : Big guns, 270°. End casemates, 135° from axial line ; others, 50° before and abaft the beam.
Height of Guns above water : Bow turret, 23½ feet ; after turret, 22½ feet.

Torpedo Notes.—6 searchlights, 6 dynamos.

Engineering Notes.—Pressure : 300 lbs. in boilers, 250 lbs. at engines. Grate area : 853 sq. feet ; heating surface : 31,440 sq. feet. Machinery by Stabilimento Technico, Triest.

Trials, 1902-3 ; 6 hours at full power ; contract speed, 18·5 knts.

Name.	Built at	Laid down	Completed	Boilers.	Trials.
Habsburg	Triest	Feb., '99	1903	Belleville	14,942 = 19·64 *mean.*
Arpad	Triest	Nov., '99	1903	Belleville	15,900 = 19·65 ,,
Babenburg	Pola	May, '00	1904	Belleville	16,230 = 19·67 ,,

General Notes.—Very fast and handy ships. 7 steering positions. Helm can be put right in over 30 seconds. 174 compartments. Very little wood used. Average cost per ship, £650,000.

HABSBURG.

Photo, Alois Beer.

Signal letter for class : D.
Differences.—All three ships are practically not to be distinguished from each other.

WIEN (1895), & MONARCH (1895); BUDAPEST (1896).

Displacement 5600 tons. Complement 469.

Length (*waterline*), 315 feet. Beam, 56 feet. *Maximum* draught, 21 feet. Length over all, 323 feet.

Guns (M. '86):
 4—9·4 inch, 35 cal. (*B*).
 6—6 inch, 35 cal. (*F*).
 11—3 pdr.
 12 Machine, &c., (Skoda).
Torpedo tubes (17·7 inch):
 4 *above water*.

Armour (Harvey):
 10½″ Belt (amidships) *aa*
 4¾″ Belt (bow) .... *d*
 2½″ Armour deck (aft).
  [Deck flat on belt.]
 Protection to vitals ...*aa*
 8″ Bulkhead (aft). ...... *b*
 10½″ Barbettes ....*aa*
 8″—5″ Hoods to these *a-d*
 3″ Lower deck redoubt *є*
 3″ Battery redoubt...... *є*
 8″ Conning tower ...... *b*
 4″ Conning tower (aft). *d*

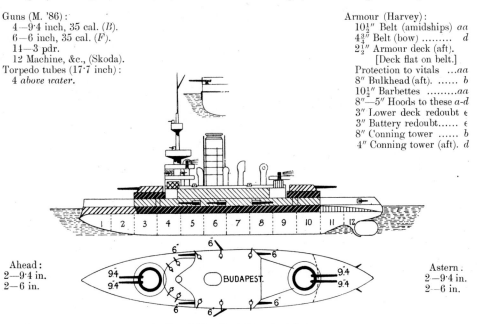

Ahead:
2—9·4 in.
2—6 in.

Astern:
2—9·4 in.
2—6 in.

Broadside: 3—9·4 in., 3—6 in.

BUDAPEST.   *Photo, Circovich.*

WIEN (also MONARCH).   *Photo, West.*

Machinery: 2 sets vertical triple expansion. 2 screws. Boilers: *Budapest*, Belleville (without economisers); other two, cylindrical. Designed H.P. 8500 = 17 kts. Coal: *normal* 300 tons; *maximum* 500 tons.

Armour Notes.—Main belt is 7 feet wide by 200 feet long; 4 feet of it below waterline.

Gunnery Notes.—End on loading positions to big guns. Hoists, hand for all guns.
 Arcs of fire: Big guns, 240°.
 Height of guns above water: 16 feet.

Engineering Notes.—All engined by Stabilimento, Technico, Triest.

Name.	Built at	Laid down	Completed.	6 hrs. at 6000 H.P.	4 hrs. at 8500 H.P.	Boilers.	Present Best Speed.
Wien	San Rocco	1893	1896	6376 = 16·7 kts.	8480 = 17·4 kts.	Cylindrical	—
Monarch	Pola Yard	1893	1897	6110 = 16·2 „	8900 = 17·5 „	Cylindrical	—
Budapest	San Rocco	1894	1897	6608 = 17·1 „	9185 = 17·9 „	Belleville	—

Differences.—

Name.	Funnel.	Notes.
Wien	Short	
Monarch	Short	
Budapest	Big and high	

KRONPRINZ ERZHERZOG RUDOLPH (1887). *Photo, Circovitch.*

Displacement 6900 tons.   Complement 492.

Length, 295 feet.   Beam, 62½ feet.   *Maximum draught, 26¼ feet.*

Guns :
3—12 inch, 35 cal. (A).
6—4·7 inch, 35 cal. (F).
15—3 pdr.
Torpedo tubes :
4 above water.

Armour (compound) :
12″—10″ Belt .... *a*
Protection to vitals .... = *ab*
10″ Bulkheads .... *b*
2″ Deck (slopes) ....
[Deck flat on belt].
10″ Barbettes .... *b*
12 Conning tower .... *a*

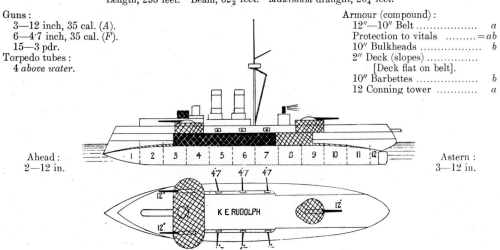

Ahead :
2—12 in.

Astern :
3—12 in.

Broadside : 2—12 in., 3—4·7 in.

Machinery : 2 sets compound.   2 screws.   Boilers : 10 single-ended return tube.   Designed H.P. 5130 *natural* = 15 kts ; 6500 *forced* = 16 kts.   Sea speed *circa* 13·5 kts.   Coal : *normal* 600 tons ; *maximum capacity* 650 tons.

Note.—Belt is 9 feet wide.

314

KRONPRINZESSIN ERZHERZOGIN STEPHANIE (1887).

5150 tons.   Guns : 2—12 in., 35 cal. (A) ; 6—6 in., 35 cal.   Armour (compound) : 9″—4¾″ complete belt (c-d) ; 8″ Barbettes forward (c).   Speed at present about 13 kts.

TEGETTHOFF.   *Photo, Circovitch.*

TEGETTHOFF (1878).   Reconstructed 1893.

7400 tons.   Guns : 6—9·4 in., 35 cal. (B) ; 6—6 in., 35 cal. (F).   Armour (iron) : 15½″—9″ Belt (b-d) ; 15½″ Battery (b).   Speed originally 15 kts.—now much less.

(Practically relegated to harbour service).

SANKT GEORG (1905).

Displacement 7400 tons.   Complement

Length (*waterline*), 384 feet.   Beam, 62 feet.   *Mean* draught, 21½ feet.   Length over all,   feet.

Guns (M. '01) :
    2—9·4 inch, 40 cal. (*AA*).
    5—7·5 inch, 40 cal. (*A*).
    4—6 inch, 40 cal. (*E*).
    8—12 pdr.
    9—3 pdr.
Torpedo tubes (17·7 inch).
    2 *submerged*.

Armour (Krupp) :
    6½″ Belt (amidships) ... *a*
    2″ Belt (ends) ....
    3½″ Armour deck ......
    Protection to vitals ∴ = *a*
    8¼″ Lower deck side ...*aa*
    8″ Barbette..............*aa*
    5″ Turret (aft)............ *b*
    5″ Double Casemates (4) *b*

Photo, A. Beer.

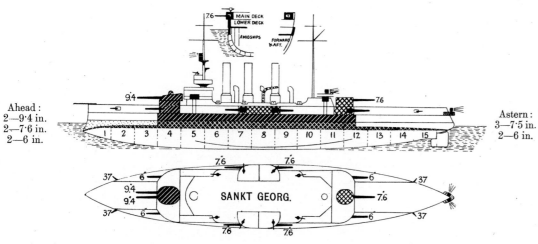

Ahead :
2—9·4 in.
2—7·6 in.
2—6 in.

Astern :
3—7·5 in.
2—6 in.

Broadside : 2—9·4 in., 3—7·5 in., 2—6 in.

Machinery : 2 sets triple expansion.   2 screws.   Boilers : Yarrow.   Designed H.P. 12,300 = 21 knots.
Coal : *normal*   tons ; *maximum* 1000 tons.

Gunnery Notes.—Loading positions, big guns all round.   Hoists : electric and hand.   Big guns manœuvred electrically ; 7·5 in. guns, electric ; 6 in. guns, hand.

Arcs of fire : Big guns 240°.

There is a special armoured position each side on top of the amidships redoubt.

Torpedo Notes.—Very complete electrical installation.

KAISER KARL VI (October, 1898).

Displacement 6325 tons.   Complement 450.

Length (*waterline*), 367½ feet.   Beam, 56 feet.   *Mean* draught, 22⅛ feet.

Guns :
2—9·4 inch, 40 cal. (*A*).
8—6 inch, 40 cal. (*E*).
18—3 pdr.
2 Machine guns.
2—12 pdr. boat guns.
Torpedo tubes (17·7 inch) :
2 *above water*
(behind 3″ armour)

Armour (Harvey-nickel)
8½″ Belt (amidships)...   *a*
8″ Fore bulkhead ......   *a*
7″ After bulkhead ......   *b*
4″ Engine hatches......
2½″ Armour deck (ends)   ϵ
1¼″ Armour deck
(amidships).
Protection to vitals ...= *a*
8″ Barbettes ....   *a*
3¼″ Lower deck redoubt ϵ
3″ Double casemates (4)   ϵ
(Total weight 1400 tons)

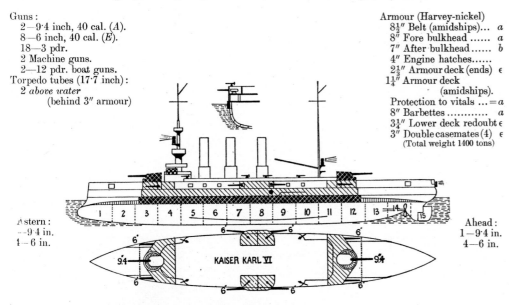

Astern :
—9·4 in.
4—6 in.

Ahead :
1—9·4 in.
4—6 in.

KAISER KARL VI

Broadside : 2—9·4 in., 4—6 in.

Photo, A. Beer.

Machinery : 2 sets 4 cylinder triple expansion.   2 screws.   Boilers : 18 Belleville with feed water heaters.   Designed H.P. 12,000 = 20 kts.   Coal : *normal*   tons ; *maximum* 820 tons.

Armour Notes.—Belt is 6½ feet wide by 241 feet long.   3¾ feet of it below waterline.   Lower edge is 6¾″ thick amidships.

Gunnery Notes.—Loading positions, big guns : all round.   Hoists : electric for all guns.   Big guns manœuvred electrically.   Secondary guns, hand.
Arcs of fire : Big guns, 260°.

Torpedo Notes.—4 searchlights (automatic) complete electric installation for all purposes.

Engineering Notes.—Machinery, etc. weighs 1100 tons.

Trials, etc. :   60 revolutions = 10·16 kts., 81 = 13·52 kts., 101 = 16·66 kts., 110 = 18·17 kts., 121 = 19·71 kts., 127 = 20·56 kts. (11,500 I.H.P.)

Full power trial (4 hours) : 129 revolutions, I.H.P. 12,900 = 20·83 kts.   Pressure is 260 lbs. in boilers, reduced to 180 lbs. at engines.

General Notes.—Tactical diameter *circa* 400 yards.   Laid down at San Rocco, 1896.   Completed 1899.   Cost £429,000.

KAISERIN-UND-KÖNIGIN-MARIA-THERESIA (April, 1893).

Displacement 5200 tons.   Complement 420.

Length, (*waterline*), 351 feet.   Beam, 52½ feet.   *Mean* draught, 21½ feet.   Length over all, 374 feet.

Guns :
2—9·4 inch, 35 cal. (*B*).
8—6 inch, 35 cal. (*F*).
18—3 pdr.
2 Machine.
Torpedo tubes (17·7 inch) :
4 *above water*.

Armour (steel) :
4″ Belt (amidships) ……. ε
2¼″ Armour deck ………
Protection to vitals …… ε
4″ Lower deck (redoubt) ε
4″ Barbettes ………….. ε
4″ Sponsons ………….. ε
4″ Conning tower ……… ε
4″ Bulkheads ………….. ε
4″ Hoods to barbettes … ε
4″ Shields to upper deck guns

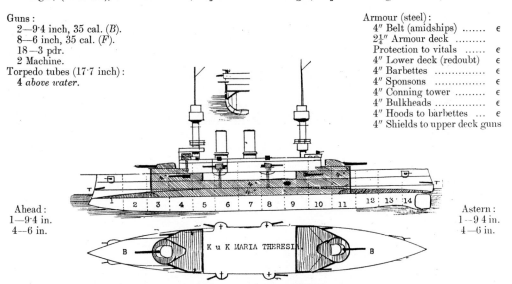

Ahead :
1—9·4 in.
4—6 in.

Astern :
1—9·4 in.
4—6 in.

Broadside : 2—9·4 in., 4—6 in.

Photo, Symonds.

Machinery : 2 sets horizontal triple expansion.   2 screws.   Boilers : cylindrical.   Designed H.P. *natural* 5880 ; *forced* 9000.   Coal : *normal* 600 tons ; *maximum* 740 tons.

Armour Notes.—Belt is 7¼ feet wide by 207 feet long ; 5¾ feet of it below waterline.

Gunnery Notes.—Loading positions, big guns : end on.   Big guns manœuvred electrically.

Engineering Notes.—On first trials (1895) she made 17·1 with *maximum* draught, and 19·3 with *forced* draught.   Present *maximum* speed over 17½ kts.

General Notes.—Built at San Rocca.

KAISERIN ELISABETH.   *Photo, Circovitch.*

KAISERIN-ELISABETH (September, 1890), **KAISER-FRANZ-JOSEF** (May, 1889).

Displacement 4060 tons.   Complement 367.

Length (*waterline*) 321 feet.   Beam, 49 feet.   *Mean* draught, 19 feet.

Guns :
  2—9·4 inch, 35 cal. (*B*).
  6—6 inch, 35 cal. (*F*).
  5—3 pdr.
  10—1 pdr.
Torpedo tubes (17·7 inch) :
  4 *above water*.

Armour (steel) :
  (Cellulose belt).
2¼″ Armour deck ...... €
Protection to vitals ...=€
3½″ Barbettes........... €
3½″ Hoods to these .. €
4″ Conning tower ...... €

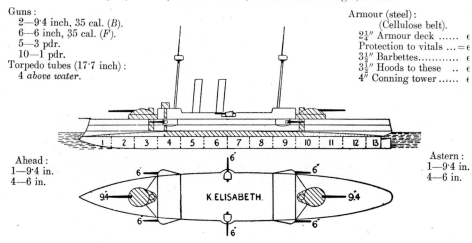

Ahead :
1—9·4 in.
4—6 in.

Astern :
1—9·4 in.
4—6 in.

Broadside : 2—9·4 in., 3—6 in.

Machinery : 2 sets horizontal triple expansion.   2 screws.   Boilers : 4 cylindrical, double-ended. Designed H.P. *natural* 6400 = 18 kts ; *forced* 9000 = 19 kts.   Coal : *normal* 400 tons ; *maximum* 600 tons.

Gunnery Notes.—Loading positions, big guns : end on.   Big guns manœuvred : hydraulically.

Engineering Notes.—The ships burn enormous quantities of coal, but can still steam at a very fair speed.   On first trials both exceeded or nearly reached 20 knots.

KAISER-FRANZ-JOSEF.

Differences :
  K. Elisabeth   Small fighting tops
  K. F. Josef   Big fighting tops

ZENTA (August, 1897), **ASPERN** (May, 1899), **SZIGETVAR** (October, 1900).

Displacement 2437 tons.   Complement 242.

Length (*waterline*), 313½ feet.   Beam, 39½ feet.   *Maximum* draught, 17 feet.

Guns :
8—4·7 inch, 40 cal. (*F*).
12—3 pdr.
2—1 pdr.
Torpedo tubes (17·7 inch) :
1 *above water*.

Armour (steel) :
2″ Armour deck
(amidships)... = ε

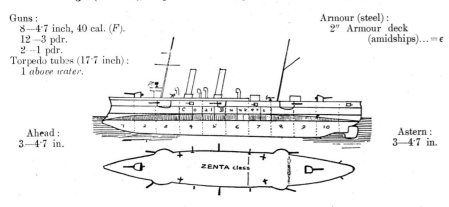

ZENTA class

Ahead :
3—4·7 in.

Astern :
3—4·7 in.

Broadside : 5—4·7 in.

Machinery : 2 sets triple expansion.   2 screws.   Boilers : 8 Yarrow.   Designed I.H.P. 7000 = 20 kts.   Coal : *normal* 300 tons ; *maximum* 500 tons.

Armour Notes.—Deck ½″—¼″ at ends.

Engineering Notes.—Heating surface 20,000 square feet.   Grate area 350 square feet.   No data of trials procurable.

General Notes.—Zenta is a trifle smaller than the later two, 10 feet shorter and of only 2300 tons displacement.   All built at Pola.   Average cost per ship £150,000.

Differences.—

Name.	Steam pipes.	Cowls between funnels.	Notes.
Zenta	before	high with low abaft	2 yards on fore, with sails
Szigetvar	none visible	low with high abaft	1 yard on each mast
Aspern	,, ,,	,, ,, ,,	

SZIGETVAR (ASPERN identical).   *Photo Symonds.*

ZENTA.   *Photo, Beer.*

AUSTRO-HUNGARIAN TORPEDO GUNBOATS.

SATELLIT.   METEOR.   KOMET.   *Photos, Circovitch.*

PLANET (1889, Jarrow). 480 tons. Complement 78.

Guns :
  2—12 pdr.
  8—3 pdr.
Torpedo tubes (T) :
  3 *above water.*

Armour :
  $\frac{3}{4}''$ over engines.

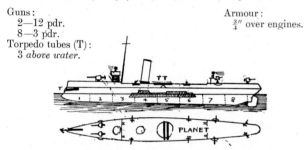

Machinery : 2 sets triple expansion. 2 screws. Boilers : locomotive. Designed H.P. 3500 = 20 kts.

TRABANT (1890). 540 tons. Complement 78.

Guns :
  2—12 pdr.
  8—3 pdr.
Torpedo tubes (T) :
  3 *above water.*

Armour :
  $\frac{3}{4}''$ over engines.

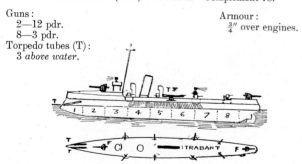

Machinery : 2 sets triple expansion. 2 screws. Boilers : 4 locomotive. Designed H.P. 3500 = 20 kts. Coal : 150 tons.

SATELLIT (Schichau 1893). 540 tons. Complement 61.

Guns :
  2—12 pdr. (*F*).
  8—3 pdr.
Torpedo tubes :
  3 *above water.*

Armour :
  $\frac{3}{4}''$ over engines.

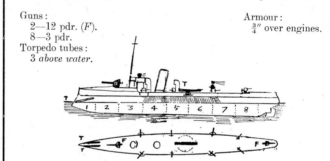

Machinery : 2 sets triple expansion. 2 screws. Boilers : 4 locomotive. Designed H.P. 4000 = 23 kts. (*trial* in bad weather 4600 = 21·87 kts.)

BLITZ & KOMET (Schichau, 1888). 360 tons.
Complement 61.

Guns :
  9—3 pdr.
Torpedo tubes (T) :
  4 *above water* (how & aft).

Armour :
  $\frac{3}{4}''$ over engines.

Machinery : 1 set triple expansion. 1 screw. Boilers : locomotive. Speed : very poor now.

METEOR (Schichau, 1887). 350 tons. Complement 49.

Guns :
  9—3 pdr.
Torpedo tubes :
  4 *above water.*

Armour :
  $\frac{3}{4}''$ over engines.

Machinery : 1 set triple expansion. 1 screw. Boilers : locomotive. Designed H.P. 2500 = 21 kts. Coal : 120 tons (bunker capacity).

(T.) MAGNET (Schichau, 1896). 510 tons.

Guns :
  6—3 pdr.
Torpedo tubes (T) :
  3 *above water.*

Armour :
  $\frac{3}{4}''$ over engines.

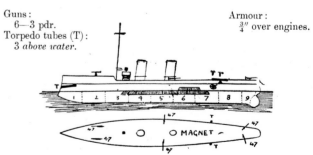

Machinery : 2 sets triple expansion. 2 screws. Boilers : Thornycroft. Designed H.P. 5000 = 26 kts. (exceeded on *trial*). Coal : 105 tons.

AUSTRO-HUNGARIAN DESTROYERS.

1+*11. Huszar* (1905) and 11 others in hand. *Yarrow* type, 390 tons. Armament: 1—12 pdr., 7—3 pdr., 2—18″ tubes. Designed H.P. 6000 = 28 kts. Complement 64.

Cobra, Python, Kigyo, and Boa ; also Viper almost identical.

Torpedo Boats.

Type.	Date.	Displacement.	I.H.P.	Max. speed.	Coal.	Complement.	Tubes.	Boilers, small tube
1+*22 Kaiman (Yarrow)*	1905-'07	200	3000	25	...	...	2	Yarrow
1 *Viper (Yarrow)*	1896	107	1800	26	30	26	2	Yarrow
4 *Cobra (Yarrow)*	'98-'99	115	1800	26	30	24	3	Yarrow
1 *Natter (Schichau)*	1896	134	1800	26	30	25	3	Thornycroft

7+*22 in hand.*

62 old boats of no fighting value retained for various local purposes.

Torpedo boats: Kaiman type.

AUSTRO-HUNGARIAN MISCELLANEOUS.

Three gunboats of *circa* 1600 tons, *Tiger, Panther,* and *Leopard* (1885-87), of which the first carries four, and the others 2— 4·7 in. guns. Speed very indifferent.

Danube Flotilla.

Type.	Launch.	Displacement.	Armament.	Armour.			Max. speed.	Coal.
				Waterline.	Deck.	Guns.		
		tons.	inches	inches.	inches.	inches.	kts.	tons.
Save Theiss }	1905	433	2—4·7	$1\frac{1}{2}$	1	$1\frac{1}{2}$	11	62
Temes Bodrog }	1904	433	2—4·7	$1\frac{1}{2}$	1	$1\frac{1}{2}$	11	62
Szamos Koros }	1892	437	2—4·7	3	$\frac{3}{4}$	3	10	62
Maros Leitha }	1871	305	1—4·7	1	$1\frac{3}{4}$	2	8	20

There are also four fast patrol boats of 30 tons for the Danube.

SWEDISH FLEET.

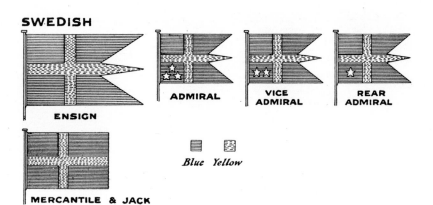

SWEDISH

ENSIGN

ADMIRAL

VICE ADMIRAL

REAR ADMIRAL

MERCANTILE & JACK

Blue   Yellow

Modern Swedish Guns (Bofors).

Nota-tion.	Designation.		Length in calibres	Model.	Weight of Gun.	Weight of A.P. shot.	Initial velocity	Max. penetration firing A.P. capped at K.C.		Danger Space against average warship, at			Nom. Rounds per minute.
								5000 yards.	3000 yards.	10,000 yards.	5000 yards.	3000 yards.	
	c/m.	inches.			tons.	lbs.	ft. secs.	inches.	inches.				
AA	25	10	42	'94	38	450	2362	$8\frac{1}{4}$	$11\frac{1}{4}$	125	340	675	$\frac{1}{2}$
A	21	8·2	45	'98	17	$275\frac{1}{2}$	2460†	7	10	100	425	600	5
C	15	6	50	'00	7	100	2788†	$4\frac{1}{2}$	6	75	230	460	9
D	15	6	45	'98	6	100	2460	3	$4\frac{1}{2}$	60	200	410	7
E	12	4·7	45	'94	3	$46\frac{1}{2}$	2427	...	...	...	...	...	10

Guns marked † in the velocity column fire Bofors special nitro-compound.

Torpedo.

Whiteheads. *Submerged* tubes (Elswick), except in Oden class. Torpedoes as in the French Navy, 18 in. (17·7), 15 in. and 14 in.

N.B.—Swedish photos all by favour of Herr Ingenior C. G. Björkman and Kapten E. Hägg, except *Oden*, by Lojt. Krook.

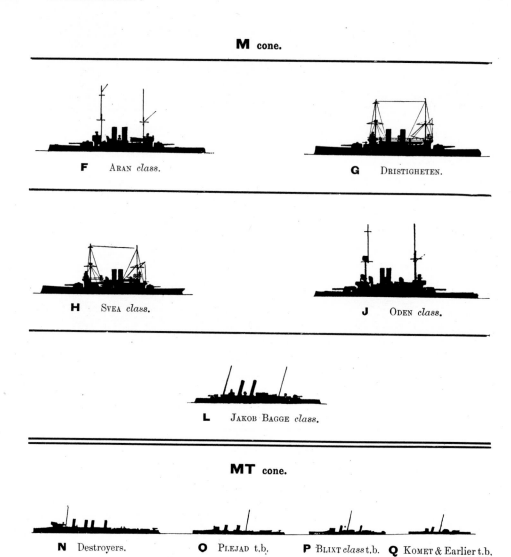

M cone.

F ARAN *class.*

G DRISTIGHETEN.

H SVEA *class.*

J ODEN *class.*

L JAKOB BAGGE *class.*

MT cone.

N Destroyers.   **O** PLEJAD t.b.   **P** BLIXT *class* t.b.   **Q** KOMET & Earlier t.b.

INSIGNIA OF RANK ON SLEEVES.

Vice-Am.	Konter-Am.	Kommendör.	Kommendör-Kapten.		Kapten.	Lojtnant	Unter-Lojtnant.
			1 klass.	2 klass.			

British or U.S.A. } „ *Rear-Ad.* *Commodore.* *Captain.* *Commander.* *Lieutenant.* *Sub-Lieut.*

Note.—Full Admirals have 3 stars (as for Vice and Rear combined).

Reserve officers have *blue* between the stripes. All civilian officers have stripes without the curl, and colour between stripes as follows:—Constructors, *Black*; Doctors, *red*; Paymasters, *blue*. Same colour on cap. Constructors also have rank designated by stars on collar lappel, which is black velvet.

Swedish Arsenals.

KARLSCRONA. One small slip. Three dry docks able to take any Swedish warship; three smaller ones.

STOCKHOLM. One slip. One dry dock, $301 \times 58\frac{1}{2} \times 22\frac{3}{4}$ feet. There are also two private docks, somewhat larger, at Stockholm.

Swedish Private Yards
(that build warships).

LINDHOLMEN. (Lindholmens Mekaniska Verkstad och Varf). Two slips, 220 and 187 feet long. One dry dock, $492 \times 58\frac{1}{2} \times 20$ feet. One 60-ton crane. Electric and pneumatic plant. Total employees 900.

BERGSUND (Bergsunds Mekanisha Verkstad och Varf). One slip, 151 feet long. No docks. One 40-ton crane. Employees 600.

FINNBODA (same firm as above). One slip, 226 feet long. No docks. 60-ton crane. Employees 700.

KOCKUM (MALMO) (Kockums Mekanisha Verkstads Aktiebolag). One slip, 275 feet long. One dry dock, $236 \times 34 \times 12\frac{1}{2}$ feet. 45-ton crane. Electric, pneumatic, and hydraulic power throughout yard. Employees 1000.

Mercantile Marine.

About 910 steamers (90 over 1000 tons, 300 under 100 tons).
About 2000 sailing (10 over 1000 tons, 1300 under 100 tons).

Principal Trade Ports.

Göteborg, Stockholm.

Coinage.

1 kron = about 1s. $0\frac{1}{4}$d. British, 24 cents U.S.A. (18 kronor = £1).

General Notes.—*Personnel*: About 3500, also about 23,000 one-year conscripts are available. *Minister of Marine*: Adolf Palander. *Chief Constructor*: H. Lilljechook. *Colour of Ships*: Brown-grey.

Efficiency is of a high order. Ships are constantly drilled in running through the difficult channels of the Archipelagos, and manœuvres against a supposed blockading fleet are frequent. Great attention is paid to both gunnery and torpedo—the drill being on most up-to-date lines. Navigating abilities are excellent: engineering very fair.

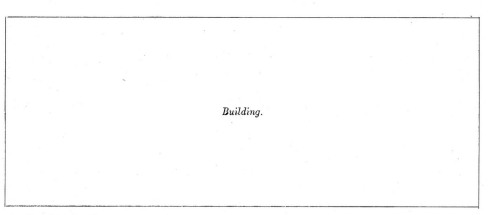

Building.

Signal letter : E.

OSCAR II. (building).

Displacement 4275 tons.   Complement 326.

Length, 313⅔ feet.   Beam, 49½ feet.   *Maximum* draught, 16¾ feet.

Guns :
2—8·2 inch, 45 cal. (*A*).
8—6 inch, 50 cal. (*C*).
10—6 pdr.
3—1 pdr.
Torpedo tubes (18 inch) :
2 *submerged* (Elswick).

Armour (Krupp) :
6″—4″ Belt (amidships) ......*a-d*
2″ Deck (slopes) ....
6″ Bulkheads .... *a*
Protection to vitals .... *aa*
4″ Lower deck redoubt ...... *d*
7½″—5″ Big gun turrets (NC) *a-c*
7″ Hoists to these.............. *a*
5″—3″ Small turrets (N.C.) .. *c-e*
7″ Conning tower.............. *a*

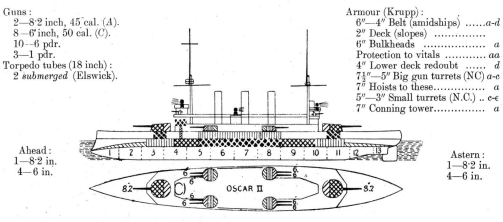

Ahead :
1—8·2 in.
4—6 in.

Astern :
1—8·2 in.
4—6 in.

Broadside : 2—8·2 in., 4—6 in.

Machinery : 2 sets triple expansion.   2 screws.   Boilers : 12 Yarrow.   Designed H.P. ·8500 = 18 kts.
Coal : *normal* 350 tons ; *maximum* 500 tons.

Notes.—Four searchlights carried—one on each chart-house, two amidships.   Building at Lindholmen.

Signal letter for class : F.

(ÄRAN CLASS—4 SHIPS.)
ÄRAN (1902), **VASA** (1902), **TAPPERHETEN** (1903) & **MANLIGHETEN** (1904).

Displacement 3650 tons.   Complement 250.

Length, 287 feet.   Beam, 49¼ feet.   *Maximum* draught, 16 feet.

Guns :
2—8·2 inch, 45 cals. (*A*).
6—6 inch, 45 cals. (*D*).
10—3 pdr.
2—1 pdr.
Torpedo tubes (18 inch) :
2 *submerged* (Elswick).

Armour (Krupp) :
7″ Belt (amidships) .... *a*
2″ Deck (flat on belt)...........
7″ Bulkheads .... *c*
Protection to vitals is .... *a*
7½″—5″ Turrets .... *a-c*
8″ Supports .... *a*
5″—2½″ Small turrets (N.C.) *c-e*
4″ Hoists, etc. .... *a*
8″ Conning tower .... *a*

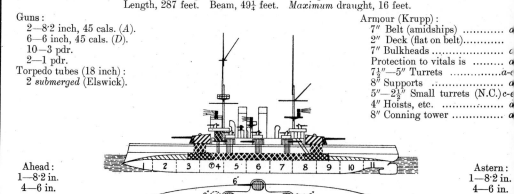

Ahead :
1—8·2 in.
4—6 in.

Astern :
1—8·2 in.
4—6 in.

Broadside : 1—8·2 in., 4—6 in.

Machinery : 2 sets triple expansion.   2 screws.   Boilers : 8 Yarrow.   Designed H.P. 6500 = 17 kts.
Coal : *normal* 360 tons.

Notes.—Where built : *Äran*, Lindholmen ; *Vasa*, Bergsund ; *Tapperheten* and *Manligheten*, Kockum.

SWEDISH BATTLESHIPS.

DRISTIGHETEN (1900).

Displacement 3500 tons.   Complement 250.

Length, 285 feet.   Beam, 48⅔ feet.   *Maximum* draught, 16 feet.

Guns :
  2—8·2 inch, 45 cal. (*A*).
  6—6 inch, 45 cal. (*D*).
  10—6 pdr.
  2—1 pdr.
Torpedo tubes :
  2 *submerged* (Elswick).

Armour (Krupp) :
  8″ Belt (amidships) ....*aa*
  2″ Deck (flat on belt) ......
  Protection to vitals .... *a*
  8″ Turrets.................... *a*
  3¾″ Battery .... *c*
  3¾″ Hoists.................... *c*
  8″ Conning tower .... *a*
  8″ Turret supports .... *a*

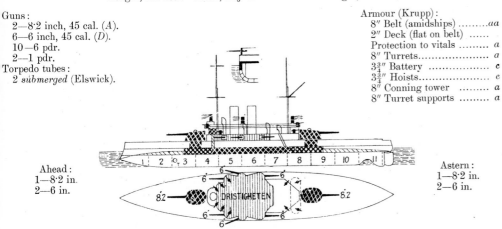

Ahead :
  1—8·2 in.
  2—6 in.

Astern :
  1—8·2 in.
  2—6 in.

Broadside : 2—8·2 in.   3—6 in.

Machinery : 2 sets triple expansion.   Designed H.P. 5570 = 16·8 kts. *natural* draught (*est*).   2 screws.
Boilers : 8 Yarrow.   Coal : *normal* 280 tons ; *maximum* 400 tons = 6 days full speed.

First trials : I.H.P. 5400 = 17 kts.

Built at Lindholmen.

(Svea Class—3 Ships).

SVEA (1886), **GÖTA** (1891), & **THULE** (1893).

Displacement about 3300 tons.   Complement 237.

Average length, 254 feet.   Beam, 48 feet.   *Maximum* draught, 17 feet.

Guns :
  1—8·2 inch, 45 cal. (*A*).
  7—6 inch, 45 cal. (*D*).
  11—6 pdr.
  2—1 pdr.
Torpedo tubes :
  1 *submerged* (bow).
  Thule 2 above water instead.

Armour (Creusot) :
  11¾″—8″ Belt ....*a-b*
  2″ Deck (flat on belt).....
  2″ Deck (at ends) ....= *e*
  10½″ Conning tower ...... *b*
Armour (Krupp) :
  7½″ fore turret (n.c.) ...... *a*
  5″ Hoist to this ....
  5″ Secondary turrets (7)... *b*
  4″ Hoists to these .... *c*

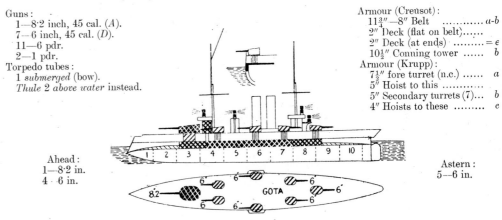

Ahead :
  1—8·2 in.
  4·6 in.

Astern :
  5—6 in.

Broadside : 1—8·2 in., 4—6 in.

Machinery : 2 sets horizontal triple expansion.   2 screws.   Boilers : 6 cylindrical.   Designed I.H.P.
4650 = 15 kts.   Coal : *normal* 200 tons ; *maximum* 300 tons.

Notes.—Completely reconstructed, 1900—04.   *Göta* and *Svea* built at Lindholmen, *Thule* at Bergsund.

(ODEN CLASS—3 SHIPS).

ODEN (1897), **THOR** (1898), & **NIORD** (1899).

Displacement 3400 tons. Complement 210.

Length, 279 feet. Beam, 40 feet. *Maximum* draught, 17 feet.

Guns (*Oden*) :
  2—10 inch, 42 cal. (*AA*).
  6—4·7 inch, 47 cal. (*F*).
  10—3 pdr.
  2—1 pdr.
Torpedo tubes :
  1 *submerged* (bow).

Armour (Harvey-nickel) :
  10″ Belt (amidships)   *aa*
  2″ Deck (flat on belt)
  Protection to vitals is   *aa*
  10″ Turrets............   *aa*
  10″ Supports and hoists *aa*
  3¾″ Battery............   *d*

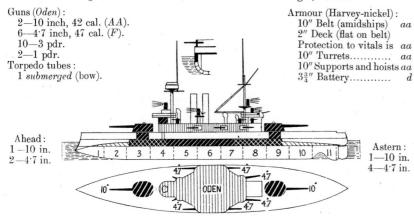

Ahead :
1—10 in.
2—4·7 in.

Astern :
1—10 in.
4—4·7 in.

ODEN.

Guns (*Thor* and *Niord*) :
  2—10 inch, 42 or 45 cal. (*AA*).
  6—4·7 inch, 45 cal. (*F*).
  10—6 pdr.
  2—1 pdr.
Torpedo tubes :
  1 *submerged* (bow).

Armour (Harvey-nickel) :
  9½″ Belt ....   *aa*
  2″ Deck (flat on belt)
  Protection to vitals is   *aa*
  8″ Turrets ....   *a*
  8″ Supports and hoists *aa*
  3¾″ Battery............   *d*

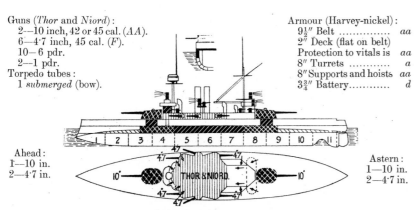

Ahead :
1—10 in.
2—4·7 in.

Astern :
1—10 in.
2—4·7 in.

Broadside : 2—10 in., 3—4·7 in.

Machinery : 2 scews. Boilers : 6 cylindrical.

Notes.—The big guns of *Oden* and *Thor* are Canet, those of *Niord* are Bofors. Two extra 4·7 in. mounted in *Oden* in 1901 ; originally only four.

Trials.—*Oden* natural I.H.P. 3700 = 15 kts. ; 6 hours *forced* 5350 = 16·82 kts.
  Thor   „   = 15·5 „ ; 6 „   „   = 16·7 „
  Niord   „   = 15·5 „ ; 6 „   „   = 16·5 „

Thor and *Oden* built at Bergsund ; *Niord* at Lindholmen.

Signal letter for class : J.   THOR & NIORD (*identical*).

SWEDISH CRUISER (*Ckryssare*).

Completing.

FYLGIA (1905).

Displacement 4060 tons.   Complement 322.

Length, 379 feet.   Beam, 49 feet.   *Mean* draught, 16 feet.

Guns (M. '00):
  8—6 inch, 45 cal. (*C*).
  14—6 pdr.
Torpedo tubes (18 inch):
  2 *submerged*.

Armour (Krupp):
  4″ Belt .... *d*
  2″ Deck (slopes) ......
  Protection to vitals ... =*b*
  5″—2″ Turrets ...... *c-f*
  4″ Hoists and supports *d*
  4″ Conning tower...... *d*

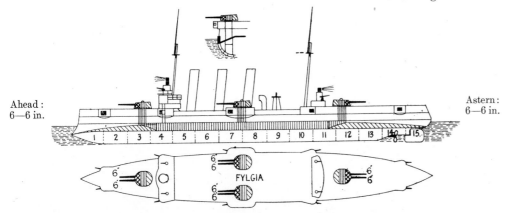

Ahead:
6—6 in.

Astern:
6—6 in.

Broadside: 6—6 in.

Machinery: 2 sets triple expansion.   2 screws.   Boilers: 12 Yarrow.   Designed H.P. 12,000 = 21·5 kts.
Coal: *normal* 350 tons; *maximum* 900 tons.

SWEDISH TORPEDO GUNBOATS (*Torped Kryssare*).

Signal letter for class: L.   JAKOB BAGGE (others very similar).

ÖRNEN (1897), JAKOB BAGGE (1898), CLAS HORN (1898) 700 tons.

Length, 223 feet.   Beam, 27 feet.   Draught, 10 feet.

ALSO

PSILANDER (1899), CLAS UGGLA (1899) 700 tons.

Length, 223 feet.   Beam, 27⅓ feet.   Draught, 9 feet = 71 × 8·3 × 2·7 metres.

Complement 99.

Guns:
  2—4·7 inch, 45 cal.
  4—6 pdr.
Torpedo tubes:
  1 *submerged* (bow).

Armour (Bofors steel):
  ¾″ Deck ....
  2″ Conning tower ....

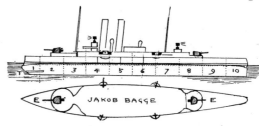

Machinery: 2 screws.   Boilers: 2 Yarrow (except *Örnen*, which has 2 cylindrical).   Designed H.P. 4000 = 20 kts. *natural draught*.

The Swedish fleet also contains 4 old monitors JOHN ERICSSON, LÖKE, TIRFING & THORDON, of about 1500 tons; 7 little monitors of 460 tons; and 10 gunboats—all of no fighting value.

Destroyers ("*Jagare*").

1 *Yarrow:* **Mode** (1902), 400 tons. Speed: 31 kts. Coal: 80 tons. Armament: 6—6 pdr. Tubes: 2 single, aft, (18 inch). *Maximum* draught, 9 feet.

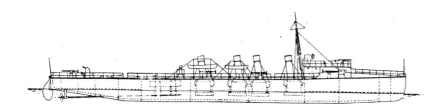

1 *Thornycroft:* **Magne** (1905), 430 tons. Speed: 30·5 kts. Coal: 90 tons (*maximum*). Armament: 6—6 pdr. 2 single 18 inch tubes, aft. *Maximum* draught, 8¾ feet.

1 other to be built.

Torpedo Boats ("*Torpedo batår*").

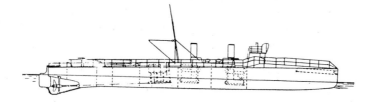

Normand: **Plejad** (1905), 97½ tons. Speed: 26 kts. 2 tubes (18 inch), bow and aft. Guns: 2—1 pdr Coal: 13½ tons. *Maximum* draught, 8¾ feet.

12 **Blixt** class (1904-1896). 92 tons. Speed: 23-20 kts. 2 tubes (15 inch), bow and aft. Guns: 2-1 pdr. Coal: 22-18 tons. *Maximum* draught, 7¼ feet.

The earliest boat *Komet* has only 1 funnel.

5 boats: Nos. 87, 85, 83, 81, and 79 (1902-05), 57-49 tons. Speed: 20 kts. 2 tubes (18 inch in No. 87, and 15 inch in the others). Coal: 22-18 tons. *Maximum* draught, 6½ feet.

OLD BOATS.

There are also 2 boats of 85 tons (9 and 11), and 20 kts. original speed (1890).
2 ,, 49 tons (77 and 75), and 19 ,, ,, (1892).
10 ,, 67-40 tons, and 18 ,, ,, ('87-'82).

Submarine (*Undervattensbåt*).

1 *Holland* type: **Hajen** (1904), $\frac{107 \text{ tons.}}{127 \text{ tons.}}$ Motive power: $\frac{\text{petrol}}{\text{accumulators.}}$ H.P. 200. Speed: $\frac{9 \cdot 5 \text{ kts.}}{7 \text{ kts.}}$ Dimensions:— 71×12×9¾ feet. Armament: 1—18 inch tube (3 torpedoes carried). Complement 6. Built at Orlogsuarfvet, Stockholm.

There is also in Sweden an *Enroth* steam submarine of 146 tons, for which much is claimed, but it does not belong to the Navy, and is a purely experimental boat of doubtful value.

NORWEGIAN FLEET.

ENSIGN

 ADMIRAL

 VICE ADMIRAL

 REAR ADMIRAL

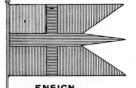

MERCANTILE & JACK

Red	Blue

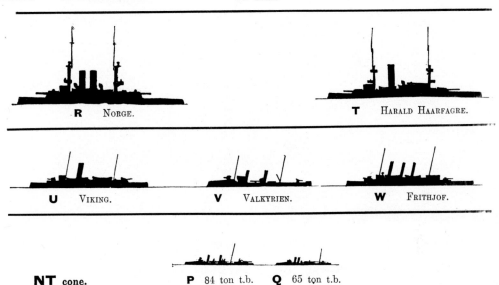

R NORGE.

T HARALD HAARFAGRE.

U VIKING.

V VALKYRIEN.

W FRITHJOF.

NT cone.

P 84 ton t.b. **Q** 65 ton t.b.

Modern Guns (Elswick).

Nota-tion.	Designation		Length in calibres	Model.	Weight of Gun.	Weight of A.P. shot.	Initial velocity	*Max.* penetration firing A.P. capped at K.C.		Danger Space against average warship, at			Nom. Rounds per minute.
								5000 yards.	3000 yards.	10,000 yards.	5000 yards.	3000 yards.	
	c/m.	inches.			tons.	lbs.	ft. secs.						
B	20·3	8	45	...	15	250	2480	6½	9¼	100	405	594	...
D	15	6	45	...	6	100	2570	3	4½	67	215	440	8
E	12	4·7	45	...	3	45	2570	...	...	...	...	...	10
F	7·5	3	40	...	⅗	12	2200	...	...	...	...	...	...

Arsenals.

HORTEN. One dry dock, 356 × 61 × 23½ feet. Also a private dock in the town about the same size. One slip at a yard here.
CHRISTIANSAND. One dry dock, 310 × 45 × 18 feet.

Private Yards.

TRONDHJEM (Throndhjems Dokelskab). Two dry docks able to take any Norwegian ship.
BERGEN: (*a*) Laxevaags Maskin & Jernskibbyggeri; (*b*) Bergens Mekaniske Verkstad; (*c*) Brunchorst and Dekke. Each has one small dry dock.

Mercantile Marine.

About 1220 steamers (150 over 1000 tons, 450 under 100 tons).
About 5500 sailing (200 over 1000 tons, 4000 under 100 tons).

Principal Trade Ports.

Kristiania, Bergen, Trondhjem.

Coinage.

Same as Swedish.

INSIGNIA OF RANK ON SLEEVES.

| Vice-Am. | Konter-Am. | Komman-dörer. | Kommandörer-Kaptien. | Kaptien. | Freimer-Lojtnant. | Second-Lojtnant. |

British or U.S.A. } ,, Rear-Ad. Commodore. Captain. Commander. Lieutenant. Sub-Lieut.

Note.—Full Admiral has 3 stars.

Reserve officers have *blue* between the stripes. All civilian officers have stripes without the curl, and colour between stripes as follows :—Constructors, *Black*; Doctors, *Red*; Paymasters, *Blue*. Same colour on cap. Constructors also have rank designated by stars on collar lappel, which is black velvet.

General Notes.—*Personnel* : About 1000 permanent, 1000 yearly conscripts, all seafaring men in reserve. *Minister of Marine* :   *Chief of Staff* : K.-Admiral Borresen. *Colour of Ships* : French grey.

Signal for class: R.   NORGE (both alike).

TORDENSKJOLD.   (Both exactly alike, except that *Haarfagre*   *Signal for class*: T.
has brass bands round big guns.)

NORGE (1900), EIDSVOLD (1900).

Displacement 3800 tons.   Complement 250.

Length, 290 feet.   Beam, 50 feet.   *Mean* draught, 16½ feet.

Guns (Elswick):
2—8 inch, 45 cal. (B).
6—6 inch, 45 cal. (D).
8—12 pdr. (F).
6—3 pdr.
Torpedo tubes:
2 *submerged*.

Armour (Krupp):
7″—5″ Belt .... *a*
2″ Deck slopes ....
Protection to vitals...= *aa*
6″ Turrets .... *b*
6″ Bases .... *b*
5″ Casemates (NC) ... *c*

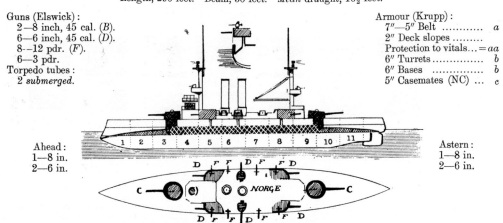

Ahead:
1—8 in.
2—6 in.

Astern:
1—8 in.
2—6 in.

Machinery: 2 screws.   Boilers: 8 Yarrow.   Designed H.P. 4850 = 17 kts.   Coal: *normal* 250 tons; *maximum* 400 tons.

Notes.—Built at Elswick.   Excellent seaboats.

HARALD HAARFAGRE (1897), TORDENSKJOLD (1897).

Displacement 3400 tons.   Complement 220.

Length, 279 feet.   Beam, 48½ feet.   *Maximum* draught, 19 feet.

Guns (Elswick):
2—8 inch (B).
6—4·7 inch (F).
6—12 pdr. (F).
6—1 pdr. (Bofors).
Torpedo tubes:
2 *submerged*.

Armour (Harvey):
7″ Belt (amidships) ... *b*
4″ Belt ends .... *d*
2″ Deck (flat on belt).
Protection to vitals is *b*
8″—5″ Turrets ...= *a—c*
5″ Bases of turrets ... *d*
6″ Conning tower...... *b*

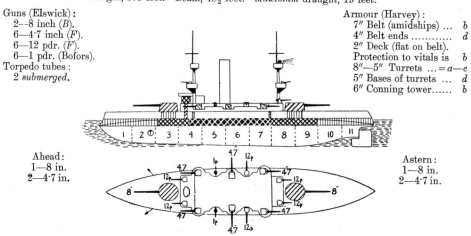

Ahead:
1—8 in.
2—4·7 in.

Astern:
1—8 in.
2—4·7 in.

Machinery: Boilers: cylindrical.   2 screws.   Designed H.P. 3700 = 17·2 kts.   (*trial* 1897).
Coal: *normal* 200 tons; *maximum* 500 tons.

Notes.—Built at Elswick.   Excellent seaboats.

NORWEGIAN TORPEDO GUNBOATS *("1 Kl. Kanonbaade.")*

VALKYRIEN.

VALKYRIEN (1896. Displacement 390 tons. Complement 59.

Guns (Krupp): 2—10 pdr.. 2—1 pdr. 2 Torpedo tubes (18 in.) 2 screws. Boilers: Thornycroft. Designed H.P. 3300＝23 kts. Coal: 90 tons.

(Officially classed as a Destroyer).

FRITHJOF (1895). Displacement 1380 tons. Complement 154.

Guns (Elswick): 2—4·7 in., 45 cal., 4—12 pdr., 4—1 pdr. Torpedo tubes (14 in.): 1 *submerged* (bow), 2 *above water.* 2 screws. Boilers: cylindrical. Designed H.P. 3000＝15 kts. Coal: 160 tons.

VIKING (1891). 1120 tons. Complement 130.

Guns (re-armed 1903): 1—6 in., 40 cal., 1—4·7 in., 45 cal., 4—12 pdr., 4—1 pdr., 2 machine. Torpedo tubes (14 in.): 1 *submerged* (bow), 2 *above water.* Coal: 140 tons.

FRITHJOF. *Photo, West.*

NORWEGIAN TORPEDO BOATS *("Torpedo Baaden.")*

Single screw boats armed with 14 in. torpedoes and a couple of 1 pdrs.

No.	Type.	Date.	Displace-ment.	Max. Speed.	Tubes.	Coal.	Complement.	Max. Draught.
			tons.	kts.		tons.		feet.
10	Schichau	1898-1901	84	24-23	2	...	...	7
7	Norwegian	1898-1900	65	19	2	...	...	7
4	,,	1904-1903	43	16	1	...	...	6½
21								

There are also 10 old boats, 40-16 tons, dating from 1873-87, originally of 20-16 kt. speed; of no present fighting value.

The Norwegian Navy includes masted training ships: NORDSTJERNEN, ELLIDA, NORNEN, all *circa* 1000 tons, 8 small gunboats (*Aegir* class), and 1 gunboat, SLEIPNER, all of no fighting value.

There are also four old monitors —THOR, SKORPIONEN, MJOLNER and THRUDVANG, *circa* 2000 tons, carrying 2—4·7 in. guns each.

DANISH FLEET.

D cone.

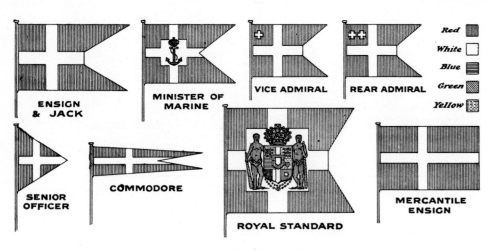

ENSIGN & JACK

MINISTER OF MARINE

VICE ADMIRAL

REAR ADMIRAL

SENIOR OFFICER

COMMODORE

ROYAL STANDARD

MERCANTILE ENSIGN

Red ▨ White ▢ Blue ▤ Green ▨ Yellow ▦

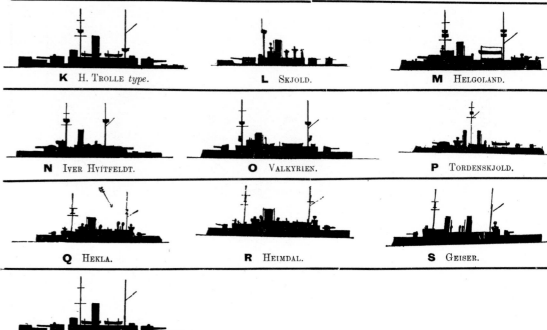

K H. Trolle *type.*
L Skjold.
M Helgoland.
N Iver Hvitfeldt.
O Valkyrien.
P Tordenskjold.
Q Hekla.
R Heimdal.
S Geiser.
J O. Fischer.

Naval Guns. (All Krupp.)

Notation.	Nominal Calibre.		Length.	Date of Model.	Weight of Gun.	Weight A. P. Shell.	Initial Velocity.	Maximum penetration A. P. *capped* against K. C.	
	in.	c/m.	cals.		tons.	lbs.	ft. sec.	5000 yds.	3000 yds.
B	14	35·5	22	...	51¼	1157½	1620	5	7
D	12	30·5	20	...	35½	725	1670	...	5½
D	10·2	26	22	...	27½	450	2000	4	6
E	10·2	26	16	...	21½	450	1640	...	4½
A	9·4	24	40	'95	25½	352	2500	7½	10½
D	8·2	21	18	...	13½	238	2020	3	5½
E	6	15	40	...	6	112	2264	...	3½
F	6	15	32	...	4½	112	1850	...	3
F	4·7	12	40	...	2	45	2460	...	...
F	3·3	8·4	40	...	...	18	2380	...	...

Guns under 40 calibres use black powder.

There are some old M.L. Armstrong in old ships. Also old short B.L. 6 inch and 4·7 inch.

Personnel: About 4000, all ranks.

Arsenal.

COPENHAGEN. Dockyard. Dry docks, (a) 288 × 59½ × 20½ feet;
(b) 106 × 40 × 27¾ feet (Floating, No. 1);
(c) 113 × 45 × 12 feet (Floating, No. 2);
(d) 412 × 23 × 25 feet (Patent slip).

Private Establishments.

COPENHAGEN. (BURMEISTER & WAIN). Two medium building slips. Dry dock 469 × 66 × 23 feet, and three patent slips.

GAMLE. One slip. One dry dock 232 × 52 × 15¼ feet.

COPENHAGEN FLOATING DOCK CO. One floating dock 296 × 55½ × 23 feet.
There are also at Copenhagen two small patent slips.

ELSINOR. Dry docks (a) 379 × 57 × 18 feet (New Dock);
(b) 335 × 43 × 14 feet (Elsinor Dry dock);
Also a patent slip.

AARHUS. Patent slip, able to take a small torpedo boat.

Mercantile Marine: About 540 steamers of about 260,000 tons. 3,500 sailing, mostly fishing craft, etc. Sea trade chiefly with England, Sweden and Norway.

Oversea Possessions: Iceland, Greenland, Faeros Islands, Danish West Indies (St. Thomas, St. John, and St. Croix).

Coinage: Krone (100 ore) = about 1s. 1d. British; 50 cents U.S.A.

Minister of Marine: Rear-Admiral Jöhncke.

DANISH COAST SERVICE BATTLESHIPS.

HERLUF TROLLE (1899), **OLFERT FISCHER** (1903) and *PEDER SKRAM* (*building*).

3470 tons. Complement 250. Length, 272⅓ feet. Beam, 49⅓ feet. *Max.* draught, 16 feet.

Guns :
2—9·4 in. (*A*).
4—6 in. (*E*).
10—6 pdr.
4—1 pdr.
5 Machine
Torpedo tubes :
3 *submerged*.
(One of them in bow.)

Armour (Krupp) :
7″ Belt (amidships) ... *a*
4″ Belt (aft) ... ... *d*
3″ Deck (forward) ...
[Deck flat on belt.]
7″ Turrets ... ... *a*
6″ Casemates (KNC)... *b*
7″ Bulkhead ... ... *a*
7″ Conning tower ... *a*

Ahead :
1—9·4 in.
2—6 in.

Astern :
1—9·4 in.
2—6 in.

Machinery : H.P. 4200=16·5 kts.   Boilers : Thornycroft.   *Trials* (1901) :
I.H.P. 3171=14·6 kts. : 4200=16·5 kts.
Freeboard, 3 feet.   Width of Belt, 6 feet.
First of class laid down 1896 and completed 1901.

HERLUF TROLLE.   *Photo, Daniellsen.*

OLFERT FISCHER the same, except that she is without fighting tops.

SKJOLD (1896).

Displacement 2160 tons.   Complement 210.

Length, 222 feet.   Beam, 37 feet.   *Maximum* draught, 17½ feet.   Length over all, 242¾ feet.

Guns :
1—9·4 in. (*A*).
3—4·7 in. (*E*).
4—3 pdr.
2—1 pdr.
Torpedo tubes :
4 *above water*.

Armour (Harvey) :
10″ Belt ... ... *a*
3″ Belt (aft.) ... ... *ε*
2″ Deck (bow) ... ... =*d*
[Deck flat on belt amidships.]
8″ Big turret ... ... *b*
5″ Small turrets ... ... *d*
7″ Bulkhead ... ... *b*
8″ Conning tower ... ... *b*

Ahead :
1—9·4 in.

Astern :
3—4·7 in.

Machinery : I.H.P. 2200=13 kts. Boilers : Cylindrical. Coal Capacity : 285 tons (*maximum.*)
Freeboard, 3 feet.   Width of belt, 6 feet.
Laid down 1893.   Completed 1899.

Photo, Daniellsen.

HELGOLAND (1878).

5370 tons.   Complement 350.   (Dimensions) L. B. D. : $257 \times 59 \times 21$ feet.

Guns (Krupp) :
  1—12 in., 20 cals. (C).
  4—10·2 in., 16 cals. (D).
  5—4·7 in., 27 cals. (E).
  10 machine.
Torpedo tubes :
  4 *above water.*

Armour (iron) :
  12″-6″ Belt ... ...   c-e
  4″ Deck (flat on belt)... ...
  10″ Battery... ... ...   d
  7″ Bulkheads to it ... ...   e
  10″ Turret and base ... ...   d

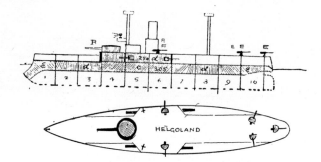

HELGOLAND

Machinery : 2 screws.   *Boilers :* Cylindrical (new in 1896).   Designed H.P. 4000 = 12 kts. (made on *trial* 1897).   Coal : *normal* 214 tons.

Laid down, 1876.   Completed, 1881.   Re-fitted 1896.

Photo, West.

IVER HVITFELDT (1886).

3290 tons.   Complement 298.   (Dimensions) L. B. D. : $242 \times 49\frac{1}{2} \times 20$ feet.

Guns :
  2—10·2 in., 22 cals. (C).
  4—4·7 in., 22 cals. (F).
  12—3 pdrs.
Torpedo tubes :
  4 *above water.*

Armour (compound) :
  11½″ Belt ... ...   a
  9½″ Bulkheads ... ...   b
  2″ Deck ... ... =f
  [Deck is flat on belt amidships]
  8½″ Barbettes   c
  8″ Hoists   c
  6″ Conning tower ... ...   d

Machinery : 2 screws.   Designed H. P. 5000 = 15·5 kts. (slightly exceeded on *first trial*).   Coal : 250 tons.

Note.—The belt is 164 feet long by 6½ feet wide.

This ship was burned in 1904, and is not yet repaired.

DANISH SMALL CRUISERS.

TORDENSKJOLD (1880) ("Torpedo ram").

2530 tons. Complement 220.

Length, 221½ feet. Beam, 43¼ feet. *Maximum* draught, 17 feet.

Guns :
 1—14 in., 22 cals. (*D*).
 4 —4·7 in., 22 cals. (*F*).
 8 machine.
Torpedo tubes :
 4 *above water.*

Armour (steel) :
 3¾″ Deck   ... ... = *d*
 8″ Barbette (compound) *c*
 10″ Conning tower   ... *b*

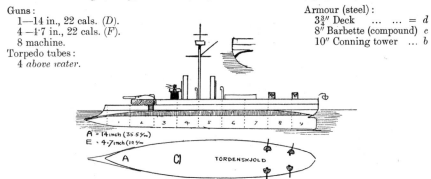

Machinery : 2 screws. Boilers : Cylindrical. Designed H.P. 2600 = 14 kts. Coal : 170 tons.

Photo, Daniellsen.

VALKYRIEN (1888).

3020 tons. Complement 300.

Length, 259 feet. Beam, 42½ feet. *Maximum* draught, 18 feet.

Guns :
 2 —8·2 in., 18 cals. (*C*).
 6—6 in., 32 cals. (*F*).
 4—6 pdr.
 10—1 pdr.
Torpedo tubes :
 5 *above water* (2 in the
  bow, 1 aft, 2 broadside).

Armour (steel) :
 2½″ Deck   ... ... = є
 3″ Engine hatches.. = є

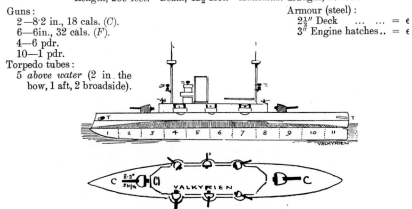

Photo, Daniellsen,

Machinery : 2 screws. Designed H.P. *forced* 5300 = 17·5 kts. Coal : 496 tons.

Note.—Valkyrien was, in her day, a very successful ship and still steams well.

Laid down, 1886. Completed, 1890. Re-fitted, 1896,

DANISH SMALL CRUISERS (PROTECTED).

(HEIMDAL TYPE—2 SHIPS).

GEISER (1892) & HEIMDAL (1894).
Displacement 1290 tons. Complement 155.
Length, 257½ feet. Beam, 27½ feet. *Maximum* draught, 13 feet.

Guns:
2—4·7 inch, 40 cal. (*F*).
4—6 pdr.
6—1 pdr.
Torpedo tubes:
4 *above water* (bow, stern and broadside).

Armour (steel):
1¼″ Deck ... ... = *f*
6″ Engine hatches ... = *b*
4½″ Conning tower ... *ε*
1½″ Hoists... ... ...
(Deck at ends is only ¾″ thick).

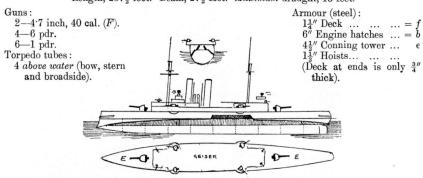

Machinery: 2 sets vertical triple expansion. 2 screws. Boilers: 8 Thornycroft. Designed I.H.P. *natural* 2400 = 16 kts.; *forced* 3000 = 17 kts. (much exceeded on *trial*; *Geiser* making 17·1 kts. with only 2157 I.H.P.). Coal 125 tons.

Note.—*Geiser* was the first ship to be fitted with Thornycroft boilers. These weigh 40 tons. *Heimdal* has only one funnel and is almost exactly like *Hekla* in appearance.

HEKLA (1890).
Displacement 1290 tons. Complement 155.
Length, 233 feet. Beam, 33 feet. *Maximum* draught, 13 feet.

Guns:
2—6 inch, 32 cal. (*E*).
4—6 pdr.
6—1 pdr.
Torpedo tubes:
1 *submerged* (bow).
4 *above water* (bow, stern and broadside).

Armour (steel):
1½″ Deck ... ... = *f*
5″ Engine hatches ... = *c*
4″ Conning tower ... *ε*
1½″ Hoists... ... ...
(Deck at ends is only ¾″ thick).

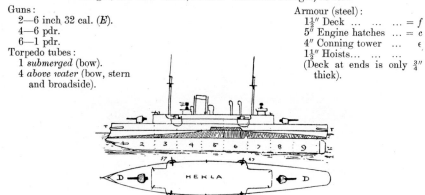

Machinery: 2 sets vertical triple expansion. 2 screws. Boilers: 6 cylindrical (weighing 60 tons). Designed I.H.P. *forced* 3000 = 17·5 kts. (hardly made on *trial*). Coal: 123 tons.

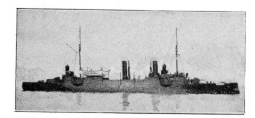

GEISER.

TORPEDO BOATS.
5 ('96-'99), 142 tons; speed, 22·9 kts.; 3 tubes.
2 (1893), 114 tons; speed, 22 kts.; 4 tubes. 7 boats, 90-60 tons. 2 of 44 tons (1901), and 13 old boats of no value.

143 ton boats. HAVORNEN *class*.

Older t. b.

The Danish Navy also contains an old masted cruiser FYEN, 4 other ships, and 7 gunboats, all of no fighting value.

Also three old monitors, GORM, LINDORMEN, and ODIN, armed with old Armstrong M.L. 10″ or 9″ of no fighting value.

DUTCH FLEET.

DUTCH IDENTIFICATION AND SIGNAL SILHOUETTES.

H cone.

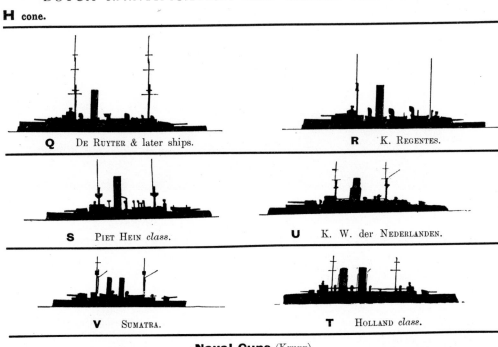

Q DE RUYTER & later ships.

R K. REGENTES.

S PIET HEIN class.

U K. W. der NEDERLANDEN.

V SUMATRA.

T HOLLAND class.

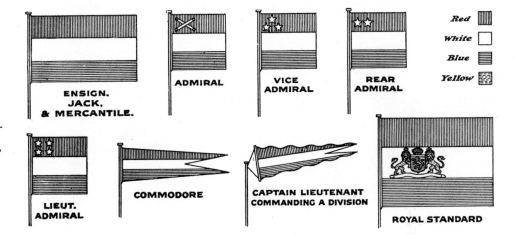

ENSIGN, JACK, & MERCANTILE.

ADMIRAL

VICE ADMIRAL

REAR ADMIRAL

Red
White
Blue
Yellow

LIEUT. ADMIRAL

COMMODORE

CAPTAIN LIEUTENANT COMMANDING A DIVISION

ROYAL STANDARD

Naval Guns (Krupp).

Notation.	Calibre.		Long.	Weight of Gun.	Weight A. P. Shell.	Initial Velocity.	Max penetration with A. P. capped against K. C.	
							5,000 yds. in.	3,000 yds. in.
	in.	c/m.	cals.	tons.	lbs.	ft. secs.		
D	11	28	35	27	474	2133	4	$5\frac{1}{4}$
A	9·4	24	40	$25\frac{1}{2}$	474	2500	$7\frac{1}{2}$	$10\frac{1}{4}$
E	8	21	35	16	$308\frac{1}{2}$	1740	—	$3\frac{1}{2}$
F	6·8	17	22	—	112	1558	—	—
E	6	15	40	5	100	2500	—	$3\frac{1}{2}$
F	6	15	35	$5\frac{1}{2}$	112	2000		
F	4·7	12	40	$2\frac{3}{4}$	45	2150	—	—
F	4·7	12	35	2	57	1804	—	—
F	3	7·5	40	·	—	12·7	2379	

Velocities of the 40-calibre guns are not service ones.   Black powder for guns under 30 calibres.
There are also a few old M. L. guns.

Arsenals.

HELDER AND WILLENSOORD. No slips. Dry docks :—
No. 1. $374\frac{1}{2} \times 63\frac{1}{2} \times 18$ ft.
No. 2. $273\frac{1}{2} \times 59\frac{1}{2} \times 16$
428 $\times 78 \times 20$ (Wilhelmena dock.)
ROTTERDAM. One slip. One dry dock—
500 $\times 78 \times 17\frac{1}{2}$ feet.
HELLEVOETSLUIS. One slip. Dry dock :—
477 $\times 54 \times 17\frac{1}{2}$ feet.·

Private Establishments.

AMSTERDAM. Yard at which warships are constructed. Five floating docks here :—
(a) 410 $\times 63\frac{1}{2} \times 17\frac{1}{2}$ (Koninginne)
(b) 410 $\times 56 \times 18$ (Koning)
(c) 200 $\times 62 \times 13\frac{1}{4}$ (No. 1)
(d) 160 $\times 62 \times 13\frac{1}{4}$ (No. 2)
(e) 160 $\times 62\frac{1}{2} \times 12\frac{1}{2}$ (No. 3)

ROTTERDAM. Yard at which warships are constructed. City floating docks as follows :—
(a) 360 $\times 89 \times 23$ ft.
(b) 295 $\times 57 \times 16$
(c) .157 $\times$
(d) 288 $\times 53 \times 13\frac{3}{4}$ (wood)
MIDDELBURG. The Prinz Hendrik dock here is—413 $\times 65 \times 15$ feet.
FLUSHING. Yard at which warships have been constructed. One dry dock—244 $\times 52 \times 13$ ft.
DORDRECHT has a patent slip 180 feet long.

Personnel : About 11,000 all ranks, navy and marine infantry (enlisted men).

Mercantile Marine : 257 steamers of about 332,400 tons ; 436 sailing of about 73,000 tons.

Principal Trade Ports : Rotterdam, Amsterdam, Flushing.

Coinage : Guilder (or florin) (100 cents) = 1s. 8d. British, or 40 cents U.S.A.

Oversea Possessions : Dutch East Indies (Sumatra, Java, Borneo, etc.) ; Dutch Guiana (Surinam) ; Curaçoa.

Minister of Marine : G. Kruijs.

2 U

K. REGENTES.   *Photo, Leijer.*
(The other two identical except that they have main top masts).

Photos by R. Ross, Esq.

TROMP (1905), & "N" (building).
Displacement 5300 tons.   Complement 344.
Length, 331 feet. Beam, 48 feet. *Maximum* draught, 18½ feet.

KONINGIN REGENTES (1900), **DE RUYTER** (1901), & **HERTOG HENDRIK** (1902).
Displacement 4950 tons.   Complement 320.
Length, 312 feet. Beam, 48 feet. *Maximum* draught, 18 feet.

Guns—(M. '01):
  2—9·4 inch, 40 cal. (*AA*).
  4—6 inch, 40 cal. (*E*).
  12—12 pdr.
  4—1 pdr.
Torpedo tubes (18 in.):
  2 *submerged.*
  1 *above water* (bow).

Armour (Krupp):
  6" Belt (amidships) .... *a*
  4" Belt (ends) .... *d*
  2" Deck (reinforcing belt)......
  Protection to vitals ....= *aa*
  8" Barbettes (N.C.) .... *a*
  4" Hoods to these ....*d*
  3" Small turrets ....*e*
  10" Conning tower ....*aa*

Guns—(M. '99):
  2—9·4 inch, 40 cal. (*A*).
  4—6 inch, 40 cal. (*E*).
  8—12 pdr.
  2—1 pdr.
Torpedo tubes (18 in.):
  2 *submerged.*
  1 *above water* (bow).

Armour (Krupp):
  6" Belt (amidships) .... *a*
  4" Belt (ends)................... *d*
  2" Deck (reinforcing belt).....
  Protection to vitals ....= *aa*
  10" Barbettes..................*aa*
  4" Hoods to these ....*d*
  10" Conning tower (fore) ......*aa*

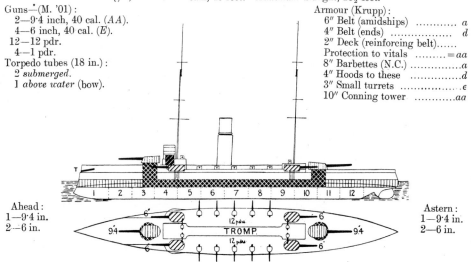

Ahead:
1—9·4 in.
2—6 in.

Astern:
1—9·4 in.
2—6 in.

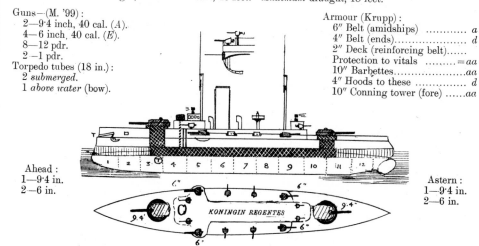

Ahead:
1—9·4 in.
2—6 in.

Astern:
1—9·4 in.
2—6 in.

Broadside: 2—9·4 in., 2—6 in.

Machinery: 2 sets triple expansion. 2 screws. Boilers: 6 Yarrow. Designed H.P. 6000 = 16·5 kts.

Trials ('06).—Tromp, 6,469 I.H.P. = 16·83 kts.

Machinery: 2 sets triple expansion. 2 screws. Boilers: Yarrow. Designed H.P. 5300 = 16 kts.
Coal: *normal*   tons; *maximum* 680 tons.
Notes.—The belt is 5¾ feet wide, and 4 feet of it is below the waterline.

EVERTSEN.   (Now carries top gallant masts).

EVERTSEN (1894), **PIET HEIN** (1894), **KORTENAAR** (1894)

Displacement 3520 tons.   Complement 260.

Length, 284 feet.   Beam 47 feet.   *Maximum* draught, 19 feet.

Guns :
3 - 8·2 inch, 35 cal. (*E*).
2 - 6 inch (*F*).
6 - 12 pdr. (*F*).
6 - 1 pdr.
Torpedo tubes :
2 *above water.*

Armour (Harvey) :
6″ Belt (amidships) c
4″ Belt (ends) .... d
2¼″ Deck (flat on belt)......
Protection to vitals ......=e
9½″ Barbette (1) .... a
6″ Hood to this............. c
6″ 8 inch shield c
3″ 6 inch sponsons .... ε
9½″ Conning tower (fore) a

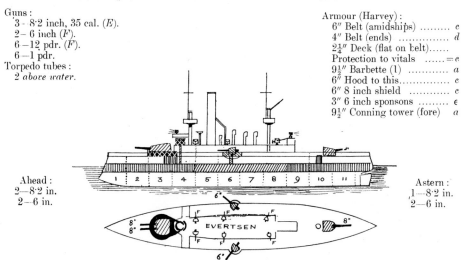

Ahead :
2—8·2 in.
2—6 in.

Astern :
1—8·2 in.
2—6 in.

Broadside : 3—8·2 in., 1—6 in.

Machinery : 2 sets triple expansion.   2 screws.   Boilers : cylindrical.   Designed I.H.P. *forced* 4800 = 16 kts.   Coal : 250 tons.

Notes.—The belt is 5¾ feet wide.

K. WILHELMINA DER NEDERLANDEN.

Photo, Geiser.

KONINGIN WILHELMINA DER NEDERLANDEN (1892) (1899)

Sheathed and coppered.   Displacement 4600 tons.   Complement

Length, 328 feet.   Beam, 49¼ feet.   Draught, 21¼ feet.

Guns (Krupp) :
1—11 inch, 35 cals. (*D*).
1—8·2 inch, 35 cals. (*E*).
2—6·8 inch, 22 cals. (*F*).
4—12 pdr. (*F*).
6—1 pdr.
4 machine.
Torpedo tubes :
4 *above water.*

Armour (steel) :
3″ Deck ....=ε
[Cellulose belt].
6″ Engine hatches ....=b
11″ B gun turret .... b
4″ Hoists to it .... ε
11″ Conning tower .... b

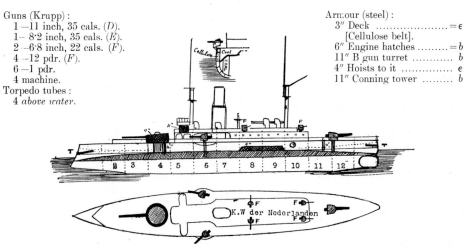

Machinery : 4 sets vertical triple expansion (new in 1899).   2 screws.   Boilers (new 1899): cylindrical.   Designed I.H.P. *forced* 5900 = 17 kts. (which she can make).   Coal : 450 tons.

(HOLLAND CLASS—6 SHIPS.)

GELDERLAND, NOORDBRABANT, & UTRECHT (all 1898).

Displacement 3950 tons.

Length, 311¾ feet. Beam, 48¼ feet. *Maximum* draught, 17¾ feet.

also

HOLLAND, ZEELAND, & FRIESLAND (all 1896).

Displacement 3900 tons.

Length, 305 feet. Beam, 48¼ feet. *Maximum* draught, 17¾ feet.

Guns :
 2—6 inch, 40 cal. (*E*).
 6—4·7 inch (*F*).
 4—12 pdr. (*F*).
 8—1 pdr.
 4 Machine.
Torpedo tubes :
 4 *above water.*
 Gelderland class have the
bow tube *submerged.*

Armour (steel and Harvey) :
 2″ Deck (steel) .... = ϵ
 4″ Engine hatches ....
 6″ Gun shields ....
 4″ Conning tower .... *d*

Signal letter for class :

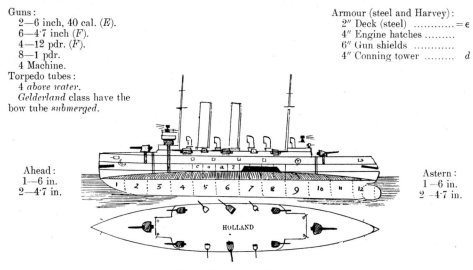

Ahead :
1—6 in.
2—4·7 in.

Astern :
1—6 in.
2—4·7 in.

Broadside : 2—6 in., 3—4·7 in.

Machinery : 2 sets 3 cylinder triple expansion. 2 screws. Boilers : *Gelderland* class, Yarrow; *Holland* class, 8 Yarrow and 2 cylindrical. Designed H.P. 10,000 = 20 kts. Coal : *normal* 450 tons; *maximum* 970 tons.

Name.		Trials (*4 hours*, 1897-1900) :		
Holland	I.H.P. 11,712 = 20 kts.	10,548 = 19·6 kts.	6236 = 16·9 kts.
Zeeland	„ 10,589 = 20 „	9818 = 19·4 „	5203 = 16·46 „
Friesland	„ 10,850 = 20 „	10,416 = 19·87 „	5982 = 17·27 „
Gelderland	„ 10,067 = 20·1 „	9867 = 20 „	
Noordbrabant	„ 10,667 = 20 „	9323 = 19·8 „	
Utrecht	„ 10,167 = 19·6 „	7311 = 17·9 „	

Differences.—

Name.	Steam pipes.	Notes.
Holland	Abaft funnels.	
Zeeland	None.	
Friesland	Before gunnery and 1 abaft fore funnel.	Conspicuous cowls.
Gelderland	Both sides both funnels.	
Noordbrabant	None.	
Utrecht	Very short abaft each funnel.	

Notes.—These ships are said to contain some of the best workmanship ever put into 4000-ton cruisers, both in construction and internal arrangements. They are good sea boats and fast, except in a seaway, when, being short, their speed falls off at once. Coal consumption usually heavy.

DUTCH MISCELLANEOUS.

Harbour Monitor.

REINIER CLAESZEN (1891). 2490 tons.

Guns (old): 1—8·2 inch, 35 cal., 1—6·7 inch, 35 cal., 4—6 pdr., 3—1 pdr.   Torpedo tubes: *2 above water.*
Designed H.P. 2000 = 12·5 kts.   Coal: *normal* 90 tons: *maximum* 160 tons.

SUMATRA (1890).   1700 tons.

Guns (old): 1—8·2 inch, 35 cal., 1—6 in., 35 cal., 2—4·7 in., 6—3 pdr.   Torpedo tubes: *2 above water.*
Armour: 1½″ steel deck amidships.   Designed H.P. 3000 = 17 kts. (present speed much less).   Coal: 170 tons.

There are also 2 very old monitors (*Draak* class) and 4 others (*Luipard* class), 2000-1500 tons, all of no fighting value.   Also several corvettes and a great number of small gunboats for police duties, etc., etc.

DUTCH TORPEDO BOATS.

4+9 *Yarrow*. **Ophir, Pangrango, Rindjani,** (1901), **Smeroe, Tangka, Wajang, Minotaurus, Python, Sfinx,** (1903), and *4 completing* (1904-05), 140 tons.   Speed, 25 kts.   Coal: 30 tons.   Armament: 2—3 pdr., and 3 Torpedo tubes (14 inch), (2 broadside and 1 stern).   *Maximum* draught, 7½ feet.

2 *Yarrow*.   **Hydra, Scylla** (1900).   90 tons.   Speed, 24 kts.   Armament: 2—3 pdr., and 3 tubes (14 inch *Maximum* draught, 6 feet.   Coal: 18 tons.

17 old boats dating 1894-1886, 90-45 tons and all under 20 kt. present speed.   Tubes: usually 2 fixed in bow (*submerged*) and 1 training aft.   Also 23 boats of 37-29 tons and very small speed, dating from 1890-1878.

SPANISH FLEET.

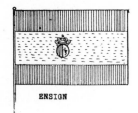

ENSIGN

ADMIRAL

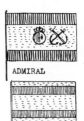

MERCANTILE

REAR or VICE

COMMODORE

Yellow
Red
Blue

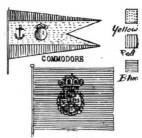

ROYAL STANDARD

Principal Naval Guns

(Schneider-Canet, or similar models made at Hontoria).

Nota-tion.	Nominal Calibre.		Model.	Length in calibres	Weight of Gun.	Weight of A.P. shell.	Initial velocity	Max. penetration A.P. capped direct impact at K.C. at		Danger Space against average ship, at			Rounds per minute.
								5000 yards.	3000 yards.	10,000 yards.	5000 yards.	3000 yards.	
	c/m.	inches.			tons.	lbs.	ft. secs.	inches.	inches.				
AA	32	12·5	...	35	47½	1036	2034	8	11	...	...	...	...
B	28	11	...	35	32½	837	2034	5½	8	...	...	...	...
AA	28	10·8	...	40	30	507	2625	8½	11¾	110	420	720	0·5
A	24	9·4	...	40	17	318	2625	7¼	9½	110	350	620	1
C	24	9·4	...	35	21	439	2034	4	6¼	60	250	500	0·5
F	15	5·9	...	45	4½	88	2625	...	3	25	200	430	5—6
	7·5	3	...	50	...	13·2	2658	...	...	...	...	...	...

Torpedoes.

Schwartzkopf, 18 inch and 14 inch.

SPANISH IDENTIFICATION AND SIGNAL SILHOUETTES.

S cone.

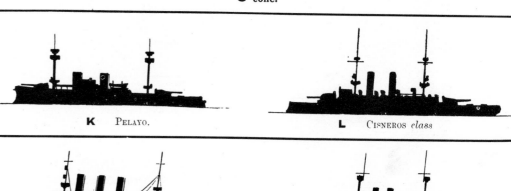

K   PELAYO.

L   CISNEROS class

M   CARLOS V.

N   LEPANTO.

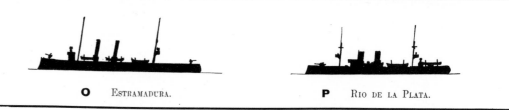

O   ESTRAMADURA.

P   RIO DE LA PLATA.

Q   D. MARIA DE MOLINA class.

R   NUEVA ESPANA class.

PELAYO (1887).

Displacement 9950 tons.   Complement 621.

Length, 330 feet.   Beam, 66 feet.   *Maximum* draught, 28½ feet.

Guns :
2—12·6 inch, 35 cal.
2—11 inch, 35 cal.
9—5·5 inch, 45 cal.
12—2 pdr.
9—1 pdr.
2 machine.
Torpedo tubes :
7 *above water.*

Armour (steel) :
16″ Belt (amidships) ......*aa*
12″ Belt (ends).............. *a*
3½″ Deck (flat below belt).
Protection to vitals ... =*aaaa*
16″ Barbettes ....*aa*
2″ Hoods to these........... *f*
3″ Battery (Harvey)......... *ε*

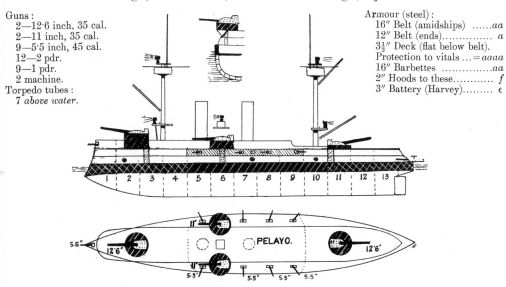

Machinery : 2 sets vertical compound.   2 screws.   Boilers : 16 Niclausse (in 4 groups).   Designed H.P. 7996=16 kts.   Coal · *normal* 500 tons ; *maximum* 667 tons.   On *trial* (1898) she made for 10 hours, I.H.P. 8000=16·1 kts.

Note.—Built at La Seyne.   Reconstructed there in 1897.

(Cisneros Class—2 Ships).   *Photo, Symonds.*

PRINCESA DE ASTURIAS (1896) & **CATALUNA** (1900).

Displacement 7000 tons.   Complement 497.

Length (*p.p.*), 348 feet.   Beam, 60¼ feet.   *Maximum* draught, 25 feet.

Guns :
2— 9·4 inch.
8— 5·5 inch.
2—12 pdr.
8— 6 pdr.
8— 3 pdr.
Torpedo tubes :
2 *above water.*

Armour (Harvey) :
12″ Belt (amidships) ......*aa*
6″ Belt (forward) .... *c*
8″ Belt (aft) .... *b*
2¾″ Deck (flat on belt).....
Protection to vitals is ......*aa*
12″ Bulkheads ....*aa*
8″ Barbettes .... *b*
4″ Hoists to these........... *d*
2¾″ Casemates(chrome steel) ε
8″ Conning tower (fore) ... *b*

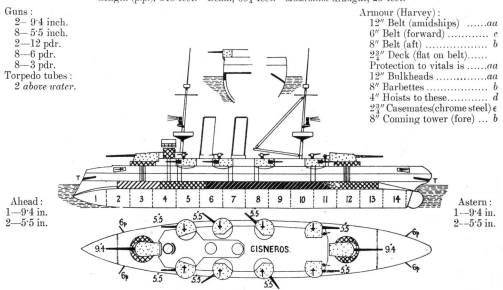

Ahead :
1—9·4 in.
2—5·5 in.

Astern :
1—9·4 in.
2—5·5 in.

Broadside : 2—9·4 in., 4—5·5 in.

Machinery : 2 sets horizontal triple expansion.   2 screws.   Boilers : cylindrical.   Designed H.P. *natural* 10,000=18 kts. ; *forced* 15,000=20·25 kts.   Coal : *normal* 750 tons ; *maximum* 1200 tons.

Note.—The belt is 5¼ feet wide and 230 feet long.   The ships took over 13 years to complete.   *Cisneros* wrecked, 1905.

EMPERADOR CARLOS V. (1895). Displacement 9200 tons. Complement 600.

Length, 403 feet. Beam, 67 feet. *Maximum* draught, 28½ feet.

Guns :
2—9·4 inch.
8—5·5 inch.
4—4 inch.
2—12 pdr.
8—6 pdr.
8—1 pdr.
2 machine.
Torpedo tubes :
6 *above water.*

Armour (Creusot special) :
2¼″ Deck .... = ε
Protection to vitals ... = ε
10″ Barbettes .... *a*
4″ Hoods to these...... = *d*
8″ Hoists .... *b*
2″ Battery................. *f*
12″ Conning tower ... *aa*

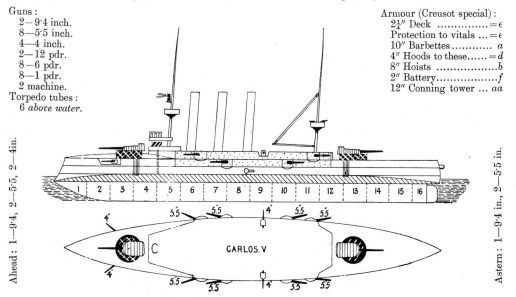

Ahead : 1—9·4, 2—5·5, 2—4in.

Astern : 1—9·4 in., 2—5·5 in.

Broadside : 2—9·4 in., 4—5·5 in., 2—4 in.

Machinery : 2 sets 4 cylinder triple expansion. 2 screws. Boilers : cylindrical. Designed H.P. *natural* 15,000 = 19 kts. ; *forced* 18,500 = 20 kts. Coal : *normal* 1200 tons ; *maximum* 2000 tons.

Note.—She cannot steam at anything like the designed speed now.

Building.
Laid down 1899.

REINA REGENTE (*building*). Displacement 5372 tons. Complement 497.

Length, 338 feet. Beam, 52½ feet. *Maximum* draught, 19½ feet.

Guns :
10—5·5 inch.
12—6 pdr.
2—1 pdr.

Armour :
3¼″ Deck.
3¼″ Conning tower

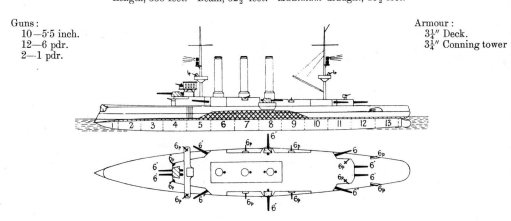

Machinery : 2 sets triple expansion. 2 screws. Boilers : (not yet decided). Designed H.P. 15,000 = 21 kts.

Lepanto. (Present rig.)

LEPANTO (1892).

Displacement 4826 tons. Complement 420.

Length, 328 feet. Beam, 50½ feet. *Maximum* draught, 24 feet.

Guns:
  4—6·4 inch (Hont.)
  6—4·7 inch (Canet).
  6—6 pdr.
  6—1 pdr.
  2 Machine.
Torpedo tubes:
  2 *above water.*

Armour (steel):
  4½″ Deck .... = c
  [Cellulose belt].
  Protection to vitals......... = c
  3″ Shields ....

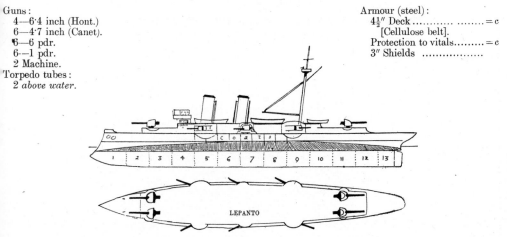

LEPANTO

Machinery: 2 sets triple expansion. 2 screws. Boilers: cylindrical. Designed H.P. *forced* 11,500 = 20·5 kts. Coal: *normal* 575 tons; *maximum* 1433 tons.

No Photo yet taken.

ESTRAMADURA (1900), & PORTO RICO (1902).

Displacement 2030 tons. Complement 260.

Length, 288 feet. Beam, 36 feet. *Maximum* draught, 14½ feet.

Guns:
  4—5·5 inch (Hont.)
  4—4 in. (Krupp).
  2—12 pdr.
  4—6 pdr.
  4—1 pdr.
Torpedo tubes:
  None.

Armour:
  1¼″ Deck ....

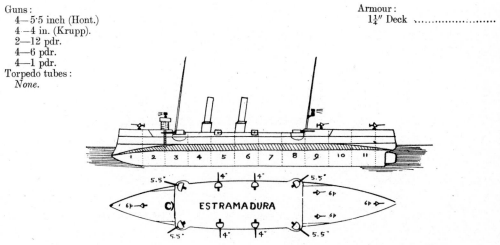

ESTRAMADURA

Machinery: 2 screws. Boilers: cylindrical. Designed H.P. *natural* 4500; *forced* 7800 = 18 kts.
Coal: *maximum* 210 tons.

SPANISH CRUISERS.

RIO DE LA PLATE (Havre, 1898), & *GENERAL LINARES* (*building*).

Displacement 1713 tons. Complement 213.

Length, 246 feet. Beam, 35½ feet. Draught, 16 feet.

Guns :
  2—5·5 inch, 35 cal.
  4—4 inch.
  6—6 pdr.
  4—1 pdr.
  2 Machine.
Torpedo tubes :
  Nil.

Armour (steel) :
  1¼″ Deck.
  [Cellulose belt.]

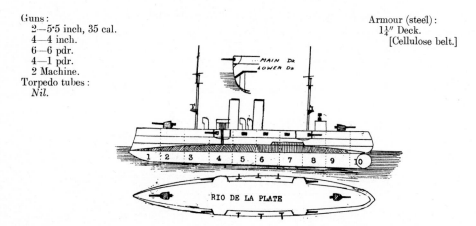

RIO DE LA PLATE

Machinery : 2 sets vertical triple expansion. 2 screws. Boilers : Normand-Sigaudy. Designed H.P. 6793 = 20 kts. Coal : *normal* 200 tons ; *maximum* 260 tons.

SPANISH TORPEDO GUNBOATS.

DONA MARIA DE MOLINA (1896), MARQUES DE LA VICTORIA (1897), DON ALVARO DE BAZAN (1897).

Displacement 830 tons. Complement 89.

Guns :
  2—4 inch. .
  4—3 pdr.
  2 Gatlings.
Torpedo tubes :
  1 *submerged* (bow).
  2 *above water.*

Armour (steel) :
  6″ Conning tower ......*d*

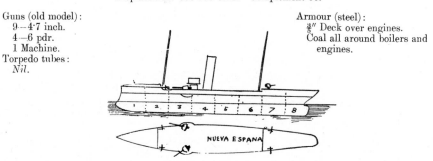

MARIA DE MOLINA

Machinery : 2 sets vertical triple expansion. 2 screws. Boilers : locomotive. Designed H.P. *natural* 2500 = 17 kts. ; *forced* 3500 = 19·5 kts. Coal : *normal* 120 tons.

NUEVA ESPANA (1889), & MARQUIS DE MOLINS (1892).

Displacement 630-570 tons. Complement 80.

Guns (old model) :
  9—4·7 inch.
  4—6 pdr.
  1 Machine.
Torpedo tubes :
  Nil.

Armour (steel) :
  ⅗″ Deck over engines.
  Coal all around boilers and engines.

NUEVA ESPANA

Machinery : 2 sets vertical triple expansion. 2 screws. Boilers : 2 locomotive + 2 cylindrical. Designed H.P. *forced* 2600 = 19·20 kts. Coal : *normal* 106 tons ; *maximum* 130 tons.

DESTRUCTOR (1886).

Displacement 386 tons. Complement 45.

Guns :
1—3·5 inch.
4 —6 pdr.
2 Nordenfelts.
Torpedo tubes (15 inch):
3 *above water*.

Armour (steel) :
1⅕″ Bulkhead (forward)
¾″ Bulkhead (aft)
Coal round engines.
39 compartments.

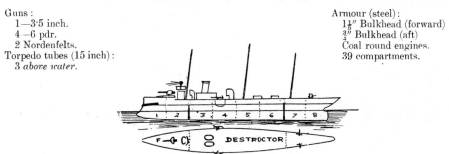

Machinery : 2 sets vertical triple expansion. 2 screws. Boilers : (1898) 4 Normand. Designed H.P. 3800 = 20·2 kts. (she has reached as much as 22·6 kts. on *trial*). Coal : *normal* 45 tons ; *maximum* 110 tons.

Note.—Built at Clydebank.

Destroyers.

1 Terror ....(1896)	450 tons.	I.H.P. 6000 = 28 kts	Boilers : Normand.	Speed now 15 kts.
2 Audaz and Osada (1897)	430 „	„ 7500 = 30 „	„ Normand.	„ once 28 „
1 Proserpine ....(1897)	460 „	„ 7500 = 30 „	„ Normand.	„ „ 28 „

$$\underline{4}$$

All built at Clydebank. All armed with 2—14 pdr., 2—6 pdr., and 2—1 pdr., and 2 torpedo tubes

Torpedo Boats.

9 old boats, 127-65 tons of no fighting value.

Submarine.

There is an old boat *Peral*, of no utility.

In addition to the ships illustrated the Spanish Navy contains an old unprotected cruiser. *Infanta Isabel*, 1152 tons. Armament 4 -4·7 inch (old). Designed H.P. 1500 = 13 kts., and 6 gunboats of 500—200 tons.

PORTUGUESE FLEET.

ENSIGN

JACK

ROYAL STANDARD

ADMIRAL

VICE ADMIRAL

REAR ADMIRAL

REAR ADMIRAL NOT COMMANDER IN CHIEF

COMMODORE

SENIOR OFFICER

Blue

White

Red

Yellow

P cone.

Indentification and Signal Silhouettes.

H Vasco da Gama.

I Dom Carlos.

J Adamastor.

K R. D. Amelia.

L S. Gabriel *class.*

Base: (1) Lisbon, 4 small docks.

Mercantile Marine: 44 steamers of 29,443 tons, 238 sailing of 56,588 tons.

Minister of Marine: A. de Sousa.

Trade Ports: Lisbon and Oporto.

Oversea Possessions: Cape Verde Islands, Guinea (Senegambia), St. Thomas (W.I.), Timor (Malaysia), Goa, Damao and Diu (India), Macao (China), Angola (Congo), Portuguese East Africa.

Coinage: Milreis 1000 reis)=4s. 5d. British, $1.06 U.S.A. ; 4500 reis=£1 English.

VASCO DA-GAMA.

Displacement 2500 tons. Complement 242.

Length, 230 feet. Beam, 46 feet. *Maximum* draught, 20 feet.

Guns (new armament):
2—8 inch
1—6 inch
1—12 pdr.
6—3 pdr.
Torpedo tubes:
2 *submerged.*

Armour (iron):
9″-7″ Belt .... *d-e*
3″ Deck (flat on it).
Protection to vitals = *d*
8″ Barbettes (Terni) *a*

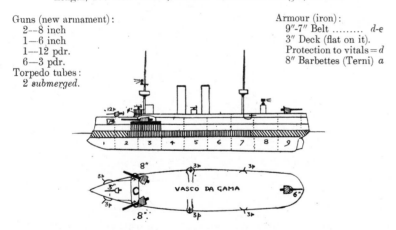

Machinery: 2 sets.
Designed H.P. (new):

2 screws. Boilers (1901-02): Yarrow
=   kts. Coal: 300 tons.

Notes.—Launched at Blackwall, 1875. Reconstructed and lengthened at Livorno 1902-3.

DOM CARLOS I. (1898).

Displacement 4100 tons. Complement 473.

Length, 360 feet. Beam, 46½ feet. *Mean* draught, 17½ feet.

Guns:
4—6 inch, 45 cal.
8—4·7 inch, 45 cal.
12—3 pdr.
10—1 pdr.
Torpedo tubes:
2 *submerged.*
3 *above water.*

Armour (steel):
4½″ Deck .... = *b*
[Cofferdam amidships.]
4″ Conning tower... *d*

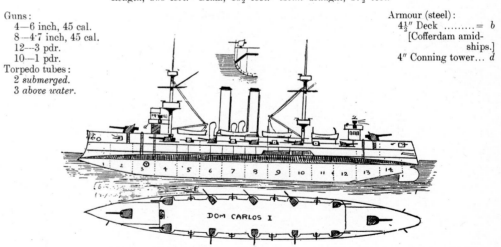

Machinery: 2 sets 4 cylinder triple expansion. 2 screws. Boilers: 12 Yarrow. Designed H.P. *forced,* 12,500 = 22 kts. Coal: 700 tons.

Notes.—On 4 hours *trial* I.H.P. 12,690 = 22·15 kts.

Photo, Symonds.

RAINHA DONA AMELIA (1899).

Displacement 1665 tons.   Complement 250.

Length, 243 feet.   Beam, 33 feet.   *Maximum* draught, $15\frac{1}{4}$ feet.

Guns (Canet):
   4—6 inch, 45 cal.
   4—4 inch, 45 cal.
   2—3 pdr.
Torpedo tubes:
   2 *above water.*

Armour (steel):
   $1\frac{1}{5}''$ Deck.
   $2\frac{1}{2}''$ Conning tower.

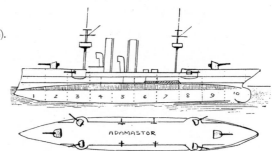

Machinery: 2 sets vertical triple expansion. 2 screws. Boilers: Normand Sigaudy. Designed H.P. 5400=18 kts.   Coal:

ADAMASTOR (1896).

Displacement 1750 tons.   Complement 237.

Length, 243 feet.   Beam, 35 feet.   *Maximum* draught, 16 feet.

Guns:
   2—6 inch.
   4—4·7 inch.
   4—6 pdr.
   4 Machine.
Torpedo tubes:
   3 *above water*
      (bow and broadside).

Armour:
   $1\frac{1}{5}''$ Deck.
   $2\frac{1}{2}''$ Conning tower.

Machinery: 2 sets vertical triple expansion. 2 screws. Boilers: 4 cylindrical. Designed H.P. *natural* 3000=16 kts.; *forced* 4000=18 kts. Coal: *normal* 220 tons; *maximum* 420 tons. *Note.*—Built at Leghorn.

SÃO GABRIEL & SÃO RAFAEL. (1898).

Displacement 1800 tons.   Complement

Length, 246 feet.   Beam, 35⅓ feet.   *Maximum* draught 16 feet.

Guns (Canet):
2--6 inch.
4--4·7 inch.
8—3 pdr.
2 Machine.
Torpedo tubes:
1 *above water* (bow).

Armour:
1⅕″ Deck ....
2½″ Conning tower.........

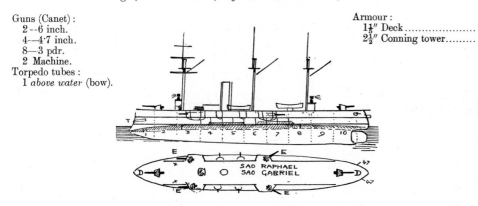

Machinery: 2 sets triple expansion. . 2 screws.   Boilers: Normand-Sigaudy.   Designed H.P. 4000 = 17 kts.

Both built at Havre.

Destroyer.

TEJO (1902).   Displacement 530 tons.

Guns:
1—4 inch.
1—9 pdr.
4—3 pdr.
Torpedo tubes:
2 *above water.*

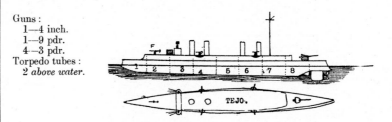

Designed H.P. 7000 = 25 kts.

OTHER   SHIPS :—

Alfonso de Albuquerque (1884) 1100 tons.   Guns: two 6 in., five 5in.   Speed originally 13 kts.
Reinha de Portugal (1875), 1120 tons.   Guns: two 7 in. M.L., four 5 in. M.L.   Speed: 13·5 kts. (Composite.)

Gunboats.

	Guns.		Nominal Speed.
Dom Luiz 1. (1895)....................................730 tons	2—4 in., 2—3 pdr		9 kts.
Liberal & Laire (1884)................................560 ,,	1—6 in. B.L., 2—4 in.		10 ,,
Bengo & Maudavi (1879) ....460 ,,	2—6 in. B.L., 2—3½ in. B.L.		10 ,,
Cacongo & Massabi (1886) ....276 ,,			11 ,,
Rio Ave (1880) ....378 ,,	1—4 in. B.L., 2—3 in. B.L.		11 ,,
Limpopo (1890)...320 ,,	1—9 pdr.		11 ,,
Vilhena (1882) ....160 ,,	1—3 in. M.L.		10 ,,
Vouga (1882) ....720 ,,	2—4 in. B.L., 2—3 pdr.		10 ,,
Thomas Andrea..⎫ 230 ,,	2--3 pdr.		12 ,,
Baptisa de Andrade ....⎭			
Chaimite...375 ,,	2—3 pdr.		11 ,,

These draw from 13 feet for the larger to 8½ feet for the smaller.

There are also 3 or 4 composite and wooden gunboats; and 23 river gunboats and 12 old torpedo boats of no fighting value.

TURKISH FLEET.

ENSIGN

MINISTER OF MARINE

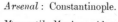

VÉZIR (ADMIRAL)

BALA (VICE ADMIRAL)

OULA (REAR ADMIRAL)

COMMODORE

IMPERIAL STANDARD

Red ▨   **White** ☐

Arsenal : Constantinople.

Mercantile Marine : About 100 steamers (58,000 tons) and 900 sailing (180,000 tons).

Principal Ports : Trebizond, Smyrna, Alexandretta, Beyrût, Basra, Jaffa, Tripoli (Africa).

Oversea Possessions : Tripoli.

Coinage : Lira (Medjidié) of 100 piastres = 18s. British, $4·28 U.S.A.   One piastre (4 cents U.S.A.) = *about* 2d. British.

Personnel : 31,000 all ranks and 9000 marines.

Minister of Marine : Djelal Bey.

T cone.   TURKISH   IDENTIFICATION   AND   SIGNAL   SILHOUETTES.

M   MEDJIDIEH *class.*

O   MESSUDIYEH.

P   PELENK-I-DERIA *class.*

V   FETH-I-BULEND *class.*

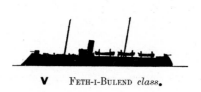

X   AZIZIEH *class.*

352

Photo by favour of C. de Grare Sells, Esq.

MESSUDIYEH (1874).

Reconstructed at Genoa, 1902.
Displacement 9120 tons.   Complement 600.
Length, 331 feet.   Beam, 59 feet.   *Maximum* draught, 27 feet.

Guns (Vickers) :
  2—9·2 inch, 40 cal. (*A*).
  12—6 inch, 45 cal. (D).
  14—12 pdr. (*F*).
  10—6 pdr.
  2—3 pdr.
  2 Field (14 pdr.)

Armour (iron) :
  12″ Belt......................... *c*
  1½″ Deck (flat on belt)......
  Protection to vitals is ...... *c*
  12″ Battery .... *c*
  3″ Barbettes (Terni) ...... *d*

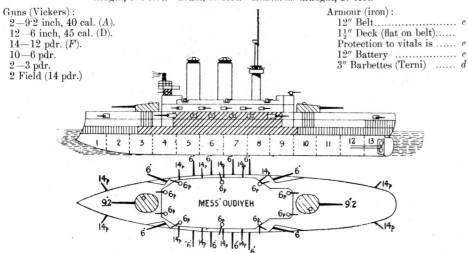

Machinery : 2 sets inverted triple expansion, 4 cylinder. 2 screws. Boilers : 16 Niclausse in 4 compartments. Designed H.P. 11,000 = 16 kts.

Note.—The old armour remains, except for the barbettes and the special protection to steering gear, &c., aft.

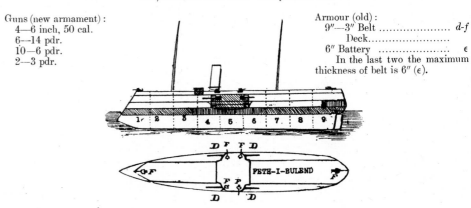

Reconstructing.
Work on all except Mukadem-i-Hair commenced early in 1903.

FETH-I-BULEND (1870), & MUKADEM-I-HAIR (1872).

Displacement 2720 tons.   Complement 220.

MUIN-I-ZAFFER & AVNI-ILLAH (1869).

Displacement 2330 tons.   Complement 220.

Guns (new armament) :
  4—6 inch, 50 cal.
  6—14 pdr.
  10—6 pdr.
  2—3 pdr.

Armour (old) :
  9″—3″ Belt .... *d-f*
  Deck.......................
  6″ Battery .... ϵ
  In the last two the maximum thickness of belt is 6″ (ϵ).

Machinery : Horizontal engines. Boilers (new) : double-ended cylindrical. Designed H.P. : *Feth-i-Bulend* type, 3250 ; *Muin-i-Zaffer* type, 2220.

Note.—Reconstructing at Constantinople by Ansaldo & Cie., of Genoa.

MEDJIDIEH (1903), & **ABDUL HAMID** (1904).

Displacement 3277 tons.   Complement 302.

Length, 330 feet.   Beam, 42 feet.   *Maximum* draught, 15½ feet.

Guns :
2—6 inch.
6—4·7 inch.
2—3 pdr.
2—1 pdr.
Torpedo tubes (15 in.):
3 *above water.*

Armour :
2″ Deck ………

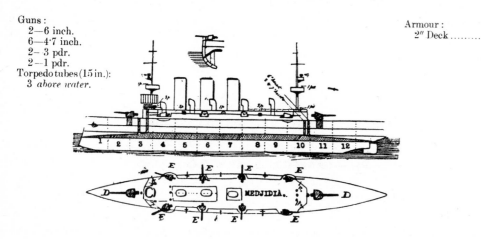

Signal letter for class : M.   ABDUL HAMID.

Machinery : 2 sets 4 cylinder triple expansion.   2 screws.   Boilers : *Medjidieh*, 16 Niclausse. Designed I.H.P. 12,000 = 22 kts. (*forced draught*) (190 revs.).   Coal : *normal* 275 tons ; *maximum* 600 tons.   *Abdul Hamid* on trial did 22·25 kts. on measured mile, and 21·1 kts. *mean* speed 6 hours trial at N.D.

Gunnery Notes.—Hoists for 4·7's are three in a row abreast end guns

Torpedo Notes.—Position of torpedo tubes uncertain, *probably* in section 3.

Engineering Notes.   Heating surface 27,882 square feet, grate surface 775 square feet.   Steam pressure 275 lbs.   Screws 3-bladed.   The full coal supply immerses the ship 12 in. more.

Differences.—*Medjidieh* has higher ventilators than *Abdul Hamid.*

354

TURKEY.

PELENK-I-DERIA & NAMET (1890).

Displacement 900 tons.

Guns (Krupp):
2—4 inch.
6—3 pdr.
Torpedo tubes (T):
3 *above water*.

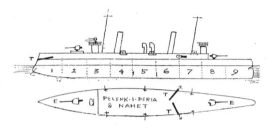

Machinery: 2 sets triple expansion. 2 screws. Boilers: locomotive. Designed H.P. *forced* 4500 = 19 kts.

PELENK-I-DERIA.   *Photo, Symonds.*

Signal letter for class: P.

There is a torpedo gunboat **SHAHIN-I-DERIA**, 450 tons, *nominal* speed 22 kts.

Guns: 1—4 in. (Krupp), 6—3 pdr.

Destroyers.

(None able to do much).

2 (**Tajjar** & **Berk Efshan,** 1894) Schichau type. 250 tons. Speed *trial* 25 kts.

4+7 **Hamidijeh** & **Abdul-Mejid,** enlarged Italian *Condore* type (built by Ansaldo, Genoa, 1901. Yarrow boilers, speeds *trial* 27·1 and 27·4 kts.; 2 others, **Eliagot** & **Ac-Hisoar,** same type (1904), with locomotive boilers: and 7 others in construction by Ansaldo, Armstrong, at Sestri Ponente.

Torpedo Boats.

21 various—none of any fighting value.

OLD SHIPS.

HAMIDIEH.   *Photo, Abdullah.*

There are also ASSAR-I-TEWFIK, ORKANIEH, OSMAINIEH, AZIZIEH, MAH-MOUDIYEH and HAMIDIEH, all without any fighting value whatever. It was proposed to reconstruct them, but they have been found not worth it.

AZIZIEH, ORKANIEH, OSMANIEH, AND MAHMOUDIYEH.

355

2 Y 2

GREEK FLEET.

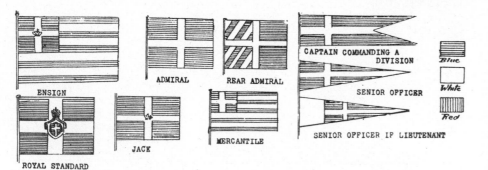

ENSIGN

ADMIRAL

REAR ADMIRAL

CAPTAIN COMMANDING A DIVISION

SENIOR OFFICER

Blue

White

Red

ROYAL STANDARD

JACK

MERCANTILE

SENIOR OFFICER IF LIEUTENANT

Arsenal : Piræus.

Mercantile Marine : 137 steamers of 115,000 tons, 927 sailing of about 184,000 tons.

Chief Ports : Piræus, Naxos.

Oversea trade chiefly with England, Russia, and Austria.

Oversea Possessions : Crete.

Coinage : Drachma (100 lepta) = about $9\frac{1}{2}$d. British, 18 cents U.S.A.

Personnel : About 4000 (conscript 2 years or enlistment).

Minister of Marine : M. Zygomalas.

O cone.

A HYDRA

B SPETSAI.

C PSARA (rig as changed 1901).

PSARA (1890), **SPETSAI** (1899), **HYDRA** (1889).

[Reconstructed at La Seyne : *Psara* (1897) ; *Spetsai and Hydra* (1899-1900).

Displacement 5000 tons.   Complement 440.

Length, 331 feet.   Beam, 52 feet.   *Maximum* draught, 24 feet.

Guns (Canet) :
  2—10·8 inch, 36 cals.
  1—10·8 inch, 30 cals.
  5—6 inch, 45 cals.
  1—4 inch, 50 cals.
  8—9 pdr.
  4—3 pdr.
  12—1 pdr.
Torpedo tubes :
  1 *above water* (bow)
  2 *above water.*

Armour (Creusot steel) :
  12″—4¾″ Belt (lower)......*a-d*
  3″ Belt (upper) .... *є*
  [Cellulose behind belt].
  2¼″ Deck (flat) ....
  Protection to vitals ......=*a*
  13¾″ Battery redoubt...... *aa*
  12″ Barbette (aft) .... *a*
  6″ Hood .... *d*
  6″ Hoists (B guns) .... *d*
  12″ Conning tower......... *a*
  [In *Hydra* deck is 2″ only].

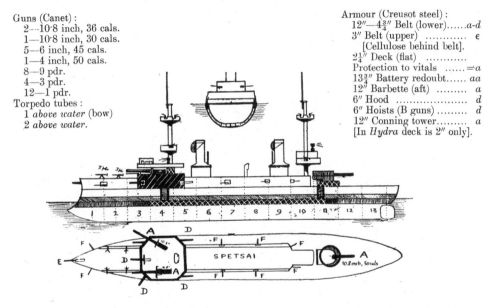

Machinery : 2 sets vertical triple expansion.   2 screws.   Boilers : cylindrical.   Designed H.P. 6700=17 kts. (on *trial*, 1890-1891, this was slightly exceeded).   Present speeds : *circa* 12 kts. or less. Coal : *normal* 400 tons ; *maximum* 600 tons.

Armour Notes.—The belt is 4 feet wide under water.   The upper belt is the same width.   The guns have flat shields to them, about 2″ thick.

(3 armoured cruisers and some torpedo craft are *projected*).

There are 20 old torpedo boats of no present fighting value ; also a few old gun boats.

HYDRA.   *Photo, Bar.*

(Spetsai identical except she has no steam pipe before fore funnel).

PSARA.   *Photo, Symonds.*

ROUMANIAN.

Personnel : About 1500.

CRUISER.

ELIZABETHA (Elswick, 1887).

1320 tons.   Complement 250.

Guns : 4 old 6 inch ; 4—6 pdr. ; 2—1 pdr ; 4 *above water* tubes.

Armour : 3″ Deck.

Designed I.H.P. 3000 = 18 kts.

(Now rigged as a full rigged ship and used for training.)

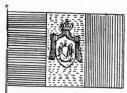

ROUMANIA ENSIGN

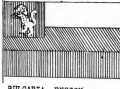

BULGARIA ENSIGN

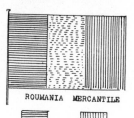

ROUMANIA MERCANTILE

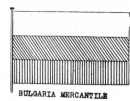

BULGARIA MERCANTILE

Blue   Red   Green   Yellow   White

BULGARIAN.

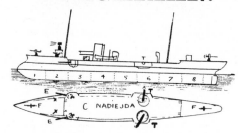

TORPEDO GUNBOAT

NADIEJDA (Bordeaux, 1898).

715 tons.   Draught 12½ feet.

Guns (Schneider-Canet) : 2—4 inch ; 2—9 pdr. ; 2—3 pdr.   2 *above water* torpedo tubes.

Designed H.P. 2600 = 17 kts.   (Did 18·85 kts. on trial.)   Boilers : Lagrafel d'Allest.   (Used as Royal Yacht.)

GUNBOATS.

Mircea, 360 tons, launched 1882. Guns : 2—14 pdr. ; 2—1 pdr. Speed, about 6 kts.
Bistritza, Olful, Gireful, Grivitza, all about 100 tons, launched 1880-88. Armed with 2—6 pdr. and 1—1 pdr. Speeds, 10 kts. *maximum.* (For Danube.)

TORPEDO BOATS.

4 Schichau boats (1894), 32 tons, 20 kts. ; 3 Yarrow boats (1895), 20 kts. ; 3 French boats (1888), 56 tons, 20 kts. ; and 2 old Yarrow (1882), 12 tons, and original speed 16·5 kts.

Projected : 6 armoured coast defence ships, 3500 tons.
8 Danube monitors, 500 tons.
4 destroyers, 300 tons.
12 torpedo boats, 80 tons.
12   „   „   40 tons.
8 torpedo launches, 12 tons.

Alexander 1. (1880).   Gunnery and torpedo school.   800 tons.   H.P. 700 = 11 kts. (paddle wheel)

Bsjen, Krum, Simeon, Veliki, of 600-400 tons.

TORPEDO BOATS.

2 old spar launches.   7 other launches.

Building : Two armoured gunboats for the Danube (Leghorn).

CHINESE FLEET.

Personnel: ?

Arsenals: (1) Foochow; (2) Taku; (3) Kiangnan, Shanghai; (4) Whampao.

Docks.		Feet.	
At (1)	*a*	480 × 78 × ?	Govt.
	b	330 × 54 × 16	Govt.
	c	390 × 55 × 15	Private.
At (2)	*a*	340 × 39 × 14	Govt.
	b	225 × 36 × 10	Private.

Docks.		Feet.	
At (3)	*a*	340 × 39 × 19	Govt.
	b	500 × 80 × 22	Private.
		400 × 57 × 11	Private.
		And three smaller.	
At (4)	*a*	500 × 85 × 14	Govt.
		350 × 59 × 18	Private.

K cone. CHINESE IDENTIFICATION AND SIGNAL SILHOUETTES.

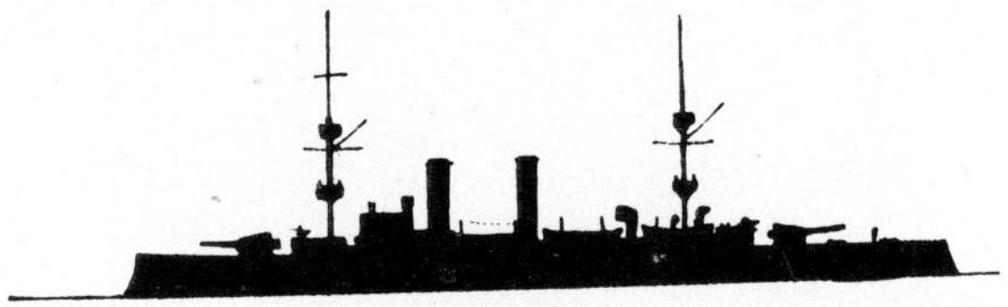

J HAI-CHI.

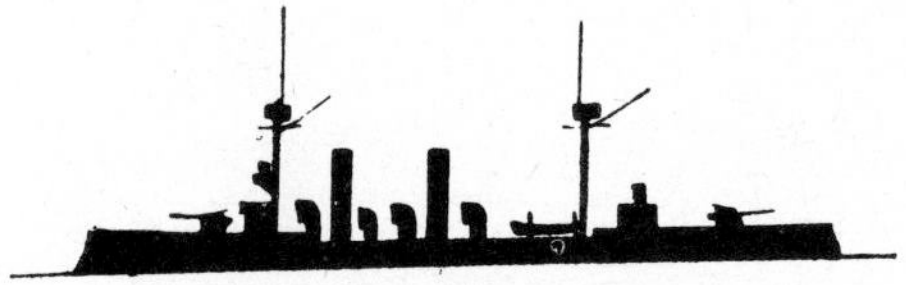

L HAI-YONG *class*.

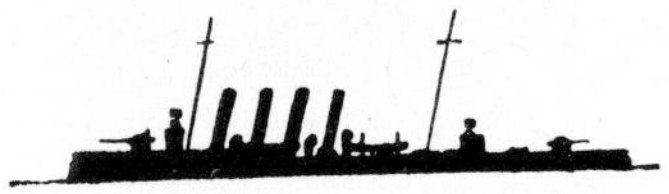

M FEI-YING.

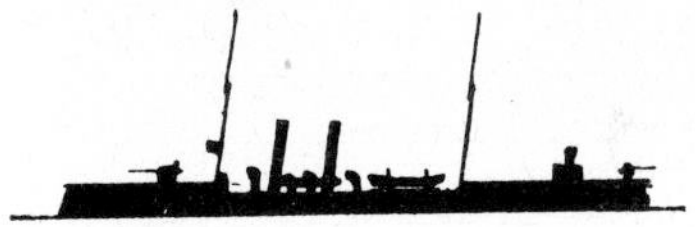

Q KEIN-WEI *class*.

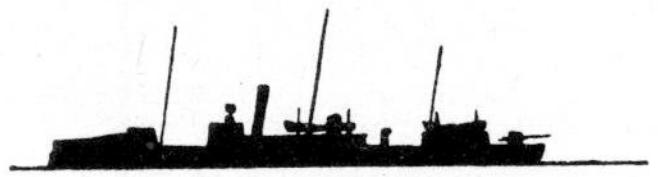

R KWANG-TING.

General Note.

The Chinese *personnel* is of small account owing to the inefficiency of most of its officers. A few officers are intelligent; the men are excellent fighting material. Under Commodore Sah the general efficiency is on a decided up-grade; and the popular idea that Chinese ships never cruise is quite incorrect.

CHINESE CRUISERS.

HAI YUNG.   (All three identical).

HAI-CHI (1898).

Displacement 4300 tons.   Complement, 450.

Length (over all), 396 feet.   Beam, 46½ feet.   *Mean* draught, 16¾ feet

HAI-YUNG (1897), HAI-SHEW (1897) & HAI-SHEN (1898).

Displacement 3000 tons.   Complement 244.

Length, 328 feet.   Beam, 41 feet.   *Maximum* draught, 16 feet.

Guns (Elswick):
2—8 inch.
10—4·7 inch.
12—3 pdr.
3—1 pdr.
6 Maxims.
Torpedo tubes (18 inch):
5 *above water*.

Armour (Harvey) :
5″ Deck................= b
4″ Hoists................ d
6″ Conning tower c
4½″ Gun shields ....

Guns (Krupp) :
3—6 inch, 40 cal.
8—4·1 inch.
6—1 pdr.
6 Maxims.
Torpedo tubes (14 inch) :
1 *submerged* (bow).
2 *above water* (section 9).

Armour :
2¾″ Deck (amidships)= d
2″ Gun shields ....
1¼″ Conning tower......

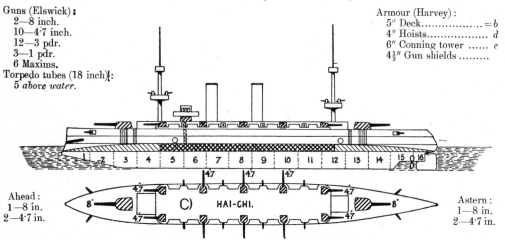

Ahead :
1—8 in.
2—4·7 in.

Astern :
1—8 in.
2—4·7 in.

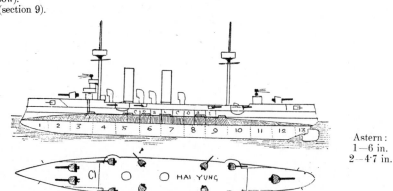

Ahead :
2—6 in.
2—4·7 in.

Astern :
1—6 in.
2—4·7 in.

Machinery : 2 sets triple expansion. 2 screws. Boilers : cylindrical. Designed H.P. *forced* 17,000 = 24 kts. Coal : *normal* 400 tons ; *maximum* 1000 tons.

Notes.—Slightly exceeded the contract speed on *trial*.   Electric hoists are fitted ; the 8 in. guns can also be electrically manœuvred.   Built at Elswick.   Sister *Hai Tien* wrecked 1904.

Machinery : 2 sets triple expansion. 2 screws. Boilers : cylindrical. Designed H.P. 7500 = 19·5 kts.
Coal : *normal* 200 tons ; *maximum* 500 tons.

Note.—Built at Stettin.

360

New cruisers *pro.* to replace Nan-Yin, Pao-Min, etc. (of Canton fleet), turned into hulks. (*Edict*, 1903) still projected.

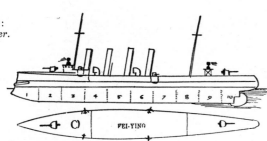

FEI-YING (1895).

Displacement 850 tons. Complement 90.

Guns (Krupp):
2—4·1 inch
6—6 pdr.
2—1 pdr.
Torpedo tubes:
3 *above water.*

Armour (steel):
2″ Gun shields.

Machinery: 2 screws. Boilers: 8 Yarrow. Designed H.P. 5500=22 kts. (exceeded on *trial*). Coal: 75 tons.

Note.—Built at Stettin.

Torpedo Craft.

KIEN-WEI (1901), & KIEN-NGAN (1902).

Displacement 871 tons.

Guns (Canet):
1—4 inch
3—9 pdr.
6—1 pdr.
Torpedo tubes:
2 *above water.*

Armour:
1″ Belt (amidships).
1″ Deck (amidships).

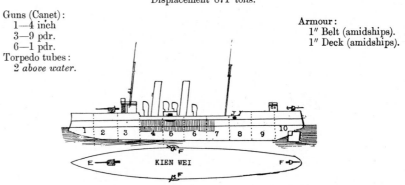

Machinery: 2 sets. 2 screws. Boilers: (?) Designed H.P. 7000=23 kts. (Machinery etc., made in France.)

KWANG-TING (1891). Displacement 1030 tons.

Guns (Krupp):
3—4·7 inch.
12 small.
Torpedo tubes:
4 *above water.*

Armour (steel):
1″ Deck.................
2″ Conning tower ...

Machinery: 2 sets horizontal compound. 2 screws. Boilers: cylindrical. Designed H.P. 2400=16·5 kts.

Torpedo Boats.

2 (Schichau, 1897), 120 tons, speed 24 kts.; 2 (Schichau, 1897), 100 tons, 24 kts.; 1 (Yarrow, 1887), 120 tons, 23 kts.; 1 (Yarrow, 1883); 2 (Schichau), 120 tons, 23 kts.; 5 small boats and 1 built at Foochow (1899), 30 tons, and 24 kts.

(Four destroyers and a torpedo gunboat Fei Ting were captured by the Allied Fleets at Taku, 1900.)

There are also a great many old gunboats, etc., including some Rendel gunboats armed with 11-inch M.L.

SIAMESE SHIPS.

CRUISER

MAHA CHAKRKRI (1902).

2500 tons.   Complement 318.

Guns:
4—4·7 inch.
16—6 pdr.
6 machine.

Armour:
2″ Deck ....

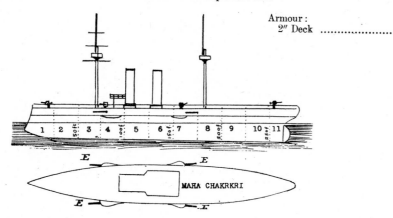

MAHA CHAKRKRI

Machinery : 2 sets triple expansion.   Designed I.H.P. 3000 = 15 kts.   Boilers : 5 cylindrical.
Coal : *normal* 280 tons.

Gunboats.

Bali & Sugrib (1901).   600 tons.   Guns : 1—4·7 in., 5—6 pdr.   H.P. 500 = 12 kts.

Murata (1898).   580 tons.   Guns : 1—4·7 in. B.L., 4—6 pdr., 5 machine.   Speed, 10 kts.

Mahut Rajakumar (1887).   500 tons.   Guns : 3—4·7 in. B.L., 4 machine.   Torpedo tube : 1 *above water.*   Designed H.P. 800 = 14 kts.   Present speed, *circa* 11 kts.

Tewa (1899).   500 tons.   Guns : 1—6 pdr., 2 machine.   Speed, 10 kts.

Yong Yot.   340 tons.   Guns : 1—4·7 in. B.L., 3 smaller.   Speed, 10 kts.

Maida.   300 tons.   Guns : 1—4·7 in. M.L., 2 small.   Speed, 11 kts.

Nirben.   180 tons.   Guns : 1—4 in. B.L., 6 small.   Speed, 9 kts.

Han Hak Sakru.   140 tons.   Guns : 1—4 in. B.L., 2 small.   Speed, 7 kts.

There are also the old wooden corvette *Thorn Kramon*, 800 tons, 4—4 in. M.L., four smaller guns ; and a floating battery, built in 1870, 950 tons (Guns : 8—4 in. B.L. ; armour : 2½″ iron).

Torpedo Boats.

1 boat, 45 tons.

Photo, West.

ARGENTINE FLEET.

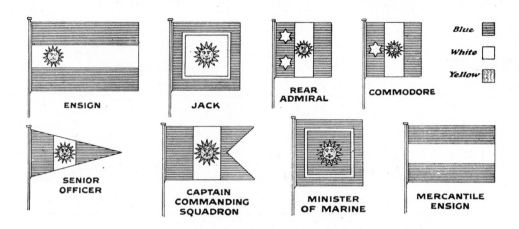

ENSIGN

JACK

REAR ADMIRAL

COMMODORE

SENIOR OFFICER

CAPTAIN COMMANDING SQUADRON

MINISTER OF MARINE

MERCANTILE ENSIGN

Blue ▨
White ☐
Yellow ▦

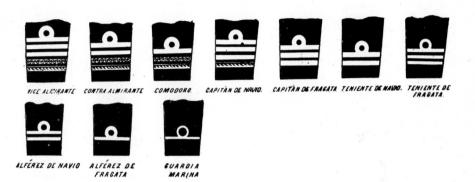

VICE ALMIRANTE · CONTRA ALMIRANTE · COMODORO · CAPITÀN DE NAVIO · CAPITÀN DE FRAGATA · TENIENTE DE NAVIO · TENIENTE DE FRAGATA

ALFÉREZ DE NAVIO · ALFÉREZ DE FRAGATA · GUARDIA MARINA

Capitan de fragata correspond to commander, *Teniente* to lieutenant, *Alférez de navio* to sub-lieutenant, *Alférez de fragata* to midshipman, *Guardia marina* to naval cadet.

Nota-tion.	Nominal Calibre.		Maker.	Length in Calibres.	Muzzle Velocity.	Weight A.P. Projectile.	Max. penetration against K.C. with capped A.P. at		Danger Space against average warship, at			Service Rounds per minute.
							5000 yards.	3000 yards.	10,000 yards.	5000 yards.	3000 yards.	
	inches.	c/m.		calibres.	ft. secs.	lbs.	inches.	inches.				
A	10	25·4	E	40	2207	500	7	9½				·6
C	9·4	24	K	35	2300	350	4½	6				·4
A	8	20·3	E	45	2660	210	6½	9				1
D	8	21	E	40	2286	210	4	6				
E	8	20	K	35	2120	200	3	5				
C	6	15	C	50	2750	88	4	6				5
D*	6	15		45	2500	100	...	4½				
E*				40		100	...	3¾				
F*	4·7	12	C	50	2756	46·3	...	3½				
F*	4·7	12	E	45	2570	45	...	2¾				
F*	4·7	12	E	40	2150	45	...	...				
F*	3	7·6	V	46	2100	14	...	...				

* = Brass cartridge case used.

In the Maker's column E = Elswick ; K = Krupp ; C = Canet ; V = Vickers.

Arsenals.

(1) BUENOS AIRES. There are two private docks here, (Eastern) 623 × 65½ × 25 feet, and (Western) 525 × 65½ × 25 feet.

(2) SAN FERNANDO. There is a shallow dock here, 330 × 64 × 11 feet.

(3) PUERTO BELGRANO.

Docks of large size *projected* at Ensenada and Bahia Blanca.

General Notes.

Personnel about 8500 all ranks.

Argentine ships are more efficient than is generally supposed, and great progress has been made of late towards efficiency.

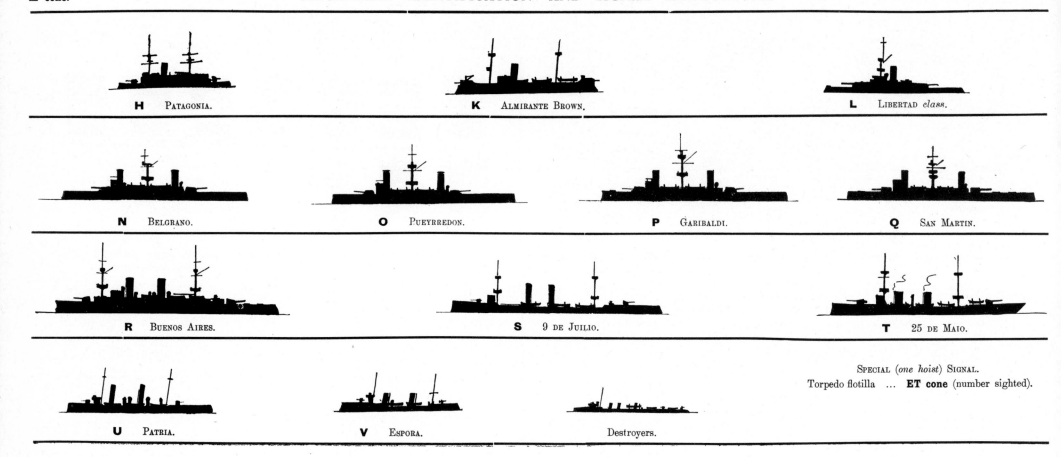

H PATAGONIA.

K ALMIRANTE BROWN.

L LIBERTAD *class*.

N BELGRANO.

O PUEYRREDON.

P GARIBALDI.

Q SAN MARTIN.

R BUENOS AIRES.

S 9 DE JUILIO.

T 25 DE MAIO.

U PATRIA.

V ESPORA.

Destroyers.

SPECIAL (*one hoist*) SIGNAL.
Torpedo flotilla ... **ET cone** (number sighted).

INDEPENDENCIA.   *Photo, Rimmattie.*

INDEPENDENCIA (1891), & LIBERTAD (1890).

Displacement 2336 tons.   Complement 225.
Length 230 feet.   Beam, 44½ feet.   *Mean* draught, 13 feet.

Guns :
   2—9·4 inch, 35 cal. (Krupp) (*C*).
   4—4·7 inch, 40 cal. (Elswick) (*F*).
   4—3 pdr.
   2—1 pdr.
Torpedo tubes :
   2 *above water*

Armour (compound) :
   8″ Belt (amidships) .... *c*
   Protection to vitals.............. *c*
   2″ Deck (flat on belt)...........
   8″ Bulkhead (forward) .... *c*
   6″ Bulkhead (aft) .... *d*
   8″ Barbettes and bases .... *c*
   5″ Shields to big guns (fronts) *d*
   4″ Conning tower .... *e*

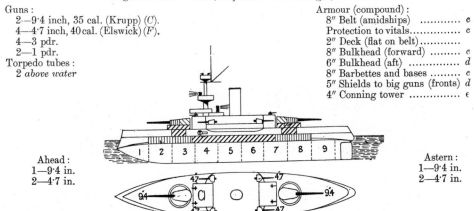

Ahead :
1—9·4 in.
2—4·7 in.

Astern :
1—9·4 in.
2—4·7 in.

Machinery : Compound vertical. 2 screws. Boilers : 4 double cylindrical. Designed H.P. *natural draught* 2100 = 13·2 kts. ; *forced* 2780 = 14·2 kts. (made on *trial.*) Coal : *normal* 230 tons ; *maximum* 340 tons.
Notes.—Built at Laird's, Birkenhead. Belt 172 feet long.

Signal letter: K.   *Photo, Rimattie.*

ALMIRANTE BROWN (1880).

Reconstructed at La Seyne, 1897.
Displacement 4267.   Complement 380.
Length, 240 feet.   Beam 50 feet.   *Maximum* draught, 22 feet.

Guns (Canet) :
   10—6 inch, 50 cal. (*C*)
   4—3·7 inch, 50 cal. (*E*).
   8— 3 pdr.
Torpedo tubes :
   2 *above water* (section 2).

Armour (compound) :
   9″ Belt (amidships) ..... *e*
   1½″ Deck (flat on belt).
   Protection to vitals... = *c*
   7″ Bulkheads........... *c*
   8″ Central battery...... *c*

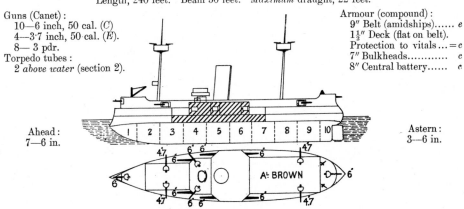

Ahead :
7—6 in.

Astern :
3—6 in.

Broadside : 6—6 in., 2—4·7 in.

Machinery : vertical compound. 2 screws. Boilers : oval. Designed H.P. 4500 = 14 kts. ; speed, 11 kts. Coal : *maximum* 650 tons.
Note.—Built by Laird, of Birkenhead.

365

ARGENTINE ARMOURED CRUISERS (19 knot).

(LATER GARIBALDI TYPE—2 SHIPS).

PUEYRREDON (1897), & GENERAL BELGRANO (1897).

About 7000 tons. Complement 500.

Length, 328 feet. Beam, 59½ feet. *Maximum* draught, 25 feet. (*Belgrano* draws 26 feet).

Guns (Elswick):
  2—10 inch, 40 cal. (*A*).
  10—6 inch, 40 cal. (*E*).
  6—4·7 inch, 40 cal. (*F*).
    (*Belgrano* carries no 4·7
    but instead 4—6 inch.
    2—12 pdr.
  10—6 pdr.
  12—1 pdr.
  2 Maxims.
Torpedo tubes:
  4 *above water* (behind armour).

Armour (Terni):
  6″ Belt (amidships) ...... *a*
  2″ Deck (flat on it) ......
  Protection to vitals is ... *a*
  3″ Belt (ends) .... *e*
  6″ Lower deck redoubt... *a*
  6″ Battery redoubt ...... *a*
  6″ Barbettes .... *a*
  3″ Hoods to big guns ... *e*
  6″ Conning tower........ *a*
  2″ Screens in battery ...

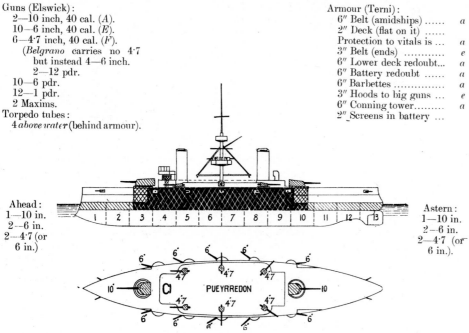

Ahead:
1—10 in.
2—6 in.
2—4·7 (or
  6 in.)

Astern:
1—10 in.
2—6 in.
2—4·7 (or
  6 in.).

Broadside: 2—10 in., 5—6 in., 3—4.7 (or 2—6 in. extra).

Machinery: 2 sets triple expansion. 2 screws. Boilers: Belleville (with economisers) in *Pueyrredon*; 8 cylindrical in *Belgrano*. Designed H.P. 1300=20 kts. Coal: *normal* 400 tons; *maximum* 1000 tons.

Gunnery Notes.—*Belgrano* has 6-inch guns mounted at the angles of the upper deck, and two 12 pdr. amidships.

General Notes.—*Pueyrredon* built by Ansaldo, *Belgrano* by Orlando, of Leghorn.

Differences—Funnels and rig. All four *Garibaldies* are easily distinguished from each other.

(EARLY GARIBALDI CLASS—2 SHIPS.)

GARIBALDI (1895), & SAN MARTIN (1896).

Displacement 6840 tons.   Complement 500.

Length, 328 feet.   Beam, 59½ feet.   *Maximum* draught, 25 feet.

Guns (Elswick) :
 2—10 inch, 40 cal. (A).
 10—6 inch, 40 cal.
 10—6 pdr.
 10—1 pdr.
 2 Maxims.
Torpedo tubes :
 4 *above water* (behind c armour).

Instead of which *San Martin* carries
 4—8 inch, 40 cal. (B).
 10—6 inch, 40 cal. (E).
 6—4·7 inch, 40 cal. (E).

Armour (Harvey) :
 6″ Belt (amidships) ... c
 2″ Deck (flat on it) ...
 Protection to vitals is c
 3″ Belt (ends) .... e
 6″ Bulkheads c
 6″ Barbettes c
 3″ Shields to B guns e
 6″ Lower deck c
 6″ Battery c
 6″ Conning tower...... c

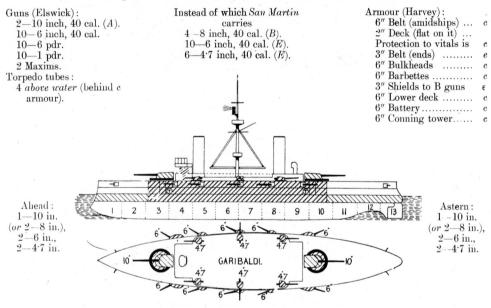

Ahead :
 1—10 in.
 (*or* 2—8 in.),
 2—6 in.,
 2—4·7 in.

Astern :
 1—10 in.
 (*or* 2—8 in.),
 2—6 in.,
 2—4·7 in.

Broadside : 2—10 in., 5—6 in., 3—4·7 in.

Machinery : 2 sets triple expansion. 2 screws. Boilers : 8 cylindrical, 32 furnaces. Designed H.P. *natural* 8600 = 18·5 kts. ; *forced* 13,000 = 20 kts. Coal : *normal* 400 tons ; *maximum* 1000 tons.

Engineering Notes.—Neither ship reached the designed speed on trial, and speed at present has sunk very considerably.

General Notes.—*Garibaldi* built by Ansaldo, *San Martin* by Orlando. Both built originally for the Italian Navy and purchased by Argentine for about £750,000 per ship.

Signal letter : Q.   SAN MARTIN.

Signal letter: R. **BUENOS AIRES** (1895).

Displacement 4500 tons. Sheathed and coppered. Complement 400.

Length (*waterline*), 408 feet. Beam, $47\frac{1}{6}$ feet. *Maximum* draught, 22 feet. Length over all, 424 feet.

Guns (Elswick):
2—8 inch, 45 cal. (*A*).
4—6 inch, 45 cal. (*D*).
6—4.7 inch, 45 cal.
4—6 pdr.
16—3 pdr.
6 Maxims.
Torpedo tubes:
5 *above water* (bow and in sections 5 and 13.

Armour (steel):
5″ Deck (amidships) ...... = *c*
5″ Engine hatches .... = *c*
Protection to vitals ...... = *b*
$4\frac{1}{2}$″ Gun shields .... = *d*
3″ Hoists to C guns ...... = *f*
6″ Conning tower (Harvey) *c*

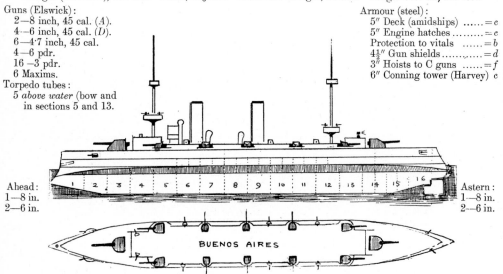

Ahead:
1—8 in.
2—6 in.

Astern:
1—8 in.
2—6 in.

BUENOS AIRES

Broadside: 2—8 in., 2—6 in., 3—4.7 in.

Machinery: 4 sets 3 stage compound direct acting. 2 screws. Boilers: return tubes, 8 2-ended and 8 1-ended. Designed H.P. 13,000=23 kts.; 17,000=24 kts. Coal: *normal* 400 tons; *maximum* 1000 tons.
Engineering Notes.—On first *trials*: 6 hours *natural* 13,000=23.2 kts.; *forced* 18,000, exceeded 24 kts.
Present speed doubtful. *General Notes.*—Built and designed at Elswick.

Signal letter: S. **NUEVE DE JUILIO** (1892).

Displacement 3500. Complement 320.

Length, 350 feet. Beam, 44 feet. *Mean* draught, $19\frac{1}{2}$ feet.

Guns (Elswick):
4—6 inch, 40 cal. (*E*).
8—4.7 inch, 40 cal. (*F*).
12—3 pdr.
14—1 pdr., etc.
Torpedo tubes:
5 *above water*.

Armour (steel):
$4\frac{1}{2}$″ Deck .... = *d*
5″ Glacis to engines ... = *c*
Protection to vitals ... = *c*
Cofferdam amidships.

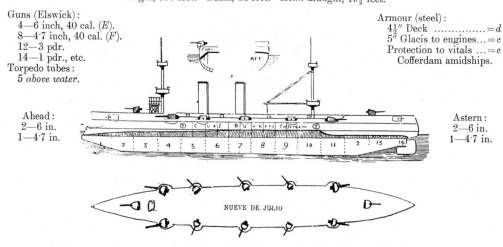

Ahead:
2—6 in.
1—4.7 in.

Astern:
2—6 in.
1—4.7 in.

NUEVE DE JUILIO

Broadside: 2—6 in., 5—4.7 in.

Machinery: 2 sets vertical 4 cylinder. 2 screws. Boilers: 8 2-ended. Designed H.P. *natural* 2500=21 kts.; *forced* 14,500=22.5 kts. Coal: *normal* 300 tons; *maximum* 770 tons.
Engineering Notes.—She reached 22.74 kts. on her first *trial*. Present speed doubtful.
General Notes.—Built and designed at Elswick. This ship has no double bottom.

Signal letter : T.

VINTE-CINCO-DE-MAIO (1890).
Displacement 3200 tons.   Complement 300 tons.
Length, 330 feet.   Beam, 43 feet.   *Mean* draught, 16½ feet.

Guns :
2—8·2 inch, old Krupp.
8—4·7 inch, 40 cal., Elswick.
12—3 pdr.
12—1 pdr.
Torpedo tubes (14 inch) :
3 *above water* (bow and broadside).

Armour (steel) :
4½" Deck....................= d
5" Engine hatches ....= c
[Cofferdam amidships].

Ahead :
1—8 in.
2—4·7 in.

Astern :
1—8 in.
2—4·7 in.

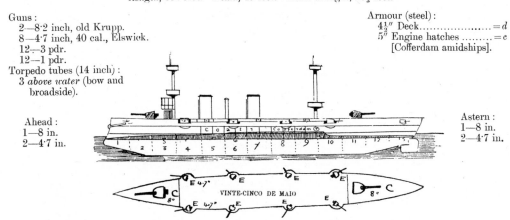

Broadside : 2—8 in., 4—4·7 in.
Machinery : 2 sets vertical 4 cylinder.   2 screws.   Boilers : cylindrical, 4 2-ended.   Designed H.P. *natural* 8500 = 21 kts. ; *forced* 13,000 = 22 kts.   Coal : *normal* 300 tons ; *maximum* 600 tons.
General Note.—Built and designed at Elswick.

Signal letter : U.

PATRIA (1893).
Displacement 1070 tons.   Complement 100.

Guns :
2—4·7 inch, 40 cal.
4—8 pdr.
2—1 pdr.
Torpedo tubes (14 inch) :
5 *above water*.

Machinery : 2 sets triple expansion.   2 screws.   Boilers   4 locomotive.   Designed H.P. *natural* 3300 = 17·5 kts. ; *forced* 5000 = 20·5 kts.   Coal : 288 tons.
Built at Laird's, Birkenhead.

ESPORA (1890).
Displacement 550 tons.   Complement 124.

Guns :
2—14 pdr.
1—8 pdr.
2—3 pdr.
2 Gatlings.
Torpedo tubes :
5 *above water*.

Armour (steel) :
1¼" Belt (amidships) ......
1" Conning tower ....

Machinery : 2 sets triple expansion.   2 screws.   Boilers : 4 locomotive.   Designed H.P. *forced* 3000 = 19·5 kts.   Coal : *normal* 100 tons ; *maximum* 130 tons.
Built at Laird's, Birkenhead.

ARGENTINE SMALL CRAFT.

PATAGONIA (1885).

Displacement 1442 tons.   Complement 210.

Guns (Krupp):
  1—10 inch (old).
  3—6 inch (old).
  6—1 pdr.
  10 machine.
Torpedo tubes:
  None.

Armour (steel):
  1½″ Deck ....= *f*
  4″ Shield, 10″ gun ε

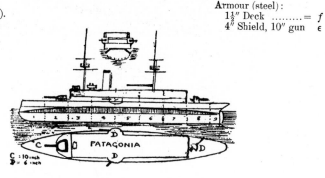

Machinery: 2 sets horizontal compound. 2 screws. Boilers: cylindrical. Designed H.P. 2400=14 kts. Coal: *normal* 200 tons; *maximum* 350 tons.

Built at Triest.

SARMIENTO (1897) training ship, built at Birkenhead 2750 tons.

Guns: 5—4·7 inch, 50 cal.; 2—14 pdr. Torpedo tubes: 2 *above water* (bow and stern). Designed H.P. 2200=13·5 kts. Niclausse boilers.

PRESIDENTE SARMIENTO

ARGENTINE TORPEDO CRAFT.

Destroyers.

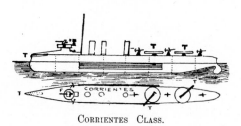

CORRIENTES CLASS.

4 *Yarrow* type (1896), **Corrientes, Entre Rios, Missiones** & **Santa Fe.** 250 tons. Designed H.P. 4200=27 kts. Armament: 1—14 pdr., 3—6 pdr., 3 tubes (18 inch).

1″ Armour protection amidships.

Torpedo Boats.

2 Thornycroft, 110 tons, speed (*trial*) 24·5 kts., 150 feet long, 3 tubes (1890).
6 Yarrow   85   „   „   „   24   „   130   „   2   „ (1890).

Also 4 old 52 tons Yarrow boats dating from 1880. Also 8 3rd class boats Yarrow, 17 kts. (1890), and 2 Thornycroft (1881), speed 17 kts. Also 4 spar torpedo boats, 12 kts. speed.

The 110-ton Thornycroft are named Commodore Py, and Muratore; the 85-ton Yarrow: Bathurst, Buchardo, Jorge, King, Pinedo, Thorne.

Submarines.

One boat (small electric) reported to exist. Argentine design.

The Navy also contains three sloops (Argentina, Parana, Uruguay); two gunboats, 400 tons, one transport, 2700 tons, speed 8 kts.; one of 1000 tons; two of *circa* 400 tons; and six small river gunboats.

BRAZILIAN FLEET.

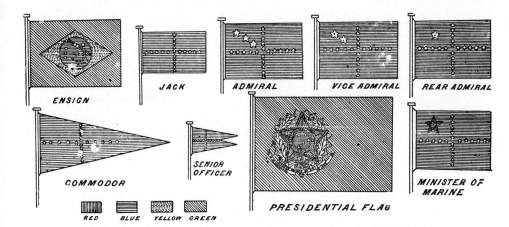

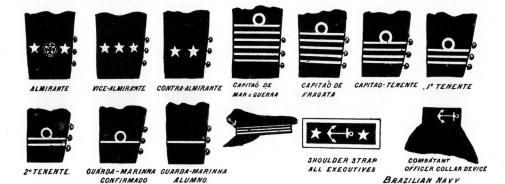

Nota-tion.	Calibre.		Length in calibres	Weight of A.P. shell.	Muzzle Velocity.	Max. penetration A.P. capped at K.C. at		Danger Space against average ships at			Service rounds per minute.
						5000 yards.	3000 yards.	10,000 yards.	5000 yards.	3000 yards.	
	inch.	c/m.	cals.	lbs.	ft. secs.	inch.	inch.				
AA	9·2	23	45	380	2700	9	11½	...	...	...	·8
AA	9·4	24	36	374	2500	8	10¼	...	...	...	...
A	8	20·3	45	210	2650	6½	8½	...	...	...	1
E	6	15	40	100	2500	4	5	...	...	...	6
D	6	15	50	100	2640	4¼	5½	...	...	...	6
F	4·7	12	40	45	2150	...	...	...	...	...	8
F	4·7	12	50	45	2630	...	...	...	...	...	8

All except the 9·4 which is Schneider-Canet, are Elswick guns.

New programme:
3 battleships 12,500—13,000 tons.
3 armoured cruisers *about* 9500 tons.
6 destroyers 400 tons.   6 torpedo boats 50 tons.
6 torpedo boats 130 tons.   3 submarines.

Capitao tenente is equivalent to a British two and a half stripe. *1° tenente* a two-striped lieutenant. *2° tenente* = sub-lieutenant. Civilian ranks have the same stripes *without* the curl, and plus colours above top stripe and below bottom one as under :

Constructors.—No colour, but a ball above the stripes.
Engineers (Machinista).—Green.
Doctors (Cirurgiao).—Red.
Paymasters (Commissario).—White.

Shoulder straps for engineers carry a cylinder, for doctors a stethoscope, for paymasters two quill pens crossed. These devices are also worn on the collar of tunic.

Caps.—Admirals have a broad gold band with oak leaf device, the other commissioned ranks narrow gold bands as on sleeves.

Warrant officers and men carry white distinctive sleeve badges, as follows :—*Torpedo*, torpedoes ; *gunnery*, two crossed guns ; *navigation*, two crossed anchors ; *signal*, two crossed flags ; *quartermasters*, a wheel ; *engine room complements*, a screw propeller.

Marine Infantry—Scarlet tunics with black insignia : five stripes for first sargento, four for second ditto, two for cabo. White helmets as the British. No commissioned officers.

Arsenals.

(1) RIO DE JANEIRO. 5 docks. *Docks a* Imperial   423 × 70 × 24
                                    b Santa Cruz   258 × 55 × 20   Government.
                                    c Sande Point   520 × 70 × 25
                            and two others rather smaller.

(2) Para, (3) Pernambuco. (4) Bahia, (5) Ladario de Matto Grosso.

Personnel about 8000.

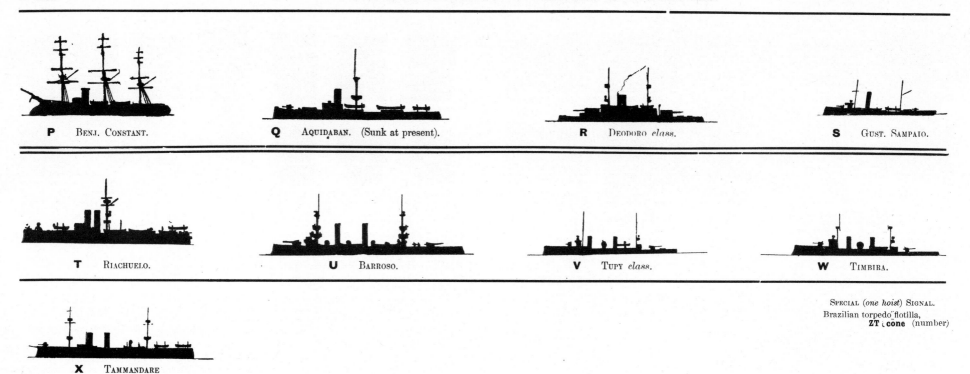

P   Benj. Constant.   **Q**   Aquidaban. (Sunk at present).   **R**   Deodoro *class*.   **S**   Gust. Sampaio.

T   Riachuelo.   **U**   Barroso.   **V**   Tupy *class*.   **W**   Timbira.

X   Tammandare

Special (*one hoist*) Signal.
Brazilian torpedo flotilla,
ZT cone (number)

Photo by favour of Teniente Porto.

RIACHUELO (1883).

Displacement 5700 tons. Sheathed and Coppered. Complement 390.

Length, 305 feet. Beam, 52 feet. *Maximum* draught, 22½ feet.

Guns:
  4—9·4 inch, 40 cal.
  6—4·7 inch, 45 cal.
  6—3 pdr.
  15 Nordenfelts.
Torpedo tubes:
  5 *above water* (stern and
    broadside).

Armour (compound):
  11″-7″Belt (amidships) *b-d*
  2″ Deck (steel) ....
  [Deck flat on belt].
  Protection to vitals is   *b*
  10″ B'kh'ds (below d'k) = *a*
  10″ Turrets .... *b*
  10″ Turret bases ...... *b*
  10″ Conning tower ... *b*

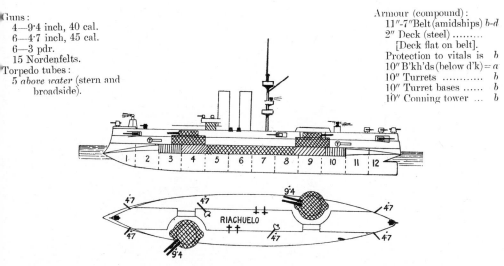

Machinery: 2 sets compound vertical 3 cylinder. 2 screws. Boilers: cylindrical. Designed I.H.P. *natural* 6900 = 16 kts.; *forced* 7000 = 16·5 kts.; present speed poor. Coal: 840 tons.

Notes.—Belt is 7 feet wide. Built at Samuda's, Poplar. Re-constructed at La Seyne, 1895. Rig altered, 1904.

AQUIDABAN.   *Photo by favour of Teniente Porto.*

AQUIDABAN (1885).
(Blown up, January, 1906. Salvage uncertain).

Displacement 5000 tons. Sheathed and Coppered. Complement 388.
Length, 280 feet. Beam, 52 feet. *Maximum* draught, 21½ feet.

Guns:
  4—8 inch, 45 cal.
  4—4·7 inch, 50 cal.
  8—6 pdr.
  10 Nordenfelts.
Torpedo Tubes (Elswick):
  2 *submerged*.
  3 *above water*.
    (stern and quarter).

Armour (compound):
  11″-7″ Belt (amidships)... *b-d*
  2″ Deck (steel) .....
  [Deck flat on Belt.]
  Protection to vitals is ... *b*
  10″ B'lkh'ds (below deck)= *a*
  10″ Turrets................. *b*
  10″ Turret bases .... *b*
  10″ Conning tower ...... *b*

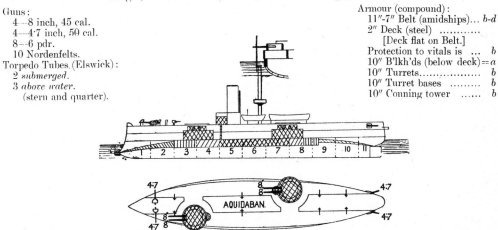

Machinery: 2 sets compound vertical 3 cylinder. 2 screws. Boilers: 8 cylindrical. Designed H.P. *natural* 5000 = 15 kts.; *forced* 6000 = 15·5 kts. (On *trial* she exceeded this, but cannot now do anything like it.) Coal: 800 tons.

Notes.—Belt is 7 feet wide. This ship was originally named *Aquidaban*, but after the revolution (in which she was torpedoed and sunk by the *Sampaio*) she was raised and re-named *Vinte Quarto de Maio*. She has since been re-named *Aquidaban* again. Built at Samuda's, Poplar. Reconstructed at Vulkan Co., Stettin, 1897. Rig altered, 1904. Blown up and sunk, 1906. Not yet salved.

FLORIANO. (*Deodoro* identical).

(DEODORO CLASS—2 SHIPS.)

DEODORO (1898) & FLORIANO (1898).

Displacement 3162 tons. Complement 200.

Length (*waterline*), 267½ feet. Beam, 48 feet. *Maximum* draught, 14¼ feet.

Guns :
2—9·2 in., 45 cal. (*AA*).
4—4·7 in., 50 cal. (*E*).
2—12 pdr. (*F*).
4—6 pdr.
4—1 pdr.
Torpedo tubes (18 in.) :
2 *submerged.*

Armour (Harvey-nickel) :
13¾″ Belt (amidships)... *aaa*
4″ Belt (ends) .... *d*
1½″ Deck (reinforcing belt).
Protection to vitals ...= *aaaa*
8″ Turrets.................. *a*
3″ Casemates .... *e*
5″ Conning tower......... *c*

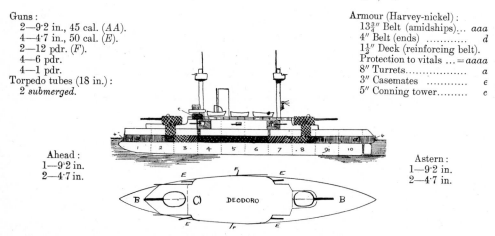

Ahead :
1—9·2 in.
2—4·7 in.

Astern :
1—9·2 in.
2—4·7 in.

Broadside : 2—9·2 in., 2—4·7 in.

Machinery : 2 sets triple expansion. 2 screws. Boilers : 8 Lagrafel d'Allest. Designed H.P. 3400 = 14 kts. Coal : *normal* 246 tons.

Armour Notes.—Lower edge of belt is only 6″ thick.

General Notes.—Designed and built at La Seyne. Laid down 1896-97. Completed 1901-02.

BARROZO Phot. Elswick

BARROZO (1896)

Displacement 3450 tons (sheathed and coppered). Complement 300.

Length (*waterline*), 330 feet. Beam, 43¾ feet. *Maximum* draught, 20 feet.

Guns :
6—6 in., 50 cal. (*C*).
4—4·7 in., 50 cal. (*E*).
10—6 pdr.
4—1 pdr.
4 Maxims.

Armour (sheet) :
3½″ Deck (amidships) = *d*
Protection to vitals ...= *c*

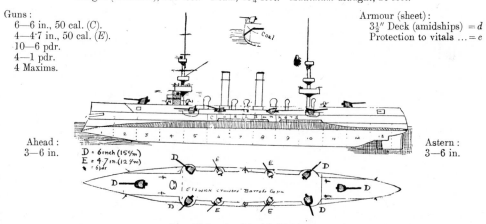

Ahead :
3—6 in.

Astern :
3—6 in.

Broadside : 4—6 in., 2—4·7 in.

Machinery : 2 sets triple expansion. 2 screws. Boilers : cylindrical. Designed H.P. *forced* 7500 = 20 kts. Coal : *normal* 700 tons ; *maximum* 850 tons.

Engineering Notes.—Made on *trials* 19·8 and 20·5 kts.

General Notes.—Designed and built at Elswick. Laid down 1895. Completed 1897.

TAMANDARE (1890).

Displacement 4537 tons.   Complement 450.
Length, 294 feet.   Beam, 46 feet.   *Maximum* draught, 20½ feet.

Guns :
10—6 inch (*E*).
2—4·7 inch, (*F*).
8 Nordenfelts.

Armour (steel) :
1¾″ Deck .... = *f*
Protection to vitals......... = *f*
3″ Casemates (4)........... = *f*
2″ Conning tower .... = *f*

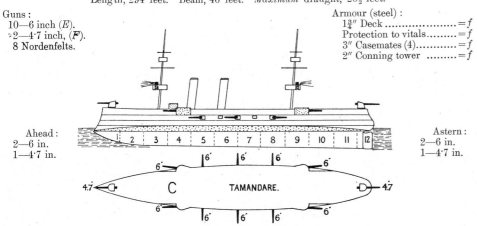

Ahead :
2—6 in.
1—4·7 in.

Astern :
2—6 in.
1—4·7 in.

Broadside : 5—6 in., 2—4·7 in.

Machinery : 2 sets horizontal triple expansion.   2 screws.   Boilers : cylindrical.   Designed H.P.
natural 6,500=16 kts. ; *full power* 7,500=17 kts.   Coal : *normal* 400 tons ; *maximum* 750 tons.
Engineering Notes.—Machinery built in England (Maudslay).
General Notes.—Ship built at Rio de Janeiro from Brazilian designs.   Laid down, 1887.   Completed,
1893.

Photo by favour of Teniente Porto.

BENJAMIN CONSTANT (1892).

Displacement 2750 tons.   Complement 380.
Length, 236½ feet.   Beam, 44½ feet.   *Maximum* draught, 18½ feet.

Guns :
4—6 inch, 45 cal. (*D*).
8—4·7 inch, 45 cal. (*E*).
2—12 pdr. (*F*).
2—1 pdr.
4 Revolvers.
Torpedo tubes :
4 *above water*.

Armour (steel) :
2″ Deck .... = ϵ
3¼″ Conning tower .... *f*
Protection to vitals......... = ϵ

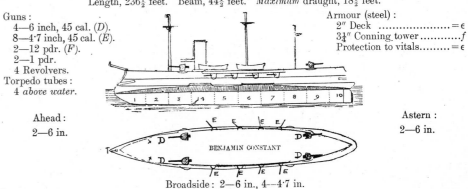

Ahead :
2—6 in.

Astern :
2—6 in.

Broadside : 2—6 in., 4—4·7 in.

Machinery.—2 screws.   Designed H.P. *natural* 2,800=14 kts. ; *forced* 4,000=15 kts.   Coal :
normal 260 tons.
General Notes.—Designed and built at La Seyne, with Elswick guns and mountings.   Classed as a
training ship, but the powerful armament gives her some war uses, and she usually serves as a
cruiser.

TUPY & TAMOYO.

Signal letter for these two : V.

TIMBIRA.

Signal letter : W.

(TUPY CLASS—3 SHIPS).

TUPY, TIMBIRA & TAMOYO (all launched, 1896).

Displacement 1030 tons. Complement 110.

Length, 259 feet. Beam, 30 feet. *Maximum* draught, $10\frac{1}{4}$ feet.

Guns :	Armour (steel) :
2—4·7 inch.	1″ Deck ....
6—6 pdr.	1″ Conning tower ....
4—1 pdr.	$4\frac{1}{2}''$ Gun shields ....
Torpedo tubes (14 inch) :	
3 *above water.*	

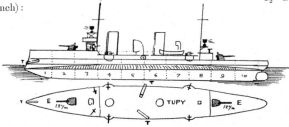

Machinery : 2 sets triple expansion. 2 screws. Boilers : cylindrical. Designed H.P. *natural* 4000 = 20 kts. ; *forced* 7000 = 23 kts. Coal : *normal* 100 tons.

General Notes.—Designed and built at Kiel.

GUSTAVO SAMPAIO (1896).

Displacement 500 tons. Complement 95.

Guns (Elswick) :
2—3·5 inch.
4—3 pdr.
Torpedo tubes :
3 *above water.*

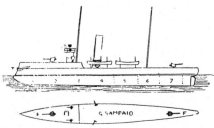

Machinery : 2 screws. Designed H.P. 2300 = 18 kts. Coal : 150 tons.
Note.— Built at Elswick.

G. SAMPAIO.   *Photo, Ferez.*

Destroyers.

6 of 400 tons, *projected.*

Torpedo Boats.

6 of 130 tons, and 6 of 50 tons *projected.* There are no modern boats. Old boats as follows :—

5 Schichau boats	(1893), 130 tons.	Original speed 28 kts. ;	3 tubes.
3 Thornycroft boats	(1891), 150 „	„ „ 25—26 kts. ;	4 tubes.
5 Yarrow boats	(1882), 52 „	„ „ 20 kts ;	2 tubes.

<u>13</u>

Submarines.

3 Holland type, *projected.*

2 *Mello Marques & Jacinto Gomez* (1903). Goubet type of about 25 tons or less. Radius about 5 miles. Speed about 6 knots on surface.

Apparently purely experimental.

The Brazilian Navy also includes wooden ships : TONELERO (1400 tons) and PAYSANDU (1900 tons), 6 small steel or iron gunboats, 5 wood or composite gunboats (all of from 700—250 tons) ; all of no fighting value.

Armed merchantmen : 1 (ANDRADA) 2600 tons, speed 14 kts., 4 guns ; 4 (MERCURIO JUPITER, METEORO, and MARTE) of 1000 tons, armed with 6-pdr. or 3-pdr. Hotchkiss, and 3 very small steamers.

Two transports of 1400 tons (paddle wheel).

One old ironclad, used as a floating battery ; 3 monitors of 400 tons (river), and two river monitors of 500 tons (building).

CHILIAN FLEET.

CHILIAN IDENTIFICATION AND SIGNAL SILHOUETTES.

CI cone.

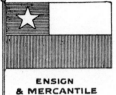

ENSIGN & MERCANTILE

JACK

MINISTER OF MARINE

VICE ADMIRAL

SENIOR OFFICER

COMMODORE

Red ▦

White ☐

Blue ▨

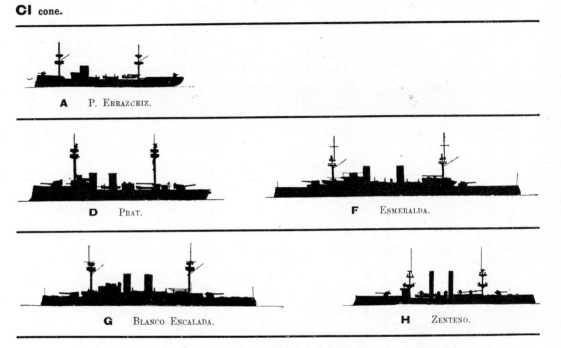

A. P. Errazuriz.

D. Prat.

F. Esmeralda.

G. Blanco Encalada.

H. Zenteno.

J. Chacabuco.

M. Simpson.

N. Lynch *class*.

O. O'Higgins.

Guns.

	Calibre.	Desig-nation.		Length in Cals.	Weight of Gun.	Weight: A.P. Shell.	Initial Velocity.	Penetration with capped A.P. against K.C. Armour, at	
								5000 yds.	3000 yds.
	in.	m/m.			tons.	lbs.	f.s.	in.	in.
A	9·4	240	Canet, 23 ton	36		374	2230	6	8
A*	8·	203	Elswick	45	17½	210	2660	6¾	8¼
B*	8	203	Elswick	40	15½	210	2570	5	7½
E*	6	152	Elswick	40	6½	100	2500	...	4½
E*	6	152	Elswick	45	8	100	2600	3	5
E*	6	152	Canet	...		88	—		
F*	4·7	120	Elswick	40	2	45	2150	...	...
F*	4·7	120	Elswick	45		45	2570	...	...
F*	4·7	120	Canet	36		36	1950	...	...
F*	3	76	Elswick, Q.F. (12 pr.)	40		12	2200	...	...

* = Brass cartridge case.

Personnel : About 8000 (conscript) all ranks.

Bases : Talcahuano. One dry dock, 545 × 80 × 28½ feet. (Out in the bay exposed to gunfire)

Valparaiso. Two small floating docks, 300 × 68 × 19 feet and 265 × 60 × 15 feet.

CAPITAN PRAT (1890).
6901 tons. Complement 480.
Length, 328 feet. Beam, 60⅔ feet. *Maximum* draught, 26⅕ feet.

O'HIGGINS (1897).
8500 tons. Sheathed and coppered. Complement
Length, 407 feet. Beam, 62¾ feet. *Mean* draught, 22 feet.

Guns (Canet) :
4—9·4 in., 35 cal. (B).
8—4·7 in., 45 cal. (E).
6—6 pdr.
4—3 pdr.
10—1 pdr.
5 Maxims.
Torpedo tubes :
4 *above water*.

Armour (Creusot) :
12″ Belt (amidships) ... *a*
3″ Deck (flat on belt)...
Protection to vitals ... =*a*
10½″ Barbettes .... *b*
2″ Barbette hoods ...... *f*
4″ Redoubt (amidships) *ϵ*
2″ Small turrets......... *f*
Conning tower (abaft
foremast) ?
(Total 2108 tons).

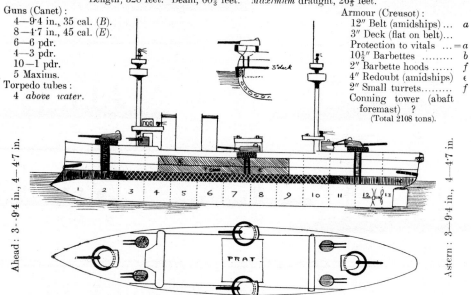

Ahead : 3 - 9·4 in., 4 - 4·7 in.

Astern : 3—9·4 in., 4—4·7 in.

Machinery : (1145 tons), 2 sets horizontal triple expansion. 2 screws. Boilers : cylindrical.
Designed I.H.P. *natural* 8000 = 17 kts. ; *forced* 12,000 = 18·3 kts. Coal : *normal* 400 tons ;
maximum 1100 tons = *circa* 4000 miles at 8 kts. *actual*. Continuous sea speed *circa* 15·5 kts.
Notes.—All guns are electrically manœuvred, and all hoists are electric. Central loading
positions. The belt is 6½ feet wide.
Laid down at La Seyne, 1883. Completed 1893. First cost, £391,000.

Guns (Elswick) :
4—8 inch, 45 cal. (A).
10—6 inch, 40 cal. (E).
4—4·7 inch, 45 cal. (F).
10—12 pdr. (F).
10—6 pdr.
4 machine.
Torpedo tubes (18 inch) :
2 *submerged*.
3 *above water*

Armour (Harvey-nickel) :
7″ Belt (amidships) ...... *a*
2″ Deck (slopes)......... =*d*
Protection to vitals ... =*aa*
[Cellulose belt].
7½″ Turrets, C guns (front) *a*
6″ Hoists to these ...... *b*
6″ Gun houses, 6″ guns *b*
6″ Casemates (6) .... *b*
9″ Conning tower ...... *a*

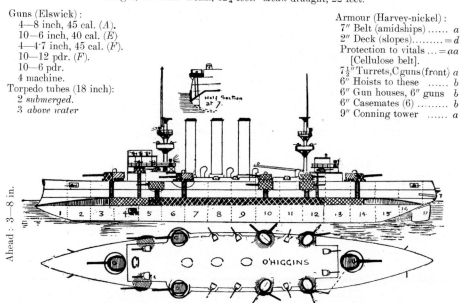

Ahead : 3 - 8 in.

Machinery : 2 sets triple expansion. 2 screws. Boilers : 30 Belleville (in 3 groups).
Designed I.H.P. *natural* 10,000 = 19 kts. ; *forced* 16,500 = 21·25 kts. Coal : *normal* 700 tons ;
maximum 1200 tons.

Notes.—The belt is 7 feet wide, and varies from 7 to 5 inches in thickness.
Laid down at Elswick, April, 1896. Completed 1898. First cost, £700,000 *complete*.

ESMERALDA (1896),

7000 tons. Sheathed and coppered. Complement 500.
Length (*p.p.*), 436 feet. Beam, 53 feet. Draught (*mean*), 20¼ feet.

Guns (Elswick) :
  2—8 inch, 40 cal. (*B*).
  16—6 inch, 40 cal. (*D*).
  8—12 pdr. (*F*).
  9—6 pdr.
  2—3 pdr.
  8 Maxims.
Torpedo tubes (18 inch) :
  2 *submerged*.
  1 *above water* (bow).

Armour (Harvey) :
  6″ Belt .... *c*
  2″ Deck..................... = *d*
  Protection to vitals .... = *b*
  6″ Bulkheads .... *c*
  4½ Shields to guns ....
  4½ Hoists ....

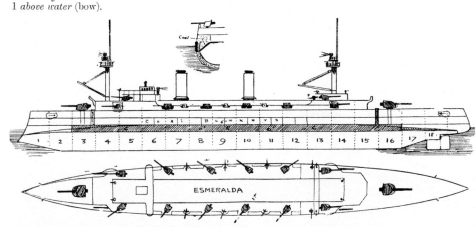

ESMERALDA

Machinery : 2 sets 4 cylinder triple expansion. 2 screws. Boilers : 2-ended cylindrical. Designed I.H.P. *natural* 16,000 = 22·25 kts. Coal : *normal* 550 tons ; *maximum* 1350 tons. *Trials* : I.H.P. 10,800 = 20 kts. ; 16,000 = 23·05 kts.

Notes.—At sea (1898) she made 21·2 knots easily. Present speed is about 19 knots, *maximum*. The belt is 350 feet long by 7 feet wide. Behind the belt the deck is 1½ inches. Laid down at Elswick, 1895. Completed 1897.

BLANCO ENCALADA (1893).

4420 tons. Sheathed and coppered. Complement 427.

Length (*p.p.*), 370 feet. Beam, 46½ feet. *Maximum* draught, 20½ feet.

Guns (Elswick) :
  2—8 inch, 40 cal. (*C*).
  10—6 inch, 40 cal. (*D*).
  12—3 pdr.
  10—1 pdr.
Torpedo tubes (18 inch) :
  5 *above water* (bow and
    broadside).

Armour (steel) :
  4″ Deck..................... = *d*
  6″ Conning tower .... *d*
  6″ Shields, 8 in. guns ......

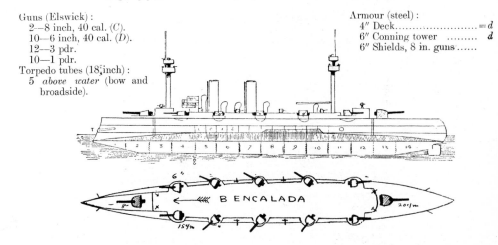

B ENCALADA

Machinery : 2 sets triple expansion. 2 screws. Boilers : cylindrical. Designed I.H.P. *natural* 11,000 = 21·79 kts. ; *forced* 14,500 = 22·78 kts. (made on *trial*). Coal : *normal* tons ; *maximum* 900 tons.

Notes.—Carries one 2nd class torpedo boat, 60 feet long. She has done 19·5 knots at sea for some considerable while, but her present speed is considerably below this. Laid down at Elswick, 1892. Completed 1894.

3 B 2

CHACABUCO (1898) (purchased 1902).
4300 tons. Complement 400.
Length (p.p.), 360 feet. Beam, 46½ feet. *Maximum* draught, 20 feet.

Guns (Elswick) :
2—8 inch, 40 cal. (B).
10—4·7 inch (F).
12—12 pdr. (F).
6—2½ pdr.
Torpedo tubes :
5 *above water.*

Armour (Harvey nickel) :
4½″ Deck.................... = b
Protection to vitals ... = b
4½″ Fronts 8 in. gun shields
2½″ Sides   ,,   ,,
2½″ Shields 4·7 in. guns
Conning tower c
Hoists .... e

Ahead : 1—8, 2—4·7 in.

Astern : 1—8, 2—4·7 in.

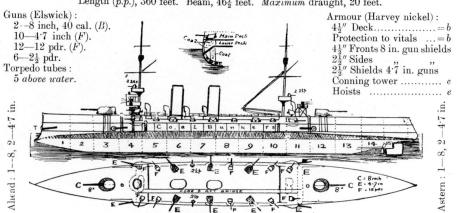

Broadside : 2—8 in., 5—4·7 in.
Machinery : Boilers, cylindrical. I.H.P. 15,000 = 24 kts. *forced.* 2 screws.
Coal : *normal* 300 tons ; *maximum* 1000 tons.
Laid down at Elswick, 1897. Completed 1902.

MINISTRO ZENTENO (1896.).
3600 tons. Complement
Length, 330 feet. Beam, 43¾ feet. *Mean* draught, 17 feet.

Guns (Elswick) :
8—6 inch, 40 cal.
10—6 pdr.
4—1 pdr.
4 Maxims.
Torpedo tubes :
3 *above water* (bow and section 11).

Armour (Harvey) :
3½″ Deck .... d
4″ Conning tower ... d

Ahead :
3—6 in.

Astern :
3—6 in.

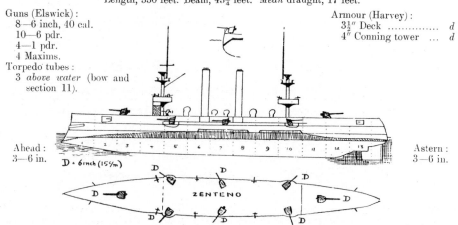

Broadside : 5—6 in.
Machinery : 2 sets triple expansion. 2 screws. Boilers : cylindrical.
Designed I.H.P. *forced* 7500 = 20 kts. Coal : *normal* 700 tons ; *maximum* 1000 tons.
Laid down at Elswick, 1895. Completed 1898.

PRESIDENTE ERRAZURIZ (1890).

Displacement 2100 tons.   Sheathed and coppered.   Complement 171.

Length, 262 feet.   Beam, 35¾ feet.   *Maximum* draught, 20 feet.

Guns (Canet) :
   4—6 inch, 36 cal.
   2—4·7 inch, 36 cal.
   4—6 pdr.
   4—1 pdr.
   2 Gatlings.
Torpedo tubes :
   3 *above water*.

Armour (steel) :
   2¼″ Deck ....
     [Cellulose belt].
   3¼″ Gun shields......

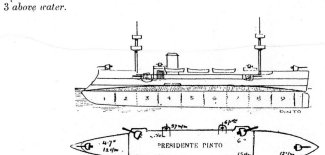

Machinery : 2 sets horizontal triple expansion.   2 screws.   Boilers : 4 cylindrical, 3 furnaces to each.   Designed I.H.P. *natural* 3500 = 17 kts. ;   *induced* 5400 = 19 kts. (reached on *trial*).   Coal : *normal* 200 tons.

Laid down at La Seyne, 1889   Completed 1892.

ALMIRANTE SIMPSON (1896).

Displacement 800 tons.

Length, 240 feet.   Beam, 27½ feet.   *Maximum* draught, 13 feet.

Guns (Elswick) :
   2—4·7 inch
   4—3 pdr.
   2 Maxims.
Torpedo tubes (18 inch) :
   3 *above water*.

Armour (Harvey) :
   1″ Belt ....
   4½″ Gun shields ....
   1″ Hood to steering gear
   1″ Bulkheads..............

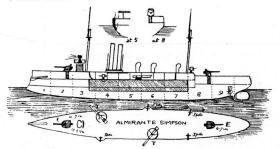

Machinery : 2 sets triple expansion.   2 screws.   Boilers : 4 Normand.   Designed I.H.P. *forced* 4500 = 21 kts.   Coal : 100 tons.

Laid down at Birkenhead, 1895.   Completed 1896.

ALMIRANTE LYNCH & ALMIRANTE CONDELL
(1890).

Displacement 750 tons.

Length, 230 feet.   Beam, 27½ feet.   *Maximum* draught, 12½ feet.

Guns :
   3—14 pdr.
   4—3 pdr.
   2 Gatlings.
Torpedo tubes (Canet) :
   5 *above water*.

Armour :
   1″ narrow belt
     (amidships)
   1″ Bulkheads.

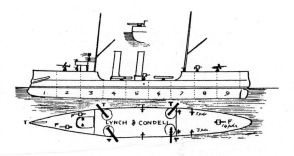

Machinery : 2 sets triple expansion.   2 screws.   Boilers : Belleville, *without* economisers (1900).   Designed I.H.P. 4000 = 20 kts. (exceeded on *trial*).   Coal : 100 tons.

Laid down at Birkenhead, 1889.   Completed 1892.   Reconstructed 1900.

Capitan O'Brien & *Capitan Merino Tarpa,*

2 boats (1902), 350 tons, Laird type.

Designed H.P. 6250 = 30 kts.   Boilers : Normand.   Coal : 90 tons.   Armament : 1—12 pdr. (*F*), 5—6 pdr., 2 tubes (18 in.), carried one amidships and one aft.

Capitan Orella, Capitan Munoz Gamere, Teniente Serano, & *Guardia Marina Riquelme.*

4 boats (1896), 300 tons, Laird type.

All details as for above, except that the draught is slightly less.

Ingeniere Hyatt, Cirujano Videla, Ingeniere Mutilla, Guardia Marina Contrerra, Capitan Thompson & *Teniente Rodriguez.*

Yarrow Torpedo boats, 140 tons (1896—1898).

Designed H.P. 2200 = 27·5 kts.   Coal : 40 tons.   Armament : 3—3 pdrs. ; 3 tubes (14 in. *Maximum* draught, 7¾ feet.

(There are also 10 old boats of no fighting value).

Also one 3rd class boat, 15 tons, originally of 19 kts. speed (*trial*) (1892); and 3 boats of 5 tons displacement.

SUBMARINE :

Urzua Curat (building).   Reported small electric type.

MINOR CRAFT :

Harbour defence ships. Old battleships *Almironte Cochrane*, 3500 tons ; and *Huascar* 1870 tons ; armed with six and two old Armstrong 8 in. B.L. respectively.

Training ship *General Baquendano*, of 2500 tons, sheathed and coppered, armed with four 45 cal., 4·7 in. guns, and two 12 pdrs. I.H.P. 1500 = 13·75 kts. Belleville boilers. Coal : 300 tons. Barque rig, one funnel, swan bow.

Also *Pilcomayo*, 600 ton gunboat (1864) ; and 12 steamers of the Compania Sud America de Vapores are held at disposal for armed transports (2300—1300 tons). speeds 15-12 kts. Also 4 or 5 smaller steamers.

UNIMPORTANT NAVIES.

(Arranged alphabetically.)

Yellow   Red   Blue   Green

BELGIUM ENSIGN

CAMBODIA

COLUMBIA ENSIGN

COLUMBIA MERCANTILE

BELGIUM.

1 *screw steamer*, 640 tons, 18 kts.; 3 of 400 tons, 17 kts.

2 *paddle wheelers*, 630 tons, 21 kts.; 3 ditto, 495 tons, 19 kts.; 1 of 419 tons, 21 kts.; 2 of 798 tons, 21 kts.; 3 of 419 tons, 16 kts.; and 2 slow boats.

Employed as packets under Government officers, and for fishery protection.

Projected: 2 coast defence monitors.
6 torpedo boats.

CAMBODIA.

Lutin (1877). 490 tons. 1 small gun. Speed originally 10 kts.

2 gunboats of 80 tons. 1 small gun each. Speed, 8 kts.

COLUMBIA.

Ex EL BASCHIR (1892). 1200 tons. Guns: 2 E (4·7 in. B.L.), 4—1 pdr.). 4 torpedo tubes *above water*. Designed I.H.P. 2500 = 18 kts.

Esperanza (1897) & *General Nerino* (1895)— (stern wheel river gunboats). 400 tons. Guns: 3—1 pdr. Armour: $\frac{1}{4}''$ nickel belt amidships. Designed I.H.P. 430 = 15 kts.

Steamer, *La Popa*; 1 sailing ship. 1 transport, *Cordova* (1891). Guns: 2—6 pdr., and 2 Maxims.

ESPERANZA & GEN. NERINO
(Columbia)   LA POPA

COSTA RICA ENSIGN
Mercantile the same
without centre device

ECUADOR

EGYPT

COSTA RICA.

1 stern wheel Yarrow boat.

1 Yarrow torpedo boat (1892). Speed, 15 kts.

ECUADOR.

Ex Papin & Inconstant (1886, French navy). 811 tons. Guns: two old 5·5 inch, 1—4 inch, five small. Designed H.P. 860 = 12 kts. Single screw, composite. Despatch vessels.

Catopari & Nuove de Julio, old and small steamers with a couple of guns.

1 Yarrow torpedo boat, 65 tons. Speed, *circa* 15 kts. Guns 2—3 pdrs. 2 Nordenfelts. 4 tubes. Named *Tunqurahua*.

CATOPARI
(Ecuador)

EGYPT.

Stern wheel gunboats *Abu Klea, Hafir, Metemneh, Tamai, El Fateh, En Naseh*, 128 tons; *Sheik, Sultan, Melik*, 140 tons. All carry one gun (usually 12 pdr.) and 2 to 4 Maxims. Some have a howitzer also.

4 other stern wheel steamers; 1 Khedive's Yacht, *Safa el Bahr*; and 1 old 3140 ton paddler, *Mahroussad*, armed with eight small guns. 1 transport, *Gharbieh*, 3700 tons; 4 other steamers; 1 tug and a small steam yacht; 10 coastguard steamers, 450-15 tons; and some sailing revenue boats.

UNIMPORTANT NAVIES.

HAYTI.

Corvette, *Dessalines* (1883). 1200 tons. Guns: 3—4 inch, Canet, 2 old 3 pdr., 2 Gatlings. *Nominal* speed, 16 kts.

St. Michael (1875). 850 tons. Guns: 1—11 in., 25 ton M.L., 8 old 30 pdr. B.L. Speed, *nominal*, 12 kts.

1804 (1875). 600 tons. Guns: 1—10 in. 18 ton M.L., 6 old 30 pdr. B.L. Speed, *nominal*, 12 kts. Can do about 6 kts.

22 Décebre (1860). 900 tons. Guns: 4 old 40 pdr. B.L. Speed originally 9 kts.

Toussaint Louverte (1886, Havre). 522 tons. Guns: 1—6·4 in. old Canet, 2 old 4·7 in. Canet, 2 Machine. *Nominal* speed, 14 kts.

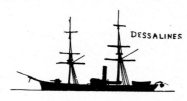

DESSALINES

MOROCCO.

1 gunboat, 450 tons. Guns: 2* (9 pdr.) Designed I.H.P. 1200 = 14·5 kts.

1 steamer, *Al Hassenah*, 1100 tons. Guns: 1—6·6 in. old Krupp, 4 Machine. *Nominal* speed, 12 kts.

MEXICO.

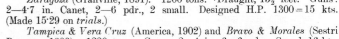

Zaragoza (Granville, 1891). 1200 tons. Draught, 15½ feet. Guns: 2—4·7 in. Canet, 2—6 pdr., 2 small. Designed H.P. 1300 = 15 kts. (Made 15·29 on *trials*.)

Tampica & Vera Cruz (America, 1902) and *Bravo & Morales* (Sestri Ponente, 1903). 1280 tons. Guns: 2—4 in., 6—6 pdr. Speed, 16 kts. Bleychenden boilers. 2 screws.

Democrata (1875), 450 tons. Guns: 2—6·5 in. M.E. Speed, about 7 kts. or less at present.

Independencia & Libertad (1874, Birkenhead). 425 tons. Flat iron gunboats, carrying 1—6·5 in. M.L. and 2—20 pdr. B.L.

Note.—Two 2400 ton cruisers, 7000 H.P. = 19·5 kts. Four 1280 ton ditto, 4500 H.P. = 19·5 kts., and 8 torpedo boats, 225 tons, 25 kts., *projected.*

ZARAGOZA.

PARAGUAY.

1 gunboat, 440 tons. Guns: 4—3 pdr. Speed, *nominal*, 10 kts. 2 smaller steamers.

PERSIAN ENSIGN

PERU ENSIGN
Mercantile flag the same
but without centre device

PERUVIAN VICE-ADMIRAL
Rear Admiral has one
sun

PERUVIAN CAPTAIN

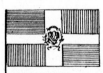

SAN DOMINGO
Mercantile the same but
without centre device

SAN SALVADOR

PERSIA.

Persepolis. 1200 tons. Guns: one 4 in. B.L., two 30 pdr. B.L., 2 smaller. Nominal speed, 10·5 kts.

PERU.

Almirante Grau (Vickers, 1906). 3200 tons. Speed, 24 kts.
Lima (Kiel, 1881). 1700 tons. Guns: 2 old 6 in. Krupp B.L. Designed I.H.P. 1800 = 16·2 kts. 2 screws.
Santa Rosa (Glasgow, 1883). 420 tons. Guns: 2 old 6 in.
Six small paddle wheel steamers.
There are also one or two small nondescript vessels, and an old monitor, *Atahualpha*, used as a hulk.

SAN DOMINGO.

Restauracion (1896, Glasgow). 1000 tons. Guns: 4 — 4·7 in., 5 smaller. Speed, 14-15 kts. originally. 2 screws.
Independencia (Glasgow, 1894). 322 tons. Guns: 7 small Q.F. Speed, originally 15 kts. 2 screws.
Presidente (old gunboat reconstructed). Guns: four 40 pdr., 4 small. Speed (in 1898), 13·8 kts.

SAN SALVADOR.

1 gunboat *Cuscatlan* (San Francisco, 1890). 75 tons. Guns: 1 small Q.F. Speed, *nominal*, 10 kts.

SARAWAK.

Lorna Doone & Aline, small screw steamers, each with 2 small guns. Also a small paddler, *Adeh.*

URUGUAY ENSIGN

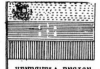

VENEZUELA ENSIGN
Mercantile the same
without arms on yellow

URUGUAY.

GUNBOATS:—
General Artigus (Triest, 1883). 832 tons. Guns: 2 old Krupp 4·7 in., 2 Machine. *Nominal* speed, 12·5 kts.
General Suarez. 400 tons. Guns: 4 old 3 in. Krupp, 4 Machine. *Nominal* speed, 9 kts.
General Rivera (1891). Guns: 1 old 6 in. Krupp, 2—3 pdr. *Nominal* speed, 12 kts.
Malvinas (Elbing, 1885). 400 tons. Guns: 2 small Q.F. Speed, about 8 kts.
General Flores (transport). 260 tons. 10 kts.

VENEZUELA.

BOLIVAR.

BOLIVAR (ex-Spanish). 571 tons. Guns: 2—4·7 in. B.L. *Nominal* speed, 18·5 kts.
GUNBOATS:
Miranda (1895). 200 tons. Guns: 2 small Q.F. *Nominal* speed, 12 kts.
Libertador (Scotland, 1883). 832 tons. 4 small Q.F. 4 river gunboats. 1 steamer, *Augusta.*

ZANZIBAR ENSIGN

ZANZIBAR.

Six small steamers, single screw. 1000—500 tons. Small Q.F. armament or old small B.L. in some.

FLEETS OF THE GREAT POWERS (in order of importance).

ARRANGED IN PARALLELS OF FIGHTING VALUE, WITH THE "DREADNOUGHT" AS UNIT.

Battleships in capitals. Cruisers in ordinary type. Ships in *italics* will not be complete for sea by the end of 1906. Approximate date of completion given in brackets.

RATE.	BRITISH.	U.S.	FRENCH.	JAPANESE.	GERMAN.	RUSSIAN. (Black Sea in brackets.)	ITALIAN.	AUSTRO-HUNGARIAN.
I.	*2 NEW ('09)* *1 DREADNOUGHT ('07)*	*1 NEW ('10)* *2 S. CAROLINA ('09)*		*2 NEW (pro.)*		*6 NEW (pro.)*		
I.-II.	*2 LORD NELSON ('07)* *2 cruisers ('09)*		*6 DANTON ('09)*	*2 AKI ('08)*	*2 ERSATZ SACHSEN*	*? A ('09)*		
II.	8 KING EDWARD *3 Inflexible ('08)*	*1 KANSAS ('09)* *3 KANSAS ('08)* 2 LOUISIANA 5 NEW JERSEY *2 IDAHO ('08)*	*4 LIBERTE ('07-'08)* *1 REPUBLIQUE ('07)* 1 REPUBLIQUE	2 KASHIMA		*2 IM. PAUL ('07)*		
III.	2 QUEEN 3 LONDON 3 FORMIDABLE 2 SWIFTSURE 6 DUNCAN *3 Minotour (07)* *4 Warrior ('06-'07)* *2 Black Prince ('06)*	3 MAINE *2 Washington ('09)* 2 Washington ('06)	1 SUFFREN 1 IENA	1 MIKASA 2 SHIKISHIMA 1 IWAMI 1 HIZEN *2 Ikoma ('07)* *2 Ikoma ('09)*	*4 DEUTSCHLAND ('07-'09)* 1 DEUTSCHLAND 5 BRAUNSCHWEIG *2 New cruisers ('09)*	1 SLAVA 1 TSESAREVITCH (2 EFSTAFI, '07) (1 PANTELIMON) *3 Rurik ('07)*	*1 V. EMANUELE ('08)* *3 V. EMANUELE ('07)* 2 BRIN *2 St. Giorgio ('09)* *2 St. Georgio ('10)*	
IV.	9 MAJESTIC 6 CANOPUS	3 ALABAMA	3 CHARLEMAGNE 2 BOUVET 2 CARNOT *2 E. Quinet ('08-09)* *1 Renan ('07)*	2 SAGAMI 1 FUJI				*1 E. KARL ('07-'08)* 2 E. KARL
V.	7 SOVEREIGN 1 HOOD 4 Drake 6 Cressy 2 TRAFALGAR	2 KEARSARGE 3 INDIANA 1 IOWA 6 California	1 JAUREGUIBERRY *1 Michelet ('07)* 3 Gambetta 1 BRENNUS 1 HENRI IV.	1 TANGO	5 WITTELSBACH 5 KAISER 1 Bismark *2 Scharnhorst ('08)*	(1 TRI SVIATITELIA) (1 ROSTISLAV)	2 ST. BON	3 HABSBURG 1 Sankt Georg
V.-VI.	6 Devonshire 2 Powerful	4 ARKANSAS	4 Gloire 3 Montcalm 2 BOUVINES 2 JEMMAPPES	2 Kasuga 6 Asama 1 Aso	4 BRANDENBURG	*3 Makaroff ('07-'09)* 1 Gromoboi (1 D. APOSTOLOV) (2 G. POBIEDONOSETS)	1 DANDOLO 3 Garibaldi	3 WIEN 1 K. Karl VI.

FLEETS OF THE GREAT POWERS (in order of importance).

ARRANGED IN PARALLELS OF FIGHTING VALUE, WITH THE "DREADNOUGHT" AS UNIT.

Battleships in capitals. Cruisers in ordinary type. Ships in *italics* will not be complete for sea by end of 1906. Approximate date of completion given in brackets.

Rate.	BRITISH.	U.S.	FRENCH.	JAPANESE.	GERMAN.	RUSSIAN (Black Sea in brackets).	ITALIAN.	AUSTRO-HUNGARIAN.
VI.	1 RENOWN 2 CENTURION 10 Monmouth	3 St. Louis 1 Brooklyn 1 New York	2 FORMIDABLE 3 MARCEAU 1 HOCHE 1 Jeanne d'Arc 4 REQUIN 1 FURIEUX	2 MINOSHIMA	2 Roon 2 P. Adalbert 1 P. Heinrich	1 Rossiya (2 TCHESMA)	3 SARDEGNA 3 LAURIA	
VI-VII.	8 Diadem	1 TEXAS 1 MONTEREY	2 COURBET 3 Desaix 1 D'Entrecasteaux	1 CHINYEN			2 LEPANTO	1 Ku. K. M. Theresia
VII.		1 PURITAN	1 Dupuy de Lôme 1 Pothuau	1 IKI	2 ÆGIR 6 HAGEN 5 Hertha	1 ALEKSANDR 2 Bogatyr *1 PETR VELIKY* ('07) (2 Bogatyr)	1 DUILIO	
VII-VIII	2 Blake 2 Crescent 7 Edgar 2 Encounter 3 Hermes 4 Arrogant 9 Eclipse	1 Olympia 2 New Orleans	2 Chateaurenault 4 Charner 1 J. de la Graviere	1 FUSO 1 Soya 2 Chitose	1 K. Augusta	1 Askold 2 Aurora		2 K. F. Josef
VIII.	8 Hermione	4 MONITORS 2 Columbia 1 Baltimore 2 Newark	4 Descartes 5 Friant	3 Matsushima	4 SACHSEN	1 P. Azova		
VIII-IX.	11 Apollo	1 Chicago	1 Foudre 1 Davout	1 Otawa 2 Niitaka 2 Suma *1 Tone* ('07)		1 Korniloff	6 Elba	3 Zenta
IX.	4 Topaze 8 Scouts 10 Pelorus	2 Cincinnati 3 Detroit 5 Chattanooga	3 Linois 2 D'Estrees	1 Chiyoda 2 Naniwa 1 Idzumi *1 Novik* ('07)	*5 Berlin* ('07-'08) 4 Berlin 3 Frauenlob 7 Gazelle 1 Gefion	1 Almaz 1 Jemtchug	5 Stromboli 1 Piemonte 1 Calabria	

NEW CONSTRUCTION.

BUILDING PROGRAMMES FOR 1906-7.

Nationality.	No.	Class.	Displacement.	Speed.	Armament.	Remarks.
BRITISH	2 / 2	Battleships / Cruisers		25	*not known*	Dreadnought improved
U.S.A.	1	Battleship	20,000	19	12-12in.	New type
FRENCH	3	Battleships	18,000	19	4-12in., 12-9·4	As described
JAPANESE	2 / 2	Battleships / Cruisers	19,150 / 14,760	·18¼ / 21¼	4-12in., 12-10in. / 2-12in., 4-10in., 8-8in.	Aki type (2 extra) / Tsukuba type
GERMAN	2 / 1	Battleships / Cruiser	17,710 / 14,760	19½	14-11in. / *doubtful*	Ersatz Sachsen / 'E'
RUSSIAN	6 / 3	Battleships / Cruisers	18,000 / 15,000	21	*doubtful* / 4-10in., 8-8in.	Rurik type
ITALIAN	1 / 2	Battleship / Cruisers	9,830	22½	*probably as V. Emanuele* / 4-10in., 8-8in.	Probably V.Emanuele type / St. Giorgio type

BUILDING UNDER PROGRAMMES 1905-6.

Nationality.	No.	Class.	Displacement.	Speed.	Armament.	Remarks.
BRITISH	1 / 3	Battleship / Cruisers	18,000 / 15,000	21 / 25	10-12in. / *doubtful, but heavy*	Dreadnought / Inflexible class
U.S.A.	2 / 2	Battleships / Cruisers	16,000 / 14,500	19 / 22	8-12in. / 4-10in., 16-6in.	S. Carolina class / Washington type
FRENCH	2	Cruisers		23	14-7·6	E. Quinet
JAPANESE	2 / 2	Battleships / Cruisers	19,150 / 14,760	18¼ / 21¼	4-12in, 12-10in. / *uncertain, but heavy*	Aki / Tsukuba
GERMAN	1	Cruiser	11,500	22½	8-8·2, 6-6in.	Scharnhorst type ('D')
RUSSIAN	1 / 1 / 3	Battleship / Cruiser / Cruisers	16,500 / 15,000 / 10,000	21 / 21	4-12in., 4-10in., 14-8in. / 4-10in., 8-8in. / 4-8in., 6-6in.	'A' / Rurik / Makaroff
ITALIAN	1	Cruiser	9,830	22½	4-10in., 8-8in.	St. Marco

COMPLETING UNDER PROGRAMMES 1904-5.

Nationality.	No.	Class.	Displacement.	Speed.	Armament.	Remarks.
BRITISH	2 / 3	Battleships / Cruisers	16,600 / 14,600	18½ / 23	4-12in., 10-9·2 / 4-9·2, 10-7·5	Lord Nelson / Minotaur
U.S.A.	1 / 2	Battleship / Battleships	16,000 / 13,000	18 / 17	4-12in., 8-8in., 12-7in. / 4-12in., 8-8in., 8-7in.	New Hampshire / Idaho (authorised 1903)
FRENCH						Work in Continuing previous programme
JAPANESE	2	Battleships	16,400	18½	4-12in., 4-10in , 12-6in.	Kashima (*completed*)
GERMAN	4 / 1	Battleships / Cruiser	13,400 / 11,500	18 / 22½	4-11in., 14-6·7 / 8-8·2, 6-6in.	Deutschland class / Scharnhorst ('C')
RUSSIAN	1	Battleship	12,600	18	4-12in., 4-8in., 12-6in.	Ivan Zlatoust
ITALIAN	2	Battleships	12,625	22	2-12in., 11-8in.	Roma and Napoli

COMPLETING UNDER PROGRAMMES 1903-4.

Nationality.	No.	Class.	Displacement.	Speed.	Armament.	Remarks.
BRITISH (7 ships) (and *2 bought*)	3 / 4	Battleships / Cruisers	16,350 / 13,550	18½ / 22⅓	4-12in., 4-9·2, 10-6in. / 6-9·2, 4-7·5	Last of K. Edward class / Warrior class / 2 battleships (Swiftsure) purchased. (*completed*)
U.S.A. (5 ships)	3 / 2	Battleships / Cruisers	16,000 / 14,500	18 / 22	4-12in., 8-8in., 12-7in. / 4-10in., 16-6in.	Kansas class / Washingtons
FRENCH (5 ships)	4 / 1	Battleships / Cruiser	14,865 / 13,644	18 / 23½	4-12in., 10-7·6 / 14-7·6 (probably)	Renan
JAPANESE (*2 bought*)						(Nisshin Kasuga) 2 cruisers purchased end of 1903. (*completed*)
GERMAN (2 ships)	1 / 1	Battleship / Cruiser	13,400 / 9,050	18 / 21	4-11in., 14-6·7 / 4-8·2, 10-6in.	Deutschland / Yorck (*completed*)
RUSSIAN (3 ships)	2 / 1	Battleships / Battleship	16,630 / 12,600	18 / 18	4-12in., 12-8in. / 4-12in., 4-8in., 12-6in.	Imperator Pavel / Ievstafi
ITALIAN (1 ship)	1	Cruiser	9,830	22½	4-10in., 8-8in.	St. Giorgio

ADDENDA TO SHIP PAGES.

U. S. A.

Chattanooga Class.

Torpedo Boats. *McKee* and *Mackenzie*.   *Photo, E. Muller.*

Destroyer. *Farragut.*

NORWAY.

Norge. Present rig.
Haarfagre class also have topgallant masts.

GERMAN.

Torpedo Boats.   3 of the S 73, etc., type.

SUBSIDISED MERCHANT SHIPS.

(Edited by W. A. BIEBER.)

BRITISH SUBVENTIONED LINERS.

CUNARD LINE (Liverpool—New York).

Photo, Adamson.

CAMPANIA & **LUCANIA** (1893). 12,950 tons gross, 4975 net. Dimensions : 620×65·2×37·8 feet. H.P. 30,000＝20·75 kts.

Photo, Priestley.

UMBRIA & **ETRURIA** (1884). 8125 tons gross, 3695 net. Dimensions : 501·6×57·2×38·2 feet. H.P. 14,500＝18 kts.

Photo, Priestley.

CARONIA & **CARMANIA** (1905). 19,594 tons gross, 10,213 net.
Dimensions : 650×72·2×40·2 feet. H.P., *Caronia*, 15,000＝17 kts. ; *Carmania*, Turbines. 17,000＝18 kts.

Will have four funnels.

LUSITANIA
MAURITANIA } 32,000 tons gross. Dimensions : 785×86× ? feet. I H.P. 72,000＝25 kts.

BRITISH SUBVENTIONED LINERS.

ORIENT PACIFIC LINE.

Photo, Gould.

ORONTES (1902). 9023 tons gross, 4622 net. Dimensions, 513·7 × 58·2 × 34·4 feet. H.P. 10,000 = 18 kts.
OMRAH (1899). 8283 „ „ 4584 „ „ 490·7 × 56·7 × 34·2 „ „ 10,000 = 18 kts.

Photo, Gould.

OPHIR (1891). 6814 tons gross, 2920 net. Dimensions, 465 × 53·4 × 34·1 feet. H.P. 10,000 = 18 kts.

Photo, Priestley.

ORTONA (1899). 7945 tons gross. 4115 net. Dimensions, 500 × 55·3 × 33·7 feet. H.P. 10,000 = kts

WHITE STAR LINE (Liverpool—New York.)

Photo, Priestley.

OCEANIC (1899). 17,274 tons gross, 6917 net. Dimensions: 704 × 68·3 × 44·5 feet. H.P. 28,000 = 20 kts.

Photo, Frith.

TEUTONIC (1889). 9984 tons gross, 4269 net. Dimensions: 582 × 57·8 × 39·2 feet. H.P. 16 000 = 19 kts.

Photo, Priestley.

MAJESTIC (1890). 10,147 tons gross, 4443 net. Dimensions: 582 × 57·8 × 39·3 feet. H.P. 16,000 = 19 kts.

BRITISH SUBVENTIONED LINERS.

PENINSULAR & ORIENTAL CO.

Photo, Gould.

CALEDONIA (1894).   7558 tons gross, 3529 net.   Dimensions: 486 × 54·2 × 34·6 feet.   H.P. 10,000 = 18 kts.

Photo, Gould.

PERSIA (1900),   **ARABIA** (1898),   **EGYPT** (1897),   **CHINA** (1896),   **INDIA** (1896).   7900-7950 tons gross, 4165-4200 net
Dimensions: *about* 500 × 54 × 33 feet.   H.P. 9400 = 18 kts.

CANADIAN PACIFIC RAILWAY CO.

Photo, Adamson.

EMPRESS OF CHINA (1891).   5947 tons gross, 3046 net.
EMPRESS OF INDIA (1891).   5934 ,,   ,,   3033 ,,   } Dimensions: 485 × 51·2 × 33 feet.   H.P. 10,000 = 16½ kts.
EMPRESS OF JAPAN (1891).   5940 ,,   ,,   3039 ,,

ROYAL MAIL STEAM PACKET CO.

Photo, Humby.

NILE (1893).   5855 tons gross, 3299 net } Dimensions: 420 × 52 × 33·5 feet.   H.P 6650 = 17 kts.
DANUBE (1893).   5891 ,,   ,,   3313 ,,

CUNARD LINE.

Photo, Priestley.

IVERNIA (1900). 14,058 tons gross, 9052 net. }
SAXONIA (1900). 14,281 „ 9100 „ } Dimensions : 581 × 64·6 × 38 feet. H.P. 10,000 = 16 kts

PENINSULAR & ORIENTAL CO.

Photo, Gould

BRITANNIA (1887) & VICTORIA (1887). 6523 tons gross, 3406 net. Dimensions : 465·8 × 52 × 34·1 feet. H.P. 6000 = 17 kts.

OCEANA }
ARCADIA } (1888). 6605 tons gross, 3510 net. Dimensions : 468·4 × 52·1 × 34·6 feet. H.P. 6000 = 17 kts.

P. & O.—(continued).

Photo, Gould.

HIMALAYA (1892). 6898 tons gross, 3700 net. Dimensions : 465·6 × 52·2 × 34·7 feet. H.P. 7600 = 17 kts.

Photo, Gould.

MACEDONIA (1903) }
MARMORA (1904) } 10,510 tons gross, 5242 net. Dimensions : 530·4 × 60·4 × 34 feet. H.P. 10,500 = 18 kts.

MOLDAVIA (1903) }
MONGOLIA (1903) } 9500 tons gross, 4930 net. Dimensions : 520·6 × 58·3 × 33·5 feet. H.P. 10,500 = 18 kts.

MOOLTAN.

BRITISH LINERS (held at disposal).

WHITE STAR CO.

Photo, Gould.

GOTHIC (1893). 7755 tons gross, 4975 net. Dimensions: 496·7 × 53·2 × 33·5 feet. H.P. 5500 = 15 kts.

Photo, Priestley.

SUEVIC (1900). 12,500 tons gross, 8108 net. Dimensions: 550·2 × 63·3 × 39·9 feet. H.P. 4500 = 13 kts.

Photo, Priestley.

CYMRIC (1898). 13,096 tons gross, 8508 net. Dimensions: 585·5 × 64·3 × 37·9 feet. H.P. 7300 = 15 kts.

Photo, Priestley

MEDIC (1898). 11,985 tons gross, 7825 net. Dimensions: 550·2 × 63·3 × 39·9 feet. H.P. 4500 = 13 kts.

ORIENT PACIFIC LINE.

Photo, Parry.

ORIENT (1879). 5453 tons gross, 3434 net. Dimensions : 445·6 × 46·3 × 35·1 feet. ·H.P. 7000 = 16 kts.

Photo, Gould.

ORMUZ (1886). 6465 tons gross, 3202 net. Dimensions : 465·5 × 52·1 × 34·1 feet. H.P. 9000 = 18 kts.

Photo, Priestley.

ORAVIA, ORISSA, & OROPESA (1897). 5321 tons gross, 3318 net. Dimensions : 421 × 48·8 × 33 feet. H.P. 4200 = 16·5 kts.

Photo, Gould.

OROYA (1886). 6297 tons gross, 3359 net. Dimensions : 460 × 49·3 × 35·3 feet. H.P. 6000 = 16·5 kts.
Transferred to Royal Mail, 1906.

ROYAL MAIL Co.

Photo, Humby.

MAGDALENA } (1889). 5360 tons gross. 2989 net. Dimensions : 421·2 × 50 × 33·4 feet. H.P. 5600 = 17 kts.
ATRATO

THAMES } (1890). 5620 tons gross, 3042 net. Dimensions : 436 × 50·2 × 33·4 feet. H.P. 5740 = 17 kts.
CLYDE

CANADIAN PACIFIC RAILWAY Co.

Photo, Humby.

TARTAR (1883). 4425 tons gross, 2768 net. Dimensions : 376·5 × 47·2 × 30·3 feet. H.P. 4900 = 17 kts.

Photo, Humby.

TRENT } (1899). 5535 tons gross, 3042 net. Dimensions : 410 × 50·2 × 32·3 feet. H.P. 5740 = 17 kts.
TAGUS

Photo, Humby.

ATHENIAN (1881). 3882 tons gross, 2440 net. Dimensions : 365 × 48 × 29 feet. H.P. 4600 = 17 kts.

COMPAGNIE GÉNÉRALE TRANSATLANTIQUE (Havre—New York).

LA LORRAINE	(1900).	11,146 tons gross, 4505 net.
LA SAVOIE	(1900).	11,168 „ „ 4529 „
LA PROVENCE	(1905).	15,000 „ „

Dimensions : 563×60×35·9 feet. H.P. 20,000=20 kts.
„ 607×61·7×38 „ „ 30,000=21 „

LA TOURAINE (1890). 8349 tons gross, 3378 net. Dimensions : 520·2×56×34·6 feet. H.P. 13,000=18 kts.

LA NAVARRE (1832). 6343 tons gross, 3231 net. Dimensions : 471×50·5×35·4 feet. H.P. 8000=17 kts.

LA BRETAGNE	(1885).	6756 tons gross, 3100 net
LA CHAMPAGNE	(1885).	6724 „ „ 3065 „
LA GASCOGNE	(1886).	7090 „ „ 3453 „

Dimensions about : 495·5×52×34·5 feet. H.P. 8000=17 kts.

LA NORMANDIE (1882). 6029 tons gross, 2947 net. Dimensions : 459·4×49·3×34·1 feet. H.P. 7000=16 kts.

MESSAGERIES MARITIMES.

AMAZONE (*ex LAOS*) (1896). 6240 tons gross, 2343 net.
TOURANE (*ex ANNAM*) (1898). 6344 „ „ 2388 „
MAGELLAN (*ex INDUS*) (1897). 6253 „ „ 2342 „
TONKIN (1898). 6364 „ „ 2327 „ } Dimensions : 445 × 50·8 × 36·1 feet. H.P. 7200 = 18 kts.

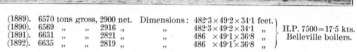

AUSTRALIEN (1889). 6570 tons gross, 2900 net. Dimensions : 482·3 × 49·2 × 34·1 feet.
POLYNESIEN (1890). 6569 „ „ 2916 „ „ 482·3 × 49·2 × 34·1 „ } H.P. 7500 = 17·5 kts.
VILLE DE LA CIOTAT (1891). 6631 „ „ 2821 „ „ 486 × 49·1 × 36·8 „ } Belleville boilers.
ARMAND BEHIC (1892). 6635 „ „ 2819 „ „ 486 × 49·1 × 36·8 „

CHILI (1894). 6375 tons gross, 2771 net. Dimensions : 462·6 × 47·6 × 36·7 feet. }
CORDILLERE (1895). 6379 „ „ 2451 „ „ 462·6 × 47·6 × 36·7 „ } H.P. 6000 = 17 kts.

DUMBEA (*ex LAPLATA*) (1889). 5917 tons gross, 2785 net. Dimensions : 463·1 × 46·4 × 32·5 feet. }
NERA (*ex BRÉSIL*) (1889). 5824 „ „ 2827 „ „ 452·6 × 45·9 × 32·5 „ } H.P. 5000 = 16½ kts.

ATLANTIQUE (1898). 6708 tons gross, 2890 net. Dimensions : 469 × 50·6 × 32·8 feet. · H.P. 7200 = 18 kts.

ERNEST SIMONS (1893). 4562 tons gross, 2162 net. Dimensions : 443 × 47 × 36·7 feet. H.P. 5000 = 17 kts

HAMBURG AMERICAN LINE (Hamburg—New York).

Photo. West.

DEUTSCHLAND (1900). 16,502 tons gross, 5196 net. Dimensions: 686×67×40.3 feet. H.P. 33,000=23·5 kts. (Fitted with Stone-Lloyd doors.).

NORDDEUTSCHER LLOYD (Bremen—New York).

(All fitted with Stone-Lloyd doors).

Very like *Deutschland*.

KRONPRINZ WILHELM (1901). 14,908 tons gross, 5162 net. Dimensions: 663×66·3×39·3 feet. H.P. 33,000=23 kts.

Photo. Symonds.

TRAVE (1886) 5262 tons gross, 2429 net. Dimensions: 437·3×48·1×34·4 feet. H.P. 6200=17 kts.

Photo. Sander.

KAISER WILHELM DER GROSSE (1897). 14,349 tons gross, 5521 net. Dimensions: 648·6×66×39 feet. H.P. 28,000=22·75 kts.

KAISER WILHELM II. (1902). 19,361 tons gross, 6353 net. Dimensions: 706·5×72·3×40·2 feet. H.P. 40,000=23·5 kts.

GERMAN LINERS (Subventioned probably).

Photo, Sander.

Name unknown. (ex *KAISER FRIEDRICH*) (1897.) 12,480 tons gross, 5147 net.
Dimensions : 581·7 × 63·7 × 37·9 feet. H.P. 27,000 = 19·5 kts.

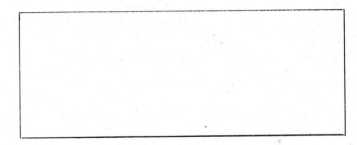

AMERIKA. 23,000 tons. Dimensions : 670·5 × 74·6 × 48·4 feet. I.H.P. 15,000 = 16·5 kts.
KAISERIN AUGUSTE VICTORIA. 26,000 tons. Dimensions : 675·5 × 77 × 53·9 feet. I.H.P. 17,200 = 17 kts.

INTERNATIONAL COMPANY (Southampton—New York).

NEW YORK (1888). 10,798 tons gross, 4643 net. Dimensions 565×63·6×39·2 feet.
PHILADELPHIA (1889). 10,786 „ „ 4577 „ „ „ 565×63·2×39·2 „ } H.P. 20,000 = 20 kts.

ST. LOUIS
ST. PAUL } (1895). 11,629 tons gross, 5894 net. Dimensions: 554×63×37·5 feet. H.P. 18,000 = 19 kts.

PACIFIC MAIL CO.

KOREA
SIBERIA } (1901). 11,280 tons gross, 5653 net. Dimensions: 550·7×63·2×40·8 feet. H.P. 18,000 = 18 kts.

JAPANESE GOVERNMENT LINERS.

AMERICA (1898). 6307 tons gross, 3460 net. Dimensions: 423×51·1×29·5 feet.
HONG KONG (1898). 6169 „ „ 3445 „ „ 431×50·7×29·7 „ } H.P 10,000 = 17 kts.
NIPPON (1898). 6169 „ „ 3445 „ „ 431×50·7×29·7 „

(Yards now removed).

RION (ex SMOLENSK), (1900.) 12,000 tons displacement. Dimensions: 500×58×(draws) 24·6 feet. I.H.P.16,500=20 kts.

(Yards now removed). *Photo, Parry.*

OREL (1889). 5074 tons gross, 2704 net. Dimensions: 452×48×24·1 feet. H.P. 10,000=18 kts.

(Yards now removed). *Photo, Parry.*

DNIEPER (ex PETERSBURG), (1894). 5432 tons gross, 1796 net. Dimensions: 460×52×31·6 feet. H.P. 10,500=18 kts.

Photo, Parry.

(Yards now removed).

LENA (ex KHERSON), (1895). 10,255 tons displacement. Dimensions: 493×54×(draught) 24 feet. H.P. 13,150=18·5 kts.

As *Dnieper*, but shorter funnels.

SARATOV (1891). 5427 tons gross, 2068 net. Dimensions: 460×50×32·1 feet. H.P. 10,000=18 kts.
Crow's nest low on fore, searchlight low on main or mizzen in all cases.

3 E 2

KUBAN (*ex AUGUSTE VICTORIA*), (1889), (lengthened 1896-7). 8479 tons gross, 3568 net.
Dimensions: 461·6 × 55·8 × 35·8 feet. H.P. 12,000 = 18·5 kts.

RUSS (*ex LAHN*). $\frac{5383.}{2449.}$ 447·1 × 48·4 × 34·5 feet. I.H.P. 9,000 = 18 kts.

As *Trave* (page 400), but mainmast removed, and wells filled in with ballooning apparatus. Topmast fitted to foremast, and two small yards high up.

DON (*ex FUERST BISMARK*), (1890). 8430 tons gross, 3226 net.
Dimensions: 504·4 × 57·6 × 34·1 feet. H.P. 16,400 = 19 kts,

Photo, Pol.

TEREK (*ex COLUMBIA*), (1889). 7241 tons gross, 2299 net.
Dimensions: 461·6 × 55·8 × 35·8 feet. H.P. 12,000 = 18·5 kts,

PART II.

THE RUSSO-JAPANESE WAR.

PORT ARTHUR.

We Russians should be ashamed of " The war from the Russian standpoint," in *Fighting Ships*, 1905.

First of all, the writer of this article is not a proper navy officer. Proofs are many. An executive navy officer would never tell that a wireless telegram can be intercepted by other ships so as not to reach its destination;[*] everyone understands that the distance from Port Arthur to Chemulpo, some 500 miles, is much too far for wireless telegraphy, especially for our home-made installations. Who can believe when he says that our torpedo boats went out *at 11 a.m.*, unobserved, and torpedoed the *Hatsuse* when weather was fine, and many from Golden Hill have seen the sinking of the *Hatsuse?* His conception that during the night from 10th to 11th August, the men have had to run from pumps—where they pumped the water out of ship—to the guns, to fire on attacking torpedo boats, is very ridiculous, etc., etc.

It is likely that the author was on *Bayan* in the first stage of the war, and his words : " I must tell the truth about this for the honour of

---

[*]It, however, appears established that a cruiser which went out from Port Arthur did endeavour to call up the *Variag* by wireless, and that this message was probably taken in by the Japanese. It does not seem to have been received by the *Variag*, which is presumably what I.R.N. intended to convey.—EDITOR.

our dear navy," gives some traces that he is connected with the navy. The perplexity and falsehood of his tale proves that he has seen nothing himself after the catastrophe of the *Petropavlosk.* Can it be that for some reason he *went away* from Port Arthur?

I make these characteristics of the author's personality and of his manner to deal with the facts, to show how much one can rely upon his stories and what could be his purposes. The principal proof against him, and that he does not really speak for the navy, are his suggestions that Admiral Makaroff was an old man and that he was himself afraid, because everyone who knew the Admiral saw him full of energy, active day and night, and rather imprudently brave. Working all day, he often spent his nights either on sentry-ship on the outer roads, or made a trip on a torpedo boat near Port Arthur, to see what means were useful to render difficult the blockading operations of the Japanese.

But his task was of an extraordinary difficult kind. He came during the war to a squadron new for him, of which the value and ability he did not know. And the latter was, it is true, not of a high standard, because all its time before the war the squadron was in reserve, with boat drills and tube shooting, and when still in commission the time was spent in parading and honouring the almighty viceroy.

Admiral Stark had no power. From shore he received every week a list of drills to be performed. For every movement or action a permission by a signal through the Golden Hill was asked. As an example of his dependency I can mention that he was on shore to receive orders from the viceroy when the battle of the 9th February (11½ a.m.) began.

The state of general passivity and oppression left from Admiral Alexeef's time, Admiral Makaroff had to overcome. Not knowing many officers or knowing them only by their former service, he had, by trials, to exclude the incapable ones appointed by the line order or by their good service to the viceroy. He had to swing the putrid marsh of the port to accelerate the repairing of torpedoed ships, and of all other ships whose machinery—by the strictly imposed before the war principal of twenty-four hours readiness for sea—was in a bad condition.

Quick outlet of the squadron in one tide out of the harbour, in which entrance the depth at low water was only 22-27 feet, was also his care, and he attained this purpose with much skill, doing on this occasion some practice to the ships in skirmishing with the enemy, and improving the evolutionary faculty of the fleet (his two sorties to Dalny and to Miaotao).

In many things he succeeded, in many he failed ; but he failed in things where no improvements could be effected in a short time and in war conditions. To cite, he failed in organisation of the most neglected torpedo-boat service,

because the training of the newly-appointed and former captains had to be produced under the guns of the enemy, and " the most likely not to return " were not " the boats which dared," but the boats whose captains had never seen the East and the East had never seen them. Such were the unfortunate captains of the *Steregushi* and of the *Strashny.*

On the Japanese beginning the bombardment of the inner roads and of the harbour, thanks to the absence of any gun on that very important place, Liaoteshan promontory, the guns were sent there ; and on the Admiral's initiative was worked out indirect firing from the ships, and the two 12 inch shells that struck near the *Fuji* (see " The War from the Japanese standpoint"), or rather struck the *Fuji* (see captain of the *Sasanami's* diary), and one cruiser, *Kasuga*, were not from the forts (which had not any 12 inch armament), but from the ships in harbour.

Admiral Makaroff's plans were clear for everyone who understood something about naval warfare, and consisted in getting ready all his disabled ships, and to give a decisive battle with all his forces, and to this purpose every officer on board was shown his fighting instructions. From this, I conclude, that the author was not there at that time.

Now as to the personal bravery of the Admiral. The words " that he was afraid " are a nasty calumny. Fear, I think, was an unknown

THE RUSSO-JAPANESE WAR.

sentiment to him. When, scouting in the night, torpedo boats were likely to be cut off from Port Arthur by the enemy, he himself clambered the nearest ship to the entrance (for example, *Novik*), and rushed out to the rescue. When he appeared in Port Arthur with his bright face, with his good humour, with his heroical bravery, with an encouraging word for everyone; it was for us all like a splendid light of the sun in the dark night. We all, oppressed by the abominable blunder of the 8th February, started new hopes.

The 12th April, we lost a truly great leader, and possibly with him the war. He was not only a great man, but a man with great will and a great heart, animated with a great love for his country. And this man died like a hero at his post. Eternal fame be with him and eternal shame with the author of the pasquil which you printed in *Fighting Ships*, and which was evidently written for some selfish and muddy purpose.

And now, why did the so broadly acclaimed Admiral Wiren do nothing during September and October? I will tell you it. A good captain is not everytime a good admiral (I do not know if he was a good captain). A captain's work mostly is the execution only.

Admiral Wiren could not ally the men and lead them to great deeds.

And his game was not lost at all. When he gave even half his men and some guns and shells for the defence of the fortress, he had still enough of all this to take in hand the newest ships of his squadron: *Peresviet, Retvizan, Pobieda, Bayan,* and *Pallada* (all with a speed at least of $16\frac{1}{2}$ knots), and some torpedo boats. All these ships were not in a hopeless condition, and needed only two or three weeks for temporary repairs, the time being favourable to this work because the Japanese still did not possess the 11 inch babies for their balistic exercises on the helplessly standing ships. The remaining ships, *Poltava* and *Sevastopol*, could with small crews have a glorious end on the outer roads (as it was with the *Sevastopol*), after drowning some Japanese torpedo boats; or, better still, could be stranded on Liaoteshan for watering and supplying purposes when the garrison drawn back from old town (easterly) forts should retreat to the last remnant of the fortress—to the Liaoteshan.

Feci quid possum. I ask you to trust that I have told the truth for the honour of our late leader, of the navy, and of my own. I zealously pray you in view of justice to rectify the Russian standpoint, and by this to amend your involuntary insult to the memory of our deceased national hero, and to degrade to the right place the writer of "The war from the Russian standpoint."

A VOICE FROM THE RUSSIAN NAVY.

MATZUYAMA, JAPAN.
October, 1905.

RAISING THE PORT ARTHUR FLEET.

Captain KUROI, I.J.N.,
Commanding Naval Brigade Battery, during the bombardment of the Russian fleet.

List of Raised Ships in Port Arthur (Between May and October, 1905).

Russian Name.	New Name.	Class.	Displacement.	When Raised.	Remarks (5th December, 1905).
			tons.		
Angara	Anegawa Maru	Volunteer Fleet Aux. Cruiser	11,700	May 12th	Commissioned as Aux. Cruiser.
Bayan	Aso	Armoured Cruiser	7,726	June 24th	Went to Japan by her own steam.
Peresviet	Sagami	Battleship	12,636	June 29th	ditto.
Poltava	Tango	Battleship	10,960	July 21st	ditto.
Ninguta	Ikuta Maru	Eastern Chinese Railway Co.'s Steamer	990	August 8th	Preparing to go to Japan by her own steam.
Pallada	Tsugaru	Cruiser	6,731	August 12th	ditto.
Gilin	Kitsurin	E.C.R.Co.'s Steamer	1,444	August 20th	Went to Japan by her own steam.
Sielnuy	Fumitsuki	Destroyer	240	August 22nd	Went to Japan by towing.
Zea	Nikogawa Maru	E.C.R.Co.'s Steamer	919	August 29th	Preparing to go to Japan by her own steam.
Blea	Yuragawa Maru	do.	919	August 29th	Serving in Port Arthur.
Retvizan	Hizen	Battleship	12,902	Sept. 22nd	Went to Japan by her own steam.
Tichikhar	Yumihavi Maru	E.C.R.Co.'s Steamer	1,028	Sept. 30th	Preparing to go to Japan by her own steam.
Gaidamak	Shikinami	Torpedo Gunboat	400	October 7th	ditto.
Pobeida	Suwo	Battleship	12,674	October 17th	Went to Japan by her own steam.
Vsadnic	Makigumo	Torpedo Gunboat	400	October 23rd	Preparing to go to Japan by her own steam.
Amur	Amakusa Maru	E.C.R.Co.'s Steamer	2,415	October 25th	ditto.

Total Displacement:—Warships, 64,669 tons; Steamers, 19,415 tons.

Besides the above-mentioned ships, 61 smaller steamers under 500 tons, and 114 miscellaneous ships (Floating crane lighters, etc.) were raised during the time.

Poltava.   Retvizan.   Pobieda.   Pallada.

Sunken ships in the West Harbour just after the surrender.

Removing 6 inch guns from turrets of *Poltava* by aid of the 60 ton crane, preparatory to raising the ship.

60 ton floating crane. This was sunk at the entrance of West Harbour. After being raised it was brought to the dock in the East Basin.

Bringing the *Poltava* into the East Basin after refloating.

The *Pobieda* ready to raise. Sand pumping dredger and salvage ship alongside.

Using the 60 ton crane to hoist out 12 inch guns from the *Retvizan's* turrets.

Damage done to a funnel of the *Peresviet* by shell fire from the siege guns.

12 inch gun hoisted out of the *Retvizan's* turret being shifted to a barge.

After turret of the *Peresviet*. The cover of the turret turned over by the explosion made by the Russians at the time of the surrender.

The *Peresviet* being got alongside quay wall of East Basin after refloating.

The *Peresviet* just up.

The *Peresviet* and *Bayan* preparing to proceed to Japan, in the East Basin. *Peresviet* to right, *Bayan* in foreground.

T. Kuroi 3 F

WAR ARTICLES.

THE END OF THE PORT ARTHUR FLEET.

By Rear Admiral Wiren.

Commanding the Port Arthur Battle Squadron from October to the surrender, and formerly captain of the *Bayan*.

———

There are some terrible stories about General Stoessel and myself in the last *Fighting Ships*, in the article about Port Arthur, by the officer who, in "The war from the Russian standpoint," writes such untruths about Port Arthur and about me. Now all this belongs to history, and only truth must be written about the war and about Port Arthur. The ships could not go out to fight the Japanese fleet, being all the time under repair, and receiving new damages after the battle of the 10th August. They could by going out have done nothing but perish, and so help our enemy to get Port Arthur sooner into their hands. When circumstances exist, one must act as is best and most reasonable in those circumstances.

After the battle of 28th July/10th August, in my opinion the best thing the ships could do was to return to Port Arthur. If they had tried to go to Vladivostok they would all have been lost, either at sea, or on the Korean Islands or interned in neutral ports, and then Port Arthur would

have been lost, maybe in August or September, for the batteries had no more shells for the six inch and ten inch guns.

The ships returned the following morning quite safely, notwithstanding they had been all the previous night attacked by the enemy's torpedo boats. Three of our ships, the *Retvisan*, *Poltava* and *Peresviet*, were so much damaged with big holes near the waterline that they could not reach Vladivostok, even without fighting and in good weather. Before the battle they had not all their guns, they lost a number during the battle, and returned with about half of their supply of ammunition on board; while at the arsenal of Port Arthur there was not a single shell left except some twelve inch for practice firing.

The *Bayan* was damaged by a Japanese torpedo ten days before the battle. She went into dry dock, and I gave away, by order of Admiral Witgeft, all my six inch guns.

Our damaged ships returned to a port which was not a safe place for ships to be repaired in. On the contrary the ships were bombarded every day and night by the enemy's batteries of six inch and 4·7 guns. But the Japanese had not then a good observation point, therefore only some five to eight per cent. of their shells struck our ships. We had no other place to repair our ships, for outside the harbour they would have been sunk by torpedoes. The workmen lived on board, and repairs were going on day and night.

At the same time, General Smirnoff asked us to

give our ammunition for the shore batteries. The enemy was preparing his first attack on Port Arthur, and so *we had only one thing to do—to help the fortress with everything we could give*, and not to allow the Japanese to take the fortress. Some of our ships were firing, too, over the hills at the enemy. With the help of our sailors, our guns, our ships, Port Arthur was not taken in August.

The repairing of our ships was going on very slowly, they frequently received some fresh damage, we lost many officers and men, and every day used some 100 of our shells and we had no other supply.

In September, by the wish of General Stoessel, one of our ships, the *Sevastopol*, was sent out of the harbour to fire from one side at the Japanese batteries, and she struck a mine, but, very luckily, did not go down like the *Petropavlovsk*, but returned to the port. She was out of service for about two months. The *Bayan* came out of the dock, but was without any guns. At this time the enemy commenced to fire the big 11 inch guns, and one of the first shells struck the *Bayan's* port engine—a month's repairs. I tried to change the place of the *Bayan*—to take her out of the harbour, but next day fifty-three 11 inch shells were fired at the *Bayan*, and five of them struck her. I took her again into the harbour where she was more hidden.

In October, the ships were in such a state that only the *Poltava* and *Pobieda* could go out, but they had *almost no ammunition for the guns*, and what could they do? Nothing!

There is a great temptation, when things are like this, when you do not know what to do, to die or perish as a hero! But we should go to battle not only for that reason; but if it be we die or perish we should do so to bring some advantage to our country from it. There is nothing easier than to "die like a hero" without use, and usually men can do that when they have lost all hope and all courage. Such a position was mine, (only I did not lose all courage), as commander of the ships, (only battleships and cruisers, for there were two more admirals, Rear Admiral Grigorovitch, captain of the port, and Rear Admiral Loschinsky, commanding the gunboats, *torpedo boats*, and all the coast defences).

I was sure that Port Arthur must sooner or later fall when all the provisions and ammunition came to an end, and that neither Kuropatkin nor Rojestvensky could come in time to save us! Of course I could have gone out in October with some of the ships without any ammunition, and so in the view of many people, perish as a hero, but *as a fool serving no purpose*, in my own opinion. Therefore I continued to help Port Arthur, considering that every *day* of life of this fortress had a great value in the war, both for the Manchurian armies and for the coming fleet of Admiral Rojestvensky.

With every day the fighting force of our ships was falling, and in November, even if they had been intact without any damages, they had no fighting crews, and no ammunition, but in reality, they were at the same time damaged and could they have gone out of the harbour, what could they do? Sink outside like *Sevastopol*, without doing any service to the fortress, expending their small ammunition against the Japanese torpedo boats? No! after much thinking I found it still better to continue our way, helping the fortress in everything as before. Just after the ships returned from the battle of 10th August, we sent on shore about two thousand men and fifteen officers, and every month, after the assaults, we had to send some more to replace the killed, wounded and sick. The gunners were one by one replacing those killed in the shore batteries, they were preparing new charges from different powder, the torpedo officers and men were preparing different mines, bombs against the enemy, the machinists were founding new shells for the six inch guns, and cleaning and repairing old Chinese shell,—in one word everybody was doing something for the fortress. If the ships

with their officers and crews had not been at Port Arthur this fortress would have fallen in August or September.

In November, when at last the 203 Metre Hill fell into the hands of the enemy, they received a beautiful observation point, and in a few days fired over three hundred shells at every ship. They damaged them all so much that there was no possibility to take them outside even for the purpose of scuttling them. During this great bombardment I was wounded and gave the order to leave the ships, taking on shore everything that could be of any use for the fortress. From this time we made preparations to destroy all the ships in case the fortress should fall. Only the *Sevastopol*, which was lying quiet inside the harbour, and unseen from the 203 Metre Hill, remained untouched. The repairing of the hole received in September having come to an end, I told the captain to go out and take the only place left alongside the gunboat *Otwajnii* in the

harbour (White Wolf). The *Sevastopol* received nets from the damaged ships in anticipation of torpedo attacks, but I knew and told the captain that his ship could not live long, and after a few night attacks she was so damaged that she could remain only near the shore touching the ground with her keel, and after the capitulation she was tugged some distance from the shore and sunk in 25 fathoms.

I had given an order for all ships to be destroyed in case I should find it necessary, but we had available for each ship only six or eight charges from Whitehead torpedoes. These were put in such places that if all exploded the ships would be really destroyed and useless for anything further except for breaking up. But it did not quite happen as I wished; some of the charges did not explode. We had only one night to do the work and in peculiar conditions; still in my opinion, the ships are so much injured that it will cost very much indeed to repair them,

and some, such as *Retvisan*, *Pobieda* and *Poltava*, are badly damaged. But at the same time I think it very interesting and also useful to have refloated them, if only for visiting and inspecting them in order to see what kind of damage they had received from torpedoes and different shells. And I am almost sure that the English Admiralty has profited on this occasion as allies of the Japanese, and gave them money to refloat the ships for permission to inspect them. But I doubt whether they can be repaired sufficiently to be much good for any fighting.

R. Wiren

WAR ARTICLES.

Class.	Name.	Original Armament.
Battleships—1st class	RETVIZAN	4—12 in., 12—6 in.
Battleships—2nd class	POBIEDA PERESVIET	4—10 in., 11—6 in. 4—10 in., 11—6 in.
Battleships—3rd class	POLTAVA SEVASTOPOL	4—old 12 in., 12—6 in. 4—old 12 in., 12—6 in.
Armoured cruiser	BAYAN	(2—8 in., 8—6 in.) (removed)
Protected cruisers	Pallada	(8—6 in.) (removed)

SUMMARY OF GUNS AT TSUSHIMA.

	12·6	12	10	12 old	10 old	9 old	8	6	4·7
Japanese	3	16	1	4	2	—	34	202	94
Russians	—	16	7	10	—	8	—	130	50

Totals.	Big Guns.	Old and Medium Guns.	Small Guns.
Japanese	20	40	296
Russians	23	18	180

SHIPS AT THE BATTLE OF TSUSHIMA.

Class.	JAPANESE.	RUSSIAN.
Battleships—1st class	MIKASA (flag) ASAHI SHIKISHIMA	(G T) SUVAROFF (flag) (G) ALEXANDER III. (G) BORODINO (S) OREL
Battleships—2nd class	FUJI	(G) OSLIABIA
Battleships—3rd class	CHINYEN	(T) SISOI VELIKY (T) NAVARIN
Armoured cruisers—1st class	NISSHIN KASUGA (D) ASAMA TOKIWA IWATE IDZUMO YAKUMO AZUMA	
Coast defence ships, etc.		(S) APRAKSIN (3) (S) SENIAVIN (3) (G) OUSHAKOFF (3) (S) NIKOLAI I (flag) (3)
Protected or belted cruisers	Chitose (D) Kasagi (flag) Matsushima Itsukushima Hashidate Akitsushima Otawa Niitaka Tsushima Suma Akashi Chiyoda Naniwa Takachiho Idzumi	(M) Oleg (M) Aurora (G or T) V. Monomakh (G or T) D. Donskoi (3) (T) Nakhimoff (G) Svietlana (W) Izumrud (M) Jemtchug (V) Almaz
Torpedo craft	About 70	About 12

D=Damaged. 3=Ships of the Nebogatoff division. G=Sunk by gun fire.
G T=Damaged by gun fire and torpedoed. T=Torpedoed. M=Escaped to Manila. S=Surrendered.
V=To Vladivostok. W=Wrecked in escaping.

THE SURRENDER AT TSUSHIMA.

By Rear-Admiral Nebogatoff,

Second in Command of the Baltic Fleet
at the Battle of Tsushima.

———

In the present article it is far from my thoughts to give a full account of the naval battle of Tsushima. I take from this catastrophe only several parts to defend myself from the heavy accusations brought against me by many critics.

After the Tsushima battle, I was condemned to the most disgraceful punishment. In ordinary life, the guilty person has the offence of which he is accused made known to him, he is listened to and tried. With me they have acted differently. I was deprived of all judicial guarantees. The judges, unknown to me, did not think it necessary to ask for an explanation from me.

In the present article, I wish to prove that my conduct as commander of the third squadron during the battle gives no occasion for any accusations. Everything that was laid upon me to do, I performed accurately. The catastrophe at Tsushima and the surrender of the ships happened through no fault of mine.

The battle began at half-past one in the day. I began the battle the ninth from the leading ship in the rear column, and in an hour I was already the fifth, as the second division drew out of the line, the battleship *Oslabia* having gone out of the ranks, and my division following me, took up the space between the first and second divisions and about five o'clock in the afternoon I was third in the column, as *Kniaz Suvaroff* and *Imperator Alexander III* left the line. During the battle we saw how the ships—coming in the first and second divisions—began to burn one after the other. It was doubtless the wood that was burning, which had not been taken away from the upper deck, also the coal and smokeless gun-powder, which burned like fire. I saw myself how the battleship *Borodino* first heeled, then straightened herself and slowly bent

to the right side, and in a minute-and-a-half sank into the water with the bottom upwards, on which crawled seven or eight men. I saw all these horrors, that have scarcely any prototype in history.

The battleship *Suvaroff*, having both her funnels knocked down and being in flames all over, left the ranks. The enemy's protected cruisers rushed upon her, I immediately took my course towards her, and fired on the enemy's cruisers. My manœuvre, undertaken to defend the battleship *Suvaroff*, gave her the possibility to recover to a certain degree. During my attacks on the enemy's cruisers I succeeded, as has been confirmed by Admiral Togo, in damaging several of them, and the flagship of Rear Admiral Dewa, the cruiser *Kasagi*, received such a serious hole that it was forced to go to the bay of Aburaya, and did not take part in the further actions. About five o'clock in the afternoon, a shell of about six or eight inch calibre, got into the turret of the 12 inch guns of my battleship *Nicolai*, the splinters killing Lieutenant Baron Mirbach, who was standing at the time in the turret. Part of the splinters flew into the conning tower, through the observation slit and wounded the right temple of post captain Smirnoff, who was led away immediately to have his wound dressed, after which I took upon myself the commanding of the ship. During the time of this battle from half-past one till six o'clock in the evening, I received no directions or orders from the commander of the squadron.

At five o'clock in the evening, finding that further manœuvring in this place was dangerous owing to the setting of the sun, after which the enemy could undoubtedly begin torpedo attacks and throwing floating mines in our way with his numerous torpedo boats, I took the course N 23, E, pointed out to me before the battle, the way leading to Vladivostok. About this time on the transport *Anadir*, a signal was made "Does Admiral Nebogatoff know"......No continuation of this signal appeared. At six o'clock in the evening the torpedo boat *Blestiashi* passed the right side of the battleship *Nicolai*, delivering with voice and semaphore, the following words

"Admiral Rojestvensky has ordered you to go to Vladivostok." After which I made the signal "Follow me," and continued to go to Vladivostok. The battleships *Apraksin, Seniavin, Oushakoff, Orel*, cruiser *Izumrud*, and some other ships followed me. All this was about seven o'clock in the evening. The sun began to set and with it ended the day battle. At this time the battleship *Borodino*, the stern of which was burning quickly, bent on the right side, and in a minute-and-a-half turned over.

The night battle consisted of ceaseless attacks by torpedo boats, the number of which reached to fifty. The ships of my division successfully avoided these attacks. I explain it in this manner that the captains of my ships were trained by me long before the battle, how to defend themselves from night torpedo attacks, by being used to manœuvring in the dark without light. The illustration of the success of these tactics is shown by the case of the battleship *Nicolai 1*, which was attacked by the enemy's torpedo boats from a distance of one cable's length. A torpedo boat fired a torpedo at my battleship, but thanks to our being in complete darkness, and turning the helm in time, according to my personal order, the torpedo passed under the stern without touching the ship. During this attack, the torpedo boats fired their guns, and with one of the shots wounded two of my men. I think if the battleships *Navarin, Sisoi Veliki* and *Nakhimoff*, had kept to my tactics, they would have avoided being hit. It is to be greatly regretted, that in this night battle, these ships made such dreadful lights with their projectors, and so betrayed their exact positions to the enemy. To repulse the attack of the torpedo boats was particularly difficult, owing to the artillery on the *Orel* being utterly unable to act, and the guns of *Nicolai 1., Sisoi Veliki, Navarin* and *Nakhimoff*, being of old pattern, firing only one shot a minute, instead of 4 to 6 shots as the new guns do. To complete all; the division of cruisers, commanded by Admiral Enkqist, left us and went to Manila, and the cruiser *Almaz* went to Vladivostok. In one word all the cruiser division with the exception of the cruiser

Izumrud, dispersed. Our torpedo boats did not help me either.

At dawn, the position of my ships was as follows:—In front was the battleship *Nicolai I.*, having on the left beam the cruiser *Izumrud*, then followed in the wake the battleships *Orel, Apraksin* and *Seniavin*. No other ships of ours were seen. Between five and six o'clock in the morning, I saw on the left beam five funnels smoking, and was soon convinced that it was the division of the enemy's cruisers of the *Matsushima* type, to which two other cruisers soon joined. I immediately made the signal, "Prepare for battle," and ordered all to turn eight points to port, having the intention of attacking the enemy from the front. But as soon as my manœuvre was noticed by the enemy, the cruisers turned their sterns to us and began quickly to go away.

Seeing that the enemy avoided a battle, and having no possibility of overtaking them, as the speed of my ships was less than the enemy's, I again took the course to Vladivostok.

Between seven and eight in the morning, behind the port beam we saw seven large funnels smoking. I immediately sent the cruiser *Izumrud* to meet them. When the cruiser returned, she reported that it was the division of the enemy's cruisers before us, and at the same time by means of signal asked my permission to go to Vladivostok separately, which she could reach easily, thanks to her speed. I answered by a refusal, as I had not yet lost hope of repulsing the enemy's cruisers, thinking the difference in force, not yet hopeless for us.

Towards ten o'clock, appeared on the horizon, six large Japanese ships and two cruisers, *Nisshin* and *Kasuga* in the direction of the port beam. After some time, more enemy's ships and torpedo boats were seen coming from the east, so that between nine and ten o'clock in the morning, we were surrounded by all the Japanese fleet, in number 27 war ships, not counting torpedo boats. All these ships, as far as we could see, seemed to be, according to their external look, in full order. Coming up to us at a distance of 56 cable lengths, the enemy's ships opened fire and firing rapidly, began to reach *Nicolai*. Several of the shells damaged the side in the water line forward, the water rushed through the hole in the forward dynamo room. The electric light went out. It was impossible to get at the magazine of this division. To my order to open fire, the gunnery officer reported to me, that firing would be quite useless as the distance between us and the enemy was 56 cable lengths, and our guns could only reach 50. We were perishing without any doubt. There was no hope, no chance of being saved. Two thousand men were waiting to hear their fate from me.

Holding the position of commander of the squadron and guarding the dignity of the Russian flag, I could not yield to the first impression, but had to consider the condition of our ships maturely and honestly, without any thought as to my own career, and after reflecting about our condition amidst the shots of the enemy, I came to the following conclusion:—

1. The 12 inch guns of the battleship *Nicolai I* were damaged the day before by the fragments of the enemy's shells. The 12 inch explosive projectiles were all used up in the battle. The remaining ammunition could not do the enemy any serious damage.

2. I have in my command four battleships and one cruiser *Izumrud*, I am surrounded by 27 big ships and a great number of torpedo boats.

3. The range of our guns is 50 cable lengths. The enemy stands at a distance not nearer than 55 cable lengths. When we try to approach him nearer, his ships, having more speed, go further away from us, not lessening the distance. In this manner we represent a target which is very easy to shoot through, and which is not able to respond to the enemy.

4. The crew of the battleship which had behaved with energy, that was above praise in the day and night battles of the day before, understood its position.

5. The enemy was firing continually, killing the men and destroying the helpless ships. A few minutes more we would perish.

Under these conditions I was fully persuaded that a battle was impossible and that further delay under the enemy's fire would bring the officers and the crew to aimless destruction. In view of all that has been stated, the moment had come when the commander of the squadron must use all his exertions to save the officers, the crew and the ships.

Were there any means in my power to save the ships and the crew?

a. We found ourselves in the open sea, having no shore near us or any ships belonging to a friendly nation.

b. Most of the rowing boats were broken, and to launch those that were undamaged was impossible under the fire of the enemy.

Beyond the rowing boats there was a total absence of life-saving means, as the hammocks had been used for arranging the protection and defence of the most vulnerable parts of the ship.

c. The total absence of time for taking any kind of measures, as the enemy's guns were devastating us.

d. The loss of physical strength from the battle that had lasted a day and a night.

There was no doubt, that in sinking or blowing up the ship all the officers and sailors would perish. Had I the right to do so according to the law or to my conscience?

The 354th article of the Navy Regulation says: "During the battle the commander shows the example of courage and continues the battle as long as possible. To avoid useless bloodshedding, he is allowed—but not without general agreement of all the officers—to surrender the ship, if all the cartridges and the ammunition are used up, the artillery destroyed, and all means of defence exhausted, and if there is no possibility of destroying the ship and the crew cannot find a way of saving themselves on the shore or in the boats."

Being persuaded of the impossibility of fighting and also of destroying the ship and at the same time saving the lives of the crew, I, before expressing my own opinion, proposed to Post Captain Smirnoff, and to the other officers that they should express their opinions. Captain Smirnoff, whose bravery and devotion to his duty no one can doubt, declared at once that he personally did not see any means of harming the enemy and saving the ship and the people in it. The rest of the commanders and officer came to the same conclusion. It is known already, that there was not one capable of forgetting the honour of a sailor. In this unanimity there was nothing wonderful, the picture was too clear to allow of any different interpretation. We were in the ocean, under the fire of a numerous squadron, threatened with death in the sea, without hope of any success. All felt and understood the same, and all saw with horror that the time had come, which is pointed out in the 354th article of the Navy Regulation. I well understood, that the claims of the law do not always coincide with all the arguments of morals, and that is why I am ready to defend myself in this affair, in compliance with every moral order. I only beg to have in view, that in deciding the question of surrendering the ships, I did not participate for one second in the selfish feeling of saving my own life. In the day and night battles of the 17th of May, I risked my life sufficiently to be absolved of any reproach of cowardice. If I had been afraid of losing my life, I could have found sufficient excuses for not meeting Admiral Rojestvensky, and with this could have finished my expedition. If I had cared so much for my life, I could have accorded my actions with the exact sense of the 109th article of the Navy Regulation. This article says: "If the Admiral's ship is very badly damaged, and is not in condition to continue the battle, or is in danger of being in the power of the enemy, the Admiral may go on to another ship according to his own judgment."

In this manner nothing hindered me; on the contrary, according to law I could have removed on to the fast cruiser *Izumrud*, and therefore had the full possibility to escape to Vladivostok. If I had had the care of my life in view, I could have made for the shore, or I could have gone to Manila, as others did. All these means were at my disposal, but I did not think of them, I went forward in the midst of the enemy's ships, with the one idea: to get to Vladivostok, as I had been ordered.

In judging my actions, it is necessary to examine the events of the past time. In contemplating the military naval actions, we always see that our foe was superior to us. I affirm that on the 27th and 28th of May, in the waters of the Pacific Ocean, it was not two equal enemies who fought, it was not a naval battle, but a definite destruction at sea, without any hope of success.

The first cause of the defeat at the island of Tsushima, was the deficiency of our ships and their bad manning. The second cause which brought us to defeat were the actions of the commander of the fleet, Admiral Rojestvensky. I will note down a few of his actions.

1. Before my joining with the Admiral Rojestvensky, I was struck with the indifference shown by him, with regard to my squadron. The Admiral was bound before leaving Noey Bey or Madagascar, to send to Djiboutly, an officer, with instructions and directions for finding me on the sea. As it is known, Admiral Rojestvensky gave no directions of this kind. I had to seek the Admiral Rojestvensky without any help from him.

2. According to the general order of things, the commander of the fleet arranges several conferences with the Admiral and Captains of ships, at which he explains the substance of the undertaking and general plan. If such conferences had taken place, those under his command would have been imbued with the plans of the Admiral and during the battle would have been active assistants. And here? I, the junior flag officer directly after Admiral Rojestvensky, the substitute of the commander of the fleet, during the whole time of our cruise, saw the Admiral only once, and was not admitted to a

conference of coming events, or even to any conversation with regard to them. I received directions every day, where to go or what course to take, and these were the only things made known to me. Wishing to understand Admiral Rojestvensky's plans, I studied his orders, and they consisted chiefly of loading coal, court martial sentences, reprimands and remarks with regard to incorrect manœuvering of the ships during evolutions and nothing else. Wishing to make these plans clear, I asked my officers to speak with the officers of the Admiral, but still could not find out anything. In this manner, I knew only one thing, that during the battle we were to follow the leading ship, replacing those which went out of the ranks, and in case the battleship *Suvaroff* went out, to follow the battleship *Alexander III* ; and at the beginning of the battle, I did not even know that Admiral Folkergam had died on the 25th of May, and that I was direct substitute of Admiral Rojestvensky. Such secrecy and uncommunicativeness of a commander of a fleet has no example in the history of the fleet.

It is possible that the Admiral did not understand that owing to accidents in the battle, he could be one of the first victims, and that it would be my duty to continue his plans.

3. One of the chief faults which brought about the destruction of the squadron, is without any doubt, the choosing of the strait of Tsushima to get through to Vladivostok. At the disposition of the Admiral there were three ways, through three straits : Tsushima, Tsugaru and La Perouse. The length of the way from these straits to Vladivostok is nearly the same, namely : about 450 miles, but in a geographical position the signification of these ways is quite different. At a very near distance from Tsushima Strait is the chief military port, Sasebo. In this manner, forcing our way through the Tsushima Strait, the Japanese fleet leaned on its chief base.

Expecting our forcing the way through the Tsushima Strait, the Japanese fleet could quietly lie at anchor near Sasebo; they could quietly prepare themselves for the coming battle, put their ships in a more advantageous condition for battle, leaving all the extra and harmful articles in the port. Thanks to their anchoring place near their base, the ships of the Japanese fleet at the time of their battle could have all their machinery and boilers in full order and cleanliness. Being near the base the Japanese were able to concentrate themselves and have in readiness a complete number of torpedo boats. At our forcing the way through the Tsushima Strait, the Japanese had the full possibility of watching the movement of our fleet at its approaching the strait, not in the least showing their presence or the place where they were stationed, or the number of their chief forces. Besides, the Japanese had the following advantage, which ought to have been foreseen :—The north Chinese sea, extending to the north, is bordered from the east by a group of islands. Tivu-Kiou, then by the islands of which Japan is formed, from the west, by the island Quelpart, by the islands of the Korea Archipelago and by the continent of the peninsula of Korea. Such a position of the Japanese permitted them to arrange on these islands many stations of observation, provided with wireless telegraphy. Cruisers and commercial steamers could continually communicate to the chief Japanese forces all the movements of our squadron. The enemy knew exactly the hour our squadron would appear, and he had only to choose the most convenient place and time for beginning the battle. To all these advantages which the Japanese fleet acquired, through our forcing the way through the Tsushima Strait, it is necessary to add several others. For example—the nearness of the base allowed the Japanese to have their crew not fatigued, and to take away the sick.

The Russian squadrons would have found themselves in another position, if they had chosen the way through La Perouse Straits, at a distance of 500 miles from the chief base of the Japanese. Here on this coast, there are no fleets, either military or commercial, and no port. In this manner of the Russians forcing their way through La Perouse Straits, both the fleets would have been in a more or less equal condition. In the month of May, in La Perouse Straits, along the coast of Tartar Strait and near Vladivostok, there are very thick fogs, which would have given us the opportunity to go to Vladivostok, even without meeting the Japanese.

At our moving through La Perouse Straits, the Japanese would have had to spend a great deal of energy and materials to defend their ships from attacks of our torpedo boats, which could come out from Vladivostok and hide in one of the numerous bays on our coast, waiting for a convenient opportunity for attacking. Without doubt coming out of La Perouse Strait, we should not have met those fresh and well-formed forces, which appeared before us in the Korea Strait. On approaching the Korea Strait, we had no news of the enemy, whereas, Saghalin gave us the full possibility of organising there several watch posts, from which by means of steam cutters, sloops and coasters, we could have instituted the delivery of news of the enemy in different places, fixed upon beforehand, along the east and west coasts of Saghalin.

If the Admiral of the fleet had effected a conference of the fleet, or some other person, he would no doubt have met with many indications of the utter impossibility of going through Tsushima Straits. I think that Admiral Rojestvensky had no moral right to use his absolute and individual power, to undertake such an important decision. Placing us in the position of blind instruments of his will. He forced many to sacrifice their lives for the Tsushima battle, and others left living, like myself, destined to heavier torments.

4. Entering the Korea Strait, Admiral Rejestvensky, sent his reconnoitring ships before him, and therefore took no precautions against any unexpected meetings with the enemy ; and no measures were taken to hinder the enemy from communicating to each other by telegraph. The 26th of May, just before the battle he forced us to drill the sailors twice, which fatigued the crew quite uselessly before the battle.

5. Overloading of ships. All the ships of the squadron, by the direction of Admiral Rojestvensky, were surcharged to the highest degree. We took in coal in such great quantities, that the armour on the water line was sunk about two feet in the water. In view of such loading, the ships were armoured on the water line only verbally.

In reality this most important part was as undefended against the enemy's ships as any merchant ship or transport. The coal was not only in the bunkers and stokers' mess deck and passages, but also in the raised floors of the crew on deck, in the officers' cabins and on the upper deck. In the small armoured ships, coal was loaded even in the captains' cabins. The battleship *Apraksin*, on the 28th of May, in the morning after the battle and after the attacks of the torpedo boats during the night, still had coal 20 per cent more than the normal quantity appointed for her. It is clear that such overloading of the ships in connection with the weed-grown parts under water, hindered the ships from going their proper speeds. For instance, the battleship *Nicolai I* with the highest pressure of the boilers and machinery, could not go more than 12 knots an hour. This is the sad condition that our ships were in during the battle. The question arises involuntary—what incited Admiral Rojestvensky always to load the ships with coal? According to our calculation—beginning the battle—we had coal for 3000 miles, whereas the way through Tsushima Strait is less than 900 miles. What sense was there in such loading, and does it not appear a shocking mistake?

6. Fires. In considering the breaking out of fires, I find that I am right in saying, that the commander of the fleet took no precaution to overcome fires. I affirm, that before the squadron began the battle, it was necessary to remove all the wooden parts of the interior furnishing of the ship, all the structures and superstructions, leaving only the necessary quantity for making up holes. All the rest of the woodwork ought to have been taken to pieces and transferred to the transport. Was this done by Admiral Rojestvensky? No, it was not! Only the ships of my division executed this, according to my order, and of the other battleships, only *Orel* was cleared from inflammable materials by the

initiative of her captain, not by the directions of Admiral Rojestvensky. The result of his attention to his work we see before us.

On the ships of my division there were no fires at all, or they were so trifling that they were extinguished immediately with water, with which all the compartments of my ships were plentifully provided. Quite the contrary happened with the other battleships. Very soon after the beginning of the battle, *Kniaz Suvaroff*, *Sisoi Veliki*, *Borodino*, *Alexander III* took fire. Especially the fire on *Kniaz Suvaroff* was great. I saw this fire personally. It began from the fore charthouse, which burned like a wooden hut. Fiery tongues rushed out of the windows. Soon the fire began to spread aft. The wooden boats, stern cabins, and woodwork gave plentiful food for the fires—a little more, and all the battleship was in flames. It is difficult to imagine what destruction a fire brings to a ship. How many people perished in the flames? From the fire all the artillery of the battleships was spoiled. Is it not clear that on the eve of the battle, Admiral Rojestvensky ought to have given orders to remove all the wood from the ships?

7. Capsizing of ships. I have had already the honour to explain, that during the battle one ship after another heeled and sank into the water, turning bottom upwards. Thousands of men perished at once without having time to harm the enemy. I am sure that our ships perished on account of their being over-loaded with coal, and also according to the directions of the commander of the fleet there were too many machines and capstans, and it is owing to this that our ships had no stability.

Besides this, to extinguish the fires, they poured water; and the absence of the scuppers gave no possibility for the water to disappear. Gradually a heavy weight formed above the waterline, and the ships turned over.

8. Only between 5 and 6 in the evening, when I was already going to Vladivostok, I received the confirmation of my decision. How must one designate this kind of commanding? Before the battle no one was acquainted with the plan;

during the battle no one gave any directions. Not one conference with us before the battle. Choosing the way to Vladivostok through the Tsushima Strait without warning us about it, even on the eve of the battle. Not one order about the battle, neither on the eve of the war operation, nor during it. The overloading of the ships, the wood not taken away, the fires, the turning over of the ships, the overburdening by the transports, the division of the cruisers and torpedo-boats wasted uselessly.

Having pointed out the actions of Rojestvensky, I shall say a few words about Admiral Enkqist, who had the duty of guarding the transports. Where did Enkqist disappear during the battle? Did he take part in it, did he help us during the night attacks against the Japanese torpedo-boats?

Reading the reports of Admiral Enkqist, we see that according to his words he tried several times to break through the line of the enemy's battleships and cruisers, to pass to the north, but had to reject this object "on account of the continual attacks."

In this manner, Admiral Enkqist "on account of the continual attacks," went away to Manila. The question is, what battleships and cruisers of the enemy stopped his way to the north?

Now it is certain that at sunset the enemy's battleships and cruisers went to the east, to the Japanese coasts, and did not hinder our ships from sailing further to the north, the best proof is the moving thither of my division. We know that during the night battle we were attacked only by torpedo boats. During such a battle the cruiser division would have been especially desirable, as the cruisers possess great speed and a quantity of quick firing artillery. If the cruisers of Admiral Enkqist's divisions had defended the end of the rear column following me, we should not have lost so many ships in the night attack. Nothing, in my opinion, hindered Admiral Enkqist from remaining with me, like the cruiser *Izumrud*. As he was under my command from six o'clock in the evening, he had no right, according to military law, to leave me and go away to Manila without my permission.

The picture of the battle, described by me is less than the reality, less than the horrors seen by me.

All that I have stated above has been represented by me not with the object of making anybody's position worse, but to prove and establish the fact that at dawn of the 28th of May, I found myself in a most fearful position through no heedlessness of mine, but by will of others and reasons independent of me. From the time I joined Admiral Rojestvensky, I was his subordinate. He placed me in the position of a blind instrument, and only in the character of a blind instrument I can be answerable before society and before the world. I declare and confess with pride that while I was independent I did not err in any way against my duty as a sailor. Leaving Libau, I safely bore with the squadron all the difficulties of sailing to the tropical sea. I avoided all complications that I met on my way. Moving towards Admiral Rojestvensky, I made the passage from Libau to Kamarahn in the shortest time, not losing one extra day. I brought my squadron to Admiral Rojestvensky in proper order. Foreseeing the torpedo attack, I taught my squadron to defend themselves from them by moving in darkness. Foreseeing the possibility of fires, I had all the wood taken off from the ships before the battle. By continual drilling and military education I brought the collected crew to know their duty as sailors. Other ships burned, turned over, perished from torpedo attacks, mine did not. Meeting the enemy the 27th of May, I made him bear a considerable loss. Not receiving any directions on the 27th of May, I did not rush towards the coast to go on shore, neither did I go to Manila. I obeyed the one order of Admiral Rojestvensky to go forward to Vladivostok and was going there without stopping.

The cruisers and torpedo boats left me and I moved alone. At dawn of May 28th all Admiral Rojestvansky's squadron, that was under his command was dispersed, destroyed, and I remained alone at my post. If there had been fogs, if the Japanese ships had had less speed, if

I had had at my disposal proper sea-going warships and not coast-ships overloaded with coal, I could have gone to Vladivostok. If I had had better guns, even equal to the Japanese guns, I could have begun the battle, and my officers and crew would have known how to die in a battle together with me. Unhappily circumstances were different. A curse lay on us for other people's guilt.

From the point of view of my judges, who have sentenced me to a disgraceful punishment, I ought to have blown up the ships in the open sea, and turned two thousand sailors into bloody pieces. I ought to have opened the Kingstons and drowned two thousand men in a few minutes. In the name of what? In honour of the Andrew flag?

But this flag represents the symbol of that Russia, which, imbued with the sense of the duty of a great nation, preserves the dignity and life of her sons, but does not send them to their death in old ships in order to hide and drown in the sea moral bankruptcy and plunder, incapable service, errors, mental blindness and dark ignorance of the elementary principles of the naval art. For the representatives of such a Russia I had no right to drown two thousand men.

N. Nebogatoff

THE BALTIC FLEET

AS SEEN BY ITS AUXILIARIES.

By Henry Reuterdahl,

Associate United States Naval Institute.

———

As very few details regarding the *personnel* of Rojestvensky's ill-fated fleet are to be found published, it may be very interesting to have recorded the impressions of some of those Germans and Dutch, who served on board the sea going tug-boats, *Russ* and *Sviet*, from Libau to the very last, the debacle at Tsushima. Last fall I had the luck to come across these men and to hear their experiences. What I have got together here is not the mere yarn of one man, but a carefully verified version of what they all had to say about their unique experiences as onlookers in the strangest drama ever witnessed. All were agreed on the main details here recorded. To them, at least, Tsushima was no surprise.

During the eight months journey they had very full opportunities to witness and observe the motley collection of Russian seamen, and the incapacity from admiral to stoker, never before perhaps observed in the whole world, unless in the Turkish Navy. For from the time the fleet left Libau, these two tug-boats were in constant attendance, pulling the destroyers, and

at other times the big ships, which often were "lame ducks" from engine room defects. This indeed was little to be wondered at, seeing that the engineers were from factories and railroads, of whom some had never before been to sea, and others not much. The sailors also were conscripts from inland towns, and of these also, to many, the sight of the sea had been previously unknown. Of the officers it may be said that they were always phlegmatic and calm when they were sober, but excited when drunk.

The *Russ*, on leaving Port Alexander III., Libau, went to Kiel for provisions, thus separating from the main fleet, and going through the Kiel canal rejoined the Russian main fleet off Brest. From there on it was a crawl towards the south, the tugs towing the torpedo craft most of the time.

During all this journey to Madagascar there was never any attempt to practice with the guns, the only practice being with tube cannon. And during the whole of the cruise from Libau to Tsushima, not once was there fired one medium or heavy gun in target practice, indeed none of the new ships had fired their guns at all since their gunnery trials.

It was during the stay at Madagascar, that the revolutionaries first appeared strongly in the fleet, several court martials being held, but the statement that they were hanged is incorrect, because the custom was to send them back to the Black Sea naval prisons. On board the flagship there was hanged one white man, who it was reported had been found to be in the pay of the Japanese and sending information to them.

The discipline here was very lax indeed, the men answering back to their officers and always very sullen, especially so when drunk. Drink was always to be obtained in abundance it seemed from the German colliers, where the market price was fifteen marks per bottle. The officers were always armed with revolvers, which they flourished conspicuously at the least sign of insubordination. The clothes of the men were in miserable condition, having no kind of uniformity, some nearly in rags. Their shoes were all worn out, and at Madagascar they obtained sandals from the natives.

For convenience of the officers there were kept on board the ships many cows and sheep with which the men herded, adding much to the dirty condition of the ships, which were in places like farmyards as much as ships.

While the fleet was here, there was a few times practice with the small quick-firers at targets, but no firing of big guns, or sign of war, except that at night when the fleet was anchored a patrol was kept with two cruisers using search-lights.

At Madagascar, the coal was transhipped from the colliers to the German liners which accompanied the fleet, and all the battleships took very large deck loads of coal, both on the upper decks and between decks in every possible place in sacks.

From Madagascar, course was shaped to the Indian Ocean, and of that there is little to say, except that the big ships could not keep station, and in bad weather were continually leaking.

The speed of the fleet in ordinary weather was about ten knots, and in spite of this slow speed the ships of the *Alexander* class could with difficulty keep station, and continually were falling behind. The stoking was always bad, most of the stokers being conscript landsmen, quite untrained. In fact the entire engine room force was poor throughout the fleet, and at Madagascar, the German engineers of the colliers and transports, were continually called for consultation, while repairs were being made, without which assistance some of the ships would never have got any further.

Sometimes in the Indian Ocean the transports would stop and the destroyers go alongside them to coal, when the big ships would proceed alone, leaving the cruisers and auxiliaries to crawl after them. In this way the fleet was often much scattered.

At Cameron Bay, Nebogatoff joined with his old ships of the third squadron, generally in a better state, so far as was noticed, than the first and second squadrons. Of the stay there is nothing else fresh to say, except that here the revolutionaries became more ugly tempered than before, growing daily more openly mutinous, without however, the officers exercising more control than before, except by showing revolvers more freely.

The best story of the battle was given me verbatim as follows :—

"It was on Saturday, the 27th of May, that we first saw the Japanese. There was a strong breeze and heavy sea, rising almost to a gale, and on the starboard bow was a Japanese cruiser which stayed there observing until eleven o'clock, when it was joined by three other cruisers, which also observed us, closing in. Our fleet then opened fire for the first time, which the Japanese answered, doing no harm to the Russian ships or receiving any damage themselves that I could see.

"We shaped course for Tsushima, the twelve armoured ships in two columns ahead, followed by the transports, and on each beam the cruisers succeeded by destroyers and the tugs.

"At 2-30 the Japanese were firing, and the Russian battleships answered. Before three o'clock the *Osliabia* and *Suvaroff* were burning, and our lines broken.

"The Japanese were quick to notice the helpless position of the cruisers and auxiliaries, and at once detached their armoured cruiser squadron to cut us off. Shot began to fall all around us, the transports being the sole target for the detached squadron.

"Till now the battle had been well ahead of us, but when the detached squadron attacked us the battle fleet turned about and came down back to us,

the heavy ships forming a circle all around the transports so as to protect these auxiliaries. Before, however, this formation could be completed the Japanese with incredible speed changed also, and formed a great outer circle round the entire Russian forces. So here were we, going round and round, outside in the fog the Japanese ships, hardly to be perceived and sometimes not to be perceived at all; inside the next circle our battleships steaming round and round, firing back at the flashes in the fog, themselves in bright light; inside again the cruisers also in a circle; inside again the transports, and behind them the destroyers and tugs, all driven together like sheep inside a fold and no ship making any attempt to get out.

"On all the Russians the sun was shining brightly, but the fog completely hid the Japanese, going round and round outside, firing very heavily, mainly at the four battleships, *Suvaroff*, *Borodino*, *Orel* and *Alexander*, and on the Nebogatoff battleship of the third fleet. The *Osliabia* steamed about without any masts or funnels, a quite bare hull burning fiercely, but still firing till she was torpedoed and sank with all hands. Then near us a Russian torpedo boat suddenly sank without a soul being saved,

Right before my eyes I saw a Japanese cruiser and also a Japanese armoured cruiser sink.[1] This has been stated and denied, but at times the small Japanese cruisers came up quite close to the Russian battleships firing, their flags plainly visible, and I distinctly watched two sink. No Japanese battleships were ever visible from the *Russ*.

About four o'clock the *Russ* was hit and began to sink, and all the crew abandoned ship in the boat, and we were later picked up by the *Sviet*.

Now the Japanese formed a circle round the entire Russian fleet, firing from every point of the compass into the mass. The Russians tried to break through but failed, for at dusk it was still the same, the Russians bunched in a heap, without much order, and several ships on fire; it was only darkness that helped the Russian transports and cruisers to escape. We could then see nothing more of the main fleet, and we knew nothing of it till we came to Shanghai, for the smoke after four o'clock became too thick to see anything in it. The *Ural* (ex-liner *Maria*

---

[1] Suggested sinking Russians which had hoisted Japanese flag. All the men stuck to this story.

Theresa) was badly shelled at half-past four, and her crew took to the boats leaving behind the wounded, but all the holy *ikons* were carefully put into the captain's boat."

The tug *Sviet*, the transports *Anadir*, *Belgia*, *Irkitok* and *Corea*, escaped to the south, conveyed at first by Enkqist's cruisers (which later went to Manila) and reached Shanghai.

The battle in my opinion was lost for various reasons, of which the following are some: because they had no scouts out, the ships were not honestly built, the crews were landsmen, they had no big gun practice, and none ever seemed to realise that they were going to battle. They were all a most hopelessly incompetent lot, with no idea about anything whatever except praying, of which they did an enormous amount at the least sign of bad weather.

H Reuterdahl

COMMENTS ON TSUSHIMA.

By Admiral Sir J. O. Hopkins, G.C.B.

It is fairly easy from the various accounts to gather the principles underlying Togo's attack, and once more we see history repeating itself, by the victor on this occasion throwing the weight of his attack upon a portion of the enemy's van, whilst threatening the rear with his lighter vessels.

And apparently Togo followed out in respect to Rojestvensky the ancient instructions of the King of Syria to his captains, "Fight, neither with small or great, save only with the King of Israel," by seeking out the Russian Admiral at the head of his column, and concentrating his guns on the leading ships, to their ultimate destruction.

The second day's disaster to the Russians—for their night losses by torpedo-boats and destroyers do not appear heavy—was the result of the able manner whereby the Japanese kept touch of their enemy and appearing next morning in force at the psychological moment, had them at their mercy, when dictates of humanity counselled surrender by the Russian Admiral.

Rear Admiral Nebogatoff's narrative of the battle of Tsushima throws a new sidelight on that action, and it must be acknowledged that from his point of view the final bloodless surrender was actuated by the noble motive of not uselessly sacrificing life by a prolonged and unprofitable struggle which could only have ended in useless bloodshedding, and his moral courage in so acting will doubtless be borne out by the verdict of posterity.

Once again we gather from this article that the head of Admiral Rojestvensky's column was the enemy's objective, and that Nebogatoff's ships (which occupied a rear position) were little damaged in the earlier stages of the action.

From Nebogatoff's showing, the "comradeship" which is so great a factor in the efficiency of fleets was conspicuous by its absence, and Rojestvensky's want of this accessory quality, his faulty dispositions, the absence of any tactical skill, and his mania for carrying in the fighting units of his fleet inordinate loads of coal helped to produce the fiasco which overtook him.

Of tactics generally there is little mention, but it is clear that the Japanese took up the positions that best suited them, were not pushed from them, and pounded their opponents as they best pleased; important factors in the case being superior speed, superior marksmanship, and better ranging guns, and further may be pointed out the enormous advantage of fighting with well-trained veterans united to the sea by the experiences of years, versus recently raised conscripts with but little experience of blue water and lacking the *esprit de corps* and cohesion of long service.

The general lessons to be deduced from the two days' fighting have been ably told by various writers, but it may be beneficial to discuss once more a few of the salient features of the combat, and particularly those which affect the devolution of the battleship in respect to armament and speed.

With reference to the former, the *Dreadnought* is undoubtedly the outcome of the school of thought which foresees the battle of the future being fought at very long ranges, and consequently aims its ship to deliver crushing and armour-piercing blows from all its weapons at extreme ranges, and if all naval battles are in the future to be fought outside 7000 yards, this armament of 12 inch guns seems common sense.

But who can guarantee this, and may not future admirals close in—as Togo is said to have done—to 4000 yards when a quicker firing and more numerous armament of lighter guns, such as the 9·2 in the *Lord Nelson* class and carried as an auxiliary to the four 12 inch, may prove more effective.

And if we accept *Dreadnought's* tonnage for future *Lord Nelsons'* they can probably be armed with six 12 inch and ten 9·2 inch, the latter a most formidable weapon, equal in range and accuracy to the 12 inch and capable of piercing at 5000 yards 10 inches of Krupp armour, or in other words, one inch more than the penetration of the 13·5 inch guns at that range.

Then in regard to speed, though certain naval writers infer that Togo did not benefit in this respect, can we ignore the fact that his superiority in this gave him the option of choosing his position, and must have added largely to the moral force which the "weather gauge" affords to every combatant who possesses it, and a large section of the Naval world will rejoice in the fact of *Dreadnought's* 20 or 21 knots as another proof of an up-to-date design.

It only remains to add a few words in recognition of the organization, patriotism, and "do or die" methods of the Japanese, which, with their sea experiences, made for special qualifications in the business of warfare, but what served them best of all was their undoubted superiority in shooting, especially at long ranges. Doubtless, too, their fire control was excellent, and the concentration at will of their guns upon any particular unit was irresistible.

Then Togo, without under-valuing his opponents apparently, realized their limitations, and, like Nelson, took full advantage of his intuitive grasp of affairs.

It is by no means clear that the smaller guns in the Japanese fleet did not materially advance the fortunes of the day, as their 12 inch guns were not numerous, and in point of fact, numerically inferior to those of the Russian squadron, which should with better marksmanship have made a more equal fight of it.

J. O. Hopkins

THE FATE OF THE RUSSIAN SHIPS AT TSUSHIMA.

Monsieur I. Bertin,
Late Chief Constructor, French Navy.

I feel very sorry to answer so unsatisfactorily the request of *Fighting Ships*. It is the lack of sure and precise information concerning the loading (*chargement*) of the unfortunate Russian ships engaged at Tsushima, as well as knowledge as to the exact nature of the damages their hulls had suffered before they capsized, which prevents my writing fully.

It is really impossible for me to determine up to what point the catastrophe has confirmed those fears which I have always expressed, especially during the last fifteen years, as to the security of this type of 'fighting ship.' I can only say that the facts seem to have confirmed my fears.

I am completely ignorant as to how much of the conception of the *Tsesarevitch* was of Russian origin, and how much belongs to French constructive ideas, and I do not think that this last ship served particularly as prototype to the other Russian battleships of the *Borodino* class, which perished at Tsushima. These battleships, in substance, represented a type common to nearly all navies up to a very recent date.

Models like the *Lord Nelson* and *République* are in each case exempt from the unhappy defects contained in the units of Rojestvensky's fleet. But do not conclude from that any advantage of priority in favour of the *République*. The improvement of English models goes back so far as the laying down of the *Majestic* after the plans of Sir William White.

Bertin

WAR ARTICLES.

THE FATE OF THE RUSSIAN SHIPS AT TSUSHIMA,

FROM A NAVAL CONSTRUCTOR'S POINT OF VIEW.

By COMMANDER WILLIAM HOVGAARD,

Royal Danish Navy.

———

IN attempting an analysis, from a naval constructor's point of view, of the causes of the destruction and particularly the sinking of the Russian ships at Tsushima, it is expedient to deal with each type of vessel separately, and to leave out of consideration all questions relating to tactics, gunnery, training of personnel, etc. In other words, we take for granted certain injuries, which the ships, according to the most reliable reports, have received during the battle, and based on what we know of the ships, it is attempted to explain how these injuries could lead to the rapid sinking of the ships.

THE OSLIABIA.

The *Osliabia* was of distinctly French type, not unlike the *Suffren*, characterised by relatively small beam (71.5 ft.), considerable tumble home and high freeboard with towering superstructions. The protection of the stability at even moderate angles of heel was imperfect, much more so than in the *Suffren*, because the heavy armour belt was not complete and not carried to so great a height above the water as in the French ship (about $1\frac{3}{4}$ feet against 3·6 ft.)

As a consequence of the small beam, the initial metacentric height was low ; judging from comparison with other ships, it can hardly have been much more than $2\frac{1}{2}$ feet in normal condition.

It has been stated (M. Lockroy) that when the Russian ships left the Saddle Islands, on the 25th of May, they had an excess of coal on board, stowed partly on armour deck, partly on upper decks. This is corroborated by a Japanese source, according to which the captured ships were found to have very large quantities of coal stowed in their upper works.* During the voyage from the Saddle Islands to the Strait of Tsushima, about 400 miles at slow speed, the consumption of coal in the large ships can hardly have exceeded about 200 tons, and this coal appears to have been taken, chiefly from the lower bunkers. It is therefore likely that the Russian ships were very nearly in their fully loaded condition during the battle, and that their metacentric height was smaller than in their normal condition.

Thus the belt in the *Osliabia* was probably less than 1 ft. above the water—perhaps nearly immersed—and the metacentric height hardly reached $2\frac{1}{2}$ ft.

The heavy belt was 9 in. thick amidships, and was surmounted by a strake of 5 in. armour extending up to the gun deck, which in fully loaded condition was about 8 ft. above the water. The sills of the 12 pdr. gun ports on gun deck were about 11 ft. above water. The 5 in. strake extended only for about half the length of the ship, leaving the ends above the belt, *i.e.*, practically down to the waterline, entirely unprotected. Thus any form of attack by gunfire was liable to produce wounds in the side near the waterline, and it is likely that the high explosive shell fire to which the Russian ships were exposed during the earliest stage of the battle opened breaches in the sides outside the high side armour which materially reduced the stability already at small angles of heel.

Due to the great tumble home, the curve of stability must, even in intact condition, have been weak, *i.e.*, the righting arms must have been small, and although the high freeboard

* See also Admiral Nebogatoff's article in the book.

secured a great range of stability, this advantage was in time of battle illusory, because the freeboard was so poorly protected. Finally the *Osliabia* possessed the undesirable feature of a centre-line bulkhead between her boiler rooms.

Early in the battle the ship received two serious wounds in the region of the waterline, apparently from large armour-piercing projectiles. The first projectile entered the orlop deck near the bow and caused the flooding of several compartments ; on the orlop deck the water reached the third bulkhead from the bow, and in the hold it reached the 6 inch ammunition room and the dynamo room. It is possible that this extensive flooding was due to an imperfect service of the watertight doors. The case brings to mind that of the *Victoria*, for as in that ship the water in the *Osliabia* reached the compartments under the turret.

Another projectile entered on the port side into the tenth coal bunker. It is probable that hereby also a boiler room was flooded, and in such case the centre-line bulkhead would contribute much to the heeling effect of the water. The ship took a heavy heel to port and settled by the bow. The starboard magazine was flooded in order to right the ship, but insufficient size of the valves made the operation too slow. At the same time the ship was on fire and the masts were carried away. The attempts to stop the leaks failed, due to the heavy sea which was running at the time, and due to the movements of the ship. Such were the facts as reported, and we have now no difficulty in imagining what next took place and how the ship finally capsized.

The water began to enter through holes in the port side above the belt, the heel increased and soon became so serious that the sills of the 3 inch gun ports became intermittently immersed by the movements of the ship and the sea. The gun ports were partly demolished and could not be closed. At a heel of about 16°-18° the sills of the gun ports became permanently immersed,

the ship then rapidly lost her stability completely, capsized and sank. This happened within one hour after the beginning of the battle, and was entirely the result of gunfire.

It appears that in regulating the stability of this ship, as also of many French battleships prior to the *Republique*, the leading idea of the designers has been to secure easy movements in a seaway. This result has probably been attained ; thus in the *Suffren* the period of oscillation exceeds 10 seconds, and also the *Osliabia* was noted for her steadiness ; but the fate of this latter ship has shown conclusively that if this quality is to be secured by small stiffness and great tumble home, it can only be had at the expense of safety in action. The smaller the beam and the greater the tumble home, the higher must be the freeboard in order to secure a proper range of stability, but the more difficult it becomes to give this freeboard an adequate protection. Also the target exposed to the enemy's fire will be greater, and the large unprotected superstructures will increase the liability to fires.

THE BORODINO CLASS.

Four ships of this class took part in the battle : *Borodino, Souvaroff, Alexander III* and *Orel*. These ships are likewise of French type, being derived from the *Tsesarevitch* and not unlike the *République*. The French in designing the *République* appear to have recognised the dangers of previous types, for not only has the tumble home been much reduced, compared with that of the *Suffren*, but the beam has been increased from 72.2 ft. to 78.7 ft., while the draught has been kept unaltered. The metacentric height thus attained is 3.6 ft. This metacentric height in a ship like the *République* may give a curve of stability, which for peace service may be perfectly satisfactory, but when the unprotected parts are damaged, the curve of stability shrinks, and if the ship is then struck by a torpedo, the stability is liable to become inadequate. This small metacentric height is indeed a feature which the *République* has in common with most modern battleships, as for instance the English, but in the French type it is combined with a system of side protection, which seems somewhat less rational than that of the English type; while in the *République* the belt is of uniform height from end to end, 7½ ft. above water, it is in English ships generally lower at the ends, but rises all along the broadest part of the ship to the upper deck. It is, however, effective as far as stability is concerned only to a height of about 11 to 12 ft. above water, where the integrity is broken by the gun ports of the secondary battery (*King Edward*, *Triumph*).

Returning to the *Borodino* class, we find that the Russians have here followed the French tendency to an increase in beam, evidenced in the *République*. Compared with the *Osliabia*, the beam has been increased from 71.5 ft. to 75.5 ft., while the draught has been reduced from 27½ ft. to 26 ft. The metacentric height has, however, hardly reached 3½ ft.

Like the *Osliabia*, these vessels have considerable tumble home, and the freeboard is very high with enormous, towering, unprotected superstructures, forming a large and prominent target for the enemy's shell fire. The side armour is arranged according to the French system, but the upper part of it is much lighter than in the *République*.

The side armour consists of two complete strakes: the lower (maximum: 10 in.) is in fully loaded condition less than 1 ft. above water; the upper (maximum: 6 in.) is covered on its top by a 4 in. armour deck, which is less than 7 ft. above water in fully loaded condition. A splinter deck, 1½ in. thick, is placed 6½ ft. below the principal armour deck, curving down at the sides to form a lateral armour bulkhead, intended to serve as protection against torpedoes.

A battery of 12 pounders is placed amidships on the principal armour deck. The sills of the gun ports are only about 9 ft. above water in fully loaded condition.

In a calm sea the heavy belt would be immersed at a heel of about 1°, the top of the upper armour strake at 10°, and the 12 pounder gun port sills at about 14°.

It has been stated that the vessels of the *Borodino* class rolled violently during the battle on the 27th.

The *Borodino* suffered much from gunfire at the beginning of the battle, and several serious fires broke out on board her during the afternoon. Fifty minutes after the fight began she was put out of action, but was, however, near four o'clock able to take the place of the *Souvaroff* at the head of the line and continue the fight. Later in the afternoon she again had a serious fire on board, and at about a quarter past seven she heeled over to starboard, capsized and sank. Admiral Togo reports that a ship, which, according to the evidence of Russian prisoners of war was the *Borodino*, was seen to become suddenly enveloped in the smoke of a violent explosion, and to sink immediately after. Presumably the fire had reached the magazines, although it is possible that the ship was struck by a torpedo.

The *Souvaroff* was soon after the beginning of the fight put out of action and had to leave the line with a great fire; at half past two the staff had to be transferred to the communication room. She lost both masts and funnels and was quite enveloped in smoke. She was subject to two torpedo attacks in the afternoon, of which it is known that the last one, at a quarter to five, was successful. A torpedo struck the ship under the port quarter and caused a heel of some 10°. In the evening she was again attacked by torpedo destroyers and sank at 7-20 p.m., after being hit by three torpedoes. The last torpedo is said to have struck at the engine rooms, after which she sank in a few minutes. It is stated by an observer in the *Aurora*, that the *Borodino*

was on her beam ends for fifteen minutes before she sank, and that he could see down her smoke stacks. However this may be, the *Souvaroff* showed considerable power of resisting torpedo attacks, which seems to prove that she had a very efficient system of watertight subdivision (probably the same as that of the *Tsesarevitch*), a feature to which the French naval architects have always given great prominence. Possibly the armoured lateral bulkheads proved useful against the torpedo explosions. The success of the torpedo attacks was made possible only by the crippled condition in which the ship was left by the gunfire.

The *Alexander III* had several serious fires on board, and suffered much from gunfire. After six p.m. she had to leave the line, she gradually took a great heel and capsized at seven minutes past seven p.m. We do not know the exact nature of the damage sustained by this ship, but it appears that she was sunk entirely by gunfire.

Orel. Although the upper works were wrecked as in the other ships of this class, the *Orel* preserved her vitality throughout the engagement. The heavy armour was unpierced, no hits were found below the waterline, and no torpedo hits occurred.

* * *

Summing up, it is seen that four modern first-class battleships were sunk in the engagement, two by gunfire, one by torpedoes and one by the fire reaching the magazines. Also in the two latter cases gunfire was however primarily responsible for the result. These ships were of the earlier French type, and all suffered more or less from the defects inherent in this type; a too small initial stability, an inadequate protection of the freeboard, a great tumble home, and large towering superstructures. Even the carefully designed French system of watertight subdivision could not outweigh these defects.

The French type of battleship cannot be said to have stood the test of battle, but it is only just to add that it was tested much more severely than was the English type.

The Smaller Russian Armoured Ships.

The *Navarin* (10,000 tons), was a reduced *Trafalgar*. She was well protected up to upper deck and had no excess of unprotected superstructures. It appears that she stood gunfire well, but she succumbed to torpedo attack on the morning of the 28th, being struck by a torpedo on each side.

Sissoi Veliki (9000 tons), had much resemblance to the *Royal Sovereign*. During the artillery fight she was struck twelve times by projectiles of large calibre, she suffered much from fire, and towards evening she had settled somewhat by the bow. During the night she was attacked by torpedo boats and was hit at least once. On the next day, in the forenoon, she heeled over to starboard and sank. Bearing in mind the small displacement of this ship, she showed considerable power of resistance.

Admiral Nachimoff (8000 tons), was in point of distribution of armour very similar to the *Amiral Duperré*, only the armour deck joined the lower edge of the belt. The belt was narrow and no armour was found above the belt, which was surmounted by an upper unprotected hull of two deckheights and a superstructure. Like the *Duperré*, the *Nachimoff* was liable to great loss of stability by damage to the unprotected side. She was struck by a torpedo on the evening of the 27th, and with the damage sustained by gunfire during the day, we can readily understand that she was found the next morning in a sinking condition. The Japanese tried to take her in tow, but after the crew had been removed she went down, capsizing. Possibly the valves were opened by the crew.

Admiral Oushakoff (4100 tons), although built as late as 1893, was of the same type as the English "Admiral class," a type which had then been abandoned for several years by the English. It was characterised by a low central belt and an underwater armour deck at the ends, covered by a cellular layer. This type was like the *Amiral Duperré*, open to the objection that damage to the unprotected parts would in a seaway endanger the stability. Both types originated during the eighties as a result of the incompatible claims to heavy guns and heavy armour on one hand and a restricted displacement on the other; but both in England and France the designers evolved what was probably the best compromises under the circumstances. Due to the great development of rapid firing guns and shellfire which took place during the latter half of the eighties and the following years, both types soon became obsolete. For service on an expedition like the one in question, ships of the Admiral class of so small displacement were entirely unsuited.

The *Admiral Oushakoff* was attacked by the Japanese armoured cruisers *Iwate* and *Yakumo*, armed with 8 in. and 6 in. guns, on the afternoon of the 28th. At the end of about half-an hour she was completely wrecked and sank.

The two old belted ships, *Dmitri Donskoi* and *Vladimir Monomach* fell as an easy prey to torpedoes.

General Remarks and Conclusions.

The first-class battleships that were sunk in this fight were in point of STABILITY somewhat inferior to most existing modern battleships. Considering, however, the way in which these ships were sunk, as also the way in which battleships of other and better type were destroyed earlier in the war, we cannot remain satisfied with even the best of existing types. If we are to continue to build large battleships,

it appears absolutely necessary that some radical change should be made in their design. A mere increase in size, if unaccompanied by a still greater increase in stability, is likely to lead to disappointment in time of war.

Hence, battleships should be given a much greater initial stiffness than has hitherto generally been given to ships of this class. The stability at moderate angles of heel should be better protected by carrying the side armour, unimpaired by the presence of gun ports, up to the upper deck all along the vitals. The tumble home should be very small. The watertight subdivision should be designed with more particular regard to torpedo attack; lateral, eventually armoured bulkheads should be carried along the vitals some 18 ft. from the sides, and the engine rooms should be reduced in size by the use of three or more propellors. Finally, compensating tanks, with a special and powerful flooding system, should be provided for righting the ship when it takes a heel.*

The advantages of a steady gun platform, so indispensable to a battleship, should be attained, not by sacrificing the safety in action, but by increasing the resistance to rolling.

While in existing battleships of 14–16,000 tons we find a metacentric height of $3\frac{1}{2}$-4 ft.; future battleships of about 18,000 tons should not have less than 6-8 ft. metacentric height, even although this feature, involving great beam, as well as the fitting of very large bilge keels may be somewhat prejudicial to speed. With a proper system of subdivision and protection, the passive power of resistance of such battleships against attack on their stability would thus be more than twice that of existing battleships.

---

* The questions here touched upon are dealt with more fully by the author of this article in two papers read before the American Society of Naval Architects and Marine Engineers in 1903 and 1904, entitled, *Watertight Subdivision of Warships* and *The Seagoing Battleship.*

In order to avoid the complete destruction of the *anti-torpedo-boat guns* during an artillery fight, these guns, and eventually their stands, should be made portable, as far as their weight and location permit, and should be capable of being housed under shelter of armour and readily mounted again. Rapid-firers of greater calibre, especially those above 3 in., which cannot be made portable without too great difficulties, should be given a protection corresponding to their importance.

The high explosive shell of the Japanese caused SERIOUS FIRES in all of the Russian battleships and widespread DESTRUCTION OF THE SUPERSTRUCTURES and all that was found in and about them. The confusion and interference with the service of ship and guns which was caused hereby can easily be imagined: communication was made difficult, the working of the guns was impeded by the debris of falling masts, funnels, ventilators, etc., as well as by the fire and smoke, the draught in the furnaces was obstructed, and the men who had to fight the fires must have been exposed in the unprotected parts of the ship to the gunfire of the enemy with consequent great number of casualities.

These numerous and violent fires came as a surprise to many, for probably the Russians had taken as complete precautions in this respect as other nations. Evidently we have still something to learn in this respect.*

In and on the unprotected superstructures of these ships were probably found a great number of inflammable objects such as furniture, hammocks, hawsers, effects of officers and crew, deck covering of wood or linoleum, etc., but these objects and materials could hardly by themselves account for the violent fires that occurred. It appears that one of the main causes of the fires were the boats, of which it is said that the

---

* See Admiral Nebogatoff's article in this issue.

Russians carried the full complement during the battle. It is worth noting that the Japanese had only a few boats on board each ship.

It has been stated that also the paint took fire; this is probably a novel idea to many, but it is a fact that even after paint is dry, the inflammable substances contained in the linseed oil are not completely oxidised, and will burn readily. It seems therefore quite likely, if the paint has been allowed to accumulate into thick layers, that it may have contributed materially to the fire and to the smoke. It may be added also that linoleum will burn freely, and is in fact much more inflammable than paint.

If the statement is correct, that the Russians during the battle carried coal in the upper parts of the ships, this coal may have contributed considerably to the seriousness of the fires.

Finally, the high explosive shells had a very great incendiary power on account of the extremely high temperature attained by the explosion.

The fate of these ships shows the necessity of reducing the extent of unprotected structures to the smallest minimum, and of avoiding more scrupulously than hitherto the use or stowage of any kind of inflammable materials in these parts of the ships.

The boats carried during action should be of steel, and should be stowed on gun deck behind armour.

In order, on the other hand, to secure the most effective offensive power, it appears premature entirely to abandon the secondary battery. The attack on lightly protected or unprotected parts, which proved so effective at Tsushima, can be better performed by a greater number of 9 in. or 10 in. guns, than by a smaller number of 12 in. guns.

W. Hovgaard.

WAR ARTICLES.

MINES AND TORPEDOES IN THE LATE WAR.

It is now possible to ascertain with some exactitude the number of ships mined and torpedoed in the war. The following list includes all large ships. An asterisk denotes that the ship was sunk.

HIT BY MINES.

JAPANESE.	RUSSIAN.
*Hatsuse****	*Yenesi****
*Yashima****	*Boyarin****
Asahi	*Petropavlovsk****
Mikasa	*Pobieda*
*Takasago****	*Sevastopol*
Chiyoda	(two or three times)
*Sai Yen****	*Bayan*
*Hei Yen****	
*Miyako****	

HIT BY TORPEDOES.

JAPANESE.	RUSSIAN.
Mikasa	*Tsesarevitch*
	Retvizan
	Pallada
	*Kniaz Suvaroff****
	*Navarin****
	*Sissoi Veliky****
	*Admiral Nakimoff****
	*Dmitri Donskoi****
	*V. Monomakh****

As regards mines, it seems quite clearly established that the *Hatsuse* was sunk by mines, and that the "sixteen Russian torpedo boats" were fictitious, so far as results were concerned.

The story of the loss of the *Hatsuse* is too well known to need repetition here. The loss of the *Yashima* at the same time has always been wrapped in mystery, and was, indeed, long kept secret. A Japanese account is as follows:—

"Five minutes after the sinking of the *Hatsuse* in the neighbourhood of the Miao Islands, the *Yashima* also struck a mine, which exploded with terrible force.

Captain Sakamoto at once ordered the ship's course to be changed, and the vessel proceeded at full speed to a certain naval base. At the same time all measures were taken to prevent the inrush of water. When she had proceeded some sixty miles and reached the neighbourhood of Yuantao, the inrush of water was so great, that the saving of the vessel was hopeless. The captain therefore ordered the crew to embark in the *Kasagi* and *Tatsuta*, and the ship subsequently sank in twenty-five fathoms of water. Even at present the tops of her masts can be observed above the surface of the sea.

"At the time of these disasters our squadron, which had been cruising off Port Arthur, consisted of the battleships *Hatsuse*, *Shikishima*, and *Yashima*, and cruisers *Kasagi* and *Tatsuta*. The *Hatsuse* and *Yashima* formed the wings, and the *Shikishima* the centre. The latter on witnessing the almost simultaneous disaster to the *Hatsuse* and *Yashima*, became conscious of the magnitude of the risks to which she was also exposed, for had she sustained a similar disaster the Japanese battleship fleet would have lost half its power. She was, however, proceeding to the assistance of the *Yashima*, when the latter signalled, "Leave us alone : seek safety." The *Shikishima* was fortunate enough to escape from the danger zone in safety."

The *Asahi* and *Mikasa* were struck under the following circumstances, which have been kept secret hitherto:—

The *Mikasa*, *Shikishima* and *Asahi*, were steaming in line ahead, not long after the *Hatsuse* disaster. Suddenly the *Mikasa* struck a mine, which, however, did not explode. It glanced from her and was narrowly avoided by the *Shikishima*. It then struck the *Asahi* amidships and exploded against the belt, damaging torpedo booms, but doing no injury of a serious nature.

From this it appears that of the six Japanese battleships, one twice ran risk from mines, and four actually struck them. That in two cases no harm resulted, was luck rather than anything else. As things were Japan lost 33 per cent. of her battle fleet by mines, but she might have lost over 80 per cent. These figures may well give food for thought. It has been claimed by the Russians that mines laid by the *Amur* were the cause of these incidents.

The Russian losses were smaller, as the Russians were less at sea, and only one battleship, the *Petropavlovsk*, was actually sunk. The *Bayan*, however, seems to have been rendered useless. The survival of the *Sevastopol* is peculiar—she appears to have been in a chronic state of mine-hitting.

The torpedo—which after all is only a mine with temporary motive power—was much less effective. The only Japanese ship actually sunk was the *Mikasa*, and she—if the story be true—was hit by a Japanese boat, which mistook her for the *Tsesarevitch* in the dark, she having dropped astern after the battle of Round Island. She was probably torpedoed somewhere forward. She was not, of course, sunk. The only modern ship actually sunk by torpedoes was the *Suvaroff*, and she had already been damaged by gun-fire. The old ships do not count.

The *Sevastopol*, though torpedoes seem to have been fired at her by the dozen, was certainly not sunk by them, and it is doubtful whether she was even hit. She is so described in "With Togo," by Mr. Seppings Wright, but as Mr. Wright pictures her with three funnels like the *Retvizan*, his account will hardly be accepted as quite conclusive. More reliable accounts suggest that torpedoes exploding in the nets and booms, caused her to leak badly, and that that was all that was accomplished. It is unwise to over-estimate torpedo results, and against modern ships they should, perhaps, be regarded as merely disabling blows.

The sinking of the *Suvaroff* is a special case. She was heavily disabled by gun fire, and probably more or less in a sinking condition when hit by at least one torpedo, and probably by three or four. How far torpedoes played a part in the sinking of the other Borodinos has never appeared, and will probably never be exactly known, and even official Japanese accounts tend to be contradictory.

There is evidence to show that torpedoes were fired at all or nearly all the ships sunk in the first day of the great battle, but little to indicate whether hits were observed. In the stress of battle these sort of incidents are apt to pass unregarded, and subsequently it is impossible to recall results with exactitude. When guns are firing heavily, torpedo explosion cannot be heard, and with shells bursting on the targets and hitting the water all round it, it is not over and above easy to detect torpedo explosions.

The night attack following Tsushima cannot be described as a brilliant success for the torpedo. The ships actually hit were the *Sissoi Veliky*, *Navarin*, *Nakhimoff*, and possibly *Dmitri Donskoi* and *Vladimir Monomakh*. In his interesting article in this edition Admiral Nebogatoff, probably quite soundly, attributes all loss to the use of searchlights, and there is every reason to believe him to be correct in this statement. Allowing that the "fifty boats" is an exaggeration, there is no doubt that at least three determined attacks were made against ships—as Admiral Nebogatoff states—ill suited to repel attack, and under conditions of demoralisation. The loss inflicted on the boats was very small, but quite as heavy as most torpedoists ever expected. Throughout the war attacked Russian ships did very small damage to their attackers. Bad gunnery may account for some of this, but the difficulty of hitting torpedo craft at unknown ranges for a good deal more. Certainly torpedo attack does not appear to come under the head of "hazardous risks."

On the other hand the Japanese had available about 150 torpedoes in their torpedo division. It goes without saying that every boat was anxious to use its torpedoes. For one cause and another, from misses, from failure to discover the target and what not, only some half-dozen of these torpedoes were used effectively—that is to say, about four per cent. The rest were either not fired or went astray. In fairness, therefore, it must be admitted that either the Japanese torpedo efficiency left much to be desired, or else an attack under real war conditions is an affair for which peace manœuvres are no criterion.

GYRO.

423

THE GERMAN WAR STORY "SEESTERN."

It was at a little inland town in Northern Germany that I first heard of *Seestern*. The town had but 6000 inhabitants all told, whose only interest in matters naval might well be supposed to be their common dependence on the weather. And yet, in response to a few flaring posters, the whole town, the whole district in fact, had gathered itself together in the large Socialist Assembly Room to listen to the Navy League address. Cinematograph scenes of life in the Navy, views of the colonies, English as well as German; then the first rate recitation of some of the stirring pages of this Book of the Great Naval War, accompanied by realistic views of the German Fleet at tactics and at Battle practice. Lastly a brief address, of which the gist was that if only every German would consent to contribute even one shilling a year more to the upkeep of the German Navy, then all these things, victory, fame, colonies, and wealth, would be theirs beyond dispute.

❄ ❄ ❄ ❄

The great War of 1906, planned by the United States, but waged by France and England against the Triple Alliance, breaks out at Samoa, where the German vessels *Möwe*, *Thetis*, and *Cormoran* destroy the British *Wallaroo* and *Tauranga*.

The only lesson to be drawn is that on foreign stations England must either have nothing at all, or else a force that can hold its own against any enemy which guile might concentrate against it. A defenceless sloop is a gift to the foe of over a hundred British lives.

Holland and Belgium join the English side, and are occupied by British troops, whereby any German advance into Northern France is out-flanked. However, during the early part of the war the British Army of occupation is success-fully held in check, and Northern France invaded, whereas in the South, the French troops, being opposed mainly to the Austrians and Italians, are able to make some headway.

The German Fleet, consisting of the five *Wittelsbachs*, the *Kaiser Wilhelm II.*, and six torpedo boats, was lying at Heligoland on March 20th, with five cruisers as lookouts to the westward.

During the night, these six torpedo boats, proceeding in the direction of England, had the luck to find the British Fleet, which was unfortunately without a guard of destroyers, and succeeded in sinking the *Pelorous* and *Diadem*, and disabling the *Cressy*, with a loss of all but one boat. It is certainly to be hoped that the Germans will cultivate the habit of firing torpedoes at the first ship they sight, instead of breaking through to the battleships which so frequently lie beyond!

Next morning the German battle fleet retreats before the combined British and French Fleets into Cuxhaven, which the Allies, being in over-whelming force, very properly proceed to attack. The minefield is successfully countermined, without doubt a most creditable performance, the outer forts silenced, and the channel is just being negotiated in single line ahead, when the German Fleet steams out, and the inner forts,

which had *pretended* to be silenced in order to save themselves for this crucial moment, open a destructive fire. Result: German Squadron not much damaged; *Ocean* and *Bouvet* drift ashore and are abandoned; numerous others of the Allies are severely mauled. This seems quite a probable action, though the chances of the above result are not so great. Cuxhaven is less strongly fortified than Kiel, and in recent combined manœuvres, in which the German Fleet, accompanied by transports, attacked the latter port, the attack was pronounced to have been *completely successful*.

With such a prize in store as the immediate destruction of the main hostile battle fleet, an attack, even on a port fortified as is Cuxhaven, would be justifiable and necessary. But such an attack would only be with an amply sufficient force, rendering success certain. The importance of being able to clear the minefield is well illustrated, as along the German Coast these "Egg Layers," as the mining boats are called, are uncomfortably plentiful. England then establishes a blockade both in the Baltic and North Sea, but the losses inflicted by the ever-recurring night attacks are surprisingly small, in view of what is known to the world of the high state of efficiency attained by German torpedo-craft. The next incident is the accidental ramming of the transport *Lucania* —invested by the author with three funnels— by the cruiser *Friedrich Karl*, then on outpost duty off Kiel. The British Fleet, which was accompaning the transports with a view to carrying out a surprise attack on Kiel, opens fire on the *Lucania*; while

the German escapes to warn Kiel. Finding themselves forestalled, the British postpone their attack until a more suitable occasion. The whole incident is probable enough. Each manœuvre witnesses at least one such case of mistaking friend for foe, and by such mischances are the best laid plans always liable to be thwarted.

Meanwhile, in the Mediterranean, pending the decision of Italy as to whether she would stand by her treaty pledges, a part of the British Fleet took up a position off Naples, where the Italian Fleet was lying, and part off Taranto, where the three *Ruggerio de Lauria* ships were stationed. It had been arranged that the French Mediterannean Fleet should similarly watch Spezia, which contained the *Regina Margherita*, *Brin*, *Emmanuele Filiberto*, *Sardegna*, *Sicilia* and *Umberto*. When the Italian Government decided to throw in their lot with Germany, the *Lepanto*, *Dandolo*, *Italia* and *Duilio* came out of Naples and opened fire. At this juncture the British Admiral is made to allow the enemy to fire the first shot, for fear of damaging the beautiful city in the background. The result is that the enormous guns of the Italian ships in the first well-aimed shots, do more damage than ought to have been done throughout the battle, which, of course, ends in the destruction of the Italians, though at a heavy cost to the British. The action at Taranto ends the same way; but at Spezia, the arrival of the French Fleet being delayed, the Italians are able to carry out a partially successful night attack, and subsequently to repulse the remnant of the French Fleet, after which the Italians return to port and refit, while pressing on the completion of the *Vittorio Emmanuele* and *Regina Elena*. Yet the author, himself a naval officer, actually conceives of the British contenting themselves with a blockade, while an Allies' defeat remains to be avenged, and while such a valuable prize as these two ships alone would be, remains to be had for the taking. Evidently the Germans with their motto "*Eile mit Weile*" have no conception of the Nelson Spirit which remains unsatisfied while a single foe remains afloat, or of the meaning of Skobeleff's maxim "STRIKE: Strike hard and strike again."

Kiel, the principal naval port of Germany, is absolutely unprotected on the land side. The military authorities are strongly opposed to permanent fortification, and hold that this, or any other position, can be more effectively protected by attention to the concentration system, and by a high state of efficiency on the part of those troops whose duty it would be to entrench and defend a threatened spot. There is, however, a considerable body of opinion in favour of the construction beforehand of suitable forts, an insurance against a surprise landing on the part of the power having the command of the sea. It was with the object of strengthening the hands of those who hold the latter view, that the account of the partially successful attack on Kiel is written so brilliantly, and with such a thorough attention to detail and grasp of the possibilities of the situation. During the early hours of April the 14th, the Saturday before Easter, the weather being foggy, the entire British

Fleet, protecting a large number of transports, approached the neighbourhood of Kiel. Well clear of the German outposts, the disembarkation was begun at a number of points; a considerable number of motor cars were safely set on shore; telegraphists cut the various wires, and reconnected them to English instruments. A small number of picked men succeeded in overwhelming the nearest outposts at the bayonet point; and as the dawn began to break, two motor cars containing gun cotton charges and torpedo men, who had been thoroughly instructed in the lay of the land, arrived at the gates of the Germania and the Imperial Dockyards. At the same moment the British storming party, 3000 strong, captured Fort Heikendorf, and from there directed Howitzer fire into Fort Korüger, which also was immediately rushed and carried before any reinforcement had time to arrive. The motor cars, which were painted and numbered to represent the German Automobile Corps, succeeded in destroying the Imperial Yard and most of the ships that were in it. Local steamboats, seized by the British near the scene of their landing, crept up to complete the destruction, but were discovered and sunk. The German Fleet sallied out, and, supported by the few uncaptured forts, compelled the enemy to keep their distance. The rapidly concentrated troops soon succeeded in re-capturing the forts, and mid-day saw the British retiring, having partially destroyed the yard, rendered unserviceable many ships which were re-fitting there, and somewhat damaged the sea-going vessels of the German Fleet, but at the cost of roughly 4000 men.

This chapter, which is intended to convey a fearful warning to the Germans, is certainly most instructive to their possible opponents; Kiel is none too strongly fortified at sea; on land it lies completely open. An attack such as this, however, would have necessitated such a detailed knowledge of the German works as Germans only may be expected to possess; but it provides us with a high ideal:—only by the most constant study of the naval ports; only by most intimate acquaintance with their works; only by the untiring practice of landing operations in conjunction with our army; and by the thoughtful provision of the largest possible number of interpreters, can such a scheme as this become a practical undertaking. Granted these things, but few ports in the world can shelter a foe from the superior British Fleet. The author recognizes this; he endows us with all these requirements. May we live to possess them.

After the attack on Kiel, the naval situation was as follows:—All the ships of the *Kaiser* class at Kiel; the remainder of the German Fleet at Wilhelmshaven. This division necessitated a corresponding division of the Allied Fleets, which kept the two ports under constant observation from balloons installed on board suitable liners.

Now for the purpose of assisting in watching a port, the help of balloons would certainly be invaluable; but though a ship could very speedily be fitted out for the purpose, yet in this, as in everything else, Preparation is better than Improvization. Probably at the present moment

the number of balloons necessary for watching even these two harbours, could only be obtained by borrowing from the Royal Engineers, who themselves are none too well equipped. The gear for hauling down, the system of communications, the gas-generating plant, all will at first be faulty; for flying at sea in a breeze of even three to four is not the same thing as being tethered over a peaceful hill on a calm summer's day in the heart of England. This is a subject well deserving of attention by us—the stronger naval power; others have experimented; but since theirs will probably not be a watching rôle, they have left the matter in this stage. England hopes to fight the enemy if he ventures out, and to watch him with an eagle eye while he lies in port. England should therefore prepare to do so.

The German aim now became this:—To unite their fleet in the western port, without the movement becoming known; then to embroil the hostile outpost ships in a small cruiser action, and to damage one of them, so as to force the North Sea portion of the Allied Fleets to engage the entire German Navy, in order to save their injured comrade. With this object in view, daily sallies from both ports were carried out; invariably the outpost ships retreated on the fleet in the rear, and the Germans then returned to port.

At length, when all the German ships were fit once more, the *Kaiser* class slipped through the Kiel Canal by night, and at dawn the British Ballooning ship reported "All as usual," the *Kaisers'* places having been taken by old crocks, which, to the telescopes thirty miles away, sufficiently resembled the *Kaisers* in appearance to convey no hint of the move that had been made.

At Wilhelmshaven the usual sally was carried out by the *Yorck* and *Kaiserin Augusta*; they closed the *Victor Hugo* and *Amiral Aube*, the lookout ships for the day, and pressed them hard as they fell back on their supports. One lucky shot, and the speed of the *Aube* was reduced to such a degree that her comrade had to stay and help her, while signalling for more support.

Now the German object was accomplished. Ship after ship came rushing out from Wilhelmshaven, and ship by ship the French and English gathered round the *Aube*. Soon the number of out-of-actions on either side was such that here was a prize too rich to leave to the advancing German battle fleet, even though they must be faced by only half the Allied Fleet. The hostile fleets closed in towards the group of fighting cruisers, and so the first and last decisive naval fight began.

Very wisely, the author refuses to be drawn into a description of the tactics on that day; but he gives us to understand that the German Fleet was fatally out-numbered, and out-ranged by the British 12 inch guns. He then takes up his station in the submerged torpedo flat of the *Wörth*, and gives a description, thrilling in the extreme, of all the scenes that there ensued. To be appreciated, this passage should be heard, not read.

Delivered in a "Tree-like" manner to a crowded house of Germans, with the German Fleet "In Battle" on the curtain on the rear, the effect was electrical.

Before many years are past, every man throughout the Fatherland will be ready to make what sacrifices may be called for, to raise *his* navy to the finest in the world. All the work of the German Navy League! Will *ours* be left behind?

When next the author comes on deck, the *Wörth* is steaming back to port. She, the *Schwaben* and the *Zähringen* are the only Germans left afloat, even the latter being hopeless wrecks. The losses of the Allies amount to eight, all told, three French and five British battleships being sunk. The impression is conveyed that the victory was mainly due to the superior power of the 12 inch guns; that the losses on the French side were attributable to their enormous superstructure and general top-heaviness, and that the Germans had the ram to thank for all the damage they inflicted.

Thus ends the naval war. The German flag has been swept off the face of the ocean. All over the world their smaller ships had done a certain amount of damage, but all over the world the end had been the same.

On land, the Germans carry all before them. France is invaded and almost over-run. The British troops prove the hardest nut to crack, but even they eventually yield before the enormous masses of the German Army. The "GREAT BATTLE"—a book demands a

"Great Battle" as a matter of course—is written with an eye to obtaining merit with the Powers that be. All the naval chapters show up shortcomings, and call for larger ships in greater numbers; here the author "makes it up" with all concerned. The great Cavalry Charge. thousands upon thousands of horsemen with their weapons shining, and the War Lord at their head, this is what will win a war!

The Kaiser himself arrives on the field to give the order, which loosens every horseman he commands upon the foe. Victory, complete and absolute, is the result; and all the critics who for years have classed the Cavalry Charge in the "Kaiser Manœuvre" as merely Pomp and Vanity, are pictured repentant in dust and ashes.

France is over-run; the British hold their own in isolated seaboard positions. The twelve thousand men, grown expert in Hereroland from years of ceaseless struggle, have invaded British South Africa, armed the Boers, and carried all before them.

The green flag is everywhere unfurled, Moslems rise against Christians; Britons, Germans, Frenchmen, all are swept away before the tidal wave of frenzied fervour; already the wave is sweeping past the Turkish borders, when the Kaiser sees the peril and appeals to all for peace. Peace is signed; disastrous for France, and humiliating for England. America and Japan have gained the commerce of the world.

Throughout the war, which lasts eight months, the *Hohenzollern* is used as hospital ship. Our

yachts might also so be used; but the first naval action will be coincident with the first hour of warfare, and it is *then* that hospital ships are needed. The provision of doctors and of nurses could be arranged for without difficulty; but whereas on land they would be wanted after *weeks*, on sea they would be vital after hours of the war. A naval medical volunteer corps might be formed; no sea training is required; only the names and addresses noted of those who are willing to take the first train to port, on receipt of wire to "Mobilize."

The only other lesson of this book, which as yet has not been touched upon, is this, that where England alone is matched against a Continental nation, that nation will, in time, be beggared without the landing of one man; but where England has a Continental ally, that ally may be a source of strength, or may be the road to England's downfall. The navy is the supreme weapon; all-sufficient for defence, and daily growing more so for the purpose of attack. Germany is recognising this. Progress is slow, but only because the conversion of the stubborn Teuton mind must be a lengthy process. But it is a sure one, and not the least of all the forward steps is marked by *Seestern*, 1906.

A BRITISH N.O.

TURBINE ENGINES.

THE principal feature of the past year has been the decision of the British Admiralty to adopt turbine engines for the propulsion of the new ships for the British Navy, both small and large.

It should be noted that the number of turbine engines now being built for vessels of the British Navy far outnumbers those being built by all foreign nations put together for turbine vessels for any purpose whatever, whether for their war navies, their merchant service or pleasure vessels, and already there are signs of an outcry of protest by interested parties against such a mark of progress on the part of the British engineering authorities similar to the agitation that was got up not so long ago when a decided step of progress was taken with regard to the boilers of the British fleet.

But because the rest of the world hangs back is no reason why British engineers should not go forward and the present heads of the engineering branch of the Admiralty indeed deserve well of their country for the decision they have come to in this matter.

Every succeeding step that has been taken with regard to the introduction of turbine engines for marine propulsion, has abundantly proved its justification, especially so in the latest and biggest installation.

This was in the Cunard steamship *Carmania*, sister vessel to the *Caronia*, belonging to the same service and fitted with reciprocating engines. The *Carmania* also was to have had engines of this type, but as soon as it was decided to adopt turbine engines for the propelling machinery of 65,000 H.P. for the still larger vessels now building at Clydebank and Wallsend, it was thought well to take advantage of the knowledge to be gained by having two identical vessels fitted with the two different types of machinery, as the experience thereby obtained would be invaluable in planning and carrying out the designs for the still larger machinery.

The dimensions of the *Caronia* and *Carmania* are as follows:—Length, 675 feet; Breadth, 72 feet 6 inches. Depth to the shelter deck 52 feet, and to the bridge 97 feet. Their carrying capacity is 12,000 tons; the gross tonnage 21,000 and the displacement 30,000 tons.

It is true that turbine machinery had already been constructed with success for a number of vessels, and amongst these the ocean going steamers *Victorian* and *Virginian* for the Allan Line, but what a considerable step in advance it was from these to the *Carmania*, is shown by the fact, that in the former the weight of the largest unit of the machinery, the low pressure turbine was 78 tons, whereas in the *Carmania*, the weight for this portion of the machinery was 340 tons, the rotors being 11 feet in diameter, with casings of corresponding size.

The trials excited great interest and were attended by the Engineer-in-chief of the British Navy and by representatives of the Japanese and Russian Navies. The preliminary trial proved so successful that it was decided to proceed with the official trial at once. This was to consist of four runs on the measured mile at full speed, and with the mean number of the revolutions obtained on them she was to continue at the same speed, so as to complete a continuous steaming trial of six hours. With the sister ship *Caronia* the results on a similar trial were Revs., 89·2.—I.H.P. 21,870 and mean speed 19·62 knots, the maximum I.H.P. being 23,500, but these results were considerably exceeded with the *Carmania*, the mean speed obtained on the four runs on the measured mile being 20·19 knots. It should be noted that the conditions of the two ships were not the same, as the *Carmania* had not been docked since her launch, nine months previously, whilst the *Caronia* had only just been cleaned before her trial.

In the case of the *Caronia* it was found that the increase in speed due to cleaning the hull was found to be half a knot, so that it is expected that the speed of the *Carmania* will be 20·6 knots with a clean bottom.

A second official trial of six hours duration was carried out on a following day, at a speed of between 19 and 20 knots, which is supposed to be the normal sea speed of the vessel, and over the whole period a speed of 19·5 knots was easily maintained. Trials were also carried out in steering and circling with satisfactory results and there was an entire absence of vibration throughout.

The advent of the *Lusitania* and the *Mauritania*, the two still bigger vessels for the Cunard fleet is looked for with the greatest interest. They are the largest vessels in the world and their dimensions are as follows:—

Length ....787 ft. 6 in.
Breadth .... 88 ft.
Depth to shelter deck 62 ft.
Depth to bridge...... 98 ft.

The gross tonnage is 33,200 tons and the engines are of 65,000 H.P. which is calculated to give a minimum average ocean speed of 24½ knots in moderate weather.

For cross-channel purposes the turbine engine is being universally adopted in England, and the practical advantages obtained in service running with the turbine engined boats would appear to have abundantly justified such a step.

The following table* has been given by Mr. William Gray, as a result of careful comparisons of the logs of the Midland Railway Co's. vessels, plying between Heysham and Belfast, those runs only being taken where the speed was maintained for the whole time that the vessels were in the open sea, and with the steamers running simultaneously, but in opposite directions.

It will be remembered that all four vessels were of the same type and dimensions with the exception of the *Manxman*, which is one foot greater in breadth than her three sister vessels.

	Antrim.	Londonderry.
No. of trips..................	48	48
Average coal per trip (tons)	35·6	35·3
Average speed in knots ...	19·7	19·5

	Donegal.	Londonderry.
No. of trips..................	42	42
Average coal per trip (tons)	36·0	36·9
Average speed in knots ...	19·2	19·8

	Antrim.	Manxman.
No. of trips..................	29	29
Average coal per trip (tons)	38·6	38·6
Average speed in knots ...	19·5	20·3

	Donegal.	Manxman.
No. of trips..................	39	39
Average coal per trip (tons)	38·7	40·2
Average speed in knots ...	19·3	20·3
Type of Engine:—	Reciprocating.	Turbine.

* Trans. Inst. N. A. Vol. XLVII, page 397.

It will be seen that the *Manxman* did 20·3 knots on the same coal consumption as the *Antrim* required for 19·5 knots, whilst to attain this speed the *Manxman* only required 35 tons against the 38·6 tons of the *Antrim*, or a saving of 9·3 per cent.

Similarly the *Donegal* for a speed of 19·3 knots required 38·7 tons and the *Manxman* only 35·4 tons or a saving of 8·5 per cent. There was also an economy in the amount of oil used for lubrication amounting to five gallons per trip, and it was found that whereas four greasers were required with the reciprocating engines, two were ample with the turbine engines.

Taking now the results of several years working of the two similar vessels on the Clyde passenger service, we again find the turbine engined boat to be the more economical. The comparative dimensions are as follows :—

	Duchess of Hamilton.	King Edward.
Length	250 ft.	250 ft.
Breadth.................	30 ft.	30 ft.
Draught	5 ft. 6 in.	6 ft.
Displacement (tons)...	638	650
Average working speed knots	16	18½
Type of Engine:—	Reciprocating.	Turbine.

The results of the running of the two boats since 1901, when the *King Edward* was first put on, have been as follows :—

	Miles run per day.	per ton of Coal.
1901.		
Duchess of Hamilton	140	8·87
King Edward........	153·5	8·47
1902.		
Duchess of Hamilton	141·5	8·51
King Edward........	142	8·24
1903.		
King Edward.........	174	8·45
1904.		
Duchess of Hamilton	153	8·90
King Edward.........	182	8·23

Captain John Williamson has also made public a further interesting comparison with regard to the *King Edward*. He stated that she steamed 12,116 miles in 79 days, on a coal consumption of 1,429 tons, at an average speed of 18¼ knots, whilst another vessel of similar type, practically of the same dimensions and the same service speed but fitted with reciprocating

PROGRESS OF WARSHIP ENGINEERING.

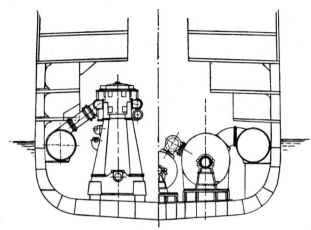

Fig. 1.
S.S. "Caronia."   S.S. "Carmania."

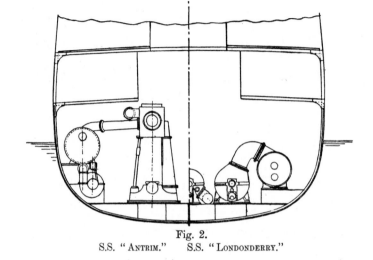

Fig. 2.
S.S. "Antrim."   S.S. "Londonderry."

engines steamed 12,106 miles in 80 days, on a coal consumption of 1,909 tons, at an average speed of 18½ knots, so that the turbine engined vessel running at the same speed steamed in all ten more knots, but with a saving in the coal consumption of 480 tons.

Another vessel specially referred to last year was the *Viking*, belonging to the Isle of Man Steam Packet Co., and placed on their Liverpool to Douglas service. On trial she made 23·53 knots, and the average speed in service has been over 22 knots. Comparisons have been made between her and a similar vessel on the same service, the following being the respective dimensions of the two vessels :—

	Empress Queen.	*Viking.*
Length	360 ft.	350 ft.
Breadth...................	42 ft.	42 ft.
Draught	11 ft.	13 ft.
Displacement (tons).....	2,940	2400
Average working speed (knots)	20	22·2
Type of Engine:—	Reciprocating.	Turbine.

The comparative results since the *Viking* has been at work are as follows :—

	Empress Queen.	*Viking.*
Total number of miles run per season	7870	8880
Coal consumed per season (tons)	4833	4206
Tons of coal per mile run	614	472

Mr. Parsons has also made public some interesting comparisons between the *Queen*, the pioneer vessel on the Channel service between England and France and other vessels on the same service.

The earning power of the *Queen* is given in comparison with three other vessels fitted with ordinary engines carrying out the same service on the same route.

The average speed of the vessels in knots per hour, is as follows :—

Queen 21,
A 18, *B* 18¼ and *C* 17½.

The results given are based on the number of passengers each vessel is certified to carry, and taking the *Queen* as the basis of comparison, the coal burnt per passenger, in the case of *A* was 74 per cent, *B* 25 per cent, and *C* 107 per cent

more than in the *Queen*, or taking the whole of the running expenses due to the machinery and engine room, that is the total cost of coal, oil, &c., and engine room staff, the figures, taking as before the *Queen* as the basis of comparison, work out as follows :—Steamer *A* cost 80·5 per cent., *B* 33·6 per cent., and *C* 105 per cent. more than the similar expenses in the turbine engined vessels.

The figures of the different vessels given above are the practical results of ordinary everyday working, extending over considerable periods of time, so that at full speed running there is evidently no question that the turbine engine is at least as economical as reciprocating engines, whilst as to cost of upkeep, it seems likely that for the new type of engine this will be very much less than is now the case with the old type.

The following advantages were claimed for the turbine over reciprocating engines on its introduction for marine use.[*]

1.—Smaller space occupied, and in the case of engines for vessels of war may be added that

---

[*] See Fighting Ships, 1904, p. 388.

---

they can be kept well below the waterline without difficulty.

2.—Lower first cost.

3.—Smaller cost of upkeep and attendance.

4.—Reduced weight of the main engines and their spare gear.

5.—No cylinder lubrication required, so that the main engine exhaust is free from oil.

6.—Economy in steam consumption, and in the case of large engines it is believed that this will be very considerable.

1.—As regards the second of these two points there is no question that it is a considerable advantage for war vessels, and what a difference there is between the two cases may be seen from Figs. 1 and 2, which show the relative heights occupied by the machinery in the *Caronia* and *Carmania* of 23,500 H.P. and in the *Antrim* and *Londonderry* of 7,800 H.P. But as regards the relation of length this is more a question for the owner of the vessel than for the engineer, and will largely depend on the view the former takes as to the percentage of power he will require provided for going astern.

2.—The introduction of such an entirely new

type of engine, of course involves a certain amount of outlay on the part of the constructors for new tools, and the new methods of work are always more costly at first. But there is no question that in course of time this advantage will manifest itself. In the case of the steamers of the Midland Railway Co., there was a difference in favour of the turbine engines over reciprocating engines amounting to 1½ per cent. of the total cost of hull and machinery.

3.—On this point practical experience has shown there to be a very distinct advantage. In the steamers of the Midland Railway Co., there is an economy in the turbine steamer in the amount of oil used for lubrication of five gallons per single trip and there was a reduction in the engine room staff, only two oilers being required in place of the four employed on the sister ships, whilst as to upkeep, so far the turbine engined vessels have cost practically nothing in this respect. And the same holds good of all the other cross-channel turbine boats.

When the *Viking* finished work at the end of last season, the upper part of the turbine casings was lifted and the rotors and spindles removed and a thorough examination made of all the blades. They were all found to be in perfect condition and the covers were replaced and the turbines closed up ready for another year's service.

4.—In the Midland Railway Co.'s boats there was a very considerable saving in weight with the turbine engined vessels, the total weight of engines, shafting and propellers in the *Antrim* and *Donegal* being 280 tons, whilst in the *Manxman* the similar weight was 195 tons and there was a saving of 30 tons in the engine seatings and other parts of the hull, making a total of 115 tons less with the turbine engines.

In the *Carmania* there was a saving in weight by the adoption of the turbine system amounting to about five per cent.

6.—As regards the economy in steam consumption the figures given above are sufficient evidence and it must not be forgotten that the experience of every day is leading to still further improvements being made in this respect. The *Onward* has precisely the same boilers as the *Queen*, but such progress had been made in the two years that elapsed between the time of her construction and that of the *Queen*, that with the latter vessel

23 knots were obtained as against the 21¾ knots speed realised with the former.

But it must not be taken for granted that the turbine engine is therefore a practical success for all types of vessels and that it can be full well adopted for warships without hesitation.

From the sketches shown (Figs. 1 and 2) it will be seen what great advantages the adoption of a turbine engine offers in the way of height, and how it can be kept well below the water line, but at the same time it takes up a considerable space in the direction of its length. A reciprocating engine that will develop its full power going astern takes up only slightly more room lengthways than a non-reversing engine and by the use of Joy's or some similar type of slide gear, it is possible to reduce the length to the bare space required for the cylinders.

But with turbine engines it is not so. If it is required that the power going astern shall be equal to that going ahead, it is necessary almost to double the length of all the engines, and if the arrangement adopted does not lend itself to running at very low powers for cruising purposes, the length has further to be added to for a cruising turbine.

Whilst the length required is thus very considerable, there is no necessity to increase the width, so that we get very long and comparatively narrow engine rooms with a corresponding waste of valuable space between the fore and aft wing bulkhead of the engine rooms and the ship's side. In some vessels this has been utilized as a reserve bunker but the difficulties involved in having to transport the coal through water-tight doors and through the other bunkers to get it to the furnaces militate against the adoption of this plan.

Another difficulty incidental to the use of large turbine engines is that the diameter of the low pressure casing is so great that even when they are kept as low in the vessel as possible, the forward end is brought up so high that the shaft has a considerable inclination aft, and is no longer parallel with the water line, with a consequent loss of power. This difficulty has been partly got over by placing the low pressure casing in the widest portion of the ship, and arranging the boilers according to the usual practice of the Italian Navy with half on either

side of the engine room. This however, has led to other difficulties being encountered, the principal being the passing the shafts through or under the after boilers. Another drawback is concerned with the wing stern brackets in the turbine ships with four screws, the amount of drag they cause being so large that a considerable amount of power has to be expended in the effort, and numerous experiments have been made to decide on the arrangement and form which best minimizes this loss. There are also the usual troubles incidental to the use of screw propellers running at high velocities.

These are drawbacks such as may reasonably be expected to be encountered in the case of new arrangements, and without doubt others will arise as the use of turbine engines increases, and which will require practical experience for dealing with them satisfactorily, so that the British Admiralty have indeed been well advised in so arranging matters that they will have the aid and experience of such firms as Armstrong, John Brown & Co., Laird, Palmer, Thornycroft, Vickers, J. S. White and Yarrow, to assist them to make a thorough success of the installations now being carried out.

There is also a new trouble manifesting itself and that is that the vessels in sea service do not maintain the speed which they proved themselves to possess on trial, nor is it yet clear why this should be the case.

On this point, Professor Harvard Biles has recently stated that the results on trial of similar vessels designed by him, show that at about 20 knots speed the turbine vessel is about 14 per cent. more efficient than the similar vessel with reciprocating engines, but that on service such results were not maintained, and the problem of the reason of such a falling off in efficiency in actual service remains to be solved.

During the past year the Vulcan Shipbuilding Co., of Stettin, have completed a turbine vessel named the *Kaiser*, which is fitted with two shafts and two independent turbines of the Curtis type, built by the Allgemeine Electricitats Gesellschaft, of Berlin, and with which excellent results were obtained on trial. The guarantees were intended to represent the performance of a first-class four cylinder triple expansion engine and called for a speed of 19½ knots on a six hours trial with a total consumption of not over 4·625 tons of coal

per hour, this to include all auxiliaries.

The dimensions of the vessel are as follows :—

Length............	310 ft.
Beam	38 ft. 2 in.
Draught	9 ft. 9 in.
Displacement ...	1,890 tons.

Each turbine is built in the form of a drum shaped shell built in sections, the shell having a length of 11 ft. 6 ins. and the outside diameter of 8 ft. 6 ins. the go-astern turbine being contained within the same casing. The weight allowed for each turbine was 70 tons, but the actual weight worked out at 57 tons.

As soon as the vessel was completed, progressive speed trials were carried out at varying speeds up to a maximum of 20·46 knots, at which speed the revolutions were 555 per minute, and the result of the six hours official trial was a mean speed of 20 knots, with a total coal consumption of 3·995 tons per hour.

The two turbines are entirely independent and in order to test their manœuvring and reversing powers, comparative tests were made with a vessel of similar type, fitted with reciprocating engines, and it was found that the turbine vessel could be manœuvred with the same facility as the other, and was brought to a full stop in slightly less time than that taken by the other vessel. Throughout the trials the turbines gave no trouble whatever and their working was altogether satisfactory.

TURBINE WAR VESSELS.

The large number of war vessels to be fitted with turbine engines for the British Navy has already been alluded to, and very valuable experience will shortly be available in the results obtained with these vessels. Meanwhile the British Admiralty is taking steps to give engineer officers experience with turbine engined vessels now in service, so that when the time comes for them to take charge, they will have acquired a certain amount of familiarity with the new type of engines and their ways.

Nearly all other nations are holding back and waiting to see the result of the venture.

As the result of the report of the special Commission, nominated by the United States Bureau of Steam Engineering to examine and report on the practicability of turbine engines for war ships, it was decided to fit the three cruisers of the *Scout* class with different types of engines as follows:

Birmingham—Twin screw triple expansion.

Salem—Twin screw Curtis turbines.

Chester—Four screw Parsons turbines.

The dimensions of these vessels are as follows: Length over all 423 ft.; Beam 47 ft.; Mean draught 16 ft. 9 ins.; Displacement 4687 tons, and H.P. 16,000, which is calculated to give a speed of 24 knots.

The propelling machinery of the *Chester* is to consist of two main high pressure turbines, two main low pressure turbines, with go-astern turbines at their after end, one high pressure cruising turbine, and one intermediate pressure cruising turbine; whilst that of the *Salem* consists of two turbines, each of 120 ins. diameter, with seven ahead stages and two astern stages. At full speed the revolutions of the Curtis turbines are to be 350, and it is computed that the space occupied in length, including the goastern engines, will be only half that occupied by the equivalent triple expansion four cylinder engine and that the weight will be considerably less. There is no end thrust due to the pressure of the steam in the turbine itself and the propeller thrust is taken up by a thrust block of the ordinary type, external to the turbine.

The German cruiser, *Lubeck*, completed her official trials in 1905, but an exhaustive series of experiments, outside the official trials, has been commenced which are still in progress. The broad results are, that by fitting to this turbine vessel screws, giving at full power identically the same speed, i.e., 23·16 knots, as her sister ship with reciprocating engines, it has been found possible to reduce the coal consumption at low powers to a figure comparing favourably with the ordinary type of engines. The *Lubeck* with this set of screws burns less coal per unit of power and has a larger range of action at all speeds from nine knots upwards, than the British cruiser *Topaze*, of the same size.

The experiments now in progress, are to determine how much faster the *Lubeck* is than the *Hambourg*, when screws are fitted to absorb the full work of the turbines at full power, and the diminution of radius of action entailed by this increase of speed is to be most carefully measured.

The large torpedo-boat, S. 125, of 400 tons, fitted with Parsons turbines, supplied like those of the *Lubeck*, by the Turbinia A. G. Parsons Marine Co., of Berlin, has also completed her official trials and been put into commission as commodore boat of her division, owing to her superior speed in service.

In December last, the Turbinia Co. received further orders for two sets of machinery for the German navy, which are now being built in the German Parsons turbine works at Mannheim.

The cruiser, at present known as *Ersatz Nacht*, is of the *Lubeck* type, but rather longer, and with extra boiler power. The displacement is increased to 3,450 tons, and the maximum speed on the mile is to be 24 knots. The machinery arrangement is to be similar to that of the *Lubeck* already described, viz., four shafts, and two engine rooms, with a dividing longitudinal bulkhead. Reversing gear will be fitted to all four shafts, and cruising turbines as usual for reduced powers. This arrangement, first carried out in the *Lubeck*, is to-day the standard one for the big turbine warships of the British Navy. The *Ersatz Nacht* may be regarded simply as an improved, enlarged and faster *Lubeck*. She belongs to the type of *O*, *Ersatz Meteor*, &c., but is modified in other respects besides machinery. She is being built by the Vulcan Co., at Stettin.

Turbine engines of the Parsons type are also to be fitted to a big torpedo-boat, G 137, having a displacement of 570 tons. Her turbine engines are to give her a speed of 30 knots, for which purpose over 11,000 H.P. is provided. She is being built by the Germania Co., at Kiel, as regards hull and boilers. This vessel, though numbered consecutively with a series of boats now building with reciprocating engines, is not really one of the same series, as she differs both in size and in power, and has 3 knots higher speed. She will be the first turbine boat to have two engine rooms one abaft the other. The forward compartment contains the high pressure turbine, the port low pressure turbine and condenser, whilst the after one contains the cruising turbine, the starboard low pressure turbine, and the second condenser. This arrangement permits of two out of the three shafts being run, even if either the engine rooms were flooded. The engine rooms are both protected by coal bunkers at the sides, which is

altogether a new feature in turbine boats.

The Ostend-Dover Belgian government mailboat *Princesse Elisabeth*, referred to last year, has been completed and has run several months in regular service. She holds the world's record for passenger steamers, being the first to maintain a speed of 24 knots.

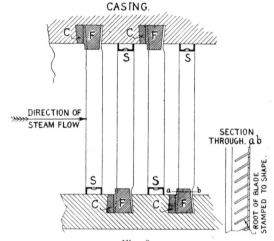

CASING.

DIRECTION OF STEAM FLOW

SECTION THROUGH. *a b*

ROOT OF BLADE STAMPED TO SHAPE.

Fig. 3.

Turbine Blading.

Willans & Robinson, Ltd.

F. Foundation Rings.　　C. Caulking strips.

S. Channel rings.

TURBINE DETAILS.

In the Parsons turbine the practice is still to fix the blades in grooves on the rotor and in the casing by means of caulking pieces or sections between each separate blade, and for blades of a certain height to fit a thin strip of brass, binding the blades together.

What an important matter the blading of a large turbine is may be gathered from the fact that in the case of the *Carmania* the total number of blades amounts to over 1,115,000. In this case to give

radial stiffness to the longer blades of the low pressure turbines, they were bound together with two circumferential strips laced with copper wire and soldered. These as first designed were in one piece, but experiments carried out at Clydebank proved that in the case of these large turbines the difference of expansion between the cast iron rotor and the brass strip caused distortion of the blades under working conditions. The difficulty was overcome by an ingenious joint whereby the binding strip instead of being in one continuous piece was divided into short lengths. The centre part of these was soldered on to a certain number of blades and the two ends were slightly reduced so that they entered into sleeve pieces which were soldered on to others of the blades, and in this way the difference of expansion was allowed for by the ends of the strips freely sliding within the sleeves, whilst at the same time the necessary stiffness of the ring was maintained.

The weak point of turbine construction hitherto has been the blading, for should the rotor from any cause come into contact with the blades in the standing part, they are absolutely destroyed.

A greatly improved system has been introduced by Messrs. Willans and Robinson Ltd., of Rugby, who have built many large turbines on this plan. A section of the blading is shown in Fig. 3 from which it will be seen that the foundation rings are of dovetail section and inserted in dovetailed grooves cut in the turbine casing and in the rotor, in which they are firmly secured by key pieces made of brass as shown in the illustration. After being driven into place these key pieces are upset into undercut grooves making a very solid construction.

The blades themselves are made of brass and are formed by special machinery. The roots are made to dovetail shape and are inserted in slots cut in the foundation or base rings, these slots also being produced by special machine tools in such a way as to exactly conform to the shape of the blade roots and to give the correct angle and spacing to the blades. In forming the blades a piece is left at the top considerably less in width than the blade so that a shoulder is produced and this projecting piece passes through a slot in a shroud ring as shown in the sketch and is rivetted over by a specially arranged pneumatic rivetter. The shroud rings are made of channel shape, the flanges in each case projecting outwardly and after being fixed in place are turned at the edges to give the required clearances. The slots in these rings are produced by special machinery in such a manner that they are absolutely accurately spaced. The flanges of the shroud rings are made so thin that although amply sufficient for stiffness, the ring does not have the disadvantage of a solid one, which would acquire a dangerous temperature by friction in the case of accidental contact between the rotating and stationary parts.

It is also claimed for this method of construction that the blades are stiffened against the effect of vibration in a much more substantial manner than by any other means thus far employed, whilst the use of a protecting shroud ring enables the working clearance to be made smaller than in the use of naked blade-tips

without danger in case of accidental contact, thus reducing the leakage to a minimum, this leakage past the blade-tips being the principal source of loss in turbines as at present constructed. As to the safety from damage in case of accidental contact, an interesting experiment was made to test this by throwing the bearings of the rotor out of line with the centre of the cylinder so as to produce contact between the periphery of the rotor and the stationary ring, but neither was damaged. Another advantage

of the rotors was balanced in detail, statically on knife edges, and dynamically in a machine specially designed and constructed for the purpose, and after the rotors were completely finished they were again placed on the knife edges for further testing and adjustment. As a final test of the accuracy of the balancing, the rotors were then put into place in their cylinders and the turbines run under steam at revolutions considerably in excess of those required under actual working conditions.

system of a series of grooves turned in the shaft into which bronze Ramsbottom rings were fitted, the whole rotating in a cylindrical gland. However, this arrangement proved unsatisfactory and the type of gland eventually adopted is shown in Fig. 5. In this gland there are a number of grooves in the rotor shaft in which the phosphor bronze fins "A" are fitted, and similar grooves and fins "B" in the casing, with four Ramsbottom rings "C" in the shaft at the outer end. A small amount of steam is permitted to leak past the first set of rings for the purpose of lubrication, and is then caught in the chamber "D" formed by a plate "E" fixed on the end of

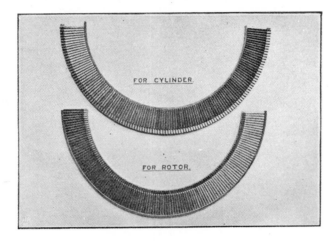

Fig. 4.

TURBINE RINGS.   WILLANS AND ROBINSON LTD.

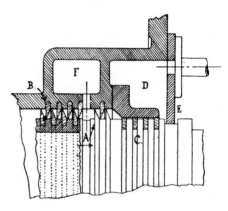

Fig. 5.—LOW PRESSURE GLAND.
"S.S. CARMANIA."

claimed for this method of construction is that if by chance a blade should prove defective, it is held in place and cannot possibly work loose and strip the other blades.

Fig. 4 shows two complete half rings built up on the system described above; these half rings are complete and ready for caulking into their respective grooves in rotor and casing.

In large turbines very special attention has to be given to the balancing of the revolving parts. In the case of the *Carmania* each component part

After the blading the next most important point is the gland where the rotor shaft passes through the end of the turbine, and as the vacuum obtained depends so largely on the tightness of the low pressure glands, experiments were made to ascertain if the form of steam gland hitherto adopted would prove satisfactory in the case of rotor shafts of such diameter as were required in the *Carmania*. These experiments extended over a long period of time, the first type tried being the Parsons

the casing whence it is led away to the condenser. In the case of the high pressure turbine, should the pressure of the escaping steam not be sufficiently reduced, the chamber "F" is connected to a place in the low pressure turbines where the pressure is below that of the atmosphere. In the case, however, of the gland on the low pressure turbine the chamber "F" is filled with steam of from 2 to 3 lbs. pressure which effectually prevents any leakage of air into the gland.

PROGRESS OF WARSHIP ENGINEERING.

Warships fitted with Turbine Engines.

	Length.	Beam.	Draught.	Displacement.	Speed.	I.H.P.	Type of Turbine.	Navy.
	ft. in.	ft. in.	ft. in.	Tons.	Knots.			
Destroyer, *Velox*	210 0	21 0	12 6	400	27·12	7,000	Parsons	British
,, *Eden*	220 0	23 6	13 9	550	26·3	7,000	Parsons	British
Torpedo Boat No. 243	—	—	8 9	92	21	1,800	Rateau	French
,, *Caroline*	152 6	15 3	—	140	26·4	2,000	Rateau	Russian
Cruiser, *Amethyst*	360 0	40 0	14 6	3000	23·63	14,000	Parsons	British
Torpedo Boat No. 293	129 7	14 0	—	95	26·2	2,000	Parsons	French
,, No. 294	126 6	13 4	—	95	—	2,000	Breguet	French
Cruiser, *Lubeck* ...	341 0	40 0	17 6	3250	23	10,000	Parsons	German
Torpedo Boat No. 125S... ...	—	—	—	400	28·3	6,300	Parsons	German
Coastal Destroyer, *Gadfly* ...								
,, *Glowworm* ...								
,, *Gnat*								
,, *Grasshopper*								
,, *Greenfly* ...								
,, *Cricket* ...	170 0	17 6	6 0	230	26	3,600	Parsons	British
,, *Dragonfly* ...								
,, *Firefly* ...								
,, *Sandfly* ...								
,, *Spider* ...								
,, *Mayfly* ...								
,, *Moth*								
Ocean Destroyer, *Afridi* ...								
,, *Cossack* ...								
,, *Ghurka* ...	270 0	26 0	8 0	800	33	14,500	Parsons	British
,, *Mohawk* ...								
,, *Tartar* ...								
Cruiser, *Ersatz Wacht* ...	350 0	40 0	17 6	3450	24	12,000	Parsons	German
Torpedo Boat No. 137G ...	—	—	—	570	30	11,000	Parsons	German
Battleship, *Dreadnought* ...	—	—	—	—	—	—	Parsons	British
Scout, *Salem*	420 0	46 8	16 9	3750	24	16,000	Curtis	United States
,, *Chester*	420 0	46 8	16 9	3750	24	16,000	Parsons	United States
Destroyer (Palmer)	215 0	20 9	6 4	370	31	7,200	Parsons	—
,, ,, ...							Parsons	
Scout	—	—	—	—	—	—	Parsons	Japanese

CONDENSERS AND AIR-PUMPS.

The absolute necessity of a high vacuum to obtain full efficiency with turbine engines has been alluded to on previous occasions, and has had a stimulating effect in inducing much needed improvements in the condensing arrangement and air pumps.

Mr. Parsons, in a recent paper by himself and Mr. G. G. Stoney, [*] refers to the matter as follows: "The question of condensing plant is such an important factor with turbines, that some remarks on this subject seem necessary. Speaking generally, with well designed air and circulating pumps, and with a condenser having an allowance of about one square foot of surface per indicated horse power, and circulating thirty times the feed at a temperature of about 70° F., a vacuum of 26 to 27 inches can usually be maintained with ordinary supervision. In order to obtain a higher vacuum the following conditions and arrangements must be observed:—

(*a*). The condenser surface must be increased to about $1\frac{1}{2}$ square foot per indicated horse power.

(*b*). It is necessary to increase the volume of the circulating water, and so to modify the design of the condenser that the velocity of water through the tubes shall be four to seven feet per second, so as to secure some measure of turbulent flow and consequently better absorption of heat.

(*c*). The tubes of the condenser should be so spaced as to allow an easy flow of steam among them; and we have also found it desirable to submerge the lower tubes in the condensed water before it goes to the air-pump. This is done by providing in the bottom of the condenser a weir, which holds up the condensed water so as to cover the bottom two or three rows of tubes. By this arrangement the condensed water is thoroughly cooled before it reaches the air-pump, and a lower air-pump temperature is obtained.

(*d*). It is generally necessary to use a larger air-pump, but the increase of power required for this and for the larger circulating pump (when the circulating water has not to be lifted more than 15 to 20 feet, and the return

[*] Inst. C. E. 1906.

main is water-sealed) will not exceed 1¼ per cent. of the total power developed.

With the foregoing arrangements it is possible to maintain a vacuum of 27½ to 28 inches, and thus to effect a saving of five per cent. on the coal consumed.

The vacuum augmenter of Mr. Parsons described last year, has now been fitted in several vessels, with very good results. In the *Virginian* and the *Manxman* the rise in vacuum due to its use was 1¼ to 1½ ins. representing an economy of from seven to eight per cent. The steam used by the jet is about 1½ per cent., leaving a nett gain of about six per cent. The effect of an increase in the vacuum of one inch, when it is about 26 inches has been found to decrease the consumption by about four per cent. and for one inch at 28 inches about six per cent.

But the plan generally adopted now, is that of dealing separately with the air, and with the water of condensation, either by a wet and dry air-pump of the Weir type, having a separate pump barrel and plunger for each use, or a pump of the Edwards type, which is found to give excellent results for the purpose. It has gradually made its way into favour and is used in many warships, and now with the advent of turbine engines it is being largely adopted as it is found to exactly fulfil the special needs of this type.

In the old type of pump the resistance due to the foot valves and the inertia of the water have to be overcome by pressure in the condenser, and the passage of the air into the pump is obstructed both by the water and the foot valves, whereas in the Edwards pump the water is dealt with mechanically, and there being no foot valves a clear air passage from the condenser to the pump is obtained.

By the action of the conical bucket, working in conjunction with the conical base and guiding edge, a regular amount of water is projected through the ports into the working barrel each time the bucket descends, and the water tends to compress the air which has already entered the barrel, and to entrain further air on its passage into the pump. It is this entrainment action which is so important when dealing with the condensing plant for steam turbines, where a very high vacuum is required and where the air consequently is extremely rarified. But its great

charm for the marine engineer lies in its accessibility, and in the fact that there is *nothing to get out of order* about it, and for boats that are hard run this is a decided and greatly felt advantage. And it is from this point of view that it is so coming into favour for warships, being a step in the direction of simplification, which will undoubtedly be a great advantage in time of war. Statistics show that the air-pumps are responsible for more than 20 per cent. of the total number of engine breakdowns, and over 11 per cent. are due entirely to the valves and buckets. But with the Edwards pumps the foot and bucket valves are entirely dispensed with, and the only valves used are the head valves, which can be readily examined, and when necessary renewed whilst the pump is at work, without any appreciable loss of vacuum. The foot and bucket valves were inaccessible in the old type of pump and consequently those parts which most frequently gave trouble, and by doing away with these, not only is the risk of breakdown completely eliminated, but the time for over-hauling and the cost of maintainance of this portion of the machinery are reduced to a minimum.

CONDENSER TUBES.

Some very serious cases of corrosion of condenser tubes that have recently occurred have forced more attention to be given to this evil and to the absolute necessity of finding out the cause and some means of remedying it. Endless trouble and expense is caused by such failures and as there seemed no way of guarding against them, they have been the most troublesome defect an engineer had to deal with, and in single screw vessels with only one condenser it became at times a most serious matter.

Some of the cases are so erratic as to be most extraordinary, and the corrosion manifests itself in so many different ways that it almost seems as if there must be more than one cause at work. Two vessels leaving the same yard, their tubes being from the same lot, and running on the same service and in the same waters may have very different results in this respect, one ship remaining immune for years whilst the other may be attacked at once, and have her tubes corroded through within six weeks of being set

to work and have to have them renewed, and possibly every voyage after. Another strange feature is that a vessel may go on for years without any trouble and yet one day, without any evident cause, the trouble may suddenly manifest itself and continue indefinitely. An exhaustive investigation into the causes of the trouble has recently been made by Prof. Humboldt Sexton and he states that as the result of his investigations it is certain that sea water is the corroding agent, but that its action may be accelerated or retarded by the presence of other materials and by the conditions under which the tube is placed, whilst as to the cause of variation of durability of condenser tubes he says that it is not to be found in the chemical composition or physical structure of the metal, nor in any variation in the process of manu-facture, nor indeed in anything connected with the tubes themselves. The specification for nearly all warship work gives 70 per cent. of copper, 29 per cent. of zinc and 1 per cent. of tin as the composition of which the tubes are to be made, whilst the requisition for most merchant service work calls for 70 per cent. of copper and 30 per cent. of zinc.

It was originally the rule to tin the tubes but that was found to give little or no protection and has been to a great extent abandoned for some time as the tin coating on the water side of the tube rarely last a month. One of the reasons assigned by engineers is impurity of the composition of the tube, but this has been absolutely disproved, nor does it get over the difficulty that one batch of tubes taken indiscriminately from a given lot will last for years whilst another batch from the same lot will fail in a few months or even less. Once this suggested cause is dismissed, there remains but one other, namely that the trouble must be due to the conditions of working, and there is no doubt that this is the truth of the matter. It seems very certain that rapid and irregular corrosion is not due alone to the ordinary action of normal sea water, but must be produced by foreign matter carried into the tubes whilst the water is circulating through them, or deposited when the circulating pump is stopped and the water comes to rest, and that most, if not all of the real mischief is done whilst the vessel is in port.

It has been held by many that the pitting is

caused by particles of carbon or the like lodging in the tubes and causing galvanic action locally, but this cannot alone be the cause as corrosion takes place every bit as severely where no possibility of such particles lodging exists, and again there are many cases where such particles have been known to lodge and no corrosion has taken place, so that something additional must be looked for. There is a recent case of a con-denser where the tubes are vertical and contrary to the usual practice the circulating water surrounds the tubes, the steam being condensed inside them. The corrosion was as usual on the water side, a set of tubes rarely lasting more than one year, and the tubes were attacked uniformly, those in the full wash of the circulat-ing water being equally attacked with the rest.

A hardworked engineer will not be pleased at any addition to his list of work in port but one way of minimizing the trouble would be to invariably empty the condenser as soon as the engines are done with, and in the case of a properley designed condenser having convenient doors for cleaning, the tubes should all be washed out as soon as possible afterwards with a jet of water and the condenser left dry until it is required again ; however, where the condensers are in use in port this of course would not be possible.

A distinct remedy has now been introduced and so far has given really satisfactory results, not only preventing corrosion, but also arresting it where it had already commenced. It is known as the "Harris-Anderson" system and the principle of it is to immerse in the circulating water a mass of metal which is electro-positive to the metal which it is desired to protect, and to connect the two metals electrically. Under these conditions the corrosive action is entirely transferred to the electro-positive protector, leaving the condenser tubes immune.

The composition of the protective metal may be altered to suit particular cases, but the one ordinarily employed is electro-positive to prac-tically all the varying alloys of zinc and copper. It maintains its protective action until completely dissolved, and is not interfered with by insoluble deposits on its surface. In some cases the apparatus is fitted inside the water end of the condenser, but this plan has the inconvenience that it is difficult to inspect the arrangement or test its activity. It is therefore preferable to have an independent vessel communicating with the water space of the condenser by two pipes and capable of being shut off at will as shown in Fig. 6. The protective metal is placed in this vessel and connected to the condenser tube plate by a conducting wire. Metallic contact between the tubes and the tube plate is ensured by means of a compressible metallic washer placed between the ferrule and the packing and screwed up tightly.

In ordinary working the connecting pipes are of course open, but if it is desired to inspect the protective mass the valves are closed and the vessel can then be opened and its contents inspected without in any way interfering with the working of the condenser. The good working of the arrangement may at any time be tested by inserting a galvanometer in the connection between the protector and the tube plate, when a more or less decided current will be observed.

The cost of the protector fitted up and set to work is about one third of replacing a single set of tubes. It requires no attention except periodical inspection and the renewal of the protective mass when it is corroded away. The life of the mass obviously depends upon the nature of the water and other circumstances, but in any case it will run several months without renewal.

It is claimed for this apparatus that in every case it has been applied it has proved a complete remedy, and one in particular is specially worth noting. The vessel in question had been remarkable for her condenser troubles, and as the result of 18 months work she had had to be supplied with her fourth set of tubes. Last year she was fitted with a protector, corrosion having already set up in the new set of tubes. The half eaten tubes were left in place with the exception of some half-a-dozen which were corroded right through and had to be changed. Since then there has been no trouble at all with her and from that time she has not lost a single tube, showing that the apparatus not only prevents corrosion but also arrests it when already in progress.

STEAM GENERATORS.

It is now becoming the practice with most of the large tube type of water tube boilers to

introduce a jet of compressed air into the furnace above the incandescent fuel thereby thoroughly mixing the gases of combustion, and undoubtedly resulting in an increased efficiency. The system was first tried with cylindrical boilers in the French Navy, in 1859, and as introduced by Bourdon consisted of a ring of steam jets placed above the fire-doors, and blowing steam along the grate. The stirring of the flame and the mixing of air and the gases

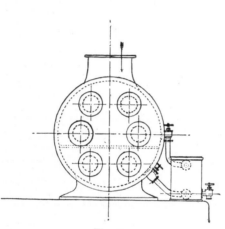

Fig. 6.
CONDENSER TUBE PROTECTOR.
"HARRIS-ANDERSON SYSTEM.

resulting from the decomposition of the steam rendered the combustion nearly complete before the hot gases were cooled down by contact with the heating surface. This system was considerably improved upon by Thierry and was used in the French Navy until 1870, when Mons. Joessel demonstrated that with return-tube boilers, where the gases of combustion have a long distance to travel, the use of this system resulted in the efficiency of the boiler being diminished rather than increased, and it was therefore abandoned.

But in the year 1881, Mons. Belleville turned his attention to the matter and for the last twenty-five years the introduction of air under pressure above the bed of incandescent fuel has formed one of the special features of his type of water tube boiler.

His investigation has shewn that even in the best fired furnaces the veins of gas ascending from the incandescent bed of fuel were very different in their composition, although they might

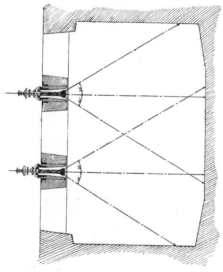

Fig. 7.
GAS MIXER. NICLAUSSE BOILER.

be side by side, these differences being due to the varied thicknesses of fuel and to the various proportions in which the lumps, small coal and dust were mixed.

As the gases left the grate they travelled in a vertical direction and rose through the tubes, the different veins travelling in parallel lines until they arrived at the uptake, and here, if the temperature was low they became simply mixed, but if the temperature at this point was sufficiently high, they combined and an intense heat was the

result of the combustion, which heated up the chimneys to a red heat. The same thing may still be seen with other types of water tube boilers when it has been necessary when running a full power trial to keep the fire hose at work and a constant stream of water on the coamings of the funnel hatches to prevent the decks being damaged.

It was thus for the purpose of producing an effective mixture of these veins of gas before their entry between the tube nests, and that they might be effectively combined and efficiently burnt, that Mons. Belleville adopted the principle of "gas mixing." He at first used for this purpose steam taken from the same boiler and this practice is still adopted and found very satisfactory for all installations on land, but for marine purposes this plan is of course not permissible owing to the necessity of making up the consequent loss of fresh water, and compressed air is used instead. There was no idea of assisting the combustion by an increased supply of oxygen in this addition of compressed air, but simply because it proved a convenient medium for mixing purposes as the use of steam was not possible in this particular case.

The system of gas mixing has been declared to be one of the "complications" of the Belleville boiler, as if the improvement of the combustion was not a thing to be sought after for its own end, and this quite independently of the type of boiler. But it has now become recognized that for effective combustion gas mixing is a necessity with water-tube boilers having their tubes in a more or less horizontal position, and whilst some adopt outright the simple and effective Belleville system, others try to effect the same purpose by forcing the currents of gas to change their direction by the introduction of baffleplates.

Reference was made last year to the experiments carried out with these latter by the British Boiler Committee in different kinds of boilers and the contradictory results obtained, and it is interesting to note that in the latest installations of the Niclausse boilers it has been decided to adopt the absolute system of gas mixing, similar to that recommended by Mons. Belleville, and in order to test it a provisional arrangement was made for the boilers of the the cruiser *Leon Gambetta* of the French Navy as shown in fig. 7.

PROGRESS OF WARSHIP ENGINEERING.

For this purpose the compressed air is introduced through the two sprayers for liquid fuel when mixed combustion is used, and an ingenious nozzle is fitted to the extremity of each sprayer having three passages in it, so that the air is injected from each nozzle in three directions and effectively carries out the mixing.

Trials with this arrangement have given good results not only as regards efficiency and economy but also it has proved to considerably reduce the troubles arising from smoke production, and it has therefore been definitely decided to adopt this system in future as an integral part of the Niclausse boiler, special pipes being fitted with a certain number of branches so as to distribute the compressed air well over the whole surface of the grate and thoroughly mix the gases.

This method of mixing must necessarily prove more efficient than the other system mentioned, for in order that the full advantage of such an operation may be gained, it must be carried out before the gases arrive at the tube nests and enter between them, that is to say, before they are cooled to such an extent as to permit but a mere mixing and exclude the possibility of a combination.

The best "mixing" effect by change of direction of the gases is that obtained in the furnace of an ordinary cylindrical boiler of the marine type, for as soon as they arise from the burning fuel they are forced to change their direction, and are fairly well mixed on their passage along the furnace, arriving at the combustion chamber in a combined state and burning there before their entry into the tubes; but in water-tube boilers where diaphragms have been introduced for the purpose of changing the direction of flow of the gases, the result of the impinging upon them of the gases already cooled by passing between the tubes often results in the production of a considerable amount of smoke. At the same time it must be admitted that there are occasions when ships fitted with Belleville boilers are as great offenders in this respect as those having boilers not provided with gas mixers, but experience has proved that this is due to the rough and ready methods that still obtain in many ships, and is not due to the apparatus itself. Little by little, scientific methods of firing are being introduced, and it is found that when

properly understood and followed out, the work of firing water-tube boilers is much easier than with the old type of boiler and the want of system that was associated with firing it. And given the Belleville arrangements of furnace, a correct regulation of the air pressure, and proper firing, it is possible to obtain a nearly perfect combustion without the production of smoke. It is true that in the later type of Belleville boiler with economizer, a means of introducing compressed air has been provided also in the chamber between the evaporating nests and the economizer, in case the combustion is not perfectly carried out in the combustion chamber proper, but where the conditions above mentioned are obtained, the use of this arrangement is not found to be necessary.

The quantity of air to be supplied for the gas mixing must necessarily vary according to the conditions under which the combustion is carried out, and the air pressure at the nozzles should be increased in proportion to the coal burnt. As the result of much experience Mons. Belleville gives the following as productive of the best results:—

Coal to be burnt per sq. ft. of grate per hour.	Air pressure in Gas Mixer.
Lbs.	Lbs. per sq. inch.
Under 15	7 to 10
From 15 to 20	10 to 13
From 20 to 25	13 to 16
Above 25	16 to 17

There are no important changes in methods of construction to chronicle this year, and but little has been done in this direction. It is greatly to be regretted that it is not more fully recognized that the weak point at present in water tube boilers of the large horizontal tube type is the casing. This casing may be beautifully designed and well made, but the fact seems to be ignored that a structure of plate only one-eighth of an inch or less in thickness and continually subject to considerable variations in temperature cannot be expected to last for ever. From the way they are constructed however, it would seem that they are expected to do so, for they are usually made and fixed in a manner which quite precludes their being readily repaired or replaced, For many ships it is becoming a very serious question, and in some cases the quickest and least expensive way of dealing with the difficulty will be to

dismount the boilers entirely, build new casings in place, and replace the generating portion. But for this the vessel will have to be put out of service for a considerable time. There is really no reason why boilers for warships should not be specially designed for the purpose, and not be merely a slightly modified arrangement of the boiler as originally designed for land service. The generating portion and the framing should be so arranged that the plating of the casing can be removed and replaced without disturbing the other parts, and if for this purpose a little extra room is required at the sides and in some cases also at the backs, more than is now allowed, it can well be afforded in most ships.

Several useful improvements have been carried out with the Niclausse boiler, and new fittings introduced which have considerably facilitated the working of the boiler.

Hitherto when it has been desired to empty the tubes of water for examination or cleaning this has been done by means of a long tube of small diameter reaching to the end and lowest portion of the boiler tube, and connected by a flexible tube to the suction side of a small hand pump, which readily extracted the water in three or four strokes. But it was found that this gradual extraction of the water resulted in the deposition of any dirt or deleterious matter held in suspension in the water on the surface of the tube and which as soon as it was dry formed a hard and dangerous coating. This difficulty has now been overcome by the arrangements

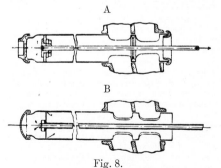

A

B

Fig. 8.
TUBE EMPTIERS. NICLAUSSE BOILER.

shown in Fig. 8 for those boilers which have tubes of the old type with separate lanterns as at A, and for the recent type of tube which has the lantern portion forming part of the tube as at B.

In the former case the opening at the mouth of the tube is rather smaller in diameter than the tube itself, and the larger of the discs shewn on the end of the small tube being made of india rubber easily passes the throat, and being pushed smartly back two or three times effectually clears the boiler tube of water.

The new type of tube however, lends itself more readily to a thorough removal of the water and the disc shewn at B is made of brass plate 2 m/m less in diameter than the boiler tube. This disc also is fixed on the end of a small tube, which is connected by means of a flexible tube to the compressed air piping if compressed air is used on board, or in default of that, to the auxiliary steam pipes. The instrument is pushed into the bottom of the tube, and the water escapes round the circumference of the disc, the communication with the compressed air or steam is then opened and the pressure blows out every drop of water from the end of the tube, and not only that but the action of the compressed air is such that the surface of the tube is left completely dry, or should steam be used it is found that the tube is sufficiently warmed for the heat absorbed by the metal to leave the surface free from moisture.

Last year, mention was made of the new system introduced by Messrs. Niclausse for cleaning the fire side of the tubes when under weigh, and it has proved so advantageous that it will probably be introduced on most war vessels having boilers of this type.

Hitherto the accumulation of soot amongst the tubes has been a very serious matter in a long voyage, causing the efficiency of the boilers to fall off very considerably, and when the point was reached at which it was absolutely necessary to do something to tackle it was rather a heavy job to tackle. The doors of the nests of tubes had to be removed, at times a difficult matter in bad weather and with a heavy roll on, and a small pipe carrying a steam jet was then introduced between the collectors and being worked from top to bottom was supposed to clear away the soot. But the space between the collectors is so small that the pipe had to be a very slight one and was easily bent, besides which its area being so reduced the force of the jet was but little. In practice it was found quite out of the question to try and clean the boiler with the fires going, and the only efficient way was to lay it off altogether, this resulting in a saving both of time and of trouble.

The arrangement now introduced is shewn in Fig. 9. A certain number of the tubes, generally

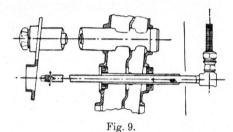

Fig. 9.

TUBE CLEANER. NICLAUSSE BOILER.

five or six per boiler, are removed altogether (see Fig. 9 on p. 426, "Fighting Ships" 1905), and their places are taken by a tube having an internal diameter of 1½ inches, the two outer holes in the collector being closed by stamped steel discs jointed in the collectors as the tubes were before, and a plate disc closing the aperture in the centre diaphragm. The centre tube projects as shewn almost to the smoke box doors and when not in use the end of it is closed by a small cap. In the smoke box door itself is a circular aperture corresponding to the position of the tube, closed with a sliding door. When it is desired to clean the tube this door is removed and a steam lance introduced, connected with a small valve on the boiler for taking off live steam, which passes through the lance and out at circumferential apertures at the inner end. The lance is moved backwards and forwards so that the steam jet can have an effect on the whole space between the back supporting plate and the collectors, and effectually dislodges any accumulation of soot and dirt. The facility with which the whole of the operation can be carried out permits the cleaning to be regularly done every day when at sea, with corresponding increase in efficiency and a considerable reduction of work

both at sea and in port. The new system has been fitted in the French Navy on the cruiser *Condè*, the battleship *Suffren*, and the destroyer *Agile*, and to the cruiser *F. Ferruccio* in the Italian Navy and has been found very satisfactory, five minutes being ample to perfectly clear a boiler.

Following on the adoption of this new system another advantage has been obtained. Now that it is no longer necessary to leave a space between the collectors for the introduction of the cleaning tube, this has been completely closed with asbestos cement, so that the flames and heat no longer have access to the large front doors of the boiler and this results in a very considerable reduction in the amount of heat radiated from the front of the boiler, and a corresponding reduction of temperature in the stokehold.

One of the difficulties found with most types of water tube boilers has been the burning away of the door frames and the supports of the tube nests, but in the latest type of the Niclausse boiler this is overcome by the supports and frames being entirely protected by fire-brick, and firebrick arches are turned over the firing holes thus forming a solid foundation for the steam generating portion of the boiler. This arrangement has been fitted in the armourclads *Patrie*, *République*, and *Ernest Renan*.

It has been decided that the new British Royal Yacht now building, is to be fitted with Yarrow boilers witth the feed heating arrangement first introduced by Mr. Yarrow in 1879, and described in a paper which he contributed to the Inst. of Naval Architects for that year.

The arrangement is shewn in Fig. 10, and it will be seen that the construction of the boiler is not varied in any way, but that diaphragms are fitted in the bottom pockets in such a way that the three outer rows of tubes on each side are partitioned off, and the feed water passes in at the right hand side of the diaphragm in the right hand leg, and at the left hand side of the diaphragm in the left hand leg, and it is claimed that the effect of this was to considerably increase the evaporative efficiency, numerous experiments made showing this to amount to as much as 15 per cent.

Mr. Yarrow's explanation of the reason of such a gain is as follows :—

"Take for example, a working pressure of 250

lbs., the corresponding temperature will be 406 deg. Fahr. Assuming that the heated gases coming in contact with the last three rows of tubes have a temperature of, say 700 deg., there will be a difference of temperature between the heated gases and the tubes of 294 deg. Now, if those three rows of tubes are supplied direct from

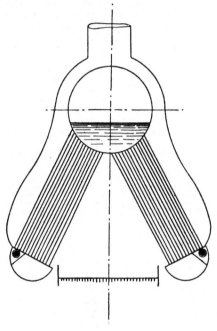

Fig. 10.

YARROW FEED HEATING ARRANGEMENT.

the feed-pump with water, say, at a mean temperature of 200 deg., there will be a difference between the temperature of the water in those tubes and the gases coming in contact with them of 500 deg. ; *i.e.*, in the latter case the difference of temperature will approach nearly twice what it was in the former case ; as the greater the

difference of temperature between the gases and the heating surface, the greater the absorption of heat, the advisability of keeping as cold as possible those surfaces which are called upon to absorb the last remnant of heat from the gases is clearly evident. The outer rows of tubes thus act, as it were, as an economiser or feed-heater of a very simple character, forming part of the boiler proper."

This system has now been in use for some years, but was not pushed as it was wished to give it a thoroughly exhaustive trial, and to see if any defects manifested themselves after it had been in use over a long period, or if it gave rise to any unforeseen troubles. However, the results have been so uniformly satisfactory that the system is now being brought forward as an undoubted advantage, and the gain in economy over the old arrangement has proved to be over 7 per cent. It has also another advantage, as it has been found in practice that any sediment that collects on the tubes settles mostly on the outside rows if the feed-water is introduced in this way, while if the sediment collects on the tubes next to the fire, they are more readily destroyed by getting over-heated when the boiler gets old.

SUPERHEATERS.

The question as to whether advantages were to be derived from the use of superheated steam has been recently revived and as superheaters are now fitted in many cases with water tube boilers, the Bureau of Steam Engineering of the United States Navy appointed a Board of Enquiry into the matter and to carry out tests with the machinery of a large freight steamer on the Great Lakes which had been lately put into service and which was placed at their disposal for the purpose by the courtesy of the owners. She is named the *James C. Wallace* and has a length of 552 ft., beam 56 ft., and depth 31 ft. She has a hold shaped like a hopper so that the cargo can be entirely removed by machine driven scoops and without hand shovelling. As is usual in this class of vessel the propelling machinery is placed in the extreme after part of the vessel. Steam is supplied by two Babcock and Wilcox boilers of the latest type, having a working pressure of 250 lbs. per square inch, and they are fitted with superheaters as shewn in Fig. 11. These superheaters consist of an upper and lower box-tube having a number of bent tubes expanded into them. The steam on leaving the steam drum of the boiler passes to the forward end of the superheater and is forced to pass three times from one box to the other, as these are divided by a partition placed in each box-tube and it is then led from the after end of

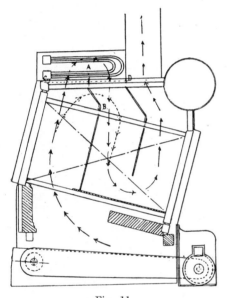

Fig. 11.
SUPERHEATER.
BABCOCK AND WILCOX BOILER.

the superheater to the main steam pipe. Piping and valves are arranged so that the steam may be taken direct from the boiler to the engines with the superheater cut out, should it be found necessary.

It is interesting to note that these boilers are also fitted with automatic stokers of the Crowe chain pattern which are driven by a single cylinder engine, 6½ inches diameter, and 6 inches

stroke, the speed of which is controlled by an adjustable ratchet device, and its rate of travel is so regulated as to maintain the required pressure of steam in the boiler. The coal is fed into hoppers at the front of the boilers and the speed of the grate is such that the coal in passing from front to back is entirely consumed.

In their Report* the Board states that they made two tests with the superheater in operation. and two with it out of use, during all of which the coal was most carefully weighed, diagrams taken at intervals from the main engines, and all the necessary engine and boiler room readings taken every half-hour.

The first two trials with the superheater in service were made with the plate A B in position as shown, and the path of the gases was as indicated by the full-line arrows, the steam passing through the superheater on its way to the engines, whilst for the other two trials the plate A B was removed, and a baffle formed of fire bricks laid on the top row of the tubes from C to D, when the gases travelled the path shewn by the dotted line arrows, the valves on the superheater being closed and the steam passing direct from the steam drum to the engines.

The Board summed up its experiments in the statement that a comparison based on dry coal, showed a net saving in fuel with superheated steam amounting to 14·5 per cent. and that this represented the increased efficiency of the machinery plant, the most important factor in which was the improved economy of the engine when running under superheated steam conditions.

The Board also stated that the automatic stokers worked perfectly throughout the voyage, and so easy was the regulation of the coal supplied to the furnaces controlled, that the fluctuations in the steam pressure were very slight indeed. The coal used was Western Pennsylvanian bituminous slack, but no smoke issued from the funnel at any time. They go on to say that "where, as is the case on the *Wallace*, the steam supply demanded, and consequently the speed developed, is fixed, and only changeable within narrow limits, there can be no question as to the decided superiority of mechanical stokers over hand firing from every standpoint. More-

_____
*Journal Amer. Soc. Nav. Engineers 1905. p. 834.

over, practical experience with stokers fitted to boilers of Lake steamers during the past few years has resulted in improving the mechanical construction to such an extent, that breakdowns are rare, and when they do occur, are usually readily and quickly remedied. In view of this success, the advisability of equipping at least one-half the boiler plant of men-of-war with mechanical stokers, is worthy of serious consideration; flexibility could be provided for by hand firing on the remaining boilers." It is perfectly true that the use of mechanical stokers on board steamers plying on the Great Lakes is an entire success, and this has led to an experiment being made for salt water work, the trial being made with a chain grate stoker similar to the one above mentioned. The coal taken on board was that for which the apparatus was arranged, and the first part of the voyage everything went very satisfactorily, and the results corresponded to those obtained in fresh water work. On reaching foreign ports, however, the fuel obtained was not only quite of a different quality, but found to be unsuitable for use with these stokers, and after many attempts to adapt the apparatus to the new conditions by adjustment, the experiment had to be abandoned, and hand firing resorted to.

The results of the trials with superheaters above noted have led to their introduction in the British Navy, and superheaters have already been fitted to some of the boilers of the *Britannia* and the tests which have been carried out with them so far give promise of a considerable increase in economy due to their use.

NEW TYPES OF BOILERS.

There has been a general tendency of late for the units of the boiler installations on board large vessels to be increased in size, and the new type of boiler being introduced by Messrs. Yarrow, permits the capabilities of the units of the ordinary type of Yarrow boiler to be doubled whilst at the same time introducing several other incidental advantages.

A longitudinal section of the new boiler is of the usual well known principle but now made double-ended, thereby doing away with the fire brick wall at the end and the necessary double casings and asbestos to protect it. There is also a

saving in space, for of course, when two boilers of the original type were placed back to back, space always had to be allowed between them large enough for a man to get between and carry out any necessary work.

It will be seen that the adoption of the new type results in a reduction of the necessary boiler fittings by one half, with a consequent simplification of the steam and feed services.

The boiler shown was constructed to take the place of a locomotive boiler in the torpedo boat *Halcyon*, built by Messrs. Yarrow for the Spanish Government 19 years ago. The change results in a saving of weight of four tons, and this together with the greater supply of steam to be obtained from the water tube boiler is expected to give the boat at least a knot more speed.

The following are the comparative dimensions of the two types :—

	Locomotive boiler.	Yarrow boiler.
Grate surface	46 sq. ft.	60 sq. ft.
Heating surface	2300 sq. ft.	3450 sq. ft.

A very interesting series of trials has been carried out by Messrs. Yarrow with the new double-ended boiler having a two-fold object.

In the first place to test the economy as compared with single-ended Yarrow boilers; and secondly to ascertain whether it would be possible under the most unfavourable working conditions in practice, with a fan in the stokehold at one end of the boiler, for the flame to come out at the doors at the other end of the boiler, assuming that that stokehold was in direct communication with the outside air.

The boiler was enclosed in a specially built shed with a stokehold at each end, and entirely shut in so as to represent the boiler in a vessel with closed stokeholds. In the stokehold A, was fitted a powerful fan, such as would be used on a destroyer for an installation of twice the power of the boiler under test. In this stokehold were also the two feed engines and all the boiler fittings, whilst in the stokehold B, the only fittings were the water gauges.

The two stokeholds were separated by an air-tight diaphragm, which fitted close to the boiler all round, thus completely shutting off the stokehold A from stokehold B. In this diaphragm were two openings, the combined area of which was 18¼ sq. ft. and through these openings all the air passed on its way from the fan to the furnace in stokehold B. This area was purposely made less than the minimum area that in practice there would be past the boiler from one stokehold to another, after every allowance had been made for obstructions, such as steam pipes, &c.

It is hardly necessary to point out that there never would be a bulkhead in this position, but the object of the trials was to get conditions similar to the worst ever possible to occur.

Each stokehold had a large door opening outwards to the atmosphere, each door having an area of 19 sq. ft. which is much larger than the usual stokehold door having generally an opening of about 11 sq. ft. in area.

The areas of the uptakes and funnel were as usual, and the funnel was cut off short just above the house so as not to get any advantage from the suction of a long funnel, which there would usually be when installed on board ship.

During the whole of the trials the fan was kept running at full speed, the fires were well supplied with coal all the time, and the stokehold A, was kept completely closed up throughout.

The first two trials were supposed to represent the conditions under ordinary working, as follows :—

1. With a thin clean fire at both ends, one fire door in stokehold B was held open and then the outer door leading to the atmosphere in stokehold B was suddenly opened, and there was no sign whatever of what is usually termed back draught, or of the fire coming out at the fire door with risk of injury to the stokers.

2. With a thick dirty fire at both ends the same test was repeated and with the same result.

The next two trials were made under conditions that might be supposed to obtain at the end of a watch, when the cleaning of the grate would of course be carried out half at a time.

3. With a thin clean fire at end B, and with bars bare after cleaning fires in stokehold A, the test No. 1 was made with the same result.

4. With a thick fire at end B, and with bars bare after cleaning fires in stokehold A, the same test was repeated with the same result.

These four experiments were then repeated with both fire doors open in stokehold A with the same result, i.e., that under no condition of the fires was there the slightest sign of back draught with both fire doors open in stokehold A, one fire door open in stokehold B and the outer door

suddenly opened in stokehold B.

Experiments were then made with the bars bare after cleaning fires in stokehold B and opening the outer door in stokehold A—only with the same result—no sign of back draught or flame coming out.

Experiments were tried with reduced air pressure and with natural draught, and also with the ashpan protection box doors held open or sealed up, but in no case was it possible to get any flame coming out of the fire doors in the stokehold remote from the fan:

The secret of the safety of the Yarrow double-ended boiler in this respect lies in the fact that the area between the tubes is very large, so that the gases having once got through the fire can easily pass on to the funnel without meeting with any serious obstruction.

Where there is a battery of boilers the conditions would be much more favourable than in the experiments described, as the area connecting one stokehold with another would be multiplied by the number of boilers, while the air-lock that could be opened would remain the same.

The second series of the experiments was to test the evaporation and the results were as shewn in the following table. The water is measured from and at 212 degrees F.

Duration of Trial.	Air Pressure in inches of water.	Coal per sq. foot of grate.	Water per sq. foot heating surface.	Water evaporated per hour.	Water per pound of coal.
6 hours Natural draft*	20·5	3·96	13,700	11·65
6 hours	0·5	40·4	7·23	25,000	11·44
4 hours	1·0	60·1	10·26	35,400	10·9

The above results are with the full area of grate and firing from both ends.

As in actual working at cruising speeds and at reduced powers it might be found advantageous to use only half the grate area and stoke only from one end of the boiler, experiments were then made using only half the bars, the other half being covered up with clinker and ashes. The results obtained are as follows, and as

* Top of chimney 16 ft. above bars.

before, the water was measured from and at 212 degrees F.

Duration of trial.	Air Pressure in inches of water.	Coal per sq. foot of grate.	Water per sq. foot of heating surface.	Water evaporated per hour.	Water per pound of coal.
8 hours Natural draft*	17·6	1·75	6,020	12·63
8 hours	0·5	42·7	4·08	14,100	12·22
4 hours	0·7	60·0	5·4	18,600	11·36

It will be seen that these latter results are a little better than the former, owing to the fact that the proportion of heating surface to grate surface was doubled. It will therefore be seen that with the double-ended Yarrow boiler a very high efficiency is obtained at cruising speeds with half the grate only in use ; and if increased speed were suddenly required the other half of the grate could be quickly brought into action. It will be obvious that the time taken in getting useful effects from the remaining half of the double-ended boiler will be much less than the time required for lighting up and raising steam in a separate boiler.

There is an appreciable reduction in weight of the double-ended boiler as compared with two single boilers, which is estimated at from 12 to 15 per cent., and it makes a much better arrangement of uptakes where a group of double-ended boilers is placed across a ship, while if there is a double stokehold, with boilers on each side of the stokehold, the uptakes are much more complicated.

Mons. Aug. Normand has recently brought out a new type of his boiler and the aim of which is the converse of that of the boiler just described.

Mons. Normand says that for ships of small tonnage the machinery space is so restricted that it is difficult and sometimes impossible to place in it more than one boiler. The giving way of a tube so that the boiler is emptied now seldom happens owing to the increased thickness of the tubes and also to the greater elasticity of the metal of the tubes, which even if overheated may be considerably deformed without giving way. However, should such an accident happen to a vessel having only one boiler, she would be

* Top of chimney 16 ft. above bars.

brought up altogether for at least the time required to plug the tube, so Mons. Normand's purpose in introducing this new type is to put two complete boilers in place of one in a given space.

The boiler is shown in Fig. 13 and it will be seen that each boiler is composed of an upper drum and the usual lower one, connected by groups of tubes of the usual Normand type and with large downtake tubes outside the boiler casing. The upper drums are placed side by side and are of just half the usual capacity, whilst the lower ones occupy precisely the same position as they would in a boiler of the usual single type.

The fire boxes of the two boilers are separated as shewn by a wall of firebrick of the same type and thickness as that generally fitted at the two ends, but if the boilers are to be used under forced draught this division is made of two distinct walls with an air space between.

Each boiler of course has its own distinct set of fittings so that each one is absolutely complete in itself. In the sketch shewn the hot gases after they have passed through the clusters of tubes escape into the funnel which is common to the two boilers. Should, however, it be found advisable, a division may be put at the base of the funnel and carried up to any required height in order to separate the draught.

This new type should come greatly into favour for torpedo boats and similar craft which have hitherto been fitted with one boiler only, and it will result in considerable economy for ordinary speeds as one boiler can be shut off when reduced power only is necessary, and in this way also the life of the steam generating plant will be considerably prolonged.

ASH EJECTORS.

The ash ejector has now been adopted for the large warships of most of the principal Navies of the world, and its many advantages over all the other systems of sending the ashes overboard have led to the overcoming of the objections urged against it in the case of armoured vessels, and no difficulty is now made about taking the discharge pipe through the armoured side.

The type generally adopted is See's hydropneumatic apparatus, arrangement of which is shewn in Fig. 14. It consists of an ejector connected by means of a copper pipe to the delivery branch of a duplex direct acting pump, so arranged that the pump can draw water from the sea and discharge through the patent combined cock and nozzle, which is shown attached to the bottom of the ejector.

The *modus operandi* is as follows :—

The non-return valve or sluice valve on the ship's side is first opened, the lid of the ejector hopper is opened ready for the ashes to be shovelled in and remains so during the operation and the apparatus is then ready for work. The donkey pump is started, drawing from the sea and delivering to the ejector cock, which latter is kept closed until the water gauge indicates a pressure of 200 lbs. per square inch, when the cock is opened quickly and the water flowing in at a high velocity passes through the special nozzle which is connected to the cock. The donkey pump is then kept running at a sufficient speed to maintain a pressure of about 150 lbs. per square inch while passing through the nozzle, the required working pressure necessarily varying according to the height to which the ashes have to be lifted.

By this means a jet of water under high pressure is forced up the discharge pipe causing a partial vacuum at the bottom of the pipe, and as a natural consequence a rush of air down through the hopper.

The ashes are now shovelled into the hopper and they are quickly drawn down towards the water jet by the rush of air and on reaching the jet they are carried up the discharge pipe and passing through the valve are discharged 20 to 30 ft. clear of the ship's side.

By the time the ashes leave the apparatus they are mixed with water so that no dust will blow back on board the vessel.

The manual labour required simply consists of shovelling the ashes into the hopper and this is all done down in the boiler room, no work on deck whatever being necessary.

After all the ashes have been put overboard the donkey pump is allowed to keep running for a couple of minutes to make sure that all the dirt in the hopper and pipe has been ejected overboard, it is then stopped and everything shut off, including the valve on the ship's side and the hopper lid closed down. This lid is provided with an india rubber watertight joint so that sea water cannot find its way into the stokehold in bad weather, even if the valve on the ship's side be left open.

A hand cleaning hole with watertight cover is provided at the lower part of hopper and also

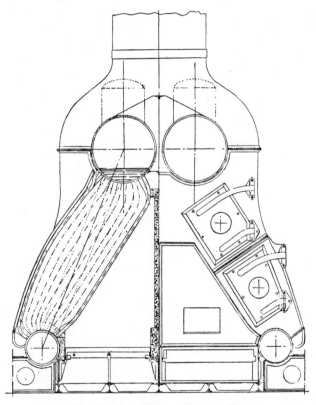

Fig. 13.—New Type of Normand Boiler.

serves for the periodical examination of the nozzle.

Of the various parts of the ash ejector, the nozzle made of navy bronze is perhaps the most important, as on this depends largely the efficiency of the apparatus. Great care has therefore been taken in designing and constructing this nozzle of the best possible shape to give a concentrated stream of water under the high pressure.

A combined cock, nozzle and escape valve possessing several novel features has been fitted to all recent ejectors and gives excellent results.

The bend at the top of the pipe next to the delivery valve is subjected to a scouring action of the ashes and water, and it is therefore con- structed with loose segments or saddle pieces, so that these can easily be renewed when after awhile they become worn thin.

These segments are constructed of a special material known as *Adamant*, combining toughness with great hardness, so that they resist wear and

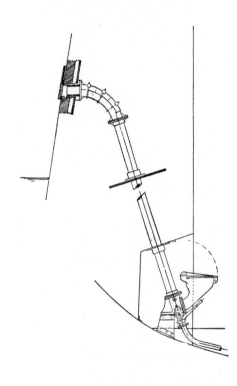

Fig. 14.

Ash Ejector (See's type).

last for a considerable period.

In some navies it is required that a sliding valve shall be fitted outside the armour so that the discharge orifice is not visible from the outside, and in that case a plate valve is fitted as shown.

ENGINE ROOM TELEGRAPHS.

One of the most important of the accessories of a warship is the means of communicating the orders of the officer on the bridge to the officer in charge of the engines and the more speedy a vessel is, the more necessary is it that this apparatus should be absolutely reliable and convey accurately to the engine room the order to which it is set on the bridge. The first type adopted was that where the revolution of a pulley on the bridge was communicated to a similar pulley in the engine room by means of wires led from the one place to the other, the place of the wire being taken by linked chain running over a flanged wheel where it had to go round corners, or at an angle from its original direction. As the wire and chains stretched the slack was taken up by stretching screws and directly this was done, the relative positions of the index on the bridge and the indicator in the engine room required re-adjusting or they did not correspond.

For some time past, it has been the rule in nearly all warships to depend only on rigid shafting and bevel wheels for the telegraph. At first the shafts were of solid bar and the wheels left as they came from the foundry, but these have now given place to hollow tubing with accurately machine-cut bevel wheels. The transmitting instrument and the receiving indicator however, have undergone but little change, being of similar type to the original instruments, one turn of the handle above corresponding to a similar movement of the indicating finger below, the complete circle being divided into a number of segments for the different orders. Experience has led to modifications from time to time in warship practice. At first the two bottom segments representing full speed ahead and full speed astern were adjoining, but a small defect in the apparatus would permit of one order being mistaken for the other with serious results, so that a blank space was placed between them, and later on a stop was fitted in this space, so that to change the order from an ahead motion to an astern one, it was necessary for the handle to pass right round the top of the dial. At first the dial of the transmitter was horizontal with a corresponding movement of the handle, but later these were changed to the vertical, the

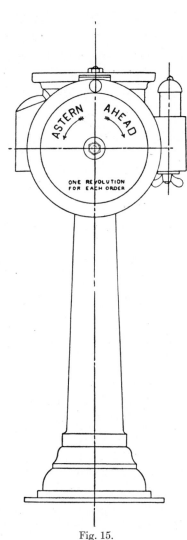

Fig. 15.

ENGINE ROOM TELEGRAPH. NEW TYPE.

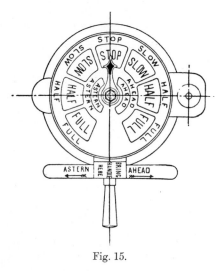

Fig. 15.

movement of the handle corresponding to the direction ahead or astern it was desired to give to the vessel by the use of the engines, and to obtain sufficient clearness in the engine room as to the order it was intended to give, the dial was very much increased in size.

But the great augmentation in the length of the transmitting shafting due to the large increase in size of modern battleships and cruisers, has led to some further modification being necessary to ensure the requisite exactitude in the indications below, for with the small size of the segments corresponding to at most one eighth of the circle, the amount of movement to go from one order to another was so small that a very minute amount of backlash in the numerous pairs of bevel wheels and a slight difference due to spring in the long shafting (with a portion of it generally at an elevated temperature where it passed through the boiler rooms), was quite sufficient to cause the order given in the engine room to be other than that intended, and indicated on the bridge instrument.

Fig. 15 shows a new type of instrument which has been introduced by Messrs. Chadburn and

adopted by the British Admiralty, and which is now fitted to every vessel on the active list of this Navy.

The regulations now in force in the British Navy prescribe that the transmitting instruments are to be fitted with a wheel handle giving an order for each revolution, the upper part of the wheel moving in the same direction as the vessel should move in and the shafting to make at least half a revolution for each change of order. The pointer of the engine room dial has to move in the same direction as the engine shaft for going ahead or astern, and separate gongs of different tone fitted for the ahead and astern movements of the telegraph.

For the reply, there is a system of electric single stroke gongs, a push being fitted in the engine room and a gong at each transmitting station.

In the instrument shown, the wheel handle makes one complete revolution for each change of order, the arrangement being as follows:

The ordinary lever handle of the bridge transmitter is replaced by a hand wheel keyed on to a spindle which carries a bevel wheel, this bevel wheel gears into another containing double the number of teeth, which is in turn keyed to the vertical spindle which runs down the inside of the column and which is connected by hollow steel shafting and bevel gearing to the engine room indicator. It will thus be seen that one revolution of the hand wheel gives one-half a revolution to the connecting shafting. In addition to this train of gearing, the hand wheel spindle actuates a geneva stop mechanism which moves a pointer from the centre of one order to the centre of the next. The pointer is moved sharply while the hand wheel travels through a small arc, whilst for the remainder of the revolution the pointer is locked in its mid position, and a stop is arranged which arrests the motion of the hand wheel when the pointer has reached its extreme order in either direction. A similar train of gearing actuates the pointer and bell movement of the engine room dial, and it will thus be seen that all the back lash of bevel wheels and spring in the shafting, is taken up during that portion of the revolution in which the pointer is not being moved. With the increased leverage of this new system it is possible to put the telegraph over from "full

PROGRESS OF WARSHIP ENGINEERING.

speed ahead" to "full speed astern" in three seconds.

Besides being fitted to every vessel on active service in the British Navy, this new type has been definitely adopted for the Japanese Navy, where it has been fitted to upwards of fifty vessels, and its advantages over the old type are so decided that it seems likely to become the regulation type for all warships.

INTERNAL COMBUSTION ENGINES.

Last year an account was given of the performances of a boat built by Messrs. Yarrow at Poplar, of 40 feet in length and which realized a speed of 26 knots on trial in Long Reach. She was named the *Napier II* and had twin screws, a 45 H.P. Napier motor driving each shaft.

In August, 1904, she took part in the eliminating trials for the British International Trophy but during her races there she commenced to leak badly, and on examination it was found that some of the bow plates had worked loose through the hammering effect of the waves upon her bottom. After the races were concluded she went back to the Yarrow yards, where many experiments were carried out with the object of overcoming the weakness. The result was a new *Napier II* which made her appearance early in 1905. The length of the hull was the same and the beam also, but the lines were somewhat altered. A radical change was made by running the same motors at a faster speed, thereby obtaining about 75 H.P. from each. In a series of trials over the measured mile above Greenhithe a mean speed of 25·98 knots was attained, and straight from her trials on the Thames she was sent to Monaco, where she won the 100 kilometre race from seven starters, making a record time for the distance. Two days afterwards she was pitted against still more formidable competitors, but her floor plates gave way during the race, and she was compelled to give up. After Monaco she was strengthened up, and during the summer made some fine runs, never once being beaten in her class, but after the Burnham races she again commenced to leak and then it was decided to scrap her.

With the experience gained from the *Napier II* of 1904 and 1905 Messrs. Yarrow have constructed a boat of the size of what is termed a

second-class torpedo boat, 60 feet in length by 9 feet beam. This motor boat is said to possess excellent sea-going qualities, being strongly built and not to be looked upon in any sense as coming under the category of a *racing boat*, which is generally built simply to win a race and then possibly collapse. It is claimed that the vessel in question is a thoroughly practical craft and in every respect quite as durable as an ordinary second class torpedo boat. The machinery consists of three sets of internal combustion engines, driving three screws, each of the two outer pro-

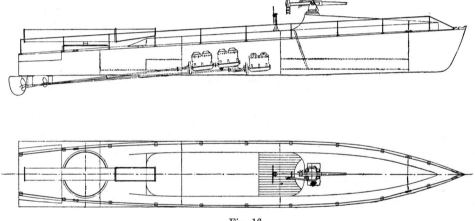

Fig. 16.
60ft. YARROW TORPEDO BOAT.

pellers being driven by engines of about 120 H.P. and the centre propeller by an engine of 60 H.P. The two outer propellers are only capable of going ahead, while the central engine can be reversed.

This vessel is shewn in Fig. 16, and appears admirably adapted to serve as a torpedo boat if fitted with a revolving torpedo tube which could discharge a torpedo over either side. The weight including the hull and propelling machinery does not exceed eight tons, so that it is quite easy to carry such a craft on board a vessel. It would

seem that such a boat fitted with torpedoes is well adapted for the defence of a port or a coast, and it is probable that given a certain amount of money it would be more advantageously expended in obtaining a large number of such craft rather than a few vessels of larger size. The cost of one modern destroyer is equal to that of about fifteen such torpedo launches, and for the purpose of defending a port from an attacking or blockading fleet it is certain that fifteen small vessels of high speed, which it would be difficult to hit, would offer a much greater means of

defence than one destroyer of large size, upon which the fire of a number of guns could be concentrated. Another important point is that the number of the crew working the machinery is about half what is needed if propelled by steam, so that in the event of such a craft being sunk the loss of life would be much less than in the case of a steam vessel.

The engines have been built by Messrs. Napier from the designs of Mr. M. Napier. There are five sets in all, one set driving the central shaft which is used for running at a slow speed, and

two sets each on the wing shafts. Each set has four cylinders of 6½ inches dia. with a piston stroke of 6 inches. The four cylinder jackets and the upper portion of the crank chamber form one large gunmetal casting to which the other parts of the engine are secured, whilst the cylinders proper consist of cast-iron liners fitting into the jackets and provided with wide flanges on their upper ends, by which they are fastened to the main casting by means of countersunk screws. The cylinder heads and valve pockets are cast in pairs, the inlet valves being placed immediately over the exhaust in the valve pockets which overhang on one side of the cylinders, and all are mechanically operated from a single camshaft. Jumpers project through the top of the covers and are depressed by rocker arms, the lower ends of which rest on the top of the valve stems. The tappet rods have large rollers on their lower ends, and are prevented from turning by a vertical slot in the bottom of the guides, which fits the squared ends of the rods. These guides are of gunmetal and are bolted to the engine body by two studs, so that they can be removed, together with the tappet rods, without disturbing other parts of the motor. The exhaust valve gear is made on an exactly similar principle except that the rocker arms are dispensed with.

The pistons are extremely light and turned with very great accuracy, and so close is the fit that they are slightly tapered off at the upper end to allow for the greater heating of that part and its consequent expansion. To give sufficient strength, webs are cast inside the pistons, and an internal flange is left at the bottom of the trunks to ensure the requisite stiffness. Both ends of the connecting rods have gun metal bushes with white metal lining. The stroke of the engine being comparatively short, the crankcase is very little wider than the outside diameter of the cylinder jackets, and the base chamber which carries the three main crankshaft bearings is very shallow, thereby allowing the centre line of the engine to be kept near the bottom of the boat and the propeller shaft to be kept almost horizontal. The crank-shaft bearings are lined with white metal, as also are the camshaft bushes.

Water circulation is maintained by a centrifugal pump driven off the crank-shaft by a chain,

PROGRESS OF WARSHIP ENGINEERING.

a non-return valve being fitted between the pump and the engine so that the jackets can be filled at starting, should the pump run dry from any cause and refuse to draw.

Splash lubrification is adopted, the supply of oil being kept up by a forced feed, entering at the bottom of each cylinder and through each main bearing. The oil pump is chain driven and of a special type, capable of working against a pressure of 30 lb. per square inch, though the usual pressure is only 6 lb. The pump consists of two segments of circles mounted opposite each other on the pump spindle and fitting the barrel fairly closely; between them is a square piece of metal mounted eccentrically in such a way, that as the pump revolves, this piece oscillates from one end to the other of the slot left between the revolving segments. When opposite the suction pipe from the oil tank, the reciprocating part of the pump is moving away from the orifice and therefore sucks up oil, and half a revolution further on, when opposite to the oil-feed pipe, the motion has become reversed, the oil being forced into the engine.

The control of all the engines is brought by rods to a small table close to the after-bulkhead of the engine room, and they can be readily adjusted so that the three shafts run at an equal speed.

By an ingenious arrangement the main petrol tank is completely isolated from the interior of the boat. The deck proper is dropped 15 inches for a length of 6 ft. from the stern, and the main tank carrying a ton of petrol is fastened on to it, so that should there be any leakage, the liquid drains direct into the water, and by no possibility can it find its way into the boat. With this amount of fuel it is estimated the boat can be run for 300 miles.

On a series of trials recently carried out on the measured mile above Greenhithe a mean speed of 26·15 knots was obtained, which is unprecedented for a boat of such dimensions, and it seems likely that for coast defence mosquito fleets will be formed of such vessels, and will prove comparatively inexpensive and give more effective protection than any other method adopted at present.

This year's successor to *Napier II* is very similar to her, but built of sewn wood on the Saunders system instead of having a steel hull.

She is named the *Yarrow-Napier*, and resembles a steam boat in that she has a funnel. The two exhaust sides of the cylinders are together in the centre of the boat, and the exhaust gases pass into a common receiver into which the circulating water passes. The exhaust can then pass down through the bottom of the boat and be discharged under water or by opening plate valves go out through the funnel.

Still more powerful engines than those above described have just been completed for the racing boat *Siola*, a craft of 40 ft. in length and 5 ft. beam. She is fitted with one engine of 180 H.P. and the six cylinder principle which has proved so successful in Napier cars has been adopted. The cylinders are all cast separate and the valves are both of the same size and operated from below, two cam shafts being employed, driven by spur gearing.

The engine has been specially designed for racing work, no attempt being made to make any part of the engine immediately accessible, since any but the most trifling repairs are practically impossible in a boat of this class, so Messrs. Napier have made the motor as simple as possible, with ample bearing surfaces, large

water jackets, and a most complete system of lubrication. The diameter of the cylinders is 8 inches, the stroke 5 inches, and the pressure in the cylinders at the moment of firing is about 600 lbs. per square inch, the number of revs. per minute at full speed being 1150.

An interesting point in the construction of this engine is that the flywheel is not fixed on the crankshaft but on a separate shaft which is driven by gear wheels at about double the speed of the main engine, this arrangement permitting the engine to be fixed much lower in the boat, and therefore the propeller shaft to be kept more nearly horizontal. For starting from cold there is a small auxiliary motor of 4 H.P. which drives the flywheel shaft and thus the main engine by means of chain gearing.

The engines have been specially designed for fast running, and the weight has been cut down as far as possible, whilst at the same time care has been taken that they are amply strong enough for the work. The total weight of the engine is about 1 ton or rather under 12½ lbs. per H.P.

There is no doubt that as soon as a really satisfactory engine is found capable of working efficiently with mazout, and which is not more

costly or much heavier than the ordinary petrol engine, it will be insisted on as the only type admissible for naval work. Meanwhile, the paraffin engine is being adopted in several navies.

Internal combustion engines are being found to be very useful on warships for driving dynamos, and Fig. 17 shows a combined electrical set supplied by Messrs. Thornycroft to the British Navy, using oil of a flash point of not less than 200° Fahr., as required by the British Admiralty. The motor is of the four-cycle type, the cylinders being 8 in. diameter, with a piston stroke of 8 in., and by using the very highest class of material the weight has been reduced to a minimum, so that any vibration is scarcely perceptible. The inlet valves are mechanically operated by cams and tappets, and all parts for the inlet valves are made identically the same as for the exhaust valves, so as to reduce the number of spare parts necessary as much as possible.

Great attention has been given to the carburetter and mixing arrangements, and they are found to run very steadily and economically. The engine is easily started from rest by means of a crank handle, and governing is effected by means of a sensitive governor connected to the throttle valve.

In the French Navy, with a view to obtaining a really satisfactory engine for the vedette boats for protection of the French fisheries, the Minister of Marine has decided to hold a competition, with prizes of 10,000 fr., 8000 fr., and 6000 fr. for the best three motors, and the engine which is adjudged to be the best will be purchased by the Navy.

The motor is to work with ordinary commercial paraffin and no other fuel of a more volatile or inflammable nature is to be permitted, and the engine must be started with the same fuel. Compressed air, however, may be adopted for this purpose, but in that case the motor must be provided with means of compressing the air and also of storing it.

The power of the engine is to be between 165 and 200 B.H.P., and the normal number of revs. at full power about 500 per minute.

The maximum weight of the complete motor with fuel sufficient for 24 hours continuous running is not to exceed 70 lbs. per H.P.

Ten minutes are to be allowed for starting up

60 ft. MOTOR TORPEDO BOAT.

PROGRESS OF WARSHIP ENGINEERING.

from cold, and attain half the normal power.

The engine is to be capable of running satisfactorily and regularly for long periods both at full power and at dead slow, and trial runs are to be made at maximum and minimum powers of six hours duration each.

Special attention is to be given to the reversing arrangements, and with the engine running at full speed, reversal must be efficiently and easily carried out in not more than 15 seconds, after which time the speed astern must be about 300 revs.

MARINE GAS MOTORS.

Messrs. Thornycroft have made considerable progress with their marine gas plant on the Capitaine system and have had wonderful results in the matter of economy of fuel. The arrangement of machinery, as fitted, consists of a suction gas producer in which the gas is generated, and an internal combustion engine working on the usual "Otto" cycle.

Either coke or anthracite coal may be burnt in the producer, and the gas is generated from a mixture of air and steam, which is drawn through the incandescent fuel by the partial vacuum created by the outstroke of the piston in the engine.

The gas is generated only as required and as no gas-holder is necessary, there is therefore no danger of explosion.

The whole producer plant working at a pressure below that of the atmosphere, there is no chance of leakage of gas.

One great advantage is that gas is produced only as it is needed by the engine, and in quantities to suit the varying loads, so that there is no waste while the engine stands idle, and at work it has been proved that the heat efficiency of the plant compares exceedingly favourably with the very best compound condensing steam engine, being 23% as compared with only 11% for the steam engine; that is to say, the gas plant consumes less than one-half the fuel which would be used in a steam engine and boiler of the same power.

A fair average consumption for different qualities of coal is 1 lb. of fuel per brake horse power per hour. If good anthracite be used this figure is slightly reduced. If the fuel be coke

the consumption is about 1¼ lbs. per B.H.P. per hour.

Messrs. Thornycroft designed, built and engined a gas motor yacht on this system, named the *Emil Capitaine* which competed in the Reliability Trials at Southampton, and was

Fig. 17.
THORNYCROFT INTERNAL COMBUSTION ENGINE AND DYNAMO. BRITISH NAVY.

awarded a special gold medal. The hull is built of galvanised steel plates, has a length of 60 feet, with a beam of 10 feet, the draught being 2 feet 6 inches.

She is fitted with a producer gas plant and a four-cylinder engine on the Capitaine system, but

with certain important improvements tending to increased convenience and economy. The engine gives 70 H.P. on the brake, enabling the vessel to travel at a speed of about 10 knots.

During the trials the fuel was carefully and officially weighed and it was found that the

consumption for 24 hours, including lighting up and burning down, as well as 10 hours running at about two-thirds power, was approximately 4 cwts. only, thus giving the consumption (reckoning the whole of the fuel as used for the generation of power in running time)

of under 1 lb. of fuel per B.H.P. per hour.

Some interesting tests have been made with two tug vessels, the *Gasschlepper*, 44¼ feet long, by 10½ feet beam, fitted with a four-cylinder, 70 H.P. suction gas plant, and the other the *Elfriede* 47 feet long, by 12 feet beam, fitted with a triple expansion steam engine developing 75 H.P.

A run from Hamburg to Kiel and back was made by these two boats during very stormy weather, at a maintained speed of 8½ knots. The consumption of fuel was as follows:—For the *Gasschlepper* 530 lb. German Anthracite; for the *Elfriede* 1,820 lb. Steam Coal. This was taken during a 10 hours' run and shows an economy of 1 to 3·44 in favour of the gas plant.

There is no doubt that in future we shall see a wonderful development with this type of engine, and especially so for such classes of vessels as tug boats and coasting craft, and the economy of fuel is so considerable that endeavours are now being made to introduce it for larger vessels.

Sets of engines on the Capitaine system are now being constructed in Scotland of 500 and 1,000 H.P., to run at a speed of about 130 revs. per minute. The smaller of these consists of five cylinders, each capable of developing 100 H.P., and is of very similar construction to those of less power already at work, the framing consisting of steel plates so arranged as to transmit the stresses directly from the main bearings to the cylinder heads. Cam-shafts are fitted on either side of the cylinders for actuating the inlet and exhaust valves, which are worked by rocking levers.

The larger set has the same diameter and stroke of cylinder but the engine is double-acting. These large engines are started by admitting compressed air through special starting valves so as to give the engine the first few revolutions in the required direction, and reversing is effected by an arrangement for shifting the cams for working the valves.

BRITISH ENGINEERING STANDARDS.

The Engineering Standards Committee is still continuing its useful work and during the past

PROGRESS OF WARSHIP ENGINEERING.

year have issued an interim report (No. 20)* on screw threads and definite report (No. 21)* on pipe threads, for iron and steel pipes and tubes. In the former of these it is stated that it was found that the terms in use amongst Engineers in different places often varied considerably in their meaning, so that it was first decided that the nomenclature and definitions to be employed should be as follows:—

STANDARD GAUGE.—A male or female gauge having plain cylindrical surfaces, or a male or female screw gauge suitable for depositing with some recognized authority, for purposes of reference.

REFERENCE GAUGE.—A copy of the foregoing Standard gauge, and intended for use by manufacturers for checking their own shop gauges. They are to be verified and their accuracy certified to by the authority in whose custody the Standard gauges are deposited.

LIMIT GAUGES.—These are for ensuring that any given dimension is within the tolerance laid down for the class of work to be produced. In the case of cylindrical work these gauges may be either double male gauges one end of which must enter, and the other end of which must not enter the hole to which it is applied, or they may be two ring or two gap gauges, one of which must pass over, and the other of which must not pass over the plug or male piece of which they are to give the size.

The Committee recommend that the Whitworth type of thread be adopted for all screws of $\frac{1}{4}$ inch diameter and upwards (B.S.W.) and that the series of pitches originally devised by Sir Joseph Whitworth be retained. The angle of the slopes is 55° and the threads are to be rounded equally at the crest and at the root to a radius of ·137329 times the pitch, so that the depth of the thread is 0·640327 times the pitch. They also recommend that from one-quarter to seven-eighths the advance in sizes should be in sixteenths of an inch, from seven-eighths to $1\frac{3}{4}$ in eighths, from $1\frac{3}{4}$ to 4 inches in quarters of an inch, and that from 4 to 6 inches the advance should be half an inch at a time. The table at present is not carried beyond 6 inches.

For screw threads below quarter inch diameter the Committee recommend the adoption of

the pitches, sizes, and form of thread of the British Association Small Screw gauge (B.A.) and give a table of twenty-five sizes, from a quarter of a millimetre to a quarter of an inch (6 m/m). In this form of thread the angle between the slopes is 47·5° and the threads are rounded equally at the crest and at the root to a radius of nearly two-elevenths of the pitch.

The Committee state that their investigations have clearly indicated that there is a wide-spread desire for a series of finer pitches to supplement the ordinary Whitworth series, for use where the screw thread is subjected to shock and vibration, or where extra strength is required in the case of a screw of given diameter, and they give a table of fine pitches for screws from quarter inch to 6 inches diameter inclusive (B.S.F.) These are so arranged that only two additional chasers are required beyond those adopted in cutting the ordinary Whitworth pitch. For sizes up to and including threads of 1 inch diameter the pitch is based on the formula

$$P = \frac{\sqrt[3]{d^2}}{10}$$

where P = the pitch of the thread in inches, and D = full diameter of the thread in inches.

For those sizes above 1 inch diameter up to and including 6 inches diameter the pitches are based on the formula

$$P = \frac{\sqrt[8]{d^5}}{10}$$

The recommendations of the Committee are entirely in accord with the best practice throughout the world, and it is to be hoped that every navy will adopt the tables now issued as their official ones. These are so complete and so adapted to meet all needs that there is no longer any reason why a manufacturer should continue to use special tables or special threads of his own devising.

For British Standard Pipe Threads for iron or steel tubes the Whitworth type has also been adopted and the threads are to be known by the nominal sizes of the bore of the tube. The

Committee also considered the size of threads of tubes made of other metals, such as copper, brass, or similar material, and they recommend that for these the form of thread should be the same (i.e. Whitworth), and that in those cases where the outside diameters agree, and the thickness of metal permits, the same pitch should be adopted.

STANDARDIZATION.

At the commencement of this article reference was made to the enlightened policy of the Engineering branch of the British Admiralty, as evidenced by their decided step of progress in the adoption of turbine engines on such a large scale. The fact of such a decision is generally known and is certainly approved by most practical and unprejudiced engineers.

But there is a step that this authority has taken with regard to reciprocating engines, which although less generally known, is nevertheless every whit as much a mark of progress and deserves as much to be chronicled, and which, although its results may not be immediately apparent, may possibly have a tremendous influence on the eventual result towards the end of a conflict, should the British Empire be engaged in a desperate and prolonged struggle.

From time to time the general idea of standardization had been given close and serious attention, as from a military point of view it held out promises of many advantages.

It is certain that outside the Admiralty itself, all professional opinion was against standardizing propelling machinery, but it must be borne in mind that not only was there no experience of its feasibility, but also that owing to the lack of any regular system of shop gauges, and absolute definite accuracy in working to dimensions with this class of work, there was in many cases an antagonistic feeling against such a practice, due to trouble already experienced in meeting the requirements of the Admiralty as to the interchangeability of the pieces of spare gear. And directly the subject was brought forward many were the objections urged against it. It must be remembered that the underlying principle of the contracts for propelling machinery, has ever been that the builders of the machinery are entirely responsible for its

fulfilling all the conditions of the specification, and also for the efficient working, durability, safety and efficiency of the various parts. The specification gives the outline of the project and also the minimum dimensions and strengths which are considered necessary, but in every case the contractor is held liable not only for any variation, but also that the conditions themselves of the contract are sufficient.

It will therefore be seen what a serious question was involved in any general standardization of the machinery for any given class of vessel, for it would almost seem that a wholesale reversal of the old conditions would be necessary, and if the several makers were to adhere to a certain dimension for any given part, it would appear as if it would fall to the naval authorities to decide what that said dimension should be, and thereby relieve the contracting firms of all responsibility in the matter so far as design and strength were concerned, leaving them only the matters of quality of material and workmanship to be responsible for.

In addition to this there was the no less serious question involved of the various practices of the different firms, each one based on its own experience, in some cases extending over a long period of time, and which of course each one considered to be better than that of other firms, and in consonance with which their shops were laid out and their business carried on.

These are but the outlines of some of the objections to such a change as was contemplated, the magnitude of which can only be properly realized by those who have had experience of the direction of large engineering or other industrial establishments.

However, the advantages of such a scheme were so very great from a military point of view, that it was eventually decided to make the experiment and to standardize the propelling machinery for the vessels of the *Duke of Edinburgh* class, which are developments of the six vessels of the *Devonshire* class.

The engines are similar to those of the cruisers of the *County* class, being four-cylinder triple expansion of 3ft. 6ins. stroke, running at 135 to 140 revs. per minute when developing 23,500 H.P., their full power. Their machinery was unfortunately decided on in accordance with the recommendation of the Boiler Committee, that a combination of one-fifth cylindrical boilers should be fitted with four-fifths of water-tube boilers, these latter to be of one of the four specified types that they favoured. Consequently the steam pressure was limited to 210 lbs. per square inch, and they carry about 140 tons more weight in machinery than they need, and with this develop some 1500 less H.P. than they would have done had a more rational policy been adopted.

When the decision to standardize the machinery had been come to, that for the *Duke of Edinburgh* had been ordered from Messrs. Hawthorn Leslie, of Newcastle, and that for the sister vessel, the *Black Prince*, from the Thames Engineering Co., of Greenwich. As soon as it was decided to make these sets of machinery identical and interchangeable, a conference took place between Admiralty Officers and representatives of the two firms, which was presided over by the Controller of the Navy, and at which the Engineer-in-Chief of the Navy was present.

It was eventually decided that the respective firms should retain the full responsibility they assumed under their contract, and they agreed to make the following parts interchangeable in the two ships.

(a) Main bearing frames and the back and front columns.

(b) Cylinders, cylinder covers and pistons.

(c) Piston rods, connecting rods, the glands and metallic packing.

(d) Slide valves, slide rods and slide valve gear, including eccentrics, eccentric rods, weigh shafts and reversing gear.

(e) The shafting, thrust blocks and tunnel bearings.

(f) Propeller bosses, and flanges and bolts of the propeller blades.

(g) Boiler fittings and steam pipes as far as possible.

Thus it will be seen that broadly speaking, the whole of the parts of the machinery which it would be at all advantageous to make interchangeable were included in the arrangement.

As the manufacture of the machinery progressed, frequent conferences were held between an Engineer officer specially appointed by the Admiralty, and the Managers of the Engineering Works and the various incidental questions were discussed and disposed of as they arose. Amongst other interesting decisions come to were the following:

(a) In all cases of driving fits, the part that is to be a driving part on another part should accompany that part, and as far as interchangeability is concerned, the two parts are to be regarded as one piece.

(b) In cases where a definite clearance or allowance for working has to be made for parts which move on one another, the work is to be carried out to interchangeable gauges for certain specified parts, leaving the constructors free to adopt their ordinary shop practice for the corresponding parts.

(c) All minor fittings, such as cocks, small valves, unions, etc., are to be regarded as a whole, and the constructors may adopt their usual design for such fittings.

But it is hard to fully realize the infinitude and large scope of the discussions that were necessary and the matters that came up for decision. Take for example the case of the connecting rod. Was it to be regarded as a whole, and in case of need was it considered that the entire rod should be changed and another substituted? or was each of its component parts to be so duplicated, that any one part could be substituted for its corresponding part of any rod, and on either ship?

In the first case one large and costly gauge would be necessary, whilst a large number of smaller ones would be sufficient in the other case. And again in the case of the brasses, would it be considered sufficient to have the diameter and length of the bearings of the brasses and their width, length, and thickness to gauge, or must they be of identical form and dimensions in every respect? Or take the bolts, was it sufficient that they should be of the correct diameter to go into place, or was it desirable that they should exactly correspond all over, and even the heads also be made to gauge? And the external dimensions of the caps, was there any reason for making these identical? And the diameter of the stump, should this also be made exactly to gauge? This will

give but a faint idea of the many questions that came up for settlement, some of which could be decided by a definite line of action laid down at the commencement and a common-sense reasoning, but there were others for which there was as much to be said on one side as on the other, and which required very considerable discussion before a decision was come to.

To put into effect the arrangements come to, over 1,800 templates and jigs of various forms and descriptions were devised and constructed by the two firms concerned, the drawings for them being sent to the Admiralty for examination and approval. But this by no means represents the extra work involved by the adoption of the new system, for the drawings of the machinery itself now had to be consulted on by the two firms, and a definite arrangement come to about them before they could be sent to the Admiralty; and as they were now based on a combination of ideas and not on the regular practice of one firm, they in many cases embodied features new to one firm or the other, so that the preparation and examination of the working drawings entailed a large amount of extra work on all concerned, and as it was imperative not to delay the actual manufacture of the machinery, it was mostly done at very high pressure. As regards the auxiliary machinery, not only were the parts of the different engines to be made interchangeable, but it was also required that it should be possible to take an engine from one ship and put it in the other, and that it should go directly into place, and be capable of being fixed and all the flanges of steam, exhaust, suction, and delivery pipes, be able to be coupled up without trouble or loss of time. It will be seen at once that this required not only a very accurate template, but also one of considerable size. This part of the work was somewhat simplified by it being decided that the practice of "handing" was to be done away with, and all auxiliary machinery made to one hand only, the arrangement of pipes on the second side of the ship being modified to suit.

The special appliances made for standardizing the machinery, ranged from templates large enough to cover a section of the main bedplate, to gauges for such small articles as condenser tube ferrules, and the actual manufacture of them was divided between the two firms, and it was arranged that whatever gauge or template

one firm elected to construct, the same firm should also make the duplicate for use in the works of the other firm, and every one of the gauges and templates was verified, both as to its accuracy and agreement with the drawings by the Engineer Overseer before it was put into use.

The various arrangements described had all been settled and got into working order, and the actual work of construction was in full swing, when tenders were issued by the Admiralty for the machinery of four other vessels of the same class, and the conditions stated that they were to be in all respects identical and interchangeable with those under construction for the *Duke of Edinburgh* and *Black Prince*, and that they were to be made to sets of gauges and templates, similar to those already in use by the constructors of these two sets of machinery, and which would be furnished by them. For the purpose of tendering, the competing firms were furnished with copies of the plans which were already being worked to, and they were asked to guarantee the machinery and the results to be obtained, in a precisely similar manner to that which had obtained before.

The orders were placed as follows:—

For the machinery of the *Cochrane*, Fairfield; for the *Natal*, Vickers; and for the *Warrior*, Wallsend; whilst for the *Achilles*, a repeat order was given to Hawthorn Leslie, and it is well worth placing on record, that within fifteen months of the putting into practical shape the decision to standardize the machinery of British warships, there were six sets of engines of 23,500 H.P. being made in five different parts of Great Britain, which were all precisely similar and identical in all their parts. Note should also be taken of the remarkable goodwill shown by the firms concerned and their officials, and the results fully prove the honest desire manifested by all concerned to make the scheme a thorough and practical success.

In constructing such large sets of engines, in which every endeavour was being made to economize space and weight, from the joint design of two firms 300 miles apart, it would not have been surprising if some fouling of parts had been found when it came to the fitting together and erecting, but thanks to the extensive and thorough examination made of the designs, both by the firms themselves and the Admiralty officials, no trouble at all of this kind manifested itself.

The placing of the repeat order with Messrs. Hawthorn Leslie was of considerable advantage in affording a very good test of the immediate benefits of the system of standardizing, and the actual value of the templates and gauges adopted to carry it into effect, and so well was their purpose fulfilled, that parts were machined and finished without any reference at all as to which place or which ship they were intended for, and thus a considerable saving of time was effected, and the construction of the second set of engines very rapidly carried out.

During the progress of the work there were of course many cases in which material that could perfectly well have been utilized under the old conditions by a slight modification of the corresponding part, had to be put on one side as it would not hold up to the required size, and therefore could not be made to fulfil the requirements of interchangeability.

It is worthy of note that the use of the gauges was found to cause a very material improvement in the standard of workmanship, and not only that, but a very considerable saving of time was effected by the less work required in fitting the various parts together, and this was very noticeable indeed when it came to erecting the engines.

When the manufacture of the gauges was completed, and the construction of the six sets of engines well advanced, a special report was made to the Engineer-in-Chief and the results of the experiment were summed up. It was stated that all the jigs and most of the templates had been found to be necessary for the special object in view, but that most of the gauges and a few of the templates were only such as should form part of the regular equipment of a modern establishment for the construction of warship engines, and therefore should not be regarded as especially necessary for standardizing.

The extra cost of the machinery due to the new system was about £10,000 per ship, which is about four per cent. on the total cost of the engines and boilers, but this amount has already been reduced to less than three per cent. in the case of more recent engines of somewhat greater power which are to be built under similar conditions, and this will certainly be still further reduced in future. It is probable that the addition of such a sum to the cost of the machinery, will lead the authorities of many navies to decide against its adoption, but given the fact that the one aim of a war vessel is that it should be an effective fighting machine, and that the object of a navy should be to prepare for the day of battle, and not for one combat only but for many, there can be no doubt that the immense advantages obtained from a military point of view, are worth considerably more than the extra outlay involved. Not only will there be very material advantages in war time, in the case of several vessels on a station having identical machinery, but even in the case of one vessel only of its kind, the advantage of the new system is very great in the facility and saving of time, in which parts could be replaced from home in time of need, and be fitted in place on arrival without trouble or loss of time.

GAUGES.

It was very evident that for such work as has been above described the old shop methods of gauges were almost worthless, and that a radical change was necessary. It was evidently essential to adopt a new method which would enable the work to be done with certainty, and thus quickly and cheaply. It was a great step in advance to put into the hands of the workman a double gauge known as a "limit gauge" and which gave a maximum and minimum to be worked to, one was to pass over the finished work, whilst the other was not to pass over. In this way any possibility of error was eliminated, and nothing was left to the individual ideas of the workman as to what a certain given diameter really represented. These gauges were made with the utmost care, and hardened, but after a certain amount of use they no longer represented the original dimension they were intended for, and something else was necessary to ensure the absolute correctness called for, for the fully carrying out of the requirements of the new system of standardization.

This necessity was met by the Newall Engineering Co., of Warrington, whose new system of limit gauges is now being largely adopted.

In the Newall system of gauges the different types of "fits" are classed as follows :—

"Force fits," which require a screw or hydraulic press, or heating to force them together.

"Driving fits," which require the use of a hammer to drive the spindle into a hole.

"Push fits," where the spindle can be pushed into the hole by the hand.

"Running fits." These comprise all classes of running work, and inasmuch as different classes of work demand different degrees of looseness, they are divided into three groups as follows :—

X. Suitable for engine and other work where easy fits are wanted.

Y. Suitable for high speeds and good average machine work.

Z. Suitable for fine tool work.

It may seem at first sight rather a complication, but it is astonishing how very simple it is in practice where properly introduced and carried out. A table is made out for the drawing office giving the allowances for the different types of fit and for the various portions of machinery, and the draughtsman gives the exact dimension on the drawing both of the rod and the bush in which it has to work. The workman gets his limit gauge from the gauge store set to the required dimension, and merely has to execute the work in accordance with it, certain that it will be correct, and without any trouble to himself. It will be at once seen what a saving of time and work there is by the adoption of such a method, and it is not until one seriously goes into the matter that it is recognised what a very large amount of allowancing is done with a file and according to the ideas of each individual workman, and when work is in a hurry or the erector not experienced enough, very serious trouble may be caused by the lack of a proper system. Cases have been known where trials of very large engines have had to be suspended and the engines dismantled in order to draw out the piston rod and ease the neck bush in the gland because this latter had been bored to the dimension given on the drawing and been slipped into place without the usual easing. And with one shaft or rod and another the same thing has gone on with nearly every marine engine that has been built. The more scientific method, however, is now being largely adopted in England, and has proved already that it pays better than the old style.

Of course, this multiplicity of fits makes a full stock of solid limit gauges commercially impossible. But the introduction of an adjustable caliper limit gauge has quite overcome the difficulty.

Fig. 18. ADJUSTABLE LIMIT GAUGE.

Fig. 18 shows the latest type of gauge made for this purpose, it is of crescent shape, and of special metal. The screws are made of hardened steel, ground true after hardening, and the holes for them are put in on a special machine which ensures that they shall be exactly in line. The locking plugs when closed make the gauge fully as rigid as a solid one, and the limit is so arranged that for any given work the outer one should freely pass over the finished diameter whilst the inner one should not.

It will be seen at once what an advantage this type of gauge has over the solid one, for any gauge must wear, and when a solid one has become worn it must be readjusted or a new one supplied. But in addition to this, a gauge made in this manner lends itself so entirely to the new system of working fits as above described. When the workman has his drawing he goes to the gauge store and gets a gauge set to the exact dimension given on his drawing, and practically it is as if a new and perfect guage were made for each job. For dead lengths the limit gauges are set to the double reference bars which are kept in the gauge store, and which are as shown

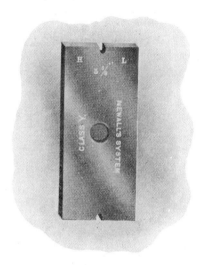

Fig. 19.　Double Reference Bar.

in Fig. 19. They are made of hardened steel, ground true to the high and low limits after hardening, and as they are not intended to be used for anything else but setting the limit gauges, the wear on them is practically nil, and they do not vary in the slightest degree from year to year. In order to set the limit gauges for varying fits the very ingenious "setting dials" shewn in Fig. 20 are used. These dials have taper shanks which fit into taper holes in the screws of the limit gauge. The screws are first adjusted to the nominal size required by means of a standard setting bar or other reliable gauge and are then locked. The dial and index are then inserted in the holes of the screws at zero, as shewn in Fig. 21, and the screw carrying the dial is released and adjusted to the required allowance either above or below standard by rotating the screw in the plus or minus direction

Fig. 20.　Setting Dials, Newall System.

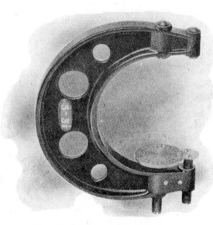

Fig. 21.　Setting Dials in Place.

as shown by the arrow on the index. When one screw has been set, it is locked, the dial and index transposed, and the second set is set and locked in the same way. The dials are divided into thousandths on the main divisions and subdivided into quarter thousandths, and they are so arranged that one pair of dials suits all sizes of external limit gauges up to 6 inches, and another pair all sizes from that up to 12 inches.

Fig. 22 shows an internal limit gauge, the long end being the "go" end and has to enter the

Fig. 22.　Internal Limit Gauge.

hole, whilst the short end is the "not go" end, and holes finished to these gauges are as near standard as it is commercially possible to make them. These internal gauges form the foundation of the system, and the rule is to make all holes absolutely to standard, and allowances for the various classes of fits above described should be made on the piece that goes into them.

The use of such gauges defining with absolute certainty the margin above or below the required size which is permissible has now become a necessity not only for those works where standardization has to be carried out on the lines of the British Admiralty but also in the class of everyday machining. Not only do they make no greater demand on the skill of the workman than the old method, but indeed the contrary is the case, for men using them work with greater freedom, knowing exactly what they have to do. Marine engine makers abroad, however, are as slow to realise the advantages of the new methods, as the naval chiefs are to realise the advantages of standardization. In many navies

now it is the rule that the pieces of spare gear carried on board shall be tried in place during the construction of the engines, and they are supposed to be able to go into place anywhere, but it is a rule that is but seldom carried out. What the state of things really is in this respect may be seen from a recent case where it was insisted that the spare gear of a large set of engines should be made to comply with the regulations as to interchangeability. It took about two months work to complete the job, and although it is true that the various pieces will now go into place anywhere, some of them will be found a very loose fit if they happen to come into conjunction with certain other parts.

DEPTH OF WATER AND SPEED.

During the past year the store of knowledge as to the influence of the depth of water on the speed of ships has been considerably added to.

It will be remembered that Captain A. Rasmussen, of the Danish Navy, first drew attention to the subject in the year 1894, and gave some particulars of the results obtained with a torpedo boat named the *Makrelen*, whose dimensions were as follows: length, 140 ft.; breadth, 14 ft. 3 in.; draught aft when fully equipped, 7 ft. 4 in., and displacement at this draught, 127 tons.

It was found that at depths varying from 18 to $8\frac{1}{2}$ fathoms the results coincided, but at a water depth of $6\frac{1}{4}$ fathoms the loss in speed in full power was about $1\frac{1}{2}$ knots, whilst at a water depth of $3\frac{1}{4}$ and 2 fathoms at full power the speed was about two-thirds of a knot greater than in deep water.

In 1899 Captain Rasmussen gave further particulars of similar trials carried out with another torpedo boat in the spring of 1898.* This vessel was of the following dimensions: length, 145 ft. 6 in.; breadth, 15 ft. 6 in.; draught aft when fully equipped, 7 ft. $9\frac{1}{2}$ in., and corresponding displacement, 140 tons. A most exhaustive series of trials was carried out with this vessel, eight runs on the measured mile having been made in the Sound at Copenhagen, which is specially adapted for such trials, as the tide there is so small that the depth of water is practically constant. The runs were carried out

---

* Trans. Inst. N. A., vol. XLI, page 12.

at four different depths of water, $2\frac{1}{2}$, $6\frac{1}{4}$, 8, and 20 fathoms, and it was found that at half-power the loss in speed in shallow water was very great, while at full power the speed was higher for depths below or above 8 fathoms, this being, of the four named depths, the most disadvantageous for the propulsion of the boat at full power.

The results obtained on these trials were as follows:

Depth of water	Speed with 2200 I.H.P. knots	Speed with 1000 I.H.P. knots
$2\frac{1}{2}$ fathoms	24·1	13·1
$6\frac{1}{4}$,,	23·8	17·2
8 ,,	22·8	18·3
20 ,,	23·6	18·6

The following year Colonel Rota, of the Royal Italian Navy, communicated the result of an exhaustive series of trials made with models in the experimental tank at Spezia, and which were specially carried out in order to ascertain with some accuracy, for any given size of vessel and at any given speed, what the depth of water should be in order to avoid the influence of the bottom.[*]

A number of models were tested of different forms and proportions, and the experiments consisted in towing each model through the tank, the bottom of which, for a considerable length, had been artificially raised by means of a smooth timber floor, giving a limited depth of water compared with the unlimited one, represented by the normal depth of water in the tank. For any given displacement, the depths of water corresponding to those relative to the model were found, these depths being those appropriate to speeds of from ten to twenty-two knots per hour corresponding to the speeds of the model, and it was found that the particular depth of water beyond which no increase of resistance is felt by reason of the influence of the bottom, would rise with the displacement and fall with the increase of the fineness of the hull, the speed in each case being constant.

But there was one peculiar case, the model being of a vessel of the torpedo boat type. The curves of resistance were deduced by towing the model at various depths corresponding to from 32 ft. to 125 ft., and it was seen that up to a certain limit of speed, the speed-resistance

---

[*] Trans. Inst. N. A., vol. XLII, page 239.

changed as is usual with ships of ordinary shape, the resistance increasing rapidly with the speed. But beyond this limit the resistance kept almost constant, and then fell decidedly below that experienced by the ship in deep water.

Taking a torpedo boat of 150 tons displacement, the depth corresponding to the least resistance worked out as follows:—

Speed in knots per hour	Depth of water in feet
12	43
14	53
16	76
18	85
20	85
22 to 30	20 (about)

With a view to testing the correctness of the formulas and results thus obtained, exhaustive experiments were carried out in the German Navy with a torpedo boat, and the greatest care was taken to eliminate any possible errors due to extraneous causes. The trials were carried out in perfectly still weather and were run over a measured distance with depths of water varying from 23 ft. to 197 ft.

It was found that at all speeds up to 13 knots per hour the power required to develop a given speed was the same as in 23 ft. of water as in 197 ft. From 13 to 20 knots per hour the greater the depth, the less was the power required, whilst when the speed of 20 knots was exceeded, there appeared to be a critical depth at which the power required to drive the vessel was a maximum, this varying from a depth of 49 feet with a speed of to 21 knots, to 82 feet when the speed was 27 knots.

Calculations had been made from the formulas enunciated by Colonel Rota of the results which should be obtained from this vessel, and the tests showed that they agreed very closely with those actually obtained.

Since then a number of other trials have been carried out with vessels of the British Navy, and the results have accorded very closely with those calculated according to Colonel Rota's rules.

Mr. Sydney W. Barnaby has given an account of the difficulties that Messrs. Thornycroft met with on the trials of the destroyers of the River class in getting the contract speed. The first trials were made in 50 feet of water on the measured mile at the Maplins, but an increase of 2 knots was obtained when running in 100 feet

of water off Dover, and when the boats were taken to the Clyde and run on the Skelmorlie mile, where there is a depth of 240 feet, there was a still further advantage amounting to 1 knot more.

Messrs. Yarrow had similar troubles with their vessels of this class, and the results of their experiments relative to the effect of the depth of water when running trials have recently been published by Mr. W. W. Marriner and Mr. Harold Yarrow.

Having failed to get their speed on the measured mile at the Maplins, Messrs. Yarrow and Co. erected mile posts on the cliffs near Dover, off which they successfully ran their first four destroyers of the River class. Although the depth available there was not the most suitable, it was much better than that of the Maplins, as the vessels were able to get into deep water outside the Goodwin Sands directly after the measured mile trials had been made, so that the greater part of each trial was made under favourable conditions as regard depths.

The East Coast firms were in the same difficulty, and after a long series of trials they added to the height of their mile posts, so that they might be seen further from the shore, and this enabled them to get through their trials. It was found that with a depth of water of 100 feet or less the guaranteed speed could not be obtained, but when the depth was 120 feet or more, the speed was realized without difficulty, and these conclusions coincided with the results obtained in the South.

MISHAPS.

The casualties connected with the machinery of warships during the past year have unfortunately been accompanied with considerable loss of life, which is intensely to be regretted, as in nearly every case they have been due to preventable causes.

Two especially of these should receive attention.

On July 12th, 1905, an accident occurred in the British battleship *Implacable*, two valve box covers on the main steam pipe in the forward boiler room being blown off by water hammer action.

In this ship there are three boiler-rooms, and the steam pipes are so arranged that the boilers in the forward boiler-room and the two starboard

boilers of the after boiler-room are connected to the starboard main steam pipe, whilst those in the middle boiler-room and the two port boilers in the after boiler-room are connected to the port main steam pipe, and there was the usual cross connection between the two main pipes in the engine-rooms. The pipes were arranged with a slight inclination towards the engine-room to allow for them being drained into the separator when the valves were open.

Previous to the accident the vessel had been steaming at reduced power, only the boilers of the middle boiler-room being used. From these, steam was taken to the starboard engines through the cross connection.

Steam was then raised in the after boilers and on connecting up the two boilers on the starboard side with the starboard main steam pipe, the water which had accumulated in this pipe was driven to the forward end with tremendous force, fracturing the covers of two main valves.

The valve of the starboard main steam pipe on the engine-room bulkhead had been opened when preparing for steaming, so that all the steam pipes were in connection, and this pipe should have had a free communication with the separator and have drained into it, but it is believed that as condensation went on in the pipe not being used, the valve being an automatic one had gradually closed without being observed and effectually prevented the water getting away.

It says much for the engineering staff of warships that there are not more accidents of this description, for with the complication of main and auxiliary steam pipes that there are now in large vessels of war, special attention should be given to the matter of draining them, and the arrangement for this purpose should be so designed as to render it impossible for any such accumulation of water as above described to take place in the steam pipes, reliable automatic steam traps being fitted in accessible positions where necessary, so that whether any given valve is open or shut perfect drainage may be maintained.

But such an important matter as this is too often left entirely in the hands of a junior draughtsman to design, who may be entirely without practical knowledge of the necessities of the case, and in many cases where, as in the *Implacable*, the pipes drain towards the separator, it is contended that no drains at all are required however many valves are in the pipe, on the ground that if the valves are open the pipe drains itself, whilst if a valve is closed it does not matter if the pipe gets full of water, and then, owing to a want of judgment or lack of experience on the part of the man who opens the valve, we have such lamentable occurrences as that being dealt with. In the absence of a properly designed arrangement, too often the question of a sufficiency of drains in the steam pipes resolves itself into a battle between the inspecting officer and the erector of the machinery as to what is or is not really required, and it is time that the only test question that should be recognised in such a matter (and this, every whit as much on the part of the constructor of the machinery as on that of the prospective user of it) should be that of absolute safety, and any arrangements and appliances necessary to obtain this should be duly provided.

Another point in design that this accident brings out is the absence of anything to call attention to the closing of the automatic valve. In every case where there is such a fitting, a pressure gauge should be fitted in an accessible and conspicuous place on the same side of the bulkhead as the valve itself but in communication with the under side of the valve, so that it may at once be seen if the pressure in the pipe beyond the valve is the same as in the rest of the steam pipes, and the valve therefore properly open.

* * * *

The other mishap which calls for special attention occurred on the U.S. gunboat *Bennington*, on the morning of July 21st, 1905, and resulted in the complete wrecking of the vessel and the death of more than 60 men. This vessel is a twin screw gunboat of 1,700 tons displacement and 3,400 H.P., having four single-ended three furnace boilers of the cylindrical direct tube type, each 9 ft. 9 in. diameter and 17 ft. 9 in. long, set end to end with the smoke boxes together and leading into one funnel, and there being two athwartship stokeholds at the two extreme ends.

The *Bennington* arrived in the harbour of San Diego., Cal., on July 19th, from Honolulu, being en route to Panama, and the boilers were in fair condition and perfectly efficient considering their age, which was about 14 years. On July 20th orders were received to proceed at once to Port

Harford, Cal., so the boilers "A" and "B" were ordered to be filled with fresh water, and steam was ordered for ten o'clock the next morning. That night the boiler "C" was being used for auxiliary purposes, and steam was raised in boiler "D" and connected to boiler "C" at 7 a.m. At this hour the two boilers "A" and "B" which were being filled showed water in the gauge glasses and the hydrokineters were started away and the fires started in the centre furnaces of both boilers by the transfer of live coal from the other two boilers, and at 9-15 when steam began to form, the fires in the wing furnaces were also started. At 9-20 the steam gauge on boiler "B" showed about 5 lbs. of steam pressure, and the water-minder ordered a fireman to close the aircock, and he climbed up and shut *something*. Almost immediately, the steam gauge of this boiler failed to register any pressure, but this was quite unnoticed either by the water-minder or the firemen, and they kept on firing-up heavily, and finally the steam gauge on the boiler "A" showed 135 lbs. of pressure, whilst that of boiler "B" remained at zero. At 9-45 the engines were turned round using steam from boilers "C" and "D" and as there was full steam pressure then showing in boiler "A," it was connected up with the others at 10-20, no pressure showing on the gauge of boiler "B," and the stokers thinking that no steam was being made in this boiler fired as hard as possible.

Just after this a leak manifested itself in the left wing furnace of boiler "B," and the water-minder sent a trimmer on deck to call the boiler-maker, but just as he had given him the message a tremendous explosion occurred. The corrugated furnace in the centre of the boiler collapsed throughout its length on top and partly so at the bottom, and the boiler itself broke from its fastenings and moved bodily aft, going right through the bulkhead, and then collided with great force against boiler "D," which it carried away in its turn from its fastenings, and the two boilers continued their motion aft, forced boiler "D" to break through the engine-room bulkhead, and finally to bring up against the forward part of the engine framing. The result was very dreadful and far worse than could be caused in war time by the explosion of a shell under the armoured deck, for boiler "B," in its progress of over 14 feet, carried away the steam connections of all four of the boilers, giving the steam free

exit from all of them, and at the same time carrying away many sea connections, both in the boiler-rooms and in the engine-room, giving the seawater direct access to the ship, and disabling the whole of the machinery. The steam escaped with terrific force into almost every part of the ship, carrying with it water, ashes and coal, and killing 62 and wounding 40 more of the officers and crew, out of a total ship's company of 197. The ship was found to be filling and settling down when a tug was obtained and the ship was towed into shoal water until she grounded.

From an examination of the collapsed furnace and the boiler, and the tests that were made, it was found that the material was of good quality, and the special court of inquiry found "that the explosion was caused by excessive steam pressure in boiler "B," which came about first by shutting the valve connecting the boiler with the steam gauge, so that it did not indicate the pressure in the boiler; secondly, by unusual and heavy firing in the boiler to get up a pressure which the gauge failed to show; thirdly, by the failure of the sentinel and safety valves to lift at the pressure for which they were set, and the pressure increased without relief until it was beyond the strength of the boiler, which finally gave way in its weakest part."

The court of inquiry also brought to light that there was no record or any evidence of the safety valves having been overhauled or examined during the previous twelve months, nor of the sentinel valve having been overhauled, and it was found that the hand gear for lifting the safety valves was not in working order, nor did it seem that the safety valves had been tested in accordance with the U.S. Navy Regulations.

The whole business seems almost incredible, and it might have been thought that men would have more regard for their own safety than to so utterly disregard the most elemental rules for dealing with steam boilers. One result of the disaster was that the old absurd cry was again raised as to the inefficiency and incompetency of the naval engineer as compared with his brother of the merchant service, but it certainly had this amount of truth in it, that such a state of affairs as was disclosed on the *Bennington* would seem to be absolutely impossible on board a merchant vessel, nor would the owner of the wretchedest old tramp steamer be so blind to his own interests as to put his machinery in charge

of men without any proper training for such a post. The disaster calls attention to a decided defect in the U.S. Regulations which require two safety valves and two water gauges, but are content with only one pressure gauge. In this respect they are probably behind all the other Navies of the world, and it is to be hoped the specifications will be amended and insist on this necessity, for all future work. For all marine boilers, large or small, it should be the invariable rule to have two safety valves, preferably separate and independent, but there is no absolute objection to having them in a common valve box; two water gauges with entirely separate connections to the boiler; and two pressure gauges each with its independent cock and line of piping. Another point that is now somewhat lost sight of, is that the sentinel valve should be fitted to act as such, and should give a shrill whistle when it lifts. This was the original intention when it was introduced, but too often now it is fixed in places where it cannot be seen, and designed only to lift and pass steam without giving a real warning, so that when by chance the pressure in the boiler reaches the lifting point it merely blows off, and no notice is taken, as it is supposed to be only a joint or gland leaking.

The U.S. regulations require that the safety valves on the boilers be lifted once a week, but it would appear that this had been totally ignored. Unfortunately the U.S. Navy is not the only one where such regulations are in force and yet are quite disregarded, and it would seem to be a matter for consideration if it would not be advisable to entrust an annual inspection of all such safety appliances to a separate office of inspection, whose sole business it would be to see such regulations carried out.

The state of things that the enquiry brought to light aroused considerable attention, and an agitation took place with a view to rescinding the new regulations, and returning to the old method of having the engineer branch entirely distinct and separate from the executive branch. However, the Engineer-in-Chief was decidedly opposed to such a step, and deals thus with the matter in his annual report:

"So much has been written in the public press advocating the establishment of a separate corps of engineers, similar to the one abolished by the Personnel Act, that it is deemed advisable

PROGRESS OF WARSHIP ENGINEERING.

to state the views of the Bureau upon that question.

The Bureau is opposed to the formation of a separate corps of engineers in the Navy, for the following reasons:—

1. Engineering, as the means of propulsion of ships, logically belongs to the line.
2. Marine engineering of to-day demands for its votaries as high rank and as great consideration, as that of the most favored branch of naval science, consequently a corps of such officers would require a certain number of positions of high rank, in order to insure a proper flow of promotion, and there are not enough such positions of sufficient dignity for high rank, to render the formation of such a corps justifiable.
3. The engineer force of a modern, high-powered ship of war, is a large proportion of the entire crew of such a vessel, and it is contrary to the ethics of military discipline that so many of the crew should be under the orders and direction of two separate and distinct bodies of officers.
4. There is a widespread prejudice throughout the service against the formation of a separate corps of engineering specialists, which prejudice can not be ignored.
5. The controversies and jealousies incident to two bodies of officers performing duties of which the line of demarcation is very vague, so happily removed from the service by the amalgamation feature of the Personnel Bill, would be restored."

Dealing with the main question of how to provide a remedy for the existing state of things, the Engineer-in-Chief reports as follows:

"Again I consider it my imperative duty to invite the attention of the Department to the critical condition of engineering in the Navy.

That this subject must receive serious and immediate attention, the deplorable accident on board the U.S.S. *Bennington* most forcibly emphasizes.

Five and one-half years ago a momentous step was taken regarding the performance of duty in the Navy. A whole corps of specialists was virtually abolished, and the duties performed by these specialists were transferred to the line. The intent of the so-called "Personnel Bill," the instrument by which the Congress authorized this change, was that all the younger officers of the Engineer Corps (the corps in question), were to perfect themselves in seamanship, gunnery, and navigation, and were thereafter to perform both line and engineering duties indiscriminately, and at the same time the younger officers of the line were to perfect themselves in engineering, and thereafter likewise perform indiscriminately the joint duties. The older officers of the Engineer Corps, although transferred to the line at the same time, were for obvious reasons to continue in the performance of engineering duty only. Thus eventually the line would be wholly composed of officers fitted to perform all duties connected with the movement of ships.

The younger officers of the Engineer Corps were given two years in which to qualify for these new duties. How well they did it the records of the examining board and the fitness reports on officers, bear striking testimony. As all midshipmen at the Academy had been given for years excellent practical instruction in engineering, no examination, other than that required for promotion, was demanded of them for qualifying for the performance of these joint duties. The intent was, however, that they should be ordered at once to the performance of this duty in subordinate capacities, as assistants of the older engineer officers.

Owing to the absence of specific instructions to that effect in the Personnel Bill, combined with powerful adverse influences within the department, for three years absolutely nothing was done by the younger line officers in acquiring engineering experience, and later, owing to the large number of ships kept in commission and the scarcity of officers, but little in that direction was accomplished.

So long as the older officers of the former Engineer Corps remained available for service at sea, supplemented by a new body of warrant officers called warrant machinists, the engineering duty of the fleet was properly performed. Credit must not be withheld also from a few officers of the line, who by their own personal exertions perfected themselves in engineering, and served, or are serving, with marked efficiency in most responsible engineering positions afloat.

The older officers of the late Engineer Corps are rapidly disappearing from active service. In my last annual report I stated that there were sixty-six such officers at that time. The number has since been reduced to forty-three, and were it not that the services of certain retired officers are available, the Bureau would already be experiencing great difficulty in finding officers for the various responsible positions both on shore and at sea.

So few officers of the line are taking up engineering seriously that the situation is becoming alarming.

That the department must do something to relieve this situation, and do that something at once, is only too obvious to the most casual observer of present conditions. Were the country suddenly plunged into war, the Navy would find itself in no condition to win battles. As necessary as good workmanship is the ability to carry our guns to the firing line and to keep them there amidst the havoc created by modern ordnance, and this will never be done with amateurs in charge of the machinery. That line officers can become good engineers has already been proved, but they must have experience to become so, and that experience must be acquired in subordinate positions. No young officer out of the Academy but a short time, who would not be given charge of the deck except under the supervision of a senior officer, should be placed in charge of the engineer department of a ship, as has been done."

The Engineer-in-Chief then outlines a scheme which he considers would furnish the Navy with a body of competent engineers.

But the Secretary of the Navy in his report to the President, is not at all in accordance with these recommendations, and states that he "does not share the views of the Engineer-in-Chief, although fully recognizing the necessity for some action to deal with the serious situation he very accurately describes," and he proposes the formation of a new corps of "Marine Engineers for shore duty only."

He says "the real difficulty arises in connection with the engineering service on shore. The situation in this respect, is already embarrassing, and will become a source of weakness and danger to our Navy, unless it shall be promptly remedied. In dealing with it, I think it must be borne in mind, that the occupations of building and repairing marine engines and of operating them on board-ship, are separate and distinct. I agree with the Engineer-in-Chief, that it is an advantage for those engaged in one of these occupations, to have some knowledge of the other, but this does not seem to me a decisive consideration.

To speedily attain the end desired, we must relinquish some theoretical advantages, and I therefore submit for your consideration and that of the Congress, the advisability of promptly organising a service of marine engineers for shore duty only, corresponding to the civil engineers now employed at our naval stations. I feel confident that a corps of this character, could be readily recruited from graduates of the best schools of engineering in the country, and that after a comparatively brief apprenticeship at our several navy-yards, under the instruction of officers belonging to the former corps of engineers, they would be fully qualified to replace these officers, upon retirement of the latter, in all forms of shore duty. It will be noted that by this suggestion, the alarming scarcity of competent officers for such posts would be remedied within a very short time, whereas the system suggested in the report of the Engineer-in-Chief could bear fruit only after a period of many years."

It will be noted that the system now proposed has something in common with that in force in several of the European Navies, but it cannot be sufficiently insisted on, that in order to obtain true efficiency, it is absolutely necessary that the engineers for sea service should be "officers who devote all their time and attention to engineering."

It is an open secret that in the British Navy also there is likely to be a similar trouble before long, owing to a dearth of officers willing to take up engineering duties, and from the very nature of the case it must be so, for given equal conditions no sane man with a free choice would opt for the life of an engineer, largely spent in artificially lighted compartments under the protective deck, with its ultra responsibility, its many drawbacks and its few marks of recognition, in preference to what is termed in comparison, the "gentleman's life" of an executive officer, in the pure air and sunlight, unless he had an actual passion for engineering.

THE PRINCIPAL TYPES OF WATER-TUBE BOILERS FITTED IN WARSHIPS.

(Revised and brought to date by CHARLES DE GRAVE SELLS, M. Inst. C.E.)

[Arranged in order as used.]

BELLEVILLE BOILER.

THORNYCROFT OR SCHULZ BOILER.

The Belleville boiler is the most used of all the various types of water-tube boiler in the War Navies of the world, and there has accordingly been great experience with it, with the result that it is to-day the most economical and serviceable boiler afloat. It consists of a series of elements arranged side by side, each element being formed by two vertical rows of parallel tubes inclined in opposite directions at about 3° from the horizontal. The tubes of these two rows are united by horizontal junction boxes, and each element is connected to the steam drum at the top by a flange joint, and to a square horizontal tube (known as the feed collector) at the bottom by a conical nipple joint.

Above the main portion of the boiler proper is a smaller copy of it known as the economizer, consisting of similar elements of rather smaller tubes, and the space between them forms a second combustion chamber. The feed water delivered by the feed pump passes through a regulating valve on the automatic feed regulator shown at the front of the boiler. It then passes into a distributing box at the bottom of the economizer, through the elements to the outlet at the top, and is led to a non-return valve fixed on the steam drum, along which latter it flows, finally passing down to the feed collector, and so into the elements which form the boiler proper.

The arrangement of the boiler in two parts as shewn is very conducive to efficiency of combustion, and the feeding arrangements are such that the circulation is certain and constant.

SMALL bent tubes are the characteristic of all the Thornycroft types. With these a few large tubes are generally associated. All Thornycroft boilers till recently had one feature in common, in that all the generating tubes delivered their contents into the upper barrel above the water-level. This arrangement, which affords large evaporating area, combined with the baffle plates or grids which the steam has to pass before reaching the internal steam pipe, renders the steam very dry, and gives, it is claimed, great security from priming, even under rapid variations of power. Another advantage claimed is, that in the event of a tube splitting, the rush of steam keeps back the water. The latter types have some tubes entering the upper barrel below the water-line. The courses of the gases are indicated by arrows—there being a slight difference of direction between the two forms illustrated.

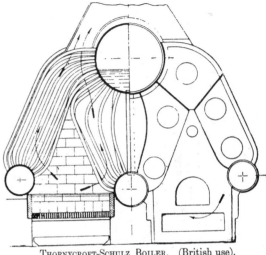

THORNYCROFT-SCHULZ BOILER. (British use).

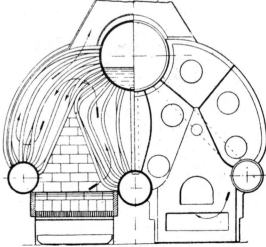

SCHULZ-THORNYCROFT BOILER. (German Navy.)

3 L 2

THE PRINCIPAL TYPES OF WATER-TUBE BOILERS FITTED IN WARSHIPS.

NICLAUSSE BOILER.

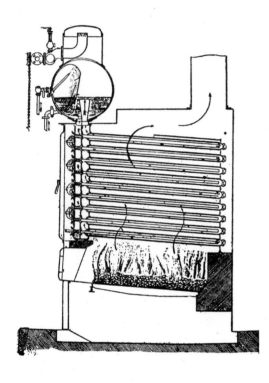

THERE is a steam and water drum at the top, fitted with a diaphragm for the entering feed water.

Inclined duplex tubes are used, the outer of which is of solid-drawn steel in a single piece, the lantern being formed in the tube itself. The tubes have conical ends, fitting coned surfaces in the headers, and are held in place by external dogs. They are interchangeable, which allows the lower tubes next to the fire to be replaced by the upper tubes. They are arranged vertically over each other, so that each group has its own header chamber, which is connected to the steam and water drum.

The collectors are now made of a solid-drawn tube without welding, rectangular in section, and with conical apertures for the tubes. The circulation is indicated in the illustration. The descending feed water passes through the internal tubes, then back through the annular space between it and the outside tube, and is separated from the ascending hot water and steam.

BABCOCK & WILCOX BOILER.

THIS boiler consists in the main of an arrangement of inclined tubes forming the bulk of the heating surface, a horizontal steam and water drum, and a mud drum at the lower front end of the elements.

The tubes are expanded at both ends into wrought steel boxes or headers, and thus form sections vertically. By means of connections with the steam and water drum at the top of these headers the steam generated in the tubes passes into the drum, and the water supplied descends to take its place.

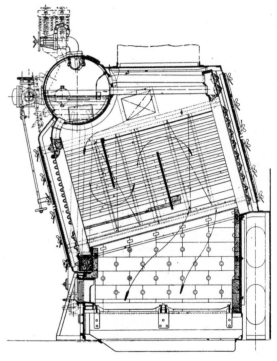

The furnace is underneath the nest of tubes and the gases come into intimate contact with all the heating surface, as is shewn by the direction of the arrows in the illustration. The furnace is lined with firebricks, or in cases where weight is a very important consideration fire tiles are used in their place, which are bolted to the side plates. The whole boiler is encased in an iron casing, lined with non-conducting material, this casing being fitted with doors for the removal of soot. Opposite the ends of the tubes are internal doors, the joints being made on the inside of the header by means of asbestos rings, and the door being drawn up to its face by means of an outside nut on a bolt with crossbar. All the steam mountings are attached to the steam and water drum, and blow-off valves are fitted to the mud drum.

The steam generated in the tubes of the boiler rises vertically through the rear headers into the steam and water drum, whence the water returns to the tubes through the short connection between the drum and the front heaters, so that there is a continuous circulation of water in one direction, giving the boiler as far as possible an equal temperature in all its parts so as to avoid undue strain.

THE PRINCIPAL TYPES OF WATER-TUBE BOILERS FITTED IN WARSHIPS.

NORMAND BOILER.

YARROW BOILER.

DÜRR BOILER.

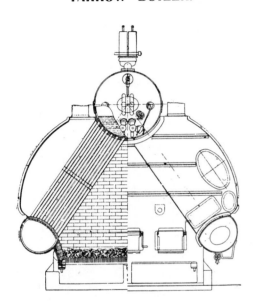

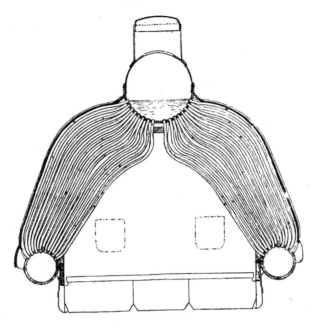

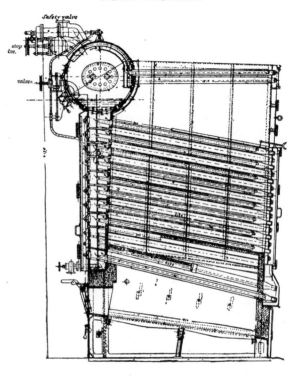

" Drowned " tubes are the chief feature of this boiler. The drum runs from back to front, and the tubes, which are straight, are expanded directly into it in two groups—one on each side—so that the boiler, with its tubes, forms a shape ∧. All the tubes of each group are expanded at the lower ends into a flat-sided horizontal drum just below the fire-level. The circulation is from the upper drum downward, either by special tubes or by the outer and less heated tubes of each group, and up again by the small tubes or those nearest the fire.

Between the large-tube type (for big ships) or the small-tube type (for torpedo craft) no essential differences exist.

The illustration shows a section of this boiler as at present fitted. In general appearance it is the same as that used since 1892, but the arrangement of the cluster of tubes is new, and is said to give a higher economic duty than the original one.

The hot gases enter the cluster of tubes on both sides of the boiler at the front end only and through the whole height; they afterwards travel horizontally to the other end, and an inverted bridge pierced with small holes forces the gases to heat the lower part of the tubes before entering the uptakes. The general direction of the tubes, especially in the more heated part, is such that the bubbles of steam will rise easily and that none of the steam produced can return to the lower reservoirs. The height of the fire-box is very great, and the greater part of the flames and hot gases remain some time in it, being obliged to come to the front before entering the cluster of tubes, and the motion thus imparted to the flames is favourable to complete combustion. The curves of the tubes are sufficient to prevent any undue strains from expansion. The upper end is under water, and the shape of them is such that the formation of " steam pockets " is impossible. The diameter of the return tubes is such that the difference of pressure between the upper and lower reservoirs is very small.

In the Normand-Sigurdy boiler the front ends of two boilers are coupled together to form a single boiler, so as to prevent as far as possible the variations of pressure and water-level when several generators are used for supplying steam to one engine.

The chief characteristics of the Dürr are a large water chamber—divided into two parts, the duplex tubes passing into the two parts of this water chamber, the collector at the top, and the superheater.

The tubes are inclined, and the rear ends rest in the rear wall, so that they can expand without limit and without bending. The duplex tube arrangement is also employed in the superheater.

The feed water flows downward in the front half of the water chamber and through the inner tubes. The steam and hot water then pass through the outer tubes, and ascend into the front part of the drum collector, where the steam enters the tubes of the superheater, and in which any water that may have been carried along is evaporated.

THE PRINCIPAL TYPES OF WATER-TUBE BOILERS FITTED IN WARSHIPS.

WHITE-FORSTER BOILER.

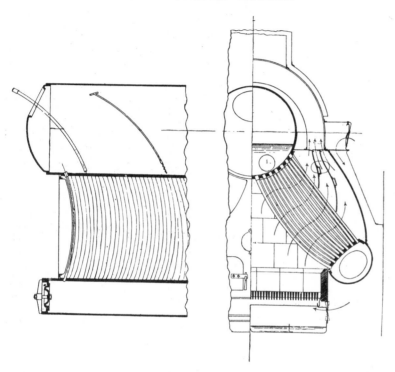

MUMFORD BOILER.

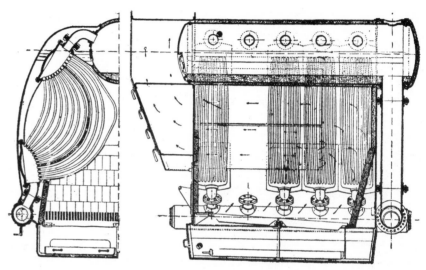

THIS boiler is constructed of elements, or groups of tubes, fitted into top and bottom boxes made of forged steel, and which have one inlet in the bottom box and one in the top box, as shewn Any of these elements or groups of tubes can be disconnected, lowered into the furnace space, and removed through the furnace front for repairs without disturbing in any way the remainder of the boiler, or necessitating the breaking of any joints, beyond the two connected with the element in question. By taking off the top and bottom covers of the tube boxes a single defective tube in any position can be taken out and replaced by a new one, without interfering with those surrounding it. There is no delay in replacing the elements, as the joints are accessible and easily made.

THE White-Forster boiler is largely adopted in the British Navy for destroyers, torpedo boats, and smaller vessels. It consists of a large centre drum and two small ones at the wings, the generating tubes are entirely drowned and are curved sufficiently to determine the direction in which they will move when subjected to heat. They are all curved to the same radius and take up in each row positions due to the converging of the tube holes as if they had been rotated on their ends through a small arc. A divided uptake is adopted, causing the gases on their way to the funnel to dip down and embrace the lower half of the tube surface. The tubes can be readily removed and replaced through the manhole as shewn.

THE PRINCIPAL TYPES OF WATER-TUBE BOILERS FITTED IN WARSHIPS.

REED BOILER.

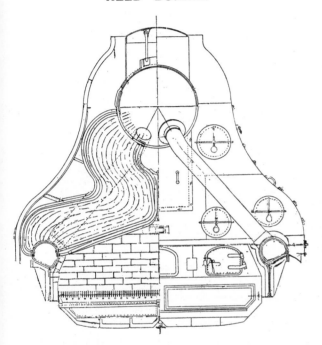

The Reed boiler has three chambers; two lower water chambers, and one upper chamber for water and steam. They are connected by four large downtake pipes, which also do duty as part of the framework of the boiler. The generating tubes are bent to a special shape as shewn, and designed to allow of an easy disengagement of the steam bubbles from the heating surfaces, and a free circulation of the water. It also provides for the necessary expansion of the tubes. The tubes are secured to the tube plates at each end by special spherical joints and nuts, so that the tubes are readily removable, and can easily be replaced. Another special point of this boiler is that it is fitted with a small steam dome, carrying inside a simple form of separator. This boiler has been extensively adopted for the British Navy with excellent results, and is fitted in many torpedo boats and destroyers, and in three third-class cruisers.

MIYABARA BOILER.

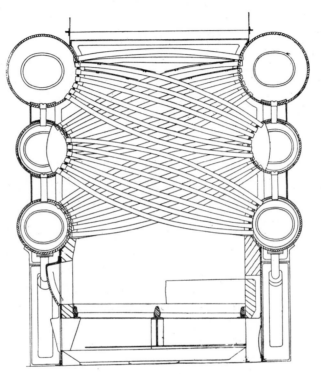

The Miyabara boiler consists solely of rivetted barrels and rolled or drifted tubes. There are six of these former as shewn, the two upper ones being considerably larger than the other four. The tubes are bent to a slight curvature, and are so arranged that there is only one change of direction in the circulation from the bottom water drums, to the steam drums at the top. All the drums are large enough to admit a man. This type of boiler is fitted in several vessels of the Japanese Navy.

LAGRAFEL D'ALLEST BOILER.

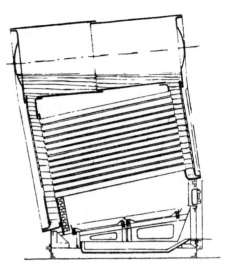

The model of the Lagrafel d'Allest boiler now used in the French Navy was introduced in 1888, and belongs to the type of water-tube boilers with flat water spaces. Like other large tube boilers, the generating tubes are slightly inclined backwards, so as to cause the generated steam to be directed towards the front. Above the generating tubes is a large cylindrical reservoir connecting the two flat water spaces, and the water level is in this chamber.

The characteristic feature of this boiler is the combustion chamber situated at the side of the grate, the boilers being all arranged in groups of two with the combustion chamber between them. Owing to its great length, equal to the length of the tubes, a small transverse width of this chamber is sufficient, and the hot gases, after passing into it, return right across the generating tubes, and escape by an opening on the opposite side of the boiler. They then pass up outside the nest of tubes, and along the top of it, embracing in their passage the lower half of the reservoir, and thence to the uptake. As the top drum is cut away in the lower half of its circumference where it joins the two water spaces, the two ends are stayed together by longitudinal stays set round in a circle.

A NEW "IDEAL" SHIP.

By Colonel VITTORIO E. CUNIBERTI, Chief Constructor Royal Italian Navy.

AFTER a period of thirty years naval artillery returns to follow exactly the ideas which guided Barnaby and Brin in their conceptions of the *Inflexible* and the *Duilio*.

During this thirty years cycle the naval gun has gone down from a diameter of sixteen inches to six in the enthusiasm for rapid firing and in the foolish idea that by multiplying the wounds to the skin it would be possible to wound mortally the heart of the ship.

If the six-inch projectiles were like so many drill points, and, one having penetrated the armour, the others would rapidly enter the same hole one after another, there might be something to be said for such an idea, and perhaps the theories set forth in books might be upheld and lead to victory in the day of battle.

Unfortunately, however, for the believers in such theories, Ito in 1894 with his many rapid-fire guns was not able to pierce the skin of the *Ting-Yuen* and of the *Chen-Yuen*, and at nightfall had to withdraw with his own ships damaged, leaving the armourclads unhurt; and from that day until now faith in the potentiality of the six inch gun (the classic type of rapid-firer) has steadily declined.

Ten years after this, another Japanese Admiral completed the discomfiture of the gun of medium calibre by adopting long range fighting which in the hey-day of rams (after that unhappy day of Lissa) no one believed to be either practical or capable of definitely deciding a battle.

We still see occasionally some isolated attempt to maintain it in favour, but the cause is hopeless, and these very attempts only serve to show how different were the fallacious prophecies of the so-called experts from the reality as demonstrated in recent actual warfare.

Three years ago, * and before the Russo-Japanese war, our contention was that there are but two methods by which one can destroy one's adversary, the one is to wound him little by little so as to weaken him, and then close in to deliver the fatal blow; the other is to save the useless expenditure of the ammunition thus inefficiently spent, and to deal but one deadly and mortal stroke.

In deference to the inquiry of Admiral Sir John Hopkins an ideal type of battleship for "Britain the Wealthy" was worked out, and it was proposed to adopt the only really reasonable method, namely the second one of these two, not to wound, but to destroy absolutely.

The proposal entirely to exclude guns of medium calibre in arming the future battleships and to adopt but one calibre—the biggest—did not meet in 1903 with the favour with which it now appears to be hailed in many navies after the result of the recent war, which showed most clearly the correctness of the views that had been put forward.

But the "Ideal Battleship" armed only with twelve 12in. guns was proposed previous to the late war; three years have passed since then, bringing many changes, and many new lessons to be learned from the events of the recent war, and it is therefore necessary to make a step forward and in future ships to seek to avoid, not only

* See Fighting Ships, 1903, p. 407.

those dangers to which they were proved in the war to be subject to, but also those others not less actual, but which were not greatly accentuated during that period owing to the absence of submarines in the Far East.

Submarine warfare has been described in a very attractive form in several technical romances. One is also able to gather some idea of it from the manœuvres more or less secretly carried out by the few navies which possess submarines and submersibles, but there has not yet been a real and actual sea fight in which this most important factor in modern warfare has played a part and been able to demonstrate its value, and from which may be gleaned an idea of the influence it is likely to have on naval construction.

It is not an easy thing to form in one's mind a really just concept of a future naval engagement neither influenced too greatly nor too little, by ideas of blockading by means of mines laid out at large, or by very swift destroyers, or by slow speeded submarines.

And it is not fortuitously that side by side we have mentioned in contrast the thirty knots speed of modern destroyers and the ten knots of the submarines. For in this lies the crux of the whole matter.

However much we may improve them, adding to their present slow speed and uniting to it the greater velocity which they would have, if instead of submarines we should adopt submersibles, we must inevitably be faced with this dilemma; when the submersible navigates on the surface she will be subject to all the perils that slow torpedo boats are liable to and from which fast destroyers are immune, whilst if she navigates under water her reduced speed will render her at least ill adapted, if not indeed useless, for attacking and striking vessels of high speed, except in exceptional cases and under special circumstances.

* * * *

It may be taken for granted that in the future very fast ships will be a necessity. Let us now see what other defence these ships should have against under-water attack besides superior speed. And here it will be well to glance for a moment at the method adopted for constructing ships of wood in days gone by.

Nature did not produce large sheets such as we now obtain in plates of six and seven feet in width, nor was it possible to obtain ribs in wood of such length as modern steel-works can now furnish us with in metal of any required section. Consequently the structure of a hull was limited by the products of nature, and had to be formed by a skeleton of transverse ribs covered with a skin, somewhat as nature had already outlined in the skeletons and their coverings in the case of animal creatures.

With the introduction of metal for such purposes, the same imitation of nature was followed; but the ideas of construction which then obtained, however well they may be adapted for resisting water, are certainly not those which should be followed if we are to consider the submarine warfare of the future. Nor can we at all rely on external protection, which has proved to be of but little service. Nearly every navy has now definitely abandoned the use of protective nets, for with the vessel in motion it is found not to be convenient to use them, both because it results in such a considerable reduction to the speed, and from the dangers of entanglement of the screw propellers during an action; whilst, after the lessons taught by the torpedoes at Port Arthur, a much better system of protection has been devised of protecting the ships when at anchor, by mooring the nets at some distance from the ships.

A construction specially designed with the idea of being able to withstand the explosion of a mine or torpedo has completely resolved this part of the problem,* the idea being of a floating structure somewhat similar to two Eiffel towers united together at their base and covered over with thin plating. But even then, the knowledge that the enemy possesses submarines, is likely to have a great moral influence over the mind of the commander of the vessel, although he may be aware that the hull of his ship may be able in a certain degree to withstand their attack.

✳ ✳ ✳ ✳

If Admiral Tōgo had found himself in Europe between the British and French Fleets, both well provided with submarines, how would he have manoeuvred?

If besides mines laid in defence of ports, he had had also to fear other mines sown before his ships in the open sea, would he not have meditated once and again on the loss of the *Yashima*, of the *Hatsuse*, of the *Yoshino*, of the *Takasago*, and would he not have come to the conclusion that submarine weapons are even more fatal than the gun?

It is therefore indispensable:—

1. To gather together all the results of the progress made in recent years in the production of materials, and to utilize it in design and arrangement of the structure, radically modifying the old (and present) system of construction.

2. To avail ourselves of the introduction of turbine engines so as to obtain the very highest

✳ ✳ ✳ ✳

---

* Fighting Ships, 1905, page 385.

possible speed, and to take full advantage of the possibility of subdividing them in several chambers of small cubic capacity, judiciously distributed at some distance from one another, thus doing away with the enormous peril of the large engine-rooms necessary for the present type of inverted engines of high power, and in which the entrance of many hundreds of tons of water may be the result of an explosion against the hull.

3. The adoption of small and light boilers, but which are very efficient, and capable of being worked at a very high rate of forced draught; these also should be subdivided and arranged in many compartments separated from one another and of limited volume as regards flooding.

4. The provision of numerous magazines, making these also as small as possible and thus of small volume, distributing them in different parts of the ship and in armoured redoubts in the central corridor of the vessel just below the water line, so that they are well protected, both from the side attack of torpedoes and from the bottom attack of mines.

5. To increase the number of steering appliances, abandoning the present system of concentrating in one place at the stern the whole of such an important feature in the command of the ship, and damage to which in the late war occasioned such serious disasters.

6. To completely protect all parts of the vessel above the water line, doing away entirely with the present protective deck, but so armouring the "lid of the box" that it is really a protection.

7. To arm the vessel with guns capable of penetrating at 10,000 yards the thickest plates of the enemy and maintaining at that distance an energy (foot tons) sufficient to damage a vessel so thoroughly that one blow would be sufficient to render it unserviceable.

Can it be said that the existing twelve inch gun is capable of such a thing? If we are to judge from the trials on shore on the proving ground, the answer must be distinctly in the affirmative, for its penetrative power is more than equal to the thickest plates that one can place on a vessel, and besides with a line of fire nearly normal the cap gives such an increase of pene-

trative power to the projectile that this largely exceeds that necessary for perforating the very thickest armour made.

It should, however, be noted that this supremacy was not manifested in actual warfare, and the *Tsessarevitch* received a dozen blows from a modern 12 inch gun without going to the bottom. And what commander of a squadron can hope in future to get in a dozen such shots on an enemy's vessel?

It is absolutely certain that the battle at long range has entirely and definitely put out of court the medium calibres, thanks to which one was able to get in many hits on the target opposed, but at the same time putting in one ship many guns of the maximum calibre of twelve inch, one would certainly have a great supremacy over actual ships afloat, which possess but four big guns.

However, is it really worth while to go to an expenditure so absolutely colossal, as we now see "Britain the Wealthy" going in for, and which it appears, other nations are preparing to take in hand, merely to abtain in actual warfare a result somewhat the same as that obtained in the case of the *Tsessarevitch*? Really the end attained appears altogether disproportionate to the means.

It was the writer himself who was the first before the war to urge the necessity of this heavy uniform armament, but now after the poor results obtained in actual warfare with the 12 inch gun it is impossible to counsel such a step.

It will be seen that it is not merely a question of merely improving this weapon, by adding, say five calibres to its length and so increasing the initial velocity; but what is wanted is to maintain this velocity at 10,000 yards, and therefore it is necessary to have a weight of projectile considerably greater, so as to guarantee at long range the same effect which, according to proving ground tests, we were certain to obtain at short range, namely the rendering of a ship unserviceable with one blow only.

✳ ✳ ✳ ✳

It is very evident that substituting for the usual (15 or 20) quick firing a much fewer number (8 or 10) of large guns, not

only is the number of successful shots reduced by half, because there are only half the number of barrels, but that number also must be again reduced by more than fifty per cent, owing to the much slower fire of the heavy guns as compared with those of medium calibre. So that it is indispensable that when on one of these rare occasions the projectile should fortunately hit its mark, the shattering effect produced by the percussion of such a mass of metal should serve not only to perforate the armour but must have so much living force remaining as to render the vessel useless, or at least to damage her so effectually as to reduce her efficiency so that her capture could be easily effected, or if necessary she be quickly sent to the bottom.

Let us see what means our predecessors adopted to attain such ends thirty years ago. Had the construction of the artillery of that day arrived at such a perfection as we now find? Was the armour of iron or of soft steel of that epoch more difficult to penetrate, owing to its great thickness, than the face hardened plates of to-day? Or finally, to justify the use of such large guns as 16 inch, was the system of protection more efficient, the cellular divisions more minute, the compartments to be flooded less capacious than those of to-day?

In the case of vessels armed with guns of one uniform calibre, the supply of projectiles is also uniform or at most to be divided between capped and uncapped shell, which can be contemporaneously adopted against the same target, so as to have ready both one and the other, those without cap, when obliged to take the risks of an oblique fire, and at the same time to be in a position not to lose a favourable opportunity of getting a shot through the opponents thickest armour, by using a capped shell, if during the evolutions, the target should happen to present itself broadside on.

Adopting one uniform calibre we in a measure increase our store of ammunition, for if we are left with but one serviceable gun, it matters not which it may be, as we can utilize our ammunition for it to the last cartridge; it also permits the introduction of many simplifications in the supply arrangements to the guns. But we must not lose sight of the fact that the total supply of ammunition provided for any one big gun, cannot possibly be so great as that which has in the past been provided for the smaller quick firers.

* * * *

It is very certain that these future combats, controlled by the desire to strike with as little risk as possible to one's self, but even more by a dread of attack from the enemy's submarines, will have a duration considerably greater than the combats at short range, and therefore the consumption and waste of ammunition will be very great indeed, due partly to the greater distance, and partly to the greater duration of the combat, so that the probable percentage of shots getting home will be very small indeed.

Let us therefore see if we cannot resolve the problem by the means of these very few good hits.

It is for this purpose that the 16 inch gun of about thirty years ago is again being seriously considered, it being well understood of course, that this is with all the improvements made during the past thirty years.

But at once an extreme difficulty arises, not only for the artillerist, but also for the naval architect, the same difficulty which Barnaby and Brin had to contend with, viz., the enormous weight of these guns and their fittings, as well as the encumbrance they cause on board and which did not permit these masters in naval architecture to place more than four of them on each vessel. They endeavoured to arrange them in the most efficacious manner, assigning to them as large a field of fire as possible, so that all four muzzles should be able to fire ahead, astern, and on either beam, but the conditions of the propelling machinery and of the boilers of that time, rendered the resolution of the problem difficult; besides, the soft armour of that day entailed enormous thicknesses to obtain adequate protection, and therefore a perilous reduction of protected area had to be resorted to; and finally the embarrassment caused by the structures at the ends of the vessels rendered more hypothetical than real, the possibility of effective firing in the line of keel,

which ought absolutely to have the pre-eminence in ships like those under consideration, whose speed greatly exceeds that possible of the adversary.

* * * *

Without doubt in a modern ship of war that portion of the armament which is best situated, is a gun of large calibre placed forward with a radius of fire absolutely free towards the bow (and not only in the line of keel as generally contemplated in theory.) If the turret is kept sufficiently distant from the central structure, this gun could have a range of about 300°. Generally this portion of the armament is the highest above the water line, and for the aggressor is certainly the most efficient.

Immediately afterwards, the arm most favoured is that at the extreme stern, which also possesses a large sector of fire, and is capable of developing those special methods of attack which are possible when one has the supremacy in speed.

For the reasons above stated, both Barnaby and Brin were not able to avail themselves of these advantages, and had to concentrate the thickest armour at the centre of their vessels, and to limit the field of fire of their guns, by placing them in echelon at the middle of the ship.

Now it is very evident that in existing ships, the two portions of the armament, forward and aft, would in any case probably be firing continuously, but should the target be either on the port or starboard side, the rest of the armament would be utilized for but the half of its weight, and (excluding the rare case of a general melée, in which it would be necessary to fire contemporaneously from the two sides), only half of the pieces could be utilized in an action at long range.

Therefore, if these guns instead of being of a medium calibre are of the maximum, it is necessary to increase their value, giving a greater importance to their position on board, and endeavouring that both the port guns and the starboard can be used contemporaneously on either side against the same target.

* * * *

Increasing the weight of the main guns forward and aft, going from a calibre of 12 inch to that of 16 inch is not an absolutely impossible thing, endeavouring of course to mitigate as much as possible their influence on the pitching of the vessel; but without going in for displacements absolutely enormous, it is not possible to arrange for other similar stations on the four extreme points of the central redoubt.

Again, it must be borne in mind that if the side turrets at the bow are brought too near the central forward turret it is no longer possible to give them a range of fire of 300°, without running the risk of seriously injuring both the forward wing turrets and those who are serving them with the blast of fire from such enormous guns, when firing aft with the forward turret.

And if, instead, the four central turrets are put nearer one another, their range of fire will be largely reduced, and especially so for those shots in the line of keel.

Therefore, theoretically, the best arrangement for the guns of the heaviest calibre, giving due importance to shots in the line of keel, ought to be that of a rhombus, keeping the pieces as far distant as possible one from the other, in accordance with the old maxim which advises us not to put all our eggs in one basket, and giving the side turrets a range of fire of 180° without interfering in the slightest degree with the fire of the guns in the end turrets. This arrangement is logical enough, but presents, however, the same difficulty as above referred to, and which is a defect of all modern ships, viz., that one obtains only half the utilisation of the side barrels which should be due to their weight. We must therefore arrange these beam turrets so that they may be utilized for firing both to port and to starboard, without however reducing their capacity for firing fore and aft on a line parallel with the keel, for such an arrangement becomes absolutely indispensable when one discards the medium calibres in favour of a fewer number of the maximum calibre. But even to obtain this end it would appear altogether inadvisable to follow the system adopted for the *Kentucky* and

Kearsage, with superimposed turrets placed one over the other on the line of keel, for the perils arising from the blast of fire, when firing one over the other, have already manifested themselves pretty plainly.

Nor is it well to adopt the arrangement of the *Brandenburg* type and afterwards used also in other ships, consisting of two turrets placed aft at the same level on the centre line of the vessel, because in that case the fire from one turret is completely masked for firing astern, which as we have said has a very great importance for fast ships, which are able to engage the enemy with their stern guns, keeping him continually under their fire.

Faced by the problem of finding the best solution of how to place heavy guns on board swift vessels, so that they may be most efficient and that we may be able to force the enemy into that type of action that we should prefer, we find ourselves after a space of thirty years following in the steps of our predecessors, for clearing the decks of the 6-inch guns, the problem which presents itself to-day is identically the same as it was in those bygone days, and by shifting the position of the beam turrets, we can arrange them in a manner which will offer the advantages that, as regards the *Inflexible* and the *Duilio*, we shall get forward and aft fire from two more stations, which has now become possible for the reasons above stated; the distance between the guns will greatly facilitate the special internal arrangements against submarine attack, to which allusion has already been made; and we shall have eight muzzles for use on the beam, six muzzles for use ahead, and six also for use astern.

However, the displacement that such a vessel would require, constructed as we have described with the internal arrangements for safety against underwater explosions of whatever nature, with efficient external defence against projectiles, and finally with such great powers of attack, being armed with eight guns of 16 inches, would be so great that we should be absolutely forced to forego the very high speed necessary for future actions in which submarines would take part, or else we should have to adopt engines of such enormous power, as would be incompatible with the structure of the vessel and with the spaces required on board for other purposes.

At the present moment, therefore, it does not appear practicable to pass with one step only to an increase of 4 inches in the calibre of the guns we propose to adopt, thus attaining once again, at one leap, the calibre of the guns of the *Inflexible*, and in that case we must content ourselves for the moment with an increase of something less than this.

The amount of such a reduction must be here left for the present, nor for obvious reasons is it possible to give more definite particulars, or to reveal the details of the vessel herself.

It must therefore, for the moment, suffice to say that in this new "ideal" vessel the conditions insisted upon as now necessary are fulfilled. The construction is such that full advantage has been taken of the advances in methods of preparation of materials to produce a structure more in accordance with the needs for modern warfare. Advantage has also been taken of the very latest experience, both for the boilers and the propelling machinery; the internal arrangements are carried out in accordance with the lessons taught us in the late war. She is thoroughly protected with very heavy armour, and her armament consists of eight guns so arranged as to obtain the fullest efficiency possible from them.

V. L. Umberti

ADDENDA TO SHIP PAGES.

FRENCH.

PATRIE.

Photo, M. Bar.

GERMAN.

AMERIKA (liner, subventioned probably).

Photo, Harris.

JAPANESE.

IWAMI (present rig).

ERRATA AND ADDENDA TO SHIP PAGES.

Page 37—Heading for BC cone should read B cone.

„ 40—Two funnel destroyers.—The boat shown as a 30 knot t. b. d. is another *River* class. The silhouette of the 30 knot t. b. d. should have come under the same head as the 27 knot, but has been omitted. It closely resembles the 27 knot.

„ 69—Guns: 2—9·2 in. should read 1—9·2 in.

„ 76—*Topaze* (1893) should read (1903).

„ 84—British Destroyers (4 funnels), Laird type.—*Wolf* should be in 27 knot list.

„ 85—British Destroyers (3 funnels)—*Skate* should be deleted.

„ 120—Armament is now fixed at 2—5 in. (1 forward and 1 aft) and 6—14 pdr. *Chester*, Parson's turbine. *Salem*, Curtis turbine. *Birmingham*, reciprocating engines.

Page 239—*Von Buelow* (building) should read *Scharnhorst* (March, 1906). New Cruisers (to be built) should read New Cruiser "*E*." 15,000 tons. No data available. Reported armament: 6 or 8—11 in., 6—6·7 in.

The sister to the *Scharnhorst* is reported to be named *Gneisenau*.

„ 298—The two sisters to *St. Giorgio* reported to be named *Amalfi* and *Pisa*.

„ 315—*Sankt Georg* (1905) should read (1903).

„ 334—*Iver Hvitfeld* is now repaired.

„ 337—Gun Table—8 in. should read 8·2 in.

„ 340—*Gelderland, Noordbrabant* and *Utrecht*—(all 1898) should read (all 1899).

Page 357—*Spetsai* (1899) should read (1889).

„ 362—*Maha Chakrkiri* (1902) should read (1892).

„ 367—*Garibaldi*—Guns: 6—4·7 in. omitted.

„ 423—Col. 3, par. 3, line 4—Instead of sunk should read hit (re *Mikasa*).

U.S.A.—Destroyer *Goldsborough* accepted into service. The two fleet colliers instead of being called *Erie*, etc., will be named *Vestal* and *Prometheus*. Four new Holland submarines under construction.

BRITISH.—Battleship *Montagu* wrecked on Lundy Island; will not be effective for some time.

Building programme.—Owing to the pressure of certain politicians it is possible that the second new battleship will not be laid down 1906-07.

JAPANESE.

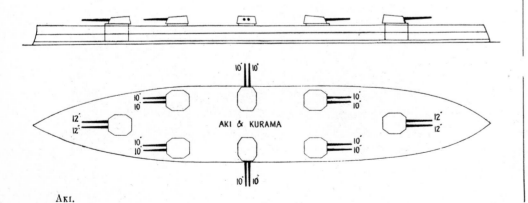

TSUKUBA.—Armament now reported to be 4—12 in. (in pairs in the turrets, fore and aft), 8—8 in. (upper deck), 12—4·7 in., carried on main deck and under forecastle.

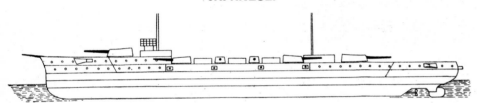

AKI.

AUSTRO-HUNGARIAN.

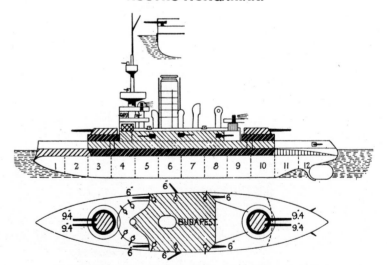

Substitute for plan of WIEN CLASS, Austro-Hungarian Navy.

FINAL SILHOUETTE INDEX.

SILHOUETTE INDEX FOR IDENTIFICATION OF WARSHIPS OF UNKNOWN NATIONALITY.

1 FUNNEL, 1 Mast.

NOTE.—This is intended for reference only when the nationality of the ship sighted is unknown.   The ships are all on a uniform scale, 1 inch = 320 feet.   The ships are arranged (1) by funnels (2) by masts (3) by rig
To identify an unknown vessel, note number of funnels and masts. Then note the rig, look down the left hand column and along the line containing all the warships in the world at all like the vessel sighted. The
strange vessel can thus be named, and compared with her silhouette, the large silhouettes (double the scale) on the index pages of each navy. N.B.—When for any reason a vessel might come under more than one
description, she will, as a rule, be found silhouetted in both places.   Important ships are printed in capitals.

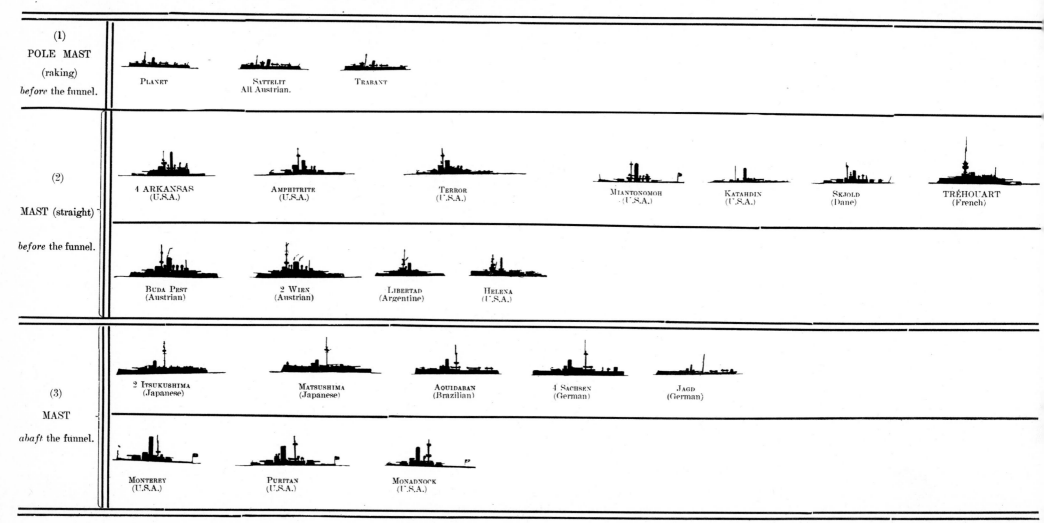

(1) POLE MAST (raking) *before* the funnel.

PLANET   SATTELIT (All Austrian.)   TRABANT

(2) MAST (straight) *before* the funnel.

4 ARKANSAS (U.S.A.)   AMPHITRITE (U.S.A.)   TERROR (U.S.A.)   MIANTONOMOH (U.S.A.)   KATAHDIN (U.S.A.)   SKJOLD (Dane)   TRÉHOUART (French)

BUDA PEST (Austrian)   2 WIEN (Austrian)   LIBERTAD (Argentine)   HELENA (U.S.A.)

(3) MAST *abaft* the funnel.

2 ITSUKUSHIMA (Japanese)   MATSUSHIMA (Japanese)   AQUIDABAN (Brazilian)   4 SACHSEN (German)   JAGD (German)

MONTEREY (U.S.A.)   PURITAN (U.S.A.)   MONADNOCK (U.S.A.)

1 FUNNEL, 2 MASTS (Raking).

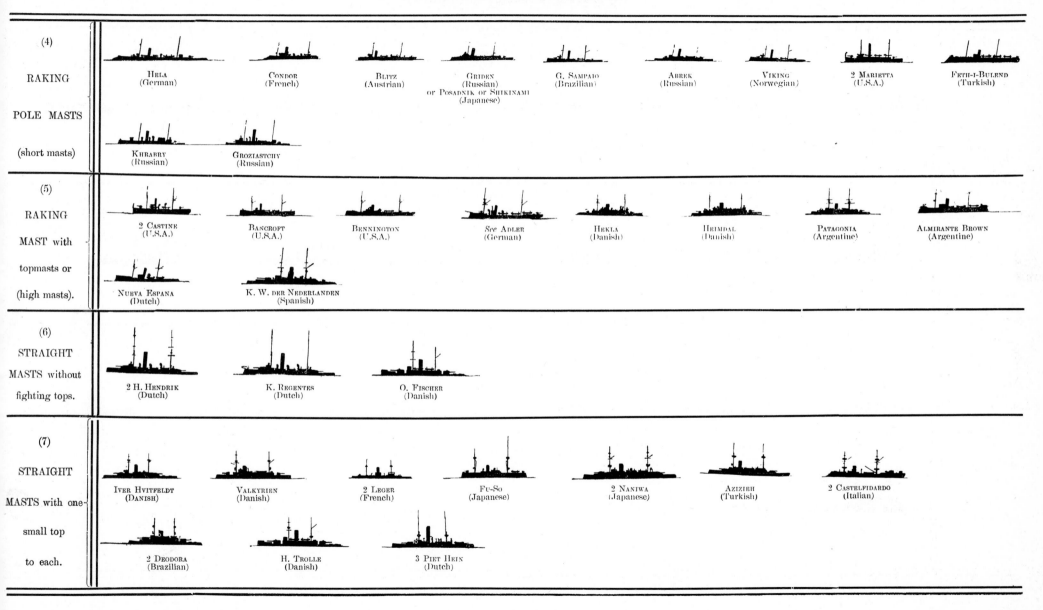

(4)

RAKING

POLE MASTS

(short masts)

HELA
(German)

CONDOR
(French)

BLITZ
(Austrian)

GRIDEN
(Russian)
or POSADNIK or SHIKINAMI
(Japanese)

G. SAMPAIO
(Brazilian)

ABREK
(Russian)

VIKING
(Norwegian)

2 MARIETTA
(U.S.A.)

FETH-I-BULEND
(Turkish)

KHRABRY
(Russian)

GROZIASTCHY
(Russian)

(5)

RAKING

MAST with

topmasts or

(high masts).

2 CASTINE
(U.S.A.)

BANCROFT
(U.S.A.)

BENNINGTON
(U.S.A.)

See ADLER
(German)

HEKLA
(Danish)

HEIMDAL
(Danish)

PATAGONIA
(Argentine)

ALMIRANTE BROWN
(Argentine)

NUEVA ESPANA
(Dutch)

K. W. DER NEDERLANDEN
(Spanish)

(6)

STRAIGHT

MASTS without

fighting tops.

2 H. HENDRIK
(Dutch)

K. REGENTES
(Dutch)

O. FISCHER
(Danish)

(7)

STRAIGHT

MASTS with one

small top

to each.

IVER HVITFELDT
(DANISH)

VALKYRIEN
(Danish)

2 LEGER
(French)

FU-SO
(Japanese)

2 NANIWA
(Japanese)

AZIZIEH
(Turkish)

2 CASTELFIDARDO
(Italian)

2 DEODORA
(Brazilian)

H. TROLLE
(Danish)

3 PIET HEIN
(Dutch)

1 FUNNEL, 2 Masts—continued.

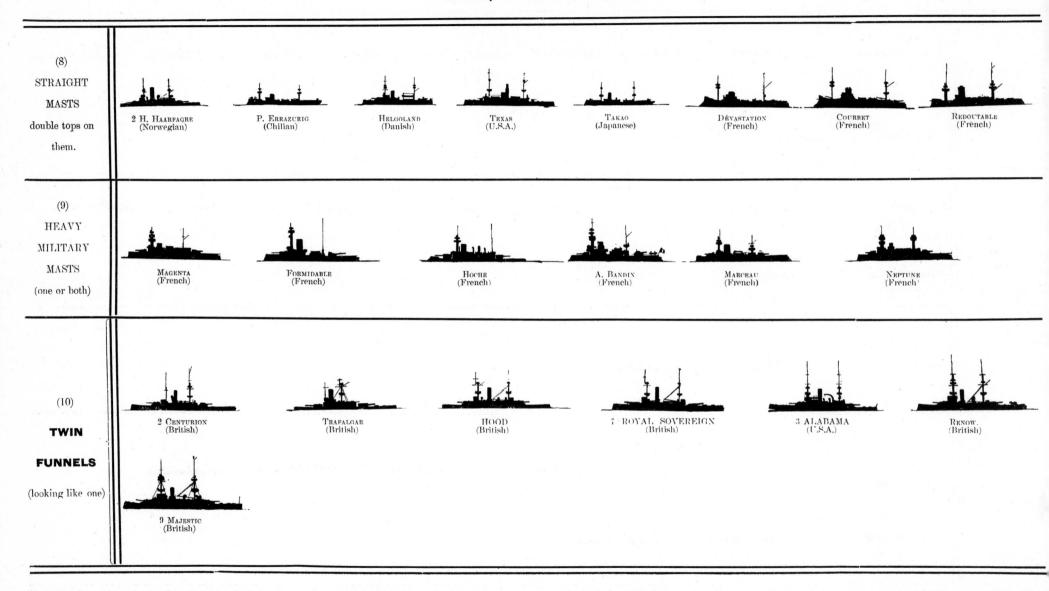

(8) STRAIGHT MASTS double tops on them.

2 H. HAARFAGRE (Norwegian) P. ERRAZURIG (Chilian) HELGOLAND (Danish) TEXAS (U.S.A.) TAKAO (Japanese) DÉVASTATION (French) COURBET (French) REDOUTABLE (French)

(9) HEAVY MILITARY MASTS (one or both)

MAGENTA (French) FORMIDABLE (French) HOCHE (French) A. BANDIN (French) MARCEAU (French) NEPTUNE (French)

(10) TWIN FUNNELS (looking like one)

2 CENTURION (British) TRAFALGAR (British) HOOD (British) 7 ROYAL SOVEREIGN (British) 3 ALABAMA (U.S.A.) RENOW. (British)

9 MAJESTIC (British)

1 FUNNEL, 3 Masts.

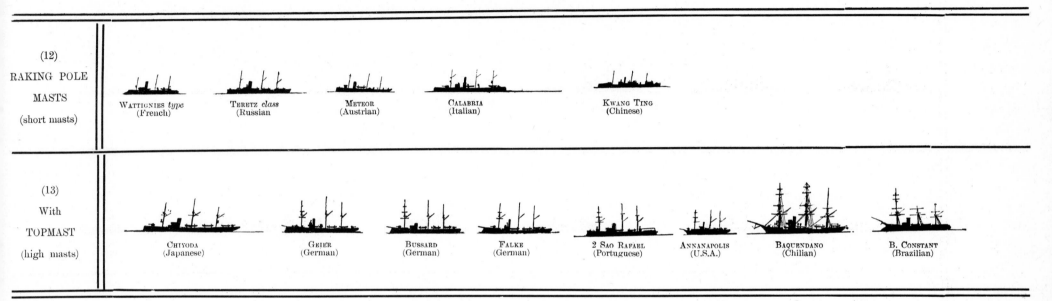

(12)
RAKING POLE
MASTS
(short masts)

WATTIGNIES *type*
(French)

TERETZ *class*
(Russian

METEOR
(Austrian)

CALABRIA
(Italian)

KWANG TING
(Chinese)

(13)
With
TOPMAST
(high masts)

CHIYODA
(Japanese)

GEIER
(German)

BUSSARD
(German)

FALKE
(German)

2 SAO RAFAEL
(Portuguese)

ANNAPOLIS
(U.S.A.)

BAQUENDANO
(Chilian)

B. CONSTANT
(Brazilian)

2 FUNNELS, 1 Mast.

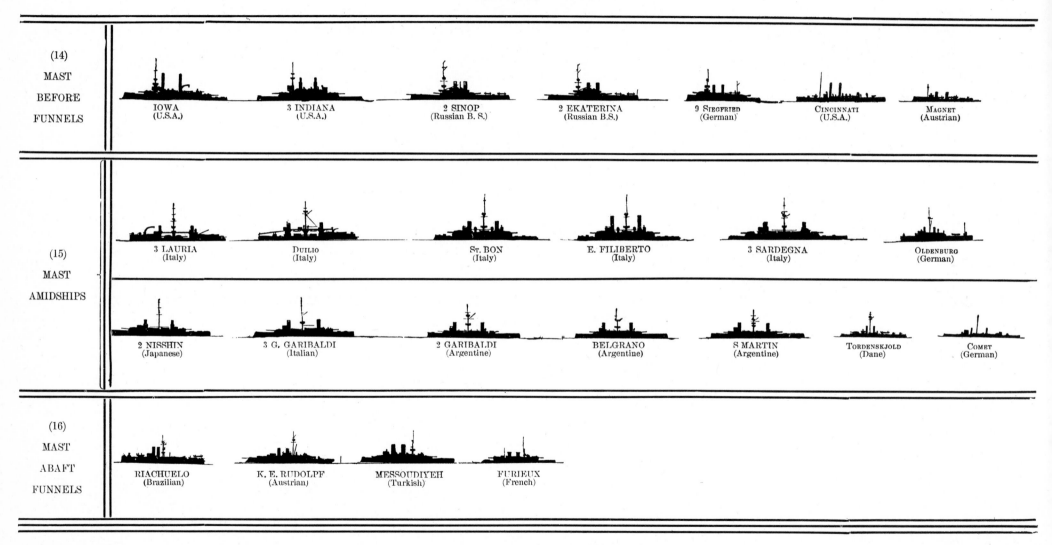

(14)

MAST

BEFORE

FUNNELS

IOWA
(U.S.A.)

3 INDIANA
(U.S.A.)

2 SINOP
(Russian B. S.)

2 EKATERINA
(Russian B.S.)

9 Siegfried
(German)

Cincinnati
(U.S.A.)

Magnet
(Austrian)

(15)

MAST

AMIDSHIPS

3 LAURIA
(Italy)

Duilio
(Italy)

St. BON
(Italy)

E. FILIBERTO
(Italy)

3 SARDEGNA
(Italy)

Oldenburg
(German)

2 NISSHIN
(Japanese)

3 G. GARIBALDI
(Italian)

2 GARIBALDI
(Argentine)

BELGRANO
(Argentine)

S MARTIN
(Argentine)

Tordenskjold
(Dane)

Comet
(German)

(16)

MAST

ABAFT

FUNNELS

RIACHUELO
(Brazilian)

K. E. RUDOLPF
(Austrian)

MESSOUDIYEH
(Turkish)

FURIEUX
(French)

2 FUNNELS, 2 Polemasts (Raking).

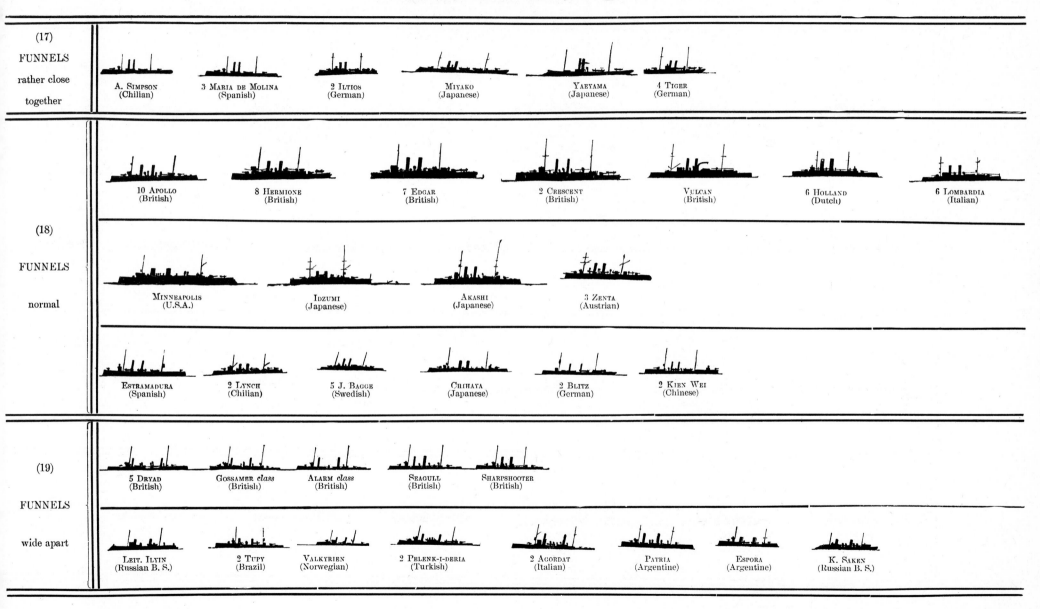

(17)

FUNNELS

rather close

together

A. SIMPSON
(Chilian)

3 MARIA DE MOLINA
(Spanish)

2 ILTIOS
(German)

MIYAKO
(Japanese)

YAEYAMA
(Japanese)

4 TIGER
(German)

(18)

FUNNELS

normal

10 APOLLO
(British)

8 HERMIONE
(British)

7 EDGAR
(British)

2 CRESCENT
(British)

VULCAN
(British)

6 HOLLAND
(Dutch)

6 LOMBARDIA
(Italian)

MINNEAPOLIS
(U.S.A.)

IDZUMI
(Japanese)

AKASHI
(Japanese)

3 ZENTA
(Austrian)

ESTRAMADURA
(Spanish)

2 LYNCH
(Chilian)

5 J. BAGGE
(Swedish)

CHIHAYA
(Japanese)

2 BLITZ
(German)

2 KIEN WEI
(Chinese)

(19)

FUNNELS

wide apart

5 DRYAD
(British)

GOSSAMER *class*
(British)

ALARM *class*
(British)

SEAGULL
(British)

SHARPSHOOTER
(British)

LEIT. ILYIN
(Russian B. S.)

2 TUPY
(Brazil)

VALKYRIEN
(Norwegian)

2 PELENK-I-DERIA
(Turkish)

2 AGORDAT
(Italian)

PATRIA
(Argentine)

ESPORA
(Argentine)

K. SAKEN
(Russian B. S.)

2 FUNNELS, 2 Raking Masts with Topmasts.

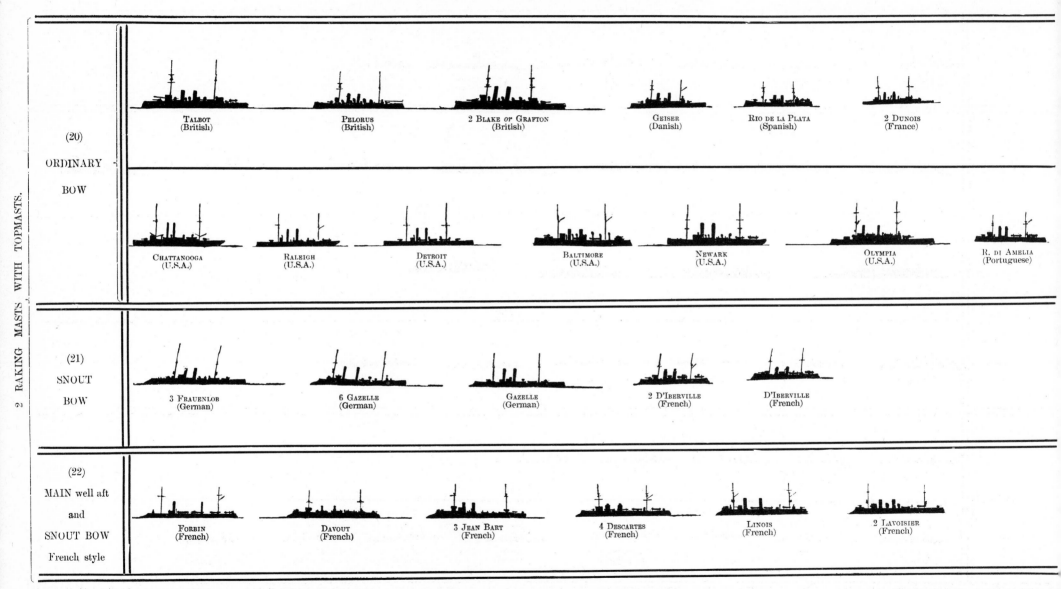

2 RAKING MASTS WITH TOPMASTS.

(20)

ORDINARY

BOW

TALBOT
(British)

PELORUS
(British)

2 BLAKE or GRAFTON
(British)

GEISER
(Danish)

RIO DE LA PLATA
(Spanish)

2 DUNOIS
(France)

CHATTANOOGA
(U.S.A.)

RALEIGH
(U.S.A.)

DETROIT
(U.S.A.)

BALTIMORE
(U.S.A.)

NEWARK
(U.S.A.)

OLYMPIA
(U.S.A.)

R. DI AMELIA
(Portuguese)

(21)

SNOUT

BOW

3 FRAUENLOB
(German)

6 GAZELLE
(German)

GAZELLE
(German)

2 D'IBERVILLE
(French)

D'IBERVILLE
(French)

(22)

MAIN well aft

and

SNOUT BOW

French style

FORBIN
(French)

DAVOUT
(French)

3 JEAN BART
(French)

4 DESCARTES
(French)

LINOIS
(French)

2 LAVOISIER
(French)

2 FUNNELS, 2 Raking Masts with Tops and Topmasts.

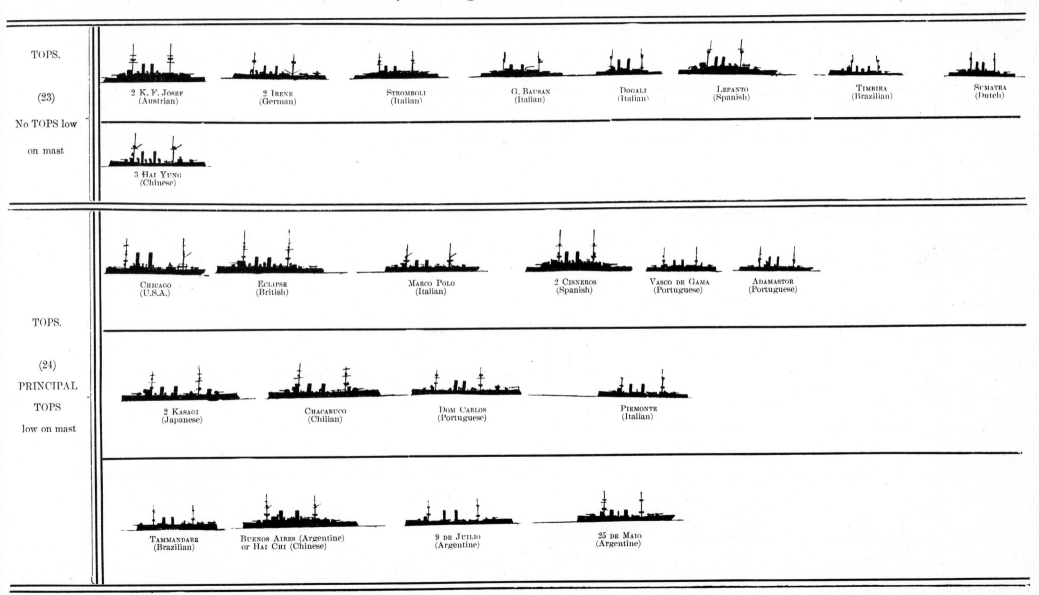

TOPS.

(23)

No TOPS low

on mast

2 K. F. Josef (Austrian)
2 Irene (German)
Stromboli (Italian)
G. Bausan (Italian)
Dogali (Italian)
Lepanto (Spanish)
Timbira (Brazilian)
Sumatra (Dutch)

3 Hai Yung (Chinese)

TOPS.

(24)

PRINCIPAL

TOPS

low on mast

Chicago (U.S.A.)
Eclipse (British)
Marco Polo (Italian)
2 Cisneros (Spanish)
Vasco de Gama (Portuguese)
Adamastor (Portuguese)

2 Kasagi (Japanese)
Chacabuco (Chilian)
Dom Carlos (Portuguese)
Piemonte (Italian)

Tammandare (Brazilian)
Buenos Aires (Argentine) or Hai Chi (Chinese)
9 de Julio (Argentine)
25 de Maio (Argentine)

2 FUNNELS, 2 Masts—Light-Looking Ships.

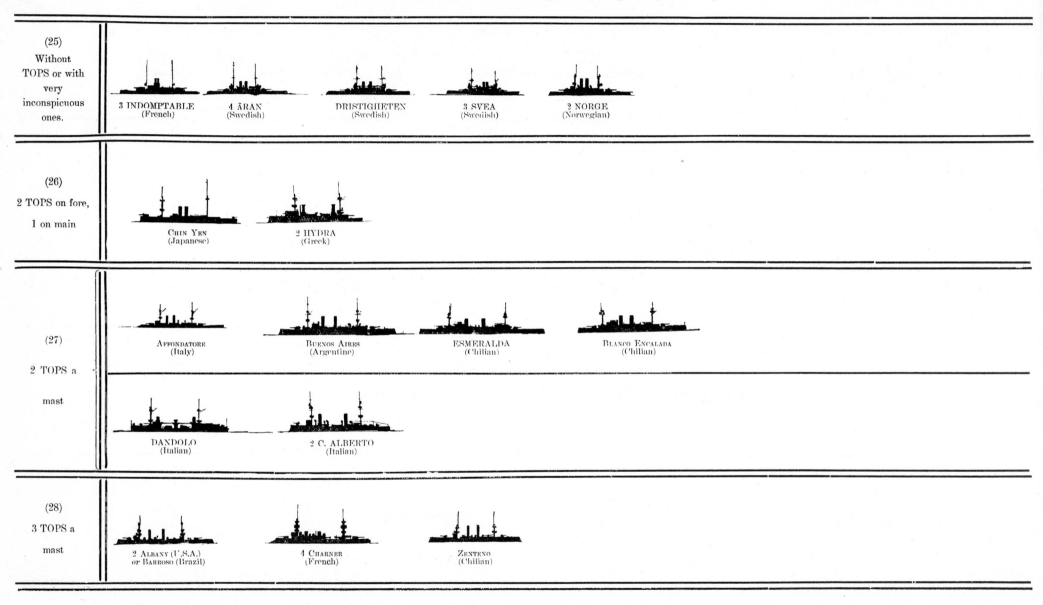

(25)

Without TOPS or with very inconspicuous ones.

3 INDOMPTABLE (French)   4 ÄRAN (Swedish)   DRISTIGHETEN (Swedish)   3 SVEA (Swedish)   2 NORGE (Norwegian)

(26)

2 TOPS on fore, 1 on main

CHIN YEN (Japanese)   2 HYDRA (Greek)

(27)

2 TOPS a mast

AFFONDATORE (Italy)   BUENOS AIRES (Argentine)   ESMERALDA (Chilian)   BLANCO ENCALADA (Chilian)

DANDOLO (Italian)   2 C. ALBERTO (Italian)

(28)

3 TOPS a mast

2 ALBANY (U.S.A.) or BARROSO (Brazil)   4 CHARNER (French)   ZENTENO (Chilian)

2 FUNNELS—Heavy Looking Ships.

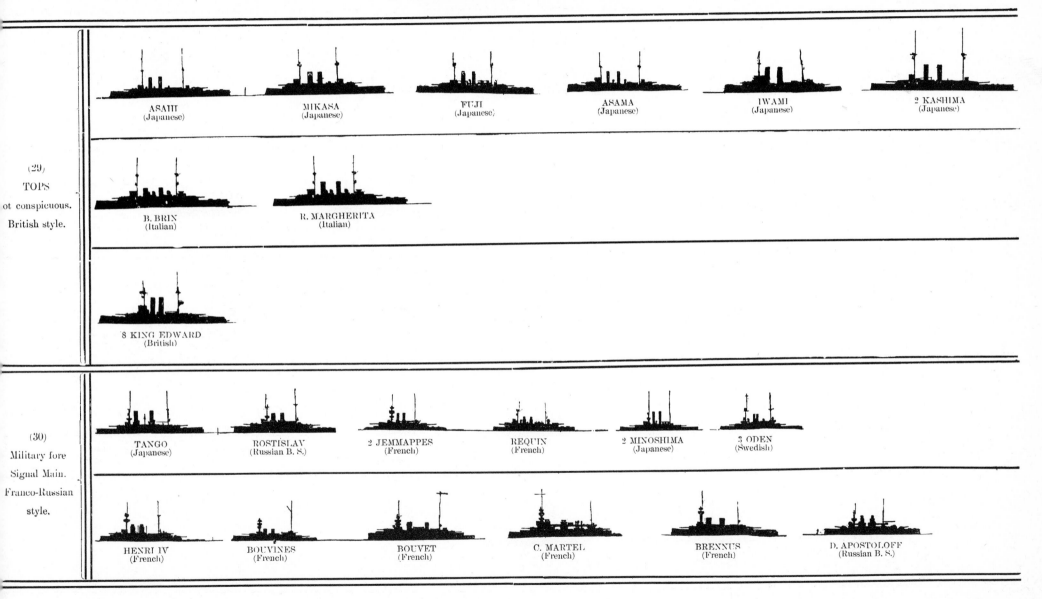

(29)
TOPS
ot conspicuous.
British style.

ASAHI
(Japanese)

MIKASA
(Japanese)

FUJI
(Japanese)

ASAMA
(Japanese)

IWAMI
(Japanese)

2 KASHIMA
(Japanese)

B. BRIN
(Italian)

R. MARGHERITA
(Italian)

8 KING EDWARD
(British)

(30)
Military fore
Signal Main.
Franco-Russian
style.

TANGO
(Japanese)

ROSTISLAV
(Russian B. S.)

2 JEMMAPPES
(French)

REQUIN
(French)

2 MINOSHIMA
(Japanese)

3 ODEN
(Swedish)

HENRI IV
(French)

BOUVINES
(French)

BOUVET
(French)

C. MARTEL
(French)

BRENNUS
(French)

D. APOSTOLOFF
(Russian B. S.)

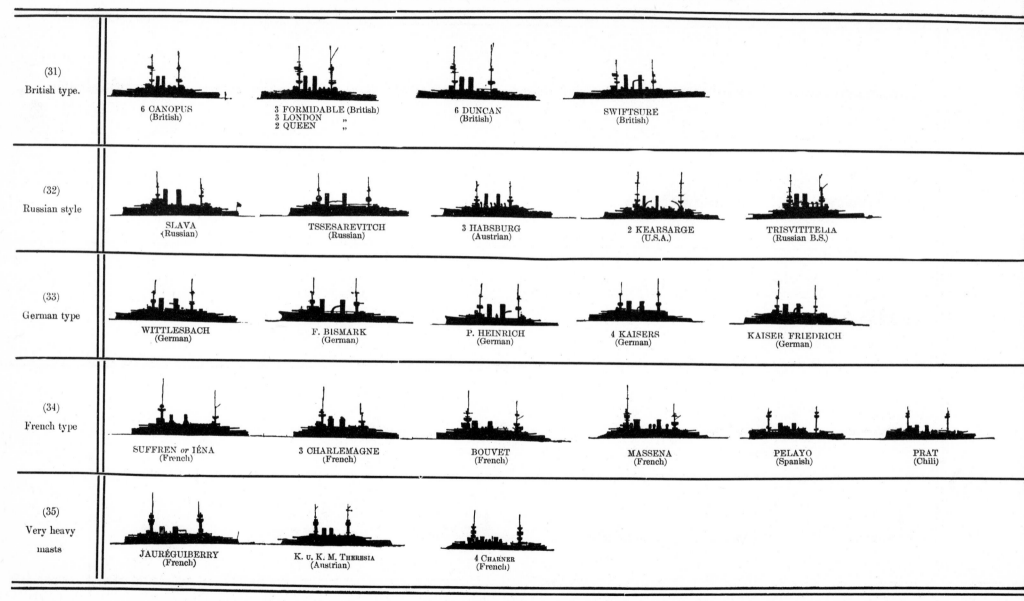

(31) British type.

6 CANOPUS
(British)

3 FORMIDABLE (British)
3 LONDON   „
2 QUEEN   „

6 DUNCAN
(British)

SWIFTSURE
(British)

(32) Russian style

SLAVA
(Russian)

TSSESAREVITCH
(Russian)

3 HABSBURG
(Austrian)

2 KEARSARGE
(U.S.A.)

TRISVITITELIA
(Russian B.S.)

(33) German type

WITTLESBACH
(German)

F. BISMARK
(German)

P. HEINRICH
(German)

4 KAISERS
(German)

KAISER FRIEDRICH
(German)

(34) French type

SUFFREN or IÉNA
(French)

3 CHARLEMAGNE
(French)

BOUVET
(French)

MASSENA
(French)

PELAYO
(Spanish)

PRAT
(Chili)

(35) Very heavy masts

JAURÉGUIBERRY
(French)

K. u. K. M. THERESIA
(Austrian)

4 CHARNER
(French)

2 FUNNELS 3 Masts.

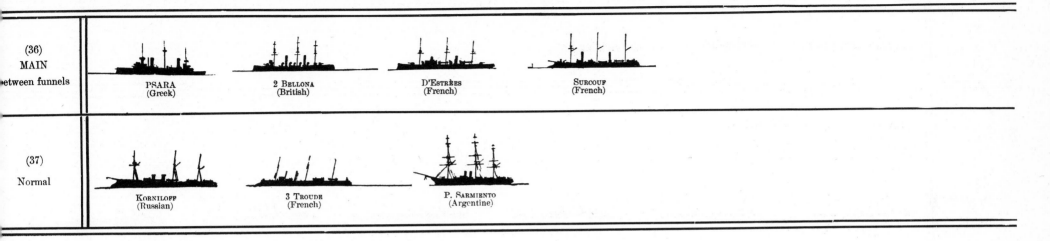

(36) MAIN between funnels	PSARA (Greek)	2 BELLONA (British)	D'ESTRÉES (French)	SURCOUF (French)

(37) Normal	KORNILOFF (Russian)	3 TROUDE (French)	P. SARMIENTO (Argentine)

3 FUNNELS.

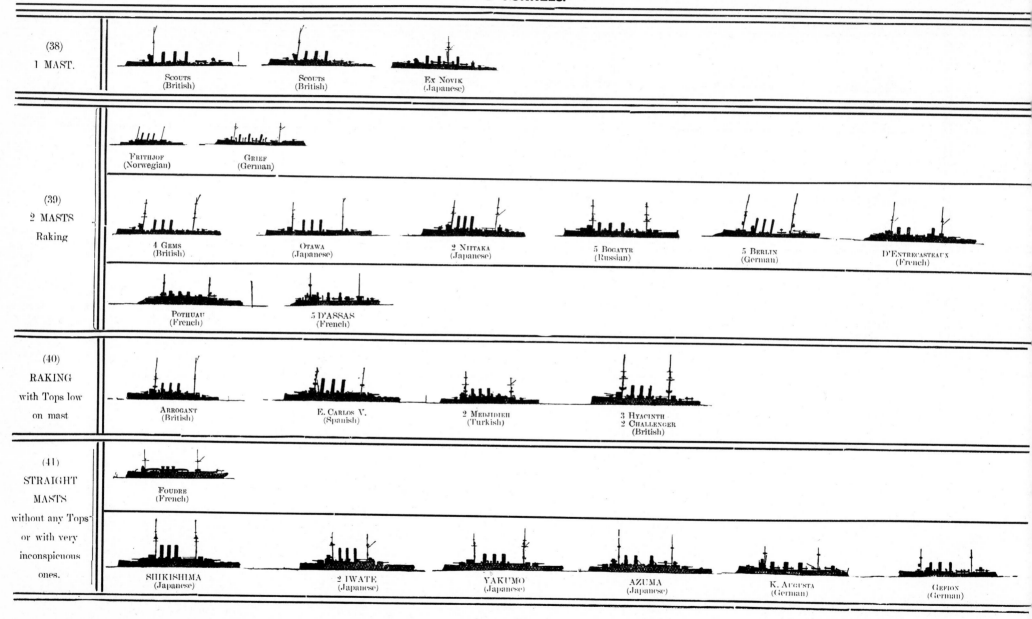

**(38)
1 MAST.**

SCOUTS
(British)

SCOUTS
(British)

EX NOVIK
(Japanese)

**(39)
2 MASTS
Raking**

FRITHJOF
(Norwegian)

GRIEF
(German)

4 GEMS
(British)

OTAWA
(Japanese)

2 NIITAKA
(Japanese)

5 BOGATYR
(Russian)

5 BERLIN
(German)

D'ENTRECASTEAUX
(French)

POTHUAU
(French)

5 D'ASSAS
(French)

**(40)
RAKING
with Tops low
on mast**

ARROGANT
(British)

E. CARLOS V.
(Spanish)

2 MEDJIDIEH
(Turkish)

3 HYACINTH
2 CHALLENGER
(British)

**(41)
STRAIGHT
MASTS
without any Tops
or with very
inconspicuous
ones.**

FOUDRE
(French)

SHIKISHIMA
(Japanese)

2 IWATE
(Japanese)

YAKUMO
(Japanese)

AZUMA
(Japanese)

K. AUGUSTA
(German)

GEFION
(German)

3 FUNNELS, 2 Masts (straight with Tops).

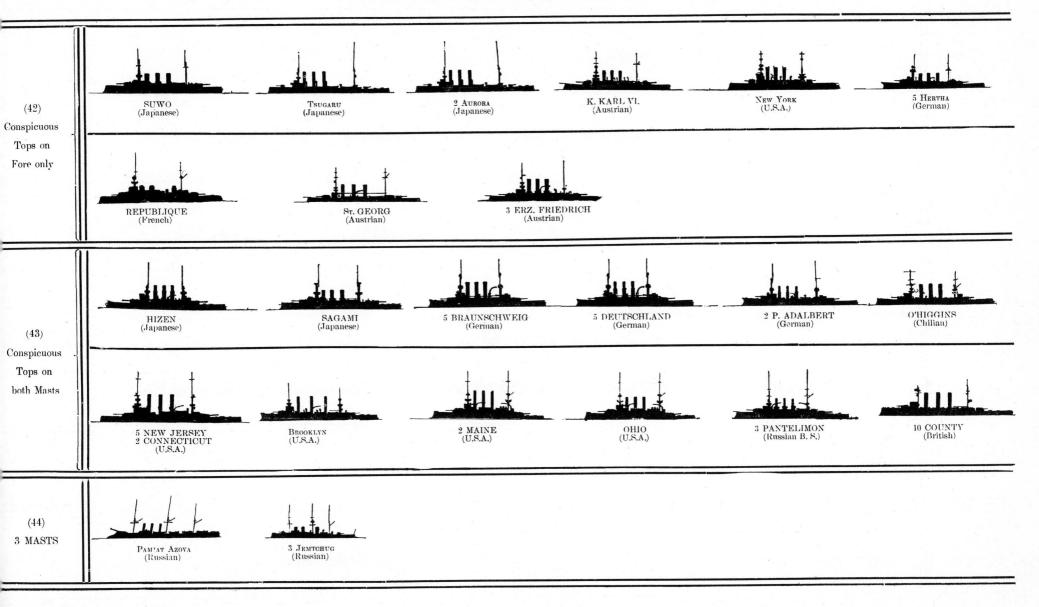

(42) Conspicuous Tops on Fore only

SUWO
(Japanese)

TSUGARU
(Japanese)

2 AURORA
(Japanese)

K. KARL VI.
(Austrian)

NEW YORK
(U.S.A.)

5 HERTHA
(German)

REPUBLIQUE
(French)

ST. GEORG
(Austrian)

3 ERZ. FRIEDRICH
(Austrian)

(43) Conspicuous Tops on both Masts

HIZEN
(Japanese)

SAGAMI
(Japanese)

5 BRAUNSCHWEIG
(German)

5 DEUTSCHLAND
(German)

2 P. ADALBERT
(German)

O'HIGGINS
(Chilian)

5 NEW JERSEY
2 CONNECTICUT
(U.S.A.)

BROOKLYN
(U.S.A.)

2 MAINE
(U.S.A.)

OHIO
(U.S.A.)

3 PANTELIMON
(Russian B. S.)

10 COUNTY
(British)

(44) 3 MASTS

PAMIAT AZOVA
(Russian)

3 JEMTCHUG
(Russian)

4 to 6 FUNNELS.

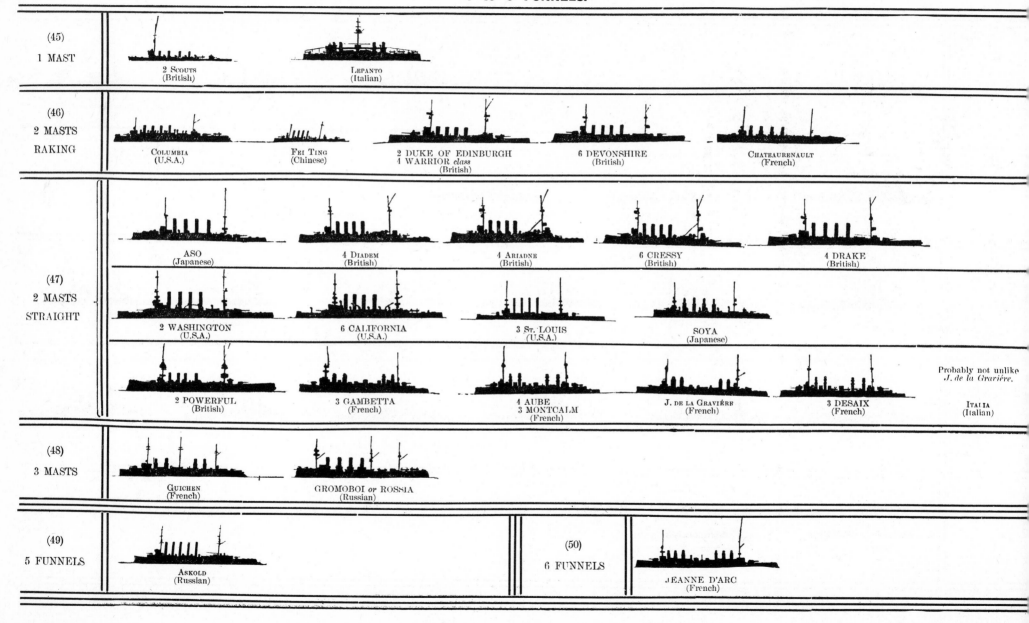

(45)
1 MAST

2 Scouts
(British)

Lepanto
(Italian)

(46)
2 MASTS
RAKING

Columbia
(U.S.A.)

Fei Ting
(Chinese)

2 DUKE OF EDINBURGH
4 WARRIOR *class*
(British)

6 DEVONSHIRE
(British)

Chateaurenault
(French)

(47)
2 MASTS
STRAIGHT

Aso
(Japanese)

4 Diadem
(British)

4 Ariadne
(British)

6 Cressy
(British)

4 Drake
(British)

2 WASHINGTON
(U.S.A.)

6 CALIFORNIA
(U.S.A.)

3 St. Louis
(U.S.A.)

Soya
(Japanese)

2 POWERFUL
(British)

3 GAMBETTA
(French)

4 AUBE
3 MONTCALM
(French)

J. DE LA GRAVIÈRE
(French)

3 DESAIX
(French)

Probably not unlike
J. de la Gravière.

ITALIA
(Italian)

(48)
3 MASTS

Guichen
(French)

GROMOBOI *or* ROSSIA
(Russian)

(49)
5 FUNNELS

Askold
(Russian)

(50)
6 FUNNELS

JEANNE D'ARC
(French)

TRIPLE EFFECT FRESH WATER DISTILLING APPARATUS. As Fitted to H.M.S. "Audacious," "Aquarius," and "Assistance." 2,000 gallons per hour. Ratio of gained water to boiler steam used, 2 to 1.

PATENT EVAPORATOR. With door removed for cleaning coils or testing joints.

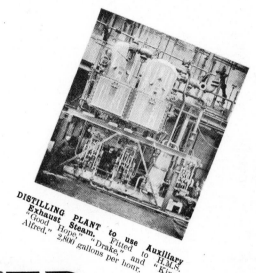

DISTILLING PLANT to use Auxiliary Exhaust Steam. Fitted to H.M.S. "Good Hope," "Drake," and "King Alfred." 2,800 gallons per hour.

SOLE MAKERS CAIRD & RAYNER ENGINEERS

ADMIRALTY CONTRACTORS,

777, COMMERCIAL ROAD, LONDON, E.

Manufacturers of

FRESH WATER DISTILLING MACHINERY for BRITISH and FOREIGN NAVIES

FROM SIZES SUITABLE FOR TORPEDO BOATS UP TO THE LARGEST BATTLESHIPS AND CRUISERS.

EVAPORATORS ARRANGED TO WORK SINGLE OR MULTIPLE EFFECT, OR TO USE EXHAUST STEAM FROM AUXILIARY ENGINES.